The Islander

A biography of
HALLDÓR LAXNESS

HALLDOR GUDMUNDSSON is an Icelandic author, a former publisher and the first director of Harpa, Iceland's main concert hall. His biography of Halldór Laxness, *The Islander*, was awarded the Icelandic Literary Prize. He lives in Reykjavik.

PHILIP ROUGHTON is a scholar of Old Norse and medieval literature and an award-winning translator of Icelandic literature, having translated works by numerous writers including Halldór Laxness and Jón Kalman Stefánsson. He lives in the north of Iceland.

The Islander

A biography of Halldór Laxness

HALLDÓR GUÐMUNDSSON

Translated from the Icelandic by
Philip Roughton

MACLEHOSE PRESS
QUERCUS · LONDON

The publishers would like to thank the following for the permission to
reproduce the photographs which appear on pages 487–490 of this book:

Halldór aged around fifty: Jón Kaldal; Halldór with his parents: Gunnhild
Thorsteinsson & Co; María and Málfríður Jónsdóttir: María Halldórsdóttir; Halldór at
Clervaux Monastery: Laxness family; Sænautasel farm: Skúli Guðmundsson; Kristín
Valgerður Einarsdóttir: Jóhanna Stefánsdóttir; Halldór in 1934: Einar Laxness; Inga and
Halldór in Nice: Einar Laxness; Halldór at the Bukharin trial: popperfoto.com; Vera
Hertzsch with Erla Sólveig: Benjamin Eiriksson; Auður Sveinsdóttir at the age of
twenty: Laxness family; Halldór at the memorial sculpture: Laxness family

Every effort has been made to contact copyright holders.
However, the publishers will be glad to rectify in future editions any
inadvertent omissions brought to their attention

First published in Great Britain in 2008 by MacLehose Press
This paperback edition published in 2023 by

MacLehose Press
An Imprint of Quercus Editions Limited
Carmelite House
50 Victoria Embankment
London EC4Y 0DZ

An Hachette UK Company

Originally published in Iceland as *Halldór Laxness, ævisaga* by
JPV, ÚTGÁFA, Reykjavík, 2004

This translation is published with the financial assistance of Baugur Group, Kaupthing
Bank and the Fund for the Promotion of Icelandic Literature.

A CIP catalogue reference for this book is available from the British Library

ISBN (TPB) 978 1 52943 373 9
ISBN (ebook) 978 1 52943 374 6

2 4 6 8 9 7 5 3 1

Designed and typeset in Garamond by Patty Rennie
Printed and bound in Great Britain by Clays Ltd, Elcograf S.p.A.

Contents

ONE

An Unwritten World

Childhood and Adolescence
1902–1919

> At that time nothing had been done; young writers arrived at
> a nearly unwritten world.
>
> *Halldór Laxness*

HALLDÓR LAXNESS WAS EUROPE'S LAST NATIONAL POET. NOT BECAUSE
the entire Icelandic nation loved him but because almost everyone in the country
took an interest in his writing. No-one was neutral. Like the Century of Extremes
in which he lived, Halldór was a man of extremes himself; extraordinarily amiable
and discreet and at the same time audacious and critical with his pen. The writer
and the man were often at odds; he was bold in his literary vision – and in his
mistakes. He had the ability to control circumstances and people to such a degree
that everything would revolve around him and his goal of writing stories. His ambition was boundless and sometimes indelicate. But he wrote out of inner need, not
in order to ingratiate himself with others. The contrast between lofty vision and
earthly existence tugged at Halldór all his life; from this tension came the sparks
of his creativity.

The Story of the Stone

"Nowhere have I found the echo of the divine voice in my heart except at one
stone in the fields of the farm at home," the nineteen-year-old Halldór writes in
the autobiographical story "My Holy Stone". The stone loomed large on the hill
behind the farm, a short distance from the cleft where the river ran down and
formed a stone pool in the gorge. It was at this stone that Christ appeared to the
narrator, one bright midsummer day when he was seven. Christ addressed the boy,
and afterwards "all things lost their radiance to that childhood memory of standing
face to face with the Redeemer".

It is often faithful children that experience visions of Christ, and Halldór pokes some fun at his youthful vision in the memoir *The Saga of the Seven Masters* many years later. It is the same vision, changed only to suit the formal demands of the narrative, as with so much else in Halldór's memoirs:

> On Easter morning when I was seven years old . . . I experienced a revelation . . . The sun had come dancing up as befits the Saviour at Easter, even when the weather is cold. I was just standing behind the house . . . feeling something of a sense of resurrection, just a touch cynical, looking eastwards; and as I was standing there I heard these words whispered from somewhere out in the universe: "When you are seventeen years old, you will die."

The memory works as an admonition to Halldór to hold fast to his writing: there is not much time left for him, even while it provides the occasion for a little self-irony, in contrast to the pious tone of the story. But common to both these narratives – sixty years apart – is their description of a youthful revelation. The boy had caught a glimpse of a higher world, which led to a new understanding: from that time on nothing mattered except his writing.

Halldór's aesthetic sense was shaped by his youthful revelation: art granted a glimpse of a higher world, of the beauty of the world of dreams. To write poems or tell stories would always be partly an attempt to capture this world, store its essence against the drudgery of human life. When Halldór was sixteen he wrote the following lines, which appear in *Child of Nature*, his first novel to appear in print:

> Dead is all without dreams
> And sad the world.

The hill where Gljúfrasteinn, Halldór's adult home, stands now was part of the farm of Halldór's childhood, and early on he had set his sights on it. He wrote to his mother from Los Angeles in 1928: "You must not . . . sell the land. If I can make some money, I will build a house up by the ravine." Seventeen years later he achieved his goal. Gljúfrasteinn means "the stone in the ravine", where the Kaldakvísl River runs down into Mosfellsdalur, where a seven-year-old boy experienced a revelation.

There was another stone that Halldór had set his sights on. In the spring of 1971 he wrote to his wife Auður Sveinsdóttir from Italy saying that he had been thinking of trying to get someone to "pull that beautiful stone unscathed from the [Kaldakvísl] and put it on the lawn". The task fell to Auður, as did most of the work at Gljúfrasteinn, and in April of that year she sent Halldór news that the stone had been removed from the river the day before, a job that required six people and two pieces of heavy machinery. One man fell into the river, and the dog Lubbi "ran off to Seljabrekka". Now the stone stands on the lawn at Gljúfrasteinn, a silent witness to the youthful dreams of the writer, an image of the beauty that compelled him to write.

———

Halldór Guðjónsson (who was to change his surname) was born in Reykjavík on 23 April, 1902. Just over seventy years later he described the circumstances of his birth as follows:

> People in the know tell me that I was not born in the wooden house on the plot at Laugavegur 32, where the maid dropped me out of the window, but rather in the stone house . . . where the cat jumped into the cradle to claw at the face of the child as it slept; and was hanged for doing so.

Halldór's parents, Guðjón Helgi Helgson and Sigríður Halldórsdóttir, were living in Reykjavík when Halldór was born. In a manuscript biography of Halldór written when he was barely thirty, Stefán Einarsson, then professor of linguistics at the Johns Hopkins University, Baltimore, records that Halldór's father came from the Mýar district in the west of Iceland

> and was raised "on the parish" at Hvítársíða, because all his people were completely impoverished. He was . . . thrifty [and] became a dry-stocksman in Reykjavík but did road building in the countryside in the summer; due to his energy and skill he was made a foreman, and he earned a good wage.

Iceland experienced as many changes in the twentieth century as other Western societies did in three hundred years. In 1900, the country was like an "unfulfilled dream", as the poet Hannes Hafstein put it; it bore the marks of centuries-old stagnation but contained the seeds of modernity. Halldór's father was born in 1870.

The term "dry-stocksman" – a wage labourer in a fishing village, one who has no farm tenancy or livestock – comes from a bygone age. Such wage labourers were also called "vacant men", because they lived in houses without land; well into the nineteenth century only men who owned land or other property had the right to vote in Iceland. Urban areas, the market economy, bourgeois culture, workers' unions: these things were only just making an appearance when Halldór himself was born.

Guðjón was a highly valued road worker. At the turn of the nineteenth century the inhabited parts of Iceland were connected only by footpaths and tracks over endless moors, creeks, grassy plains and bare sandy wastes, cut here and there by glacial rivers that could become impassable at the slightest change in the weather. The main means of transport, for those who did not walk, was either horse or horse and cart. Guðjón and others like him built roads in teams of twenty to thirty young men using horses and carts to transport the tools.

By the time his son was born, Guðjón owned a small stone house at Laugavegur 32, along with a large garden. By then he had been living in Reykjavík for almost ten years, having married Sigríður Halldórsdóttir, who had lived for some time at a little farm Melkot in Reykjavík, on 7 November, 1896. Sigríður was born in 1872 to a farming family in the south of Iceland. Her mother, Guðný Klængsdóttir, whom Halldór would later immortalize, had been widowed when Sigríður was only ten years old. She had then moved in with her sister, Guðrún, who lived at Melkot on land belonging to one of the old estate farms in Reykjavík. Guðrún lived with her husband, Magnús Einarsson. Melkot became for Halldór a symbol of the lost paradise of his youth, and the model for the farm Brekkukot in the novel *The Fish Can Sing* (1957).

A detailed description of Reykjavík in 1900 is given by the poet Benedikt Gröndal. The inhabitants numbered just over six thousand, and the city could not exactly be described as elegant, dogs and street urchins being the "dominating element". The city had two policemen and, says Benedikt, would have been completely overrun if a crowded foreign ship had docked in its harbour.

Anything urban about Reykjavík was brand new. Well into the 1800s inhabitants had to fumble along from house to house in pitch darkness during the winter; the first street lamps were not put in until 1876, and when the municipal government received an offer from an English company in 1888 to light the streets with electricity, it was quickly rejected: people had never heard such a ridiculous proposition. In 1870 there was a total of ten two-storey houses in Reykjavík, and the inhabitants numbered around two thousand, but in the next thirty years the population tripled and the town centre actually started to resemble a city. These decades were extremely difficult out in the countryside, and thousands of people, mainly from the east and north, emigrated to North America. Guðjón and Sigríður, however, were among the many who moved from the west and the south to Reykjavík.

Good fortune visited the household at Laugavegur when Halldór was born; the couple had previously had a stillborn girl. In 1903 Guðjón wrote his sister a letter that testifies to the young parents' daily concerns:

There is little news . . . except that we feel tolerably well, thank God. Little Halldór is quite energetic and behaves himself well; he was weaned two weeks ago and was peculiarly nonchalant about it . . . his mother . . . has been ill on and off since before Christmas . . . although for the most part she has been able to be up and about . . . Guðný has stayed with little Dóri [a nickname for Halldór] during the nights since he was weaned . . .

Guðjón also mentions that he was seeking out as much work as he could get, since, "my position in life demands that I not miss any opportunity". At the time he was doing piecework as a stone worker, but reckoned on going west to do road work during the summer.

Guðjón and Sigríður were swimming somewhat against the current of the times when Guðjón sold his house in Reykjavík in 1905, bought the Laxnes farm in the Mosfell district, about twelve miles from the town, and moved there with his family. This meant a change in the family's fortunes, because now Guðjón was at home much more often. He generally did road work for between five and seven weeks during the summer, never too far from home.

It was in June, 1905, that the household of six travelled on horseback from Reykjavík to Laxnes. The group included Halldór's grandmother Guðný Klængsdóttir, and two workers. Once on the farm, there were usually more people about: servants, day labourers during haymaking and guests. Halldór considered it his great fortune to have been raised in such a busy household. There was a great deal of work to be done improving the land, and both sheep and cows were kept there; later a small telephone exchange was set up. New guests were always arriving – not least because of the farm's location on the path over the Mosfellsheiði heath. Guðjón quickly became swamped with work for the local church (he held a seat on the parish council from 1907 until 1919).

Although Halldór grew up in excellent conditions according to the standards of the time, Laxnes was not considered a particularly good farm. The hayfields were in bad condition, tussocky and wet. But the previous occupant had built a house out of wood and corrugated iron. At the time, the Laxnes house lorded it over others in the area because they were made of turf. Guðjón put his road-work experience to good use and built a road leading to the farm, thought to be the first raised, paved "drive" in the valley. He also renovated the house, installed water pipes and drains, and built an extension. The neighbouring farmer, Jónas Magnússon, described Guðjón's house in 1915 as "one of the best and most spacious homes in the district".

Guðjón worked at improving the land, most importantly by attempting to level the tussocks; all the work was done with hand tools. A description of the farm given in the *Property Valuation Book of the Kjós District From the Year 1918*, compiled by Björn Bjarnason, a farmer near by, says that the farm's hayfields were on lowland, some of them quite marshy, but that they were "almost completely flat", suggesting that Guðjón had not been careless in his work. The same description also gives the following information under the excellent heading "Crew": "7 cows, 6 horses, 130 sheep; for haymaking 5–6 people."

The image that Jónas Magnússon creates of Guðjón, in an article written many decades later, has a saintly air about it. Guðjón was constantly at work though not particularly strong; he was energetic and likeable, and had a knack for getting others to work hard without raising his voice. He was prudent, and always had enough work, as one can see from a letter that he wrote to his sister on 23 June, 1910:

> I am mainly going east to the Þingvellir area, and will be improving roads there, and also to Mosfellsheiði, Laugardalur, and Biskupstungur; I wish that I had wings to fly between teams.

Jónas describes Halldór's mother as "always happy and genial in her daily occupations, but at the same time quiet and reticent by nature". She is also said to have been an entertaining conversationalist in familiar company and particularly good with children.

One could say that Jónas gives an idealised portrait of Halldór's parents; yet it is clear that Sigríður and Guðjón had a strong sense of morality and the work ethic; one suspects that people then took more pains to live well than they do now.

Halldór wrote in a letter to his biographer Stefán Einarsson that there had always been a feeling of good accord at home, and in his memoir *In the Fields of Home* (1975) he writes:

> In those days warm-heartedness, scrupulous behaviour and respect for one's neighbours were to be found where we now have computerized justice; there was a beauty in human relations that people could not live without despite everything else.

Jónas describes how Sigríður in fact had no special liking for farm work and took no pleasure in raising livestock, since she had not grown up doing such things. But she took on farm work anyway.

The circumstances of an artist's youth might not be as significant as how he responds to and takes advantage of them. In Halldór's case one particular thing made a huge difference: his father was a musician.

Like other aspects of bourgeois culture, playing musical instruments at home did not have a long tradition in Iceland. In the first half of the nineteenth century there were only seven pianos in Reykjavík, and a foreign visitor suggested that a European composer would have had a hard time recognizing his own music due to Icelanders' lacklustre musicianship. There were violins, guitars and other instruments available, but ensemble playing was unknown until the Horn-playing Society of Reykjavík was founded in 1876, the same year that the first street light was put in and Wagner's *Der Ring des Niebelungen* performed in full in Germany. But Icelandic musicianship gained ground, and it became more common for young people to take harmonium or organ lessons, not least so that they could play in church; and of course every member of a church congregation could sing, for better or worse. Guðjón started a choir at Lágafell Church, for which he played the organ and violin; he was considered a talented violinist. When Halldór was seventy he remarked in a television interview that his first memories were of lying on the floor at home, snuggled up near the organ's foot-pedal. In *When I Left Home* (1952), the autobiographical novel he started in 1924, he gives this description of his father's violin playing:

> He played daily, whenever he returned from work, and when evening came on he sat in the twilight by the living-room window and played, and I can still see his cheeks silhouetted in the window, and outside the gleam of the new moon, and autumn clouds in the west creating strange shadows. As a child I learnt to play the violin a little, but gave up quite early. But my father thought me suited to singing and gave me a harmonium. I was eleven years old. We got an uncle to come to the farm to teach me the fundamentals of this instrument; ever since then music has been my most blissful delight, and when I die I want to hear music.

Halldór was twenty-two when he wrote this description, but he could have written it much later on in his life. In many of his writings he calls music the highest art, and music is a symbol of the dream visions of a higher world. Music seems for him to be the stuff of revelation, of something entirely different from everyday life. It is in music that one detects the connection between father and son, the inheritance from the ever-struggling farmer and road builder in the writer who never did an honest day's physical work.

Guðjón was also a good storyteller, and could – when time allowed – tell an entire corpus of anecdotes, along with "character descriptions of peculiar men" with whom he often had to do business. Guðjón had an animated and prepossessing narrative ability; he told his stories in a quiet voice, with a gentle wry smile and a delivery "as if he were a trained church-reader", says Jónas Magnússon. There is much to suggest that Halldór was closer to his father than his mother, although Sigríður would show him invaluable support on his path towards becoming a writer. But that path was not within his sight as a child in the first decade of the new century.

*

Halldór did not remember much of his infancy, but he was often ill as a child, sometimes dangerously so, for instance, when he contracted polio. The Surgeon General Guðmundur Björnson saved his life when he was three. Later he became quite strong, but he was sure that he bore the marks of his childhood polio, among them his hesitant speech, which impressionists never grew tired of imitating after he had become famous.

Halldór was an eccentric child. "I started to live my own intellectual life at a very early age", he wrote to Stefán Einarsson. Testimony to youth is found primarily in a letter written to Stefán towards the end of Halldór's stay in America in 1929 (similar in style to the chapters on his youth in *When I Left Home*) and in the memoir *In the Fields of Home*. The latter is bathed in a gentle clarity, reflecting the warm mood of old photographs, the disasters of youth turning into humorous incidents. In the letter to Stefán, on the other hand, Halldór consciously distances himself from the countryside, and the arrogance of the newly moulded cosmopolitan peeks out:

> Of those members of my family who are now living, not a single soul among them has earned a higher education or won any sort of recognition for anything, as far as I know . . .

He felt so completely different from his family in so many things that only the word *mutation* would apply if one were searching for a biological explanation. He certainly honours his parents in his letter to Stefán, but his heart is bent upon expressing his own detachment:

> I had deep respect for my father, deeper than I have had for any other man, and this feeling dug itself so deep into my soul that even today I often still dream of my father with the same original sentiment. My mother did not have much influence on me in my youth – at least not overtly . . . One of the deepest sorrows that I have ever experienced was when my mother burnt a great deal of my writing, stories and poems that I was constantly composing when I was about seven. Afterwards I always treated my writing as I would

a murder – I was always writing, but as soon as I wrote something I would put it under lock and key and allow no living person to see it, and I never spoke to anyone about what I wrote . . .

Quite frequently in Halldór's books one encounters a lonely, artistically inclined boy who has a limited number of things in common with the other members of his family. The letter exaggerates: Halldór's parents were incredibly tolerant of their son's long vigils over his books, writings, drawings and dolls. Halldór was something of an outsider, however. Many years later Þorsteinn Magnússon recalled his old playmate Halldór in an interview, saying:

Halldór did not come out to play very often . . . He was always thinking about things and of course writing, but he wasn't a show-off. He never enjoyed ball games or any of the other games that we played . . . He came across early on as being a bit peculiar . . .

Halldór probably sums up most people's opinions from that time:

The boy at Laxnes sits ten hours a day scrawling in notebooks. He can't be stopped from doing this. He isn't like most people. It must be a great hardship for his parents. The parish must feel sorry for them.

It must not be forgotten that well into the twentieth century Icelanders spent nearly all of their time working to survive. The writer Þórbergur Þórðarson, who was slightly older than Halldór and grew up in an isolated district, was no less "peculiar" as a child. He described the prevailing view as follows: "To mess around drawing, map making and minting coins, and waste time in idiotic surveying and shipbuilding – that was not work, but rather pauperism, cursed beggary."

Halldór's narratives about his youth in the countryside, written fifty years apart, are disparate in tone. His statements from the 1920s are dramatic and critical, whereas *In the Fields of Home* is far more good-natured. Earlier, Halldór says that he feels closer to his father, later, closer to his mother. For these discrepancies there is a simple explanation: during the 1920s he was still trying to distance himself from Laxnes, attempting to break free from the bonds of Icelandic xenophobia, whereas during the 1970s he was making his way back home.

Guðjón describes his nearly nine-year-old son in a letter to his sister:

My Dóri has started doing a few light jobs outside when the weather is good, and when he is inside he most often likes being with books or a paper and pen; he is a very bright and pleasant boy, remembers what he reads and can retell it in an entertaining way.

Guðjón pride is obvious despite the fact that farm work did not capture the child's attention. In *When I Left Home*, the narrator describes himself as follows:

It's as if I have an innate aversion to labour. I shall soon be twenty-two and have never, to this day, done an honest day's work, as they say in the countryside. When I was a child at home, there were few odd jobs that I did without sulking, even moaning. My parents probably found it difficult to understand me although they would certainly have liked to. My eagerness for reading indicated that I was not a complete lazybones, because if I had the opportunity I would sit diligently over my books from morning until night, paying heed to nothing else. When it became fairly clear that I would never "be inclined to farm work", I was no longer required to do any more physical work, and I can be eternally thankful that my parents were so understanding and did not make me tear my child's shoes to tatters in contemptible slavery.

Everything concurs on one detail: Halldór wrote constantly from the time he was seven. He writes to Stefán Einarsson that he had been a "commonplace errand boy and milkman in others' eyes, but a very uncommon philosopher 'before God'". Until his two sisters, Sigríður and Helga, were born in 1909 and 1912, the fact that he was an only child must have increased his feeling that he was special.

There were numerous books at home, and in *In the Fields of Home* Halldór describes the first book he remembers, which he called *Bótólfur*; he heeded his grandmother's advice and paid attention not to the text but to the mysterious illustrations, and did not come to realize until much later that the book was a collection of excerpts from Grimm's fairy tales in Danish. He delved into Andersen's folk and fairy tales, but throughout his life remained dubious about the Danish writer due to Andersen's schoolmasterly moralising. Halldór also read some translated novels and other literature, and became acquainted at an early age with the *Felsenburg Stories*, German romantic literature from the eighteenth century, in Icelandic translation.

The day before his tenth birthday, Halldór wrote and dated "Bylaws of the Children's Club of Mosfellsdalur", including the following statement of purpose:

To cultivate good conduct in words and deeds. Members of the Club may not swear or use foul language, neither at their meetings nor elsewhere. They shall make a habit of using fair speech, and speak pure Icelandic.

The club held its meetings on Sundays, and members had to be under fourteen. By 1915 club members were being encouraged to participate in sports, and the maximum membership age was raised. A list of thirteen members exists from the same year, written in the hand of Ólafur Þórðarson from Æsustaðir, one of Halldór's childhood friends. They wrote to each other on and off for several years, among other things concerning club matters. It is in these letters that Halldór first describes his idea of adopting a pseudonym, the name Lax.

Having seized him at an early age, Halldór's passion for writing never left him. In a letter to Stefán Einarsson, he said:

> I wrote thousands of pages at home in Laxnes and had trunks full of finished notebooks – novels, stories, poems, magazines and newspapers (which I "published" for myself), essays about religion, politics, philosophy – everything between heaven and earth, and finally diaries.

What shaped this inclination? A youthful revelation, an innate gift of genius? Clearly Halldór was a talented boy who had a rich need to create and who was happy in his own world. He played with dolls – there was a feminine side to him as to many male artists – and strong female characters later became one of his trademarks.

A storyteller must have room inside him for many different characters and the characters that he creates reflect parts of him. It has been suggested that what distinguishes artists in their youth is not particularly their surpassing talent, but rather their unquenchable thirst to express themselves. Halldór was raised on a farm in a country in which literature was the only cultural inheritance of any worth; was it not natural for him to try his hand at becoming a writer?

What did he write in Laxnes, before he moved to Reykjavík at the age of thirteen? His writings from the time are not preserved, but he described them in this way much later:

> I think that the concoction that this totterer came up with in his father's house from the age of seven to twelve was the product of an immature inclination to express himself, which is innate in certain people even if they do not unburden themselves in books. It is precisely this healthy inclination, or perhaps unhealthy passion, which learned men feel to be most appropriately named in German, and which is called in that language *die Lust zum Fabulieren.*

At a young age Halldór found contentment in weaving narrative webs. The parents of this blond, bright dreamer provided him with the best opportunity they could: the year after Halldór finished elementary school, he was sent to Reykjavík to study drawing and music.

*

It always proved difficult for Halldór Laxness to write about his parents; he was generally not open about his feelings. On the other hand there was one woman in Halldór's youth whom he loved, and about whom he had no qualms in speaking: his grandmother. Guðný Klængsdóttir, who was born in 1832, lived with Halldór's parents at Laxnes to an extreme old age, and Halldór spoke of her so often that for a time other Icelandic writers felt that they too should invent such a grandmother, an old woman with an inexhaustible well of stories and wisdom from days long past.

Halldór spent a great deal of time with this old woman when he was young. He says in *When I Left Home*: "I . . . was raised at the feet of the nineteenth century . . . among folk from the part of the Icelandic people that was cut from the cliffs of antiquity." As an example of his grandmother's views about the modern world, he describes her reaction to the telephone: ". . . although that monstrous telephone rang endlessly in her ears . . . she died with the full conviction that telephones were nothing but vanity and chasing after the wind".

Halldór's grandmother was the line that connected him with Iceland's past. She had an independent, strong, ancient grasp of the language, knew an incredible number of stories and was typical in being accustomed to relentless, uncomplaining drudgery. She has her own place in his books: in *Independent People* (1934–5), for example, Halldór creates a portrait of a young man saying farewell to his grandmother before he travels out into the world armed with his grandmother's good advice; and in *The Fish Can Sing*, the grandmother is the personification of charity and the soul of the common people. His grandmother was both sufficiently beloved and sufficiently distant to become story-material, a symbol of the best of Icelandic popular culture, to which he remained faithful all his life.

Adolescent Years in a Small Town

As Halldór's adolescent years approached, he read almost everything he could get his hands on. The elementary school for the Mosfell district was a "mobile school", which meant a school that moved from farm to farm. This arrangement was common throughout the country, and well into the twentieth century there were still journeyman teachers who travelled between farms. Halldór fondly recalled the influence that elementary school, and especially his first teacher, a young woman, had on his development:

She was . . . a spiritual encourager, an inspirer of goodness, and an extremely energetic leader in our [youth] club, Miss Guðrún Björnsdóttir from Grafarholt. The patriotism that she inspired in us children was contrary to all tepid patriotism. The best of the culture of the world was not too good for the Icelanders, according to her beliefs. She never missed an opportunity to exhort us concerning what was noble and magnificent in the history of Iceland and its educational traditions. She was a conservative woman according to the standards of the time, which meant that she wanted all foreign contamination wiped clean from the country unconditionally. She strengthened this spirit of Icelandic conservatism within us.

Iceland had not yet achieved independence from Denmark; the country was both sparsely populated and poor, and its self-image was cloudy. In schools, social organizations and newspapers Icelanders constantly exhorted each other to educa-tion, to great deeds, to independence: people were shoring up their self-confidence in order to take on the new age alone and unsupported. In Halldór's first writings this childish exhortative spirit is occasionally apparent. In his thirties he contested nationalism in a grandiose way, but he returned to it in his fifties: the conflict between being an Icelander and a man of the world stayed with him all his life.

Halldór's first trip away from home was not a long one: in the autumn of 1915 he went to study at the Technical College in Reykjavík. This was the only school at which it was possible to study anything resembling the arts in Iceland. Guðjón's foresight is revealed in his choice of this course of study for Halldór; in order to gain his son admittance, he contacted his supervisor, Chief Engineer Jón Þorláksson, later Iceland's Prime Minister. Halldór described the interview as follows:

Jón thought the world of my father and came frequently to stay with us at Laxnes. He was a remarkable man. Father told him that I read quite a lot of books, was sometimes writing and always playing music. He needed to enrol me into some kind of art course and because of this he had his eyes on the Technical College for me . . . Jón . . . had been a spokesman for the Technical College for several years, knew the right people and could ensure this boy a place.

It was quite a change for the short, pale and, by his own admission, skinny secretary of the Children's Club of Mosfellsdalur to find himself surrounded by students who were mostly grown men, studying wood-, iron- and stone working, or even baking or printing.

Halldór attended courses in various subjects, but mainly in drawing. His teacher was one of the pioneers of Icelandic painting, Þórarinn B. Þorláksson. Þórarinn held the first exhibition of work by an Icelandic painter in Reykjavík in 1900. One of Halldór's schoolfriends, Ásmundur Sveinsson, significantly older than him, would become one of the greatest Icelandic sculptors. Fifteen years later, Halldór called Ásmundur his first intellectual companion.

The coursework did not really suit Halldór: it was too regulated and uninteresting, and he may also have discovered that his talents did not lie in this area. It is difficult to judge now. One drawing from that autumn exists: a picture of Lord Byron that Halldór copied from a printed original, neatly done. In any case, his thoughts were not firmly fixed on the course, and as the year went by his interest ebbed away.

During the winter of 1915–16 Halldór also studied the organ and piano with the support of his father, benefiting from the instruction of another pioneer, Eggert Gilfer Guðmundsson, who, along with his brother, was one of the first professional musicians in Iceland. "Everyone thought I had the makings of a musical virtuoso," Halldór says in *When I Left Home*, though this statement must be read with caution. It is certain that he cultivated his piano playing throughout his life, and he especially enjoyed playing Bach, as we shall see. But in his adult years he seldom played for others, because his desire for perfection was too strong. Among Halldór's other teachers that winter was his Icelandic teacher, Jakob Jóhannesson Smári. Smári was a poet and widely read aesthete to whom Halldór would turn for advice about his literary attempts during the next few years.

*

There was more to learn than the arts in Reykjavík. The Industrial Revolution had finally reached Iceland in the shape of trawler fishing, which was begun there in earnest in 1907. Alongside the development of trawler fishing the labour-union movement began to gain strength, and the trawlermen's strike in 1916 had extensive influence – these were the first organized disputes between workers and management in Iceland. In the same year, the Federation of Labour Unions, the Social Democratic Party and the Progressive Party were all founded. Reykjavík experienced a housing shortage due to the steady stream of country folk coming into the town; people were gathered into unsanitary hovels, and poverty was marked.

Not that these factors in his immediate environment had a deep influence on Halldór. He had other things on his agenda, namely, his writing:

After I was sent south . . . I wrote a novel in opposition to Redemption theory. It is one of the longest novels that has ever been written in Icelandic, compared to *Lightning* by Torfhildur Hólm, whom Þórður Sigtryggsson used to call the Sappho of Iceland when poking fun at his compatriot. Torfhildur's book was about the victory of Christianity in ancient Iceland. For emphasis I called my book *Dawn*.

This is a curious story, whether it is true or not. In any case Halldór says in a letter to Stefán Einarsson in 1929:

In the winter of 1915–16, before I was confirmed, I was for a time in Reykjavík. There I wrote *Dawn*, a novel of six hundred thick pages, which still existed in tatters at home the last I knew of it.

Of the manuscript not one tatter remains, whether because his mother burnt it along with other old writings or because it was lost when he left Laxnes for good in 1928. It is noteworthy that Halldór took it upon himself as a thirteen-year-old to write a novel as a kind of showdown with one of the most renowned Icelandic novelists up to that time. Torfhildur might not have enjoyed much critical favour, but she had a significant readership and was the first Icelander to work as a professional writer. Decades later Halldór would become the second.

What sort of novel was *Dawn*? Its existence is corroborated in a short narrative in *When I Left Home*. There the novel is called *Daybreak* (the handwritten paper of the Youth Club of Mosfellsdalur was called *Dawnlight*) and is said to be nearly a thousand pages in length. The narrator recalls little of the book,

except that I tried to imitate the narrative style of Bjørnstjerne Bjørnsson. The characters I had my heart set on most were stately men and idealists, who praised rationalism, performed charitable works, walked in the paths of God . . . The optimism and joy of life in *Daybreak* had to be absolutely intoxicating; these two things were the mightiest powers I knew. Many great events occurred in the book, such as murder, catastrophes, house burnings, thievery, engagements, marriages and divorces. There were meditations – and attacks – on everything that I knew to exist.

The young writer most likely adopted a rationalistic stance for his moderately anti-clerical novel, since Torfhildur Hólm's book was about the victory of Christianity in Iceland. The most remarkable thing about this huge manuscript – if in fact it was so long and filled with events – is the way in which it reveals that Halldór had discovered his abilities as a writer. He had succeeded in spinning a story from within himself, and in his letter to Stefán Einarsson he says that the novel is more "genuine" than the books that came later, unspoilt by scholarly pedantry. The writing of *Dawn* was Halldór's first ambitious conflict with another writer, and the novel was the apex and conclusion of his youthful obsession with writing.

In fact one man had managed to look at this manuscript: Jakob Smári. The writer Guðmundur G. Hagalín, who was Halldór's good friend in the years that followed, bears witness to this in his autobiography. Hagalín tells of how, when he was eighteen, he paid a visit to Smári to ask the poet's opinion of his writing. Smári told him that a fifteen-year-old boy had come to him with a long novel; this would have been Halldór (although the age is wrong). Hagalín asks if the novel is any good:

> It is understandably not a piece of art, but in it several threads are woven together. The writer makes an attempt to give each person his own particular characteristics, and he presents ideas that bear witness to unusual flights of fancy and wonderfully complex issues.

During his first winter in Reykjavík Halldór did not spend much time socialising; for the most part he kept to himself, writing or practicing on the piano when he was not attending courses at the Technical College. He lived at Vegamótastígur 9 with some distant relatives, Davíð Jóhannsson and Guðrún Skaftadóttir. In the spring he returned to Laxnes to prepare for his confirmation, which he made in the church at Lágafell in May, 1916. But Halldór was not the same boy who had left the countryside the previous autumn. He cared little for his catechism and played the prince by reading Georg Brandes and Tolstoy, as well as by quoting from the great work by Ágúst H. Bjarnason, *A Conspectus of the History of the Human Spirit* (1905–15).

As Stefán Einarsson wrote in his biography:

> Halldór was not the only one of those young Icelandic confirmation candi-dates who went to the altar during those years with the catechism on their lips and the books of Á.H. Bjarnason in their minds; what that man gave to Icelandic youth through his writings represents a remarkable educational achievement, although they were not popular with all of the priests.

Bjarnason wrote his great work on the history of Western thought in Icelandic, a strong factor in its popularity and influence. He was no radical, but his works were written in the spirit of nineteenth-century rationalism and scepticism: they explained ideological movements within a narrative context without passing judgement from a Christian perspective. His book thus raised suspicions among many rural folk, although they affected young readers strongly.

Halldór was one of these young readers. That he had been a religious child is clear, but he had quickly lost interest in Bible stories and traditional family readings and started seeking other goals. He was "searching for higher values", as he put it later, and this search was as ingrained as his passion for writing. Halldór was never content with what was generally accepted; he had to find his own way, and he cultivated this attitude early on in his writing style. Above all, he wished to avoid using clichés that would fail to make an impression on his readers, even if they contained grains of truth. The rebellious yearning evident in his writing was at odds with the courteous and charming man, and this "discrepancy" would puzzle many of his political opponents later on.

Although Halldór enjoyed making a show of himself by quoting from writers who made at best only a middling impression on his Lutheran instructors, and had even threatened that he would not accept confirmation, he changed his tune uncomplainingly when he sensed his mother's disappointment: "She said that she could not believe it of me that when it came down to it I would disgrace my family."

Halldór's music studies benefited the congregation at Lágafell Church. When Guðjón was away, he had to find a substitute to lead the choir and play the organ. Halldór sometimes took over this task, most frequently during the year in which he was confirmed. He did, however, play down his musical accomplishments in an interview many years later:

> I saw quickly that the trick of playing the organ in church was simply to play
> slowly enough. If I sailed too quickly through the hymns the congregation
> would quite simply lose the melody . . . This was naturally not due to any sort
> of musical gift of mine . . .

When Halldór was growing up, books and newspapers specifically intended for children were only just beginning to be published in any significant way and teenagers simply did not exist; they were just small adults. Childhood did not last long at that time in Iceland. It is enough to look at Halldór's confirmation photographs to see the child playing the man. The same quality can be seen in his first work, when he tries to write like a middle-aged man. He does not truly indulge in "being himself" before *The Great Weaver from Kashmir* (1927), an extremely pretentious book.

On 19 March, 1916, a work by Halldór Guðjónsson appeared in print for the first time, not under his own name, but under his initials. The article, "Hot-Spring Trout and Hot-Spring Birds", was published in the daily newspaper *Morgunblaðið*, which had been in circulation for just over two years. The piece could almost have been written by an eighteenth-century naturalist. "H.G." strikes a pose and informs his readers about creatures that live in hot springs:

> Within the Landmanna highland pastures are so-called "baths". These are boiling hot springs, in a tiny hollow. Visitors to the Landmanna area often camp on the hills by the banks of these "baths", and it is convenient to get kettles of hot water from just in front of one's tent; these hot springs are said to contain many . . . fish. The hillmen once caught a fish there with a pole. It weighed approximately 1 pound. It was reddish in colour but pink where it was wounded. This fish must have been quite poisonous. They gave it to one of the dogs, and the dog fell down dead upon eating it.

The writer of the article suspects that readers might not believe his story and cites his sources in footnotes, naming *Book on Iceland* (1746) by the German Anderson, the eighteenth-century Icelandic poet and antiquarian Eggert Ólafsson and *Journal of the Icelandic Literary Society* (1887). What's more, an anonymous old woman is cited as a witness to the existence and behaviour of hot-spring birds. The concluding words of the article can hardly be doubted: "This phenomenon and many others in nature need to be studied further." It is difficult to see now what compelled Halldór to publish this article, except the basic urge to see something one writes in print. In any case the editors of *Morgunblaðið* seemed somewhat perplexed and introduced the article with the rare parenthetical statement that they had been asked to publish it.

The first step had been taken. That year Halldór Guðjónsson from Laxnes published several other articles in newspapers, under either a pseudonym or his own name. In the June issue of the magazine *Youth*, he published a letter about the children's paper *Sunshine*, which was then being printed as part of the second-most popular newspaper for Icelanders in North America, *Lögberg* (the *Tribune*). This article is thought, along with the letter ("Sunshine Children") printed in *Sunshine* in Canada on 15 June, 1916, to be the first material Halldór published under his own name. He had written to *Youth* "so that young people in Iceland could become somewhat acquainted with their little compatriots – the Icelandic youth in North America". His tone is not that of a child writing for children but that of someone who considers himself to be both experienced and educated. He says about *Sunshine*:

It is written mainly by children, for children. It is amusing to see their childish, innocent writing styles . . . It is clear . . . that these children are quite clever; they write in an orderly manner, although they are young.

The greeting to the "Sunshine Children", beginning with the words, "Good day to you, dear children", is also written in a fatherly tone remarkable for a fourteen-year-old boy. Halldór encourages the children to love their fatherland at the same time that he expresses his appreciation for the Icelandic sagas, mentioning that he had read them all by the time he was eleven. The article shows some spirit, especially when Halldór describes the arrival of spring:

When the snow melts from the mountainsides and the hollows, when ice and cold flee from the dells, when the sun inches its way higher and higher into the sky, when the nights start to shorten and the days to lengthen – although the heaths are still snowy and not an iota of spring warmth is reflected on the mountain peaks – when green needles start to spring up from the ground for the sheep to graze, when the ewes start to lamb, the lambs to play in the fields, the children to bring out their toys and build houses, when grown-ups start to put in order that which the winter has left disordered, when everything is on the upswing in Iceland, when everything seems to rise from its winter sleep, then it is spring.

That same autumn Halldór sent the "Sunshine Children" another greeting, in which he tells them how things are when autumn comes to Iceland, clearly with the previous epistle in mind:

When the wind and the rime draw nigh, when the sun inches its way back down from heaven each day, when the nights start to lengthen and the days to shorten, when the grass starts to fade, the tiny Icelandic birch forest to shed its leaves, when everything seems to be on the downswing in Iceland – then it is autumn.

Why was Halldór interested in this connection with children in Canada? One reason might have been the influence of his father's foster-brother, Daníel Halldórsson, who had moved to Canada in 1912 and who offered to support Halldór if his father wanted to send him to Canada. It is likely that such a journey had crossed Halldór's mind, since a large number of emigrations were still occurring at the start of the twentieth century.

*

June, 1916: there was something in the air of those bright, early summer days in the countryside: "The world [was] like a stage where everything [was] set up for an extravagant opera," as Halldór put it in *The Great Weaver from Kashmir*. And once again he appears to have experienced a revelation, which is described in *When I Left Home*:

> That night I did not come home. I continued eastwards to the mountain slopes where the birch grows and the sun first shines in the mornings, my soul one sea of joy and hymn of praise. The spring world and my youth, all was an angelic poem, I and nature one, eternity like harp-song in my heart. God, God! Bliss overwhelmed me . . . You are powerful and inexpressible, and I who am nothing but a breath of dust have received from you glorious gifts. I wish to perform great deeds and create with my hands unforgettable monuments to the glory of the one who granted me these gifts!

The perception of the divine was incredibly strong in this boy, despite the half-hearted way in which, several weeks earlier, he had been confirmed with the words of learned sceptics on his lips. The experience of another world, the world of beauty, was always a factor in Halldór's artistic creations.

That June Halldór published some poems for the first time. They appeared in *Morgunblaðið* on 13 June, under the heading "Poems"; the poet called himself Snær the Wise. The compositions in the elegiac style of the time consisted of two quatrains, one entitled "Ditty" and the other "Waiting by Angry Old Women"; a short piece called "Motto for Stories and Songs"; and a lyric called "Morning Songs of the Shepherd Boy". Snær the Wise – the clever, bright man ("snær" means "snow"): the name says something about Halldór self-image. And the talents of the fourteen-year-old poet are clearly displayed:

> Though love be blazing in the morning,
> Misfortune chills at the setting of the sun.
> Of hatred beware, dear friend of mine
> – now winter has come, though summer was here.
> The Spinners of Fate do you harm,
> You weep, and leave, you flee your land.

Halldór used the pseudonym Snær the Wise several times during the next few years, and his friends were quite familiar with the name. But he was not interested in promoting the poetry of the clever Snær. On the other hand, he did mention an article published under his own name in *Morgunblaðið* in the autumn of 1916, "An

Old Clock". Magister Sigurður Guðmundsson, one of Halldór's secondary-school teachers during the winter of 1917–18, had the piece in mind when he told the young man who had come to visit him for the first time:

> We have known about you since last year, when you walked up to Bragi's door, and, like an ancient Icelander, announced your name and whence you came, as well as what clock you own.

*

In the autumn of 1916, Halldór returned to Reykjavík, where he spent the next two years studying for the exams for his secondary-school diploma from the Reykjavík Lyceum, sitting them in the spring of 1918. He lived at Laugavegur 28 with one of his father's friends, Árni Einarsson, a merchant, and his family. Now he was staying in a respectable middle-class home with three rooms, good-quality furniture, paintings on the walls and a grand piano that he was sometimes allowed to play. And there was the merchant's daughter and her friends, all of a similar age, awakening premonitions of adventures to come.

The war in Europe was a distant rumbling to the young people in Reykjavík. What did get them to prick up their ears was the idea that Iceland was going to become a free and sovereign state. Little by little a kind of cultural stage was taking shape in Reykjavík. During the First World War the town became the headquarters for the publication of Icelandic books and journals, taking over from Copenhagen and Winnipeg. Respectable journals were transferred home and new ones founded; in 1917, eighteen journals were published in Iceland, a number that increased significantly during the 1920s. This development allowed greater breathing space for debate about the future of Iceland; nothing was off limits in the papers. At the same time a tiny group of academics was being formed. According to the 1910 census almost a thousand people were working in so-called "intellectual work"; of these most were teachers, but thirty-three were listed as journalists and writers, although none of them could precisely have been called professional writers of belles-lettres. A year later the University of Iceland was established, and thereafter the number of academics increased steadily.

Despite a temporary setback in the economy during the 1910s, a large percentage of young people were convinced that spring was in the air. Young men met at the youth and debating clubs of Reykjavík to discuss the future. Although the first telegram was sent from Iceland to the outer world in 1906, the country was still accustomed to ships bringing news and ideas from further south; the telegraph was for emergencies. In the debates held by young Icelanders during the war years, movements that people their own age on the Continent had abandoned years earlier sometimes found new life. Nordic Naturalism was most influential in the field of prose, while young poets wrote in a late Romantic style that was occasionally somewhat abstruse. The next poetic composition that Snær the Wise published was an excellent example of this misguidedness.

At this time Jakob Smári was the editor of a newspaper called the *Country* and supported a branch of the Independence Party. Icelandic political debates during the war often focused on complicated policy issues concerning the relationship with the Danish king and government, issues that are difficult to understand nowadays. It was in the *Country* that Snær the Wise published his next poem, on 13 April, 1917. It was written in honour of Kaiser Wilhelm of Germany and bore the title "On the Birthday of the Kaiser", although the Kaiser had turned fifty-eight several months earlier. The poem begins with the words: "Hail, Wilhelm the Bold!/ Stouthearted kinsman, brother and friend." In defence of the fourteen-year-old poet, it should be said that his wish is that the heroic fight waged by Wilhelm and his forces should end in brotherhood and peace. It is undeniably peculiar that Halldór should have published a poem in honour of the Kaiser in the same year that the historical event occurred that would shape his political thought later on – the Russian Revolution – and that his poem should be published in a paper founded in response to the clash of opinions concerning Icelandic special interests within the Danish government.

In 1917, Halldór became acquainted with a group of young men who shared his interests. He met Tómas Guðmundsson, who would become one of the greatest Icelandic poets. Tómas and Sigurður Ólafsson, later an engineer, lived together one house away from Halldór on Laugavegur. Tómas and Sigurður decided to fast-track their exam preparation by taking private lessons and finishing a two-year course in one winter. They advertised for a third man to share the cost of the lessons and received a number of replies. Tómas says: "Among the applicants was a certain young man, bright of appearance and slim, with thick, long blond hair, who introduced himself as Halldór Guðjónsson, a writer from Laxnes." The three became good friends. About their shared interests, Tómas said:

> At that time I was gripped by a relentless passion for poetry, whereas Halldór himself had already become a productive writer. I don't think it's too much to say that he came to town that autumn with almost an entire trunkful of original compositions: novels, poems, essays, and diaries. That winter he'd also sit most days writing, for longer or shorter periods of time, if I remember rightly; he was, in short, the greatest workhorse I've ever seen when it came to writing.

With Halldór's thoughts so firmly fixed on writing, it must have seemed particularly expedient to take private lessons for the secondary-school exams. One of the
teachers hired by the three companions was Magister Sigurður Guðmundsson,
later principal of the Akureyri Lyceum and one of the best-known Icelandic
schoolmasters. Among Halldór's other teachers that winter were Árni Sigurðsson
and Ingimar Jónsson, who both became clergymen. But Halldór was distracted
and did not attend lessons regularly, prompting his father to intervene. Guðjón
contacted Halldór Kolbeins, another future minister and later a good friend of
Halldór. Gísli Kolbeins, Halldór Kolbeins' son, said:

> Guðjón said that his son's laziness was causing him some concern. Halldór
> needed to be educated. He said that he'd arranged for him to study with
> others, but that Halldór didn't turn up for his lessons. He just forgot about
> them.

Despite making promises, the young writer also "forgot" to attend lessons with
his namesake, and he had Halldór Kolbeins' persistence to thank when he passed
his exams; Kolbeins would catch him out walking when he was supposed to be at
school and drag him to his lessons. Halldór himself described the situation:

> I was extraordinarily undisciplined when I first started studying with private
> tutors. I only went to the class when I felt like it, and otherwise wrote and
> composed poetry for the newspapers. I thought about everything except for
> scholarship, and was a worry to everyone.

He nonetheless earned his secondary-school diploma from the Reykjavík
Lyceum in the spring of 1918.

The main problem Halldór faced as a boy was the problem he wrestled with all
his life: how to find a balance between artistic creation and everyday living. Art
was always foremost to Halldór, but he needed a kind of equilibrium to be able to
work at it. In the next decade he found it difficult to achieve any sort of balance,
and the psychological stress he experienced because of this might be considered
the "growing pains" of the poet-to-be. He had trouble unifying his inner and outer
lives, finding for the latter the form within which the former could find fulfilment.
He often felt as if his inner life was suspended on the edge of a precipice; his
childhood bliss had dwindled, and revelations about a higher purpose thoroughly
disturbed him.

Sometimes Halldór tried to prove to himself and others that he was not having
difficulties with these sorts of things, that he was a responsible and upright young

man. A good example of this can be seen in the article "Diaries and Accounts", which was published in *Vísir* on 10 December, 1917. It begins with the words: "Young students, and all young people in general, should keep both diaries and accounts." It is as if a grown and slightly boring man is holding the pen here; he exhorts people to keep diaries because of how entertaining it can be to recall events from one's youth, memories that take on "an alluring and comforting aura of innocence", and he goes on to say that diaries can be particularly useful for older people writing their autobiographies. Account statements are no less important:

It is very useful for itinerant labourers, for example, to be able at each month's end to take account of their status and see to which side they lean. I am acquainted with many cases among my peers and even among older people in which their accounts have saved them from unnecessary waste. This can also help form useful habits in other areas and has various other beneficial effects.

It did not occur to Halldór to follow his own advice, as he admitted to a girl he knew at that time:

Never in my life has it crossed my mind to keep a diary . . . even less an account book. If I happen to come into possession of a króna I spend it immediately.

In his teenage years Halldór was in fact far from being the awkwardly responsible boy he pretended to be in his article. He gained good marks in his exams, but they meant the end of his career in terms of academic accreditation. He started at the Lyceum in 1918 and was placed in its fourth grade, but was frequently indisposed. He described this in a letter to Stefán Einarsson ten years later:

I have never lived through anything so miserable as my year in the fourth grade. I could not focus my mind on anything, never slept until it was nearly morning, had no appetite. Once I was blind for two hours! . . . closer to death than life from mental anguish, *Weltschmerz*, hypochondria, angina and insomnia and I was constantly thinking that I would die or lose my mind!

He was plagued by the disquietude that grips creative people when they feel they are wasting their time, and it should not come as a surprise that he dropped out of school early in 1919.

The Red Booklet, a manuscript housed in the National Library of Iceland and containing the first draft of the book that later became *When I Left Home* and, later

still, *The Great Weaver from Kashmir*, confirms this anguish. It is not autobiographical in a strict sense, but bears witness to its author's hesitancy and soul-searching,
as Halldór pointed out to Stefán Einarsson. Morbidity often gripped Halldór
during the years following his confirmation, and he spent many sleepless nights
brooding over the futility of everything, sometimes so intensely that he thought he
was going mad. School did not save him. He writes in *The Red Booklet*:

> My nights that winter were what I would call hellish. And then my room-mate
> would wake me up for school . . . I was tired and stiff after my insomniac
> night, had studied nothing, and because of this felt sick about everything
> having to do with school.

He often got himself a doctor's note at such times.

Not all of his days were like this, however, and that year marked a turnabout for
Halldór; his resolution to become a writer became fixed in his mind, and his interest
in others' poetry, his friends and his surroundings increased. He continued to publish while he studied for his exams, and his first short stories appeared in the journal
Animal Rights. The very first, "Wages", was published in two parts, in the autumn of
1917 and at the start of 1918; the second, "Zeus", was published in the autumn
of 1918. Both appeared under the pseudonym Snær the Wise. The animal rights
movement was popular at the time. Tryggvi Gunnarsson, the founder of the SPCA
in Iceland, wrote about animal rights in the *Almanac of the Patriots' Society* in 1904;
any encouragement to Icelandic farmers to treat horses and dogs properly was
useful at the time. "Wages" deals with the shameful lot of horses and "Zeus" with
the fate of dogs; both stories are quite sad. The writer's conclusion in "Wages" is
clear: "Animal rights have a long way to go in this country."

"Zeus", on the whole a better story, is the first draft of another story, "The
Poet and Zeus", that Halldór published several years later in *Berlingske Tidende* and
again in Icelandic in the collection *Several Stories* (1923); it was finally used as the
basis for a film script called *Kari Karan* in 1928. The first version of the story tells
of a young philosopher who owns a dog but betrays it for a woman. The dog
wanders far and wide and is treated poorly everywhere it goes, but the woman
betrays the philosopher, who finally runs across the dog again, frozen to death. A
strong sense of sympathy for the powerless, and an antipathy toward betrayal,
underline both stories.

Although Snær the Wise published poetry, it is clear that Halldór was more
inclined towards writing stories. During his youth there was little in the way of a
novelistic tradition in Iceland. *Boy and Girl* by Jón Thoroddsen, which may be said

to be the debut of the Icelandic novel, had been published in 1850, but the novel did not come into its own until the last quarter of the nineteenth century, and then under the influence of naturalism and Georg Brandes. The short story was more common and well past the nineteenth century poetry commanded more respect than the writing of prose fiction; this was still apparent in the works of Halldór's peers. A pioneer among Icelandic novelists was Torfhildur Hólm, and at the time when Halldór published his animal-rights stories, two novelists (both realists) were already quite popular with Icelandic readers: Jón Trausti and Einar H. Kvaran. Jón Trausti was the pen name of the printer Guðmundur Magnússon. His novel *Halla* (1906) marked a turning point: a romance, it gave at the same time a broader description of everyday life than had ever appeared in prose. Jón Trausti did not have any formal education, and in fact had been raised in the most wretched poverty, but he was intimately acquainted with the people around him, and *Halla* was the first of a great series of novels focusing on Icelandic rural life. This fictional world was, however, foreign to Halldór. In 1918, when Halldór was struggling to complete what became his first published novel, Jón Trausti published his final one, *Old Bessi*, a conservative work that had no appeal whatsoever for the young writer.

It was a different case with Einar H. Kvaran. Einar was influenced by radical Brandesism, but later professed milder ideals of Christian charity and forgiveness; early in the twentieth century he became captivated by the latest fashionable movement, spiritualism, devoting himself to it for the rest of his life. With *Higher Power* (1908), he published the first true novel of Reykjavík, later writing more novels, and plays and essays. Halldór wrote his first book review about Einar Kvaran and spoke warmly of him later. He respected Einar's clear style, his use of everyday language and avoidance of archaicisms, his desire to improve social conditions through his writing, and, as Halldór expressed it in an essay written on the occasion of Einar's death in 1938, the way in which he allowed "himself to choose his protagonists from among the wretched and the downcast".

To begin with Halldór was most heavily influenced by the Scandinavian authors who were popular in Iceland at the start of the twentieth century. In his memoir *The Saga of the Seven Masters* (1978) he relates how in the spring of 1919 he read Norwegian writers such as Henrik Ibsen, Bjørnstjerne Bjørnson, Jonas Lie and Alexander Kielland, all of whom had only recently died. They belonged to a different age from Halldór, and later he seemed both ashamed of their influence and reluctant to discuss novels about Scandinavian rural life.

Other Norwegian writers that Halldór read included Sigbjørn Obstfelder, whose works were introduced to him by Guðmundur Hagalín in the winter of 1918–19; their influence can be seen in *The Red Booklet*, as can that of books by the writer with whom Halldór would share a love–hate relationship for the next several decades, Knut Hamsun. The works of these Scandinavian authors laid the ground-work for the novel that Halldór wrote during his year at secondary school, and which became his first and only contribution to pastoral literature, *Child of Nature* (1919). When his style started to develop independently, it was in opposition to such literature. Although he had grown up in the countryside and read books about the countryside, he divorced himself completely from both. He did not wish to be considered a Scandinavian writer, and even in his old age he turned up his nose if he was called a poet of the countryside.

There were advantages to the fact that the novel, the literary form of bourgeois society, was so undeveloped in Iceland when Halldór was taking his first steps as a writer. In an interview with Ólafur Ragnarsson seventy years later, he observed: "At that time nothing had been done; young writers arrived at a nearly unwritten world."

*

Despite the peace accords in Europe and the granting of sovereignty to Iceland, the autumn of 1918 was a sad one. A deadly influenza epidemic ravaged the country, beginning in late October. Almost five hundred people died from this flu, half of them in Reykjavík (and among them the poet Jón Trausti). It was a huge loss of life for such a close-knit society. Halldór, who contracted the flu along with his room-mate, Sigurður Einarsson, described the situation in his memoir:

> Friends of ours who were not susceptible to the flu came to visit and said that people in town were dying like flies and were being laid out two by two in the church's makeshift morgue, where it was possible to see the corpses through the windows; besides this every meeting place was filling up with bodies, some in trunks, some under sheets.

An undated message from Halldór to his parents, written around the time that he was finally able to rise from his sickbed, says:

> I just wanted to let you know that I am still the best of a bad lot today from the influenza. I was quite bad yesterday, but the fever had gone down greatly this morning. Everyone is in bed: the shops and bakeries, schools and dance halls are closed. The printers and papers have stopped publishing.

Just before this, the room-mates at Laugavegur 28 had, like other Icelanders, witnessed a great natural disaster, when the Katla volcano erupted violently on 12 October, covering almost the entire country with an ashy cloud. The cloud did nothing to diminish the young writer's intimations of Doomsday, and, according to *The Red Booklet*, he tried one night to wake his room-mate and talk to him about this: "'Don't you think it's terrifying to see the earth burning?' 'Oh, we'll let it burn!' he answered as he lay down again. 'We probably can't put the fire out anyway!'"

When Iceland was declared a sovereign state within the Danish kingdom on 1 December, 1918, the news was received rather dully by the residents of Reykjavík. Halldór writes of the formal ceremony held that day in *The Saga of the Seven Masters*:

> It took place in the bitter cold of late autumn; I remember the mud and slip-pery ice under the sky's low clouds. In this bleak weather everyone who wasn't dead gathered together to celebrate our sovereignty at Bakkarabrekka and Lækjargata and to have a look at the Ministry Building. A brass band played. A Danish officer parading a little group of sailors marched up carrying an Icelandic flag and raised it over our Ministry Building, to symbolize that the Danes were hereby handing over to us Icelanders this cursed land; he then saluted and marched to his ship with his sailors.

Halldór's description, written sixty years after the event, is an example of how he liked to satirize all things ceremonious – and to write ceremoniously about things that other people found banal. His description of the weather does not agree at all with contemporary accounts. The daily newspaper *Fréttir* gave this account of the ceremony:

> Yesterday the town was rollicking. People cast off the plague-nightmare and joyfully shook the two hands that the day extended to them. The weather was most beautiful, perfectly clear and dry. The sun shed its rays over the town shortly before the ceremony was to begin.

The speeches, the band music, the beautiful uniforms and the flag-bearing are described, and the article concluded solemnly: "The ceremony was perfect. Everyone present participated wholeheartedly and celebrated Iceland's newly received sovereignty."

Halldór made some other good friends in 1918, including Sigurður Einarsson, who became his room-mate the following winter. Sigurður, born in 1898, was four years older than Halldór and had a strong influence on him, as indicated in *The Saga of the Seven Masters*. It was primarily Sigurður's eloquence, in both poetry and prose, that affected Halldór, along with his vigorous imagination, his aristocratic bearing and his confidence. Halldór viewed Sigurður as a "fabulist, whom I shrink from calling a fantastic liar". Sigurður could not do anything without it ending up as an extraordinary adventure, and poetry poured out of him all day, every day. In the manuscript of *When I Left Home*, the protagonist of *The Great Weaver from Kashmir*, Steinn Elliði, appears, and there he resembles Sigurður Einarsson to some degree:

> His speech shimmered; ideas and metaphors thrust themselves forth from all directions like strange birds, seven swords in the air; his voice dulcet and measured, puns tripped from his lips like young doves, power blossomed in his eyes, freedom laughed in his movements.

In the 1940s Sigurður would become one of the first and most popular Icelandic radio announcers and, according to Halldór, put his talents to excellent use, always sounding like a man of experience when delivering news of brilliant discoveries in the sciences and arts. One does not have to look far to see bits of Sigurður's personality in many of Halldór's characters, from Garðar Hólm to Godman Sýngmann.

The Reykjavík Lyceum was the only such school in Iceland at that time, and thus the student body was comprised of people from different backgrounds and varying ages. An interest in poetry brought many of Halldór's fourth-grade classmates together, and early in the autumn of 1918, Halldór, Sigurður Einarsson, Tómas Guðmundsson and others founded the poetry club Milky Way, which held just one meeting. At this meeting Halldór read an elf-ballad he had written. A long poem from *Child of Nature*, it is without question the best poem he had written up till then; it resembles folk poetry, and is sincere and unpretentious. This was, however, not the style Halldór adopted for all of his poetry that autumn. On 31 October he published under his own name, on the front page of the daily newspaper *Fréttir*, a poem called "The Sea Wave". This poem is undeniably morose, with lines such as "The booming of the waves/ gnawed at the roots of my heart," and also displays Halldór's penchant for archaic language. Halldór said that the editors revised this poem, but he was extremely proud of seeing his poetry in print, and in *The Red Booklet* he writes of the happiness he would feel when this happened:

> One day a poem that I wrote was printed on the front page of one of the Reykjavík newspapers, and was criticized fairly by several intelligent people with whom I spoke.

Those were the days when newspapers in Iceland printed poetry on their front pages. *Fréttir* was short-lived; it had been founded the previous spring for a specific purpose, "to work tirelessly to make it known to all the peoples of the world that Iceland is a sovereign state". The paper's editor was a poet, Guðmundur Guðmundsson, known as the "School Poet", and that autumn Guðmundur Hagalín, Halldór's friend, had been appointed assistant editor. Halldór's poem took up the central column of the front page; the day before, a love poem by his friend Sigurður Einarsson, "Smile", had taken up the entire front page, leaving room only for the paper's name and an advertisement for Politicos cigars and Embassy cigarettes.

Other members of Halldór's class at the Lyceum included, besides Sigurður Einarsson and Tómas Guðmundsson, Richard Beck, who became a professor of literature in America, and Sveinbjörn Sigurjónsson, later school principal and the brother of Ísleifur from Copenhagen, who would go on to play a part in Halldór's life. The Lyceum's fifth grade included Guðmundur G. Hagalín and Jóhann Jónsson, and in the sixth grade was Davíð Stefánsson, who won the hearts and minds of young Icelanders with his book of poetry, *Black Feathers* (1919).

Davíð was seven years older than Halldór, and they did not get to know each other that winter. Jóhann Jónsson later became one of Halldór's closest friends. In his 1929 letter to Stefán Einarsson, he wrote:

I did not spend much time with poets during my secondary-school years – I had too much respect for them to push myself to approach them. Tómas Guðmundsson and I, however, were good friends. He had great poetic fancies and later published a book of poetry.

Tómas was a country boy like Halldór. Halldór later said of him: "Tómas and I were the same vintage of unnamed wine. We read each other's poetry and understood it. We were, I hope, like wine that has just started to ferment."

Jóhann Jónsson was introverted, lame from tuberculosis, and reflected the image of a late Romantic poet so well that his friends called him Lord Byron. Guðmundur Hagalín also wrote poetry during those years, but was a happy and playful storyteller by nature, with a background in the fishing culture of the Westfjords. In 1952 Peter Hallberg was assembling a book about Halldór's youthful writing and sent him a list of questions in which he asked whether it was true that Halldór had sometimes been called Halldór the Singer during those years. Halldór answered:

I have no knowledge of ever having been called a "Singer". But because I knew a little bit about music, I probably attracted some attention on my

travels in the countryside – I was able to play and sing for audiences in places
where such things were quite out of the ordinary . . .

Hagalín describes in his memoirs how Halldór sometimes sat at the pedal organ
in the rooms that they shared with Sigurður Einarsson and got the group to sing
if he thought their conversation had run its course, although none of them was any
good at singing except Jóhann. Hagalín adds this description of Halldór, the
youngest boy in the group:

> Halldór was especially courteous and quiet, sat for long periods and listened,
> but seemed sometimes to be distracted, with a dreamy expression as if he was
> looking at something in the distance. Anything coarse or vulgar was clearly
> not to his liking. He was not an eloquent speaker, he stammered and his voice
> was peculiar, but he was always cheerful and pleasant if the conversation
> turned to him. He was unjudgemental and always tried to add something
> positive, always tried to find a peaceful settlement when the debate got too
> heated, which did not happen often among these friends.

Halldór seems to have been something of an outsider, just as he had been in the
countryside. These men could perhaps be called his acquaintances rather than his
friends, with the exception of Tómas. Halldór was shy in their company and kept
his dreams to himself. All of them became prodigious writers, and they had
different points of view about the Cold War. Seldom have the effects of the Cold
War on Iceland been better described than when Halldór wrote in a 1983 epitaph
for Tómas Guðmundsson that they had "lived in an atmosphere in which best
friends meet each other as strangers".

During the winter of 1918–19, the paths of the poets in the fourth and fifth
grades led to the Future, the Debating Club of the Scholarly Department of the
Reykjavík Lyceum. Club members held meetings, read for each other, judged each
other's poetry and published their works in an occasional journal, *Skinfaxi*. In that
winter's first issue Halldór published the short story "Ingólfur".

The narrator describes his youthful friend, Ingólfur, with whom he shares a
passion for poetry. Ingólfur has blue eyes that can penetrate all dreamlands, and
"fairer masculine locks" than the narrator has ever seen – the boys' world of
Halldór's secondary-school years was not free from sexual ambiguity. Ingólfur's
characteristics are derived from Halldór himself: "I never saw him doing anything
but playing the piano and messing around with poetry – I never saw him look at
a school book." Ingólfur, however, falls for a girl called Helga. She goes to America,
and Ingólfur goes after her but does not find her, because her father, a rich

merchant, will not hear of it. The narrator says nothing more of Ingólfur, except when he imagines him overseas:

It may be that he is searching for Helga – searching for her across the breadth of America, searching for her in the blind despair of love. It may also be that he is locked in some asylum, or that he is lying somewhere, unknown to anyone, beneath an indifferent gravestone in an American churchyard – dead along with his hopes and dreams.

The story, dated 15 September, 1918, is said to be from the unpublished collection, *Portraits*. It is related to the story about the philosopher and the dog Zeus – both Ingólfur and the philosopher become lost in their pursuit of a girl. In the same issue of *Skinfaxi* there is a story called "The Maggot", described as the first chapter of *Child of Nature* by Snær the Wise, and the minutes for the meeting of the Future reveal that Snær the Wise is Halldór Guðjónsson. *Child of Nature* is the work that mattered most to Halldór from the summer of 1918 to the spring of 1919.

*

Child of Nature was Halldór's response to the revelation he had when he was seven years old that he would die when he was seventeen. In his memoirs he says that the revelation had prompted him to finish the novel by the spring of 1919. Very likely he felt that the huge *Dawn* was unsalvageable, and that if he wanted to prove himself he would have to write a better book. *Child of Nature* was the first manuscript Halldór brought to a publisher, the bookseller Arinbjörn Sveinbjarnarson. Iceland's book business resembled that of eighteenth-century Europe, since those who published books were most often also booksellers or bookbinders. Arinbjörn would not take a risk on Halldór's book, so he did what many other Icelandic writers did well into the twentieth century: he took his manuscript to a printer. The managers of the Society Print Shop, the brothers Steindór and Þorleifur Gunnarsson, agreed to fit the job in when they got the chance, as long as Halldór's father was responsible for the cost. By the time the book was finally ready for printing, Halldór had gone overseas and Guðjón had died, and Sigríður Halldórsdóttir was left with the printers' bill, along with other debts that Halldór had accumulated.

Nearly two hundred pages long, it was printed in a small, well-crafted volume; its author calls himself Halldór from Laxnes. In the preface to the second edition Halldór says that the novel was mostly composed during the summer of 1918, when he was sixteen and going around the town dressed "according to the fashion of a

precocious lad fascinated by the facial portraits of most of the geniuses from the
previous century shown in the *World History* and the *Encyclopaedia*".

He goes on to say:

> The book is at the same time the précis, the conclusion and sum of all that
> I wrote later; all my later books were simple expositions of the conclusions
> that I had come to in *Child of Nature*.

A romance that bears the marks of the Scandinavian pastoral literature Halldór
read while growing up, the novel tells the story of Randver and Hulda. Randver is
a young man who has travelled out into the wide world and returned home richer
for his experiences; in him there is something of Steinn Elliði or Arnaldur. Hulda
is a child of nature, independent and revolutionary, and her qualities are present
in both Diljá (in *The Great Weaver from Kashmir*) and Salka Valka (in the novel of the
same name, 1931–2). Randver wants to become a responsible, respectable farmer,
and for Hulda to become his wife, but when she hears this she shouts: "'Never!
With what you have said tonight, you have spread cow dung on the hopelands of
the child of nature, and covered her dreamlands with ice! Never!'" For a time the
prospect of love seems dim, but finally they do come together, and on Randver's
terms, farming and avoiding trite indulgence and foreign vanity. Hulda has come
to understand that "Randver had wished to honour her. He had pointed her toward
the highest goal of life: joy in the toils of the day." The concept of joy in the toil
of the day comes up again and again in Halldór's novels

Two reviews of the novel proved to be both kind and prophetic. On 6
November, 1919, the *People's Paper* published a review saying that a reader should,
despite the work's shortcomings, "admire the dedication and daring of the young-
ster; and I think that we can expect the best from him when he matures in age and
wisdom". It concludes with these words: "And who knows, Halldór from Laxnes
might turn out to be the promised child of the Icelandic people." On 10
November, 1919, *Morgunblaðið* published a review by the journalist and writer Jón
Björnsson, which did not beat around the bush:

> This is the story of a child of nature by a childishly young man. The story is
> also quite childish. And art does not put up with childishness. It requires
> experience and knowledge. It demands a secure grip. It condemns groping.
> It is never content with bloodless sacrifices. But this is a bloodless and
> marrowless book.

Björnsson nonetheless gave the seventeen-year-old author some hope:

"And yet . . . this young man might perhaps write something of more artistic value."

Halldór had gone to Copenhagen and did not see the reviews until later, but Björnsson's review stung him and he never forgot it, any more than he did any other negative review – he was always sensitive when it came to reviews. It must have allayed his distress, however, when, the following year, Jakob Smári – who always thought highly of Halldór – wrote a review for the journal *Skírnir* in which he said that here was a writer who would likely "become quite accomplished after maturing and experiencing more of life". No watershed was reached when *Child of Nature* was published, and it did not sell very well either; the remaining stock passed from one speculator to another, until Halldór received a final statement in 1944, the year Iceland became a republic.

A Love Story was the novel's subtitle. Was Halldór so familiar with love that he could write a novel about it at sixteen? Not if one accepts his statement in the preface to the second edition that the subtitle must have been based on a misunderstanding "to lure people to the book – like when Eiríkur the Red christened the glacier Greenland". But in fact he had added the subtitle himself, and had started to show interest in girls. In a letter to his friend Einar Ólafur Sveinsson from the summer of 1924 he wrote:

> I have never been more proud in my life as I was six years ago when I kissed a young woman for the first time. This was a young and rosy girl living on a farm here . . . She was wearing a green dress.

Country girls seemed to like Halldór. His playmate, Þorsteinn Magnússon, said in an interview much later:

> I have heard that a young girl at Skeggjastaðir was in some ways the model for "the fair maiden" in *Iceland's Bell* [1943–6], and I'm not sure that's not correct. I remember the girl. Her name was Fríða. Beautiful girl. The girls liked Halldór.

Skeggjastaðir is on the northern side of the hill visible from Laxnes, suggesting that Fríða Einarsdóttir was the first girl Halldór kissed. There is also this amusing testimony from Guðmundur Hagalín, who went with Halldór to Laxnes early in the summer of 1919 and stayed with him for a while. On a hike up on to the heath,

> . . . Halldór entrusted me, in a low and mysterious voice, with the news that just ahead lay the path to a blonde-haired maiden, who had the fairest blue

eyes of any woman, white skin, and red, rosy cheeks, innocent like the first
flower of spring on earth and so beautiful and delicate in her blossoming
youth that one might not touch her – only thoughts, pure and clear like unsul-
lied springwater could play around her – even from an immense distance.
That he considered going to meet her – no chance. He only wanted to go as
far north as the heath, so that he could see her farm.

"Perhaps then I will sense the aura of the smoky vestiges of the ling that
she has picked with her slender white fingers."

During the years leading up to his trip to Denmark in 1919, however, Halldór's
romantic adventures most likely occurred in the same place as so much else did:
inside his head. Corresponding later with Peter Hallberg about this time, he says
that his phobias and fancies were the same as other boys'; what distinguished him
was that he had put them down on paper. But Halldór *was* different: he had an
intense internal disquietude and an unquenchable need to express it. He spent time
with men who were significantly older than him, and he did not develop personally as quickly as his writing did. Love must have been a matter for contemplation
long before it became a practical problem. This mismatch continues: throughout
the 1920s, as Halldór slowly gained more experience in love, he was enormously
preoccupied with "woman" as a writer's topic, whether he turned to Strindberg,
Weininger or Freud. It was thus not surprising how well he was able to describe
the contradictions of love later on. In his memoirs there is only one little love
story from these years. Halldór is walking a young girl home from Laugavegur,
and it is raining:

We could not say anything, nor could we disentwine our hands in the rain. I
am certain that our combined heart was beating quite strongly. The rain came
down on our warm, entwined fingers. But soon it had stopped.

Halldór lost interest in *Child of Nature* as soon as he finished it, and immediately started his next book. In March, 1919, he gave up on school entirely and
moved back to Vegamótastígur 9. Apart from his walks into town and his meetings with friends, he was writing all the time. On 10 May, 1919, an advertisement
appeared in *Morgunblaðið* that read: *"Halldór Guðjónsson from Laxnes* will read a
chapter from his new, unpublished novel, Saturday evening the 10th of this month,
9 p.m. . . ." Tickets could be bought for 1.50 krónur at the Ísafold bookshop or on
the door. "A smattering of people came, but I certainly gained little or nothing
from it," wrote Halldór in a letter to Hallberg, later on indicating that he had
thrown out the novel he had read from.

The reading gained him both some publicity and some kind reviews, although he described the experience as nightmarish in his memoirs. But the facts remain: a boy of seventeen advertised a reading in Reykjavík on a Saturday evening and charged an admission fee. No matter how reserved he was during his adolescent years, how tormented his soul was or how insecure he was in the company of other poets, two characteristics are evident here that became the key factors in his breaking free from his fear of the world into world literature: self-confidence and ambition.

A month later Halldór became involved in publishing a newspaper. He and Tómas Guðmundsson decided to publish a humorous periodical in Reykjavík, which after some deliberation they named *Láki*. Neither of them was old enough to accept responsibility for its printing, so they asked one of Halldór's childhood teachers, Pétur Jakobsson, to become the official editor. When the four-page periodical was published, the only name that appeared in it was Pétur's. The articles were published under pseudonyms.

The paper introduces itself like a spring blossom:

Láki is the many-sided man of spring. He lets his light shine for the first time one day in June, when springtime is in full bloom, precisely when the sorrels have sprung up and the angelica is green and the spring rains bellow with tremendous might, and form dark, muddy rivers in the gutters, which break out over all the banks – exactly like the thoughts of the youth.

In the second issue Icelanders are said to have in a thousand years

become fair of form and fearless under the nurture of severe frosts and savagery – phlegmatic and frugal under the protection of stupidity and narrow-mindedness, and niggardliness and scrimpiness have prevented them from being led astray in the whirlpool of life.

Although Tómas and Halldór put their hearts into their project, they lost interest quickly: the second issue of *Láki* was printed, but never circulated.

That summer Halldór reached a turning point: Reykjavík had nothing more to offer, and the impatience that was driving him away can be seen in *Láki*. A few days after his novel reading he wrote to his mother in Laxnes:

I want very much to travel across the sea. It is necessary for a man like me to become acquainted with life in as many forms as possible. You think perhaps that I am not sufficiently mature . . . but this is certainly a misunderstanding. I am more mature than many who are twenty or older . . .

One thing that helped to expand Halldór's horizons was his acquaintanceship with Erlendur Guðmundsson and the boarding house called Unuhús (literally, Una's House). Halldór went there for the first time in the spring of 1919, in the company of Guðmundur Hagalín, and Unuhús would become his refuge in the 1920s. Halldór's writings about Erlendur and Unuhús have a mythological aura: Erlendur became for him something of a saviour, as well as the model for one of his first "Taoist" characters, the organist in *Atom Station* (1948). Halldór never wrote a plain word about Erlendur, according to an agreement they made, until after Erlendur's death. In the manuscript of Stefán Einarsson's biography, Halldór crossed out Erlendur's name and wrote in the margin: "Erlendur does not want to be written about."

Unuhús was a unique refuge for artists and writers, along with people who had nowhere else to go, as it had been since the turn of the century. In this red house at Garðarstræti 4, Erlendur's mother, Una Gísladóttir, rented out rooms and ran a cafeteria. She offered her services at a lower price than anyone else did, and therefore many people who had little money looked to her; it would be the greatest of understatements to say that mother and son did these individuals a good turn. The folk who gathered there must have seemed a "ragtag lot", to quote from Pétur Pétursson's interview with María Guðjónsdóttir, who as a young girl helped Una out.

That spring Halldór met Þórbergur for the first time. Þórbergur recalled this meeting in an article commemorating Halldór's fiftieth birthday in which he described their lives "since we met first in Unuhús, the hospital of the soul, where the paths of all Icelandic geniuses led for half a century". The paths of these masters of narrative fiction were to cross frequently.

At Unuhús Halldór became acquainted with the idealistic currents of the time. People there preached spiritualism and theosophy, embraced the so-called "New Theology" and Rudolf Steiner's theories and read up on yoga in the *Bhagavadgita*. Some, like Þórbergur, tried to bring together all of these things. Around this time Halldór first heard, from Erlendur, about the Tao-te-ching, or The Book of the Way and its Power, by Lao-Tzu. In *The Red Booklet* one of the narrator's friends resembles Erlendur, and Halldór refers to the Tao for the first time:

I don't recall having known any man who was as chaste and pure and rich with the Tao. He listened to every word that was said and never turned a deaf ear to anything; he understood everything, like a sage.

When Halldór went to Unuhús for the first time, it was to visit Stefán from

Hvítadalur, the poet who had written *Songs of the Traveller*, one of the most talked-about books of poetry published during Iceland's "sovereign year". Stefán had wandered everywhere despite having suffered from tuberculosis. Halldór thought him somewhat cold and tormented at first:

> But when he started talking, in a hoarse whisper, his eyes became softer; and when he laughed at us with his hoarse laughter a bright and gentle gleam shone forth from his blue eyes, like an unexpected gift.

It fell to Stefán to wrench Icelandic poetry free from the melancholia of the war years with his sincere, plaintive, unaffected verse. It was good for Halldór to meet such a man, and he immediately wrote to his mother: "Stefán is doubtless one of the greatest poets the Icelanders have; he himself is so interesting and peculiar, and so mysterious, that a man could never grow tired of him."

This sums up precisely Halldór's problem during the spring and summer of 1919. He had grown tired of the company he had been keeping in Reykjavík, needed something different against which to measure himself and his will to work as a writer. The morbid thoughts of his youthful years were still strong, and the search for a "higher value" was beginning to impel him, as it would for the next decade or so. *The Red Booklet* is a good indicator of this. The protagonist has just left secondary school, publishes poetry in the newspapers and is tormented by depression, fear and disquietude:

> I was surrounded exclusively by half-educated people, young like myself, people who studied and planned to become leaders of the people and flag-bearers of the nation if they could. One could have said a lot of good things about them – previously I saw them only in the best light. I had believed in many of these companions of mine as demigods, but now my vision of them had suddenly darkened; their heedless behaviour brought antipathy into my heart, yes, almost disgust.
>
> They sit most hours of the day in cafés, their conversations are nothing but meaningless noise, they do not walk gently through the doors of joy, but shout with laughter and rage and slam their fists on the table. For hours on end they discuss with undivided attention the glories of their last drinking binges.

The country boy who had experienced a revelation and planned to become a writer and improve the world with his books could not remain content with this company for much longer. Reykjavík was merely a sketch of a modern society.

Everyone knew one other, and business was conducted according to family relationships and proximity. Industrialization had made little progress. In 1919 the Gutenberg print shop was the largest manufacturing enterprise in Reykjavík, with forty workers; society, on the whole still based on agriculture, was uniform and isolated. And no Icelandic writer could make a living from his books.

*

Then came a shock that would further erode Halldór's relationship with his homeland – his father died. Guðjón contracted pneumonia and died on 19 June, 1919. Halldór was at Vegamótastígur the week before, busy with *Láki* and the proof-reading of *Child of Nature*. He received the news in a letter from his mother delivered by someone from his district.

In October Halldór wrote his mother a long letter from Copenhagen, in which he describes how much he loved his father:

> I think so exceedingly much about blessed father, and I feel that now, after his death, I know best what a great and good man he was, and how much I have him to thank, because it was always he who encouraged me and always awakened in me beautiful and noble thoughts.

He also explains that he had not cried when his father had died because he had known that it was just the body that had gone; his beloved father's memory would live on. He had not been too concerned that people might think that he did not care. Quite the contrary: he had not wanted to discuss the loss with his mother because he had no desire to upset her further.

Like many of the letters Halldór sent his mother later on, this one contains food for thought. It is likely that he never spoke to her in the same way that he wrote to her. Those who knew Sigríður in her later years agree that she was loving but reticent and terse, and Halldór himself says that she had been averse to sentimentality. She and his father had scarcely talked about their feelings.

But in his letters to his mother Halldór could be genial, frank and sincere. He had become a man of written expression; it was in writing that he felt most comfortable, and writing opened the window to his inner life. In his manner he was most often disciplined and impeccably courteous – but in his writing he could be as frank, brusque and passionate as he wished to be. Distance formed the foundation for his sincerity.

From Halldór's first trip abroad and the next quarter-century an enormous quantity of letters remains in which he frequently expresses his thoughts in unpretentious terms and sketches his feelings in bold strokes when the time is right.

These letters are unique in that they display his tormented psychological state. Long before he started to cloak his life in his fiction, he started to turn his life into a story.

In the aforementioned letter to his mother he tells about the last meeting that he had with his father:

It was the Monday after Whit Sunday. My book was being printed, and I was supposed to read the first proofs the next day. The weather was gorgeous, sunshine and spring warmth, with light showers every now and then. Around midday I started thinking that it might be fun to run up to Lágafell, where a communion service was to take place. I got three of my friends, Hagalín being one of them, and we drove up and had quite a good time, as you might imagine. We arrived at the church in the middle of the sermon and stood at the back for the remainder of the service. I looked around for Father, and although I did not see him I reckoned that he was probably there, and that I would find him afterwards. And then at the end he came to us as we stood there at the door, on either side of the loft stairs. He greeted us as easily and gladly as ever . . . [H]e . . . went in with us and gave us all coffee and cakes and sat with us and talked with us so amiably and kindly, as was his way. And then he left, because there was a congregational meeting . . . that he had to attend, and he asked me to come there and say goodbye before I left.

I went back into the church, and the farmers were all sitting there, he in an innermost pew. We didn't have the faintest idea then that seventeen days later his body would be dead, carried out of the church and laid down in the ground. I asked whether he wanted to talk to me a bit outside the church doors and we walked there. I asked whether he could help me pay for the car-trip, and he gave me 10 krónur. So I thanked him happily and said goodbye and bade him say hello to everyone at home. He extended his hand to me in a friendly way, which I never have forgotten, and said: "Bless you now, dear Dóri."

We said farewell in the church porch and I never saw him again.

Don't you think that this is beautiful, Mother? I have thought about this so much ever since.

This meeting is also described in *The Saga of the Seven Masters*, but in a different way. According to the book, Halldór had gone to ask his father for financial help with *Child of Nature* and Láki. "He smiled . . . and spoke only these words . . . and nothing more: 'You will be looked after, dear Dóri.'" In between these two versions are sixty years, and sixty books.

*

On Thursday, 31 July, 1919, Halldór Guðjónsson from Laxnes boarded the *Iceland*, a United Danish Steamship Company ship, for Copenhagen. His mother had sold some property to pay for his journey. One of the first things Halldór did when he arrived in the big city was to have a business card printed, taping one to the door of the house where he was staying:

HALLDÓR FROM LAXNES

POËTA

TWO

The Monocle and the Cross

Travel Years
1919–1929

> You are Iceland's brightest hero. You have done many great
> things, but your own life is probably the most remarkable
> novel of all.
>
> *Ísleifur Sigurjónsson,*
> *in conversation with Halldór Laxness*

WHAT A CHANGE FOR A COUNTRY BOY FROM ICELAND TO COME TO
Copenhagen, "where the screeching of cart wheels and the smoke of the factories
blinds the eyes and ears", as Ísleifur Sigurjónsson put it. In our time of constant
travel, it is impossible to imagine the vast difference between the lives of people
in the capitals of Denmark and Iceland, the feeling of freedom and the incredible
giddiness that many young Icelanders must have experienced in entering into the
hustle and bustle of city life for the first time. Ísleifur, for example, felt as if now
he could pour oil

> on long-cooled embers and let the fire of life burn; I myself a young arrow,
> thirsty for pleasure, and this the first day that I am able to let my feelings
> burst forth from their cold shackles, darkness and dependence.

Copenhagen was an ancient city, and one could still see its numerous old
churches and splendid halls despite the great fires of previous centuries. But it was
also new in the sense that it never broke out of its walls until the middle of the
nineteenth century. In 1900 its inhabitants numbered around four hundred and
fifty thousand, people living in cramped conditions like the inhabitants of Paris and
London. By the end of the First World War the population had increased by more
than a hundred thousand people. To an Icelander the city must have seemed overwhelming: the noise, the crowds on the narrow streets of the city centre, the smells,

the screeching of the trams, the cars and motorbikes, the cries and shouts of merchants hawking their wares, the life and energy of the almost two thousand bars and restaurants – in addition to the multinational population.

Denmark had not participated in the war, and actually profited a great deal from the sale of foodstuffs and industrial goods while the disaster played out south of its border. Yet the country was near enough to the war and contemporary revolutionary movements to wipe the gleam of belief in turn-of-the-century progress from the eyes of its inhabitants.

Halldór's attitude towards Denmark was ambivalent. He travelled quite often to Copenhagen, making it his "home from home"; sometimes he even kept a car there. Almost all of his foreign publishing contracts in the four decades after the Second World War were drawn up by a law office in Copenhagen, and for a long time his books were nowhere better served; more or less everything that he wrote was published, and his was a household name in Denmark. He had numerous friends among Danish writers and artists, was highly respected and was a sought-after interviewee for newspapers and other media. Nevertheless he did not think very highly of Danish literature, and used to say that the Danes were much better at baking pastries than producing literature. Nevertheless, he always praised them for their *joie de vivre* and their enjoyment of food and drink. His attitude was comparable to praising someone for his physical accomplishments while suggesting that he is lacking in intellectual capacity. This attitude was partly shaped by national pride and partly by Halldór's dislike of Lutheranism.

Halldór's ambivalent attitude is apparent in *When I Was Young* (1976), which describes his first winter in Copenhagen. But his letters to his mother in the autumn of 1919 reveal a deep enchantment with the city. He arrived in Copenhagen on Tuesday morning, 5 August, 1919, aboard the ship *Iceland*, which had set out from Reykjavík the previous Thursday. Slow modes of transport gave people more time to acclimatize, and ships were always Halldór's favourite way of travelling – he found such journeys comforting. He had promised his mother a full account of his trip, and he did not let her down. The letter reveals Halldór's keen and humorous power of perception, not apparent in his earlier writings but later one of his critically important tools; few could match him in sketching clear and vibrant characters with just a few strokes.

It cannot be said that the great city received Halldór with open arms. When he disembarked wearing his finest clothing ("a boy in disguise", he said later), his belongings in large trunks, he had nowhere to stay. Hailing a taxi, he asked to be driven to the nearest hotel, but there were no vacancies. He then remembered that the merchant Árni Einarsson had given him the address of a friend with whom he always stayed in Copenhagen. Thus it happened that Halldór knocked at the door of Oskar Wilhelm Scheuermann, a brewery foreman, at Store Kongensgade 96, where he was allowed to set himself up in one of the sitting rooms, a separate room not being available.

Halldór cautioned his contemporaries against taking his memoirs from the 1970s at face value, calling them novels in essay form; in them he adjusts the image of himself and his circumstances to one he prefers. In *When I Was Young* the taxi driver started making all sorts of threats until Halldór finally came up with the address on Store Kongensgade. The driver refused to wait while Halldór introduced himself: "He would not stand for any further delays, and instead threw my things up the staircase, grabbed the money from me and drove off in a foul mood." In a letter to his mother written on the day that these events took place, the story is told differently:

> We carried up the trunks, the driver and I, and I thanked him for his services; he was extremely honest and helpful, and I paid him 10 krónur for his work and bade him live well.

Like other authors of memoirs, Halldór uses memories from his youth to construct his self-image as an adult. At one time or another, everyone invents a story that he imagines to be his life, as Max Frisch put it.

Scheuermann and his wife received Halldór extraordinarily well. He was not only offered lodging at a decent price, but Scheuermann offered to take him round the city, of which Halldór sent his mother the following description:

> Many things . . . are different than in Reykjavík. First and foremost are the towering huge houses on every street, blocking the sight of everything so that all one can do is look up into the clear blue sky. Then there are tall birch trees and oaks peering out everywhere, with their broad, thick, leafy crowns and powerful, stout trunks. And not least is this excessive traffic on the streets. In some places it is dangerous to walk across the square: it is full of all sorts of motorized carriages, horse-drawn carts, motorbikes and different types of delivery vehicles, which are always dashing around at tremendous speed.

That same evening Scheuermann took his twenty-five-year-old daughter Alette and Halldór to the Tivoli amusement park, a kind of Scandinavian dream of lands to the south and east, offspring of nineteenth-century colonialism. This must have kindled the young poet's imagination, because he wrote his mother a long letter that ended with these words: "And such unexampled beauty was there when they lit up all the multicoloured lights around the lake, up in the trees and around the rose bushes." Out of a sense of duty he added:

> All the same, I thought that Icelanders could thank God that they do not have a place such as the Tivoli, for such places tend to encourage a mob mentality and all sorts of foolishness.

In the late summer and autumn of 1919, the anguish and insecurity that had so often beset Halldór the preceding winter disappeared. A letter he wrote to his mother at the start of October shows this well:

> It is clear to me that this journey of mine is a great step in the direction that I have been seeking, namely, to gain knowledge of people and the world, so that I can become a real writer, which is where my heart truly lies.

The death of Jóhann Sigurjónsson on 30 August also had an effect on him. Jóhann was, along with his friend Gunnar Gunnarsson, the best-known Icelandic writer in Denmark at that time. Like many other Icelandic writers at the start of the twentieth century, he wrote in both Danish and Icelandic; he had gained a foothold in Danish theatrical life and was widely known. Highest praise was accorded to his play *Eyvindur of the Mountains*, which was previewed in Reykjavík at the end of 1911 and performed in Copenhagen in the spring of 1912. The play attracted a great deal of attention. Halldór had seen it in Iceland and enjoyed it. It is not hard to understand that a writer like Jóhann would have appealed to him: an Icelandic writer who had achieved success abroad! Halldór's description of Jóhann's crowded funeral in *When I Was Young* is extremely effective, but the narrative is designed no less to show readers that Halldór never intended to write in Danish: "Somehow I did not care about his foreign 'victories' at all."

This is not entirely true. In the autumn of 1919 Halldór seriously considered writing in Danish, working on short stories and a novel in that language. In a letter to his mother early that spring he writes of a friend, Karl Sigvaldason, who will

> find me a publishing company for the story that I am writing now, both in Danish and Icelandic, and plans to try with Gyldendal, the largest publishing house in Scandinavia, for whom Icelandic writers have worked . . .

Halldór was determined to support himself as a writer, although that autumn he had to send his mother both a telegram and a letter asking for money. Halldór confirms his plans in a letter to his mother written at the end of 1919:

> I have considered asking a good Danish writer to look over the language in
> my Danish version of the novel before I take it to the publisher . . . All of
> the Danes are eager to help an Icelander in such matters, because they gener-
> ally have good faith in Icelandic writers and respect them, and do everything
> they can to get them to write in Danish – the Danes are currently experi-
> encing something of a shortage of writers.

He tells his mother that he will not be coming home until he has "succeeded"
in Danish. Halldór contemplated taking Jóhann Sigurjónsson as his model after
witnessing his funeral. He planned to establish himself by writing novels in Danish,
and had also started to think seriously about the practical aspects of writing: proof-
reading, getting published, earning a living wage. He never finished the novel that
he worked on that year, and it is now lost. Most likely his first attempt to write a
great rural novel in the spirit of Knut Hamsun's *Growth of the Soil* (1917), it was to
be called *Salt of the Earth*, and it is significant that Ísleifur Sigurjónsson remembered
it later under the Danish title, *Jordens salt*.

Halldór settled comfortably into the Scheuermanns' sitting room. Among other
enjoyable things were the plentiful fruits and vegetables at the dinner table, rare
commodities in Iceland. He worked hard reading and writing, played the
Scheuermanns' piano and studied languages.

Always a great linguist, Halldór began studying Russian that autumn, finding it
challenging: "It would be interesting to travel to Russia . . . after the Bolsheviks have
got everything in order," he wrote to his mother. His stay with the Scheuermanns
influenced his thoughts concerning the Danes. Not literary folk, his hosts were
extremely kind and enjoyed the finer things in life; he called them "princely
workers" in *When I Was Young*. Halldór seems to have charmed them. The daughter,
Alette, sent Halldór a letter in May, 1966, after seeing him on television, saying that
it was almost like meeting him again.

Halldór kept in touch with the Scheuermanns and sent them copies of his
books. Sigrid Scheuermann, a relative of the family, received a small amount of
financial assistance from him in the 1950s, for which she thanks him in a letter:

> Certainly no-one dreamed when you came first to Copenhagen . . . that you
> would eventually be accorded such great honours; and I know that . . .
> Scheuermann . . . would have rejoiced that you have been able to push your-
> self in such a way, because that is rare.

Halldór's money quickly ran out, and it was Karl Sigvaldason who suggested
that he try to sell one of his stories to a newspaper. The description of Karl in
When I Was Young is ambivalent: his helpfulness is non-committal, his interest in
literature superficial; he is, the memoir says, "discreet and dreadfully boring". Karl
is one of the few characters who does not appear under his real name; he is called
Björn Hannesson, the name that Gunnar Gunnarsson used for him in the final
part of *The Church on the Mountain* (1923–8). Following Karl's advice, Halldór wrote
a short story in Danish and sent it to *Berlingske Tidende*, Copenhagen's most
respected newspaper. The story was accepted, as far as can be seen, without the
intercession of agents, and was published on the front page of the Sunday paper,
along with a drawing of Icelandic country folk by Gerda Ploug Sarp, a well-known
illustrator. The story had the solemn title "The Thousand-year-old Icelander" and,
as he had before, Halldór adopted the tone of a much older man, no doubt
preventing the editors from guessing that they were publishing the work of a
seventeen-year-old. When he translated the story into Icelandic and published it in
Morgunblaðið several years later, it was called "Child of Nature", the title retained
in *Several Stories*, although in later editions of the collection it is called "Heiðbæs",
after its protagonist, to avoid confusing it with Halldór's first novel.

The literary scholar Kristján Albertsson, who lived for a time in Copenhagen,
later described in an interview how the Icelandic community there was thunder-
struck by this novice who managed, while still a complete unknown, to get
something published in a place others could only dream of. The story suited the
Danish paper because it resembled a formulaic advertisement for Icelandic
tourism: it takes place on a farm and has as its hero a working man called Helgi who
is in touch with what is most splendid in Iceland's history. There is also a beautiful
girl on the farm. The plot is set in motion by the visit of the wandering and foppish
intellectual Heiðbæs. The backdrop consists of nothing less than a volcanic erup-
tion, thus enabling the test of manhood that the faint-hearted artist does not pass.

The story is vivacious and belongs to the same world as *Child of Nature*, but
what is remarkable is the fact that its love-triangle would appear again and again,
in various forms, in Halldór's works for a long time, its basic elements more developed and ambiguous: a refined intellectual who has lived abroad but is perhaps a
weak character, an Icelandic girl who is closely connected to nature and strong-
willed, and finally – although Halldór often omits this character – the intellectually
weak but ethically strong third wheel, in this case the worker. Both *The Great Weaver
from Kashmir* and *Salka Valka* foreground an unsteady intellectual and a strong girl,
but one can see the whole triangle, for example, in *Atom Station*, with modifications

in *Under the Glacier* (1970) – and in some ways turned inside-out in *Iceland's Bell*. Although the story of the thousand-year-old Icelander was clearly written to appeal to foreigners, Halldór's writing was starting to take on the characteristics of his later work. As we shall see, the triangle is connected with his own life.

It is noteworthy that Halldór wrote the story in Danish after having been in the country for only a few months. In *When I Was Young* he calls forth erudite Danes as witnesses to his having always written impeccable Danish, almost as if he had mastered the language unconsciously; he did, in fact, find it amusing to suggest that Danish was innate to Icelanders. The truth was not so simple; the *Berlingske Tidende* subeditors corrected his errors, something Halldór admits in an interview for the paper in 1951. After the story was published he was invited to a meeting with one of the editors and asked to write for the paper at appropriate intervals, for quite a good sum of money. He published two more stories in the paper that winter.

The editor of *Berlingske Tidende* may not have understood how young Halldór was because, among other things, he knew how to dress. Along with his hat, cane and glasses, he wore a respectable overcoat and jacket with a broad tie and silk collar that extended to his shoulders. On his move to Reykjavík he had adopted the habit of dressing himself as a significantly older man, according to the custom of the time, and the fact that he kept company primarily with older men helped to add a certain maturity to his bearing. Throughout his life Halldór dressed well and carefully. The art of writing is also the art of disguising oneself.

Halldór quickly became acquainted with the dashing group of Icelanders living in Copenhagen, many of whom met at the Café Himmerige. Ten years later Halldór wrote:

> In Copenhagen I kept company with Icelanders, Jónas from Flatey, Jón 'the worse' Norland, Friðrik Brekkan (the writer) – various painters, bohemians, students and vagabonds of all imaginable types; merchants, fishing-boat owners, ordinary seamen, all sorts of editions of Danish bourgeois and such rabble; workers and restaurateurs, drunkards, and even thieves.

That first autumn he met Jón Helgason, who was on a master's degree course in Scandinavian Studies and who remained his closest friend, besides being one of the very few who had unshakeable confidence in everything that Halldór wrote. In *When I Was Young* Halldór tells of their long debates about literature at Café Himmerige; they gave little weight to contemporary Icelandic writers except for Þórbergur Þórðarson. This was remarkable, since by that time Þórbergur had not published anything except two small books of poetry. If Halldór is correct, this shows how he and Jón were listening out for new voices in Icelandic literature. A new age was at hand, demanding new expressions. They desired originality and bold language, not to mention humour. Halldór was becoming more conscious of distinct authorial and stylistic qualities, and would later work hard to develop such things within his own oeuvre.

Halldór's other good friends that autumn, such as Ísleifur Sigurjónsson and Jón Pálsson from Hlíð, were more inclined towards adventure. Having grown up in the countryside in Iceland, Ísleifur became enamoured of Copenhagen's nightlife and entertainments. As he says in his diary, he started to spend whole weeks in the quayside bars, in "that deep night-ditch of human life, where seamen from most countries in the world sit drunk, embracing demi-monde wenches". He would later settle down in Copenhagen and become an expert in "living on social security". The seaman Jón Pálsson from Hlíð was deeply interested in culture, especially music and literature, but inclined towards drink.

Halldór never followed the others into excessive drinking. Another kind of disquietude attacked him: an inextinguishable need to create, combined with a heightened sense of anxiety that caused him seldom to be content with his work; he was always looking for new angles, trying to find his own way. It was from this "nervousness" that his incredible renovative power as a writer sprang, which can be perceived in everything he wrote. He had come across a book by August Strindberg, *Inferno* (1897), in one of the Copenhagen bookshops, and the Swedish writer seized him with an unbreakable grip. Few books could have suited Halldór better at this time. *Inferno* is a feverish portrayal of a horrendous psychological state, which must have reminded Halldór of his worst days at school. The novel is written in the first person, and the story – which seems to have been Strindberg's own – is built on the idea that the narrator is exceptional but at the same time alone and hounded.

It has been said that *Inferno* is an attempt to "uncover the crimes that have merited the punishment inflicted upon the narrator". Strindberg's novel would influence Halldór's writings in the 1920s, not least *The Great Weaver from Kashmir*, and Halldór admitted this in later years. This rare admission is more remarkable for the fact that those who evaluate the importance of other writers to Halldór must often beware of putting too much stock on what he himself says. He was not fond of admitting the influence of his contemporaries and even wrote that he had never met a literary scholar who had detected Strindberg's influence on his work. But in 1919 nothing else would do: Halldór had to go to Sweden to read more Strindberg.

The young writer in the sitting room bade farewell to the wonderful Scheuermanns, boarded a train and made his way to Hälsingborg.

*

In Hälsingborg Halldór took lodgings in a small hotel and set to work, writing chapters of *Salt of the Earth* and reading Strindberg in the library. He was living once again in the world of thought; he isolated himself, worked diligently, met no-one, and, before he knew it, had no money left. In *When I Was Young* he beautifully describes how he suddenly discovered that he had no money for his trip home, and barely enough for a meal:

> And so it happened that a world-famous violinist, the Hungarian von Vecsey, advertised a concert in St Mary's Church in Hälsingborg. I decided to go and listen rather than eat, and sat alone in my room wearing two overcoats and gloves, writing that fine book *Salt of the Earth* (about Þórður), and the hoar-frost on the windowpanes was as thick as the plush in those world-famous Swedish Rya tapestries.

He did not regret going to the concert: "I had certainly never heard such music before; had truly never imagined that such playing existed." This is one of the snapshots from Halldór's memoirs that does not need to be taken literally; it is written more in the spirit of an exemplum: the cares of the world fade before the glories of art; something always comes to the aid of the young writer who chooses art over worldly things. Thus the memoir tells how Ísleifur Sigurjónsson appeared at Halldór's door the next morning, having decided to pop over to Hälsingborg

> because he knew that his friend from Laxnes was sitting in the glorious light of poetry writing famous books for the world. He paid for my trip to Copenhagen and bore my household things on his back.

The story agrees for the most part with the testimony of Ísleifur himself:

> When we boarded the ferry, Halldór said to me: "Because you are so strong, I would like to ask you, my dear Ísleifur, to carry my luggage on board." "It shall be my true pleasure," I answered, "and I will remind you of it when you win the Nobel Prize for Literature."

It was December, 1919. There exists a version of the story that is more down to earth, perhaps in tune with the weather at that time of year and in that part of the world. It is from the memoir of the painter Ásgeir Bjarnþórsson, who was

living in Copenhagen at the time and put Halldór up for several days on his return
from Hälsingborg:

> Now it ought to be mentioned that a boy by the name of Halldór Guðjóns-
> son from Laxnes had wound up penniless in Hälsingborg and lay there
> destitute and starving. He wrote to one of his acquaintances in Copenhagen
> – I no longer recall whom – and asked for assistance out of this difficulty.
> We collected some krónur so that he could come home to Copenhagen.

This is most likely correct; Ísleifur must have been chosen for the mission. Sadly
the facts deprive the story of its fairy-tale aura.

Ísleifur himself described his trip to Sweden as follows:

> Halldór wrote to me and asked me to come to visit him . . . When I arrived
> in Hälsingborg I had a hard time finding him, so I went to the police and
> asked the way to his hotel.
>
> They knew immediately whom I meant because they had everyone under
> surveillance. They were worried about spies, you see, because this was actu-
> ally just right after the First World War.
>
> They were somewhat suspicious of Laxness and started asking me all sorts
> of questions about him, and told me that he did nothing but write all day.
> They found this to be extremely peculiar behaviour.
>
> I assured them that the boy from Iceland was absolutely harmless, that he
> had been gripped by the delusion of writing stories about Icelandic shep-
> herds, so they had nothing to fear. Most of their fears were allayed and a
> ribbon-bedecked police officer with a sword on his belt was ordered to
> accompany me to Laxness' hotel.

Halldór did Ísleifur some favours later in his life. Ísleifur tells of their reunion
in 1949 in a letter to his brother:

> . . . I heard one day that Halldór Laxness was staying at the d'Angleterre
> and I went there to talk to him after all those years of war. It was at the
> beginning of October, early in the morning, in raw, cold weather, and I
> wandered into the most elegant hotel in Scandinavia and asked after Iceland's
> most renowned hero, and gold-sashed, pompous servants and doormen
> looked at my torn raincoat in scorn, and when I asked after the honourable
> writer Laxness they asked whether my interview with him had been arranged,
> and I said that it hadn't, but would they most kindly ring his room and tell
> him my name. They did this with obvious sulkiness but were quick to hand

me the receiver when they heard the response of the poet and cosmopolitan on the upper floor. So I said hello to Halldór on the phone in jingly, cloddish Icelandic, surrounded by all sorts of glitzy folk who came and went, as if I had arrived in . . . the banquet halls of Constantinople . . .

Halldór's friendship with Ísleifur stood out vividly in his mind when he was writing *When I Was Young*. Remembering that he still owed Ísleifur for the trip from Hälsingborg to Copenhagen, he rang Ísleifur's niece and asked for his address. Then, according to Ísleifur, Halldór sent him a considerable sum of money, which Ísleifur took as a birthday present. In this way his costs for the trip were repaid an ample sixty years later.

Conditions at Ásgeir Bjarnþórsson's were cramped, so Halldór and Jón were forced to search the streets for lodgings. Ásgeir advanced them money; Halldór was expecting some from both his mother and *Berlingske Tidende*. After various adventures, including a murder in their first hotel, upon which all the guests were questioned, Halldór rented a decent attic room and started writing again, among other things stories for *Berlingske Tidende*.

Jón Pálsson dreamed of going to work for an estate farmer in Jämtland who was helpful to Icelanders. The only catch was that he did not have enough money for the trip until just before Christmas. But Jón was mugged and robbed, only to be taken in and nursed by a prostitute. This event – which Halldór describes differently in *When I Was Young* – became the inspiration for "A Poem", published in *Several Stories* (and called "A Christmas Poem" in later editions). Like many of the shorter stories in this collection it is more of a sketch – of a lonely man wandering around in the pre-Christmas bustle of the city – and the fact that it is written in the first person, besides being set on Christmas Eve, makes it even more sorrowful. Halldór is practising his narrative techniques, but of course the event itself affected him deeply. In the memoir and a Christmas letter to his mother he states that following the mugging he lent Jón money for his trip to Jämtland.

Early in the new year Halldór sold *Berlingske Tidende* another story, which was published on 15 February. In *Several Stories* it is called "The Story of the Folk at Kálfakot", a terribly poignant tale about a destitute farmer with a large family, who, following a storm, is found dead along with his wife and stillborn twins. The story, partly written in Hälsingborg, is noteworthy in that it represents the first draft of what would become the great rural novel *Independent People*. Halldór was investigating ways in which he could compose a work about a farmer on an isolated farm that would fly in the face of traditional pastoral romance – the same thing he was trying to do in *Salt of the Earth*.

Of course Halldór had not yet found his voice, and his stories could be considered writing exercises. That he was moving away from the traditional models of his youth is apparent from his interest in Þórbergur's originality, his admiration for Strindberg's audacity and, not least, his doubts concerning the vitality of artistic life in Denmark, especially in the visual arts. A large number of Icelanders were studying painting there, but painting in Copenhagen did not impress Halldór any more than did Bertel Thorvaldsen's cold marble:

> Concerning the painter's art I do not think it an exaggeration to say that I have never in as few days set eyes on as many scenes of gleaming pastoral bliss beneath queasy sunsets, in addition to hopeless mountain profiles and slices of the sea.

Halldór was in search of modern art and was sharply critical.

Every writer of fiction, in order to master his or her craft, must have a strong grasp of the variety of human life and gather many different character types in a mental "portfolio". Halldór was given great opportunities to do just that during his year in Copenhagen, as when he got to know the herring speculator Óskar Halldórsson. The first six chapters of *A Song on God's Gifts* (1972), which are closely related to the memoirs he wrote several years later, are based on Halldór's memories of a spring day in Copenhagen in Óskar's company. Óskar was a corpulent and stately man who wore a waistcoat and a bowler hat, reminding one of Oliver Hardy; he was open and sincere one minute, a stiff-necked fox the next. His wealth might have been a hoax or in danger of disappearing like dew in the sun, but such a man was precious material for a fiction writer, and he appears in different forms in many of Halldór's books.

*

Although his attic room suited Halldór well and he was working almost non-stop at his writing, he quickly began to thirst for new experiences and perceptions. Now he wanted to visit the Danish countryside. He had got to know one of the founders of the Danish–Icelandic Friendship Society (founded in 1916), the writer Åge Meyer Benedictsen. Åge's father was a Jew, his mother was of Icelandic descent, and he himself was a true cosmopolitan, well versed in languages, exceptionally well travelled and greatly concerned with the rights of small nations. In *When I Was Young* Halldór says of him:

> To tell the truth I thought that such a good man could not exist; that he was at least insane. I forgot that tradesmen of Åge Meyer's type are cultural prodigies reaching back to ancient times – from countries to the east of the

Mediterranean sea, for example, Phoenicia, where the alphabet was invented. We Scandinavians are pitiful addle-heads compared to people that enjoyed high culture three thousand years before us.

Åge encouraged Halldór to see more of Denmark and experience spring in the countryside, and got him a room on a farm in southern Sjelland, where he spent March and April "in great celebration and eternal feasting, as is the custom there". But Halldór was not happy; he experienced his first serious writer's block and could not make progress on *Salt of the Earth*. Spring came, nature blossomed, but for the writer everything was inert.

But then Halldór experienced something for perhaps the first time, something extremely encouraging that he would often experience later. He met an admirer, a reader who was enchanted by one of his works. A supply teacher in the area, she was so deeply affected by the story about Þórður from Kálfakot that she sat for long hours in quiet conversation with Halldór, or so he says in *When I Was Young*. Enchanted by her enchantment, he told her stories, including the one that he was writing and which would be the last short story he would sell to *Berlingske Tidende* for a while: "Digteren og Zeus" (2 May, 1920). When its Icelandic version, under the title "The Poet and the Dog", was printed in *Morgunblaðið* in the spring of 1923, this dedication preceded it: "Bögesö, April, 1920. To Miss Ch." Perhaps Halldór and Miss Ch. shared more than an adoration of literature – no-one knows for sure now – but it is clear that the story is a revised, expanded version of Snær the Wise's "Zeus", except that the dog's owner has been changed from a philosopher to a writer. Halldór's "Christmas Poem" has the same root in compassion for the downtrodden. This sensibility is found throughout his works, although in time he learnt better ways to incorporate it into his narratives.

In late spring Halldór returned to Copenhagen, only to discover that he had had enough of the Danish capital. Perhaps he also was having difficulty getting support from home. Before he returned to Iceland he decided to visit Jón Pálsson in Sweden, where he went in May.

According to the farmer, Lars Larsson, with whom Jón Pálsson had worked (he was interviewed by a Swedish newspaper in 1954), a "stately and extremely comely boy" came to visit Jón one day. This was Halldór from Laxnes. As might be expected, Lars had no stories to tell of Halldór's aptitude for farmwork, but he said that the friends held lively discussions on Whit Sunday, when everyone had a day off.

They discussed the forests in Jämtland, ancient and modern literature, and – not least – Lars' special interest, Nordic languages. Jón and Halldór apparently expressed their admiration for the Swedish language, while considering Danish meagre, although Halldór did cite one exception, possibly with Miss Ch. in mind, when he said that Danish was "almost beautiful in the mouths of young girls". The article portrays Halldór as having been curious about everything he saw, as well as cheerful and optimistic, if something of a know-all. He could discuss poetry, nature and languages day in, day out.

The fate of Halldór's close friends from his first year in Denmark turned out differently. Jón Pálsson gave up the struggle against Icelandic apathy, became a drinker and later drowned: it was probably suicide. Ísleifur Sigarjónsson died shortly after receiving Halldór's money in a retirement home in Copenhagen, as his relatives in Iceland only found out many weeks later.

Halldór's first stay overseas came to a close with those good days in Jämtland. He had experienced the modern culture of a great city, gained a better idea of his career path, perceived the blessings and anguish of being a writer, and collected a great deal of material. After stopping at Trondheim and Stavanger, he returned to Copenhagen in June, travelling back to Reykjavík on the flagship of the new Icelandic Steamship Company, the *Gullfoss*.

From Dilksnes to Dresden

When I arrived home I adopted the same kind of bohemian lifestyle for which I had acquired a taste during my trip abroad. I was either in the cafés in Reykjavík or out gallivanting with my friends in the countryside, was of course always writing something, but actually had no "plan" for life other than that I wanted to be immortal. I was thinking about sailing abroad again in the autumn, somewhere out in the world, and made enquiries into trips to Greece on fishing boats and official posts in the Faroe Islands, became engaged to the young daughter of a wealthy farmer and spent time with her in the countryside.

This is how Halldór described the summer of 1920 for Stefán Einarsson nine years later. The memoir he wrote sixty years later is called simply *The Greece Year* (1980), because his idea of going to Greece became symbolic of that summer, which was characterized by aimlessness and disquiet. The trip home itself had been pleasant: the *Gullfoss* was the most elegant transport Icelanders had ever had, and there were many passengers on board. The writer Friðrik Brekkan helped Halldór with his luggage, of which he always brought a great deal on his journeys, including a trunk full of books. In his memoirs written nearly half a century later, Halldór reproduces a conversation he had with Friðrik concerning the problems of writing:

"When is a story perfect?" I asked.

"Never," said Brekkan.

"Does it mean anything then to be doing this?" I asked.

"No," said Brekkan.

"Doesn't that then apply to one's whole life?" I asked again.

"Yes," said Brekkan. "But that doesn't change anything."

This attitude appealed strongly to Halldór in his later years, whether this conversation actually took place or not.

From the voyage Halldór particularly remembered Helgi Pjeturss, that peculiar, imposing, immensely learned geographer, who was dedicated to a complicated and extremely odd doctrine he'd created about life on other planets. This eccentric man often talked to Halldór on board the *Gullfoss* and endeared himself to him. Although Helgi's cosmobiological theories did not appeal to Halldór, he praised the geographer's books for their language. It was often Halldór's habit to look up to "unlikely" contemporary Icelandic writers and praise them for qualities that were not immediately evident. At work in such cases was both his lifelong endeavour to avoid the readily available and obvious and a defensive stance that made it difficult for him to heap too much praise on writers with whom he was in close competition.

On the way home to Iceland Halldór also met Einar Ólafur Sveinsson, who was studying Scandinavian languages and literature at the University of Copenhagen. The two remained close friends during the next decade or so, and Halldór's letters to Einar Ólafur contain some of the best examples of his train of thought in those days. Einar Ólafur was well read and later introduced Halldór to Freud and Jung, as well as to the classic works of Nietzsche and Thomas à Kempis. Their intellectual camaraderie during Halldór's formative years was as close as it could be between two souls searching for the highest explanations for existence, and Halldór frequently entrusted Einar with his deepest thoughts, although the tone the friends adopted in their letters is not free from superficiality and waggery.

After Halldór's homecoming he kept one foot in Laxnes and the other in town, and sometimes stayed with Einar Ólafur's parents. Although Reykjavík had grown into a little town, in the eyes of the experienced traveller it had also diminished, seeming little more than a village to someone who had lived in a huge city. The opportunities that Reykjavík offered Halldór had not increased; there was still nothing to tempt him to become a professional writer in Iceland. His determination had somewhat petered out, and he spent his time negligently during the summer and autumn. His mother was taking paying guests at Laxnes, and he felt as if he did not entirely belong there – his childhood home was disappearing. He was of course always writing, but the salt in *Salt of the Earth* had lost its flavour. He went to cafés with his friends and took part in discussions with the residents of Unuhús, but the theoretical soup served there did not taste good enough. People discussed esoteric subjects in which few of them had a good grounding. Halldór had not yet become overtly political, although the suspicion had doubtless started to grip him after his trip abroad that the war had put other ideas and ideals on the world's agenda.

Halldór's self-image as a writer was unclear at this time and his confidence prone to oscillation. He knew that his stories in *Berlingske Tidende* reflected an earlier literary style from which he preferred to distance himself. Although people complimented him on *Child of Nature*, he had left that book behind him. He did not refrain, of course, from paying back Jón Björnsson for his review of *Child of Nature*, publishing his own review of Jón's collection of short stories, *Infertile Earth* (1920), in the *People's Paper*. To say that Halldór's criticism is vigorous would be an understatement; he called one particular story

the purest hermaphrodite, too mediocre for it to be called a sin against the holy spirit of Icelandic narrative art, a living witness to the spiritual mediocrity that we Icelanders hate, but must fear like the plague or the devil.

Here one can distinguish something of the ostentatious tone that characterized many of Halldór's contributions to newspapers from the 1920s onwards.

In thinking about going to Greece, Halldór imagined himself as a character he had once seen in a painting: a carefree man leading a donkey, his luggage on the donkey's back. Halldór went to a saddler and asked for the same kind of packsaddle, then requested passage on a cargo ship headed for Piraeus. He was telephoned at Laxnes when the ship was ready to depart, but when he arrived at the ship with his fine packsaddle the captain turned him away with several choice words about

idlers who are burdens to their mothers, penniless widows, besides the fact that they are nuisances to themselves and banefully annoying and a shame to all Icelanders wherever they go, yes, wherever their names are heard spoken. This ship is not a cruise ship for ne'er-do-wells and barbaric renegades who live off of others' goodwill.

In his memoirs Halldór says, most likely in all earnestness, that he is eternally grateful to this man for his vitriolic criticism. Relentless toil was an Icelandic commonplace, but although many Icelanders found poetry and stories entertaining, the general view was that people who spent time composing them were useless. There was an ongoing debate in journals and newspapers about the ethical dangers posed by people who did nothing other than hang around in cafés, and even the few members of the intelligentsia were wary of the rapid growth of urbanization and the book market.

Autumn arrived, and Halldór's prospects for travelling abroad looked dim. His mother, who had probably spent too much supporting her son during the previous winter, had taken up knitting to earn money. Halldór did not know what to do to improve his situation. In October, 1920 he wrote a little sketch at Laxnes (published in *Several Stories*) entitled "Chanson Triste", which expresses his mood at that time. The sketch tells of a farm that is crumbling to ruins on desolate land, and concludes with the words:

> Century after century he has sat on a lopsided doorstep, this age-old man, with thin grey wisps of hair beneath his tattered hat, in a torn jerkin and frayed breeches, holding a rusty iron stick in his blue-black, bony hands.

He stares helplessly out into the lifelessness and the desolation, as if he is ceaselessly puzzling over his fate, whether he will become either a stone statue or a pile of dust.

Halldór wrote in the margin of the manuscript of Stefán Einarsson's biography: "I think that the 'Chanson Triste' was one of those ominous insomniac visions that I had so often in those days." These were visions similar to the ones that had prevented him from sleeping during his year in the Reykjavík Lyceum; their strength varied according to his circumstances. Such visions, and the anguish and panic attacks that accompanied them, had plagued Halldór since childhood. People forced to cope with such violent anxieties try to avoid the circumstances that seem most to cause them. Some do this by trying to stabilize and order their lives to an obsessive degree, while others travel constantly in search of new conditions. This could partly explain Halldór's restlessness during those years. To write becomes a fight against death. It also becomes a struggle for psychological health in the face of other dangers. One of the redeeming qualities of the writer's art is that it is a stage upon which both the storyteller and the audience can experience these dangers at one remove. It is the fire-simulation exercise in the school of life.

It having been made clear that nothing was to become of Halldór's hoped-for trip abroad, in October he took a job that, in his old age, he would have considered unlikely: he became a home teacher on a farm at the instigation of Þórbergur Þórðarson. The commercial manager of the Hornafjörður Cooperative, Björn Jónsson from Dilksnes, had been looking to hire a home teacher for his six children. Hornafjörður was not only a long way from Reykjavík; it was extremely difficult to get there by land, since the area was situated between unbridged glacial rivers. Halldór booked a passage on the coastal ship *Sterling* with two friends who were also going out to teach in the countryride; they sailed to Djúpavogur with a stop at the Westman Islands. From there the two Halldórs, Kolbeins and Guðjónsson, continued to Hornafjörður, for the most part on foot, although horses carried them across the glacial rivers. This was the longest trip he had ever taken in Iceland.

For the next five months Halldór taught at Dilksnes, although Björn's offspring were no longer "children". Halldór's memoirs do not paint a glorious picture of the experience; he admitted in a letter to Stefán Einarsson that he thought he would die at Dilksnes of the same afflictions that had troubled him at secondary school. As before, however, he did manage remarkably well to keep some distance between his psychological torments and his behaviour, and the people at Dilksnes were pleased with his work. But it is easy to imagine how poorly suited he was for it. Though he worked hard on *Salt of the Earth* he did not make much progress. It still seemed to him as if his life was aimless. Quite important, however, was his friendship with Halldór Kolbeins, whom he visited sometimes at the village of Höfn.

At Dilksnes Halldór became more familiar with rural life. In *The Greece Year* he mentions the father of the wife at Dilksnes, Eymundur, a well-read man who had tried his hand at many things. Halldór listened eagerly to his stories, cultivating his feel for character and dialogue. This sensitivity can be seen in the one work that survives from this time, the short story "Labouring Men", which begins with the words: "I know these poor labouring men, who each day contend with the forces of nature; I have seen them with my own eyes, yes, lived amongst them." But this does not change the fact that while at Dilksnes Halldór had "no presentable picture to hang up on the wall of my soul", as he puts it in *The Greece Year*. No doubt pleased when the job came to an end, he set off for Reykjavík the day before his nineteenth birthday.

In Reykjavík the cafés and his friends welcomed him with open arms, but he did not spend much time there. Halldór Kolbeins had been appointed pastor for the parish of Flatey in Breiðafjörður, but it seems that his journey there was delayed, and he waited for Halldór to go on ahead as if to announce his coming, like John the Baptist and Jesus, as Halldór amusingly put it sometimes. Halldór arrived at

Flatey early in the summer in time to discover another side of Iceland, a side that is long gone. No longer the trading station that it had been for most of the nineteeth century, Flatey still showed signs of affluence. The village was made up of handsome wooden houses, and had a church and a library. The island had been home to a robust reading club as well as publishing activity, and buried there is one of the greatest Icelandic historians of the old school, Gísli Konráðsson; men like him appear in the novel *World Light* (1937–40). Halldór became friends with the outgoing minister, Sigurður Jensson, nephew of the hero of Iceland's struggle for independence, Jón Sigurðsson.

In *The Greece Year* Halldór tells of sitting at his window watching a girl sunbathing, and it is likely that he enjoyed some sort of romantic adventure on Flatey, although no sources confirm this. At one point he reluctantly agreed to give a "concert" for the island's inhabitants, accompanying himself on the organ at the elementary school, performing "Leise flehen meine Lieder" and other beautiful songs by Schubert. It must have been like attending a concert given by Álfgrímur before he went overseas in *The Fish Can Sing*.

Halldór Kolbeins arrived to take up his post later that summer, and he and his namesake travelled round the parish, which extended beyond the island. Among the places that they visited was the cottage called Svínanessel (Sel) at Kvígindisfjörður. In an interview with Matthías Jóhannessen many years later, while talking about whether Bjartur from Summerhouses in *Independent People* had been modelled on someone from the Eastfjords, Halldór said:

> When I was a teenager and travelled around with my friend, Reverend Halldór Kolbeins, there in the west, I became interested in "the Icelandic cotter", and wanted to write a heroic saga about him. So I paid special heed to all the small cottages and their inhabitants . . . The original model for Summerhouses was the cottage called Sel in Múlasveit.

Sel was a rather destitute cottage. The farmer there, and the poverty and difficulties experienced by him and his family, are described in the memoirs of Reverend Árelíus Níelsson. The buildings consisted of three connected turf sheds, all old and dilapidated, and there were

> fifteen ewes, two goats, no cow, and two old women sick with cancer . . . It was only after the famous young man Halldór Laxness . . . sat down in a tent to write about Sel that people seemed to take notice of that isolated part of the country.

Halldór's visit to this farm affected him deeply and strengthened his determination to write a great novel about life in an isolated cottage in the Icelandic countryside. But it also affected the people on the farm who met him. Jón Jóhannesson from Skáleyjar heard from the farmer at Sel that he had thought Halldór's behaviour somewhat peculiar: "When he went to sleep at night, he wound his clothes up, tied a string around them, and hung them from a notch in the rafter over his bed." Halldór did this to avoid lice, just as he bathed in the sea every morning to keep fit. He was definitely a peculiar man, but congenial and interested, as the farmer says:

> He was very gentle and pleasant, although he was unlike us here in the fjords. There was a huge difference between him and the bailiff, who came here once. He hardly said a word to us and wouldn't come in. And the minsters have never kept company with us, as you know.

The writer and his people were becoming acquainted. According to Halldór's *Abbey Diaries* (1922–3), which became *Days with Monks* (1987), he even remembered the people of Sel in his prayers. Later they were to form the basis for characters in *Independent People*.

The blessed days on Flatey came to an end, and Halldór set out for home. On the way he received permission to read at the church at Hjarðarholt in Dalir. There he read, according to *The Greece Year*, mostly from the poems of Rabindranath Tagore, among the most "trendy" of works at that time, if one can judge by the fact that Tagore was awarded the Nobel Prize in 1913. After his next trip abroad, Halldór bade farewell to Tagore's optimistic pantheism.

*

Halldór stayed for most of that late summer in Laxnes, but he longed to go overseas. He remained, of course, constantly engaged in literary projects. But then he met with some good luck. His father's foster brother Daníel Halldórsson in Canada sent him a considerable sum of money in dollars so that he could visit him. Instead of going immediately to North America, Halldór first went to Europe.

At the beginning of October, Halldór, his friend Jóhann Jónsson and Jóhann's new wife Nikkolína Árnadóttir sailed to Copenhagen, from there continuing on to Germany. This was a peculiar trio. Halldór and Jóhann were great soulmates, although they could also be somewhat roguish if they were in the mood. Nikkólína was the most vibrant of women but had a contentious disposition and sometimes refused to do anything for weeks at a time.

The trip did not start off well because, as Halldór describes in *The Greek Year*, he and Jóhann had so much to discuss that they completely forgot about the bride below deck:

> It was not until we got to the steak that Jóhann remembered his wife. "She can come if she wants," he said. But she did not come. All the same our conversation became stiffer after we remembered the woman; by the time dessert came round Jóhann stood up and went to get his bride. But it must have been too late.

From Denmark Jóhann, Nikkólína and Halldór took a train across Germany, Halldór planning to go to Dresden and the couple to Leipzig. In a letter to a friend Jóhann says that he did not enjoy the train ride at all, trains being unknown in Iceland: "It is completely exhausting to be thrust along in such a raving mad fury. The carriages bump and sway beneath one, shaken by the vehemence of the steam engine."

During most of the winter of 1921–2, Halldór stayed in Germany and Austria, and his time there had no less of an effect on him than his first year in Denmark. In the cities of Germany immediately following the First World War he beheld grandiose cathedrals and palaces; the devastating effects of the war were obvious everywhere, as, in some places, were the consequences of the revolutions or civil conflicts that came in the war's wake. When Halldór walked about the wide streets, he encountered handless and legless veterans his own age or slightly older lying on the ground. In a letter to Einar Ólafur Sveinsson he says that it would be better to sell the victory columns and church towers and buy bread

> for these uglier-than-sin invalids whose legs have been cut out from under them and whose eyes have been torn out of their heads in the war, these abominable remnants of people who pose with beggars' bags and placards reading "Eighty-five per cent incapacitated" and who are not a damned shame to the state, but rather to all mankind.

In Germany Halldór began to contemplate social issues in earnest. In the same letter he says that he is gathering material for a philosophical essay. This is the essay that became *The Red Booklet*. The manuscript is egocentric and wide-ranging, full of emotional outbursts and fits of despair, in many places resembling Strindberg's *Inferno*. It is here that Halldór starts to realize himself as a writer. Rather than rework old stories from the countryside, he writes about his own concerns and experiences. This is the first developmental step for many novelists:

they must write a self-centred work about their formative years before they can
begin to write books about others.

The narrator of *The Red Booklet* is a nineteen-year-old secondary-school pupil
from Reykjavík, suffering from malaise and depression. His nights are desperate
and sleepless, he calls out to God for help, turns for comfort to an old woman, tries
to compose poems but says about them: "The situation overwhelmed me; everything became remote garrulity; if there had been any thought involved anywhere,
the words themselves would have killed it." This sharp criticism can occasionally
be applied to the manuscript itself. The writing seems premature in places, but it
is remarkable as the forerunner of what is to come, no less because of how
completely different it is from contemporary Icelandic prose: Halldór was finding
his own voice.

Although the narrator towers over all the other characters, in the first part of
The Red Booklet there appears a certain Miss R., a highly cultured married woman
who is sympathetic to the much younger narrator during a difficult time. We do not
know whether her character was based on an actual person, but it is certain that
various women were prepared to give Halldór the sympathy he craved. That winter
he wrote several letters to Kristín Pjetursdóttir Thurnwald, the sister of Helgi
Pjeturss, who lived in Germany; Halldór had met her there and in Copenhagen. In
one letter he says that it gave him strength on his own among the thousands "to
have in mind fresh recollections of a woman who understands, who has a soul
filled with Icelandic fire" – although he does add in parentheses: "Oh, forgive me
if I am starting to jabber like an idiot."

On his way to Dresden, where he stayed for most of the autumn of 1921,
Halldór passed through Berlin, where he was able to show off a bit thanks to the
dollars in his pocket. The decline in the German mark benefited everyone who
had exchangeable currency, and tourists streamed into the country, as did a number
of Icelanders who went there to study. In a letter to Einar Ólafur Sveinsson written
at the end of October Halldór wrote pompously:

> I present myself as the Icelandic Baron *von Laxnes* here at the opera and at
> other fine places when necessity demands . . . I live for the time being at the
> Hotel Stadt Weimar and live luxuriously, as a baron should.

But he is not impressed by the art galleries, inspired neither by Rafael nor the
modern art, which he considers an attempt to imitate nature using misshapen
forms, as one finds in folk tales about the devil trying to create man.

His guide to the museums and cafés of Dresden was Emil Thoroddsen, a musician and painter, who lent Halldór books that he read eagerly. Halldór also borrowed books from Arnfinnur Jónsson, whom he met when he took a short trip to Leipzig at the end of October. Arnfinnur was there studying pedagogy, and he and Halldór became good friends. Halldór was particularly enamoured of one author that autumn, Otto Weininger,

> an Austrian Jew who wrote a huge work (over six hundred pages), which discusses "that ancient concept" (as the writer himself says): man and woman . . . The man is radiant with wisdom, as erudite as the devil.

Weininger became world famous for his book *Gender and Personality* (1903), in fact nothing more than a high-flown attempt to give a philosophical underpinning to gross misogyny.

Why did Weininger appeal to Halldór? For one thing, the young philosopher located all of his ideas within a metaphysical system, besides taking his reasoning as far as it would go, without fear of deflection by even the most difficult of questions: "Man is completely alone in the universe, in eternal, horrendous loneliness," he says. For another, his misogyny was related to Strindberg's, who also admired him. Halldór was himself experiencing what has been called the "cultural crisis" of Europe following the First World War. He felt that the goal of man should to seek out higher values and serve them, and this naturally led him to contemplate everything that stood in the way: stupidity, mankind, beastly nature, woman and the temptations of the flesh, all earthly toil. These contradictions shaped his writing throughout the 1920s.

Halldór took both his reading and writing seriously that winter; he was outrageously industrious, usually working at least ten hours a day. He read literature, but concentrated on scholarly and philosophical books. He also worked on *The Red Booklet* and spent time revising his short stories, since Arnfinnur Jónsson had offered to get them published if they could raise the funds. A printer had offered exceptionally good terms. Halldór wrote to Arnfinnur enthusiastically from Dresden: "It is clear that what is at issue here is a hugely profitable venture . . . " But he was tempted by more than profit: ". . . it would be fun to show the damned idiots at home that I am not dependent upon them." He added that: "The manuscript and the copyright are available for nothing whenever anybody wants them, because . . . it has been predicted that I won't ever become fat-chinned from writing."

Nothing came of this project, however, though *Several Stories*, published in Iceland two years later, had essentially the same contents. Halldór also wished to see his stories published in book form in Denmark. Karl Sigvaldason had one of his manuscripts and tried unsuccessfully to convince a Danish publishing company to take it. Halldór also worked on having his stories published in Germany, but nothing came of this either. The only material published that autumn was the story of Heiðbæs, translated into German and published in the paper of the German Friends of Iceland, *Mitteilungen der Islandfreunde*, under the title "Child of Nature".

Halldór continued to write, leaving Dresden for Munich at the end of November. Munich enthralled him; it had an air of southern elegance and grace. Halldór referred to it in a letter to Arnfinnur as "a place of glory, which surpasses any other that I have yet seen".

From Munich Halldór travelled to Innsbruck, at first staying in a hotel but then moving to a boarding house in the mountains. There he found himself in working conditions that suited him well and which he later sought out at different times during his career: staying on his own away from the city.

Alone in the Tyrol he contemplated his position and plans, as can be seen in a letter he wrote to Arnfinnur on 23 December. He first tells his friend that he has gone to live in the mountains

> not in a way that corresponds to our ideal of house sharing, but rather as a hermit. This has come about because I have not given myself time to cultivate female relations.

Halldór crossed out the last sentence in Stefán Einarsson's manuscript, just as he did most sentences about such matters, and this suggests, that he was unable to get Helga Jóhannsdóttir, with whom he had had a short-lived affair, to come to visit him from Copenhagen. His writing thus had to take priority:

> I have a whole galaxy of ideas in my head, and since I reckon that I will be able to write them all down, I have decided to leave all my writing work on 23 April, 1922 (my twentieth birthday) for an indeterminate period of time and devote myself to study.

In fact Halldór intended to finish two manuscripts before that date.

This was incredibly audacious for a nineteen-year-old boy living in a foreign country and shows how firm his determination had become, as well as his devotion to study and reading – he even planned to take courses, which until then had not appealed to him. Yet one annoying practical matter is revealed in the same letter: the fact that he had no excuse for spending the money sent to him for a trip to North America "on rambling around here in Europe". Halldór wrote to Arnfinnur: "Can you find out whether I can make it to America, somewhere in America, for . . . 100 dollars?"

Halldór was not plagued by moral concerns during the next year, however. Alongside his determination to write, he became convinced that others would always offer to assist him, without question, whether with money or other gifts. He continually asked people for loans without any guarantee that he would repay them, just as he considered it obvious that Arnfinnur would know the details concerning trips to North America, rather than finding them out for himself. The following in a letter sent to Kristín Thurnwald that autumn tells the same story: "If perhaps you might be so kind as to write me a few words, tell me what you think you might be able to do for me."

This attitude is evident in the marginal notes he made in Stefán Einarsson's manuscript almost ten years later, where Stefán described how Halldór lived in extreme poverty during the winter of 1924–5 in Reykjavík:

Actually, not more than usual; I was constantly broke, but always well-dressed, and I was always able to get something to eat. I have never in my life had actual concerns about money; I have always muddled along, carefree. I have never owed more than a few dozen krónur to any particular lender, but have often "made deals" knowing full well beforehand that I would never repay the money – and no-one who ever gave me money expected that I would repay it!

Here Halldór tempers the despondency that occasionally accompanied his poverty, but the situation is clear: he got from others whatever he needed to devote himself to his calling, and never promised repayment – except through his work.

On his trip south Halldór continued to write *The Red Booklet*. Its narrator declares that he has travelled throughout Europe, "this barren playing field of the insensible cultural world", where he has "gazed on [his] soul made lame by human need, the aftermath of the greatest human indignity that history has ever witnessed". The narrator believes that all men must, under such conditions, practise charity. Halldór himself was moving closer to religious faith, although that faith had not yet taken on a definite form.

At the same time his social consciousness was strengthening, and that winter he published his first great political article. Published in parts in the *People's Paper* beginning on 15 February, it was called "Letter from the Alps". The article was written in response to the conflict that occurred in Reykjavík at the end of November, the "White War". This conflict arose when the authorities decided to deport a Russian boy who suffered from an eye disease. Ólafur Friðriksson, the leader of the Social Democrats, had brought the boy home with him from Russia, where he had gone to acquaint himself with the progress of the Revolution. Ólafur considered the deportation to be a political gesture and refused to surrender the boy. The government gathered its supporters, Ólafur's followers organized themselves, and hundreds of people fought each other in the streets of Reykjavík, an event without precedent.

Halldór's article, sympathetic to Ólafur, is written from a metaphysical perspective, warning that Icelanders should on no account fight amongst themselves. He also says that arresting Ólafur and his men would solve nothing, because Icelanders were fighting against ideals, not men. Halldór would voice his convictions concerning the power of ideals in many different forms. In the last part of the article he says: "One thing I know: socialism, Communism, anarchism, all of these have more of a future than we suspect." It appears that what Halldór had written to Kristín Thurnwald earlier in the spring had come true: "I will more than likely become enthralled by a revolution (depending on the appearance of a revolution, of course) or something even worse."

Following his trip to the Alps, Halldór went to Copenhagen to visit his girlfriend Helga, and when the relationship fell apart he returned to Germany. He went back to Berlin, and despite all his ethical admonitions he became enamoured of "the corruption" there. In the middle of March he wrote to Einar Ólafur:

> Berlin can be incomparably elegant, and it is a pure wonder how the world can be so devilishly delightful on the side of it that shows – I have in mind those beautiful and bejewelled women and those well-groomed and manicured diplomat-types and repeat the same expression: devilishly delightful.

But as always the contradictions within him were at work. In the same letter he thanks Einar Ólafur for having introduced him to a book that he kept close at hand for the rest of his life: *De Imitatione Christi* by Thomas à Kempis.

On the Imitation of Christ came into Halldór's life at the right time. He read this five-hundred-year-old book first in English and, after he learnt Latin, he always reread it in the original. It was the only book on Halldór's writing desk when I visited him in 1983. Thomas à Kempis wrote about the dangers inherent in loving earthly life, and about the necessity of humility.

Humility appealed strongly to Halldór precisely because it represented the opposite of the superman concept that sometimes gripped him. Immense ambition combined with unbelievable self-confidence were contradicted by humility and submission for the sake of high ideals. When Halldór's religious period ended, the Book of the Way and its Power by Lao-Tzu met this same need to be reminded of the soft and weak as opposed to ambition and struggle.

Through his reading of Thomas à Kempis he discovered what a consolation it could be for a restless writer to deny himself, plagued as he often was by doubts about his vocation. When Kristín Thurnwald wrote to him concerning what a gift it was to be a writer, Halldór replied:

No . . . let me go to hell if it is good to be a writer! It is perhaps better for some people to read a good book (and best, easiest, most sweet for women who have mastered the art of letting it go in one ear and out the other with just as much pleasure) than to write a good book, to be condemned to this by all the merciless, horrific powers of the world, condemned to untie such a Gordian knot as creating a work of art, to be an intermediary who interprets the revelations of something beautiful and powerful, no heavier cross has been laid upon another man's shoulders, no more painful torment in any man's breast.

Thus did Halldór waver between arrogance and meekness. Although Thomas à Kempis had sown a fertile seed in his mind, his work as a writer continued to have the stronger hold. Having decided to go to North America, he had started thinking about the artistic form most popular there: the motion picture. At the end of March he wrote to Kristín Thurnwald from Leipzig: "Otherwise the most interesting thing to tell of me is that I am writing a film script in English – it is one of the things that will conquer the world." Here once again Halldór's grandiose way of thinking is evident.

On Easter Day, 1922, he arrived in Hamburg, informing Einar Ólafur by post that he was writing the script and that the Lord wanted to send him to Holland and from there to New York: "I do not agree with this but it is useless to argue."

On 23 March he sent Erlendur Guðmundsson a remarkable message:

What I mean is, that since I plan to live abroad, perhaps ultimately for the greater part of my life, and do not want to have to resign myself to having others always call me by my paternal name (according to the customary, universal naming system), I plan to adopt a *characteristic* family name as my *Rufname* for use when among foreigners. The name that I am thinking of adopting is the possessive form of Laxnes, i.e., Laxness.

He asked Erlendur to take care of the necessary paperwork, and his name was formally changed and listed in the *Government Gazette* approximately one year later.

His pen name prepared, his film script in the works, Halldór felt ready to try his luck in North America. Embarking in May, 1922, he travelled to New York, and although his dollars sufficed only for the trip, he was convinced that everything would work out. But things did not go as planned: he had not acquired the authorizations necessary for entry, and the authorities on Ellis Island quite simply turned him back – he was not allowed to enter the United States. According to Hannes H. Gissurarson, a phone call was made to Daníel Halldórsson in Canada, but Daníel would not take responsibility for Halldór – he was extremely displeased that all the money he had sent had been wasted on the young man's rambles through Europe.

Helga Kress has shown that Halldór continued to try, with the help of friends, to acquire the necessary paperwork from Canada later that same year and the year after. Nothing came of it until the summer of 1927, however. On his way back to Hamburg, he wrote the short story "Júdith Lhoff", the best story in *Several Stories*. The main character is a charming Russian girl who goes to Iceland by chance, and while there agrees to marry an Icelandic labourer, a true Viking as well as a faithful soul. The reader quickly realizes that she is playing the labourer for a fool, but he refuses to believe it: "He knew, in other words, the Icelandic saga; not the foreign novel." She betrays the labourer's trust and marries an American businessman, "so incredibly thin and limpid, his chest so narrow, his neck slender, his shoulders so weakly built and his hands powerless". While the story resembles that of Heiðbæs, it contains a variation in that the narrator has sight of two worlds, thus reflecting Halldór's own situation. Throughout his life he was pulled in two directions, to be an Icelander and a man of the world, and it was never easy. "Júdith Lhoff" is the first evidence of this dichotomy.

To the Cross

In the village of Rønne on Bornholm in Denmark lived the mason Julius Schou and his Icelandic wife, Sigríður Jónsdóttir. Julius had gone to Iceland from Bornholm in 1880, living in Reykjavík for forty years, and had only recently moved back to Denmark when Halldór looked to him for help after a short stay with friends in Copenhagen. Julius and Sigríður were acquaintances of Halldór's parents, and since he was now completely penniless he turned to them.

Even though Halldór was well received at Rønne, the usual afflictions plagued him and he did not feel well. One reason was his poverty. He had numerous debts and could not see any way to repay them, in fact could not even see a way to buy stamps, as he wrote to Einar Ólafur:

I am extremely depressed at the moment because just a few minutes ago, when I went down to drink coffee, the householder started asking me when I would be able to pay for my lodging. Luckily the man does not know how accursed I feel because of this, how it has completely ruined my day, and I even feel since coming up to my room again as if the sun there in heaven holds absolutely nothing for me.

This was a difficult situation for a man as proud as Halldór. He was trying to sell stories to *Berlingske Tidende*, but the editors there seemed reluctant to buy them. On 30 June he asked Jón Helgason to send material to another journal, and whether he might expect help from the Danish–Icelandic Society:

It has caused me no little anxiety to be in such a state of need that I am not able to pay you the money that I owe you, as things stand now. I do, however, have everything that I need to live here . . .

That Halldór was lonely at Bornholm is revealed in a long poem he deftly composed in Danish on the evening of the feast of St John, called "Sankt Hansilden blusset" ("St John's Fire Blazes"):

> St John's fire blazes in the night.
> See the bonfires all around!
> I walk here alone in the sand,
> a wanderer, a foreigner.

He sought comfort from a servant-girl at the farm, Málfríður Jónsdóttir, who was six years older than him. Their romance must have been short, but it was still long enough for Málfríður to have become pregnant by the time Halldór left Rønne, although he did not hear of this until the autumn. Their daughter, Sigríður María Elísabet, was born on 10 April, 1923. Halldór received no news of his daughter until six months later, though the agency of the Catholic Prelate Meulenberg in Reykjavík, and Reverend Árni Sigurðsson, who christened Maria when she was five months old. Halldór was thus no longer able to hide the fact that he had become a father, but did not write to Málfríður until 20 December, 1923. He reveals in this letter that he has little experience of babies, because he asks about his daughter: "Can she walk? Can she talk? Can she sing?"

Born in 1896, Málfríður Jónsdóttir went only to elementary school, because she had to start work at an early age. A pretty woman, she was rather reticent, and had certainly not been the instigator in her relationship with Halldór.

Although Málfríður had from the start brought up the child alone, with the help of her parents and sisters, she remained fond of Halldór. Their daughter believes that they spent some time together in the spring of 1925, before Halldór went to Sicily. A letter Halldór sent to Málfríður from overseas in the autumn suggests this:

> Thank you very much for our last meeting; I can express perfectly my grat-
> itude for what you did for me that last evening. That was very beautiful of
> you. I do not have any relationships with any women, and you are the only
> woman that I have ever touched. I will never be enamoured of women and
> am not fond of any except for my mother and the mother of my child. I am
> certain that I will never marry. I can never do anything for a woman, have
> nothing to offer.

María spent her summers at Laxnes from the age of two until Halldór's mother could no longer look after the house. His sisters were good to her, though. Halldór was not very fatherly when he visited. María remembers him this way:

> I knew that this was my father, but I viewed him just as I would a stranger.
> He was, that is to say, my father – but nothing else; I did not feel any attach-
> ment to him.

Málfríður raised María and lived with her for forty-two years until she moved to a retirement home. She died on 7 November, 2003, then the oldest of all Icelanders, aged one hundred and seven.

*

During his summer on Bornholm, Halldór thought more and more about matters of faith. The Schou family belonged to the island's sparse Catholic congregation, and Rønne was visited by a number of priests to whom Halldór talked. He was of course mulling over what he had seen in Germany, what he had read in philo-sophical works, and not least his own anguish and uncertainty. In a letter to Einar Ólafur dated 3 July he writes about his religious development: he had never prayed as much as now, because little by little he was coming to grasp the meaning of the words "Thy will be done":

> I feel the inexpressible near to me for only a fraction of an instant, and that
> is precisely what I long to discover next. My spirit has cried out and shouted;
> it is this nearness that I yearn constantly to feel, because without conscious-
> ness of such a divine presence it is certain and absolute that a man can never
> become truly useful to the world or descry the greater truth.

It was as if Halldór was searching for the perception and presence of something higher, and that if he had found it he would have been prepared to deny his own will and ambition. Besides Thomas à Kempis he read the famous autobiography of the most widely recognized Scandinavian Catholic writer and poet, Johannes Jørgensen. The Danish Jørgensen had converted to Catholicism in 1896, and in the autobiography, based on diaries he kept beginning in childhood, he details his youth and upbringing, his first marriage and his conversion. Halldór was moved by what he read that summer and viewed Johannes as a role model: here was a respected writer who had accepted the Catholic faith.

In an article Halldór wrote for the journal *Catholic Youth* early the next year he said that Johannes outshone his paltry contemporaries. Later on he wrote to Johannes directly: "In a very sensitive period for me [your books] have given me tremendous strength; you have played a great role in helping me find the path to Catholicism." Halldór held the Danish writer in great esteem for virtually his entire life and kept a photograph of him on his desk.

There were also literary reasons for the fact that Halldór found inspiration in Johannes Jørgensen: Strindberg's *Inferno* closes after the narrator has become acquainted with Johannes' work and is waiting to enter an abbey to find psychological and spiritual peace. Precisely twenty-five years after *Inferno* was published, Halldór wrote to Jørgensen in Assisi to ask if he could help him find a place in a monastery. By the time he received an answer, Halldór had left Bornholm and was staying with a priest, Torkil Skat Rørdam, whom he had met by chance in Ryslinge on Fyn and who had invited Halldór to visit him. Halldór accepted gladly, penniless as he was, and went to Fyn early in the autumn. Torkil Skat Rørdam was not a Catholic, but he was extremely religious and led a separatist congregation that was in conflict with the Danish national church.

Halldór was in Ryslinge in September, 1922. According to him, he worked fourteen to sixteen hours a day, trying to finish *The Red Booklet* in the hope that Guðmundur Hagalín, who had become the editor of a newspaper in Seyðisfjörður, would be able to get it printed. But Halldór could not stay in Ryslinge past 6 October, and he asked Einar Ólafur to send him 8 krónur so that he could pay his way to Copenhagen. He also asked Einar Ólafur to find some work for him there, for example, copying old manuscripts.

While in Ryslinge Halldór received two fateful letters. He remained silent about the first of them until he wrote the introduction to *Days with Monks*:

I . . . received . . . a letter with news that I had made a girl pregnant in Rønne earlier in the summer. I was worried that it would put a black mark on my record.

This letter seems only to have served to strengthen Halldór's determination to enter a monastery – it was as if he refused to accept the fact that he had a child. The other letter was a reply from Johannes Jørgensen in Assisi, in which the Danish Catholic says that he has arranged for Halldór to visit the newly built abbey of St Maurice de Clervaux in Luxembourg. The only problem was that Halldór had no money to get there.

Halldór made it to Copenhagen and then to his friend Jóhann Jónsson in Leipzig. It is not known precisely how he paid for these trips, but he always managed to find ways to procure money in the 1920s. Halldór's grandchild, Auður Jónsdóttir, said that Halldór's mother had sent him a gold medallion that the Danish king had given to Halldór's sister Sigríður after she had played the organ for him as a child. Sigríður kept the medallion in a special box, but one day it was gone: their mother had sent it to her big brother as travel money. Halldór's friends in North America had also continued to collect money for him to visit them there. A mutual friend of Halldór and Jóhann Jónsson, Friðrik Friðriksson, took out a 200-dollar loan that winter and sent it to Halldór, who had yet to repay it sixteen years later.

In Leipzig Halldór stayed for a time with Jóhann and Nikkólína, and redrafted the story about Júdith Lhoff. He entered the abbey in Luxembourg at the end of November, 1922, as a guest. Established in 1909, the abbey had been completed in 1910. That same year Pope Pius X had established a prayer network there, its goal being the reconversion of Scandinavia to the Catholic faith. As an errant Scandinavian soul, Halldór was a welcome guest. In a newspaper article published two years later he described his arrival:

The Abbey of St Maurice is located on a mountaintop and looms large when seen from down in the village, and it is blissful to come there as a guest just when the vesper bell is ringing. The path to the abbey from the village consists of steep steps that lead up a hillside covered with evergreens, then along the abbey wall for a while, until one finally reaches the hilltop and a large gate. The guest opens a low door in the wall to one side of the gate and stands the next moment on a narrow lawn, closed off on all sides, and opposite him tower the main doors of the abbey and the church, with columns in front and impressive towers above. He ascends the steps to the abbey's main doors, broad and wide, and rings the doorbell. A long time might pass before anyone comes to the door. Finally a tiny hatch at the top of the door is opened and a face peeks out. It is Brother Paul, in his cowl with his hood hanging over his ears, who greets you . . . The custom of the Benedictines is to greet a visitor as if he were Christ himself. And that is because one is never certain, when one meets a stranger, that it might not be Christ himself in disguise.

Much has been written concerning Halldór's stay at the abbey, there being a number of sources on which to draw, including the diary he kept while there, memoirs and numerous detailed letters to his friends. But why did he enter a monastery in the first place? Although he thought that he was following in the steps of Strindberg, Halldór's reasons seem in fact to have been ideological, psychological and financial. He was, in every sense of the phrase, seeking refuge. Ever since his childhood the idea of a higher world and values had worked upon him strongly, and ever since his confirmation he had considered Lutheranism to be a "lukewarm" religion at best. He wanted to discover whether a life devoted to Christ, under the terms of Catholic monasticism, could bring him closer to lasting values. Doubts frequently assailed him as to whether human life could be reconciled to higher spiritual values. He knew perfectly well that Iceland still had a long way to go towards "modernity", and had also beheld the terrible consequences of the war in the countries that were the supposed champions of the concept of modernism.

Of course there was a literary influence; Halldór's determination had been strengthened by his reading of European *fin-de-siècle* literature, in which the self or ego stands ever alone against the universe. As Giovanni Papini, one of Halldór's inspirations for *The Great Weaver from Kashmir*, put it: "The universe is divided into two: me – and the rest." This self-centred world-view appealed to the writer in Halldór.

When fear and anxiety are added to the assault upon one's self-image, causing one to doubt one's ability to make choices, release can be found in devoting oneself to some higher power. Halldór was penniless, unsuccessful in getting published at home and abroad, and had no idea how to react to the fact that he was a father. Could not the abbey support his reading and writing, help him to rebuild his strength and regain his self-confidence without his having to worry constantly about his finances?

His first reactions upon arrival were light-hearted and happy. After a week he sent Einar Ólafur a postcard:

> Good friend. In this place I have for the first time in my life entered into the company of educated men. The days pass by one after another divided between work and prayer. The wisest and most amiable elder that I have ever met, Father Beda, is my teacher in the ecclesiastical sciences, and will hopefully be my baptismal father.

The abbey welcomed the young visitor with open arms, brought order to his days and nights, and calmed the waves of his soul. Each day began at five with morning services, which took two hours, followed by the so-called silent masses, wherein each priest said his own mass at a little altar, and, finally, chanting, which ended around eight-thirty; then there was breakfast, and high mass at ten. High mass was the most ceremonious part of the day, on holy days celebrated with all the accoutrements at the Church's disposal. Next the monks had time free for work, with vespers at four, followed by more free time until evening services at nine. Thus the monks' days and nights were entirely planned out.

As a guest Halldór was not required to attend all the holy services, but he chose most often to do so anyway – he was the kind of person who could do nothing in halves. Now he sank himself into study to discover whether Christ would determine his fate. Was it possible that he could divorce himself from the world outside and gain spiritual peace?

Pater Beda von Hessen, a German priest nearly eighty years old, who had lived almost all his life in monasteries, became Halldór mentor. In a letter written to Einar Ólafur at Christmas, Halldór said about Beda:

His experience and understanding of the soul of man are startling; when I sit before him I can feel how he reads every one of my thoughts before I speak a word, and perceives every movement of my mind down to its roots. I have not seen a more beautiful old man; his sincere, childlike smile never disappears from his face, nor do his nobility or quietude.

Beda von Hessen became not only Halldór's baptismal father but also his father figure, a man whom he admired for his vast learning and no less for his humanity and tolerance.

Beda was not only an acute perceiver of the oscillations of a restless soul, he also became for Halldór a symbol of men who had successfully followed the call to humility. This is why Steinn Elliði's alter ego in *The Great Weaver* is in some ways modelled on Father Beda, and in the same sense Beda is – along with Erlendur Guðmundsson – the predecessor of Halldór's Taoist characters like the organist in *Atom Station* and Pastor Jón Prímus in *Under the Glacier*. These are men of clemency and charity, entirely unconcerned with worldly advancement. Even in *The Book of the People* (1929), when Halldór accepts faith in humanity over faith in God and presents himself as an advocate of social reform, he pays respect to Father Beda. Halldór described his own return to the abbey in the late autumn of 1925 when he felt like a deranged woman staring into the grave of her child. Of course its eternal gates were closed to my soul from that time on, but I knew that, although all the channels were closed, the friendly embrace of the monk Beda would still be open to me.

He was not disappointed – Beda welcomed him, he said, as a true friend who would never betray him although he might betray them.

During his first weeks Halldór took his work seriously. In his Christmas letter to Einar Ólafur he wrote the following about the Abbot, Dom Alardo, though he crossed it out in Stefán Einarsson's manuscript:

Some of the most blessed moments that I have ever lived occurred when I was allowed to kiss the hand of this highly venerable man, and when he placed the palm of his hand on my head and spoke some fatherly words.

The seeker had found refuge with the fathers; his aberrance was at an end. Halldór was baptized a Catholic on 6 January, 1923. He adopted the name Halldór Kiljan Marie Pierre Laxness (Kiljan being an Irish saint's name and the closest he could find to an Icelandic name; he used it in his pen name for the next forty years).

Halldór was impressed by the fact that many of the monks were exceptionally learned men, who, he thought, had had careers and plans for worldly advancement that they had sacrificed according to St Benedict's weightiest rule: *Operi Dei nihil præponatur*, "Let nothing be preferred to the work of God." His childish admiration for these men was sometimes mixed with fear, and sometimes revealed his need for adoration and obedience. Thus he admitted to Jón Helgason, in a letter dated 8 May, that he had discovered yet another superior being: the Prior, Alexander Ely:

If I were a novice under his guidance I would fear him somewhat, as I did Jón Ófeigsson in the old days. One novice told me that he was eternally strong in an eternally gentle way. They all love him and admire him limitlessly. He knows everything, they say.

Halldór was deeply affected when, several weeks later, the Prior left to become a novice in the much stricter Carthusian order: "He left the abbey yesterday morning, as completely destitute as Jesus Christ himself, with nothing but a staff in his hand," he wrote to Einar Ólafur. Halldór reused this event in *The Great Weaver*, and in all his works one can see his respect for men who dedicate themselves selflessly to their callings and turn their backs on honours and advancement.

The forces that had compelled Halldór to enter the abbey continued to battle within him, however, no matter how much admiration he had for the monks, as can be seen in his diary and letters. Humility did not come naturally, and from the beginning of 1923 he began to send his friends what he called "universal letters". He said that he was giving his friends the opportunity to follow his spiritual development, and that he was determined to defend himself against their criticism, whether it was directed against Catholicism or based on suspicions that he had entered the abbey for economic reasons. One can see traces of the flippant attitude that characterized his letter writing throughout his life, however. For instance, he tells Jón Helgason of how well off the monks and their guests are with regard to food, drink and intellectual conversation:

I am thankful for the prevision that has now spirited me away from the world and all its women and all that other damned idiocy in which it is richest. Because as far as my "respectable me" is concerned, the ultimate truth is that it hates women, despises and fears the same (NB: with the exception of my friends' wives, whom I love).

But in the letter's postscript he adds: "I am wearing leather trousers."

Despite his occasionally informal tone, there is no question that Halldór was serious. He was thinking about attending a seminary in Rome and becoming a Jesuit priest, and wondered how he could gain his matriculation first. Stefán Einarsson's biography says that Halldór had planned to enter the Propaganda College in Rome, the Vatican department dedicated to preaching the faith, not least in countries that were not Catholic. Halldór wrote often, and with deep sincerity, about his yearning for the Lord and a pure faith, as well as his wish to devote himself to the preaching of the truth of Jesus Christ. There was no middle ground: "One either gives oneself to the devil completely or sacrifices one's life and soul to a divine idea," he wrote in one of his "universal letters".

At the same time he was learning French and Latin, adding them to the languages he already knew: German, Danish and English. He read voraciously, mostly religious works and scholastic philosophy, including the works of Thomas Aquinas, but also novels by Catholic writers. Among these the novel *Le Disciple* (1899) by Paul Bourget had the greatest influence on him, perhaps because it is about a young man who loses his ethical perspective due to his riotous ambition and scientific pursuits. Knowledge of French allowed Halldór access to a wider literary world because the abbey's library kept a variety of French cultural journals on its shelves. It was there that he first became acquainted with Marcel Proust and heard of the latest trends in French avant-gardism. If one takes *The Saga of the Seven Masters* at its word, the monks allowed him to order modern literature of the widest variety, as long as he took the books with him when he left the abbey. It is more likely, however, that contemporary literature was on his reading list more often during his second stay, in the winter of 1925–6.

Halldór did not stop writing at the abbey, although he did perhaps slow down to some degree. At the start of March, 1923, he described for Einar Ólafur what he had been doing during the previous three months:

> . . . I have written more than a thousand pages in all of my novel. Out of that, four hundred pages (half as large) clean-copied twice. In addition, I have written three extremely difficult essays, one in Danish (whether they will be printed at some time I do not know). Have written around seventy letters, some quite long, as you know. Have learnt French, of which I knew only one word when I arrived here (that was the word *dans*, which I learnt from you!). I am now reading all the French literature that I possibly can. Have learnt a considerable amount of Latin. Have read at least a dozen books in different languages, mostly theological works, some extremely difficult. Besides that I have spent an average of three hours a day in prayer and worship.

Halldór's obsession with writing was just as incurable as when he had sat as a boy in his small room at Laxnes, and apart from the time that he spent in prayer there was little that drew his mind away from his writing. The novel that he mentions in the letter was his one and only attempt to write a Catholic novel, *At the Foot of the Sacred Peak* (1924). The first draft, written at the abbey, was one thousand three hundred pages long. Although it was just one-third of that length when it was published, it did not comprise a unified whole. Halldór had strong doubts about it, which he expressed to Einar Ólafur: "I hate and despise myself for this chicken-hearted task, yet must continue the damned rubbish since I have spent so much time and energy on it." He feared that he was losing his Icelandic because of his prolonged stay in foreign lands; his subject-matter was hardly worth the effort; his novelistic writings showed precisely how far he still had to go, and how he was still devoted to vanity. Perhaps he felt that his writing and his faith would never harmonize, and this weighed heavily upon him, as his concluding words in one letter written in the spring indicate: "I feel terribly ill. But Christ is risen."

Sometimes he was plagued by doubts about what he was doing, by the feeling that he had no power over his writing or his faith. On 5 March he wrote in his diary:

> Idler, ragamuffin, impossible person. I have experienced the greatest anguish due to my exiguity and worthlessness in everything. I am a perfect example of a wretch. Foolish, ingenuous, cowardly, void of character.

And he adds: "With the exception of being prideful and having empty dreams of being a superman, I am nothing." There is a fine line between ostentation and self-pity, and both of them tugged at Halldór during those weeks and months. Industriousness was innate in him, but he was not sure that he was on the right path. His youthful fears plagued him now and then as well, as can be seen in his diary entry for 18 April:

> Last night I was paralyzed by the fear of death. I woke up again and again almost screaming with fear at the thought of having to die sometime, and prayed loudly in utter darkness. This morbid anguish is the most horrid visitor. And scarcely a day passes when it does not fill my soul for longer or shorter periods of time.

Much of what he wrote in this diary should be considered the natural struggle of a young man who wishes to turn to God, as this entry dated 9 March shows: "God grant me the strength to do something great and vital for the world, and to deny myself entirely! I prayed a great deal for chastity as well." The last-mentioned item must have proved difficult for Halldór, because time and again the diary mentions the beautiful and tempting women who were giving him the eye. Once when a noble-looking young woman in black sat down a short distance from him at mass it was enough to prevent him from receiving the Eucharist, since he imagined that she had been sent from the Inferno (19 February). The girl who sat at her window in a village house did all she could to seduce him when he passed by, but he was careful not to look up, except very quickly (22 February). And on 8 April he wrote: "I am often engaged in an enormous struggle with my flesh and the worship of vanity." But, if we take the diary at its word, nothing more serious happened than a shy glance and an unclean thought or two, and for the most part Halldór passed his time in prayer and writing, as well as in conversation with the monks and guests.

Besides the older monks, Halldór became acquainted with the abbey's other guests; he particularly enjoyed the company of the young Portuguese prince Duarte de Braganca, who had been driven into exile when his father had been overthrown in 1910. They discussed many things on long walks together. Halldór also found soulmates in two young Danish brothers, Bengt and Jan Ballin, and his most painful experience in the abbey occurred when Bengt suddenly took ill and died – Halldór wrote that he wept for a long time and prayed for Bengt's soul. Jan persuaded Halldór to write an article about his conversion to Catholicism for the Danish journal *Catholic Youth*. Another good friend in the abbey was the Norwegian Arne v. Juell-Skielse, who at that time used the paternal name Skjelsö. Halldór prayed often for his Icelandic friends, that they might be freed from the Lutheran heresy, and not least among those was the good pastor Halldór Kolbeins, as the diary shows.

The most memorable guest at the abbey was the unusual Danish scholar Dr Konrad Simonsen. Simonsen, who held a doctorate in comparative literature, had lived an eventful life and had travelled far and wide in his search for the truth before arriving at the abbey in August, 1923. He was much older than Halldór; they nevertheless became good friends. On 1 September Halldór informed Einar Ólafur by letter that Dr Simonsen had been at the abbey for a fortnight, and that they often took long walks and argued in Danish about philosophy:

> Dr Simonsen is endlessly genial and I spend a lot of time these days laughing with him (otherwise I have not laughed for ten months). He buys boxes of chocolates to give to the novices and laughs and chatters in the abbey hall-ways, and he holds discussions with everyone in the house.

From Konrad Simonsen's diaries it can be seen that the pleasure had been mutual. On 10 September he wrote that he learnt a great deal from his daily walks with the young Icelander, since Halldór had trained himself to keep a tight rein on his desires; from his entry several days later it can be seen that he considered Halldór to be extremely talented. Halldór held a place of honour on a list Simonsen kept of his friends that winter, and when Simonsen was baptized a Catholic at the end of September Halldór was his sponsor, although he was a quarter of a century younger than the Danish scholar.

Both Halldór and Simonsen left the abbey in the autumn, but they kept in touch. Simonsen later returned to the abbey, remaining there until the summer of 1924. Like Halldór, he sought out the company of the old priest Beda. In June, however, the gifts of chocolates and pious prayers came to an end due to a "scandal". A Danish newspaper reporter, Knud Holmboe, who was a guest there, felt obliged to make Simonsen's homosexuality public, and suggested that he was there to make advances to the novices; he cited the chocolates as evidence. After Holmboe was unsuccessful in having Simonsen driven out, among other things because Father Beda defended him, he convinced Johannes Jørgensen to join him, and together they were able to get Simonsen expelled for crimes against morality.

Halldór received news of these events and was deeply hurt. He sent Jón Helgason a letter about the affair in the late summer of 1924:

> Dr Konrad Simonsen has been subjected to the most horrific accusations, and I consider the article in *Politiken* even more disgraceful, since I am better acquainted with the truth of this affair.

Halldór cited a letter received from Father Beda that said that it was nothing but Simonsen's philanthropy, his openness and gullibility that had led to this situation. Halldór added:

> Johannes Jørgensen made one of the most miserable and ignoble trips to Clervaux that I have ever heard of, and was fairly driven back out of the abbey . . . I pledge on my honour that Dr Simonsen is as innocent as a child of this disgraceful calumny, and you should reiterate that whenever you hear anything to the contrary.

A serious blow had been dealt to Halldór's sense of justice. Although he himself never felt the need to put up fences around his private life, he was always suspicious of those who rebuked others for their lifestyles or preached "average Christian behaviour", as he called it. Nearly a decade later he wrote an entertaining narrative about this case, "The Search for the Truth", in *A Day's Journey in the Mountains* (1937), in which Konrad Simonsen is called Knud Sörensen and Johannes Jørgensen Professor Sacristan. Halldór's sympathy for Simonsen is clear, but he also does not hide the childishness and the occasional naiveté of his friend in his search for truth.

*

In the spring of 1923 Halldór's short stories were finally published in Iceland, first in a series in *Morgunblaðið* from March until summer, and then collectively in the volume *Several Stories*. Although it is never expressed openly, it is clear that the story "Sir", written in Copenhagen in the autumn of 1919, describes a young man's visit to a prostitute: "Tonight I have quaffed from the cup of pleasure, all the way down to the last drops." Halldór is no more outspoken about sexual matters in this story than in his other writings, but its subject is clear, and many in the small town of Reykjavík would find it scandalous.

At the start of September Halldór received a letter from Prelate Meulenberg, in

Reykjavík. Meulenberg said, among other things, that "Sir" had done immeasurable damage, that he had never seen such immoral writing in an Icelandic newspaper, before and that everyone was scandalized, Catholics most of all. Halldór reacted in a very unusual way. In "an open letter to Icelandic readers" published in *Morgunblaðið* on 6 October, 1923, he asked for forgiveness and expressed his regret that the story was published. He says that he had written it at the age of seventeen, at that time an atheist engaged in a struggle with "artistic dabblers and poetic loafers", and that "the lewd narrative mode" bore witness to the atmosphere in which he had lived. He says that he had sent *Morgunblaðið* the stories in the summer of 1922, and then not given them another thought, in fact had no idea what had become of them. This was not entirely correct, since his sister Sigríður had written to him when they were published in the paper. As a Catholic he found the story abominable: "It is with blushing cheeks and painful shame that I recall this filthy work."

It seems that two factors were at play in Halldór's apology: he was seeking absolution but was not as remorseful as he made himself seem for the fact that the story was published. A notice from the editor of *Morgunblaðið* followed, in which he confirmed Halldór's statements regarding the story's publication and also pointed out that the story was perhaps not so dangerous now. The pettiness and priggishness of the Icelandic literary world in the years after the First World War appear nowhere more clearly than here.

Halldór was correct in saying that by that time he had come a long way from the short stories of his youth; he was completely occupied with the novel *At the Foot of the Sacred Peak* and was wondering how to gain control of Icelandic as it gained a hold on modernity. He wrote to Einar Ólafur:

> The Icelandic that we have to work with at this time is the purest abomination of the language. In it we find the same awkwardness and spinelessness as we do in modern Icelanders in general, in their character and culture, that is; they can never be either one thing or the other.

Here, for the first time, Halldór was expressing the ideas that compelled him to establish the foundation for modern Icelandic literature with *The Great Weaver from Kashmir*. Traditional Icelandic literature did not grasp reality, and he was also convinced that the language of the sagas would never do for modern writers. This was a view he expounded often, in various forms, during the 1920s.

That year and the next Halldór considered seriously whether he ought to write in a foreign language, or even settle in a foreign country. The longer he stayed at the abbey, the more earnest he became in asking himself whether he should continue to pursue his goal of being a writer. In a letter to Einar Ólafur he wrote:

> I have finally rid myself of the disease that has plagued me from childhood – namely graphomania. I am done with being "a writer". I woke up to that realization one fine day last week and suddenly felt alive again.

Several weeks later he described the same event to Jón Helgason, but then immediately started to distance himself from his decision, adding that he had been struggling for months to rewrite *At the Foot of the Sacred Peak*:

> I then discovered that I . . . was a chronic graphomaniac, since my entire life for twenty-one years had never been anything but the outpouring of my insane passion for writing. At this discovery I became so terrified that I hurried to direct my poetry towards the cross, although I had by that time finished rewriting a third of the first volume, or nearly that much. I sent this third of the manuscript to Iceland and burnt everything else that I'd written, hid my pen and ink, and wandered about God's green earth for more than a week trying to convince myself that I was cured of the writing disease.

In a continuation of this letter he summarized the novel for Jón and his wife, and was obviously quite proud of himself; it was clear that his writing disease was not entirely cured. *At the Foot of the Sacred Peak* was published a year later, but it suffered from the fact that Halldór never really finished it.

Home and Away

> I am created from the fates of men and women, nations and entire centuries. During the day I walk up to a hilltop and stretch out my arms and feel like dying from the knowledge that I am composed of so many different fates.
>
> *Halldór Laxness in a letter*

Halldór sent Jón Helgason the letter about his writing obsession from Paris. Through the agency of Jan Ballin he had received a French grant and so had left the abbey on 5 October. A day before, he had reaffirmed his faith by becoming a Benedictine *oblatus sæcularis*, pledging to maintain a Christian lifestyle in the spirit of St Benedict. Taking this vow was the closest that Halldór ever came to becoming a monk. But in doing so was he devoting himself even more to Catholicism? He described the event to Stefán Einarsson eight years later:

I was consecrated an *oblatus sæcularis*, and was given the name Maurus, but the consecration was in my eyes something of a "joke." I did it mostly out of courtesy to the monks and "for sport", because by that time I had already almost completely lost my faith and rarely received Holy Communion, except for propriety's sake.

Halldór's explanations after the fact should always be taken with a pinch of salt, but he did – as is common for religious people – endure intense psychological struggles the whole time he was at the abbey. Clear testimony for this is seen in a comment he made in one of his letters: "If there is any creature in the world that suffers and struggles relentlessly day and night, it is Halldór Kiljan Laxness." His soul was pulled in two directions: to the Church and unconditional service to God, and to his writing and thoughts of worldly advancement.

From both points of view Paris seemed a good destination, not least because the most famous of Icelandic Catholics, Jón Sveinsson, lived there. Jón, known as Nonni, had left Iceland at a very young age and become a Jesuit. He was also the best known of Icelandic writers because of his children's books, which he wrote in German. Enormously popular in Europe, they were printed in huge numbers, although Nonni of course did not profit from this, since he was obliged to donate his earnings to the Jesuit order.

Halldór was interested both in the teachings of the Jesuits and in meeting an Icelandic writer who was popular outside Iceland. When he first wrote to Nonni from the abbey in the spring, he was quite clear about this.

Although they became friends during the 1920s and wrote to each other a great deal, there could hardly have been two more dissimilar men, one huge, elderly, yet childlike and sincere, the other young, ambitious, impatient, optimistic and slim. Many years later Halldór said about Nonni:

He was one of those few men who are absolutely, perfectly magical. He became more interesting to me the better I got to know him – and I could hardly say that I knew him very well.

In Paris Halldór lived in a large house under the supervision of the Benedictines in Anteuil. It was there that he first met Nonni. That autumn he wrote an article for *Morgunblaðið* in which he suggested that it was high time that the Jesuit was invited back to Iceland. When Halldór met him, Nonni had not been to Iceland for more than half a century. Two days later Halldór wrote to Jón Helgason in much the same spirit, saying that he was mostly keeping company with the Jesuits, which he found a unique pleasure.

In the interim both Prelate Meulenberg and Reverend Árni Sigurðsson had written to tell him that he had become a father. He wrote to Jón Helgason: "As far as my paternal history is concerned, it is certainly all true, except that I have had a daughter rather than a son," adding in a carefree tone: "If you and Ásta have a son, we should marry them." But he was concerned that the situation could affect his plans for the future:

Otherwise this paternal mess is the greatest nuisance, and puts numerous obstacles in my path, since I intend to become a priest. But my friends the monks in Clervaux are all on my side, and are as firm as can be that I as a Catholic do not bear any responsibility for the blunders that I have committed as a Protestant.

The last statement shows in any case that Halldór had acquired some understanding of scholasticism.

Although Halldór might have found it entertaining to dispute with Jesuits about waywardness in a Paris suburb, he wanted to travel further south, in the footsteps of Catholic pilgrims. Nonni procured some money for him to go to Lourdes in Southern France and on to Loyola in Spain, where the founder of the Jesuit order had lived. Halldór set off on 19 October, 1923, travelling mostly by train.

Interest in wonders and miracles went hand-in-hand with the spiritualist movements of first part of the twentieth century, and almost a million pilgrims went to Lourdes during the summer of 1923. He was very interested in stories about the place and read as much as he could about the miraculous healing that occurred there. That the town had an effect on him can be seen from a postcard he sent Einar Ólafur:

The place is very supernatural, the air thick with prayers and wonder-works and the fragrance of incense and hymns of praise and worship and blessings and holiness. It is teeming here with pilgrims from all nations, who do nothing but pray to God from morning until night, from night until morning. Night and day masses are said, sometimes many masses at once, and also around every altar (there are more than seventy altars in the pilgrims' churches here) . . . Before the grotto . . . lie rich and poor, clerics and laymen face down in the dust, weeping. Within the grotto almost a thousand candles burn night and day. Here one stands face to face with the supernatural.

Although he promised in a letter to Jón Helgason to give lectures about Lourdes in Reykjavík, it is probable that his visit increased his doubts rather than the other way round; he later became critical of everything having to do with mediums and miracles, in fact. In an interview with Ólafur Ragnarsson he said of his visit to Lourdes: "I found it obvious that this was all a kind of swindle."

After ten days in Lourdes Halldór made a trip to the monastery at Loyola. Despite his contemplation of divinity and his own life calling, it should be remembered that he was only twenty-one and acquainting himself with new wonders all the time. He often radiated joy, as when he took a two-day car trip over the Pyrenees; in those bleak mountains his thoughts returned to Iceland.

During the trip south Halldór re-experienced the joys of earthly existence. At the same time the trip triggered a sort of poetic frenzy, and he composed numerous adroitly crafted, clear, often humorous poems. This was the kind of poetry that appealed most to Halldór, and that he came across later in a collection by Bertolt Brecht, *A Manual of Piety* (1927). Although Halldór never dreamt of being a poet, his poems, many of which he included in his novels, fill a volume of a hundred and sixty pages: *Collected Poetry* (1930).

The celebration of humanity that Halldór permitted himself on this journey was a mere diversion. When he returned to Paris he went straight on to London, with plans to go to a Catholic college in England.

For the next two months Halldór was in England, engrossed in Catholic studies and worship. He was first admitted to a Jesuit college in Osterley, Middlesex. His timetable there was extremely rigid, beginning at a quarter past five in the morning and continuing until ten at night. Besides English, Halldór studied Latin, Church history and theology, and for two hours a day the former farmboy from Laxnes worked in the garden. Added to this were readings and prayers. Despite his busy timetable, Halldór found time to continue writing.

Having put *At the Foot of the Sacred Peak* aside for the time being, he started on a new book that he described in a letter to Einar Ólafur:

It so happens that I am now gathering material for a new book that will be called *Between the Millstones* (shut up about the name!) In Danish it would be extremely well translated with the words: *I trædemøllen* [*In the Treadmill*]. This is a *Bildungsroman* about a young man who is nurtured at the breast of fashionable culture, and whose path leads later, in a remarkable way, to the foyer of the Holy Church, where he becomes a Catholic. In other words, it's my story.

Halldór was planning to write a universal apology for his conversion in the style of Johannes Jørgensen; in other words, his own saint's life. Benedikt Gröndal, another Icelandic writer whom he read that autumn, influenced him; he wrote an essay about Benedikt and published it in *Morgunblaðið* a year later, praising Gröndal's autobiography *Pastime* (1923), which was unique in its frankness and colourful characterizations. Halldór wanted to write the story of his own soul, just as he had attempted to do in *The Red Booklet*. The novel he described to Einar Ólafur was later entitled *When I Left Home*, but he stopped writing it in 1924, and it was not published until 1952. It was the predecessor to *The Great Weaver from Kashmir*.

At the Jesuit college Halldór read diligently about the Carthusians. On 18 November he wrote to Einar Ólafur: "No contemplative order moves me in such a way as this one, and if I wanted to become a contemplative monk I would without delay become a Carthusian." The chief guiding precept of the order is: "Although the world might change, the Cross remains." Halldór admired the order not least because its members had turned their backs on the world and dedicated themselves to God. He was allowed to visit their monastery in Sussex on the day after Christmas, after he attended mass at Westminster Cathedral, and he stayed there for ten days, living under the same conditions as the monks.

The order also includes laymen, and one such lay brother received Halldór. Complete silence reigned in the house, however. After Halldór was shown to a room the lay brother came to him and said that he could speak to him for a quarter of an hour. He asked Halldór whether he would like to be treated as a guest or if he preferred to follow the rules of the house, and asked: "What can you tell me of your soul?" The conversation came to an abrupt end after the fifteen minutes were up.

Because Halldór chose to follow the rules of the house, he was always sought for services, including three hours during the night; frequently the monks only partook of bread and water, and Halldór's letters reveal how much this strained his nerves. He tried to bear it well, writing to Einar Ólafur on 2 January, 1924:

My stay here has granted me no mental respite at all – four hour vigils at night in the church (from eleven until three) are not conducive to relaxation. On the other hand they work to pacify my soul. Absolute silence reigns here, and a man breathes in the fragrance of prayer with every step . . . I have spent my days here in constant prayer and meditation. The maturation that this week has granted me is more than my total maturation during the past year. I will be a different man when I come out of here again.

In the same letter, he apologizes for his moodiness and brusqueness in previous letters:

I have recently been terribly irritable, due to far too much spiritual strain (for example, for two nights in London I had to *be dragged* from my work to my bedroom); I have slept poorly, have had to struggle with various things.

Halldór returned to the Jesuit college, but his stay there soon came to an end. A letter he wrote to Jón Helgason from London on 12 January is filled with the contradictions that plagued him. First he tells of all the religious works he is reading, but then he adds:

I certainly work far too much, am emaciated, sleep poorly, am nervous and morbid. (For ten days after Christmas I stayed near the English Channel with the Carthusians, and did almost nothing there but pray, attended all the choir services . . . I have never at any other time in my life developed so incredibly much as during those ten days; I have beheld clearly the truth in many things that were previously hidden from me.) Despite the benefits of this life, I count the days until I can free myself from this place, because I fear that this will kill me or drive me insane.

Halldór had discovered the truth about himself: any decision to turn his back entirely on the world would lead him to insanity or death. This realization forms the basis of the opposition between Steinn and Diljá at the end of *The Great Weaver from Kashmir*. After Steinn has isolated himself in the monastery in Rome, Diljá says:

How he is holy and terrible in his Church, this God! His Church is even more powerful than the laws of nature and calls to itself the souls of men from east and west, north and south, calls them from all of the cardinal directions so that they might rise against the nature of the created and lift themselves from the dust to eternal life. Jesus Christ is a bizarre tyrant: his enemies crucified him, and he crucifies his friends in turn.

Halldór's faith was most likely never more passionate the Christmas and new year 1922–3. He found refuge at Clervaux, although his stay with the Carthusians the following Christmas marked both the apex of his monastic life and the beginning of its end. He comported himself as a Catholic for the next two years, but his thoughts were directed elsewhere. In the article he wrote about his stay with the Carthusians, he says:

I would like to add that although the paths shared between me and Christianity have diverged for the time being as distinctly as can possibly be expected . . . it is my experience and conviction that the most finely made, most excellent, and in most things most outstanding type of man of whom stories are told on earth is the particular type of ascetic that some canonical orders of the Holy Church have been able to create.

After London Halldór stayed for a time with acquaintances in Brighton, where there lived a woman from his own district, Valgerður from Hraðastaðir, who had married an elderly English millionaire by the name of Wall. He then gratefully accepted Jón Helgason's invitation to stay with him and his wife in Copenhagen. He left England for Copenhagen at the end of January 1924.

Halldór was both tired and mentally run down when he arrived at Jón and Þórunn's home. He read from *At the Foot of the Sacred Peak* at a meeting of Icelanders in Copenhagen, conversed a great deal with his hosts, Einar Ólafur and other acquaintances, and made contact with Danish Catholics. He had volunteered to lecture on the Carthusians at the Catholic Academy but bowed out at the last minute, saying that he was "in a state of shock after all the excitement in England".

Halldór travelled back to Iceland via Norway, arriving on 3 March: "We came to Reykjavík early in the morning in sunshine and frost, the mountains as white and radiant as saints' garments, the sky as blue as the mantle of God's mother," he wrote to Jón and Þórunn several days later. He thanked them for their hospitality and financial assistance, but said that he could not repay them for the time being. It was vital for him to conserve his energy; the stay in the monastery had affected him deeply. He had never come closer to admitting defeat before the power of the Church than when he was with the Carthusians, and just a few years later he viewed this stage of his life with revulsion, perceiving how close he had come to a tremendous abyss. While he was with Jón and Þórunn he had composed his most beautiful religious poem, "Hymn to Maria", which remained in their guest-book until much later. The poem is characterized by a genuine air of humility, beginning with the lines: "Help me, holy and kind/ bright Mother of Heaven!/ Lay my humble prayer/ at your child's heart!" His stay at the abbey was a kind of catharsis, and afterwards he mentioned his indisposition and panic attacks much less frequently.

Halldór joked about friends who were café philosophers and academics, some of whom he met as soon as he stepped off the ship from Denmark; it did not take long for his old arrogance to return. He felt like a man who, after escaping from some life-threatening danger, meets people who understand nothing. But he was convinced that others were interested in what he had to say:

Otherwise everyone in Reykjavík wants to eat me up. It's as if people here think that I'm hung meat, when in fact these poor people thirst after spiritual values; this has in some ways given me an unshakeable faith, as if I could easily expel from them all of their conceitedness and insipidness.

After having been at home for a week, Halldór says almost the same thing in a letter from Laxnes to Einar Ólafur in Copenhagen. He finds the cultural situation poor but cannot hide his pleasure at how often people ask after him and about Catholicism, and it is difficult to see which pleases him more. Of course he found it good to be home at Laxnes, where the dog Laxi recognized him and his ninety-two-year-old grandmother welcomed him warmly, having filled the cake tin twenty days earlier. He used this reunion later in his books. Guðný Klængsdóttir died a few weeks later.

People may have been curious about Halldór the Catholic and Halldór the writer, but he was not back in Iceland to waste his time idling, rather to attend to business. He contacted the rector of the Lyceum about his plans to take the exams for his matriculation in the autumn, since he was still intending to study at a seminary in Rome. He also met Þorsteinn Gíslason, the editor of *Morgunblaðið*, to discuss having both his short stories reprinted and *The Red Booklet* published. He was in contact with the most important publisher in Reykjavík, Ársæll Árnason, who was planning to publish *At the Foot of the Sacred Peak*. This happened in May of that year, two and a half years after the publication of *Child of Nature*.

At the Foot of the Sacred Peak is one of Halldór's least known works and has never been translated. It is divided into two segments, which are so unlike that the novel can be said to fall apart. The first segment, the shorter of the two, tells of the schoolfriends Snjólfur and Kjartan and describes their different views of life. Snjólfur betrays his dreams by opting for a bourgeois existence, but Kjartan is carried along by the current of the times. In the second part Kjartan has become a priest in the countryside and his son, Atli, is the protagonist, a revolutionary artist who learns to bow to Christ in humility. The novel shows signs of its author's having lost interest in it halfway through, having realized that it was far from the modern literature he had started to read, and he never tried to write its great continuation, the idea for which had begun to take shape at the abbey.

Although the work is not characteristic of Halldór's oeuvre, it does contain some good chapters and a lively narrative spirit, and several of its descriptions and stylistic qualities resonate with his later work. The reviews were favourable, for the most part. "There is an energy to this novel, unrest, gripping incidents and adventures. Halldór Kiljan Laxness is one of those from whom we can expect great things," said one reviewer in the daily newspaper *Tíminn*. Halldór was considered promising, progressive and perceptive; to have a power that was as yet untamed. But the literary clique in Reykjavík did not have a huge membership. Thus Halldór's childhood friend Guðmundur G. Hagalín wrote in *Vísir* that he was certain that the book would gain attention and be bought, but he also criticized it sharply. Jón Björnsson was disparaging in *Morgunblaðið*, like Hagalín citing the work's use of language.

In his own defence Halldór felt obliged to publish a special essay that autumn about the intentions he had had for the book, first in the *Book Lover*, which was published by Ársæll Árnason, and then in *Morgunblaðið*. In the essay he says that he had not intended to write the novel in a traditional manner, as any idiot could have done, but rather to introduce his readers to his personal artistic methods. He would never bind his art within a rigid form, since he always wished to call forth what he termed "living thought". It is true that Halldór did from that time on follow such a path, but when the essay was published his ideas were thought to be evidence of incredible foppishness. As Kristján Albertsson wrote in *Vörður*:

Whether he writes about Hamsun or describes a mass in Westminster Cathedral in London – one feels first and foremost that he is writing about himself, about Halldór Kiljan Laxness. And sometimes nothing looks more likely than that he is standing on tiptoe every other sentence – Look at me, notice me, I've travelled round the world, I'm a Catholic, look at me, me, me!

It seems as if one of the traits of modern writers, boundless egotism, had reared its head. Many years later the famous German critic Marcel Reich-Ranicki said in his biography that he had never met a writer of any worth who was not vain and egotistical. But Halldór could hardly let Kristján's criticism go unanswered, and claimed that he was devoid of any sort of arrogance and that his words were free from bourgeois cant. And he was not going to keep his opinions concerning Icelandic literature to himself: "We are all literary backwoodsmen."

The writer was neither in Laxnes nor in Reykjavík when *At the Foot of the Sacred Peak* was published, but instead had gone to Flatey to see Halldór Kolbeins. "The sun hangs over the straits, calm over the inlets," he wrote to Einar Ólafur; "a boat sails by, just in front of my window." He found it supremely beautiful on the island, and although he was not inspired by life there he adored the scenery, the birds, the lapping of the waves, even the kelp on the beach. Not surprisingly, he was also receptive to love on Flatey. Just as had happened in the summer of 1921, he found himself involved in a romantic adventure, this time more than likely quite serious – but here the sources fail almost completely. Halldór does, however, explain to Stefán Einarsson that what took place was "a romance with a married woman, which consequently led her to leave her husband and divorce him". This suggests that the woman was Solveig Pétursdóttir. Solveig was very much in love with Halldór for several years and tried to follow him to North America in the autumn of 1927. This romantic adventure caused him to write these noteworthy remarks in a letter to Einar Ólafur from Flatey:

> I have lived an adventure here that has filled me with deep joy and deep sorrow at the same time. God help those who love. Man's fate is extremely dramatic, but not nearly as dramatic as the fate of woman. I am created from the fates of men and women, nations and entire centuries. During the day I walk up to a hilltop and stretch out my arms and feel like dying from the knowledge that I am composed of so many different fates.

If Kristján Albertsson had discovered the egotism of the future master novelist that summer, Halldór had for his part discovered another side to the psychology of the novelist; the ability to accommodate the fates of many persons, men and women, old and young. In a television interview in his old age Halldór said that every writer housed a specific number of people whom he used again and again in different forms. During the 1920s Halldór was absorbing his gallery of characters, and love gave it a deeper colour.

Halldór travelled a great deal with his namesake throughout the parish, as they had done their first summer there. Returning to Reykjavík at the start of July, 1924, Halldór met Valgerður Wall, with whom he had stayed in Brighton. She encouraged him to come to Þingvellir,

> and that I did, and was there for ten days, surrounded entirely by women who spoke of nothing but spiritualism and theosophy, and I would have lost my mind if I hadn't had one book of poetry with me.

Halldór used his stay at Þingvellir in *The Great Weaver from Kashmir* for descriptions of scenery as well as in the excellent chapter (eighty-three) in which Steinn Elliði speaks about the theories of Helgi Pjeturss and related topics. There one can see, just as in Halldór's letters, how ridiculous he found Icelanders' interest in spiritualism, theosophy and cosmobiology. On the other hand, the book of poetry he had with him, Christian verse by Stefán from Hvítadalur entitled *Holy Church* (1924), appealed to him, and he wrote a genial essay about it for *Morgunblaðið*.

Among those whom he met at Þingvellir was the sixteen-year-old girl who, six years later, became his wife: Ingibjörg Einarsdóttir, from a well-to-do bourgeois home in Reykjavík. Inga, as she was called, remembered their first meeting in a letter five years later:

> I remember precisely the first words that you spoke to me; we were at Brúsastaðir along with Mrs Wall and others, and you needed a match to light your cigarette. You were in a fuss about it, complaining that there was never a match at hand when you needed one! But suddenly you pointed at me and said: "Little girl, you can light my cigarette – with your eyes!" I think I knew right then that you were the right one.

Halldór truly knew how to charm young girls – his attractive clothing, his cosmopolitan manner, as well as a phrase here and there that they would never forget. It did not matter at all that the girl was staying at the Hotel Valhöll, as was then the fashion for those who could afford it, and Halldór was staying in a tent (Inga actually first saw him with his mother and was amazed that he wore nail-varnish!). Nothing more came of their association until later.

After a short stay in Reykjavík, Halldór went to Akranes for a week, to see his daughter for the first time. He met her only briefly, however, and felt no connection, as he says in a letter to Jón Helgason: ". . . I still can't clearly conceive of this daughter of mine as a real person." He was still rejecting his parenthood and wanted his mother to bring up the girl so that he might pursue his studies.

Late in the summer Halldór spent time between Laxnes and Reykjavík preparing for his matriculation exams. A recent graduate, Þorgrímur Sigurðsson, later a priest, went with him to Laxnes on the advice of the rector, and they read Latin together and made good progress, finishing a two-and-a-half-year course in eight days:

> Of course I am terrible to this man, because I wake him at seven in the morning and do not stop until ten at night, but I have this one good quality of being unwilling to grow tired.

Although Halldór might have been showing off to his friend Jón Helgason, it is clear that his work habits were incredible when he put them to good use. It is equally clear, however, that he was perfectly unable to learn things that did not awaken his interest. Although he went to Reykjavík in September and took tutorials in Latin poetry, biology and mathematics, he was as uninterested in the latter subject as he had been at secondary school five years earlier. He took the exam at the start of October and achieved satisfactory marks in everything except maths, and because of this low mark he failed the exam. Stefán Einarsson wrote that Halldór did not take this to heart; the young writer added, "since I had only studied it for a few weeks". But of course this put a black mark on his record; it was clear that he would not go to the seminary in Rome that winter, and he sent word of this to the Abbot in Clervaux, since he still considered himself to be under the latter's guidance.

Halldór was thus condemned to life in the small town of Reykjavík for the winter. Financial troubles continued to haunt him, but he was once again writing constantly – in fact had become known in the town as a writer – and had a large group of friends. All the same he was restless and let the miserliness and small-mindedness of Reykjavík trouble him a good deal. The jingoism, the indiscriminate glorification of rural culture and a lack of knowledge of modern cultural ideas got on his nerves. "Here in Iceland local conditions are so mediocre that cosmopolitans are tempted to make jokes about the insipid whining of the apostles and prophets," he wrote to Einar Ólafur, and it was no secret as to who one of the cosmopolitans was.

Halldór's impatience regarding Icelandic cultural dialogue is understandable. The country was so peculiarly out of touch that a sensitive man would have felt it deeply. Icelandic society was quickly becoming urban and market-based, although in a minor way, and class politics took over after the struggle for independence. In the country's numerous cultural journals and papers, influential intellectuals, who had often spent years abroad at school, such as Sigurður Nordal and Guðmundur Finnbogason, held firmly to rural culture as the foundation of society and further development, often promulgating an idealized image of such culture. To this was added an obsession with the idea of guidance. Icelanders were viewed as children whose best option was to bow to the authority of the fatherly intellectuals so that they would be protected from the dangers of foreign culture. Mass culture and class struggle were poison in their veins, and some commentators went so far as to drag parliamentary democracy into doubt, even imagining the resurrection of a Viking-age society controlled by priest-chieftains.

During the next few years Halldór would write numerous polemical articles opposed to such ideas, and his antipathy, although not yet clearly defined, can be seen in the work he was writing that autumn, the manuscript he had introduced to Einar Ólafur under the name *Between the Millstones*. When it was published many years later, it bore the subtitle *A Youth's Self-Image*, which suited it well. Following his ill-fated exams, Halldór threw himself completely into this work. The publication of *The Red Booklet* had again been delayed, prompting him to give up on it entirely and take the manuscript back in order to determine what parts of it he could use in his new book.

At the end of November the manuscript was given the title *When I Left Home*, derived from the Old Icelandic *Saga of Hervar and Hreiðrekur*. The work has a strong autobiographical element, developed after Halldór had gone to Laxnes to rummage through a large chest containing his manuscripts and letters. As he told Einar Ólafur:

> Here in Laxnes is stored a large chest, red and very heavy. If you wanted to write up my history, you would have to come here and sit down by this chest, because it is bursting with documents. I have been searching through it today. There are diaries from around the time when I was confirmed, and novels up to several thousand pages long from when I was a child. There are the most high-flown poems. There are letters from people who were once best friends of mine, but whom I have now forgotten. And there are endless love letters from women that I have loved and who sacrificed to me all the holiest things in their possession, as if I were God, but who are now married somewhere, I do not know where. Memories flood my heart, making it difficult for me to breathe. I grow hungry and thirsty but I long for neither food nor water.

While searching through this chest, Halldór discovered that his childhood, and the Laxnes and Iceland he had grown up in, had deserted him completely. But he was also prompted to write to his friends, in the hope of collecting his own letters. Stefán Einarsson benefited from this when he was writing Halldór's biography in 1929; he and Halldór continued to collect as much material as possible, and this material later became invaluable for Peter Hallberg when he wrote his books about Halldór.

When I Left Home, like *At the Foot of the Sacred Peak*, was supposed to have been a major work, but Halldór only finished its first part. The book is replete with images from his childhood: his grandmother, his life at Laxnes, the abrupt finish to his schooling. But there is no pastoral romantic spirit in the work, no triumphant Icelandic labourer, no piety regarding Icelandic heritage: "Is not the conclusion of all Icelandic sagas the burning of Njáll?" asks the narrator, who is obviously much more interested in contemporary foreign novels. This book is a much better showcase for Halldór's style and audacity than *At the Foot of the Sacred Peak*. At one point the narrator launches into a diatribe against traditional values:

> This is the land of old age. Ancient fools and overrated misers, who would

never dare to be without their dog's share, are called men of mark and are elected to Parliament.

The book is, however, first and foremost a journey through the wide expanses of a single soul. Halldór's style here is more powerful than ever and his Icelandic more succulent; he had taken to heart the criticism against the language in *At the Foot of the Sacred Peak*. *When I Left Home* was intended to be the narrator's *Bildungsroman*, tracing his anguish and despondency and concluding with Catholicism, but at the same time it was designed to show the narrow-minded pedants of Iceland what genius Halldór possessed.

This twofold intention is made clear in an interview with Halldór published in *Morgunblaðið* on 13 December in connection with a reading from his forthcoming book the next day. The interviewer enquired about the reading, because although Halldór was controversial, no-one doubted his talent, Halldór answered:

> I never actually intended to do readings here, but it is mainly due to the challenges of various good men that I let myself be persuaded into it. I actually scarcely reckoned that people in Reykjavík would be interested in listening to someone who is in the first place Catholic, in the second place has been accused of being arrogant, in the third place is personally unknown to most people here – I have not lived here for any extended period of time since I was a child – yes, and in the fourth place not all of the reviews of my books have been worded in such a way as to awaken people's interest in me.

Halldór's answer is a good indication of his disposition during those years: a combination of showiness and delicacy verging on an inferiority complex. As the interview continues, his pride gains the upper hand, and it ends with some famous remarks:

> "Have you settled back in Iceland for good?"
> "No, no, no. I have no home here at all. I just wanted to stay here for six months for my pleasure, but now it seems most likely that I will have to stay here until spring, to my degradation."
> "Where will you go then?"
> "South – for good. I don't believe in the polar climate."

Apart from the reading and an excerpt published in *Morgunblaðið* just before Christmas that same year, Icelanders heard nothing more of the new book for a time. Halldór put it aside after finishing its first part; the idea for *The Great Weaver from Kashmir* was taking shape, and he decided to use in that book what he discarded of *When I Left Home.*

When I Left Home was finally published in Halldór's fiftieth year, when he spoke of the reasons why he had been unable to complete the work earlier. Having nearly finished with the first twenty-five chapters, he had realized that the work was defective; the two main characters "only dragged each other down, cleaving the work in two". Steinn Elliði had sneaked his way in and threatened to take centre stage away from the narrator, and it became clear to the writer that such a bulky man needed his own book, although both characters were parts of Halldór himself.

Three days after the reading something happened that must have influenced Halldór. Þórbergur Þórðarson published *Letter to Lára* (1924) at his own expense on 17 December. Contrary to what the rather conservative intellectuals of the 1920s had hoped, modern Icelandic literature did not come into being as a rebirth of the sagas in the cradle of rural culture, but rather as a reaction against traditional prose fiction and a society based on farming: "Spiritual death begins with tranquillity, an ever increasing dullness of mood, ruination of ideals and love of rural life," according to *Letter to Lára*. The book is a radical confessional, richly revolutionary both ideologically and in its narrative methods and language. Nothing is sacred to its writer: the book is egotistical and extroverted, its composition characterized by extravagance and irreverent humour. In an article about *Letter to Lára* written several years later, Einar Ólafur Sveinsson said that it displayed the rapaciousness of the imagination when it could find no gratification in external reality.

With this book Icelandic prose was opened up to completely new dimensions. Icelandic society lacked the complexity to provide new literary movements with material. The uniform and sparsely populated farmers' society would never suffice, and urbanization was incomplete. A talented writer with the ambition not to lag behind his foreign counterparts had to conduct a wider search for material: in the depths of the imagination, like Þórbergur, or in the crucible of foreign culture, like Halldór.

Letter to Lára came crashing into the rather peaceful Icelandic literary world, and Þórbergur actually lost his job as a teacher as a result of the debate about the book, which caused such a scandal precisely because of how ostentatious it was. Its author did not shy away from sensuality. He was also supportive of socialism, and even though the book made a spectacle of mysticism and spiritualism, it also levelled sharp rebukes against Christianity, not least the Catholic Church.

Letter to Lára must have put Halldór in something of a quandary. He was sympathetic to the work's audacity, since he had been expecting something great from

Þórbergur for a long time, but Þórbergur's criticism of Catholicism bothered him. In the end Halldór answered *Letter to Lára* with a little book called *The Catholic View* (1925), which he wrote at the direct request of Meulenberg, the shepherd of the Catholic congregation in Reykjavík. Halldór's apology was thus in a certain way made to order, and was also poorly paid, as he told Stefán Einarsson later:

> After the new year 1925, Prelate Meulenberg came to speak to me and asked me to write an apology for Catholicism in response to Þórbergur's attack on the Church ... I was very poor that winter, lived with acquaintances, ate for nothing. The apostolic representative did not want to pay me as much as the typesetter for composing this apology, yet all the same I delved deeply into Catholic writings before writing it.

The book was published at the beginning of April, after Halldór had already held a well-attended lecture in defence of the Catholic Church at the New Cinema. Although he stated that he disagreed with Þórbergur on all accounts, he did acknowledge the latter's talents: "The power of the man's imagination is incredibly expansive and the cloak of his language is richly colourful." However he deftly satirized various errors in Þórbergur's logic, mocked his simplistic sources and suggested that he would do well not to blame others for heresy and superstition.

In other respects the book is an orthodox defence of Catholicism and its claim to preach the one truth, and the writer equates freedom of thought with prejudice; it is the one truth that sets people free. Compared with Halldór's ever-increasing daring in his articles and poems, the tone is, by his own admission, rather stiff. He wrote to Einar Ólafur: "I have finished my little devil of a booklet about the Catholic view (puny, banal, beneath my abilities), and am having it printed; I shall send it to you."

Although Halldór took up the defence of Catholicism at this time and argued with his friends about it, he was nevertheless moving away from it; he did what was required of him as the most literate member of the sparse Icelandic congregation, but his matriculation and seminary course had been quietly removed from his life plan. There was also a distinct change of emphasis in his articles: Dostoevsky had taken the place of Catholicism and Nonni, and the writer's craft was all that mattered. In an article entitled "From the Carnival of Culture", published in *Morgunblaðið* in December, 1924, Halldór was outspoken about modernity and its manifestations, and considered no problem more pleasurable and no puzzle more laughable than the chameleon known as modern man. No writer up to that point had described that chameleon better than Dostoevsky. Halldór was thinking like a writer, not like a candidate for the priesthood.

*

In the winter of 1924–5 Halldór spent a great deal of time with Erlendur from Unuhús. Every time that Halldór mentions Erlendur in letters during these years he suddenly stops showing off and instead adopts a deferential tone, calling Erlendur the wisest man in Iceland and describing him almost as a saint: "The one man in whose company I find the most genuine pleasure is Erlendur Guðmundsson," he wrote to Einar Ólafur. "He resembles Jesus Christ; you most likely know him – he works as a police cashier, is an exceptionally wise man, unsuited to the world and all of base desires." Halldór tells Nonni that he lets Erlendur read everything he writes, and the same goes for Þórbergur and Stefán from Hvítadalur; though he never takes a public stand on anything, Erlendur has more influence on Iceland's spiritual life than anyone else. This is how Halldór describes him:

> Erlendur Guðmundsson is now thirty-two years old. He lives a strictly chaste life, has an auburn beard down to his chest, hair down to his shoulders, and blue eyes that are unforgettably fair and intelligent. He reads most European languages and one gets the feeling that he knows everything; he plays instruments gloriously and is said to be the best chess player in Iceland.

Erlendur appears as both the wise and true friend in *The Red Booklet* and as Master Ásgrímur in *When I Left Home*. The same kind of portrait is drawn of him as the organist in *Atom Station*, although the admiration accorded him is not as childish.

There is no reason to doubt Erlendur's radiance and intelligence, but Halldór's view also displays his own deep need for a father figure. Erlendur occupies the place Father Beda had at the abbey; he is the incarnation of idealism, the representative of higher values in a banal world, and Halldór follows him as a disciple. It is not certain that this role suited Erlendur, because he appears in his own letters as a rather down-to-earth and intelligent man with a good sense of humour and a sincere love of culture and the arts. But a writer arranges the people around him in the same way that he does his gallery of characters – as it suits him. Halldór had lost his father at precisely the time when he could have found a soulmate in him, and others had to fill that enormous gap.

The other people gathered at Unuhús did not radiate much holiness, being for the most part young, jovial and radical. Halldór met them sometimes at Unuhús and sometimes at the house of Hallbjörn Halldórsson, the editor and printer of the *People's Paper*, and his wife Kristín Guðmundardóttir, who ran the Hollywood beauty salon. The couple became great friends of Halldór. Hallbjörn was an enthusiast for Icelandic language and literature; he was also a trained printer and a talented artist, both of which crafts were greatly valued by Halldór. Halldór wrote in an obituary of Hallbjörn that he had been attracted to the ideal of work for work's sake, had seen the "perfection of a mortal man in this one thing: performing his work as well as was humanly possible, without consideration for all the trappings". It might have made a difference that Hallbjörn was, according to the same article, one of those few people in Iceland who were never in a good mood, "but instead were always in the best of moods".

The couple at Spítalastígur 7 took pains to make their acquaintances feel at home there. This can be seen, in the following description of gatherings there sent by the writer Sigurjón Jónsson to Stefán Einarsson:

> We had a lot of fun there. We came night after night, year after year, Guðmundur G. Hagalín, Halldór Kiljan Laxness, Stefán from Hvítadalur, Þórbergur Þórðarson . . . Everyone sat in the kitchen; Þórbergur always lay on a sheepskin on the floor. There new poetry and politics were discussed . . . Everything was criticized and torn asunder with red-hot irony. New truths were discovered, new aphorisms invented, new types of daring, new viewpoints. Kristín doled out coffee and dried fish, constantly refreshing the spirit of joy.

Company of this sort was a great encouragement to Halldór, who during those years was inclined to think to the limits in his search for higher values.

By this time Halldór had spent a whole year in Iceland, for the most part in Reykjavík, and he had had enough. His purpose had become clear: writing had won out over the priesthood. Writing to Einar Ólafur on 19 March, 1925, he mentioned the numerous books that he was thinking about or planning to write. Among them were what he would call "expressionistic experiments" following current trends in literature, as well as a great novel in the classical style, and in the summer he was going to write "an Icelandic potboiler in ten weeks, which some obscure men in Reykjavík plan to buy from me for 200 krónur . . .". Nothing became of Halldór's potboiler – which certainly would have been a curious work – but he had started *The Great Weaver from Kashmir*. Later in May, after he had set out on his travels again, he informed Nonni that he had put the theological course on hold for the time being: "I cannot start to study anything, no matter what, until I have finished this story."

Early in the spring Halldór attempted to obtain a public grant to support his writing, telling Einar Ólafur that he was busy "intriguing" (in other words, plotting), "since I am offering my writing talent for sale to the public, and threatening otherwise to leave the country". Halldór's somewhat simplistic plan of attack included publishing an article in *Morgunblaðið* at the end of January, in which he resolutely urged professionalism in writing. He considered the gregariousness of Icelanders unsuited to the demands of prose fiction, saying that they could never devote themselves to a particular topic but were

> bound to a boring passion of wishing to gloat over everything ... in general, there are no writers here, people with an unshakeable interest in writing as a career, but rather gnatish dilettantes who turn writing into a kind of fiddling around done in one's free time.

Here Halldór presents himself as the spokesman for contemporary attitudes towards the writer's work, emphasizes his own proficiency, his extensive education and his work ethic. These views were not common, and Halldór suggests that the problem lay in the nature of a small society that still had not made many advances in technology and the division of labour: "People here tend to see writing a work of fiction as some kind of divine fidgeting, which happens in a splendid environment." He knew what was needed to lay the foundation for serious writing: "It would be most natural for the state to pay its artists, no less than its officials, a secure, yearly wage."

Halldór's application, signed in Reykjavík on 25 February, 1925, for a grant of 3,000 krónur for travel and writing is stored in the archives of the Alþingi and is a remarkable testimony to both his plans and his self-image. In the application he says: "I have pursued writing since my childhood, and have had only one goal my whole life: to become an Icelandic writer." He also says that by the time he was twenty he had written six long novels, as practice, but had discarded all of them except *Child of Nature*. He had then lived abroad, "but had always lived under the strictest of conditions, since I was completely helpless financially". He then lists his books, *Several Stories* and *At the Foot of the Sacred Peak*, tells of the good reviews they received, and says that he had not received a single penny for them, with the exception of a few krónur from *Berlingske Tidende*. He wishes to point out, with respect, that things would have been different if he had been writing in Danish or some other foreign language. Finally he says that he is writing a great novel and needs to collect material in Italy and elsewhere, but that his conditions would become even more cramped and troublesome if he did not receive a grant:

On the other hand I am as determined now as ever to devote my energy to Icelandic literature, no matter how things go, since I know no other work or industry that could support me throughout my life if I were to stop writing. It is my most earnest wish that my talents (which I do not have the least reason to be ungrateful for), be put to their greatest use for my people . . .

At first Halldór's application was given a favourable reception (it should be borne in mind that the Alþingi granted an annual total of 8–10,000 krónur to writers and artists). The decision-making process took time: each of the two houses of Parliament had its own committee for financial assistance, and applications were reviewed and discussed three times before being approved or rejected. The lower house agreed at first to award Halldór a 1,500-krónur grant, but the upper house rejected this plan.

The case was returned to the lower house for further debate, but now the majority of the grants committee agreed to reject the application; the minority objected, and Bjarni Jónsson from Vogur delivered two speeches in support of Halldór. He emphasized Halldór's great talent, which poverty would keep him from cultivating: "He seems to have been born for the arts and to be one of those independent-minded men who must develop in their own particular field or else nowhere . . ." The representative for the majority, Tryggvi Þórhallsson, spoke out against the grant, and in the end the lower house followed the precedent set by the upper house and defeated the proposal by fifteen votes to twelve.

It was of course no great news that a young writer had been denied a grant, and the decision seems not to have been made along political lines, although Halldór did enjoy the support of various Conservative Members of Parliament. But why did the Alþingi change its decision? Halldór was convinced that it was because of one of his "expressionistic experiments" that was published in the journal *Eimreið*, the poem "The Youth in the Forest". This was a truly audacious work according to the criteria of the times, prose broken up by bits of poetry about love, either in a high-flown style or rich with puns and other linguistic distortions. A short preface to the poem written by Halldór made his intentions quite clear: "Expressionist poetry is mostly designed to produce emotional effects through the musical use of language, rather than to provide anyone with any definite resolutions."

The poem was discussed in the halls of Parliament and the staid older gentlemen and lovers of rural culture – which, it is safe to say, meant the majority of the Members of Parliament – doubtless had no idea what to make of a poem in which the speaker says that he is a "skámáni from Spáni/ from Skámánaspáni/ and I'm coming to get you, get you". However, the transcriptions of the Alþingi's sessions do not reveal an inclination towards literary criticism. Another concern did became apparent in an address given by Ásgeir Ásgeirsson, later President of Iceland:

> Now I come to Halldór Kiljan Laxness. It is my understanding that support for his application is greatly diminished because of the fact that he is a Catholic. And this would be because people consider the Catholic Church to be more of a superpower and thus in a better position to help him than the Treasury of Iceland.

Ásgeir points out that Halldór and Stefán from Hvítadalur do not get paid more for being Catholic. On the other hand Halldór might end up becoming a Catholic priest or monk:

> But it would be my wish that this does not happen; that he buttons up his poetic muse in a cloister, or yields her up to Thomas Aquinas or other such men. I think that such a cohabitation would hardly be fruitful.

It was thus likely that there were three main reasons for the denial of Halldór's grant: the general conservatism of Members of Parliament; their lack of under-standing of his avant-gardism; and their vague notions that the Catholic Church should provide for its own.

What Halldór said in his grant application, that he was resolved to write even though he might not receive the grant, was correct. Now others stepped in to help him travel abroad, first among them Árni Jónsson, a Member of Parliament for the Eastfjords. This is revealed in a letter Halldór sent to Nonni from England on his way south. The letter is curious in the way it shows Halldór putting the best spin possible on the rejection of his application, perhaps specifically for the Jesuit father:

> They had agreed to a 1500-krónur writer's grant for me in the lower house of the Alþingi, but the upper house rejected the grant, because I was Catholic and would get enough money from the Catholic Church, they said. Because of this I fell into a foul mood and left the country.
>
> One of my friends who had supported me in the Alþingi, the M.P. Árni Jónsson, offered me money – "I'll get you some money," he said, and gave me 800 krónur several days later. He had collected it from several rich men who were well disposed towards me, and had received a promise of more.

Before Halldór left he sent *Morgunblaðið* a remarkable article in defence of modern literature. Called "Fashion and Culture", it had the subheading "On Poetry". Its main theme was this: "The development of culture in Iceland is characterized by the greatest reluctance, putting poets in danger of becoming the voice of an older time . . ." Here he expounds on what he has perceived on his trip to Germany, that the Western world was changed completely by the First World War and that modern art should reflect this. He mentions a book of poetry by his friend Tómas Guðmundsson, *By the Blue Straits* (1925), and commends the poems, but points out that they could have been written fifty years earlier and would have been better suited to that time: "A poet who is behind the times is like a dinner guest who comes late to the feast."

Although Halldór had been preoccupied with the search for God and higher values during the preceding years, the birth of European avant-gardism had not passed him by. The conception of beauty had been radically changed; now people found the roar of cars or the racket of factories more beautiful than classical sculptures or Homer's epic poems, as the Futurists put it. Halldór was to become a determined spokesman for modernism and progressivism in fashion, social issues and the arts.

The Journey South

> There is a danger that a man will start thinking too peacefully
> if he dwells too long in the same place.
>
> *Halldór Laxness in a letter*

Halldór set off for Italy in May, 1925, planning to travel all the way to Sicily, where a part of the novel he was working on was supposed to be set, with a stop in Rome. Although he certainly thought about visiting some of the Church's holy sites, the trip was made primarily because of the novel. After spending several days with Valgerður Wall in Brighton, on 15 May he wrote to Nonni in Paris:

> I am now writing a great and remarkable book for the whole world. It is a Catholic novel, a novel about sacrifice, asceticism and the soul's peace, a novel about the glory of self-denial, etc. etc. Although the book is mainly about Icelandic characters, it is not bound to Iceland, *but rather is written for the entire world*, and besides that proclaims the newest movements that characterize our time in the art of form. The novel takes place in Reykjavík and at Þingvellir, in a monastery in France, in Rome and Sicily, and I myself am now on my way to Sicily (Palermo), to do research for this book.

Complaining about the Catholic congregation in Iceland he says that he is on his way to the Catholic fatherland. At the same time he asks Nonni whether he can arrange housing for him with the Jesuits in Palermo.

Something in the letter's tone, a certain shortage of humility, did not escape Nonni's notice. His reply caused Halldór to respond angrily in his next letter, sent from Brighton five days later. Nonni's has not been preserved, but from Halldór's answer it seems that he felt that Halldór should have continued to work with the Catholic congregation in Reykjavík, and that he was putting the Lord to the test with this rash trip to Sicily, indeed that he had lost his innocence. Of course from Nonni's viewpoint, this was correct, but Halldór was annoyed: "I do not understand how one could possibly lay a moral judgement upon a trip any more than on sequestration!" He sees nothing ungodly about his trip, describes how the Alþingi was making him pay for his Catholicism, and tells Nonni that he need not trouble himself by contacting the Jesuits in Sicily. One statement goes to the heart of the matter: "It seems that you have no idea just how strongly I feel the calling to be a writer."

Nonni calmed his friend down and Halldór met him in Paris, where they settled their dispute. But Halldór's innocence was lost, as Nonni had suspected, and although Halldór often wrote to him in utter sincerity in the following years, their relationship became somewhat strained, until in 1930 Nonni finally said that he did not wish to meet Halldór in Iceland, at least not in public. At the end of May Halldór wrote to Nonni again, from Taormina in Sicily, thanking him for his hospitality and describing his trip. He had gone to the holy city of Rome and met a Catholic prelate whom Nonni had mentioned to him, as well as the Dane Knud Ferlov, a translator and friend of the Italian writer Giovanni Papini, and a group of Icelandic Catholics on pilgrimage under the guidance of the Prelate Meulenberg. He said that he had taken the opportunity to visit St Peter's. Further, he told Nonni that he had gone to Taormina because he had heard – and here he switches to German – that it was the most beautiful place on earth. His wording is precisely the same as Otto Weininger's when describing Taormina, a place that Weininger also adored. It is possible that Halldór's trip had a literary inspiration, just as his stay at the abbey had done.

A week later Halldór sent Nonni a much more detailed letter. He had found good accommodation, had started writing and had not been very inspired by his stay in Rome. In 1925 the city celebrated a jubilee, marking the holy days in style and canonizing martyrs. But such things no longer touched Halldór; he was invited to attend a canonization ceremony but declined: "I take little pleasure in these liturgical *jongleur*-events; they represent something completely different from what I admired in Christianity," he wrote to Nonni. And although he certainly thought it wonderful to see St Peter's, he admitted that he took no pleasure in so-called "places of interest", that is, places that everyone went to see: "I always find it most pleasurable to see things that no-one else notices". This is the way a writer thinks, and for Halldór there was only one reason to be in a good mood: "What I find, however, most delightful to tell you, is this: namely, that I have started to write my book – and not just one, but two." This was the novel about the great weaver and a collection of essays about the state of culture in Iceland that he had sold to Kristján Albertsson, editor of *Vörður*, a conservative weekly newspaper.

Halldór wrote to Nonni about various practical difficulties. As soon as he had arrived in Italy, he had had to phone Árni from Múli for more money, but the transfer had gone badly, because he received paper lira instead of the so-called gold lira: paper lira were worth much less. Halldór experienced more troubles of this sort while he was in Sicily, and he either sent a telegram to Árni or Erlendur Guðmundsson. On 27 May, he did not even have enough money for a train ticket from Rome, and had to charm two English women into "lending" him enough for it. In Taormina he went to a hotel that was actually closed for the summer, but the Danish woman who owned it let him have a room and gave him money for food at first, because she said that

> she had never in her life known an example of such daring as to come penni-less to Sicily, and started laughing her heart out at this ridiculous behaviour, and naturally I also laughed, although I found it anything but funny.

In a short time, however, money was wired from Iceland to Sicily; everything worked out just as it had done when Ísleifur Sigurjónsson had saved him from starvation in Hälsingborg.

Most remarkable about Halldór's letter to Nonni of 7 June is his attempt to explain his new novel. He says that *At the Foot of the Sacred Peak* had been about "the feast behind the day", but that the new book is about the "world's essential resplendence". Although Halldór says that no-one can understand this explanation, *At the Foot of the Sacred Peak* was about the magnificent world of faith that opened up to those who looked behind the commonplace. *The Great Weaver from Kashmir* was about the glory inherent in earthly life. Halldór also admitted to Nonni that he was very interested in fashionable French literature and asked whether Nonni could find some of these works for him in Paris. So it happened that later that summer the Jesuit priest sent his progressive friend works by the greatest modernists in France: Louis Aragon, Philippe Soupault, André Breton and Guillaume Apollinaire.

*

"Midway between Catania and Messina stands Taormina on hills by the sea, and the hills are covered with cactus hard as stone, shaped like futuristic images of Scandinavian trees," wrote Halldór in an article he sent to *Morgunblaðið* from Sicily. It becomes clear almost immediately that he was enchanted by this place, which at the time was one of the most popular resorts in Europe. Halldór describes both of the town's faces: the Italian village with its strong sense of family unity in the embrace of the Catholic Church, and the tourist trap with its colourful nuances. His description of the Italian part of the village is friendly, but it is obvious which side of the town enchants him more. He writes about both men's and women's clothes with insight and familiarity, and when he describes the Old India restaurant, where he was in the habit of eating, his words display the same fluctuations as in *The Great Weaver from Kashmir*:

> Here all the world's languages blend together in one cacophony: Chinese
> potentates clink glasses with prudish girls from America and wealthy painted
> Mesdames from Fiume and Marseille extend the backs of their hands to the
> lips of half-destitute artists from the northern part of the world and receive
> kisses, as old English ladies who look like hundred-and-forty-year-old Indian
> chiefs take out cigarette boxes and offer cigarettes to homosexual dance
> teachers from Naples, and while all of this is going on the foxtrot and tango
> are danced, there is singing and joking and laughing, or whispering, touching
> or stroking, and the jazz devil leers at everything with power akin to that of
> the loading cranes in Leith.

Although as a Catholic Halldór doubtless felt obliged to keep his distance from this international decadence, he was clearly enthralled. The zeitgeist had him in its power, and it was given a prominent place in the articles he sent home that summer.

Most notorious was "A Boy's Head and the Icelandic Woman", which appeared in *Morgunblaðið* in early August. This is the first indication of what was to come in *The Book of the People*; although Halldór's radicalism was not very political, he did by now approve of women's liberation. He reprimanded his countrymen for their egotism, setting up an opposition between youth and old age, and the short haircut for girls called "a boy's head" becomes a symbol of the distinctive perspective of youth. Halldór sees the features of the modern age in fashion. Against this the entire Conservative Party bestirs itself under the leadership of virtuous scribes, "who wade in the blessed error that it is possible to raise youth on soul-killing blather about morality and Christian behaviour". Conservatism fights against the radically changed position of women, against what Halldór calls companionship between the sexes, and against women becoming like men in work as much as in dress, pushing them back into motherhood and child-rearing and redirecting their capacity for work into idling and handicrafts. Although Icelanders had not missed out on the women's emancipation movement at the start of the century, thanks to Briet Bjarnhéðinsdóttir and other pioneers, they were not used to such radical statements:

The past raised women to be *sexual beings exclusively* – so that they were made into the most readily marketable childbearing machines; when a man established his home, his wife was the furniture of furniture.

Men were allowed to do real work in the public sphere, but women stayed at home with the children and "gave orders about the porridge, hysterical, uneducated, and pregnant". Halldór recommended day nurseries for the childcare of the future.

It is not surprising that phrases like "childbearing machines" shocked many people, and the housewife and writer Guðrún Lárusdóttir, later a Member of Parliament, answered Halldór immediately in *Morgunblaðið*. She was especially angered by a Catholic attacking the housewife and the home, which were in her mind sacred institutions. A short time later there appeared a resolution in support of Guðrún from "some girls from the Eastfjords", and others who had been scandalized spoke up in protest. Halldór replied to Guðrún in an article published in *Morgunblaðið* on 12 September, suggesting that he had simply been describing the characteristics of the age, not revealing his personal opinions. It is apparent, however, in everything that Halldór wrote that summer, that what he wanted was to establish his own position with several strong brushstrokes. His views on equal rights did not have anything to do with Guðrún Lárusdóttir. In a letter that he sent to Erlendur later that autumn he wrote: "I have recently written this Guðrún a private letter, and urged her to keep her mouth shut the next time I speak." Although not everything he wrote to his friends can be taken literally, he seemed truly to have felt that inexperienced Icelanders should keep quiet when he had something to say.

In one of Halldór's letters to Nonni it becomes clear that Nonni did not like the article. Halldór says that he had expected more sympathy from him regarding the characteristics of the modern age:

But certainly the reason why the poorly educated petit bourgeoisie in Reykjavík went into a frenzy over my article is because they do not know what time the clock is striking in the world.

He was wrestling with one of the classic difficulties faced by a writer: taking a stand. He wanted to look reality in the eye. In the newspaper articles he wrote during the next quarter-century, he avoided commonplace language and phrasing; he wanted to awaken his readers by coming at them from unexpected directions.

In the collection of articles "On the Icelandic Cultural Situation" that was published in *Vörður* from the middle of the summer until December he took the same tack. The first part covers the primitivism, poverty and lack of education in the countryside, his rebuke directed not least against the intellectuals and writers who had celebrated Icelandic farm culture. In its place he promotes Reykjavík, which he feels has "suddenly come to possess everything that suits a city of the world, not only a university and cinemas, but also football and homosexuality". Later in the series he criticizes Icelanders' rusticity, especially in their drinking habits, a thorn in his side all his life. Here is a man grabbing his people by the collar in part because he realizes that his writing career has scarcely any foundation in his homeland. Halldór is never timid, and in the last part of the series he focuses his criticism on his benefactor, Árni Jónsson from Múli, who had objected to his views of rural life. Although such people supported Halldór, they had not bought him.

Icelandic cold and toil must have seemed far away indeed in Taormina. It was extremely hot around noon, when Halldór would always sit inside and write, lightly dressed, sporting a fashionable monocle, although sometimes he lay out in the sun by the sea or took in the human flora at Old India. According to his letters to Erlendur he felt very well during the first part of the summer, but by the end of July it had become extremely hot. The vegetation was scorched, most of the visitors had gone, and he was alone at the guest house. Besides that he was utterly destitute; his credit in the shops had run out, and thus it seems that in the first week of August, 1925, Halldór had – contrary to what he always said later – simply gone hungry. He says in a letter to Erlendur:

These eight days of death have already taken on a very occult aura in my memoirs, and I do not understand how they passed by. I sat the whole time in a deep easy chair in my room, without having the energy or inclination to read; most often I slept, my thoughts in restless flight, all in a dream or half-dream.

In the end he took matters into his own hands and accepted a loan from a young Italian he knew. The temperature became cooler, and he had good friends with whom he sat long into the night, discussing politics and cultural issues.

The young man who rescued Halldór from his financial straits was Benedetto Parfumi, one of his three best friends that late summer. About Parfumi he said:

He is a Southern European in hair and skin and a modern man through and through. He is excellently educated, speaks and reads five–six languages easily (everything from Danish to Arabic). He runs a huge antiques shop and travels all over Europe collecting his wares.

Parfumi was married to a Danish woman and had lived in Denmark. But what Halldór found most intriguing was the fact that the antiques dealer had

on his shelves a whole library of perverted poetry in Italian, Spanish and French, and I was amused to discover the other day that perversion is completely indisputable in his eyes; it is to him the one and only natural reality. *À notre temps tout le monde est pervers* [In our time everyone is perverted], he said with a look of surprise when I shrugged my shoulders at the cursed pornography in one of the poems.

If Parfumi was remarkable, another Italian-American was entertaining and intelligent. Bambara Salvatore, whose name Halldór borrowed for a character in *The Great Weaver from Kashmir*, was a doctor of literature in his forties,

who went around in silk stockings, with a meaningful ironic smirk, a monocle, a large dog on a lead and strong revolutionary ideas on politics, which he dared not entrust to anyone but foreigners, because he suffered from paranoia.

Halldór learnt a great deal from Bambara Salvatore, not least about Italian politics, and had gone to visit him at his home: "He seems to have enough money; lives luxuriously; treats his guests generously; his face and clothing bear witness to his thorough (if not innate) elegance, down to the finest detail."

Some of Halldór's friends in Taormina were homosexual, and his treatment of homosexuality in his newspaper articles was designed to provoke his Icelandic readers. Taormina had been a popular destination for homosexuals ever since the turn of the century, and had become famous because of a series of nude photographs of young men made there by the German Wilhelm von Gloeden, a friend of whose was called Salvatore Bambara. Could this have been Halldór's friend? If so, Bambara's paranoia was not completely without cause; several years after von Gloeden's death the Italian Fascists destroyed most of his works.

Halldór's closest friend in Taormina, and the only one with whom he kept in contact afterwards, was a German artist and professor by the name of Richard Becker. Halldór wrote to Erlendur:

> He is in appearance a living twin of Trotsky. It was an outstanding stroke of luck for me to get to know this erudite and talented man . . . who says with the self-confidence of the superman: "I do not think. I know. I do not examine. I see through."

Becker was an Expressionist and sketched and painted Halldór. Becker had a huge influence on *The Great Weaver from Kashmir*, not least its ambivalent attitude towards women; he admired slender young girls but fled if they got too close. Halldór and Becker left Taormina together in the autumn and stayed for several days in Naples; they never saw each other again but kept in contact until the Second World War.

*

The Great Weaver from Kashmir was the focus of Halldór's attentions in Taormina. It did not matter that he sometimes had no money or was engaged in polemical debates with people at home. He wrote to Erlendur time and again about the progress of the work, full of energy and optimism:

> I am bursting with power, and when I walk here in the moonlight in the evening, and look at the green moonshine haze over the Mediterranean . . . I find that I am not a man at all, but something entirely different . . .

In the same letter he says that this is "a story about a creation when it is absolutely new, steaming and smelling like warm loaves from a baker's oven."

Why should Halldór have found such inspiration in Sicily? The most likely explanation is that there his desires and his intellect finally came together. All his life he had longed to become a writer, but while he was at school and later at the abbey his mind had set itself other goals. At the end of June he wrote to Erlendur:

> There is one thing on my mind right now, and that is to send a sample of the novel in Danish in the autumn to a publisher in Copenhagen, for example, Gyldendal; I dare to assert that it would be an absolute success. No matter what, it is nothing other than foolish sport to be writing in Icelandic as things stand now; one simply cannot afford it, nor is it the right soil in which to sow seeds.

These statements well reflect Halldór's grandiosity and the growing conflict within him between the Icelander and the cosmopolitan. Whether he tried Gyldendal or not that year, the book was not published in Denmark until half a century later. Danish critics then lamented the fact that this "ragged masterpiece from the time of the great cultural depression" had not been published earlier.

Halldór felt that things were going well with *The Great Weaver from Kashmir*; no matter what happened regarding its publication, he was writing himself into contemporary European literature. It was also clear to him that Icelanders would be lost for words on reading the book: ". . . then everything will be turned topsy-turvy . . ." Around the middle of September he had finished drafts of five of the parts – there were to be eight in all. With relentless pleading and cablegrams to Erlendur and Árni he also managed to get himself out of financial difficulties for the time being. He wrote to Erlendur:

> In the end hitting up the rascals back home turned out well. I have actually collected a total of 1,900 krónur from here and there. Now I will go into retirement for several months, but do you think it might be possible to get a new collection going when winter comes on? In other words I trust you to butter those fellows up, when you have the chance.

It was not a pleasant job that Halldór asked his quiet friend to do, but he didn't let it worry him.

Despite the fact that things were going well, Halldór began thinking about a change. Even at his best, he would be overcome by the urge to travel, continuing to do so throughout the 1930s even though he had a home in Reykjavík. This disquietude had its roots in his psychological state, but was also connected to his unquenchable curiosity. As Halldór put it in a letter to Erlendur: "Because there is a danger that a man will start thinking too peacefully if he dwells too long in the same place." If he sat back in one place, his mind would grow numb. And then nothing would ever happen.

*

Halldór left Taormina on 12 October, 1925, travelling to Clervaux, where he planned to stay as a guest for a time and finish his book. En route he stayed for several days in Naples, a week in Rome, two days in Florence. Where he did not go is perhaps more noteworthy, however. He did not visit the centre of the Benedictine order at Monte Cassino, nor did he stop at the home of St Francis near Florence, nor accept an invitation to visit Johannes Jørgensen in Assisi. About his visit to Rome and St Peter's he wrote: "I felt as if I had met the ghost of my former self." He did stop in Switzerland, to visit in Arlesheim the most famous scholar of Scandinavian and Icelandic studies in the Germanic world, Andreas Heusler. Language had moved nearer to his heart than faith.

When Halldór arrived at Clervaux on 21 October, he was received with affection. He was given his old room, and the next day he sent Nonni a few lines to express his joy at having returned to the abbey, as well as his opinion that the Benedictine way of life was the fairest of them all. But his friend Beda von Hessen and Halldór both realized that nothing would ever be as it had been. Halldór wrote to Erlendur several days later: "In fact there is no reality for me except for *The Great Weaver from Kashmir*. Everything else is similitude and shadows." On 11 November he sent Erlendur a detailed summary of the book, from which it can be seen that he was considering it in its totality. He explained that the book's language was new, because it focused on things that had never been written about in Icelandic before.

During the next few months he worked hard on the novel at the abbey, in comfortable conditions and without the interruptions of prayers and masses. At the abbey he wrote himself away from Catholicism. After several weeks there, however, he had become more moderate and humble in what he said to his friends; he is especially genial to Einar Ólafur in a letter written on 8 December.

When Halldór secluded himself with his writing, he found his own thinking more real than everyday events. He spent a lot of time reading foreign literature, as he told Einar, especially works by contemporary writers in the Romance languages, including Pirandello and Unamuno, both of whom were preoccupied with the disintegration of human identity.

That year saw the publication in France of a book that Halldór used unsparingly in *The Great Weaver from Kashmir*, *The Devil Leads the Dance* by George Anquetil. This work was based on quotations from newspapers and poetry about the moral decadence of modern times. Halldór was not interested in the book's message, but rather in its depiction of western decadence and corruption. He had begun to see that if he wished to move his readers he would have to be as skilful at depicting evil as he was at preaching good.

His next letter to Einar Ólafur, airing his prejudices regarding mutual friends in Iceland, shows that distance had given Halldór a clearer view of the culture at home. He attended a number of masses over Christmas and went out of his way to show interest in the world of the monks, reconfirming his own monastic vow. Nonni came to visit the abbey and gave some talks; Halldór was delighted, feeling a sense of pride in his famous countryman. Discussion occurred about establishing a monastery in Iceland, and Halldór wanted to lend whatever assistance he could. In a detailed letter to Nonni on 16 February he underlined the following statement: "This is more of a matter of national interest to Iceland than anyone can suspect." Later that same month he wrote to Nonni and informed him that he was working on the matter with Meulenberg and taking counsel from Father Beda.

It is not entirely clear why Halldór became so fascinated by the idea of a monastery in Iceland; perhaps he saw it as a place where he could take refuge, and where he would have access to a library when he was at home. The French monks did not like the idea of moving to Iceland, and the plan fell through.

In the latter part of January Halldór took a trip to Belgium and visited, among other places, the monastery in Averbode, where his companion from his previous stay at Clervaux, Jan Ballin, was a novice. He wrote an article about the trip for *Morgunblaðið*'s weekly cultural magazine, *Lesbók*, that was less about faith than it was about the writer's trip, with Halldór's tone bordering on arrogant. For instance, he says that he disliked travelling in a train full of workers who were constantly spitting and hacking:

> It is frightful to spend time with people who work for the sake of their wages, people who do nothing unless they are paid for it. The faces of such men can be extremely ugly, and they think like useless ruffians.

Statements such as this show just how distant Halldór was from waged labour. His work was artistic creation, and no price could be put on it. The grants and loans he received were something completely different in his eyes. During these years it was unclear whether he actually used such funds to support himself. For example, he had his clothes specially tailored in Belgium, thus making him, by his own account, extremely foppish in the eyes of the monks. Everywhere he went he stood out from the crowd.

Foppish is also a word that can be used to described the poem cycle Halldór composed later that winter and which he titled *Rhodymenia palmata*. He boasted to Nonni that he had written the cycle in thirty-five minutes, which may well have been the case. An unbelievable variety of material is mashed together in the cycle, with parts bearing titles such as "Behind the Calling Card" or "Solo for Three Accordions". Halldór said that it was written in the spirit of surrealism, but the overall effect is amusing rather than deep. Several skilled Icelandic poets amused themselves by imitating these poems when they were published in *Morgunblaðið*'s *Lesbók* on 4 April, 1926.

After a three-month stay at the abbey Halldór had made so much progress on

The Great Weaver from Kashmir that it was time to go home. On 12 March, 1926, he wrote to Einar Ólafur as follows:

> I am actually ready to travel back to Iceland; but I cannot tear myself from the biblical apothecary . . . I stroll around there the whole day, feeling like a diver at the bottom of the sea; the days pass without anyone noticing . . . The peace is as absolute as in heaven, and I can do nothing but thank God for every little thing that has come into my head.

It was of course uncertain as to what awaited him at home and how his book would be received, if in fact it would be published at all. He did receive a 400-krónur grant from a fund established by the Alþingi, but he told Nonni: "Iceland is ruled by a type of conservative politics whose only goal is to reward soulless speculators and capitalists while killing poets and artists and the nation's culture."

Halldór left the abbey at the start of April, 1926, and said farewell to Father Beda for the last time. "We shall see each other later, somewhere else, if not here," Father Beda said. Six decades later Halldór wrote:

> When I said farewell for the last time to this becowled philosopher, my dear friend and father confessor of old, I greeted a new life. I have often wondered whether these farewells and greetings have not been the most consequential moments of my life.

He had come to Father Beda with anguish in his soul, and bade him farewell with a great modernist novel in his suitcase.

Coming to Terms with the Nation

> I recently said in a letter to Halldór Kiljan that we two were the only Icelandic prose-writers who had anything new to say. All the rest was piss, which by accident had become the bathwater of the nineteenth century.
>
> *Þórbergur Þórðarson in a letter*

Halldór's trip home took him first to Ostende in Belgium, and from there to Brighton, where he stayed with Valgerður Wall for several weeks until he took the *Gullfoss* to Leith and then Reykjavík, arriving home on the morning of 28 April. *Morgunblaðið* announced the writer's homecoming the next day, and also stated that he had brought with him the manuscript of *The Great Weaver from Kashmir*.

Halldór's name was now well known to the literary clique in Reykjavík, even though he had not got much published or sold many books. His arrogance and grandiloquence had been the subject of a great deal of discussion, and *Morgunblaðið* felt that readers should be allowed to follow his travels. A month later came more news, this time of his plan to read from *The Great Weaver* on 24 May:

And now the people have seen Kiljan here on the streets, tall and slim, with huge glasses and a wide-brimmed hat, loping along with long strides, emaciated from digging in the depths of human existence and embracing and enclosing all the newest forms in the poetic arts.

Large spectacles had replaced Halldór's monocle, and their dark, broad frames had strengthened the appearance of his face, which was crowned by his hat. It mattered how people saw him – he belonged to the world of modern art, symbolized by Baudelaire and his Parisian contemporaries more than half a century earlier, including the *flâneurs*, who drew attention to themselves through various types of outrageous posturing, like strolling around with turtles on leads. Halldór was intensely industrious and would never have wasted time simply sauntering around town, though he was inclined towards behaviour designed to create and maintain an image, to gain attention, pretending at the same time that nothing was out of the ordinary. The artist in a capitalist society is not just a creative thinker, he is also his own publicist; image meant a great deal, and Halldór knew it.

In the *Morgunblaðið* piece he explained the title that he had given to his novel. He had been told that Kashmir meant "the valley of roses"; the great weaver was a man who had been born in the valley of roses, and his weaving was "created with the view of life of the fashionable man as the warp, and the one true faith as the weft". The book was about everything that might cause a young man to have sleepless nights: politics, the meaning of life, religion, the role of women. Halldór succeeded in arousing sufficient interest for his reading to be repeated several days later.

The reading was an attempt to provide for himself. The publisher of his last novel, Ársæll Árnason, did not want to take on *The Great Weaver*. Even if young and arrogant writers inspired attention, the market was small, and outside Reykjavík interest was even more limited. Þórbergur had printed *Letter to Lára* at his own expense, with a first run of three hundred copies, though with subscriptions he was soon able to print an additional one thousand five hundred. Halldór quickly realized that he would have to publish *The Great Weaver* in the same way and signed an agreement with the Acta printshop. He worked hard typing the manuscript during the summer, and printing was scheduled to start in August; it was delayed until the beginning of 1927, however.

At the start of July, 1926, Halldór delivered a radio talk about the problems of being a writer in Iceland. Early in the spring the telegraph engineer Ottó B. Arnar had set up the first radio station in Reykjavík; it lasted for about a year. Weather reports and religious services were the most common programmes. Halldór's outspoken talk was an exposé of the poor conditions endured by Icelandic writers and an exhortation to the state to secure them financial support, since the way in which a nation treated its great intellectuals was a measure of its worth. Halldór mentioned that distribution of books in Icelandic was poor compared to that enjoyed by foreign writers, and that only a small percentage of the country's hundred thousand souls understood literature. Culture was the one measure of the value of a nation:

If we do not wish to use our facilities to shape culture, then it is useless for us to be here, because we have no other calling than the cultural. Do we want to be part of a nation with nothing else on its agenda than to live like beasts?

That summer Halldór read Freud, Jung and Adler; these psychoanalytic texts were to make their mark on *Salka Valka* and *Independent People*. Although Halldór later rejected Freud, for instance in *A Poet's Time* (1963), he was preoccupied with these theories during the 1920s and well into the 1930s. Halldór was interested both in the ways that new movements in literature like surrealism drew heavily on psychoanalysis and its theories about the unconscious, and, as might be expected at his age, in types of sexual behaviour, including homosexuality, sadism and transvestitism. He had not been in Copenhagen for more than a week as a seventeen-year-old before he bought himself one of the most popular nineteenth-century books on sexuality, by the Frenchman Auguste Debay, *Women and Sexual Hygiene for and in Marriage*. It is not certain that he finished reading it, but he did underline one sentence about flogging in the Middle Ages.

By the middle of August Halldór had finished preparing the manuscript of *The Great Weaver from Kashmir* for the printers and took a long trip to the east and north of Iceland. This journey, from which he did not return until around Christmas, renewed his interest in the circumstances of Icelanders. The trip inspired poems, a series of essays and short stories, and laid much of the groundwork for *Salka Valka* and *Independent People*, in addition to increasing Halldór's political radicalism.

*

While visiting Eskifjörður, where his old friend Arnfinnur Jónsson lived, Halldór was introduced to Halldór Stefánsson, who told him the story of an old woman who slaved away her whole life salting herring and could not be dragged away from it except by force. This inspired Halldór to write the short story "The Herring", which he read in public while there. A dark tale about a lonely, out-of-touch individual, it is similar to some of his earlier stories but better composed, more convincing in its realism and with a broader narrative scope. It was, however, considered so harsh that the *Icelandic Journal of Literature* rejected it, but it was published in 1930 in *Berlingske Tidende*.

From Eskifjörður Halldór continued to Egilsstaðir, where he worked on a draft of a poem that he completed on 26 August at Hallormsstaður, and that became perhaps his most famous poem, "The Hallormsstaður Woods". This is a poem about reunion. The form is traditional, but displays a sheepish humour and unexpected images. Halldór was composing himself into the land, seeking as his model the foremost Icelandic poet of the nineteenth century, Jónas Hallgrímsson, whom he admired for his clarity, his romantic spirit, his sincerity, and his lack of pretentiousness. Two years later he wrote one of his most famous essays about Jónas, making it clear why he identified with him:

Although it might ring false in Icelandic ears, it was a huge city [Copenhagen] that fostered the poetic genius of Jónas Hallgrímsson and brought it to maturity, and in this he is no exception . . . Great poets are always influenced by urbanity or other conditions that are contrary to rural life . . . A man of the countryside cannot compose poetry from a deep, clairvoyant consciousness of nature, his work and life's struggle until the major cities of the world have given him perspective and impregnated his soul with wisdom and artistry.

Seldom had Halldór revealed himself so clearly. On 1 September he wrote to Nonni from Skriðuklaustur:

What a difference there is in my life now than at the same time last year when I sat in boiling heat down south in Sicily and muddled over *The Great Weaver*! And what a huge difference there is in this Icelandic rural setting compared to Clervaux . . .

No-one who did not take an active interest in other people could become a good novelist – even if he only looked at those people as material for his work. In the autumn of 1926 Halldór found himself listening to the farmers and workers: "They thought it fun to get Laxness to visit, because he had so many things to say, but asked about so much more," said one man he met.

Halldór felt quite comfortable in Hérað, where he stayed for the most part with an old schoolfriend, Bjarni Guðmundsson. In "Travelogue from the East", written at Skriðuklaustur on 9 September and published in two parts in the weekly *Vörður* in October, he ranges widely throughout the cultural spectrum. But his main focus was urbanization. He considered the beggarly farming of the "dry-stocksmen" in their hovels as hopeless impoverishment, each man crouching over his measly fireplace, "with bitten lips and wrinkled forehead", inventing his own idea of independence. Such descriptions give a foretaste of *Independent People*, the story of one proud individual's struggle to work his own farm at the risk of bringing destruction upon his family. Isolated farming changed people's essence, according to Halldór, making them "outcasts from society, eccentric, unhappy, and ugly".

Halldór had planned to go north, over the heaths on skis. However, winter came early in 1926, and he and his companions encountered deep snow and storms. The trip took a huge amount of time and when they lost their way, they were only rescued by Halldór's little compass. It is most likely because of the compass that he first described this trip in the Christmas paper of the Scouts, *The Outdoors*, although the article was reprinted in a later collection of essays.

Jökuldalur, a sparsely populated district, was a place where Halldór could contemplate the conditions of Icelandic farmers, and he stayed there for almost a week. A worker named Júlíus Jónasson, whom Halldór thought a remarkable man, later told Matthías Jóhannessen in an interview:

I think that Laxness stayed ... for a fortnight, and the better part of his days there he spent writing. I thought to myself: What kind of rubbish is that, that men think they have to be writing there in the south. But I didn't say anything, because I was a worker.

Júlíus and another man accompanied Halldór over to Möðrudalur, but the desert was impassable and they were forced to turn back due to the weather. The worker saw that Halldór was a hearty traveller:

I thought that he was, for an inexperienced man, very industrious and quite strong, and there was no doubt that he had undergone many difficult journeys in order to achieve his goals. That was worthy of respect.

Eventually they made it to Grímsstaðir in the mountains, the highest and most remote farm in Iceland. En route the companions sought shelter at a little farm on the Jökuldalur heath, Sænautasel, staying overnight. Halldór was fascinated: nothing is as tempting for a storyteller as people living on the outer edge of human civilization.

❧ *The Story of Sænautasel* ❧

Skúli Guðmundsson is a car mechanic who has for decades worked for the National Roadworks, but his special interest is the people of the Eastfjords, about whom he has written in local journals. He spoke to this author in the spring of 2004 about his interest in the history of the Eastfjords. He and his siblings may perhaps be called the victims of the complicated interplay between fiction and reality in the tiny country of Iceland. Skúli was born in Sænautasel and lived there until he was six.

Halldór Laxness came with two other men to Sænautasel on a freezing November day in 1926, because their intended route to Grímsstaðir was impassable. They were received well and given food and drink, as well as lodging overnight. This would hardly have been memorable if Halldór had not written an article about his visit, "A Short Day's Night on Jökuldalsheiði", which first appeared in the *People's Paper* in March, 1927, and then in *A Day's Journey in the Mountains*. The article would most likely have faded from memory had not everyone thought that it held a key to one of Halldór's most celebrated novels, *Independent People*. Halldór wrote:

> There was no difference in appearance between the cottage and the glacier, but my companions and I made it there by following a specific direction. It was many steps down the glacier before we came to the door of the farmhouse . . . downstairs were hay and sheep. Here lived the farmer and his wife, their son and the farmer's mother, a decrepit old woman. The farmer . . . had slaughtered the one cow so that the sheep would have enough hay to eat. He said that it mattered little that the people had no milk and very little food: the point was that there was enough food for the sheep. The people were very sickly looking, especially the boy and the old woman. She . . . groaned and whined constantly and said that she wanted milk . . . "just a tiny drop".

> No effort was spared for the guests, because "the proletariat are the most aristocratic creatures on earth"; meat from the cow was boiled and there were stale doughnuts.

> The farmer rocked back and forth and smiled a broad smile from wordless joy. I thought: I wonder if this man finds the meaning of life and centre of the universe to be here on the heath?

Sænautasel is not named in the article, and reaction was fairly mild, but after *Independent People* was published and became one of the most talked-about Icelandic novels, eventually a world bestseller, it became widely known that the farm at Sænautasel was the model for Summerhouses in the novel.

Although Skúli had not yet been born when Halldór came to the farm, he has written a long, unpublished essay about this visit. Skúli's father lived at "Sel" from 1907 to 1943 with his family. In the autumn of 1926 the farmer's elderly mother also lived with them, which corresponds to Halldór's account. But Skúli questions almost everything else Halldór says. For instance, Sænautasel was not as far from other human habitation as Halldór had implied, unless the people of Jökuldalur were not considered human; there were still quite a few farms on the heath, and Sel was "only" a sixteen-hour train journey to Vopnafjörður. The bedroom was larger than Halldór had indicated, the farmwork more pleasant, the food much more varied and the crop of hay greater; the sheep were not kept in the farmhouse. Skúli has, what's more, determined that no card games were played that night. The three men had slept in the couple's bed, since the farmer and his wife had lent it to them.

Taking everything into consideration, Skúli makes a strong case for Halldór's having exaggerated heavily. If one looks at it from more of a distance it becomes hard to deny that heath-farming had been incredibly difficult work: the heavy snows and the isolation during the long dark winters were unbelievable, and it was in many ways heroic to farm in such conditions and survive for nearly four decades.

The conditions had shocked Halldór; the poet who had recently lived in Southern Europe found them unacceptable. Radical changes were to be preached. All this was fresh in his mind when he wrote the novel, and to the newer material he added his memories from his stay at the other Sel in the Westfjords. Both farms became for Halldór symbols of what was unacceptable in Icelandic society. In the interwar years the situation was drastic enough in some places for men to choose to farm for themselves under difficult conditions rather than work for wages that were paid in kind.

Halldór's depiction of such farms as primitive and marginal distorted their particular realities and insulted the proud folk of Sænautasel. Halldór later said:

I cannot unfortunately give the [real] location of Bjartur from Summerhouses, any more than I can my own. I have never met him, either to the east or the west of the glacier, except in myself.

In this regard, fiction that searches for a general truth collides with history that looks for facts. The hurt took on various forms: Skúli tells how his father had a scuffle with one of Halldór's companions in the mud at Vopnafjörður because of this and wrestled him down, and Skúli had for a long time been unwilling to tell anyone where he came from. In later years he learnt to appreciate *Independent People*, although he is still uncomfortable with much that is in the book. As he put it to the author:

> One can imagine that if Kiljan had not come to Sel . . . my father and his family would have been left in peace, since there was no reason at all to talk about him and his farming any more than anyone else who is now forgotten and whom no-one thought to humiliate.

Halldór moved on, meeting his old friend Reverend Halldór Kolbeins along the way and finally arriving back in Reykjavík on 23 December, 1926. He did not sail on the ship on which he had first booked a passage; which was just as well since the *Balholm* sank off the west coast that December, with all its crew and passengers.

Everywhere he went on his trip, he talked to people, scraping together information about their lives and opinions. But he never made it to the place he had originally intended to go: the birthplace of the poet Jónas Hallgrímsson.

*

In the new year Halldór's thoughts turned to fresh exploits. He chose a new arena: the *People's Paper*, the mouthpiece of the Social Democrats. In January and February, 1927, he published a two-part article entitled "About Reviews", and in March a series of articles "Electrical Lighting of the Countryside", which included "A Short Day's Night on Jökuldalsheiði". The two-part article shows conclusively that his self-confidence was strong, and was being shaped by his work ethic and professionalism (he speaks of the "business of the novel"). He feels that Icelandic fiction has been characterized by dilettantism for too long, and that the critics have been too kind:

> It is nothing but an abnormality of the times that the pursuit of a hobby qualifies a man to become a critic, especially since every sort of "business" has now become so complicated and variegated, that is to say, demands deep study and a great deal of diligence.

Halldór's attitude towards writing is beginning to approximate its later form, and his comparison of writing and the study of history is noteworthy:

> The value of a story does not generally depend on whether it is true or false, but rather on how it is told, and naturally on how its vision opens itself to the dimensions of human life.

He himself judges writers according to how effectively they deal with character.

Halldór sets his goals high, whether that means practical knowledge of a particular literary genre, his familiarity with it, or its social impact. It should have been clear to Icelandic readers that this was a man who intended to become an author for Iceland.

If Halldór's dreams were to come true, his country would have to embrace progress. His political views had become considerably more focused. "Books are nothing but vanity. Culture is first and foremost built on the defeat of poverty and powerlessness," he writes, adding that culture meant "creating one's own environment, as best one can, so that spiritual values can be relished when the day's grind is at an end". In order to create culture, Iceland needed more urban areas and electricity. "A rail line to the east! Cultivated land! Electrical lighting of the farms in the countryside!" Halldór remained a fighter for modernity, although modernity could no longer be measured by cultural standards alone but also by technological ones.

Halldór wrote these articles just before he turned twenty-five. In them he laid out his goals: to become a novelist in earnest according to the standards of the world, and to work for improving the lot of the people so that they could enjoy his books and other people's. No matter how one assesses his performance, these goals were achieved.

*

The Great Weaver from Kashmir was finally published in early 1927. The author's friends had not yet managed to find a hundred subscribers, as the printshop had wanted them to. Nor had a publisher accepted the work, so Halldór published it himself with help from some others, as he says in *A Poet's Time*. No-one did more to make it possible for Halldór to devote himself to his writing during these years than Erlendur Guðmundsson and Kristján Albertsson, either by lending him money or trying to procure grants for him from the Alþingi.

The Great Weaver was published in seven parts (though it was divided into eight). This was rather inconvenient – the seven parts were sent to subscribers and sold on the streets – but the book actually did better than anticipated. It was discussed in the papers, although more calmly than might have been expected. *Morgunblaðið* spoke without a doubt through the mouths of the more prudent Reykjavík academics when it said on 11 March, after the publication of the first four parts: "In general it is agreed that the author has, both in his characters and narrative techniques, overstepped the bounds of what is reasonable." It is likely this little notice conveyed the public's opinion of the book, since Icelanders had not read anything of the kind since the publication of *Letter to Lára*.

Then things became more complicated. Because of the good relations between *Morgunblaðið* and Halldór, and because of the sympathy that Kristján Albertsson, the editor of the Conservative weekly *Vörður*, had shown him in the past, many assumed that Halldór was a Conservative himself. The *People's Paper* said nothing about the book, even though the paper's editor, Hallbjörn Halldórsson, had proof-read it in its entirety. One man saw the controversy as an opportunity to advance his own position: Jónas from Hrifla, the leader of the Progressive Party. A ruth-less election campaign was being waged in the papers that spring; the Conservatives were in power, but the Progressives were making their attack. On 23 April Jónas cited several statements in *Tíminn* from *The Great Weaver from Kashmir*, for example, concerning whores, homosexuality and sodomy, and called Halldór the "poet of the government", which he claimed had taken upon itself "the unbelievable fostering of this work".

On the next day *Morgunblaðið* replied: "Jónas from Hrifla quotes several of Kiljan's most fanatical obscenities, thinking he can cash in on them. Most appro-priate. He would certainly know – the slanderer smacks his lips on the pornography." But if there were anything that Halldór would never allow himself to be accused of, it was writing pornography. He immediately brought libel charges against *Morgunblaðið*, demanding that the comments be rescinded, even though it was clear that he had ended up in the middle of a mud-slinging contest. The case was settled out of court, and *Morgunblaðið* published an article on 10 May stating that their attack had been made on Jónas from Hrifla, not Halldór.

Halldór was then able to explain his position in *Morgunblaðið*, vehemently denying even a trace of pornography in *The Great Weaver*, and defending the case for being frank:

> . . . when a serious writer undertakes the task of describing the over-whelming life of the soul, paying heed to the ways that it swings back and forth between the angelic and the demonic, he simply cannot avoid giving descriptions of the various types of moods that might take on fantastic shapes in the eyes of readers who have commonplace intellects and souls, and that might even have a disagreeable influence upon them. It does not pay for a writer to be wary when he makes it his point to express his thoughts as thoroughly as possible with unaffected earnestness, humility, and candour.

Halldór also attempted to publish a response in *Tíminn*, but was denied. He did not want *The Great Weaver of Kashmir* to become some sort of footnote to the dialectics of Icelandic government, although these debates were not entirely useless to him, as one can see in a letter he sent to Jón Helgason: "I'm said to be a pornographer and homosexual and all sorts of other things. On the other hand all this babble has its advantages when it comes to publicity." A writer's need to advertise himself had quickly become clear to Halldór, and the debate also revealed that he was distancing himself from the Conservatives. As far as publicity was concerned, when it became clear how controversial *The Great Weaver* was, Ársæll Árnason, who had published *At the Foot of the Sacred Peak*, hurried to advertise it, calling it "without doubt the best book that this young, sharp-tempered writer has written; it has been debated less than his other books because it is not possible to dispute its worth."

In *The Great Weaver from Kashmir* everything that Halldór had learnt during his six years away from Iceland came together. When one reads the book now, one finds its structure loose and its cultural commentary stuck in a time warp. And although the book is written in the third person, a significant portion of it consists of an enormous monologue. But, along with *Letter to Lára*, *The Great Weaver* marked the start of modern Icelandic literature. For decades young Icelandic authors and readers considered the book to be both enlightening and redemptive.

Its uniqueness was due in great part to its writer's audacity in his use of language and metaphors. Icelandic nature had never been described this way before:

The first whimbrel cried out to the south-west like a young, sleepless drunkard. Otherwise the birds had not yet stirred. Two sheep, staid and respectable like old housewives, stepped leisurely along a narrow path a short distance away, their gait gentle and notable; they were thinking. The gentle breeze had given way to a dead calm; everything had begun to glisten with dew. The birch-grown foremost edge of the lava field smelt sweet, like the bosom of a prudish foreign girl.

The unusual language conveyed unusual opinions that mocked both the ingrained ideas of Icelanders concerning their own excellence and all conceptions of the beauty of rural life. The central character, Steinn Elliði, is like a modern man sprung from the egotistical literature of the turn of the century and shipwrecked on an isolated island:

What . . . business do I have amongst these rustics . . . where the vanguard of culture is comprised of beggars, grannies, fortune tellers, and retired bailiffs? I'll never be the main character in a romance with a setting and characters such as these!

Steinn searches for perfection, and his search leads him both to a monastery and into magnificent modern literature, as well as occasionally into megalomania. In the spirit of Strindberg and Weininger, God and woman compete for his attention. From the same direction come two characters that are able to dig Steinn out from under his egotism: Father Alban, with his Christian humility and charity, and the girl Diljá.

With *The Great Weaver* Halldór left Catholicism behind, as he pointed out in *The Book of the People* two years later:

> If God is everything and man an illusion, vanity, then it is obvious that it would be best for man to go off and die, so that God could "be everything" in peace.

Halldór had no alternative other than to turn to something else. After *The Great Weaver* he wrote, as he said, nothing significant for several years: "*The Great Weaver* was like a stone where I stopped and looked around for a long time."

Around this time, Icelandic literary culture was gaining strength, due not least to the journals *Iðunn*, *Eimreiðin* and the newly founded journal of conservative intellectuals, *Vaka*. These published detailed reviews of the book, but Halldór had already left the country. His old friend Jakob Jóhannesson Smári wrote in *Eimreiðin*: "It is easy to become scandalized by this book. But it is better to contemplate it, to go to the heart of the matter." In *Iðunn* another old friend, Tómas Guðmundsson, defended the book, pointing out the miserable state of Icelandic fiction and the need for new blood. Tómas thought that Halldór was the first serious Icelandic post-war novelist.

Vaka's editors were in disagreement and published two reviews. Kristján Albertsson was on the whole very favourable: "Finally, finally, an imposing work of fiction, which rises like a mountain castle from the flatness of Icelandic poetry and fiction of the last few years!"

In general, however, the conservative intellectuals were sceptical, although no-one went as far as Guðmundur Finnbogason, the National Librarian, whose review, published in the same issue as Kristján's, consisted of a single phrase (just two words in Icelandic): "Well-churned imp's butter." Although his wording was abstruse, his meaning was clear: *The Great Weaver from Kashmir* was a perfect deception.

Halldór never forgot negative reviews and would sometimes take his revenge much later on. Thirteen years later he wrote about Guðmundur Finnbogason's translation of a collection of essays:

It makes matters no better that upon the translation of these essays Guðmundur Finnbogason has laid his dead hand. Of him it has been said that his language shows signs that he has never listened to anyone other than himself. Although this translator is a man who has some skill in using particular words, he has never had the fortune of putting two words together in such a way that is remembered by anybody.

Two words together: Guðmundur's review had remained in Halldór's mind.

In the spring of 1927 Halldór had been in Iceland for nearly a year, but he was not ready to settle down. Now he planned to fulfil his old dream of going to North America, and at the same time to visit the headquarters of the new mass culture: Hollywood.

In the interim, though, Halldór had become better acquainted with Ingibjörg Einarsdóttir, the girl whom he had once asked for a light at Þingvellir. Her mother, Sigríður Þorláksdóttir Johnson, ran a sewing workshop in Reykjavík for a time, while her father, Einar, had studied law in Copenhagen and became a professor of law when the University of Iceland was established in 1911, a Member of Parliament and government minister in the war years, and a Supreme Court judge from 1932. Ingibjörg had been born in 1908. When Halldór met her, the family were living in a handsome middle-class home.

Inga was a happy and enterprising girl. She had studied for two years at the Reykjavík Business College, but had left in 1924. She and Halldór did not start spending time together until early in 1927, since Halldór was often overseas, and Inga worked as a domestic servant in Scotland from April until December, 1926. Inga says in her autobiography that she was afraid that she had ruined Halldór as a Catholic, but their meetings had an air of innocence: "We promenaded together ... in all directions. There was no kissing-fever in those days, just walks and chats!"

Halldór made it a habit to go to Iaga's house for coffee, to the delight of her mother, who was a book-lover. Although Einar, according to his daughter, might have wished for a different son-in-law, he did not interfere. Halldór presented Inga with the parts of *The Great Weaver from Kashmir* as soon as they were published, inscribing the first volume with these words: "To Inga. In memory of the desire for higher values." She was a lively modern woman with a sense of style, and her home had the bourgeois air that Halldór had so often described in his newspaper articles. He was, however, not sure about what he wanted from the relationship; on his way overseas again, he was not certain that he would return. As he put it in a letter to Inga later:

I was so incredibly afraid of taking any sort of determined step when we were together in the winter of '27, because I was still planning to stay for a long time abroad, much further away from Iceland than I had ever been before, and I did not dare risk being bound to you from fear that I would surely lose you later.

A prolific exchange of letters began as soon as the two parted. Halldór's love was strengthened by distance, as was so often the case throughout his life: a period of separation from the one he loved was always necessary. It was as if Inga took on the form of Diljá in his mind. This is clear from a letter he wrote to her at the start of May, 1927, when he was still in Iceland and Inga herself had gone abroad:

My dear Inga,

When I walk along the streets here and think that I have no further hope of meeting my little girlfriend again when least expected, as I always had hope of doing during the winter, then I find everything here to be much emptier and more impoverished than ever before. It is, moreover, a comfort to me to meet your friends . . . they remind me of you. I am full of lyrical sorrow these days, but no-one knows it. My name is officially connected to nothing other than litigation, polemics, and criminal novelistics . . . But when I think about this farce, I'm convinced that it is entirely vanity, and that there is likely nothing more real to me than the memory of one little girl, who has gone away . . .

No matter how it goes, I will cherish the memory of you as you were in the winter: a sprite of a girl, cold and fiery at the same time, who desired something great and inexpressible. I felt as if you could never put your desires into words, Inga, they were so powerful. Perhaps it had been a misunderstanding of mine that you were passionate, but I admired you for it in my mind. I have only managed to hold your hand a few times . . . and that is in fact all that I know about you. But why am I speaking in such a way, when I cannot imagine that you understand me at all . . .

I do not say farewell to you – I only send you the sorrow in my thoughts. Your friend, Kiljan.

Halldór would go on to write Inga many beautiful love letters; it was as if she sometimes became a symbol of the nation to which he was accountable. These letters become key sources for his ways of thinking and his work during the next decade: Inga became his closest confidant. Of course the woman to whom he wrote so often from America was in some ways his brainchild, but the passionate admiration that one can detect in her letters intensified his thoughts about her. Halldór's letters also shed light on another side of him, confirmed by the fact that he always signed them "Kiljan", something he did not do otherwise.

Despite their newly kindled love, Halldór's writing career was more important. Although the publication of *The Great Weaver* had secured him some travel money, his financial standing in Iceland was uncertain. Halldór was not ready to decide whether he would become a character in a romance set in Iceland, as Steinn Elliði puts it in *The Great Weaver*. Halldór wrote to Jón Helgason on 10 May: ". . . I have no further business in this country. It is undecided where I shall go . . . I have new, great novels in mind, and all sorts of plans for the future." Two weeks later he boarded the *Gullfoss* on his way to the land that he had been prohibited from entering five years earlier, North America.

Happy Days in Hollywood

I often feel in my heart like a man who is rowing for his life
on a little boat out on the open sea.

Halldór Laxness in a letter

For I desire only two things: love and fame, and from neither
have I yet found satisfaction, nor will I ever find it.

Balzac in a letter

Halldór travelled to Leith and from there to Glasgow, where he booked a passage on the *S.S. Montclare* to Montreal in Canada. From there he would still have a train journey of several days before arriving in Winnipeg, where he planned to spend time among the numerous "Western Icelanders" (as Icelandic emigrants to Canada are called) who lived there. Upon his arrival in Glasgow he wrote to Inga to say that they had to see each other again:

You have a power that stimulates me every time I think about it. One feels almost as if life is worth living if one has been granted the fortune to get to know a little girl like you. Inga, once (perhaps more often) we spoke about meeting beneath the palm trees in a city rich with sunshine; we spoke about this in the darkness and the cold, one Icelandic winter's night.

Halldór challenged them both to make this dream come true.

As always happened during his travels in the 1920s, Halldór's poetic side emerged. The poems are often joyful and amusing, just like those he wrote on his trip south in the autumn of 1923. For example, he inserts a line in English into a poem called "*S.S. Montclare*": "I am the happiest Charleston man on board." Singing, dancing and other amusements were part of Halldór's youth; he was not constantly mulling over eternal life. The poem displays at the same time his newly awakened love for people: This was of course somewhat abstract, because the poet particularly mentions how bored he is with the crying of the children on board.

Halldór composed a poem about the Atlantic Ocean and sent it to Inga from Winnipeg on 17 June along with two love poems. One of these, "Evening – Stanza Antica", he says he wrote for her: "Give me that which you do not guard/give it to none but me so that they might my deceased body/lay at your feet." There is a kind of tormented undertone to this poem that is even more discernible in a third poem, "Nameless", which was included in *Rhodymenia Palmata*. This is a poem that one could imagine Steinn Elliði writing for Diljá: "Can you not suffer, woman,/suffer for me?/Can you not hate, hate,/hate for me?" In the poems' distinct voices we are given a glimpse of Halldór's internal struggles.

The train journey took the writer "through amazing cities, over wide plains, agriculturally blessed grazing ground, day-long wild forests, sparsely grown mountain land, over prairies that seemed endless and along lakes that resembled seas", as he says in an article entitled "Nationalism", written about a year later and included in *The Book of the People*. He tells how the trip inspired observations on nationalism, and about how he awoke one day in Ontario and "felt more like a foreigner in the eyes of God and men than I had ever felt before". He contemplated why so many people had left Iceland in the last quarter of the nineteenth century to settle on the isolated plains of Manitoba or Saskatchewan. Had they not lost their nationality without gaining anything in its place? Halldór's double-edged view of Western Icelanders throughout his life could be explained by such musings.

*

Halldór was cordially received when he arrived in Winnipeg on 13 June. He was given a room by the mother of the writer Lára Salverson, and his arrival was described in one of the Icelandic-Canadian newspapers, *Heimskringla*:

> Mr Halldór Kiljan Laxness, who is without doubt one of the most talented young writers in Iceland, plans to stay here in Canada this summer, and then to go west to California during the winter. He is here mainly to do research on children's education.

Halldór visited villages near Winnipeg Lake in the area called "New Iceland". It cannot be said with certainty how much Halldór learnt about children's education; the Icelandic settlement in Canada was only somewhere he thought he could raise funds through lectures and readings to travel south. On 20 June he wrote to Kristján Albertsson, his friend and benefactor with whom he was constantly squabbling:

> I have an incredible project in mind, which I cannot entrust to anyone as things stand, but I promise you that after several years you shall hear me shout from the rooftop in a great city – most likely from a skyscraper.

He expresses this somewhat differently in a letter to his mother, telling her that he intends to go to the Pacific Ocean that autumn and learn English:

> I plan during the next year to test the conditions here, to see if it is possible for a man like me to earn any money here in the west, and if it turns out to be little or none . . . then I will settle down in Iceland for good.

It only remained to be seen how much of a will he had to achieve his goals.

Halldór's life in North America was controlled by his ambition to succeed as a writer. The Icelandic-Canadian community was just a soft landing in an alien world. He planned to go to Los Angeles, not to study, since it had been shown how poor he was at studying, but to bring himself closer to the world of the cinema. He wrote to Erlendur in July:

> I discovered within myself a completely uncontrollable calling to go to Hollywood to write ten movies. I am convinced that nothing is more suited to me than the motion picture. I have eyes for nothing as much as the cinematic. I am convinced that I can earn millions of dollars by making movies in a considerably short amount of time.

Around then he wrote Inga an even more dramatic letter. Telling her of his motto never to give up, he goes on to say how enchanted he is by the world:

> I speak about the world like a drinker about wine because of my irresistible longing to conquer it. I am completely wild with power! Iceland could never satisfy half of the ambition that fills me. For me there exist only two options: either to conquer so memorably that I own the world in every respect or else to go perfectly to the dogs. And even if I go to the dogs, I will return from them! There is nothing in me that can be called giving up.

Halldór viewed himself as a resolute representative of modern culture, so it may have seemed natural that he should try his hand at that most modern of arts, the cinema. This was the medium that reached the most people, and Halldór wanted more than anything to conquer it.

First, however, the Icelandic-Canadians were given a dose of his arrogance and provocativeness. On 1 August he delivered a lecture in Hnausar called "From the Hearth to the Community", a defence of both the labour movement and modernity, and especially of youth against the traditional values of the older generation. Much of this was written in the same tone that he uses later in *The Book of the People*, only more light-hearted. By the time he wrote *The Book of the People*, he had seen how unrestrained capitalism could destroy modern society, but in this lecture he was still optimistic about the benefits of mass culture.

Halldór did not just preach to the Western Icelanders, but also learnt about their history and lifestyle. Just as in Eskifjörður the previous year, he wrote short stories based on the tales told to him by people he met; he found material everywhere. Much later he made a great deal of the opposition to his readings and lectures in Canada; it came, he said, in the form of loud protests and scuffles. In the "American Letter" Halldór sent to *Morgunblaðið* in the spring of 1928, however, he praises the reception he received, though he jokes that after his reading in Riverton the owner of the trading station there launched into an invective against him, as had happened in Árborg. But Halldór must have anticipated that there would be some who would oppose his idea that the Western Icelanders had lost their nationality without having gained anything in return.

The short story "New Iceland" was written in the spirit of Halldór's older proletarian stories, and is not dissimilar to Einar Kvaran's famous "Hopes". Halldór's tale portrays a farmer similar to Þórður from Kálfakot, but is told with more confidence, although the journey to Canada made by Torfi Torfason happens too quickly. Torfi's old farming techniques do not serve him very well in the endless barren expanse of Canada. And in the end this big strong man weeps – "this proletarian who had sacrificed his children to the hope of an outstanding future, a better life". Halldór's concluding words in the "American Letter" to *Morgunblaðið* were:

> ... I shall not conceal the fact that next to the plague I consider no sorrow more tragic for the history of the Icelandic nation than the emigration to Canada during the last quarter of the nineteenth century. The difference is that those who died from the plague went to heaven, but those that went west disappeared into the British Empire or the humbug culture of the United States.

Halldór's circumstances in North America were different from those of his earlier travels. He was determined to succeed – but as an Icelander – and he was more critical of contemporary foreign culture. The Icelandic settlements could not be more than a stop along the way, and at the end of October he left for California with a rich acquaintance who became his benefactor. Halldór Halldórsson (who spelt his name "Haldor Haldorson" in America) came from a poor family, an adventurer who was said to have become rich by selling water in the deserts of Australia, and now he was furiously building condominiums in Los Angeles. He invited Halldór to travel with him by train and told him that he could get him an apartment when they arrived in California. In *A Poet's Time* Halldór wrote:

> He was a splendidly amusing companion: he never grew tired of quarrelling and never left any subject alone. We argued sometimes for days on end over things that he knew nothing about and I even less . . .

On the way the two Halldórs stopped in Utah, where Halldór found himself thinking about a popular writer whom he had long admired, Eiríkur Ólafsson from Brúnir. This Icelandic farmer had become a Mormon, gone to Utah in 1881 and written a travelogue about his journey. Halldór said later:

> In the autumn of 1927 when I stood for the first time opposite the temple in Salt Lake City with its lofty, needle-straight towers, with the square on the other side, where the tabernacle cowered, convex and oblong, its interior shaped like the Mouth of God, there came to my mind the story that I had read by accident as a child, about the pilgrimage of an insignificant man throughout the world in search of the Promised Land, and if it were possible, even more about the chilling trials that befell his family after he had gone. Before I knew it I had started to connect this story with my own reality. The idea continued to visit me for more than thirty years.

It was not until Halldór had travelled his own long road in search of the Promised Land that he could write that story, the novel *Paradise Reclaimed* (1960). Halldór also found himself thinking of Inga. He sent her a letter from Utah to tell her that he was on his way to Los Angeles, sick of the banquets in Canada, and added: "Remember that I desire you no less than you me, and my desire for you increases by degrees with the growing distance between us." A day later he had arrived in Los Angeles, where he wrote to her: "Palm trees grow here, Inga" . . .

Haldor Haldorson found Halldór a small but comfortable apartment in one of his condominiums near the centre of Los Angeles. This new residence could hardly have been more different from the isolated villages of the Canadian plains. Halldór wrote, somewhat in amazement, on 4 December: "Last year around this time I was on skis north in the Icelandic wilderness; now I am here surrounded by nothing but roses." But this was a huge American city, rich in people of numerous nationalities, an industrial city with deep rifts between rich and poor, pervaded by the rotten sweetness of prostitutes, as Raymond Chandler put it. And it was in the suburb of Hollywood that film production had its headquarters – not just for America but for the world.

Halldór immediately got down to business. After a week in Los Angeles he took stock of his situation in a letter to Inga saying that he was writing a novel in English, working at it six hours a day. It was supposed to be short and Halldór planned to finish it in a few weeks. In the meantime he was also thinking of something else:

> I have been in contact with a damned great woman about becoming an agent for me; she has been an agent for various well-known men in the film world. I have personally met Crysander, who is a director for Laski, and they have some of the largest studios in Hollywood. On the same evening I was with Cody, the actor famous in every hemisphere, and a script writer whose name is Durlam. I plan to meet Cody again soon. The cinematic world here is extremely interesting and I have the greatest hopes of working my way into it, as soon as I have prepared something in English. Life here in Hollywood is enormously entertaining during the evenings.

He had also got to know several Icelanders, including two nurses, young country girls who studied nursing in Europe, "very energetic girls and afraid of nothing". These were friends from Borgarfjörður, Ástríður Jósepsdóttir and Kristín Valgerður Einarsdóttir, a minister's daughter from Reykholt; she went by the name of Valgerður and signed her name "Vala Poulsen". In 1920 she and Ásta had gone together as nineteen-year-old girls to Scotland to train as nurses, had then worked in Canada before setting in Los Angeles. According to letters from this time, Vala had been an adventurous woman, independent-minded and emotional, interested in music and literature, and had quickly fallen in love with Halldór.

Halldór's energy and optimism these first weeks had no limit. He wrote to Einar Ólafur on 17 November:

> Have been here for a month. Wrote *Kari Karan*, a synopsis of a photo-drama [film script]. My name is Hall d'Or – in movie circles. Was today finishing an

essay (a draft) that is called "Cinematography and Creative Art". I plan to
have completely finished it in the next two weeks. Then I plan to send it to
the ten largest newspapers in the world . . . My mood at this time is such that
I feel as if my powers have no limit.

Two days later he told his friend Ragnar Kvaran in Canada about how he was
learning film-making. He visited the studios, tried to teach himself scriptwriting and
attempted to involve himself in the business side of the film world. It was only in
the autumn of 1928 that he finally became tired of such activities.

Most of the film companies had moved to Los Angeles during the 1910s, among
other things because of the year-round sunny climate and the variegated landscape. A great amount of money was poured into this young industry and
thousands flocked to Hollywood to try to break break into films. The first talking
picture, *The Jazz Singer* with Al Jolson, came out the same year that Halldór went
to Hollywood, but the large production companies hesitated to invest in talking
pictures, among other things because of how expensive it would be to set up sound
systems in cinemas throughout the country. Directors and actors from around
the world tried their luck in California, since speaking was not necessary on the
big screen.

It did not take Halldór long to get to know the Icelandic-born movie actor, Bill
Cody, who acted in the most famous genre of the 1920s, the cowboy film. Halldór
wrote an article about Cody, "The Cowboy Actor from Skagafjörður", on 4
November, and it was published in both *Heimskringla* and *Morgunblaðið*. What was
being produced in Hollywood was a commodity, not art. Halldór wrote about Cody
with admiration for a man descended from dirt-poor Western Icelanders. Halldór
played the reporter's role, describing his visits to Cody and his interviews with him.

Halldór also met other Icelanders who were trying to break into the film business, including the comedian Bjarni Björnsson, whom he remembered from
performances in Rekyavík. Bjarni, who worked under the name Barney Bronson,
was not successful despite landing several small roles, and supported himself
mainly as a doorman at a film studio. The two men spent time together in Los
Angeles and became good friends, but Bjarni gave up on Hollywood and returned
to Iceland. Halldór wrote an article about him for *Morgunblaðið* in 1928 in which he
encouraged Bjarni to return home, "because it is better to be unforgettable in a
smaller nation than to disappear within this gurgling bird's nest of millions of
nations". Halldór had certainly contemplated this for himself.

That he hoped to work his way into the world of cinema is clear from an article
he wrote about American film and mentioned in a letter to Inga, though it was

never printed in English. He is critical of the industry, although he admits that the motion picture is the "most democratic form of entertainment that has ever been invented". And he goes on to assert that any form of art that did not reach someone, no matter how incredible it was, did not have social value. The article is an exhortation to creative artists to become involved in cinema. Halldór says that he is content with the high-modern spirit of film-worship, and he celebrates the technological achievements of film-making: "The redemption of mankind from the tyranny of the word grants us the right to believe in a beautiful millennium ahead." And he describes his admiration for the works of Asta Nielsen, Charlie Chaplin and Emil Jannings. However, the motion picture's art, he believed, was drowning in profiteering, technique and trends.

Halldór claimed that he gave up publishing this article in English since it could have given him a bad name in the film studios. On the other hand, he did want to publish it in Europe, so he sent it to his most famous acquaintance, Nonni. Nonni's reaction was favourable; he also told of his dream that his own books would be made into films. He asked whether Halldór could help with this.

Halldór responded and explained how difficult it was to make any headway in American film. Meanwhile Nonni got Halldór's article printed in a rather conservative Catholic weekly magazine, *Das Neue Reich*, published in Vienna.

Halldór gained no attention in the major European newspapers for his views on cinema, and Bjarni and Cody were unable to advance his cause in Hollywood. Halldór shifted his focus to trying to establish contacts with foreign film-makers and took up writing scripts. At the turn of 1927–8 he wrote to Inga:

> I am . . . working on two magnificent film scripts. One of them is called *Kari Karan* or *Judged by a Dog*, and the other, *Salka Valka* or *A Woman in Pants*. They will both take time and effort to complete. But if a man does his job in the spirit of perfection, his works will be talked about longer than he lives.

These scripts, one of them based on an old short story, the other the first draft of a larger novel, were the weapons Halldór thought he could use to succeed in Hollywood.

It was long thought that the scripts had been lost, but it turned out that they had been in the keeping of Stefán Einarsson, who had given them to Halldór's son, Einar. They are written in English, and it would perhaps be more correct to call them drafts of novels; *Salka* is more detailed in its descriptions of settings and camera shots. Halldór was not well versed in the technicalities of film-making and both films were to have been silent.

Kari Karan is basically the same story as "The Poet and his Dog", which Halldór
had written during his first year in Copenhagen. The script reflects the exaggerated
style of silent films. For example, Kari, a Scandinavian writer, is described as
follows: "His expression is a mixture of lunacy and extreme pain."

Salka Valka is no less dramatic, but is a better composed story with more interesting characters, as one can see from the novel that it became. It is set at the
seaside in Iceland, and it bears the marks of much that preoccupied Halldór at
that time: the struggles of Icelanders in seaside villages, the lot of women, a revolutionary spirit and the torments of love.

Salka herself is described as follows:

She is tall and strongly built. The chief ingredients of her facial expression:
rustic virginity, dare-devilry, primitive charm. She is dressed like a fisherman:
wide pants, the boot-legs reaching up over her knees, a pipe in her mouth.

Having decided to "escape the fate of women", she becomes the captain of a
boat, but her crew turns on her: "Wild with terror, she runs to the shore, where
she finds a small boat, jumps in, rows out and disappears in the furious breakers.
Night. Blizzard."

Halldór is bolder here than in *The Great Weaver from Kashmir* in his descriptions
of tormented passion, drawing from the works of Freud and his followers, as well
as from what he had heard of the range of human sexual behaviour, for instance,
from his friends in Taormina. In the end Salka goes to her lover's cottage and takes
his beautiful Icelandic whip down from a hook on the wall: "She folds out before
her the double leather straps of the whip, kissing it with all the voluptuousness
and pathos of the primitive." Halldór imagined Greta Garbo – known in
Hollywood for being a cross-dresser – in the title role.

*

Halldór's rent seems to have consisted of helping his landlord, Haldorson, write
poetry. The artist and musician Magnús Á. Árnason, who met Halldór the
Christmas of 1927, remembered that, when visiting him, the telephone had rung
and Halldór had had a long conversation with Haldorson:

He was letting Laxness hear his latest poetry, but Halldór recomposed the
poem on the telephone and added a great deal to it. I understood that they
did this almost every day . . .

The arrangement recalls the relationship between Pétur þríhross and Ólafur
Kárason in *World Light*.

Haldorson and Halldór took car trips and played golf together. Halldór and Magnús Á. Árnason became good friends and in Magnús' memoirs there is a curious but convincing description of Halldór:

> ... he was a nearly average-sized man of height, very thin and exceptionally erect; his hair was blond but not thick, his forehead high, his eyebrows pale, his nose quite large and his lower lip somewhat jutting. His eyes were especially beautiful, light blue and sparkling and radiating an attentive thoughtfulness, goodwill and humour. His hands were particularly beautiful and long and his fingers slender, and would have suited a pianist no less than a writer. He was trim, joyful of expression, not pretty, but exceptional in many ways, with an engaging personality.

Many doors must have stood open to such a man.

Halldór wrote frequently to Inga during his first months in Los Angeles. At one point he felt compelled to make a confession:

> I have to tell you something rather serious . . . *In order to come to you, I need to commit the most horrific of sins.* I must sacrifice the dreams of happiness of a person who loves me with all her heart . . . and now I receive word that this same person is setting out over sea and land in order to make me her prisoner again.

Inga questioned him repeatedly about the woman. Halldór writes:

> I would never imagine saying anything bad about her. She has divorced her husband in order to follow me here . . . and by the end of last month she had made it all the way from Iceland to a city . . . in Canada. There she was prohibited from travelling any further. She was sent back over the sea . . .

In Halldór's archives one can find several letters sent to him by this woman, Solveig Pétursdóttir. They have the aura of a long-lost love: old photos in an envelope, dried roses, flowers that Solveig had gathered at Þingvellir. From the letters it is clear that Solveig and Halldór had had a relationship, which had probably started on Flatey in the summer of 1924.

Solveig's letters from 1928 show her hope of their being reunited, and then her sorrow when she perceives Halldór's apathy and hears about Inga. It was probably necessary for Halldór to set her right. Reykjavík was a small town, and Solveig, together with Kristín Guðmundsdóttir, owned the beauty salon called Hollywood where Inga had her hair done. Inga's letters reveal that she and Solveig found each other annoying, but the annoyance did not cut deep enough to prevent them from occasionally meeting. Inga was enchanted to be made a member of the Holy Milk Club, to which Solveig also belonged; she felt as if she came closer to Halldór through his friends.

Halldór often found himself in tight romantic spots. Nonetheless he spent a lot of time convincing Inga that she was his first true love. Several days after Christmas, 1927, he sent her this description of his love life up till then, at the same time a kind of apology:

I often had crushes on girls from when I was a boy for as long as a day, sometimes several days, but these did not affect me as time went by; they were instead as wind blowing past me. I was sometimes frivolous and negligent . . . and my negligence often led to unpleasant consequences; there were girls that took my frivolity too seriously, as, for example, this last one. Once I grew tired of all of this and sat in an abbey for two years! Don't you think that your old abbey-dweller wasn't sometimes ridiculous in the fight?

Although Halldór had no rent to pay, he did need to earn some money. The woman he referred to as his agent in the film business, Harriet Wilson, was able to find him work as a lecturer. Around the new year Halldór wrote to Inga:

In the next few months I will most likely go to San Francisco for several weeks . . . Harriet Wilson . . . has . . . arranged for me to deliver paid lectures about Scandinavian literature in four "millionaire's clubs". I am to be paid 100 dollars for an evening . . . Otherwise I have no interest in this type of "job".

Remaining in Los Angeles in January, he wrote to Inga on 23 January to tell her that in the preceding weeks he had experienced one of his spells of depression, and that Hollywood's soulless attitude towards money was taking its toll: "Success here means only two things: either it is piled up around people in foolish praise in disgusting newspaper articles – or else people's lives are poisoned and destroyed by money."

And something else was burdening him. He had received a telegram advising him of the death of his best friend:

I often thought [he wrote to Inga] that when he was dead I would have no-one else to look to throughout the wide world. He was a monk in France. If you remember Father Alban in *The Great Weaver*, then you know this friend of mine who is now dead. There is no other man for whom I have more to thank.

Father Beda and Halldór Laxness had not met again since their farewell at Clervaux in the spring of 1926. Halldór's sorrow was so profound that he saw no-one for two weeks.

In the end he gladly accepted the offer to lecture in San Francisco. He travelled there by car at the end of January, accompanied by an acquaintance of his, a Bulgarian sculptor by the name of Katchmanaikof. In addition to lecturing, he planned to start translating *The Great Weaver from Kashmir* into English with the assistance of Magnús Á. Árnason. Halldór stayed with Magnús for the next four months. As always, he was quick to adjust to his new surroundings: he visited restaurants, the cinema and concerts, met resident Icelanders and was invited to parties, including one with the daughters of Jack London: "One of them is a writer, a bright girl and a red Bolshevik." Significantly older than him, Harriet Wilson also lived in San Francisco, and they spent some time together while he was there. Many years later Halldór described her in an epitaph for Magnús as "the kind of grandmother I had never imagined existed except in Iceland". He was still plagued by the restlessness that resulted from his overwhelming depression, as he worded it memorably in a letter to Inga:

> Is it not amazing that around a man as cold as I am there should always be fire? Sometimes it tries to burn me: but I usually collect my things and leave. *I have not been able to flee from you.* You are everywhere that I am.

Shortly before this he had confided to his mother that he and Inga were engaged.

Around the middle of February he informed Inga that he had been written up in the papers because of a lecture that he was going to give to the "Berkeley League of Fine Arts", which meant that it would be attended by the best people. A Danish paper published in San Francisco praised the lecture, and mentioned that he and Magnús had sung Icelandic folk songs afterwards. These were the first public concerts that the writer had given since he sang Schubert on a bright summer evening on Flatey.

Halldór spoke in many other clubs, and in *A Poet's Time* good-naturedly satirizes himself as an uninspired lecturer at the Housewife's Club for the Elation of the Spirit. But he earned 50–100 dollars each time, and this was his main means of support during his two years in California. One of his lectures, written in English, survives: it is a kind of introduction to Icelandic literature, a dramatic presentation of the sagas. Halldór never hesitated to describe the poverty and hardship faced by Icelanders throughout the ages, as well as his admiration for his nation's literary endeavours. Although his interpretation of history is rather traditional and nationalistic, we can glimpse his personal opinions. At the end of the lecture he draws attention to some younger writers who had written in foreign languages, and also compliments several who wrote in Icelandic, even though only a hundred thousand people could read their work. Nowhere else did Halldór praise his fellow Icelandic writers so unreservedly.

*

The months that Halldór and Magnús spent together in San Francisco were good ones; their memoirs agree on this, and they remained close friends ever afterwards. Magnús had a studio attached to his apartment and they often received visitors or went out, ever curious about their surroundings. Halldór wrote some poems, and Magnús, who was an excellent musician and had a piano in his studio, set them to music. Magnús described their friendship that same year in an article in the *People's Paper*, his words reflecting the opinions of many who came to know Halldór at that time and later:

> As far as this young troublemaker is concerned, it has always turned out that those who approach him with enmity and suspicion quickly turn to celebrating him as a friend, their enmity changed into admiration, their suspicion into trust. This is because the man is gentle and peaceful, pleasant and popular, and he is loved and admired by all who meet him.

After Halldór had been in San Francisco for nearly a month, he received a letter from Vala, the nurse he had met earlier that winter:

> Today I went up on to a hill and sat there for a long time. Everything was so pure and charming after the rain . . . To the south-east Mount Baldi stood proudly but there on the tussock sat I, thinking about the man who had perhaps awakened the best in me or, no, I do not believe that I have anything stronger or better than the love that I have for you.

Vala's letters bear the marks of her passionate feelings, which surely must have been mutual.

Halldór did not write much fiction during his years in North America. He had abandoned Catholicism, adopted radical views and become ever more critical of iron-cold mercantilism, as he called it. All the same he had not given up his hope of advancement in the chief fortress of the marketable arts. He enjoyed life in Southern California, a land, as he wrote to his mother, that reminds one of the most perfect ideas about heaven. The worst thing about Los Angeles is that a man can absolutely not long to leave the place. The eternal sunshine and pleasant breezes, the cool nights, and from every handful of desert grow colourful flowers.

Halldór did write a short story in San Francisco – "And Sweet Smells the Lotus Blossom" – which sheds light on the unrest in his soul. It is about a little boy who manages to stay alive by collecting cigarette ends on the streets, beneath the city's huge billboards, while also taking care of his seriously ill mother. Radical ideals clash at her sick bed, each with its own spokesman, a Russian atheist and a Catholic priest. Despite the story's determined criticism of capitalism, it contains a remarkable resolution, when the boy in his destitution takes out a violin and plays Mozart. Here the reader senses the coherence in Halldór's thinking ever since childhood, his belief in a higher world that art – not least music – can convey.

Halldór's inner struggles are clearly displayed in the letters he sent to Inga that spring. At the end of March he told her that he was turning into an idiot, and that if he did not pull himself together he would become a rootless wreck. Two weeks later he sent her a long meditation about whether it was better to have the support of a small nation than everything inherent in the idiocy of a huge nation. The same question assailed him when Harriet Wilson invited him to a dinner in honour of Mexican intellectuals:

Did you know, Inga, that when I found myself in amongst all of this glitziness in foreign banquet halls, I sometimes trembled at the thought of going north to Iceland, where I would end up encountering nothing except for misunderstanding and enmity.

A short time before he left San Francisco he summarized these concerns: "This is my tenth year in foreign lands – I have no refuge anywhere, no home anywhere – a foreigner, a foreigner to God and men, even a foreigner to myself." These fearful waverings, along with his relationship with Vala, occasionally caused the tone of his letters to Inga to be quite miserable.

That spring, however, he was constantly coming into contact with new people and environments, and he had good friends. His views were becoming clearer, with his politics approaching a kind of radical socialism. This became evident when he received a letter from Inga containing a photograph of her and Prelate Meulenberg:

Just how amazed was I when out from your other letter fell a photo of you at the side of Monsignor Meulenberg – my supervisor in religious matters (!)

– and the Catholic Church behind you! That was truly a photo of my old and
new loves side by side. Once I loved the Catholic Church like someone insane
and kissed the Prelate's ring. Now it is a different time. I am, that is to say,
completely bored with all religious rote; cannot hear it named. (All the same
I must admit that I am more fond of the Catholic Church than bourgeois
society! Oh, yes, there once was a time that I shed pious tears in the shadowy
stone cells of European medieval monasteries. So many horrible and intense
adventures have I experienced – but it is certainly best to read about adventures in books!).

Halldór was handicapped by the fact that his ambition was finding insufficient
outlet; he was uncertain about his position and future as a writer.

At the end of May, 1928, he returned to Los Angeles, even though he and
Magnús had only finished translating half of _The Great Weaver from Kashmir_. That
he felt better there is revealed in a letter he wrote to Rannveig Þorvarðardóttir
Schmidt, an Icelander who worked at the Danish consulate in San Francisco:

Here I live like an egg yolk. My friend, Mr Halldórsson, has during the time
that I was gone built a huge building containing eighty apartments, and he
has given me one of them to live in. Southern California is so heavenly that
I have difficulty contenting myself with the thought that I might need sometime to leave this place – oh, I had grown so tired of the "studio" life.

He wrote to Inga:

Look, Inga, if I succeed here with the film – _which is just a matter of time_ – then
I will be safe. Then all my troubles will be over. I cannot run away from this
half done. I must succeed. I cannot go and settle down at home as things
stand and vanish into small-town life, not now, while I am so young and full
of victorious energy.

In the summer of 1928 Halldór came as close as he ever would to selling the
script of _Salka Valka_ to M.G.M. In a letter from the famous Swedish film director
Victor Sjöström (he spelt his name Seastrom) to Halldór written on M.G.M.
stationery and dated 25 May, Sjöström says that unfortunately he has little if any
information for Halldór, and asks Halldór to call him at a particular time, which
he did. He says in a letter to Inga:

Right after I arrived the other day I called Victor Sjöström at Metro-
Goldwyn-Mayer Studios. This morning he called me before I had got up and

asked me to come down to the studio on Thursday, to be present when they started filming a new movie with Greta Garbo.

Halldór admired no other actress as much as Garbo, who, like Sjöström, had left Sweden for Hollywood during the 1920s.

After this wheels started to turn. On 20 June he told Inga that he was haggling with the film companies, and that it was enormously difficult to attract their attention to an Icelandic theme. Competition was unbelievable; in one instance, Paramount sponsored a competition and received forty thousand scripts in response. Even though Halldór had got interviews with some of the industry bigwigs, it was very difficult to achieve any kind of result:

> I have come furthest with the Metro-Goldwyn-Mayer company – received a letter from them today, in which they explained to me that they had discussed taking up my script with Greta Garbo, but at the moment they are using her for another project. This . . . letter does not in any way reject the script but opens various possibilities . . . Oh, it is exciting, I tell you. If it happens then I am "made".

Two days later he wrote Inga a letter full of optimism:

> As I write these lines, everything seems to indicate that my "game" here in Hollywood is achieving some results. It even looks as if I shall set off for Iceland within a few weeks with four film people in tow: "male lead" (who at the same time is the business manager of the trip), "female lead", director and camera man. In other words I have succeeded in getting Hollywood interested, *and there are 50,000 dollars at hand to film a script written by me.* I am to take care of all the practical details. If we do not set out within three weeks, we will not arrive this summer, and if we arrive in September we cannot possibly expect enough sunshine for filming in Iceland. We have to arrive in Iceland by the first few days in August, otherwise everything will be useless. There has been talk of going by plane over the mainland of America to New York. You can understand that it is quite exciting to know within the next few days whether we will be able to prepare for the trip or not.

It is easy to imagine how excited Halldór must have been. Thus it was a huge disappointment when nothing came of the idea. The man who was to direct the film would not be free before the middle of July. Halldór wanted a contract, but M.G.M. would not give him one until shooting commenced. M.G.M. said that it was interested in reading more of Halldór's scripts, so he worked hard at typing up a new one in a week (it might have been *Kari Karan*). But nothing came of this either; Halldór reacted gruffly to the studio's idea of moving the setting to Kentucky, telling them that he had not come there to make a fool of himself. In August M.G.M. told Halldór that someone would contact him again in January, a way of putting him off. Halldór had had enough and wrote to Inga:

> I do not intend to hang around in Hollywood; it does not suit me! This is humiliation. Here it is not possible to do anything with genius. What they ask for is idiocy.

Luckily his dealings with M.G.M. seemed not to have weakened his confidence. Interestingly no documents pertaining to this matter exist in the studio's archives.

*

Halldór went to America early in the summer of 1927 with a plan to make it in the world of cinema in his sights. He worked energetically for nearly a year without any success. The consequences of his defeat are more remarkable than the defeat itself: an increasing disgust with film-making as a commodities industry, a renewed vow to become a writer in Icelandic and a belief in the necessity of the struggle, whether that meant the struggle for higher values or the struggle for himself and his creativity. He worded it this way in a letter to Inga late in the summer, after she had innocently admitted to him her love of luxury, money and travel:

> Do you know, Inga – *there are no adventures apart from this struggle!* Luxury and comfort signify lack of struggle, lack of adventure, a "dead" life. The value of the individual is only contained in his capacity for the struggle – not in the victory or the defeat, but rather in his ability to struggle against great odds. Defeat is a rule, victory is an exception, an accident.

Here Halldór describes the course his life would take for the next fifteen years. He let neither victory nor defeat drive him off course.

Halldór enjoyed the summer in Los Angeles, however. He continued to meet people and worked on a collection of essays. He was frequently with Vala; they went to concerts and to the beach. She had waited impatiently for him to return to Los Angeles. He had not spent much time with Inga before leaving Iceland; perhaps their relationship had developed into a deep epistolary friendship rather than anything else.

In September, 1928, Halldór and his benefactor, Haldorson, had a falling out, and he moved for a time to a beautiful apartment that was far too expensive. He told Erlendur in a letter that he was used to asking the rich Australian-Icelander for loans, but he was terribly stingy. Halldór asked his namesake for money for a journey to Europe, "but he told me to go out to work . . . Of course I would rather try to steal the money I need than start 'working'." Halldór then asked Erlendur whether he could get travel money for him.

But his plans changed, and at the start of October he wrote to Inga:

I am thinking about renting a room with two Icelandic girls who live a short distance from here, and about letting them feed me as well, because it is much too expensive to be constantly eating at restaurants (and here I have no kitchen). These Icelandic girls . . . have just arrived here and occupy an entire house. They are nurses, very likeable.

Halldór moved in with the girls and lived with them for the better part of the next six months while he wrote *The Book of the People*. There was no doubt that his relationship with Vala made him decide to remain, and she supported him for the most part while he composed his essays on social struggle. She enjoyed Halldór's company, even though some might have been scandalized by the fact that they were living together.

Halldór, however, always seemed to have a strong need to describe his plans to Inga, to tell her of his dreams and ambitions. They were both modern personalities and fond of big cities, and Inga herself travelled abroad while Halldór was in America, among other places to London. But postal communication moved at a snail's pace. Letters took at least twenty-five days to arrive, sometimes as long as six weeks. A question asked in a letter could take two to three months to receive an answer, and it was not possible to telephone Iceland from America.

In his letters Halldór often expresses his love and longing for Inga, but he does not conceal the fact that it is entirely up to him whether and when he will return to Iceland:

I cannot explain my instincts. There is a kind of insatiable desire for knowledge that drives me on through life – for knowledge, which gives me power over the world. It is this tremendous passion that is the strongest of all my urges.

At the same time he became uneasy if there was a large gap between her letters. On 28 May, 1928, Halldór wrote impatiently: "Has Iceland sunk into the sea? Where are you? Or have you crossed me out?" The next day a letter from Inga arrived and Halldór noted that he felt blissful. That year he even started to make plans to bring her to Los Angeles, but later he dropped the idea.

Inga was no homebody. Nor did she refrain from teasing Halldór, writing, for example, from London that she had met a boy there who was "awfully cute". Halldór replied as soon as he received the letter: "My dear, don't use such foul language as to tell me that some Englishman is 'awfully cute'. How can an enlightened girl such as you say such a thing!"

In the autumn of 1928 the letters became more serious, since Halldór was involved with Vala and nothing about his future was clear. Inga perceived his coldness, and of course Halldór did not feel comfortable with the situation. He nearly admitted everything to her when he added this handwritten sentence to a typewritten letter: "Do you know, I find that I have been squashed to bits like a worm, half of me rooted here, half at home with you . . ."

The pair managed to rekindle the embers of love in their letters, however. Halldór identified Inga with Iceland and when he finally decided to return home his faith in their future together became stronger:

Once you were like a little bird who came into my life – you alighted on the hedge and started to sing . . . and little by little I forgot everything but this song, and everything around me seemed to be false compared to that – my entire life a false note without this song . . .

From July, 1928, until January, 1929, Halldór worked on the collection of essays that was published in November, 1929, under the title *The Book of the People*. He was thinking seriously about going home. He told Inga: "I will never become even half a man abroad. I have decided to throw myself into politics when I come home, and my new book is thus all about politics." This was the book that made Halldór famous, even notorious, in Iceland. *The Great Weaver from Kashmir* had, despite all the hubbub, not really worked its way beyond the literary and intellectual circles in Reykjavík; *The Book of the People*, however, was an extremely vigorous polemical work and many people discussed it. Reverend Emil Björnsson, later news director for Icelandic National Television, was a teenager when the book was published, and he recalled the harsh reactions to it:

It was especially, I think, the essay in *The Book of the People* called "On Hygiene in Iceland" that made people's hackles rise, although it was evidently written to awaken self-respect.

The Book of the People expressed Halldór's new agenda and covered the territory he was most interested in at the time. Printed on the cover of the first edition were these arrogant words:

This book shines with all those topics most dear to the Icelandic people: social issues, literature, the arts, gender issues, religion. A new revolution has taken place in the writer's psychology, and he invites the Icelandic people to taste of its fruits.

The book begins with a chapter on books – to be more precise, with the declaration that the truth is "not in books and not even in good books, but rather in people who have good hearts". Halldór cares little for writers who write for small audiences, even less for the delusional snares of the New Testament, but he praises Þórbergur Þórðarson, who proved in *Letter to Lára* that he was both better informed about divinity and the soul than the apostle Paul, and a better stylist.

The tone is set. Halldór is fresh and radical, and still finds it amusing to tease his readers, but now his messages are more cohesive. The chapter on nationalism shows how optimistic Halldór is about Iceland's future; here Halldór is heavily influenced by Spengler's *The Decline of the West* (1918). The essay on hygiene is reminiscent of earlier articles about the state of culture in Iceland, and he is just as ruthless in his position regarding rural culture.

Film-making in America received its share of criticism in a two-part essay that he wrote at the end of 1928, and that was published, like his previous essay on the topic, in the Viennese journal *Das Neue Reich*. The optimism that had pervaded the previous article had disappeared: "The motion picture is a tool of misanthropists, used to make a commodity of the desire for excitement in that portion of the American people that can be called imbeciles." There was in fact only one real man in that desert, and that was Charlie Chaplin; no man had made as many friends of the helpless. Radical artists throughout the world admired Chaplin.

In *The Book of the People*'s preaching about social reforms an appeal is often made to various scientific and technical developments, and emphasis is laid on the fact that radicalism touches most spheres of human activity, among them the position of women:

> The whole object of the division of labour, which aims at making woman an ornamented and ignorant sexual slave, as is common among better placed citizens, or a slovenly skivvy, as is the custom among the working class, is savagery.

Halldór had no faith in marriages built either on this division of labour or entirely on sexual passion. He believed that a married couple must act in unity with respect to a cultural goal if their cohabitation was to last. It is tempting to read such comments in an autobiographical light. Halldór considered passion exceptional, but time-bound:

Our demands and longings change at every period of our lives; that is, for instance, a woman whom I loved for several years now means nothing to me at all . . . The view changes according to where we are situated – before we are aware of it our emotional life plays on other strings – our taste changes, another aura pervades our conscious life overall.

At the end of the book the writer delineates his experience of religion, and how his path to earthly contemplations has been found through a rejection of the vanity of the heavens. He describes his new faith:

MAN is the joyous tiding of the new culture: man as the most perfect biological species, man as social unit, man as a symbol of life and idealism – the one true man – YOU.

These remarks, which removed any lingering doubts about Halldór's renouncing of Catholicism, caused his dear friend Nonni to feel that he had had enough. On 10 May, 1930, he informed Halldór that he felt certain that he could continue to be his friend even though Halldór had enlisted with another army, but from that time forward they could only cultivate that friendship privately. Nonni seemed to think that Halldór would understand his position. But Halldór must have been hurt, and in the event Nonni did not stand by his resolution.

*

While he was in America Halldór continued to read contemporary literature. He and Magnús read, for example, *Ulysses* (1922) by James Joyce, and even though Halldór respected this great work of European modernism, he knew he would not try to follow in Joyce's footsteps. His dabbling in avant-garde literature had concluded with *The Great Weaver from Kashmir*. His attitude was aloof towards *The Magic Mountain* (1924) by Thomas Mann; he was much fonder of *Buddenbrooks* (1900) and *Death in Venice* (1912). The literary movement that Halldór liked most in the United States was social realism. Three of its best-known representatives during those years were Theodore Dreiser, Sinclair Lewis and Upton Sinclair, and Halldór read as much of their work as he could, besides becoming personally acquainted with Sinclair. Lewis, best known in Iceland for *Babbitt* (1922), had the greatest appeal for Halldór, probably because he had the most talent for bringing social issues and the art of storytelling together, which was what Halldór intended for himself; for a long time he had a great essay about Sinclair Lewis in the works, as he told Stefán Einarsson.

Halldór's acquaintance with Upton Sinclair had unpleasant consequences. At the time Sinclair lived in Long Beach, a short distance from Los Angeles, and was at the apex of his career. He was a radical socialist with a distinct American flair, and his novels sometimes read like colourfully camouflaged newspaper reports in the service of a cause. They were read and discussed throughout the United States. Halldór attached great hopes to their acquaintance, because they shared the same political views, and because he thought that Sinclair could advance him in the American literary world. They met first in the late summer of 1928, and in September Halldór wrote proudly to Inga that he had lunched with Sinclair twice and had gone with him to a socialist meeting at the Trinity Hotel. Halldór took advantage of the opportunity and told Sinclair about *The Great Weaver from Kashmir*; he was planning to finish the translation with Magnús and trying to get it published in America, having become convinced that he had no future in cinema.

Later in the autumn Halldór wrote a short article in honour of Sinclair's fiftieth birthday, which was published in the *People's Paper* on 27 December, 1928. The article is somewhat sloppily written, as the writer himself says; in it he heaps praise on Sinclair because he did not write in the service of capitalism and was not owned by the powers controlling the market economy. He also mentions their acquaintance and describes Sinclair as being

> vigorous like a teenager, utterly charming and pleasant; his face is the most noble and promising that I have seen in America and the most aristocratic. In its hue it is similar to the face of Þórbergur Þórðarson.

He follows this description with praise for Sinclair's political struggles, in general observing that Americans were prevented from obtaining information that would increase their knowledge of social issues: "In this case every one hundred per cent American is a complete idiot." He recommends several works by Sinclair, especially *Boston* (1928), which was about the Sacco and Vanzetti case.

It is unlikely that anyone would have remembered this article if it had not been reprinted in *Heimskringla* on 30 January, 1929. The comment about the idiocy of one hundred per cent Americans did not sit well with Icelanders living in Canada and the United States (Western Icelanders) and a furious debate ensued in their newspapers. After several months *Heimskringla* refused to print any more of Halldór's rebukes, since the paper had by then lost many of its subscribers Stateside. Several Western Icelanders under the leadership of G.T. Athelstan (Gunnlaugur Tryggvi Aðalsteinsson), who by some ironic twist of fate worked in pest removal, filed charges against Halldór in Washington, presenting the Sinclair article as proof that it was Halldór's intention to harm the United States. On 2 June, 1929, Halldór wrote to Inga from California:

The day before I came here to Ojai, I was taken by policemen and brought to the police station in Los Angeles, where they conducted a private inter-rogation with me – I saw that the documents that they had already gathered about me had become four–five thumbs thick. I was told that I had dangerous political views, which aimed at toppling the reigning social order, and that I had written articles about the United States, in which I said that the Americans were "idiots" etc. Then my passport was taken from me. I was given the opportunity of seeing the translation that my friends in Winnipeg had made of one of my articles, and I stated straight away that it was a false translation. I was then given a small amount of time to get hold of the article and produce my own translation of it.

Halldór was angry and surprised and turned to Sinclair for help. Sinclair put him in touch with the American Civil Liberties Union, which promptly took up his case, refuting the charges and seeing to it that the case was publicized in the papers. Little by little discussion of the charges dwindled, and it became clear that Halldór would not be deported, but it was not until 4 October, 1929, that his pass-port was returned "at the urging of the lawyer that the Civil Liberties Union had persuaded to take my case", he told Inga:

> The United States has similar morals regarding thinking men to those Russia had in the days of the Tsar. The American authorities are nothing but a flock of inveterate thieves and murderers.

His experience of being called before the police because of his political writ-ings had a great effect on Halldór, and he never forgave the Western Icelanders for filing charges against him. This affair did nothing to detract from his radicalism, and in the autumn of 1929 he wrote another article about Upton Sinclair for the journal *Iðunn*, more detailed and ordered, with sharper opinions. He called one hundred per cent Americanism, by which he meant the supporters of the American powers-that-were, "Western idiocy", choosing the most abominable adjectives. At the same time he praised Sinclair for having rattled the cage of the mercantile powers.

It appears that in the winter of 1928–9 the translation of *The Great Weaver from Kashmir* got bogged down. Magnús Á. Árnason went bankrupt, lost his home and then moved to the state of Washington, where he was able to build a house on his sister's land. Halldór decided to visit Magnús in Washington and see if they could finish the translation, because he did not want to leave America until he had found a publisher for *The Great Weaver*. His confidence received a boost when Stefán

Einarsson announced that he wanted to write Halldór's biography. Halldór was enthusiastic and wrote to his mother and various friends at the start of 1929, asking people to send Stefán their letters in order to make the work easier for him. It is remarkable that an Icelandic professor in the United States, and a linguist besides, should have taken it upon himself to write a biography of a comparatively young writer who had not been published outside his own country. The collection of letters became invaluable for all later books about Halldór, although Stefán's own book was never published.

Halldór had nearly completed *The Book of the People* in January, 1929, and sent the manuscript to Erlendur, whom he viewed as a kind of agent. After doing this, and before going up to Washington, he stayed for several weeks in San Diego with a rich Icelandic woman, Ms Curry, whom he had met in Winnipeg. Halldór longed to go to Mexico and made a short trip to Tijuana but got no further because of the civil war. His main business in San Diego was to meet a world-famous medium, Mrs White, who was highly respected by Icelandic spiritualists. He was able to attend a séance conducted by her and thoroughly enjoyed the experience, describing it in an article published in *Heimskringla* and, later, in *A Day's Journey in the Mountains*. He refrained from passing judgement, but no-one who reads the article can have any doubt that he thought the interaction between the medium and the other world absolute rubbish. This was not the last time that he satirized spiritualism.

During his final year in America, Halldór was eager to learn as much as he could. He attended concerts at the Hollywood Bowl, and on his way north in March went to a concert in Oakland, writing to Inga:

> I listened to the world-famous black singer, Roland Hayes – perhaps one of the greatest artists in the world. When he sang about the trials of the Negro slaves in America, I felt as if he was singing the whole time from my own heart. I have never listened to a singer who gripped me so strongly. I am like a black man in America!

Halldór also wrote in detail to the Icelandic composer Jón Leifs about the strong effect that Hayes' singing had had on him: "You may not speak disrespectfully about American Negro music – it is the only music in America that is of any worth, and its worth is in fact great." Twenty years later Halldór heard Paul Robeson sing in Moscow and was just as moved.

Halldór arrived in Point Roberts, Washington, at the end of March after a short stop in Seattle, where he met the woman whom he considered to be the greatest

Western Icelandic poet, Jakobína Johnson: At Point Roberts he and Magnús got down to the business of translating, and were nearly finished by April. Since it was impossible to sell lectures in that remote area, Halldór was once again penniless, but Valgerður sent him money from Los Angeles.

By this time Halldór had told Valgerður about Inga, that he would be returning home and that they could no longer be anything but friends. Her letters to him reveal her love and despondency, but at the same time her devotedness and determination never to stand in his way. All the same, she clung to hope. On his advice she attended a Roland Hayes concert, writing at the start of April:

> One song that he sang I felt to be a message from the future and the past. It was like a whole man's life or a sleepless night, full of hopes and hopelessness, sorrow, trials, suffering, terror. Our relationship came to mind: did it have to be so painful? At that moment R.H. walked into the hall and said that he intended to do an encore: "Love Finds a Way" . . . I shall never forget it.

While Halldór was staying with Magnús, a representative of the Census Bureau visited Vala and Ástríður to find out why a man was living with them without his address being legally registered. It became clear that Vala would lose her residence permit if this cohabitation was investigated further, which meant that Halldór had to move elsewhere when he returned from Point Roberts. Since he had settled his dispute with Haldorson in the meantime, the latter let him use another of his apartments.

The Nobel Prize-winning writer Tagore delivered a lecture in Vancouver, a short distance from Point Roberts, in early April, and Halldór and Magnús went there to see their former hero before Halldór returned to California. Magnús had translated Tagore's *Song Offerings*, the same poems that Halldór had recited at his reading in Dalir in 1921. Halldór wrote an article, "Rabindranath Tagore in Vancouver", which was published in *Iðunn* in 1929 and reprinted in *A Day's Journey in the Mountains*. He still respected Tagore but found him too distant from contemporary social reality: "The views of the dreamy Indian wise man seemed to be somewhat disharmonious, or might I say, rather childish . . . his social criticisms are the tamperings of silk-clad aristocratic hands." Writers could no longer ignore the conflict between the working and the upper class, Halldór believed; they had to take a stand.

On 24 April Halldór sent Upton Sinclair the first three parts of *The Great Weaver from Kashmir*, along with a letter of explanation in which he admitted that the work's idealism did not reflect his current train of thought, but claimed that the novel would introduce him well to the English-speaking world. He asked for leniency regarding the translation, since he did not have the necessary command of English to render the stylistic genius of the Icelandic original.

When he returned to Los Angeles at the end of April he went straight to Long Beach to confer with Sinclair, staying there for a week at the beginning of May. He had decided to return to Iceland in the autumn, as he informed Inga: "Home, Inga! Home to my land and yours – home from the enchantments of the south, home to the reality of the north!" Around the middle of May he told Inga that Sinclair liked *The Great Weaver*

> and he has taken personal charge of trying to get the manuscript published, and has written Knopf (one of the largest publishing companies in New York) a personal letter about me and the book, and asked me in addition to write an introduction for its English edition. He assures me that such a book would be published straight away – it remains to be seen whether he is in fact a true prophet.

In a letter to Halldór dated 25 May Sinclair says that a skilled reader could easily correct the translation, and that the text was already good enough for a publisher to form an opinion of the work. A copy survives of the letter Sinclair sent to Knopf on 8 May along with the first three chapters of *The Great Weaver*. He says that he finds the book remarkable and the style powerful, but is not convinced regarding the book's overall structure. This was kind of Sinclair, because *The Great Weaver* was not a novel of the kind that would appeal naturally to him. Although Knopf did not accept it, Sinclair continued to assist Halldór with letters to other publishers and interceded for him with agents.

But all this came to nothing. Many years later Halldór made a good-natured joke about it, although he had been quite earnest at the time, and recited the letter of rejection he received from Knopf, who felt that American readers would not be particularly interested in the work's Catholicism: "I am afraid that many of these good people would have difficulty getting to the bottom of all of the musings on the Pope in your book." Clearly the publishing company had not felt that there would be a market in America for such an egotistical work about the cultural crisis in Europe. But Halldór was undeterred. He wrote to the Dorrance publishing company in Philadelphia at the end of October, 1929, citing Sinclair's comments and pointing out that although various American publishers thought that there would be no market for the work, and he had met with similar misunderstanding from Icelandic publishers, he had published the work himself and broken all sales

records. Halldór's salesmanship was not good enough, however, and his and
Magnús' translation lies untouched in the archives of the National Library of
Iceland to this day.

These were not Halldór's only attempts to publish his work in 1929. He had
three manuscripts awaiting publication besides a collection of poetry, then called
Parodic Songs, and one of short stories, *Men's Footsteps* (1933). He entrusted Erlendur
with the task of getting them published but was annoyed by how slowly things
were going, as he told both his mother and Inga. Early in 1929 he came up with a
plan to send Erlendur *The Book of the People* as a gift for the Social Democrats, on
the condition that it be published immediately: "I was given food, clothing, and
shelter while I was writing it, so it would be nothing but fair for me to give something back." But this too was delayed, and Halldór wrote to his mother that
summer: "It is sloth that my books should not have been printed in Iceland, yet
there is absolutely nothing that I can do about it until I come there myself." He sent
Erlendur a telegram: "Why are my books not printed. Give explicit answer."

As 1929 drew to a close Halldór was most concerned about publishing *The Book
of the People*. In a letter to Kristín Guðmundardóttir, the wife of the printer
Hallbjörn, he said, quite nonchalantly, that he had lost his talent for writing:

On the other hand I have adopted a new view of life, which is that they
should light the farms in Iceland electrically and make them into collectives,
demolish the cottages by law, and only build huge condominiums. This view
has been taking form within me since I crossed Iceland in the winter of 1926.

He made plans to hurry home: "I have no use for America and America no use
for me". He further observed that "Icelandic loitering and limping is a legacy . . .
from Icelandic slavedom, and most of the energy of the people goes into blowing
their noses and spitting, as is well known."

When Halldór returned to California from Point Roberts in the spring he took
the opportunity to visit Krishnamurti, who at that time was the most famous Asian
philosopher in the world. Krishnamurti was considered by some to be a new
Buddha, and every now and then he held outdoor conferences where his disciples
and other interested people could listen to him. One of these was held in the Ojai
Valley, May–June, 1929, and Halldór went as a kind of newspaper reporter, telling
of his trip in *Eimreiðin* in 1930.

The effect Krishnamurti had on him is evident in his letters to Inga: "I do not
find him to be more than averagely talented, and his education seems to be somewhat one-sided, but he has good intentions." A day later he added a note to the

letter, saying that he had conducted two detailed interviews with the guru, and considered him one of the most remarkable men he had ever met. Halldór was convinced that he was a man of peace and understood the conditions of the working class, although that understanding did not run very deep. Even though Halldór thought the ideals of socialism expressed mankind's most noble goal, this did not decrease the value of other ideals, as long as they were not expressly opposed to socialism.

Back in Los Angeles Halldór was once again able to earn some money delivering lectures, although he had grown bored with this and his mind was focused on other things. It is likely that he spoke that summer to the best-known radical workers' union in the United States, the I.W.W. (Industrial Workers of the World). His account of this event in *A Poet's Time* is somewhat ironic and conveys a sense of the huge gap between lecturer and audience. But he was proud of having been asked if the following comment in a letter to his mother refers to this particular meeting: "Yesterday I held a lecture in a huge hall downtown for a labour union, and it was extremely pleasant. My lecture was on political topics."

Halldór finally collected his thoughts and started writing a new Icelandic novel. The farmer Þórður from Kálfakot, from the earlier short story, knocked on the door of Halldór's psyche, suggesting a tale about an Icelandic farmer living on an isolated heath. The draft that Halldór wrote that summer, called *The Heath*, is today in the National Library of Iceland.

The Heath was the first version of *Independent People*. Much more primitive than the novel, it had been reworked from earlier versions and was based on his travels and his opinions about the hopelessness of independent farming. Halldór had finally started to write the type of fiction that suited him best. That his inspiration was great is revealed in a letter to Inga from the start of July:

> I have recently started writing a new novel – a new Judgement Day for myself – oh, it is appalling, my dear child Inga, to take upon oneself so intensely the fates and sufferings of numerous people, but I must, I ought – because the sufferings and struggles of my characters are my own sufferings, my own psychological battles.

The tale of the solitary farmer who fights against powers through a misconceived sense of heroism was supposed to have been longer; on the title page of the manuscript it is revealed that *The Heath* was only intended to be the first volume in a trilogy; the next was to have been called *Of the West* and the third *The Icelander from Winnipeg*. The latter two parts were never written.

When Inga wrote and told Halldór of a car trip that she had taken over Mosfellsheiði, he replied to her in late summer:

Oh, I know Mosfellsheiði so well. My father built much of the Mosfellsheiði road, and when I was a boy I went with him for four summers to help the men do their work, and was supposed to cook for my father, although that only proceeded by fits and starts. I know all of the bends and curves in the Mosfellsheiði road. I have slept on Mosfellsheiði many summer nights. I also herded sheep there during the spring and autumn, when I was a boy . . . It would be my heartfelt wish that at some point I could drive with you alone over the heath late one summer evening, even in the rain. This barren heathland is so perfectly connected to my own psychological state. It has played its part in raising me, in making me an Icelander. No man could love Icelandic heaths more passionately than I. The last time that I was home I crossed at least seven heaths in high winter, and that was the most entertaining journey that I have ever taken.

Halldór was ready to return home. He had no money for the journey, but his mother sent him some. At that time the most efficient route to Europe was by way of the Panama Canal. Halldór booked a passage on 1 November aboard the German ship *S.S. Portland*; he would take the *Goðafoss* home from Hamburg on 1 December.

Halldór's time in Southern California was at an end. He had experienced defeat there, and his ideals were calling him home. But he had felt well there and, many years later, wrote that those three years had been the happiest of his youth. On the other hand, he could not have left at a better time. On 29 October the great Wall Street crash occurred, thus marking the start of the Depression. Many years later Halldór described the event to this author:

In California everyone was happy and rich and fortunate until the Great Depression hit. It happened in one day, and I actually watched it happen. I walked around the streets, which were full of lost people and crying women with children; they had lost everything. People thought that capitalism was dead and no-one was satisfied or happy any longer. They had lost everything that they had in banks and stocks, and a friend of mine lost his home, and there was no longer any need for a young man to speak about Iceland at afternoon parties.

Halldór also said goodbye to Vala Einarsdóttir. He wrote to Erlendur in the autumn saying that he was desperate, "because I have more difficulties with my soul and life now than I have ever had before". He felt as if he was tugging at a knot. Vala left for New York and worked there as a nurse for nearly a year before she returned home and became a farmer's wife in Borgarfjörður. She never mentioned her love affair with Laxness to anyone. She did, however, write to Halldór several times from New York, wishing him everything good and hoping that her memory did not make him sad. But it was cold in the big city and the post box was usually empty: "It is long, long past midnight; I heard a clock somewhere strike two. The night is so silent: there is only this peculiar moan of the big city that never ceases." On his journey home, off the coast of Mexico, Halldór wrote two love poems, "She Was Everything" and "Our Final Day Has Gone". There one finds these verses:

> And the sunburnt hills droop
> Beneath the heaven as pale as wine:
> It is I who bid you adieu with a kiss,
> My dearest beloved.
>
> Because we were created to part:
> We part . . . and never more . . .
> The life that once dies
> Never returns.

THREE

The Switchboard of the Feelings of the World

The Years
1929–1939

When one is writing, one has to think that one is not in the first, but rather in the last instance writing on paper. Beyond all else the writer must keep it fixed in his mind that he is writing upon a human heart.

Halldór Laxness in a notebook

The Bird on the Beach

HALLDÓR'S FIVE-WEEK JOURNEY HOME PRESENTED HIM WITH A GOOD opportunity to calibrate his spiritual and intellectual compass. His cinematic dreams had come to an end, and he no longer fantasized about becoming a writer in a foreign language. His intention was to write in Icelandic, about Icelandic subjects – but hopefully for the world. And he intended to participate in the struggle to improve living conditions in Iceland.

Halldór was no longer the same man who had gone to California. He was no longer as childishly curious, no longer as convinced that he would conquer the world, no longer as certain what business he had with it. But his courage and his determination to become a great writer were undiminished, as was his belief in high ideals.

Halldór's soul was set to rights by the idea of seeing Inga once again, and she of course was waiting just as impatiently for him. On 12 December, 1929, Erlendur Guðmundsson went to tell her that Halldór had arrived. Inga was working for her uncle, Ólafur Johnson, at the time:

I leapt up excitedly, threw everything aside and went straight up to Unuhús with Erlendur – and there he sat! I sat down by him and I will never forget how I was squeezing his fingernails until he shouted: "Ouch! Stop hurting me, stop hurting me my dear Inga!" I was so rough with this voyager to America.

At first Halldór lived with his mother and sisters in the apartment Sigríður had bought after selling Laxnes, though Inga and he spent all their time together. Now that they were officially engaged, they were physically affectionate with one another, though Inga did not want to have sex before they were married.

Around the turn of the year Inga was bedridden with a fever. Halldór sent her messages saying that he could think of nothing but her. On 2 January, 1930, he told her how everything seemed empty without her, adding that he wished that he could always have her near him, "especially in the evenings, after I have finished working, because then I feel so lonely".

The 1930s were to be one of the most fertile periods in Halldór's career. He published a collection of essays, a book of poetry, short stories, travelogues, a play and three of his most acclaimed novels. If *The Book of the People* is included, he published a total of fifteen books in just over ten years. At the same time he travelled constantly and often stayed overseas for long periods because, although he had come home, he was still a man of two worlds, an Icelander and a cosmopolitan, and he was not prepared to choose between them. He never appreciated the small-town mentality of Reykjavík, and whenever he felt it oppressing him he left. This was nevertheless the time when he was most involved in the political and cultural life of Iceland, writing articles, lecturing and becoming a member of various clubs. Failure was simply not an option.

Reykjavík began to resemble a city during those years: its population increased to around thirty thousand, and life was much more multifaceted. Compared to Los Angeles and Copenhagen, of course, it still did not have a lot to offer. The national theatre had not been built, cafés and bars were few and not particularly varied, and cultural life was monotonous. What did young, thoughtful people do in the evenings, when they hadn't worked themselves to the point of exhaustion? They visited each other, drank coffee and conversed. Halldór's friends continued to meet at Unuhús, at Erlendur's home, or at the home of Kristín Guðmundardóttir and Hallbjörn Halldórsson.

Halldór took a lively part in these conversations. He was thinking seriously about diving headlong into politics, having taken his first steps in that direction with *The Book of the People*. The newspaper *Tíminn*, controlled by Jónas from Hrifla, who had made such brusque comments about *The Great Weaver from Kashmir* and was now the country's foremost political figure, made favourable comments, calling the book unusual and daring. Although the conservatives naturally did not like it, their protests did not spark any battles.

The book inspired a greater degree of private discussion. Some of the author's acerbic comments caused consternation, for instance his statement that the middle-class wife was "the purest species of harlot that has ever been produced here on earth". Inga had been extremely displeased with this chapter when she had read the book in manuscript, asking Halldór in a letter:

> Why do you always write such disgusting things about women? Are women in your eyes nothing but beasts or cheap whores – is that something that men think in general? Is there then no such thing as love, can men never love, can there never be any pure and earnest love between a man and a woman?

In fact Halldór's comments were conceived in support of the women's move-ment, but the audacious way in which they were expressed shocked some of his readers to such a degree that they could not grasp what he was actually saying; sometimes he lost sight of this himself.

His old friend Kristján Albertsson continued to reproach him for his writings. In a letter sent from France at the start of 1930, he thanked Halldór for *The Book of the People*, and said that he had enjoyed it very much although he was ashamed to admit it:

> But why, dear friend, do you stick with this eternal, roguish, boorish language – do you think that it will impress anyone but unread teenagers? Do you think that obscene language is power – or brilliance?

Behind these comments is something more; with *The Book of the People* it became clear to Iceland's bourgeois establishment that Halldór was lost to them. He had of course often satirized such people, but liberal conservatives like Kristján had chosen not to take his comments too literally. It took the right-wingers time to come to terms with the fact that Halldór had become a socialist. Even Inga wrote to him at the end of October from London: "You say that you're wrapped up in politics – what side are you on? Don't tell me you're a Bolshie?!" Halldór answered her immediately in no uncertain terms:

> Well then, my dear, so you know me no better than this, understand me so little that you are not able to imagine that I am something other than a

Bolshie? How did you ever get the idea that I was a conservative? Do you think that a young man or woman at this time who is not either stupid or evil could be anything other than a Bolshie?

' Halldór's new platform as outlined in *The Book of the People* was absolute in most respects. But it must not be forgotten that grandiloquence was the rule rather than the exception in Icelandic politics during the interwar years, and the newspapers often published malicious statements about their adversaries. Additionally the lines between the political parties were not as clear. When Halldór returned from America Jónas from Hrifla, the leader of the Progressive Party, was in power having won the 1927 election.

Jónas had played a role in the establishment of the Progressive and Social Democratic Parties in 1916, imagining that inhabitants of the countryside would find refuge in the Progressive Party and the Social Democrats would muster the workers in the villages. The bourgeois powers that came together in 1929 with the founding of the new Independence Party viewed Jónas as a dangerous radical and fought against him tooth and nail. For instance, Kristján wrote to Halldór in America:

> Occupying the Minister's seat now is the first-ever socialist in Iceland – Jónas from Hrifla – who steals steadily from the Treasury to line the pockets of his Party brothers so that they can entertain themselves in foreign countries; who himself spends nearly the entire year on pleasure trips at the government's expense; appoints Pálmi Hannesson, an inexperienced man, newly emerged from his exams, as rector of the Lyceum, because he is a Social Democrat etc.

Nevertheless Jónas had Halldór's support.

Politicians like Jónas disappeared for the most part after the Second World War. He was a determined idealist, a nationalist who fought with businessmen and ship owners and applied government power unscrupulously if necessary. In some matters he took the same course as the socialists, in others his behaviour resembled that of the Italian Fascists, causing King Kristján X to say in 1930: "So you are the one who plays the little Mussolini here in this country?" But Jónas was no Fascist. He wanted to keep capitalism and urbanization in check; his political base was in rural areas, and as their importance diminished so did his influence.

Nowadays it is hard to imagine Halldór and Jónas as allies, but they were for a time and both reaped the benefits. Halldór did not hesitate to defend Jónas in one of the most famous debates in Icelandic politics in the years between the wars, in the course of which Jónas' opponents started suggesting that the politician was mentally ill:

> I do not hesitate to assert that Jónas Jónsson is, in most respects, one of the most splendidly gifted and best suited for leadership of all of those men I have got to know at home and abroad . . .

Halldór received a scolding in *Morgunblaðið*, in which he is called "the well-known religious simpleton and wencher, café-philosopher, Halldór Kiljan Laxness".

Kristján Albertsson was displeased that Halldór should defend Jónas, writing to him from France:

> J.J. is a strange blend of a good man and a rascal, a superman and a tattered rag, a bold warrior and a wretched liar, an idealist and a leader of bandits – just as the parliamentary majority that supports him is a blend of a political party and a company of knaves . . . May you be eternally shamed for your support of this riff-raff!

At this, Kristján and Halldór formally parted political company, although they did continue to have contact until the Cold War period, when the battle lines were dug so deep they could not be crossed.

Halldór's article about Jónas is testimony to both his talents and his shortcomings as an essayist on contemporary affairs. He was more eloquent than most journalists, but he preached too much and had difficulty maintaining his critical distance from causes or people he supported, though he often approached them from unexpected directions in order to attract readers' attention. Halldór's ability to understand people's dissimilar fates – and views – found expression in his fiction, which never became entirely propagandistic. There he had room to express the doubts that were out of bounds to an essayist.

Although Halldór had proclaimed his admiration for Jónas from Hrifla, he himself was a socialist rather than a progressive. His article "They Come to You in Sheep's Clothing", which he wrote in January, 1930, displays his characteristic combination of political idealism and religious evangelism; it is difficult to avoid the thought that he was practising the art of political rhetoric. The long paragraphs are structured as if written by hypnotic orators, replete with figurative language in the spirit of the Bible. Of the spokesmen for conservatism, the article says:

> These malicious beings . . . behold their vanguard, the bacteria of pestilence cultivated with bribes in the leprous dens of the capitalist papers here in

town and appointed by the bloodsuckers of the workers to champion the development of the workers . . . have decided to . . . spread their fingers over all the argumentation of civilized men, yes, every effort to debate wisely any political issue; they have now gone too far . . .

Halldór had written more audacious articles but never anything this acerbic. Just as he occasionally did in other polemical articles, Halldór became intoxicated by the poisonous concoction of his own words.

Einar Arnórsson, Inga's father, was a candidate for the Independence Party in the city council elections that inspired Halldór's journalistic attentions, and one can only imagine his reaction to the writings of his eldest daughter's suitor. Halldór was certainly not buttering up his hoped-for in-laws. It did not help that a decade before this Einar had been the victim of a fanatical personal attack made by Jónas from Hrifla. After Halldór and Inga were married it fell to her to see to it that politics were not discussed in the family, since the young couple owed a great deal to her father:

It was as if I were between two fires, always trying to prevent arguments — because both of them could argue, my father and my husband, and they were great adversaries and things could have turned ugly if nothing had been done.

Though Halldór had gone home penniless from America, he now, for the first time, received a public grant of some real worth. Early in 1930 the Ministry of Education awarded him 2,000 krónur through the agency of the Progressive and Social Democratic Parties. The matter sparked significant opposition from the Independence Party and so Halldór' received 1,500 krónur in the end. He was by no means wealthy, but he was saved for the time being.

*

On 1 May, 1930, Halldór and Inga were married by the Municipal Sheriff. They immediately boarded the passenger ship *Lyra* for their honeymoon in Norway, where Halldór had been invited to a Nordic writers' conference. Inga describes the trip this way:

Both of our mothers accompanied us to the ship and we stood on the gangway and waved to them. Then a man strolled up to Mother and said: "Do you know, Mrs Arnórsson, what kind of man your daughter has married?" She of course said little but the man continued, telling her that this son-in-law of hers had had a child with a girl in town. I felt Halldór grow cold

with terror at my side and I pushed him ahead of me down into the cabin.
There he said that he had not dared to tell me of this out of fear of losing
me, but I said: "As if I haven't known that for ages! And it doesn't matter
at all."

The conference in Oslo ran from 1 to 6 June. There Halldór was in the company
of several of Iceland's major writers, all of whom were in good spirits as a result
of Iceland's newly attained sovereignty. They included Sigurður Nordal, Þórbergur
Þórðarson, Kristmann Guðmundsson and Gunnar Gunnarsson, who was the head
of the Coalition of Icelandic Artists. Time was divided between lectures and
banquets, and Halldór wrote to his mother that he found the latter tiring, on a par
with the most difficult labour.

Halldór never liked to spend much time at banquets. No teetotaller, he was only
a moderate drinker and did not like drunks. His distaste for gatherings that went
on into the night was also connected with his work habits, which he wished to
have disturbed as little as possible. He became impatient if he was unable to write
almost every day, and his old disquietude attacked him if his work plans went awry.
On the other hand he did not like having to stay in the same place for too long,
and thus he accustomed himself early on to working while travelling and in hotels
according to a rigid schedule. But he attended banquets and gatherings if they
could help him advance his work.

Halldór used his time well at the Nordic writers' conference. In an interview
with the *People's Paper* he tells of his meeting with Sigrid Undset, whom he considered to be the most interesting of all female Scandinavian writers; this is a different
tone from the one he adopted later, when he could not bear to hear that she had
influenced him.

In Oslo Halldór met the "revolutionary" Danish writer Martin Andersen Nexø
for the first time; the two had a lot of contact in the years that followed, particularly when Halldór sought Nexø's advice about making himself known in the
Soviet Union. Halldór was enamoured of other radical writers at the conference
and went to a meeting of Clarté, an international society of socialist writers.

From Oslo Halldór and Inga went to Copenhagen to visit Jón Helgason and his
wife Þórunn. Following Jóhann Jónsson's death in 1932, Halldór had no friend
who was more devoted to his work than Jón. Jón gave him ideas for his books, and
was the first to direct him to the story of Jón Hreggviðsson, which became the
catalyst for *Iceland's Bell* in 1924. During the 1930s Jón was Halldór's main adviser
in matters of language and proved to be an extremely important reader when
Halldór wrote *The Happy Warriors* (1952). Halldór frequently asked Jón to read

proofs of his books and even to go over earlier books of his before they were reprinted. Halldór trusted no reader as much as Jón because of Jón's extensive knowledge and his critical opinion of and disregard for easy truths. Though they shared the same sense of humour, their relationship was not always easy; there was sometimes a comical stiffness between them, especially in the presence of other people. But the friendship was a long and close one.

Halldór also used his time in Copenhagen to visit Gunnar Gunnarsson, who was among the most popular novelists in Denmark during the 1920s and whose auto-biographical masterpiece, *The Church on the Mountain*, he particularly admired. In an article Halldór wrote a year later he makes a direct connection between Gunnar's financial situation and his artistic achievement:

> ... in the same way that increased recognition changed his position in society and made his financial concerns disappear, he was granted the freedom and leisure required for the achievement of equilibrium, rich maturity, and glorious works ...

Halldór had experienced enough of a financial struggle during his own ten-year meander around the world to reject all romantic theories about the nobility of the starving poet.

Halldór and Inga returned to Iceland on 23 June. There was a lot going on there in preparation for the Alþingi Festival, the first great celebration of the young sovereign state which would mark the millennial anniversary of the establishment of the Icelandic Parliament.

Halldór and Inga attended the festival along with thirty thousand other Icelanders. Inga's father had a fine car and it fell to her to transport them and some acquaintances over Mosfellsheiðir to Þingvellir, where they stayed in the tent village that had been set up there: "It was a pulsating sea of people and as far as I remember everything went well. But I was naturally so happy that I hardly noticed it". The young couple went several times to Þingvellir that summer; the place had always been important to Halldór, as can be seen in *The Great Weaver from Kashmir*. But the happiness they felt was not shared by everyone present. Malfríður Jónsdóttir worked at Hotel Valhöll during the summer, cooking and waitressing. Her and Halldór's daughter, María, though only eight years old, knew how miserable her mother was after Halldór and Inga were married: "All her life she loved my father."

Although the newly-weds were happy at Þingvellir, the author of *The Book of the People* did not join in the festive atmosphere the organizers attempted to create with special poems and ceremonies in honour of the Danish king. Halldór was entirely too iconoclastic to take the festival seriously. He did, however, compose a great poem about it, "Alþingi Festival Cantata – for Singing after 1930", in which he paid homage to the Mosfell District and the beauty of Þingvellir. Concerning the festival's other contributors, he observed: "Your poems are like the noisy cackling of hens."

"Alþingi Festival Cantata" was included Halldór's in next book, *Poems*, which was published in September, 1930, and in which he collected poems composed during the 1920s, many of which had been published previously in magazines. He did not take himself very seriously as a poet. At first this book was to be called Mock Poetry, which was Halldór's translation of the word "parody", and many of the poems are precisely that, as Halldór says in the preface:

> Attempts at lyrical methods, investigations into the elasticity of the poetic style, a kind of land survey, both in the world of the practical and the impractical, the usual and the unusual, the commonplace and the absurd, the concrete and the inconcrete."

In fact Halldór's poems are uneven: there are ingenious lines, flawless poems about love and nature, distortions and awkward messes all at once. Lyrical form demanded a sincerity that he was afraid to display under his own name; later he attributed many of his most moving poems to characters in his novels. When he could hide behind them, his pretentiousness disappeared. At the start of 1931 he reviewed the books of the year, including his own, for the *People's Paper*:

> H.K. Laxness has in a little volume of poetry tried to make pure attempts . . . at finding a less dilapidated form than is normal for him, but in general it can be said that he has worked in vain, and the poems are just as boring by old or new standards.

Nonni was among the guests at the Alþingi Festival, and he and Halldór spent some time together despite Nonni's hesitation after reading *The Book of the People*. Halldór later commented that they had travelled together at the time and that Nonni had visited him at home, yet Halldór is not mentioned by Nonni; as a Jesuit, he could not discuss in print his interaction with men who had left the Catholic Church. Halldór was faithful to Nonni all his life and sent him a copy of *Salka Valka* inscribed "To my dear old friend". Nonni thanked him and added that Halldór's faithful friendship was particularly dear to him. They rarely discussed matters of faith, which is not surprising, since Halldór had declared in *The Book of the People* that he had lost faith in God and discovered faith in man.

Halldór wrote an enormous amount in 1930, his greatest work being *O Thou Pure Vine*, the first part of *Salka Valka*, which he completed before Christmas and which was published in March, 1931. The second part, *The Bird on the Beach*, was published a year later, but it was not until the publication of the second edition that the whole novel was given the name *Salka Valka*.

His next three great books, *Independent People*, *World Light* and *Iceland's Bell*, were also published in multiple volumes, often with a year-long interval between them, and it was far from evident to Halldór when one volume came out what the next volume would be like. He would perhaps have written a rough draft, but he wrote each part independently, and each was published as soon as he finished it. He put an enormous amount of work into each volume, researched locations and sources, and rewrote several times.

Halldór visited fishing villages in the east and west while he was working on *Salka*. He stayed for a time in Ísafjörður, at the home of the mayor, Ingólfur Jónsson, and his wife, the actress Ingibjörg Steinsdóttir. Ingibjörg's brother, Steinþór Steinsson, lived with the couple, and the family was convinced that the character with the same name in the book was modelled on him. Ingibjörg's granddaughter, Ingibjörg Sigurðardóttir, investigated this:

> Laxness often read from his novel for the people at home, but always avoided the chapters in which the character Steinþór Steinsson appears. When the book was published they were rather surprised and were for a time angry with the author, to whom they had given free food and housing.

This story reveals something of Halldór's working methods. Wherever he went he collected material, familiarized himself with local conditions, discovered interesting characters and wrote down vocabulary in notebooks he always took with him. This had been his habit from an early age. Luckily he kept a lot of the notebooks; the National Library of Iceland holds a collection of them spanning half a century. Most are from the 1930s. In them he wrote draft chapters, ideas for novels or clever remarks he thought he might use later. Much in the notebooks awaits investigation. In a letter to Inga from May, 1931, Halldór says:

> One naturally uses a great part of the day letting the material "grow inside oneself" e.g., I am always writing in my notebooks, wherever I am. The material continues to be developed and shaped in my head.

The first notebook from the *Salka* period contains a draft of a speech that Halldór delivered at the writers' conference in Oslo in 1930, and also notes made during the summer. He reminds himself that he planned to let oppositions tug at the character of Arnaldur. Then, suddenly, there is this description:

> Give Steinþór a philosophical aspect in the rewrite, let him be a kind of completely uneducated ruminator who comes up with all kinds of crazy ideas about existence, always ends up in difficulties and contradictions and later cuts vengefully at all the knots.

Also in the notebook are glosses on Salvation Army song books and quotations from the works of Theodore Dreiser and Sinclair Lewis. In the midst of these comments are observations on literature: "The novelist uses 'life', 'reality', as much as he can – that is to say, to such a great extent that it clashes with the laws of the novel." But just as clearly he wants his books to become part of reality:

> *Literature that has nothing to say to the people is not literature.* When one is writing, one has to think that one is not in the first but rather in the last instance writing on paper. Beyond all else the writer must keep it fixed in his mind that he is writing upon a human heart.

In the first *Salka* notebook one finds an unexpected comparison with a book Halldór admired all his life, *Don Quixote* by Cervantes. Thus it is possible to see in Arnaldur the dolorous knight who fights with windmills, and in Salka the down-to-earth squire Sancho Panza.

And in the next notebook he says about Arnaldur and Salka: "They understand at the moment they love most passionately. Tragic perspectives on the incomprehensibility of human feelings." Readers of such comments might recall how Halldór left Valgerður in California. In the same notebook he says:

> Momentary love never perishes, it remains eternally fixed in the universe – we pass away, but the moment of our love is absolute, it can never pass into nothing. Its time was and is.

In this sense, love never dies. With *Salka Valka* Halldór was, among other things, distancing himself from his relationship with Valgerður and his decision to leave her. He had certainly betrayed her, but the ideas that the betrayal served were greater than him. He also contemplates his situation as a writer, observing that planning to live as a writer in Iceland is like being a great merchant and setting up an office on a heath.

The third notebook from the *Salka* period, marked Paris, June, 1931, shows how widely Halldór searched to understand his craft, for instance, when he remarks that he must read Joyce's *Ulysses* for style. The notebook also contains an outline of a book about a man who intends to become a singer for the world (later to become *The Fish Can Sing*). Then suddenly there appears this unostentatious sentence: "Write a little book, called *At Home*, memories from childhood and descriptions of life at Laxnes (for children, full of poems and strange stories)." Halldór wrote this book forty-five years later, and called it *In the Fields of Home*.

Halldór's trips to the fishing villages in 1930 were not just for social research: he was also interested in linguistics. For instance, he wrote in Stefán Einarsson's manuscript, in a section on the style of *O Thou Pure Vine*: "The language in *Pure Vine* is not *einheitlich*, but rather a rehashing of the speech habits and dialects from here and there around the country." Part of his repatriation consisted of strengthening his grip on the Icelandic that was spoken at home. For a decade he had been mulling over a great rural novel, but he was discontented with the draft he had written the previous summer in Los Angeles. With *Salka*, on the other hand, he created a great novel from the manuscript that the cinematic world had rejected, and at the same time wrestled with topics that interested him: love, women, the role of the intellectual, the lot of the common people. In December he wrote to Jón Helgason in the nonchalant tone they often shared:

> On the 11th of the month I completed one of the most pitiful potboilers that have ever been written in the history of the world. It is about penniless folk, and I plan to send it to you as soon as it appears in printed form, not least because I understand that you receive more income in a month than all my characters do in lifetime, and some of them have even made it into their eighties. At the same time I plan to send you a volume of poetry as a kind of excuse for the fact that I have written a good novel. I hope that it befits the Cultural Fund to publish this potboiler, so that your sons have will something edifying to read next year.

Conditions were good for Halldór to cultivate his art in 1930. At first he and Inga lived rent-free in an apartment on Laufásvegur 25, where her father owned a duplex. The apartment being small, they stayed for only a year; having rented for a time, they moved back to Laufásvegur once Einar had renovated the apartment substantially. Inga had lost her job because the company did not want to employ married women, but she got a job with Ólafur, her half-brother, in the wholesale firm Ólafsson and Bernhöft, where she did the accounting, among other things.

O Thou Pure Vine was published by the Cultural Fund, the government agency that Jónas from Hrifla had established in 1928. This meant a great deal to Halldór's career, since Icelandic publishing companies were both few and weak. He received some royalties, which, along with the public grant he had received, made it possible to live comfortably and devote himself to writing.

O Thou Pure Vine received good reviews. There was no longer any question as to whether Halldór was a genuine novelist or simply a judgemental fop. The beginning of the book shows Halldór's return to the stories of his homeland:

> When one goes by boat along these coasts on these freezing mid-winter nights, one can't help thinking that there can hardly be anything in the whole wide world so tiny and insignificant as a little village like that, glued to the foot of such immense mountains. God knows how people live in such a place! And God knows how they die!

In an interview published in the *People's Paper* he says that the book shows, among other things, "how a poor individual in a little village lives and dies with the trading post on the one hand and the Salvation Army on the other". The main character is Salka's mother, Sigurlína; hers is a painful story with strong religious references, as it is from the Salvation Army that Sigurlína seeks support in her trials. The village is entirely under the control of the merchant Jóhann Bogesen, and life is dependent on fishing, as can be seen when the story turns to illegitimate children:

> This was the subject of gossip for a fortnight, over the fish, both raw and cooked, round the fish-tubs, on the drying-ground, and round the everlasting fish-pots in the kitchens, for life in Oseyri was lived in fish and consisted of fish, and human beings were a sort of abortion which Our Lord had made out of cooked fish and perhaps a handful of rotten potatoes and a drop of oatmeal gruel.

The narrator is clearly unafraid to express himself: he is liberal with his pronouncements and commentary. Halldór was trying to harmonize the boldness of *The Great Weaver from Kashmir* with social criticism, and the material he had chosen was highly suitable, since conditions in Icelandic fishing villages at the start of the Depression were mostly wretched.

Several days after *Pure Vine* was published, Halldór travelled overseas to write its sequel. He had been invited to represent the Coalition of Icelandic Artists at a huge international writers' conference in Paris at the end of May, and planned to use the opportunity to stay in Leipzig and Paris for two months and write. One of the main topics at the conference was copyright. No Icelandic artist had taken as many vigorous steps in awakening his colleagues to the necessity of international agreements in this area as the musician Jón Leifs, one of the founders of the Coalition in 1928. Halldór was registered as one of the group's original members. In letters that Jón wrote to Halldór during the 1920s he mentions the necessity of Iceland becoming party to the Berne Convention on authors' rights: "We artists are trying to return to Iceland its respect and fame, but we are kicked in the teeth." Halldór always supported the Coalition's position, although he was not always active in it. He also became a member of P.E.N., which had been established in 1921 in order to ensure authors' rights and freedom of speech.

Halldór wrote to Jón and asked him to support his sister Helga, who at the start of the 1930s was contemplating studying the piano in Germany; she had talent, and Jón was happy to help. In the spring of 1931 she went to Leipzig to study, and thus Halldór could enjoy her company, as well as that of his old friend Jóhann Jónsson, while he was there.

Immediately after Halldór's departure from Iceland he started to write Inga remarkable letters in which his musings and plans can be seen clearly. In fact he needed to think more about the future than he ever had before, since Inga was expecting a child. It is clear that Halldór was not prepared to settle down and become a responsible family man in Iceland. In a letter to Inga from Leipzig dated 12 April, 1931, he professes his love, declaring at the same time his annoyance that she had not been able to come with him on his trip and that they would not be able to live overseas the following winter since she was now pregnant. Even so, this does not cause him grave concern, because he had spent the day with Jóhann Jónsson, who was dying of consumption.

In the same letter Halldór says: "An extraordinary amount of ideas have come to mind in the last few days – my whole psyche gains new impetus on trips . . ." He wanted to keep track of events at home and asked Inga to send him newspapers. The letter ends with these remarks:

> I long for nothing more than for us to be able to live together in a foreign country in the future – I absolutely cannot stand constricted circumstances – nothing but the huge world can fuel my writer's talent.

In Leipzig Halldór thought constantly about two things: the book and his career as a writer. Even his warm greetings to Inga are so self-absorbed that it would have been remarkable if he had not noticed this himself. On 16 April he wrote:

We *shall* live overseas in the future, there's nothing more to it, nothing is as dangerous for my career as becoming locked up in Iceland – and if there is anything that I fear and hate, it is becoming a provincial, a yokel in my art. I cannot exist as a writer without having living contact with the world, with the throbbing pulse of culture. It is such damned bad luck that you could not be with me Inga, *now*: I have such a great need for your companionship . . .

But Halldór used his time well. He wrote, caught up on contemporary literature, and went to the theatre and concerts with his sister. He reread Mann's *Death in Venice*, this time in German, and reprimanded Inga when she said that she could not see what was special about the book:

It is one of the most divine odes that have ever been sung to beauty, comparable only to Roman epos and Greek art. Aesthetics have never reached a higher level in the novelistic form.

Most of all he was enamoured of Chaplin's film *City Lights*, which he saw three times: "I think that it is one of the most solid works of art that I have ever seen. It is tremendously well structured and the execution is absolutely divine."
Once again he realized how difficult it was to become an authentic Icelandic writer of world standard. And he writes to Inga on his birthday, expressing his wish that they could be together:

And you could be content with helping me to live in my books – because that is the only thing that a creative artist desires for his life, while the child is the limit of the rustic, simplistic common man; the child becomes a kind of image of eternity – he imagines that he lives on in the child, while the artist lives only in art that he creates for human society . . .

His view about child-rearing and Inga's role must have caused tension in the marriage. Inga went home to her parents, though she defended herself in her letters: what was Halldór talking about when he said that it would be horrible to have a child? "You should have thought of all of this before you took the stupid step of getting married!" She says that she is not asking him to sacrifice his career, does not want that on her conscience, but understandably she is disappointed that he never considered that it might be painful for her to read his thoughts. Here two absolutely different points of view are at work. Halldór is of course full of confidence and ambition, but his position is still weak and his finances tight; he is quite lucky that Inga's parents are willing to extend a helping hand. But Halldór is not prepared to change his opinion one bit:

Cares of the belly are abominable . . . this solemn earnestness over one's bourgeois future – nothing is more grotesque and banal. It is not right for us, Inga! I can never have that quality, and if I have that quality – then I am finished.

Salka Valka was the first of Halldór's novels to be translated into a foreign language. It is as if he had foreseen this when he was writing the book: he would not let anything distract him and there was no way that he was going to lose the fight as he had done in Hollywood. He wrote to Inga from Leipzig: "And if I am lucky with the second volume, then I am *made*, then I will have written a novel for the world." In the same letter he says determinedly:

And I *shall* become a great writer in the eyes of the world or die! There is no pardon here, and nothing that can be called giving way, not even an inch.

His strength of will was unbendable. But he did not know what he wanted from everyday life.

*

While he was in Leipzig, Halldór decided on his next project. He had taken "The Heath", the story about the farmer that he had written in the summer of 1929, with him and read from it to Jóhann, but thought that he might discard it. But Jóhann "was completely enthralled with it and said: 'This is the best that you have written. I would murder you if you destroyed this.'" Jóhann's encouragement and Halldór's reappraisal of the work helped him decide to take up the thread again after he finished the second part of *Salka*.

In mid-May Halldór went to Paris, with a stop in Berlin. He was impressed with Berlin, as he told Inga in a letter, among other things because the city "was red" – Communist ideas flourished there. Inga's cousin, Friðþjófur Johnson, met Halldór at the station, and he took the opportunity to look up compatriots, including Stefán Pjetursson, "our great Communist philosopher there in Berlin".

In Paris, Halldór saw Kristján Albertsson, who praised *O Thou Pure Vine* and promised to support another application for a grant from the Alþingi.

But Paris impressed Halldór less than Berlin: he thought the city old-fashioned and dirty, art and culture in decline, and the French hostile to foreigners. He and Kristján attended the international writers' conference and spent the evenings in the Café Rotonde in Montparnasse.

Halldór experienced strong mood swings. He missed Inga dreadfully, found it nearly impossible to traipse around alone, longed to have her near him and said that he would not have believed that he could be such a monogamist. But there was another reason for his depressed mood: he was penniless again. At first he asked Kristján for money, but Kristján turned out to be broke himself, so he was forced to ask an Icelandic physician, Dr Niels Dungal, for money for both of them. Halldór wrote to everyone he knew: Tryggvi Þórhallsson, Jónas from Hrifla and Guðbrandur Magnússon. Finally he sent Erlendur a telegram. Although the money transfer should only have taken a day, it took some time and Halldór became more depressed with each passing hour. He could not participate in the conference because he had neither a clean shirt nor socks, no money for a taxi, and would surely die of hunger, he claimed.

In his next letter he asked Inga to forgive his sulkiness and said that he could not live without her. His premise was clear:

> . . . help me to succeed *as a writer*. Some great men have so much to thank their wives for, they have done so much for them, sacrificed themselves for them – in the same way that they sacrifice themselves for their writers' ideals, and I have longed so much that you were such a woman.

Inga had suggested that he find work teaching in order to provide for them, but he did not take this well.

> As it happens I am *nothing* in the writers' world, for example at this conference. Help me to become *something*; one day in the future I can become something, if you help me; do you know that Hamsun was thirty when he walked hungry and dirty through the streets of Copenhagen, and no-one would look at his work . . . The time could well come, Inga, when I am as great as the other great men – I cannot betray my writer's ideals for any price.

Of course Halldór did go to the conference; he and Kristján dressed up with the latter's last francs and attended the banquets. Halldór spent most of his time with his fellow Scandinavians but got a good look at the most famous participants: Heinrich Mann, the Italian Marinetti, father of Futurism and devoted friend of Mussolini. Halldór described Marinetti to Inga this way: "He looks like a horse shying."

Originally Halldór had thought about staying in Paris and going to another international conference sponsored by P.E.N. in Amsterdam in June. The Icelandic writers had asked Nonni to act as Iceland's representative, and Halldór was to attend with him. But he had had enough and asked Kristján Albertsson to attend in his place, returning home at the start of June.

But he did not stay at home in the embrace of his family. A friend of Inga's had a brother who had a place in the small fishing village Grindavík. Halldór stayed there for a time that summer and made great progress on *The Bird on the Beach*, the second volume of *Salka*, which is why this excellent combination of geographical locations is listed at the end of the first edition: Leipzig–Paris–Grindavík.

Halldór was in Reykjavík when his son Einar was born at home on 9 August, 1931. Although Inga went back to work soon after, Halldór was unable to leave the bourgeois cares of the belly behind him completely. The Alþingi having been dissolved, the completion of the 1932 budget had been delayed, and it was not certain that there was a grant in it for Halldór. Jónas from Hrifla had been elected again, but the Progressives held only a small majority. When Parliament was convened during the summer, it was rumoured all the way to Copenhagen that some M.P.s wanted to revoke Halldór's grant. There Professor Jón Helgason wrote:

> . . . no matter what might be said about much in [Halldór's] writings, no Icelandic man under the age of thirty has, since this country was inhabited, been able to produce, along with everything else, two books of the calibre of *The Great Weaver* and *O Thou Pure Vine*, as proof of his outstanding talents.

It would be a disgrace if literature, "this one thing that Icelanders can pride themselves on having tried to maintain during times of hunger and degradation, died out during a prosperous era of independence".

In the event Halldór kept his grant. But it was scarcely sufficient to maintain a family and allow him an annual trip overseas. Halldór wrote to Jón and thanked him for his support:

> Naturally it is far too low for me to . . . have a so-called home like other people – my wife has had to go and live with her father (who of course always works against me as much as he can), and I myself am like some kind of *perpetuum mobile*.

There is no evidence to suggest that Einar "worked against" Halldór; in fact he and his wife helped their daughter tremendously with her young son, besides everything else. On the other hand the relationship between father- and son-in-law could not have been easy.

Halldór came to the realization that he would have to work harder to guarantee his family's future, and so, for the first and only time in his life with the exception of his stint as a home teacher, he took a job. From 1 October, 1931, until the end

of May, 1932, he worked as a receptionist in the offices of Icelandic National Radio.
Halldór said later:

> This required little effort; in fact it was easy. My main task consisted of
> bending and bowing and saying "Good day" over and over again to the V.I.P.s
> and geniuses that came to the radio station to allow the nation to enjoy their
> wisdom and wit.

Only good stories survive about Halldór in this job. One of his colleagues, the
musician Þórarinn Guðmundsson, said he was surprised that this big mouth in
print was urbane and courteous in the flesh, and actually shy in his dealings with
others. The poet and farmer Guðmundur Friðjónsson, with whom Halldór had
often quarrelled, wrote him a letter at the end of 1932, concluding: "I wish to thank
you for your genial courtesy this winter in the rooms of Icelandic National Radio."
But it is hardly possible that Halldór enjoyed his job, and he seldom mentioned it
later. It was the only time in his life that he earned a wage.

Halldór's letters to Inga leave no doubt that he loved her and that she was his
confidante for many – not all – of his deepest thoughts and feelings for twelve
years or so. But this did not change the fact that his career as a writer took precedence. He let Einar stay with his grandfather and grandmother for long periods
when he wanted to take Inga with him on his trips, even though she found this
extremely difficult. This irresolute position concerning his family never left Halldór
completely. He was fond of them and wanted to have them near by, but not too
near, or for too long. Even in his old age he needed to disappear now and again,
to make a solitary trip or to be alone to work. As a writer he often showed how
sensitive he was to his surroundings, which also meant that he was sometimes too
sensitive and could not stand too much intimacy. A telling statement he made in
his autobiographical novel is perhaps correct: his inclination to tell stories arose
"from an allergy to the phenomena of the times".

Halldór would not let others get too close to him. Stefán Einarsson had finished
the better part of his manuscript about Halldór's youth. Although Halldór had
always been kind and generous to those who wrote about him, he did not entirely
like Stefán's manuscript. As he wrote from Leipzig:

> This biography of mine is very unsympathetic, if one looks at the sources,
> I mean, my letters . . . It is quite incredible how unsympathetic a figure I have
> been, and very peculiar that I have always had good friends.

Halldór tried to convince Stefán to take a more literary approach, to distance himself from the intrusiveness of biographical commentary. Stefán was recalcitrant, saying that he was writing a psychological appraisal. He thought he could prove that Halldór was gripped by an inferiority complex that he shored up with delusions of grandeur, but that he had the marks of a genius.

So Halldór had something of a problem. He found fault with details in the manuscript, although it appears that they planned to publish the book in the spring of 1932, on Halldór's thirtieth birthday. He asked Stefán to consider whether they could not call the book an "introduction to his literary works" rather than a biography. Stefán accepted that idea but changed little else. At the start of 1932 Halldór finally passed judgement:

> I am . . . of the opinion that the time is not right for the biography to be published the way things stand now, but a literary study of my works would be extremely useful.

Though the book was never published, Stefán sent Halldór's biographer Peter Hallberg his material twenty years later.

While Halldór waited for the publication of *The Bird on the Beach* in the late winter of 1932, he prepared to publish one of his most brilliant literary essays, "Introduction to the Passion Hymns", on the poet Hallgrímur Pétursson. It appeared first in *Iðunn* that same year, but Halldór revised and republished it in the collection *The Contemporary Scene* (1942) a decade later. Of the literary studies Halldór wrote between the wars, the essays on Hallgrímur and Jónas Hallgrímsson are most likely the ones with the greatest longevity. His new grasp of social issues and a strong historical consciousness are combined with earlier thoughts on religion and poetic genius. Thus Halldór's old vision of the higher world of beauty survived within him even when his leanings toward's Marxist historicism were at their peak.

Halldór read from the essay about Hallgrímur on National Radio during Lent, 1932. The radio board received letters from influential men like Árni Sigurðsson, a Congregationalist minister, who recommended that any further readings be cancelled. The next day the station received a defiant letter signed by eight people, among them Vilmundur Jónsson, the Surgeon General, saying that the station should not submit to such demands. One of those who defended Halldór was his father-in-law, Einar Arnórsson. After some debate National Radio's directors allowed the readings to continue.

*

To go or to stay, to love or to betray, to have ideals but not to live up to them: all are themes of *The Bird on the Beach – A Political Romance*, which was published by the Cultural Fund on Halldór's thirtieth birthday. Halldór had, while holding down his receptionist's job, used his time to make changes to the book and felt happier with it than with the first part of *Salka Valka*. To the depiction of folk life in *O Thou Pure Vine* he had added the theme of social conflict, which brought the work closer to contemporary reality, as well as the romance between Arnaldur and Salka. Readers recognized current political oppositions: the character of Kristófer Torfdal was, for example, a blend of Ólafur Friðriksson and Jónas from Hrifla. Halldór allowed himself numerous parodies, even of the labour movement:

> It must be said that it was really a delightful strike. There was daily progress in Bolshevism and world revolution, red flags, frequent meetings, attended especially by the young, brilliant speeches, fine singing and loose living.

But if Halldór had become a socialist, why was he making fun of the labour movement? The paradox is noteworthy: Halldór had not converted to faith in mankind, but to faith in man "as a symbol of life and ideals". "Ideals are higher than men," says Arnaldur, and this is one of the key points of the book. Arnaldur is not capable of practising what he preaches, and so the description of the common people's struggle thus becomes distant and somewhat ironic, the sense of fatalism stronger than the hope that people can change the world. Halldór's characters nevertheless are – perhaps precisely because of this – vividly drawn. Various elements from the Hollywood film script live on in this novel, among them the strong sexual undertones. Salka is, as before, the most strongly conceived character, the girl who refuses to bow to the fate of women.

Arnaldur is a portrait of the idealist and intellectual in a little fishing village – Steinn Elliði as a socialist. And in his ideals and loves Arnaldur has much in common with his creator. He longs to do something useful but makes little progress, he longs to remain but also to leave and go out into the wide world, he longs to love but must betray his lover. Although he betrays Salka, their short affair is passionate, and never more so than when he leaves her; did Halldór feel the same way when he sailed through the Panama Canal? Salka Valka has watched Arnaldur tilt at windmills and she has suffered, but the reader feels that she will live on, just like Diljá in *The Great Weaver from Kashmir*.

The reception to *The Bird on the Beach* was a response to the political and social saga rather than to the love story, as might be expected. There had never been as aggressive a description of contemporary Icelandic society as the one the writer of the *The Great Weaver* created here. The reviews were generally good. Kristján Albertsson was extremely impressed, although he chastised the author for turning "the representatives of the upper class in the village into a collection of good-for-nothings, the dregs of society, or villains", since this caused the novel to lose its validity as a neutral and truthful description of a fishing village. Kristján believed that the novel would become, despite its shortcomings, a masterwork of Icelandic literature. On the other hand, Einar Olgeirsson, the leader of the Icelandic Communists, criticized Halldór for his obvious vacillation in his portrayal of the progress of the labour movement, suggesting that the image was caricature, traceable to the fact that he approached socialism as an idealist, without understanding the workers' struggle. Einar felt that this could be explained by Halldór's own life history and the state of the Icelandic labour movement, which was still to a great extent "bourgeois". The book was nonetheless a masterpiece in Einar's opinion; interestingly and he called his article "A Writer On His Way to Socialism".

Somewhat later *Morgunblaðið* published a long article by Reverend Benjamin Kristjánsson, whose opinion would be widely shared by Icelanders, not least after the publication of *Independent People*. He says that *Salka Valka* awakens the feeling "that human life is actually one universal boorish rubbish-heap of boffins and criminals". The most inspired article, however, was written by Kristinn E. Andrésson, a specialist in Nordic studies who had been educated in Germany and who would become one of Halldór's closest colleagues and friends. Kristinn wrote that Halldór was a unique writer whose mind showed the contradictions of his time in various, unbalanced proportion, especially those contradictions "contained in the words 'Icelander' and 'cosmopolitan'".

He was right, of course.

The Promised Land

As things stand now, the social system is far more perfect
than the people that live within it.
Halldór Laxness on the Soviet Union

Before Halldór's "political romance" was published, the Icelandic left wing underwent a transformation: in accordance with the strategy of the Comintern – the Third Communist International – the Communists broke with the Social Democratic Party and established the Icelandic Communist Party in late autumn, 1930. Since 1928 the Comintern had waged a war against the Social Democrats, calling them "social fascists". There were not many Communists in Iceland; the Reykjavík Chapter of the Icelandic Communist Party numbered fifty people when it was established. But they exerted some influence and were eager for a fight, and their numbers included men who would become influential in Icelandic politics decades later.

Halldór did not join the Communist Party. His position was made clear in an interview with the organ of the Communists, the *Workers' Paper*, published in May, 1932, on the occasion of his thirtieth birthday – the Icelandic Communist leaders being so young that birthday tributes were made to thirty-year-olds. An introduction states that the labour movement does not enjoy the understanding it might expect in the writer's books. On the other hand Halldór has "in the last few years developed in such a way that the Icelandic upper class has had little comfort from it".

Halldór is asked for his views of capitalism, which he reviles; on parliamentary democracy, in which he has little faith; and on the reformist policy of the Social Democrats, which he rejects. He considers those who support capitalist society, with its worldwide depression and preparations for world war, spiritual wretches and moral nobodies, and adds this declaration:

> I respect any party that adopts the difficult task of taking power over these idiots and ruling them according to macroeconomics, which is built on a scientific foundation, on an empirical system from the roots up, on sound human knowledge.

This declaration cannot be taken as anything other than support for the Communist Party, and he is asked why he does not join. Halldór answers that he is sick and tired of joining parties too early: "I do not dare now to declare myself a Communist before I have been able to formulate my opinion of it at first hand . . ." He then announces that he will take a trip to Russia later in the year.

It is difficult to harmonize Halldór's direct support for the dictatorship of the Communist Party with his character and experience: freedom of speech is the prerequisite for the writer's work, and for him freedom was, beyond all its obligations, as essential as oxygen. Here the chasm between Halldór the writer and Halldór the person is confirmed. It is tempting to explain this from the key word in the interview: *scientific*. From the time that Halldór wrote his articles on the electrification of the countryside, his thinking about society had been characterized by strong scientific and technological interests. The same thread runs through *The Book of the People*, where among other things he preaches scientific methods of raising children. It followed from the position that Marxist economics provided scientific formulae for a new and better society, so that there was no need for governmental opposition. For Halldór scientific thinking had taken the place of religion.

Since his Catholic period Halldór had often expressed the opinion that ideals were of greater significance than people. This might well have led to a vision in which a new society had to be built on an empirical foundation, thus rendering parliamentary democracy obsolete. Of course this was not simply a case of mental acrobatics: the problems that needed to be solved were very real. Halldór had seen the pitiful consequences of war and depression, was aware of the growing unemployment in Iceland as well as in the United States, and knew of Icelanders' poverty in the fishing villages and the countryside. He was convinced that capitalism was responsible for these problems. Just like Steinn Elliði in *The Great Weaver*, Halldór was in search of the truth; both desired certainty and a universal theory, and both hoped that the revolutionary movement would be based on these things. Besides this, Russia had always held a mysterious attraction for Western intellectuals.

Halldór's interest in Russia was not new. On his first trip abroad he had told his mother that he wanted to go there to learn Russian. And he had not been in Los Angeles for very long before he wrote to Inga: "Russia is the only one of the great lands of culture in which I have still to live, and I have thought about living there for a year sometime soon." To this was added an increased interest in the Russian Revolution. When he started *The Book of the People* he wrote to Inga:

When I come home I will have my new book printed, deliver lectures and write articles for the papers about my political interests. Then I would like to live in Russia for six months or so – with you!

With the interview in the *Workers' Paper* Halldór's political position became more absolute. The idealistic porridge of *The Book of the People* had been made according to more recipes than could be found in Marxist cookbooks. But in 1932 loyalty to the Soviet Union became the cornerstone of Halldór's political views, as it would continue to be for the next twenty years. In the Soviet Union, he believed, attempts had been made to develop a social system based on justice and equality, to eradicate hunger and poverty, and thereby to lay the foundation for people to enjoy the benefits of culture. It was no bad thing for the Icelandic Communists that one of the country's most renowned writers should express his support for their aims.

Although Halldór did not join the Party, he quickly became active in subsidiary organizations formed according to foreign models. Some of them did not have many members, while others existed in name only so that Icelandic Communists and their supporters could take part in the movement's international work. "The October Revolution produced by far the most formidable organized revolutionary movement in modern history. Its global expansion has no parallel since the conquests of Islam in its first century," as the historian Eric Hobsbawm put it.

The first letter that Halldór is known to have sent to the Soviet authorities was written in the name of the Icelandic Clarté Society. Clarté was not a functioning society in Iceland, but Halldór and his companions used the name to gain access to Soviet organizations, until in 1933 Kristinn E. Andrésson helped to establish the Union of Revolutionary Writers as a branch of the International Union of Revolutionary Writers, which had its headquarters in Moscow. In April, 1932, Halldór wrote to a man by the name of Stillmarck, who supervised cultural transactions between the Soviet authorities and foreign citizens. Halldór started his letter by thanking Stillmarck for the booklets and magazines about the Soviet Union that he had sent to the Icelandic writers. Halldór's primary business, however, was to discuss whether his own books could be published in the Soviet Union. *Salka Valka* was the first one he recommended. A young German scholar who lived in Iceland, Max Keil, would translate several chapters into German, and Halldór was thinking of sending them to Stillmarck to see if he could find an interested publisher in the Soviet Union.

Thus Halldór's interest in the Soviet Union was twofold: he was excited about the new society and the worldwide movement that was being directed from there, and he was investigating a possible new market for his literary work. This is even more apparent in Halldór's next letter to Stillmarck, written at the beginning of June. He had sent Stillmarck a short story as a sample and described his hopes for the future: "I want to go to Russia to write in my native language a propagandistic work about what I see." He has been negotiating with Norwegian and German publishers, but it is difficult to find translators from Icelandic, besides the fact that capitalist publishers are suffering under the Depression. The letter closes with these prophetic words:

> It is unlucky for a writer to be born in a tiny isolated country, condemned to a language that no-one understands. But one day I hope that the stones in Iceland will speak to the whole world through me.

Halldór sent his second letter to Stillmarck from Leipzig, where he and Inga had gone in the summer of 1932. *The Bird on the Beach* had been published, and the story about the farmer on the heath was back on track. At the same time Halldór made plans to promote *Salka Valka* overseas. Einar remained behind with his grandparents.

Inga was often left to herself to take in the sights when they travelled together, since Halldór was always working, but sometimes she helped him type his manuscripts, for instance, at their guest house in Leipzig. The place was run by two widows of academics, Dr Schumann and Professor Hartmann: Halldór tells of the women in *A Poet's Time*.

In the evening they went to bars or cafés, sometimes with Haukur Þorleifsson, who was studying in Leipzig and later became a bank clerk, or visited Jóhann Jónsson and Elisabet Göhlsdorf; Halldór's sister Helga had returned home. Halldór had met Haukur in Leipzig in the spring of 1931 and had often gone out with him in the evenings: "He is an extremely dear young man, very intelligent, studying mathematics here at the university, an extraordinarily great gentleman and a Communist of the finest sort". Halldór could scarcely pay a higher compliment during those years than to say that someone was both an intelligent gentleman and a Communist. More often, however, Halldór and Inga visited Jóhann at home; his consumption was getting the better of him.

Halldór and Inga were in Leipzig in June and Berlin in July. Inga was especially nostalgic about their stay in Berlin, which she found a refreshing and lively city. She tells among other things of the time a corpulent woman sat down next to her in a café and tried to kiss her. Halldór had chased her away: "I was not scandalized at all. It was so fashionable to be a homosexual or lesbian at that time . . ." Inga also found it pleasant to go shopping, although their finances did not allow for much beyond looking. The couple went to the theatre, concerts and the cinema whenever they could, as is revealed in a letter from Halldór to Erlendur:

> Yesterday we saw in the cinema the so-called *Dreigroschenoper* [*The Threepenny Opera*] by Brecht, with music by Weill; it was one of the greatest films that I have seen of that sort, the songs absolute masterpieces, both as literature and music. Brecht is doubtless the most talented Communist poet in Germany.

Halldór wrote to Jóhann from Berlin admitting that he was bored with the Kurfürstendamm, however. The reason for this was simple: in his mind he was in an Icelandic heath-cottage, but he was not making sufficient progress, perhaps only two pages a day, and the political unrest in Berlin was troubling. Such was the way that Halldór kept his political ideals and his work separate; that summer the Weimar Republic was rapidly approaching its end.

In fact another Icelandic writer was getting in the way of Halldór's work:

> Gunnar Gunnarsson has made it impossible to write an Icelandic rural novel: he has in fact emptied the coffers and set a record doing it at the same time, in such a way that I do not dare to describe anything that Gunnar describes, and have to be careful not to end up in court with Gunnar, because his mark

of ownership towers so high. The more that I write, the better I see what a great work the first three volumes of his *Church* are. It would be a terrible catastrophe for me if Gunnar and I were more similar than we actually are. I have chosen to maintain a ballade tone in my book.

At that time Gunnar was at the peak of his fame as a novelist; he was very popular in Denmark and even more so in Germany. He was not, on the other hand, published in Iceland between 1922 and 1938.

During the summer in Berlin Halldór made further arrangements to go to the Soviet Union, using the leverage he had gained by becoming chairman of the Icelandic chapter of the International Workers' Relief (I.A.H.). This affiliate of the Communist International had been founded in 1921 to combat famine in the wake of the civil war in Russia, but became one of the international organizations that worked on behalf of the Soviet government to strengthen its position throughout the world. The Icelandic chapter had been founded in 1930 and its original members had included Social Democrats, Communists and independents. In 1933, however, a conflict between the Communists and the Social Democrats led the latter to abandon the I.A.H., after which it became a Communist support group.

The leader of the international I.A.H. was Willy Münzenberg, a German Communist who had been a colleague of Lenin and was a major publisher of newspapers and magazines on behalf of the Party in his homeland. Münzenberg fled to France after the Nazis took power. Called to Moscow in connection with the show trials of 1938, he refused to go, fell out of favour and was found dead in a forest near Grenoble in the summer of 1940. But in 1932 he held a great deal of power. Halldór wrote to him requesting prepayment for his trip to Russia, and was invited to meet the revolutionary leader. He later described in *A Poet's Time* the huge crowd of people streaming into Münzenberg's offices in Berlin when he arrived there: "There was bustle and excitement in people's faces; each and every one of them appeared firmly fettered to his or her role in the regeneration of the world." Halldór had to wait a long time and was shown from one clerk to another, until he finally met Münzenberg:

> "*Du willst nach Russland gehen*," he said without introduction, and placed his arm quickly over my shoulders to create brotherly familiarity as he walked by. He had certainly already received detailed reports about me, because he did not ask me any personal questions . . . He stopped near one of his secretaries and started to dictate a letter. Then he asked me when I wanted to leave and I answered, "In the autumn," because I had to go to various other places

first. The letter was finished in just a moment, he signed it, folded it, handed it to me and told me to show it to the Russian ambassador in Berlin, or Stockholm if I preferred, said farewell to me . . . and followed me to the door with his arm over my shoulder to place even more emphasis on our brotherhood; and the meeting was finished.

For Halldór, this letter would open all doors to Moscow.

Inga left for Copenhagen in August but Halldór returned to Jóhann Jónsson in Leipzig. Halldór tried to find a German publisher for *Salka*, with Jóhann's help making contact with Kippenberg, the director of Insel, for whom Jóhann and Elisabet Göhlsdorf had translated Gunnar Gunnarsson from Danish into German.

Halldór wrote to Inga on 22 August to say that Kippenberg wanted to take the book although he had not read it. They signed a contract for *O Thou Pure Vine*, with Halldór to receive 10 per cent of the price of each copy sold, along with 500 marks against anticipated royalties. If *O Thou Pure Vine* sold well, Kippenberg would publish *The Bird on the Beach* immediately. Kippenberg would come to an agreement with Jóhann Jónsson and Elisabet Göhlsdorf for the translation; Jóhann had already come up with a German title, *Die Fahrt nach Süden* (*The Journey South*), a title that Halldór liked very much.

This was to be Halldór's first contract for an edition of one of his novels outside Iceland. He had tried to sell Gyldendal in Denmark *O Thou Pure Vine*, and in December, 1931, had received a telegram from Hasselbalch expressing an interest in publishing the book in both Norwegian and Danish. Nothing came of the idea at that point, however.

Fate proved ill-disposed towards the Insel contract. They never published *Salka*; Nazis took control of the publishing house, Kippenberg was pushed to one side, and the book was banned.

Only a few days after Halldór left Leipzig for Amsterdam, on 1 September, his friend Jóhann Jónsson died. That autumn Halldór wrote a short piece called "My Friend", giving a powerful portrait of their time together in Leipzig and their friendship, which went back to 1921:

> My friend lived in this city. We rambled back and forth throughout its streets on the foggy days of autumn, without feeling fatigue, walked to bar after bar, without being drunk. We were like two eternal men; between us burned the light of the world.

Halldór and Jóhann were united in their antipathy to war, their vision of a socialist future, and, not least, their love of literature, music and beauty. With the death of Jóhann, Halldór lost a part of himself and his innocence. With him he had embarked on his first reconnaissance expedition through contemporary foreign literature, with him he had discussed the most profound questions about life and death, beauty and poetry. Halldór also took notice of what Jóhann said about his work, although Jóhann could be very critical of Halldór when necessary.

Friendship is never easy when strong characters are involved. There are two letters from Jóhann Jónsson to Skúli Þórðarson from 1927 in which Halldór figures. In the first Jóhann says that *At the Foot of the Sacred Peak* is a childish work, but adds: "Yet I love Halldór and always expect something good from him." The second letter discusses *The Great Weaver from Kashmir*, among other things, and reveals Jóhann's clear perception of Halldór's weaknesses:

> Halldór's main defect is the chief peril of all true writing geniuses: an affected wit and knowledgeable arrogance . . . He has been given good talents, but he uses them badly, because he has too little respect for genius; on the other hand he is too eager for the praise of this world.

Jóhann himself never completed any of the great books that he planned. Halldór said of him:

> He communicated "His Books" only to his closest friends, expressing in conversation his poetic flights of fancy on quiet nights; afterwards we felt as if we had lived in the shadows of the wings of genius itself; written language was vain in comparison with his dusky golden-braided voice . . .

Halldór paid his debt to his friend twenty years later by writing a beautiful preface to his poems. Jón Helgason wrote to Halldór on the occasion to say that it was unnecessary to publish the book: "Jóhann is a man of one poem and that is enough for him many can be satisfied with less."

*

In Amsterdam Halldór attended the I.A.H. World Conference, organized by Münzenberg. Writing about it in the *Workers' Paper* on 13 September, Halldór stated:

> The goal of the conference was to agree on a method for fighting against the singlemost outrageous disgrace of the capitalist social system, the slaughter of the masses, that is to say war.

Discussing the conference in *A Poet's Time* thirty years later, he speaks of himself as one of the intellectuals who could not imagine joining the Party but who were prepared to work with the Communists against impending fascism in central

Europe, which had declared war against intellectuals. This attitude is a later construction, as can be seen from Halldór's article in the *Workers' Paper*, which he wrote in an orthodox Communist spirit, heaping praise on the Revolution and denigrating the Social Democrats, who would plunge the workers into war whenever it pleased them. The danger of fascism was not his main concern at that time.

A letter that Halldór sent Inga from Amsterdam expresses the same opinion. He was looking forward to meeting some of the group's most famous members, such as the writer Henri Barbusse and the renowned German revolutionary Klara Zetkin. The best-known representatives of the Soviet Union, Karl Radek and Maxim Gorky, had been denied visas and had to turn back in Berlin.

Halldór left Amsterdam for Copenhagen, travelling with Martin Andersen Nexø, whom he had met at the conference in Oslo two years previously. His description of their journey to Hamburg in *A Poet's Time* is double-edged. Halldór tells of how he himself, a poor young writer, chose to travel in one of the train's better-class carriages, while the Danish patriarch, who had been rich for a long time, chose the hard third-class seats giving the explanation that "while there were still people who travelled third class he would be their companion". Halldór gives a description of Nexø in Copenhagen, saying that he recorded all his expenditures in a notebook, even when buying an *Ekstrabladet* for 8 aurar, causing the reader to question whether it was stinginess or idealism that determined the writer's behaviour. Børge Houmann, who wrote Nexø's biography, objected to this description, pointing out that all the members of the Danish delegation had had to travel third class, and that the writer – who for most of his life had been a pauper – had of course travelled with his colleagues. Halldór's account may suggest, more than anything else, that by the time he wrote *A Poet's Time* he had become doubtful about the merits of political ideals.

Inga awaited Halldór in Copenhagen and they travelled together to Stockholm, where Halldór was a delegate at a special "Iceland Week" that started in mid-September. Describing the week in *A Poet's Time*, he made a good-natured joke about the grand conventions of courtesy and complicated etiquette at Swedish banquets, "these quotidian-cold but banquet-glad people". And he warmly recalled the contributions of two other Icelandic participants: Sigurður Nordal's lectures on the thousand years of Icelandic literature, which had been delivered eloquently and with a strong sense of national pride, and the reading by a young actress who later became a star in Denmark, Anna Borg. Her recitation made Halldór feel as if he was understanding poetry anew, as an art in which silences were key. As his life went on he found the ability to remain silent over the most important things to be the chief talent of a good narrator, but in his books from the 1930s this conviction is not yet evident.

At the end of the week in Stockholm Inga returned home; Halldór wrote straight away to say how much he missed her. In the same letter he describes how the Icelandic delegation was introduced to the Swedish royal family and went to the opera to hear *Tosca*, but even though Halldór had always been a great lover of classical music he was no fan: ". . . I slept during the opera as I often do at such opportunities, and listened to its howling in my sleep."

Halldór delivered Münzenberg's letter of recommendation to the Soviet embassy. When he received his visa on 25 September, he wrote to Inga to say that he was thinking of travelling through Finland to Leningrad. He asked for news of Erlendur and their little boy, and added: "My dear Inga, I think so much about you and I am never able to value you better than when we have been away from each other for a short time." On the same day Halldór wrote to Jón Helgason, seeking his opinion on a sensitive matter. The letter is one of the few sources from this time that show Halldór allowing himself to joke about Soviet Communism:

> Here I have with me one huge container full of philistine clothing, including two white vests, and I fear that I will be hanged as a counter-revolutionary if I bring it with me to Russia. Because of this I beg you to please accept it if I send this container and its dangerous contents to Copenhagen, and thus save my life.

It was not always easy to be an elegant gentleman and a Communist, and it was safer to leave the elegance at home when travelling to the fatherland of Communism. Several days after Halldór wrote to Inga and Jón, his youthful dream was achieved. On the morning of 30 September he arrived in Leningrad.

*

In fact Halldór took two long trips to the Soviet Union during the 1930s, the second in the winter of 1937–8. He wrote books about both, published them shortly after returning to Iceland, and also described the two journeys in *A Poet's Time*. There is a huge difference between the later descriptions and the contemporary sources – the reader might think these were not the same trips or that it was not the same man who had made them. Of course the Halldór who wrote about the trip in *A Poet's Time* in 1963 was not the same man who had gone blue-eyed over the border with a letter from Willy Münzenberg in his pocket; history had played cruel tricks on him in the interim. The path of a man, like Halldór, who participated in the battles of his time, must always cross the path of history at some point, and this intersection invariably calls for re-evaluation. Perhaps this intersection is precisely that: one little punctum, as Roland Barthes says, can be seen in some photographs; one moment on an evening in Moscow in March, 1938, in a grey apartment block of a female German exile, as we shall see.

One is inevitably led to ponder how Halldór, a man who truly wished the best for his countrymen and who interpreted their lives and fates with more sympathy and artistry than has ever been done since, could have become a defender of Stalin. Whoever investigates Halldór's life cannot be content with easy presuppositions but must try to come to terms with how it happened, what it was based on. It helps that there are not only printed sources, but also numerous private letters, as well as documents in Soviet archives, especially regarding his later trip.

In 1932 fifteen years had passed since the Russian Revolution. Stalin and his men had total control but the notorious Moscow Trials had not yet begun, although all political opposition had been quashed. The restructuring of the economic system accomplished under the first Five Year Plan was being concluded. Collective farms having replaced private farming, millions of people in the countryside had been reduced to begging; the Ukraine, which Halldór visited, was suffering famine. In fact the overall situation was horrible. The author of *A Poet's Time* did not let this go unnoticed:

> I have perhaps not at any other time been so surprised as when I suddenly found myself standing on a street in Leningrad one mild autumn day in 1932, with a fresh image in my mind of nearby cities like Berlin, Amsterdam, Copenhagen and Stockholm: I felt as if I had arrived on another planet.

He could never have imagined the bedraggled throng that filled squares and streets, stations and public transport in Russia that autumn.

Halldór must have experienced a cultural and political let-down. Or did he? In the book he wrote about this trip, *Going East* (1933), he gives no indication of this. The travelogue, published by the Soviet Friendship Society, is one of the dullest works Halldór ever wrote, in style and narrative leagues behind his later *The Russian Adventure* (1938).

Halldór himself said at the start of the book that he regarded it as a work of civic duty. He had gone to the Soviet Union unattached to any party and wanted to tell his countrymen what he saw there and how he had modified his views. Of course he had always intended to write a propagandistic work, as is revealed in the letter to Stillmarck, and no doubt few readers had expected anything else. The work thus hardly bears Halldór's imprint. Its first hundred pages are summaries of booklets by Lenin and Stalin, in part translated from the German by Arnfinnur Jónsson; only then does the actual travelogue begin. It makes for lively reading but is at the same time peculiarly distant and biased. Halldór does not say how he reacted when he came to Leningrad. He does not deny that the streets were full of ragged wretches, but he feels that overall the country is developing in the right direction. His final words are these:

> That the U.S.S.R. has become a paradise, as the papers here say some people feel, is naturally untrue. And that the Great Plan, which was a logical and inevitable continuation of the Bolshevik Revolution, has laid the foundation for a wiser and more productive social system – that is absolutely no lie.

Going East is not unique. Travelogues about the Soviet Union were common during those years, the authorities there having realized early on the benefits of getting sympathetic writers to laud the achievements of the Revolution. Such narratives developed from collections of extensive descriptions and even critical observations into defensive tracts with a religious air. In certain ways *Going East* was more like earlier travelogues, where devotees of the Soviet Union would supply detailed economic figures as proof of beneficial developments while not denying the poverty they witnessed. The modern world was being observed through the spectacles of the future; people saw what they wanted to see.

The later travelogues become stories of pilgrimages to the Promised Land. They are composed according to the methods Halldór describes in *A Poet's Time* when discussing his Catholic writings: believers "testify to their faith through the vision of its holy places: it is impossible to see from the description that they have actually gone there." This is the devotional approach taken in *Going East*.

Throughout the 1920s Halldór had vacillated between the human and the idealistic. His writings from the 1930s show the human increasingly taking refuge in fiction, while in his non-fiction Halldór writes with idealistic aims, some of which are so distant from humanity as to become adversarial. These ideals become his measuring stick for humanity, as when, in the 1932 interview with the *Workers' Paper*, he says that he considers those who do not subscribe to a scientific social system to be nobodies. As he says in *Going East*: "As things stand now, the social system is far more perfect than the people that live within it."

In *A Poet's Time* Halldór describes his companions on sightseeing trips in the Soviet Union – since he had travelled there alone he was put together with delegations according to circumstances – as having "the blessed dream in their eyes when they arrived and they did not abandon it no matter what they saw". In the same book he sometimes comes across as if this had nothing at all to do with him. But his letters written during the trip show clearly that he saw what he hoped to see. This was not unlike what had happened when he had written about his trip to Lourdes. This is how he describes his first reactions to Inga at the start of October:

I have never seen such a sea of humanity as the one that I beheld in these cities, Leningrad and Moscow. They are so incredibly densely populated; every small station that one stops at is also swarming with people. The first sound that I heard after I crossed over the border from Finland was the roaring of the tractors. Everywhere, wherever a man looks, they are working, tearing down and building, driving, carrying, dragging, constructing, building walls, manufacturing machines, and Leningrad looks as if it is completely under construction – except that the old palaces are allowed to crumble, those that are not possible to use for schools or public buildings. The workers would rather live in modern houses. In Leningrad one-and-a-half million peasants from the countryside have flocked to the city in the last six to eight years, an ugly and unkempt bunch, uncultured, but the workers here, especially the factory workers, are fine folk, and extremely handsome, and the same goes for the soldiers and Soviet state workers, and they are all well dressed although not in the way to which we are accustomed.

This is the same kind of description one finds in *Going East*, except that it is followed by an entertaining addition: "The majority of the working women wear lipstick." When Halldór writes to Inga he often thinks of practical matters:

I have here a double room, and I have been thinking how wonderful it would have been if you had come. On the other hand I am glad that you did not come, because everything here is different than in bourgeois societies, and I am certain that you would often have been impatient and found this boring; everything is done here with endless amounts of red tape and hassle, and it is not possible to duck into a bar and order a coffee or a beer, and if one wants to go on a tram, one has to fight against hundreds of people to get in, because the cities are so packed with people.

Halldór discovered that Leningrad had no I.A.H. office. He was not, however, completely lost, since Red Aid, another international organization founded by Münzenberg, had an office there. This organization provided Halldór with a huge office in a palace that was occasionally used for foreign delegations, and there he was allowed to sleep, alone among all the paintings, as he told Inga. He also

received vouchers for meals at restaurants and rubles for travelling. He was invited
to dinners in the evenings and spent his days mostly with Professor Beloussoff, an
old colleague of Lenin who talked to him about the numerous problems facing the
government. On 2 October he took an overnight train to Moscow, went to the
I.A.H. office there, and got the feeling that it worked almost as well to name Lenin
or Stalin as it did to name Willy Münzenberg:

> The people at the I.A.H. telephoned Berlin immediately and spoke to
> Münzenberg, although I did not know what they discussed, but an elegant
> Rolls-Royce was sent for me straight away and I was driven to the Intourist
> Hotel, and told to live there like a god in France.

Halldór was in Moscow for the month of October. The I.A.H. put him in touch
with the agency that oversaw cultural exchanges between the Soviet Union and
foreign countries, V.O.K.S., which provided him with interpreters to accompany
him around the city. He was energetic in his sightseeing, visiting the Stalin Factory
and the Museum of the Red Army, and also went to concerts and the theatre; he
was impressed by the arts in Moscow. He had enough work to do, since he wrote
his book about the trip while he was there, "so that when I came home I could
work as hard as possible at completing the first volume of the novel I'd been
writing that summer". He was also becoming tied to the propaganda wagon; he
wrote to Inga that he'd promised to write an article for the international journal of
V.O.K.S. and an overview of Icelandic literary history for the great Soviet encyclopaedia. In addition he had been invited to deliver an address in Icelandic on
Radio Moscow around the anniversary of the Revolution, 7 November.

It appears that Halldór was allowed to travel extensively around Moscow with
his interpreters, but his letters to Inga indicate that he had fallen completely for the
propaganda directed at him:

> This Soviet Union has the appearance of an American town that has
> suddenly experienced a "boom": where a new mine has been discovered, or
> something along those lines. The stories about hunger and unrest here are
> absolutely groundless fabrications; it is possible that there is no place on
> earth where people are as content with their government, since they govern
> themselves – the workers' councils control everything; and the army is also
> composed of workers, both women and men, so that there is no danger that
> they will fight among themselves or shoot each other as the army does to the
> workers in Germany. Everyone here seems to love their Red Army, and I
> have never seen such a close and energetic relationship between the people

and the soldiers . . . And the *joie de vivre* here! Everywhere people sing . . . the children, the workers, the youth groups, the soldiers, everyone sings. It is truly refreshing to experience a nation that is so perfectly fortunate in its dreams of development – one witnesses the most unbelievable dreams becoming reality in its hands.

When Halldór wrote to Inga he had no reason to write the propaganda he put into his book, unless, of course, he believed it – or wanted to convince himself of its truth.

Faith is the key word here. On this trip Halldór's faith was both more childish and more sincere than on the later one. For example, he wrote to Jón Helgason, who was much too ironic a man to allow himself to be deceived by propaganda:

I see Russia as the Promised Land, and its advances have gone far beyond what I could have imagined. Naturally the Russians have a long way to go; they have not yet succeeded in making the uneducated rural mob, which has been sleeping among swine, into men. But the Communists proceed like prudent farmers; they do not begin by buying fine clothes, but rather tools with which to utilize the earth's resources.

But when Halldór puts himself in Inga's shoes and tries to imagine how everyday life in the Soviet Union would appear to his youthful, cheerful, bourgeois wife, the propagandist slips away, the songs of praise are hushed for a time:

You find it somewhat distasteful that the I.A.H. did not invite you as well. I on the other hand am so certain that you would have found this incredibly boring. There is nothing here resembling anything in the countries that you know – no pomp, no refinement, people's thoughts are not concentrated on anything but achieving records in industry . . . Everyone is working and in between they are studying. There is no café life or dancing – only endless political meetings with reports on industry and the swearing of oaths about achieving this or that production goal (although there might be a solo dance performance or instrumental music afterwards). I am certain that you would have found this extremely dull.

This is the human dimension, not the idealistic one; here Diljá is speaking, not Steinn. But Steinn still had a strong hold on Halldór. At around the same time that he wrote this letter he composed "Fifteen Years of the Workers' State in Russia" for publication in the *Workers' Paper*. All that he expresses are political vows: honourable men think with respect and admiration for the common people of this country who have wiped the leeches from their hands and founded in huge parts of both hemispheres a state based on cooperation and collective ownership, in which the workers are the controlling class.

Halldór did try to free Inga from her bourgeois perspective, to get her to see things from his point of view. At the beginning of November he sent her a long letter from Moscow, remarkable as evidence of his political thought at the time:

It pleases me, my dear, that you spend time with Communists; for my part, I feel that people who do not have a Communist way of thinking are lacking something, each and every one of their observations is disoriented. You say that you have felt a certain man to be absolutely horrendously boring because he saw everything from a Communist point of view – did you not know, my dear, that there are only two views of things, the Communist and the bourgeois? Nothing in between exists. It is not the Communist view that is "boring", but instead, and naturally, various individual Communists. You say of the I.A.H. that generally you "are bored" with all "such" company. I know that you find more entertaining bourgeois company like sewing clubs and such things, but if you attach any importance *to being my companion*, then I know that you will not think any longer like those women whom I have most despised and fought against – those sheep, or better put, savages in society, who have no idea where they stand. And certainly there would never have been any improvements made to the lot of the people if what we are talking about were not a powerful organization, which all good men and good women have supported. Otherwise we would still be subject to a medieval social system even today. All changes for the better have come from below, from the people ... And of course one of the strongest fortifications of the bourgeois class is apathy, and the dullness of women, who have been systematically idiotized under the capitalist system.

Halldór's tone is not unlike the one he adopted in letters he wrote from the monastery; if people wanted to be his friends they'd have to become Catholics; that was the only way to live. In the same letter he expresses his joy that Inga was not drinking and carousing, feeling that it was only right she should spend her time reading books about Communism. This is even more remarkable considering that Halldór himself was never much of a diligent reader of Communist books.

Halldór's vision is never more childish than when the discussion turns to children and education. He asks Inga about little Einar and adds:

When I visit the nurseries here, I always think of him. The other day I asked the woman in charge at one nursery how often the children wake up during the night, and she answered: "The children here never wake up during the night." I asked: "Are the children never given any between-meal snacks?" "No," she said. "Such things make them capricious and destroy their character. We view all between-meal snacks as poison." . . . I have come to the conclusion that one child in a private house cries and wails more than two hundred and fifty children in a scientific state-run home.

Halldór was so happy with this theory that it found its way into the book about his trip. That was remarkable, since his own childhood had been characterized by extremely unscientific freedom and pampering.

These letters also contain Halldór's ideas about the next step in his writing career, which he keeps suitably separate from his idealistic battles. He tells Inga that Gunnar Gunnarsson had written to him and it was certain that Gyldendal would take *O Thou Pure Vine* and *The Bird on the Beach*, and he encourages her to spread the news; it would trump his enemies at home. Then he tells her that he needs to return to Germany to conclude some business with Insel, and that he must finish his next novel before the autumn. Apparent here is not only Halldór's desire for advancement, but also his concerns about his financial future:

. . . yet there is one thing that makes me fearful – that I will be forced to have to work to support myself, i.e., that I will have to hire myself out somewhere for money in a pinch, which would take necessary time from my writing and thus destroy my future. I know that the bourgeois class at home would in fact do anything to keep me from writing, and are prepared to bribe me into accepting some "position" or other.

Beyond all else Halldór's thought was: Do not adapt, do not become a piece of the small-town puzzle.

Halldór was supposed to have taken a trip to the Ukraine in October, but he was ill for a week and the trip was postponed until 7 November; at midnight he spoke on Radio Moscow, and the speech was broadcast on both longwave and short-wave in the hope that it could be heard at home. Published at the end of *Going East*, it discusses the Five Year Plan, industrialization and electrification, and is a kind of ode to Dnieprostroi in the Ukraine, where a huge dam was built, along with a power station and factories – in fact a whole new city. Dnieprostroi becomes for Halldór a symbol of the future, and he eagerly cites Lenin's famous words: "Communism is Soviet power plus the electrification of the whole country."

The *Workers' Paper* reported as follows: "Halldór Kiljan Laxness' speech on the radio in Moscow was rebroadcast by the radio here . . . This excellent speech . . . has awakened a great deal of attention throughout the country." Several weeks later the paper added "All the bourgeois and the snobs tore their hair from anger . . . because they view all cultural programmes in the country as their own possession".

After this speech Halldór was attached to a delegation; events were scheduled from morning till night and there was very little free time left over. He also had been assigned a room-mate, the German revolutionary Hermann Duncker, a well-known Marxist scholar, one of the organizers of the German Communist Party and its Member of Parliament. According to *A Poet's Time* Halldór was present when Duncker was engaged in confidential negotiations to conduct an interview with Bukharin, now a falling star; Duncker had, besides this, long conversations with a German comrade who had lived through horrific experiences in Siberia. That Halldór was already aware of internal Party struggles is revealed in a notebook he kept on this trip. On 13 October he wrote that it was cold in the hotel in Moscow because the room was unheated, and that he had met a group of Communists who were not orthodox and found them quite useful; in order not to mention them accidentally in the travelogue he crossed out the lines about them in his note-book. Halldór makes no mention of any of this in his letters to Inga except to say that he is sharing a room with Duncker.

According to *A Poet's Time*, another personality from the German Communist movement met Halldór at a banquet in Moscow: Sophie Ryss, the widow of the revolutionary leader Karl Liebknecht. Sophie was a specialist in art and a Russian Jew, and their conversation had been memorable to Halldór. He was just about to leave for the Ukraine and optimistically asked this elegant woman whether the collective farm was not the most important achievement of the Revolution; she looked somewhat sorrowfully at this foolhardy man from the north and told him that he needed to keep his idealism in check, because Russian villages, *Mir*, were sad places:

> And she added a comment that was so small that it could not be seen except under a microscope, but yet was deeper than most of what was said to me in Russia: "Either a man loves the Russian *Mir* or it makes him unhappy."

Halldór found it tiring to be tied to a delegation for which every hour of the day was planned. He certainly did not, despite shared ideals, have much in common with representatives of Belgian labour unions. Yet he found it amusing when the entire group was sent to the ballet and given seats in the Tsar's box. In the same letter he describes people's appearance and dress in Russia. Women from the countryside all had "shawls around their necks and were ridiculously gullible and idiotic"; yet he commented that the Bolsheviks would set things straight after they had "eliminated the difference between the city and the countryside". He adds: "You ask what I am wearing. I am in grey trousers and a dark-brown jacket . . . My new jacket I sent along with other bourgeois clothing to Jón Helgason in Copenhagen."

Several days later Halldór finally went on a sightseeing trip to the Ukraine with the Belgian delegation; from Dnieprostroi he sent Inga a long letter, enamoured as he was of the brand new industrial city. He does not believe that there was a famine in the countryside, eagerly swallowing the propaganda that is fed to him:

Now in the Ukraine everything is collectivized, there are no (or very few) private farms remaining; the largest collective and state farms of Russia are here, and large industry has developed, with the biggest power stations in the world. Can you imagine the difference! And all of this in just three to four years! It is like the story about Aladdin's lamp in *The Thousand and One Nights*. Never in my life have I experienced anything so much like a fairy tale.

On this note he concluded his last letter to Inga written during this trip, and again readers of *A Poet's Time* must be amazed: there this same trip is described as a pointless interminable train journey; Halldór's carriage is sometimes disconnected and made to wait at a station out in the countryside, where thousands of people clad in tatters loiter in eternal patience. Although the delegation was certainly invited to banquets in the large cities, in some places there was nothing to be had but tea from samovars on the train, and endless revolutionary songs and shouting of "Hurrah" led by a middle-aged guide.

Such descriptions are found neither in *Going East* nor in the letters. Of course the delegation did not see the true famine in the Ukraine, but on this trip Halldór did see much that was difficult to harmonize with the public image. In *A Poet's Time* he mentions his faith apologetically:

There is nothing more common in psychology than when someone denies belief in what he sees with his own eyes and sees what actually does not exist . . . where faith rules, wisdom keeps its mouth shut.

Interestingly Halldór's colleague Kristinn E. Andrésson described his own views nearly forty years later, without having changed his own opinion:

In my eyes the people's poverty there, which was not so different from what we saw during the Depression years here, the tattered rags of clothing, was temporary vanity in the light of historical experience and the sublime perspective of the future.

Halldór left the delegation in Kharkov and made his way alone back to Moscow, where he spent one night before taking a train to Germany. After something of a delay with his visa application he was allowed to go to Berlin, arriving there at the end of November, according to *A Poet's Time*:

It was bliss to return to an effortless place where life proceeded normally, like at the Hotel Excelsior in Berlin, where I sat back in the warm and tasteful accommodation and where no-one raised their eyes if one asked about everyday sorts of things and everything was replete with the cheap delights that accompany the normal life of modern man.

Summerhouses, That Is the World

> This play is of course not suitable for weak or nervous
> audiences, but it is thus more generous to those who enjoy
> literature in proportion to the wealth of fate that it contains.
>
> *Halldór Laxness in a theatre review*

When Halldór was in Leipzig in November, 1932, Insel was still optimistic about the publication of *Salka*. Halldór felt somewhat depressed there; this is when he wrote "My Friend" about Jóhann Jónsson.

From Leipzig Halldór continued on to Copenhagen and met Jón Helgason and Gunnar Gunnarsson, who assisted him as before with publishing matters and seemed to have returned to the opinion that Gyldendal would publish *Salka*. Halldór was in his old haunts, and at the end of the Russian travel diary he wrote notes to himself: "Have clothing tailored, meet G.G." However, he was not able to reach an agreement with the Danes and early in December he returned to Iceland.

Halldór's comrades received him with open arms. While he was gone vigorous fighting had occurred when labour unionists had supported a demonstration at a city council meeting in Reykjavík. The council wanted to decrease the minimum wage paid for relief work, which had supported many people who had been hit hard by the Depression and unemployment. The meeting disintegrated into fighting – the so-called "Gúttó Fight" – and court cases, but the protesters can be said to have won since relief-work wages were not lowered. People felt that with this incident a waymark had been set up on the road to victory for the radical labour movement. Halldór later wrote a story about the incident.

Other changes had taken place while Halldór toured Russia. The Communists had set up a new subsidiary organization, the Friends of the Soviet Union, part of the International Friends of the Soviet Union. Magister Kristinn E. Andrésson, recently returned after a two-year course of study in Germany, was persuaded to become its director. Up until that time Kristinn had not been a party-bound leftist, but rather a philosophical-minded aesthete. But the Soviet Union had found a truly powerful supporter, because Kristinn remained faithful to it until his death in 1973.

One of the first major projects of the Friends of the Soviet Union was the publication of *Going East.* The *Workers' Paper* published an interview with Halldór on 13 December, in which he was modest to start with, recalling the enormous difficulties with which the Soviet government had to contend, how progressive the society had been, and how people had to guard against thinking that there was a kind of perfect world there. He added that it was precisely in the light of this that industrialization of the country could be achieved, this "collective struggle of the masses under the direction of the Communist Party": counting victories over difficulties that could be called insurmountable. The interview concluded with Halldór citing Maxim Gorky: "'When a man comes out of Russia and looks around, only one thing seems probable to him, which is that things in the West are controlled by absolute idiots.'" Not Halldór's first thought when he had arrived at the Hotel Excelsior in Berlin en route back to Iceland.

When Halldór returned home, he lived with his family at Hotel Borg, after which they moved back to the apartment that Einar Arnórsson had renovated. Through the hotel window Halldór would sometimes see several funeral processions in a single day, since funerals in Reykjavík took place at the cathedral. This sight inspired one of his best-known proletarian stories, "Lily", about a nameless man from Ólafsvík whose body remained for only one night in the churchyard: "I imagined that the man had been sold to people at the university, and . . . they removed his bones from his body for scientific research and put stones in his coffin," says Halldór in *A Poet's Time.* The Ólafsvík connection was no coincidence: Jóhann Jónsson was from there, and his death was still fresh in Halldór's mind.

Impatience had built up inside Halldór as it always did when he took time off from his writing. After "Lily" he wrote a hundred-page story, "The Honour of the House", which became the main feature of the collection *Footsteps of Men* (1933). Like so much of Halldór's fiction, "The Honour of the House" was based on actual events; the preface to the second edition says that he heard about them from a good friend. This was the Surgeon General, Vilmundur Jónsson. Vilmundur's nephew suggested that Washington Irving's "The Spectre Bridegroom", in the translation by Benedikt Gröndal, had exerted a great influence on the style of "The Honour of the House". As had happened before, people who thought that they could recognize themselves in Halldór's story were not impressed.

"The Honour of the House" is the only one of Halldór's stories from the 1930s in which the main characters are "better people", as they were called. This is a story about the insincerity and hypocrisy of individuals who want to maintain the honour of "the house" in a small village, and yet are unable to control their own urges. Although real events doubtless formed the skeleton, Halldór also utilized his own experience, including his first trip to Copenhagen. But although the story is finely executed and full of narrative joy, it is as if Halldór were trying to compress a novel into short-story form; he does not take time with the material, and puts little effort into the settings and conversations. But the techniques of letting the reader hear of the main events indirectly and of putting silences at just the right places lift the narrative. Halldór said later that "The Honour of the House" had in fact been a draft he had put aside in order to work on *Independent People*.

The great story of the heath farmer had now become clearer, thanks to Lenin and Stalin's teachings about the difference between large-, small- and medium-scale farmers: "Then finally the problem of Bjartur in Summerhouses was solved, and I composed the story about the smallholder in one go in two years." The idea was that these groups had nothing in common. Small-scale farmers were cheated continually, either by being made to struggle financially to become "independent" like large-scale farmers, or by being tricked into joining the cooperative movement under the illusion of becoming medium-scale farmers. These theories made their mark on *Independent People*, proving that dubious doctrines can be used to produce good fiction.

It is understandable that the idea of collective farming appealed to Halldór. And he wanted the book to capture the essence of the Icelandic people. The direction of his fiction had become more determined, following his decision to write books about the fate of Iceland that would appeal to the whole world.

Notebooks from 1933–5, when Halldór was writing *Independent People*, show how disciplined his working methods had become. He wrote down words from Þorbergur Þórðarson's collection that he thought he could use, things said by people he met, and curious things from books he read. He went through newspapers from the book's period, researched economic developments, tried out sentences and ideas, or travelled to get a better idea of conditions on the ground. He wanted above all to be careful with details so readers would feel that the story was "genuine". One spring he went through Rangárvellir District with his friend Guðmundur from Miðdalur and visited various poor farms. In one place he makes the comment: "Young people on the farms must live with an enormous sexual hunger."

In the first part of 1933 Halldór travelled throughout Iceland. He says in *A Poet's Time*:

> It rained an enormous amount throughout the south; hardly a single stone was dry the whole summer. From the final weeks of winter until well into haymaking I meandered around isolated farms both in the west and north, viewing the land and chatting with the people.

In May he and Inga went to Laugarvatn, a popular resort for people from Reykjavík, and stayed there for the better part of June. Halldór worked constantly at his writing. A new version of "The Heath" was taking shape.

It is possible to trace the creation of *Independent People* from the writer's manuscripts and notebooks. "The Heath" had been dependent on what Halldór saw and experienced on his trip to the east of Iceland in 1926. The events described in it are horrific, and the attack against poverty is strong, but the manuscript never takes flight, as Halldór himself admitted. Knowing that he had to do better, he decided on writing in Southern Europe.

Around the middle of September, 1933, Halldór set off for Spain on his own. *Going East* had recently been published in a run of one thousand two hundred copies; its reception depended on the political views of its readers. At that time there was widespread interest in the Russian Revolution among Social Democrats and their radical colleagues, and many were eager to hear what Halldór had to say. Earlier in the year he had published a speech in the first issue of the journal of the Friends of the Soviet Union, the *Soviet Friend*, warning travellers to Russia against thinking that everything would be like it was in capitalist countries:

> When you look at the shoes of the Russian workers, which are of course far from being anything equal to the footwear of the fine bourgeoisie in the capitalist countries, then you should recall that before the Revolution there were two million workers in Russia who had never in their life seen shoes.

At the start of October, 1933, Kristinn E. Andrésson called for the establishment of the Union of Revolutionary Writers in Iceland, a chapter of the international organization of the same name. This organization's main task was to "support the development of radicalism in writing". Halldór was pronounced a member even though he was abroad. This marked the start of his energetic participation in leftist literary activities, and he became the country's best-known "red pen".

In the autumn and winter Halldór was overseas, however, with politics put on the shelf for the time being. He sailed first to England and wrote to Inga from London on 20 September:

> I was seasick and depressed for nearly the whole voyage, sorrowful about having parted from you and little Einar, but I felt and still feel that it is absolutely necessary for me to get a change of atmosphere.

Halldór took lodging in a hotel in Barcelona on 23 September, after nearly a three-week voyage from Iceland, having also stopped in Paris, where he visited a professor of Scandinavian literature, Jolivet, who seemed likely to translate *Salka Valka* into French. The delegation that met Halldór in the capital of Catalonia included the trade commissioner Helgi P. Briem, Halldór's schoolfriend from the Lyceum, and Jónas from Hrifla, who was there on holiday with his wife. Helgi found Halldór a room, went to the beach with him, and promised other types of entertainment, as Halldór told Inga in a letter: "Helgi has invited me to a bullfight tomorrow; six bulls will be killed. It should be quite entertaining to see."

In the same letter Halldór told Inga of his delight in the sunshine and that he was convinced that things would go well for his work in Spain. Inga had wanted to go with him, but they did not have enough money for both of them, and the book had to come first:

> If I am unable to finish it here during the next couple of months, we will have little to live on next year, not counting the grant, and if the story turns out to be boring (despite the *horrendous* amount of work and effort that I try to put into it), then it is certain the Cultural Fund will want nothing to do with it. And besides that, the Cultural Fund is bankrupt!

Halldór tells Inga that he wishes more than anything that they will be able to spend future winters together on the Mediterranean.

At the start of October Inga went with Einar to Copenhagen to stay with her parents. Halldór's work was going well:

> In the last six days (since I started here) I have typed twenty-four pages of this draft of the novel; I of course work on Sundays as well. I am extremely nervous that the novel is not coming along as well as *O Thou Pure Vine* and

The Bird on the Beach; the material is far more cold and barren. I feel that it is not written well enough. I have to rewrite this entire worthless thing one more time before I can begin to think about sending it to a publisher. Yes, a writer's work consists of little else but problems and drudgery; I am . . . convinced that there is no other type of life's work that causes such difficulties and headaches – and all of this a man has to do alone, of his own responsibility, with nothing to trust but his own strength. No other work demands as much self-denial.

The first volume of *Independent People* would be divided into two parts. These letters reveal that although he is working at it so carefully, typing the first two hundred pages of the manuscript for the fifth time, he still cannot see the work as a unified whole. In numerous letters to Inga, he tells of how he gives up now and then, feeling as if he has lost the gift of writing:

> You do not know how often I feel bad, Inga, how I am alone, how I am forced to experience such great internal battles over my work I wish that you could understand this, Inga, and that you could take part in it with me. My work is so infinitely serious to me, and at the same time sacred.

The last words rang true. Halldór had fled from the atmosphere at home, which was making him sluggish in his work and sick in his soul and body, according to his own account. Inga was concentrating on their son and their financial situation, and the tension this caused is obvious from their correspondence. The same concerns seem to have caused Halldór not to want to join the Communist Party: the work required a discipline and devotion he would have never been able to give, although he supported the movement wholeheartedly. All the same, as soon as Halldór was far from Inga his longing blossomed:

> Inga, I love you absolutely uncontrollably; after I have spent some time away from you I feel as if our "courtship" has begun again, except I find that I love you much more than I did . . . now I feel strongly that you are a part of me, a part that will belong to me as long as I live . . .

Halldór needed distance to be able to express his feelings in this way, just as he needed to be on the Continent in order to write about life on the Icelandic heaths. And at the start of November he finally started to feel that the first part of the first volume of his novel had become something. But then the next struggle took over:

I have now been trying for a fortnight to come up with the form for the beginning of the second volume. It has been endless headaches and rewrites, over and over again. I have finally finished rewriting it for the seventh time, but it is not nearly good enough, I have to give it yet another look – and this is nothing but thirteen worthless pages. Such are my working methods, my dear Inga – it doesn't seem like much compared to all the work that I put into it, and to tell the truth the coming year is a complete mystery to me, financially speaking! We will see what happens!

The first part of the second volume of *Independent People*, "Winter Morning", is one of the greatest prose chapters in Icelandic literature. Beginning with the words: "Slowly, slowly, the winter day opens its Nordic eyes," it describes a winter morning on a farm seen through the eyes of a little boy. Hoping to earn some money, Halldór decided to send the chapter to *Iðunn*, and it was published shortly before the novel itself was. "It is somewhat well written," said Halldór, "but not exactly exciting." Many years later he said that he found this chapter "forced and pretentious, even a bit affected", though he did not allow other people to say so.

Halldór found it expensive to live in Barcelona even though he did not indulge himself very much, and at the beginning of November he was broke yet again. He sent a telegram to Erlendur and asked him to send money, but this took time, so Halldór stayed in his room like a ruffian cursing his lot.

In *A Poet's Time* there is a chapter on his stay in Barcelona, describing the destinies and romantic embroglios of the *pensión* guests. He lived there like a fly on the wall and enjoyed observing the people around him. His letters to Inga show little of this interest, however. Here *A Poet's Time* most likely gives a more truthful account, since in his letters Halldór had the habit of magnifying his own loneliness and nervousness so that Inga would not think she was missing anything.

It seems that Halldór did not inform himself regarding current affairs in Spain. Democracy had only recently been established, and the course of events that led to the Civil War had commenced. He was not fond of Spanish society and wrote to Inga:

"The life here is incredibly constrained and dull as it is everywhere in Europe, the women are horrendously unemancipated, and the men are *"caballeros"* – gentlemen louts – they cannot be seen carrying anything. The difference between the classes is so huge that the situation in Scandinavia pales before it, and particularly innate to Spaniards is their hatred of all work – but to sit in cafés and chat all day long, that is their thing.

Halldór commented several times on the role of the sexes in his letters. As in *The Book of the People*, he came across as a staunch supporter of equal rights, even though this had little to do with his own life.

The day before elections were held in Spain, he wrote to Inga:

Here everything is in an uproar . . . there are shootings on the streets and labour strikes, the army patrols on horseback and there are policemen on every street corner prepared to shoot at the workers whenever they get the chance.

It is possible that these events prompted him to leave, because his anxiety and desire to travel had returned; he also wanted to rejoin his family. He had written what he had intended to write, and besides it had started to rain. At the end of November he went to meet Inga and Einar in Copenhagen.

*

While Halldór was in Barcelona *Footsteps of Men* was published by Þorsteinn M. Jónsson, in Akureyri. Some of the stories had been published previously, and the collection attracted far less attention than the novel about Salka Valka. Benjamín Kristjánsson and Halldór argued in the press about the place of moral preaching and religion in literature. "Does the author make this detour into the rubbish heap simply because it is in the nature of the swine to delight in rooting about in it?" Halldór replied that there was no human subject that was off-limits in good books, and he wanted to prove that Icelandic was a living language that could capture the new reality of modernity. This was the trail he and Þórbergur Þórðarson blazed. But when critics like Benjamín Kristjánsson appeared in respectable places Halldór shuddered. He had staunch supporters, however, and later in December his old friend Sigurður Einarsson wrote in a review of *Footsteps of Men* for the *People's Paper* that Halldór had borne the brunt of a "poisonous and ill-willed attack simply because he was a genius with words".

Halldór used his time in Copenhagen to pursue his publishing interests, and on 3 January informed his mother, to whom he always wrote from abroad, that Hasselbalch had bought both *O Thou Pure Vine* and *The Bird on the Beach*, and that Gunnar Gunnarsson had agreed to translate them into Danish. Another Icelandic writer whose works Hasselbalch published, Kristmann Guðmundsson, arranged to have Halldór invited to his first lunch with his publisher; in *A Poet's Time* Halldór says that a writer enjoyed this honour "when he was in . . . the good graces of the company, one of its favourites". Halldór also gives this excellent description of Steen Hasselbalch, an influential publisher in Denmark in the interwar years:

Steen Hasselbalch was violet in the face with clear eyes, very perky. He was easily recognizable, funny and witty, and had been a military officer. He greeted me with an uppercut, which is a boxing blow beneath the chin, and said, "We are colleagues," meaning that we both had large, protruding chins.

Now the dream that Halldór had mentioned to his mother on his first trip to Copenhagen fourteen years earlier, and that he had worked on steadily with Gunnar's help from the time he came home from North America, had been achieved. A notebook from 1933 contains notes Halldór wrote to himself in Danish, such as answers to interview questions. These clearly show that he had begun work on what was to become his speciality: giving off-the-cuff and unlikely answers to questions in such a way that his answers would be remembered. He wanted to attract attention but not let his interviewer get too close. In that spirit he wrote: "In general I do not read books," and "I have learnt to write from drunken people, the mentally insane and vagrants."

Halldór and Inga had a single room in the apartment that Inga's parents were renting; this suited them, since they were completely broke. But they enjoyed Copenhagen, spending a great deal of time with Jón Helgason and Þórunn, and somehow Halldór always had enough money for a beer in the evening. During the day they sometimes ate at an inexpensive restaurant. With the same ship that took the letter to his mother, Halldór sent the manuscript of *Independent People* or, more precisely, the first part of the first volume, to the Cultural Fund, hoping that he would be paid well for it. But this time the Cultural Fund let him down, pleading lack of financial means. By the end of 1934 the Fund's publishing activities had almost ceased. Halldór asked Erlendur to try to make a deal with Þorsteinn M. Jónsson but it was a young bookseller in Reykjavík, Eggert Briem, who published *Independent People* in the autumn.

After Halldór sent his partial manuscript home, he spent a week in January writing his first play, *Short Circuit* (1934). He had always been interested in the theatre, and in the spring of 1932 he published several reviews in the *People's Paper*, discussing, among other plays, Strindberg's *Miss Julia*:

> This play is of course not suitable for weak or nervous audiences, but it is thus more generous to those who enjoy literature in proportion to the wealth of fate that it contains.

Peter Hallberg has suggested that *Short Circuit* is closely related to *Miss Julia*. The plot is a classic one: people are forced to look their suppressed desires and hidden pasts in the eye when they in the course of a long, stormy night are locked in a fishing hut. The electricity goes off – short circuit – and so the characters are completely isolated. The dramatic effects are excellent, and the dialogue is bold: the playwright clearly had read Freud and Weininger. But the characters aren't quite convincing: they do not gain insight into their own lives, but instead are mouth-pieces for different moral viewpoints.

The Reykjavík Theatre Company previewed the play in November, 1934; it was considered scandalous and the staging daring. It was directed and staged by the Danish thespian Gunnar Hansen. Many people thought it audacious of the company to hire a foreign director, but Halldór had defended the act in a harshly worded article. He thought it was absurd to question Gunnar Hansen's presence: "Are we Icelanders in such a dismal state that we can no longer understand that normal people should want to try their hand here?" But the director himself quickly felt the effects of the small-town mentality, writing home: "They are plotting on all the street corners – my Lord! What can they possibly plot in a little town, platitudinous and abysmal!"

Although another *People's Paper* critic, Ragnar Kvaran, was rather positive about *Short Circuit*, the play was not well attended and was only performed five times. In fact Inga – who had always wanted to act – had rehearsed the part of the young girl during the summer and was supposed to act in the play, but Halldór wanted to return to the Continent and take her with him. The couple were thus far away when the play was previewed, and its author never saw it performed. However, his old friend Erlendur sent him an entertaining review in a letter:

One might say that almost all of what you feared most has indeed occurred. First the staging. I was surprised when the curtain was raised . . . The living room itself made all the descriptions that are given of its jauntiness, its orna-mentation and fragrance, laughable. God be praised that the audience could not smell it. The living room mostly gave the impression of a decent apart-ment rented by a music student. With this the play was localized unnecessarily and the class of people that it describes was made distant. The fishing shack was much better . . . I would prefer not to have to speak of the men. Þorsteinn [Ö. Stephensen] manages to make Vestan absolutely common-place, absolutely dull, asexual. He probably wears Álafoss clothing and has a snuffly voice. His movements are cumbersome, clumsy. At one point in the third act he weaves around looking extremely anguished. I thought of an exhausted, impatient farmer searching for his tobacco box. Indriði [Waage] . . . looked as if he had slept in his clothes for the last fortnight and it was time for him to get his trousers pressed . . . the audience applauded after every act, the curtain was raised three times at the end. But there has been no attendance since then.

Erlendur's letter ends with comments on various financial matters. There seems to have been some sort of difficulty with a bank manager regarding foreign currency, but Erlendur was a prescient man:

I spoke about you as if you owned a business and your books were for export, and suggested that this might turn round and you would import currency to Iceland.

Around mid-February, 1934, after Halldór had finished writing *Short Circuit*, Inga had gone home with Einar. Remaining in Copenhagen, Halldór helped Gunnar Gunnarsson translate *Salka Valka* and worked on the second part of the first volume of *Independent People*, intending to finish the book before the summer. At the end of February he seemed to be doing well. He had meals with Inga's mother, did not go out much except to the cinema (he went, for example, to see *Three Little Pigs* again, so that he could hear "Stormy Weather"), and wrote with all sincerity: "Although I am . . . a bad 'husband' and have an uncontrollable inclination for being free and independent, I quickly become miserable when I am away from you, my dear Inga . . ." As always, he was concerned about his appearance, saying that he had bought himself a hat in the finest shop in Copenhagen: "I don't know how you'll like it, but I find it somewhat dapper, as you women say." Even when Halldór was penniless, he always permitted himself a touch of elegance.

In Copenhagen Halldór wrote a long article about an old friend who had died a year earlier, Stefán from Hvítadalur. The article was both meticulous and inspired, not just because Halldór had known Stefán well, but also because he was writing about the conditions in which Icelandic poets worked and the danger of their being lost to pauperism. Stefán had become a penniless, solitary farmer; his straitened circumstances had left their mark on his psyche: "The eternally fickle currents in the arts world . . . the fiery struggle of life in inconstancy, the fiery struggle that adds fuel to all the timely achievements in the spiritual world – these were to him a closed book." The message was clear: ". . . Icelandic poverty had again managed to cut the fruit from the Icelandic spirit . . . and rob Icelandic literature at the same time of inestimable value." Halldór's own struggle against such a fate paved the way for other Icelandic artists, in fact.

In March Gunnar Gunnarsson and Halldór were engaged in something of a contractual stalemate with Hasselbalch; such things would often prove problematic for Halldór. It was difficult to find good translators, and he sometimes had to give up part of his royalties to pay them. During this time he occasionally met compatriots in Copenhagen; the leader of the Icelandic Communists took him to one of the most elegant restaurants that Halldór had ever seen in that city. He always kept open any political contact that could be of use to him.

*

Halldór returned from Copenhagen in the spring of 1934. Gunnar had finished translating both volumes of *Salka Valka*, and Hasselbalch planned to publish the book in the autumn, as Halldór could tell his countrymen with pride in an interview with the *People's Paper* on 14 April. He still had a significant amount of work to do on the first volume of *Independent People*. For most of the summer the family stayed with Stefán Þorláksson at Reykjahlíð in Mosfellsdalur, where Halldór finished the book and Inga helped with the typing. Stefán, about whom Halldór writes in *A Parish Chronicle* (1970), had recently bought Reykjahlíð, and the two summers that the family spent there were possibly their happiest days. Halldór was more at ease, the first foreign publication of one of his novels was in sight, and he was finishing a masterwork; as with most serious writers, he knew when he had done a good job. Things were fine between him and Inga. He also spent more time with his son than he ever had, frequently taking him swimming.

Inga was fortunate that the greatest living Icelandic actress, Soffía Guðlaugsdóttir, was also staying at Reykjahlíð that summer. Soffía agreed to tutor her, teaching her the fundamentals of acting and helping her with her part in *Short Circuit*.

Halldór wrote several short articles at this time, including one about a poetry collection, *Beautiful World* (1933), written by one of his old friends, Tómas Guðmundsson. Tómas had not followed his friend into political radicalism: a lawyer by profession, and a bourgeois, he worshipped beauty in his poetry. Halldór could never resist beauty in poetry, and so put aside his political yardstick, praising Tómas' handiwork and displaying his own understanding of the arts: "Beauty is an independent element; it is a goal. The struggle is about whether beautiful things are reserved only for the few." But beauty did not necessarily need to be revealed sensitively. Halldór had translated a short story by Ernest Hemingway, "The Light of the World", and had written a short introduction in which he compared Hemingway to Joyce as a master of the contemporary novel who allowed himself to break established rules. Halldór would later translate *A Farewell to Arms* (1929), and if there was one twentieth-century novelist Halldór respected all his life it was Hemingway. In one of his notebooks for *Independent People* he writes that he needs to rework the novel's dialogue in the spirit of Hemingway.

Halldór also wrote about politics. In the summer the *People's Paper* published an article of his entitled "Appreciation Speech" and addressed to "Herr Reichskommissar Doktor Metzner". The German agricultural commissioner had delivered a long speech to Icelandic farmers in the spirit of the "newly awakened German rural culture greeting the ancient Germanic rural culture". This gave Halldór an excellent opportunity to tear into the Germans' racialist programmes. The article was doubtless in the files of the German authorities when they prohibited the publication of Halldór's books several years later.

Halldór also continued to defend the Russian Revolution, with an article published in *Soviet Friends* in the autumn of 1934. Here he raises strenuous objections to reports in *Morgunblaðið* about famine in Russia, and sets the tone for his dealings with that paper for the next twenty years:

> I travelled throughout the Ukraine . . . during the "famine" of 1932. It was a wonderful famine. Wherever one went everything was on the ascent. The collective and state farms were becoming more secure . . . New cities were being built on the plains.

In 1934, Halldór's fiction took precedence over his political articles. His short story "Napoleon Bonaparte", one of his proletarian tales, is based on an account he had heard of a destitute farmer who thought he was Napoleon. When the farmer comes to his senses and starts to count his blessings, it is too late. This same theme became the foundation for the novel *Paradise Reclaimed*. In his articles Halldór continued to preach ideals; in his fiction his focus was humanity.

In the autumn Halldór and Inga travelled overseas so that he could continue writing. All his life he avoided being in Iceland when his books were published. But this time he had other business to attend to. When the couple arrived in Copenhagen at the start of October, Gunnar Gunnarsson and Hasselbalch met them at the harbour, "and then photographs of us were taken for the papers, interviews were held and things of that sort", as Halldór wrote proudly to his mother. *Salka Valka* had been published in Denmark and had received good reviews, although it was hard to say how well it was selling. Although he did not say that he was happy, he must have been, and he also was thinking about his daughter; he tells his mother that he has asked Erlendur to collect the 200 krónur that he is to receive for *Short Circuit* "and have it signed over to you to give to little María".

Banquets were held for days after Halldór's arrival in Copenhagen. In *A Poet's Time* he says that his first foreign publisher had been a munificent entertainer who frequently had his parties photographed for the newspapers. He lived in a huge palace and all Denmark's smart set went there:

Financiers, editors, industrialists, chic doctors and women jockeys in jodh-
purs, and the writers were invited to dance with them, including the bestseller
Korch, who in Copenhagen itself was the most despised Danish writer, his
books reviewed not even once in the major newspapers; he was a pleasant
and happy old man and certainly a greater man than those who looked down
on him.

When Halldór secluded himself on Amager to write, Inga used the opportunity
to visit relatives in London. Working on the second part of *Independent People*, he
thought he would finish it within the next year, although progress was slow. At the
same time he continued his correspondence with foreign publishers: he wrote
to Stanley Unwin in London, contacted an agent in Stockholm, wanted to go to
Leipzig to meet Kippenberg and to Paris to meet the French translator Jolivet. It
was clear to Halldór what he needed to do in order to reach the world with his
stories. Many years later he often claimed that publishers had first made contact
with him, but in fact it was quite the opposite during those years; his first foreign
publications were the result of his own tireless efforts.

Halldór wrote to Inga from Amager on 18 October, enclosing a letter that
Kristinn E. Andrésson, who had taken over Halldór and Inga's apartment on
Laufásvegur, had sent him:

I rushed out and got married . . . Tell Inga that nothing happens in the
kitchen because our poverty is so great that we do not even make coffee
there except during holidays . . . I cannot get any work, the radio is uncertain, substitute teaching is my only hope.

These comments say something about the position of Communist intellectuals
in Iceland in the 1930s. As the historian Þór Whitehead puts it:

It is doubtful whether anyone joined the Party for his own private interests.
The members had been voluntarily made into something like exiles from the
country in which they nevertheless had to live.

But the situation also says something about Icelandic society: Kristinn was
staying at the home of a Supreme Court judge and former leader of the
Independence Party, and while there he and others prepared a "Soviet Exhibition":

There were often about twenty people working at gluing pictures to placards, writing explanatory texts and drawing up diagrams – it could get quite
crowded there in the hall and on the stairs . . .

Halldór and Inga had discussed Halldór's travelling to the Soviet Union from Denmark, but he decided against it: "I am certain that I would not have endured an eight–ten-day train trip now, least of all in a half-civilized country like Russia." Inga returned from London at the end of October and they continued southwards together, through Germany to Rome, stopping in Innsbruck. Around mid-November Halldór wrote to Jón Helgason to say that they had arrived in Italy, happy to be free of the Icelandic winter:

> Otherwise my work has gone decently these past few days, as it always does on my trips, and yet went best today, our first day in Rome – it makes a differ-ence to work in a room full of sunshine, with both windows open. Inga has never seen such a beautiful city as Rome, and we both say: Here I would like to spend the rest of my days etc., whether that sentiment lasts longer than a week or not.

In the meantime a great deal of work was being done on Halldór's behalf in Iceland. As the chairman of the Alþingi's grants committee, Jónas from Hrifla made sure that Halldór's grant was doubled to 5,000 krónur per year. The proposal was approved after intense debate. The grant lightened Halldór's load considerably; although it was not exactly a high annual salary, it was more than a worker earned in a year. From Italy he wrote to his mother:

> . . . this is the first time that I have ever felt that I need not have fears for the next day. For so long I have had to press on without being certain that I could provide for myself.

And there was more good news. The first part of *Independent People* was published at the end of October, and was one of the year's bestselling books. *Morgunblaðið* did not hold back: "Halldór makes such remarkable advances with every book that he writes that it is astounding." Helgi Hjörvar wrote about Halldór's narrative art and stylistic genius in the *People's Paper*, and *Iðunn* and *Eimreiðin* published long and favourable reviews. In *Lögberg* there were traces of the tone that would be struck in many more places after the remainder of the work was published. There Hjálmar Gíslason said that the novel was "more bereft of beauty, less virtuous, and more inhuman than human life itself".

In *Independent People* Halldór does not paint a beautiful picture of life in the coun-tryside, but his identification with his characters and their fates is evident throughout the work. He had impressed this upon himself many times. "Make all the characters more sympathetic than they are in this draft," he wrote in the margin, and the same exhortation can be read in his notebooks. He reminds himself never to forget "for one second the feeling of sympathy with everything that exists". Halldór wanted to fight Knut Hamsun's pastoral romanticism and create a different image of the Icelandic countryside from Gunnar Gunnarsson's; he also wanted to popularize his vision of society, but knew that the trick would be to awaken sympathy for the characters in his savage story with its rugged setting.

The struggle continued in Italy, where he and Inga spent most of December. They enjoyed Rome, where they saw Marie Dinesen, a Danish woman who ran hotels there for more than half a century; Halldór stayed most often with her during his later trips, and they became good friends. Inga also had acquaintances in the city. Throughout the remainder of his life Rome was Halldór's favourite city, and some of his later books were written there.

Halldór's publishing affairs continued to proceed slowly, and at the start of December he informed Jón Helgason that he had agreed a contract for *Salka Valka* with a highly respected publishing house, Allen & Unwin, in London. Shortly before Christmas he and Inga travelled to Positano, a short distance from Naples. Inga wrote a magazine article describing the journey and the places they stayed, although she did not say much about their financial situation. Halldór wrote to Jón in Copenhagen on the day after Christmas:

> For the moment we are far from the much-esteemed civilization, in a kind of little medieval pirates' den, full of peculiar architectural pieces, hanging here on a sheer mountain slope on the Sorrento River.

He was shocked at the poverty in a place where the sunshine was the one blessing the inhabitants enjoyed, and felt that little had changed in Italy in the preceding nine years, "except for how the nonsense coming from Mussolini's mouth has increased by leaps and bounds". Jón appears to have berated Halldór for his poor grammar in *Short Circuit*, and Halldór replied that he could well believe it. It would have been much better if he had seen the proofs: "Usually geniality comes over me at the third proofreading." But Halldór also says that Inga is bored; she was a socialite and found the trip rather dull. Halldór spent most of his time sitting on the balcony writing, and some of the most poignant descriptions of snowsqualls and rough weather in all Icelandic literature came into existence in the serene winter heat of Southern Italy.

From Positano Halldór and Inga returned to Rome, where he knocked on the doors of Italian publishers, and from there their path led back to the Mediterranean, where they visited Monte Carlo and Nice. This was the arrangement Halldór had wanted when he was in Barcelona: to be in Southern Europe with Inga during the winter; he would write and she would be there to assist him and keep his spirits up but at the same time would not disturb him when he needed to be alone. Of course this was easier said than done. It was often difficult to be near Halldór when he was writing. He admitted in his letters that he was both hypochondriacal and nervous, as he put it, and irritable to boot. Inga gave up for the time being and went to Paris. She had hardly left before Halldór wrote a letter of longing:

> I have been thinking that I may have driven you away from me, because of how poorly I have treated you, and I feel badly because of it; yes, that is my ugly, weak disposition, my dear Inga.

Halldór is not the first writer to have had difficulty harmonizing his creative career and his everyday existence in a bourgeois society. Multifarious, sometimes even intolerable tensions and bad feelings can arise. It was not until much later that Halldór came up with the pattern that might be termed a peaceful cohabitation of the poet and the everyday man.

With his work on *Independent People* going well, however, he asked Inga to forgive his poor behaviour and met her in Paris. They travelled home to Iceland in February, 1935. The trip had taken its toll financially, so Halldór shook the dust off an old short story, as he told Jón Helgason:

> The other day we uncovered an old short story of mine, the one that I always considered my best; it was found in the rubbish that was going to be thrown out of Unuhús, and had become hard to read. I brushed it up a bit and gave it to Eggert Briem as payment for my debt.

The story, published under the title "Mirrors" in the journal *Contemporary Times*, in later editions has the title "Phantom from the Deep". This is a snapshot from Taormina, based on a story that Halldór's friend Richard Becker had told him, about the love of a man for a young girl upon whom he is spying. The story's strong sexual undertones and background show that it belongs to Halldór's *Great Weaver* period; he had in fact sent it to Erlendur from Sicily ten years earlier.

*

For the next five years Halldór was more actively engaged in political debates than at any other time in his career, with the exception of the period following the Second World War when he joined in the opposition to the establishment of a foreign military base in Iceland. He wrote numerous articles and delivered speeches and lectures in the service of the left. He supported all the activities of the

Communist Party, without, however, joining it formally. Halldór's presence at home was felt keenly by the readers of the *People's Paper* when it printed an article of his concerning Steinn Steinarr's writer's grant on 3 March, 1935. Steinn had just published his first book of poetry, *The Red Flame Burned*, and Halldór wrote favourably of the book. About one poem he said: "The man who has seen this sight has come to possess the most precious gift: the longing for beauty, but not just for beauty itself, but also for justice." For the remainder of the twentieth century Steinn was the poet Halldór regarded most highly. In the article he tells of how this destitute boy had tried to get a writer's grant, but had been denied. And on the day when the grants were announced, he had been sentenced to two months in prison for having been one of a group of young men who had, two years earlier, taken down a Nazi flag and torn it to pieces.

It was Halldór's hope that the Communists and the Social Democrats would join with liberal democratic powers in opposing fascism. This policy, originated by the Communist International in Moscow in 1934, marked a distinct shift in policy from 1928–33, when cooperation with the Social Democrats was considered impossible.

Halldór had been living abroad during the most intense period of internal Party struggles. It is easy to imagine that this new popular-front movement was more appealing to him than the earlier leftist movement, and that spring he unexpectedly became an influential participant in the struggle of the left for the leadership of the labour movement. The Social Democrats were understandably doubtful about Communism and were wary of the popular front, but both parties wanted, to display their pride in the writer Halldór Laxness. Because of this he was asked to read at meetings commemorating May Day: at the meeting of the Social Democrats on the day itself, and at that of the Communists on 30 April. It is clear from a description of the events published in the *People's Paper* on 3 May that he had been in something of a bind, but he seemed to have promised to read the same story to both parties ("And the Lotus Blossom Smells So Sweet"). The Communists wanted to hold a popular-front march on 1 May, but the Social Democrats did not. In the *Workers' Paper* on 29 April Halldór declared his support for the march, but all the same his comrades were not pleased that he would be reading at a meeting of the Social Democrats that same day.

Halldór tried to help himself out of trouble by writing a new story, "Lame Old Þórður", which he read without prior announcement at a meeting of the workers' unions held by the Social Democrats on 1 May. This is the only short story of Halldór's that can be categorized as purely political. It tells of a peaceful old worker who does not want to have anything to do with the Bolsheviks, but is forced to take part in the fight of 9 November, 1932. The Gúttó Fight, with its legendary significance for the labour movement, is used for the first time as a symbol of a united workers' front opposed to so-called reactionary forces. The struggle for control of the movement was also the struggle for control of its legends. The Social Democrats got Halldór's message loud and clear, even before he had finished his reading. As he described it twenty years later:

> There must not have been many workers enjoying themselves there, since the leader, Jón Pétursson, came up on stage and ordered the reading to be stopped, and then he himself finished the story, using some well-chosen words about its writer, guaranteeing for himself at the same time a special place in the history of Icelandic literature, though a small one.

It was of course clear to Halldór that those holding the meeting would see his story as a threat, but the matter was not that simple in fact. The brother of Jón Axel Pétursson, Pétur, was present at the event:

> That was one of the most memorable readings I have ever attended, and it is actually a unique event in the history of Icelandic literature, because the writer was not allowed to finish his story. The leader of the Federation of Labour Unions, Jón Axel Pétursson, stopped the young revolutionary writer with the message of the popular front on his lips and said: "Now you will stop and I will take over." I was sitting on a bench with others towards the back of the room. Several members of the audience stood up. I recognized some of them, including Erlendur from Unuhús.
>
> They followed Halldór Kiljan to the door and out, saying some offensive things at the same time, and went to . . . the Communists' meeting. This event . . . sparked a long-running argument.

Kristinn E. Andrésson was present at the Communists' meeting when Halldór arrived:

> There's no need to describe the reception he got, the joy we felt at his joining us. Halldór sat with us for a while and then went up to Unuhús, and a large group followed him singing revolutionary songs, and the weather was beautiful, spring was in the air, and when they arrived at Unuhús there was a fourfold shout of hurrah for the poetic hero.

Needless to say, events of that night were interpreted differently by different parties. The *People's Paper* published a long article about Halldór's "unartistic slandering of the Social Democrats". The article concluded:

> With his appearance yesterday evening Halldór Kiljan Laxness has in the eyes of the overwhelming majority of the working class in the country placed an ineradicable stain on his honour as a writer.

The Communists felt that they had won a great victory, and the Union of Radical Students sponsored a meeting at which Kristinn E. Andrésson lectured about the event and Halldór reread his story. "At the conclusion of the reading the cheers of joy would not cease," said the *Workers' Paper*.

"Lame Old Þórður" was published later in a booklet that sold extremely well. Perhaps the most entertaining witness to these events is Halldór himself, in a letter to Jón Helgason written on 7 May:

> There has been somewhat of a tumult here at home recently, from which I have profited in the main, although others have experienced it as a tragedy. I send you now a little book in which the main event is told in small letters and footnotes. This book has had the most luck of all my books; I wrote it in precisely two hours, and on the same evening that it was written it became famous throughout the country, although no-one had heard it all the way through. I have earned almost twice as much from it than from all the stories in *Footsteps of Men*, which took many years to write. The market is capricious.

Thus are political legends born.

When it came to his career as a writer Halldór waged his own party struggle. On that same eventful day, 1 May, 1935, an article of his was published in *Tíminn*, entitled "Jónas Jónsson and the *Beaux Arts*" to commemorate the fiftieth birthday of Jónas from Hrifla. Halldór praised Jónas highly, particularly for the establishment of the Cultural Fund which is remarkable in the light of their later dealings – before a year had passed Jónas would write a series of articles against *Independent People*.

Yet there was a hitch: Jónas, like most other Icelandic politicians at the time, had little concern for what would now be called the abuse of authority. Whoever had power could without any hesitation apply it in the service of what he believed and in support of the men whose causes he admired. At the same time the government's leaders could "rightfully" withdraw their support from people of whom they did not approve. It was this situation that would cause a complete disintegration of the friendship between Jónas and Halldór several years later.

Throughout his life Halldór was a determined spokesman for public support of artists, but he had no enthusiasm at all for the government telling artists what to produce. Some of the government's policies did not appeal to him, such as granting Gunnar Gunnarsson and Guðmundur Kamban honorary professorships, most likely conceiving of them as the equivalent of an honorary doctorate today. Halldór said in an interview with the *People's Paper*: "To call a working poet a 'professor' is in my eyes as logical as calling him, for example, a ship's captain or a priest."

*

Halldór and Inga spent the summer back in Reykjahlíð and at Laugarvatn, while he worked on completing the second part of *Independent People*. After the book had gone to the printers, he went to London to talk to Stanley Unwin and a translator by the name of Lyon about *Salka*. When Halldór went over the English translation, which was made from the Danish, the problem that accompanies many translations became more apparent to him, as he tells Inga in a letter:

> The translation is solid and even-handed, but is very simplistic . . . 50 per cent of my style has disappeared, a huge amount lost, whatever was most entertaining. But there is nothing that can be done about this – this is a translation from another translation. If the book were to be translated from Icelandic it would have to be completely redone, but I have to content myself with correcting the translational errors in the manuscript and letting the fates decide whether the volume and the structure hold the work up in the English world, in place of the style, which is such a fundamentally important part of the work in Icelandic.

For a long time Halldór had to content himself with the fact that translations outside Denmark were made from the Danish, sometimes the German – and there was always a danger that much would be lost.

From London Halldór went to Copenhagen. Gunnar Gunnarsson could not take on any more translation work for the time being, and Halldór was proud when Hasselbalch and his main adviser, Arne Stevns, praised his Danish and asked whether he could not translate *Independent People* himself. But it would have taken far too much time and energy to do this, with the result that a young Icelandic scholar resident in Copenhagen, Jakob Benediktsson, was given the task. Halldór went over the translation and felt that it was rather good.

At the end of September Halldór's proofreading was completed and Inga joined him in Copenhagen, where they stayed throughout the autumn, probably at Goldsmith's House in Nyhavn, which Inga discusses in her biography. The house had been occupied by a goldsmith, but was now a hotel; they had a room up in the attic. Halldór had started to conceive the story of Jón Hreggviðsson that would later become *Iceland's Bell*. Jón Helgason had first told him this story of an Icelandic failure in 1924, and from time to time Halldór would ask Jón to send him advice and information. Halldór would use Goldsmith's House in the final volume of *Iceland's Bell*, making it the setting for the last meeting between Snæfríður and Arnas Arnæus. But Inga did not enjoy being there:

> . . . Almighty God, the surroundings were so horrible. I dared not step outside the house alone after it grew dark, with bars all around and that pack of madmen, prostitutes, bums and robbers. But when Halldór finished his reading we would go together to the bars, and that was alright.

More than anything else, Halldór was in Copenhagen to relax. He and Inga spent a lot of time with Jón and Þórunn, and he and Jón went together to listen to lectures by Bertrand Russell. "It was a huge event for me," he wrote to Erlendur, though unfortunately he gives no details. He went to concerts, heard Elisabeth Schumann sing and Igor Stravinsky play his music. The first part of *Independent People* was published in Danish at the beginning of October, and Halldór spoke to reporters and attended banquets with Hasselbalch; apart from this he worked on writing articles. He had started to create a name for himself in Denmark and met a number of writers and intellectuals there. Besides Martin Andersen Nexø he met, for example, the poet Paul la Cour, an adviser at Gyldendal who played a part in Halldór's moving there after several years with Hasselbalch; he also met the novelist and critic Tom Kristensen, who later wrote an essay about him. As the 1930s went on Halldór also spent time with the greatest Communist writers, such as Hans Kirk.

Halldór also paid fairly close attention to Danish literature in the 1930s. Indicative of this is a letter he sent to the writer Harald Herdal, who had been subjected to criticism for his novel *Onion* (1935), which was considered frank on sexual matters. Halldór encouraged Herdal, praised him for his sincerity and said:

> But we live in a hypocritical democratic society, in which it is disgraceful to speak directly about the sexual needs of youth – and the sexual hunger that is caused by this type of society – as disgraceful as it would be to say anything about a shortage of fat under the rule of the fascists.

Halldór exhorted Herdal to do great deeds and at the same time advised him not to fall into the trap of being too one-sided in his novels.

At the end of October 1935, while Halldór was in Denmark, the second part of *Independent People* was published in Reykjavík. Now the reviewers could discuss the work in its entirety. Halldór's genius as a writer was apparent to most of them, but not all the reviews contained only praise, as those of the first volume might be said to have done. Fierce debates arose early in 1936 and continued until the next year. Halldór had made his reckoning with Icelandic rural culture, its self-image and legends. He should have expected adversaries.

The subtitle of *Independent People* in its first edition was *A Heroic Tale*, and it was no secret to its readers that the words were used ironically. Bjartur is a hero but his heroism has tragic consequences, because he is devoted to ideals that are not in accord with reality. His ideals are in this way similar to those of Don Quixote, but the consequences of his persistence and stubbornness harm not only him, but also those closest to him. This may explain why *Independent People*, of all Halldór's great novels, delivers a clear message: the era of the independent farmer in Iceland has come to an end, and Icelandic rural culture is nothing but an illusion: "Bjartur of Summerhouses' story is the story of a man who sowed his enemy's field all his life, day and night." As source material Halldór used news items, folk tales, poems and events he had witnessed or heard about. He tore down the fences of reality with exaggerations and touches of the supernatural when it suited him. The narrative joy touched his readers, the unforgettable observations, the sharp humour, the thorough character delineations.

In contrast to Bjartur, Halldór created Ásta Sóllilja, through whom he wanted to express the book's underlying theme of sympathy. Ásta's brother Nonni, on witnessing her breakdown

> felt and suffered with her. In the years that were to come he relived this
> memory in song, in the most beautiful song the world had known. For the
> understanding of the soul's defencelessness, of the conflict between the two
> poles, is not the source of the greatest song. The source of the greatest song
> is sympathy.

The relationship between Bjartur and Ásta Sóllilja is complicated: she is his foster-daughter, and although he loves her he baulks at taking advantage of her when she cuddles up to him in the hotel on their trip to town. He touches her just for a moment:

> She had never known anything like it. All her fear was suddenly gone. The
> shiver that now passed through her body and soul was of a kind altogether
> different from the cold shivering that had kept her awake all night . . .

Nothing, nothing must ever separate them again. She gripped his body fiercely and passionately in the intoxication of this impersonal, importunate selfishness that in an instant had wiped everything from her memory.

Then Bjartur pushes her away, puts on his clothes and rushes out. Halldór accomplishes what he had planned, according to his notebooks, that is, to make Bjartur's love of the girl both beautiful and tragic.

Everything is changed in this version of the novel by the introduction of Ásta Sóllilja and her point of view. Halldór's sensitivity to the character of Ásta also applies to sexual matters, as can be seen in his treatment of her reaction the morning after the teacher has taken advantage of her. Halldór's understanding does not come from having read psychology, not even Freud and his disciples. It is poetic insight, coupled with an ability to store up the fates of others inside himself. It was Halldór's habit to ask the women he met searching questions about their thoughts and feelings.

In *Independent People* Halldór wanted to set his sights on the highest peaks of literature, writing in direct opposition to the pastoral novel *Growth of the Soil* by Knut Hamsun.

"Hamsun's Last Book" was the title of a lengthy article written by Halldór and published in *Morgunblaðið* on 15 September, 1921. In 1920 the Norwegian Knut Hamsun had received the Nobel Prize for Literature, not least for *Growth of the Soil.* Here Halldór was writing about Hamsun's newest novel, *The Women at the Pump* (1920), and admitted the Norwegian's stylistic genius without hesitation, but said that the book had the "flavour of unparalleled contempt for mankind, which breathes over us everywhere through his characters".

This article is Halldór's first declaration concerning the role of literature, emphasizing its ethical aims, and his view of Hamsun was to remain ambivalent. In *Independent People* he travels the paths that Hamsun marked out in *Growth of the Soil,* with comparable characters and events but with contrary conclusions. In the epilogue to the second edition of *Independent People,* Halldór wrote:

It has been suggested that *Independent People* was written partly in imitation of Hamsun's *Growth of the Soil.* That is correct in the sense that I ask the same questions . . . although the answers I give are of course completely contrary to Hamsun's. I am not saying that all the conclusions concerning society – or anything else – in *Independent People* are correct, but their place in the composition of the book was dependent on my conviction that Hamsun's conclusions . . . were, in general, wrong.

Later, in his memoirs, Halldór remains respectful of Hamsun's style and narrative methods, but his basic stance has not changed:

> I felt that a writer who mocked old people and wretches was no artist, no matter how well he could write, and this is what Hamsun did whenever he had the opportunity.

Knut Hamsun was much older than Halldór; nevertheless these two were the greatest masters of Scandinavian literature for half a century. They never met.

Just as Halldór used one of the most famous contemporary novels as a frame of reference, he chose, as Vésteinn Ólason has pointed out, the form of classical tragedy and divided the work into five parts, with a conclusion. At the end of each part Bjartur loses something that means a great deal to him. In the end the reader sees him returning to the heath with his daughter dying in his arms. This scene is reminiscent of Einar Jónsson's sculpture, "The Outlaw", which had a strong effect on Halldór when he was young; it is also reminiscent of *King Lear*.

With *Independent People* Halldór accomplished his goal of letting an Icelandic setting symbolize the world. *Independent People* has been translated into twenty-nine languages, and with *Atom Station*, is his most popular book. Most nations are familiar with the stage when private farming under straitened conditions is made obsolete. And it is one of *Independent People*'s strengths that the setting of the heath represents the boundary-line between civilization and wilderness. In fact, the harshness of life in the Icelandic countryside, considering the time when the novel was written, was exaggerated, and would certainly have inspired a reaction. But in the end Bjartur's longevity depends precisely on his heroic struggle on this boundary.

In this book the modernist Halldór created an unforgettable image of a man who refused to enter the modern world. Several years later he expressed this idea in *The Russian Adventure*:

> The abnormal growth of personality has its paradise in half-civilized countries . . . In countries where civilization is widespread and relatively evenly distributed, often at the expense of culture, hypertrophic personalities become rare, causing the public to look involuntarily upon such personalities as insane and frightening. Civilization does not have room for the hysterical, bigoted emphasis that individuals in a small society place on their personalities, words and deeds.

Here can be seen a fundamental difference between Halldór's work and Hamsun's. They both write stories about strong men, heroes, who forsake civilization. But Hamsun is pessimistic about culture and society, and thus the main mood of *Growth of the Soil* is comedic. Halldór, on the other hand, is optimistic about the possibilities of human life, and thus writes a tragedy.

Many positive reviews appeared, but not everyone was pleased with the novel's language, and in an article in the *People's Paper* the poet and farmer Sigurjón Friðjónsson commented on the roughness and incongruity of the novel's style. The censures of the work's idealism were more serious, however. Dr Snorri Halldórsson published an article in *Morgunblaðið*, saying that the book had been written in support of Communism, and sharply criticized Halldór's image of Icelandic rural culture. Although he expressed his admiration for the work's poetic genius, he felt that Halldór's descriptions of the misery and squalor of the countryside were far from the realities of the modern world and could, what's more, do harm to Icelanders' reputation abroad. For a long time this became the refrain in public and private discussions.

No-one doubted that the leader of Iceland's farmers would speak up, and this is precisely what Jónas from Hrifla did, with his remarkable series of articles, "Folk in Tatters", the first of which was published in the *New Daily* in February, 1936, as well as in *Tíminn*. Jónas was often blamed for his harsh attacks on Halldór, since most felt that it was Jónas himself who had raised Halldór to honour and glory. Therefore one must keep in mind that in fact Jónas lauded Halldór's abilities, and praised *Salka Valka* and much in *Independent People*. Jónas was fond of the character of Bjartur, much of which derived from Jónas' own ideas:

> Bjartur is courageous, but is a massively exaggerated and distorted image of the Icelandic farmer as the struggle for existence shaped him in former centuries. The novel's central topic is of course splendid, but the working method of the writer, to blend exaggerated and often disgusting characteristics, gives the entire story of Bjartur a peculiar feel.

It is precisely this disgusting quality that Jónas rejects so strongly: "Because of this the nation feels that this genius writer, who spends so much time raising old and lost banners of oppression and debasement, is working against his own people."

There are always problems when political authorities write reviews. Jónas' review boiled down to a command that the writer learn to accept his countrymen and see the beauty in their achievements.

By this time Halldór had learnt that it was not sensible for a writer to respond to reviews and try to explain his work to insensitive readers, so others took in the task. Kristinn E. Andrésson saw the weaknesses in Jónas' literary analyses, and connected them to his political blindness in a sharp rebuttal, "The Madam of Rauðsmýri Speaks Out", published in the *Workers' Paper*. But in a certain way it was inevitable that the old rural culture and the politicians who supported its image would turn against *Independent People*. A year later, one of its best-known representatives, Guðmundur Friðjónsson, took up where Jónas had left off and published an entire booklet, *The Barbarism of the Countryside in the Mirror of the Writer from Laxnes*.

Reactions to the book had not yet been made public when Halldór and Inga returned from Copenhagen in November, 1935. Halldór was in the mood for a fight, as was clearly shown on 1 December, when he was asked to be the main speaker at the celebration of the anniversary of Iceland's sovereignty. The speech was delivered from the balcony of the Parliament Building and broadcast as well; it was no daily occurrence for radicals to be aired on Icelandic National Radio. Halldór seized the opportunity to preach the gospel of the popular front, using as the basis for his speech the Icelanders' age-old struggle for independence and freedom, but saying that although sovereignty had been achieved it was a long way to economic freedom. Like a true political leader with the rhetorical arts at his fingertips, he said:

> Now the struggle for the freedom of the Icelandic people is at its peak: Icelandic men, Icelandic women, join the struggle today, keep this day of your independence and freedom holy by joining the ranks of the people's front, the alliance of all those powers that have some small piece of the cause of the people on their agenda, the union of all the spiritual and physical working men of all parties against the foreign and domestic powers of oppression in the image of capitalism, financial capital, this most horrid enemy of the living and fighting man on earth, which moreover in these days seeks to lay its claws upon our land, upon every single living breast.

That Halldór's political position was clear was doubtless one reason why reactions to his books were often strong. The other was that those who had the ability to estimate language, no matter what party they belonged to, saw that in him they had a world-class writer; people wanted to fight for and against him at the same time.

Red Pens and Other Pens

> There is no literature against freedom, because there is no
> literature against the spirit.

Jules Romains

In December, 1935, the first volume of the annual *Red Pens* was published under the auspices of the Union of Revolutionary Writers; its editor was Kristinn E. Andrésson. Left-leaning writers had a good showcase in *Iðunn* as well as in the journal dedicated to national affairs, *Réttur*, which was controlled by the Communists. It was a matter of urgency to its founders that *Red Pens* be brought out in 1935 to connect it with the centenary of *Fjölnir*, the journal of the romantic pioneers, which in many minds marked the renaissance of Icelandic culture. Along with the struggle for the popular front, nationalism had again been in the ascendancy within the Communist movement, following similar developments in the Soviet Union.

Many well-known Icelandic writers published material in *Red Pens'* inaugural issue. Foremost among them were Halldór Laxness and Þórbergur Þórðarson, although their ranks also included Halldór Stefánsson, Jón from Vör, Gunnar Benediktsson, Örn Arnarson, Steinn Steinarr, Ólafur Jóhann Sigurðsson and Jóhannes from Katlar. Most of these were young men from the countryside who felt that they were living in a magnificent new era, in which even poor farmers' sons on an isolated island could participate in a powerful worldwide movement, as if they were, in the words of Kristinn E. Andrésson, "growing up in an age of idealism, the old dreams of freedom of the colonial nation coming true, bright hopes ahead". The passion and devotedness that characterized the literary movement in Iceland during its first years cannot otherwise be explained. Writers held up burning candles of idealism, even if these writers were later to become lost in the dark wood of Stalinism.

The literary sensibility displayed in the first volume of *Red Pens* is uniform, and nearly all of the writers that the journal introduced were loyal Communists. There were works by Anna Seghers, Alexander Fadeyev, Ernst Toller, Nordahl Grieg, Maxim Gorky and Bertolt Brecht, even a translation from *The Good Soldier Svejk* (1923) by Jaroslav Hašek. Kristinn contributed a long introductory article about the new literary movement, which, although it remained without strict definition, was said to be based on the revolutionary movement of the working class.

Halldór published four articles in the first issue of *Red Pens*, most of which he had written in Copenhagen in the autumn. They show that he was trying to harmonize his political position with his artistic insights, which were much more versatile than socialist realism, the precept of the day among the Communists. He was of course not always in harmony with himself, and made a number of hasty judgements, but tried to legitimize art that was not highly regarded by the puritans in the Soviet Union. For example, he wrote in "The Chosen and the People" about two famous Russians: "They are of course both counter-revolutionaries, but never-theless are among the greatest geniuses in the world: Rachmaninov and Stravinsky."

Two themes were particularly evident. He felt that it mattered most that people received the education and obtained the standard of living that made it possible for them to enjoy the arts; they could not be limited to the chosen few. And he felt that artists should find the core of their creativity among the people, and should not seek the role of outsider, as many bourgeois artists did.

Thus in an article on folk music Halldór encouraged composers to find material in Iceland's folk heritage, instead of imitating foreign composers. In "Modern Bourgeois Literature" he criticized what he called the analytical novel:

With this method the writer does not try to build from the material that he has in front of him, but rather tries to analyze and criticize it, to conceal it, and never set his eyes again on any edifying central power

He admits that this movement had begotten some true masterpieces, such as Mann's *The Magic Mountain*, but says that all such works are characterized by pessimism and desperation.

In this context it is interesting to note how little Halldór cared for the new book by Karen Blixen (Isak Dinesen), *Seven Gothic Tales* (1934). According to him, it was merely another representation of the frequently reawakened ghosts of Boccaccio and chivalric romance: "It works on me like a spruced-up American corpse, to which is applied make-up, powder, and lipstick, and which is then clad in a suit and put on display on a bier." It is unlikely that Karen Blixen ever saw this article, because later she paid homage to Halldór. Another work received the same treatment: *Point Counter Point* (1928) by Aldous Huxley, which he called redundant parlour twaddle. He summarizes his understanding of modern bourgeois literature as follows:

This is the refuge of the bourgeois in modern literature: to drag oneself away from the life of the living and settle down in a foul mood on some "cruise ship" (or sanatorium, or sitting room), stare down at one's navel and fuss over the uselessness of it all; and wait for the ship to sink. All connections with the life of the people are cut, and at the same time all the moral foundations of life are lost. What is left is painful ennui, which leads to hatred of life.

What had become of the staunch advocate of modern literature? It is likely that Halldór's admiration of avant-gardism during the 1920s was simply that: admiration. The storyteller was always his strongest part; epic narratives with clear and wide views were closest to his heart. When Halldór decided to return home and become a storyteller for his people, he parted company with the avant-garde, and in this the nature of Icelandic society played a part. For most creative artists of the non-European world at that time, as the historian Eric Hobsbawm says, "the major task seemed to be to discover, to lift the veil from, and to present the contemporary reality of their peoples. Realism was their movement." This suggests that artists belonging to societies that were not as developed as those in Western Europe were frequently more traditional in their work.

From this point of view contemporary literature and realism were not adversaries. Halldór always wanted to be modern: he did not want to compose his songs using old fashioned harmonies; he was a man of meaning and context, not of analysis and emptiness. He never viewed himself as a realist in the strictest sense: plainness was far from him, but "art for art's sake" was also not his motto. And, as we have seen, one of the things that protected his art from proclaiming a kind of simplistic socialist message was that he always saw beauty as an independent element, and writing as the guide towards its higher world.

Nowhere was this more evident than in his next great work, *World Light*. It was no accident that the subject Halldór chose after the girl in the fishing village and the farmer on the heath was the poet in the world. Somewhere deep in his heart doubts stirred about *Red Pens*; in a notebook that mainly contains comments for the first volume of *World Light* he wrote the following: "Critique of R.P.: propaganda on the primitive level . . . meaningless." Four issues of *Red Pens* were published, but the other three did not contain as much of his material as did the first one.

Halldór wrote the initial part of the *World Light* trilogy in 1936, although this part was not published until early in 1937. The year 1936 was a very productive one: Halldór took several long trips and wrote a large number of articles, starting in January with a series for the *People's Paper*, "Several Cultural Phenomena". These were written in the spirit of the articles on the Icelandic cultural spirit that he had written in Sicily, although their tone was more political. Halldór was civilizing his people at the same time that he was advancing his own position. He wrote about Icelanders' alcoholism in the context of the police being called to twenty-two homes in Reykjavík on New Year's Eve. Throughout his life Halldór regretted the fact that Icelanders could not enjoy wine and beer like cultured people to the south. He also wrote about the disquietude among Reykjavík teenagers, a classic topic of concern.

The longest articles, and those that elicited responses and then replies from the writer, were on so-called spiritual investigations and mediums. Halldór found little more despicable than this craze; worst of all was that respected colleagues such as Einar H. Kvaran and Jakob J. Smári had jumped on the spiritualism bandwagon. In opposition, Halldór appealed to the tenets of Freud and Pavlov. The former Catholic considered discussions of the afterlife almost nonsensical. In a rebuke to Jakob Smári he wrote:

> . . . it has never crossed my mind . . . to deny the existence of "life after death". . . The afterlife could very well exist. And it may well be that there is no such thing . . . I have no idea one way or the other . . .

Halldór reached a new level in his career in Februrary when *Salka Valka* was published in England. The *Evening Standard* chose it as its Book of the Month, publishing a glowing review: "No beauty is allowed to exist as ornamentation in its own right in these pages; but the work is replete from cover to cover with the beauty of perfection." Such reviews were proof to Halldór that his struggles abroad were achieving results.

In the latter part of May Halldór took one of his trips to remote parts of Iceland to find new material and vision, although as usual he would have to go to Southern Europe to work these things into shape. He tells of his meandering journey in *A Poet's Time*: first he sailed to Stapi on Snaefellsnes, then stayed for several days on Hamrendar in Breiðuvík, and from there crossed the mountains to Ólafsvík to visit Jóhann Jónsson's mother:

> She was like a woman I had known but who had died a long time ago and now appeared to me in a dream: for some reason we had no point of contact. She did not know who I was, and in fact I did not know who she was, but she gave me coffee, and we looked at each other – in silence.

The situation is similar to Ólafur Kárason's meeting with his mother in *World Light*; in fact the first draft of the first volume of *World Light* was written at Hamrendar. Halldór thought the conditions in Ólafsvík incredibly poor and used the village as a model for Sviðinsvík in *World Light*.

In the spring he continued with his political dealings, concentrating on the struggle for the popular front. The Society of Radical Students invited him to write an article for its paper, publishing "Popular Front is the People's Cause" on its front page at the end of April. According to Halldór the next Conservative government would inevitably resort to fascist methods, such as increasing the numbers of state police and doing away with the right to strike:

> The workers can feel this coming, and the intellectuals can also see where things are heading. The entire nation can clearly see the pressing need for the unification of the left into one popular front against the capitalists, Conservatism and impending fascism.

An interview with Halldór was published in the *Red Flag*, the organ of the Young Communists at that time. That paper was also the first to publish "The Final April", which became the most popular of his poems under the name "May Star". The last stanza about the coming of the sun in May, the bond of unity and the country's future points clearly to its being a fighting anthem; his supporters interpreted it as an ode to the popular front. However, like most good poems it had different frames of reference, and can easily be read as a love song; Halldór used it later in *World Light*, and there it can be read both ways. Jón Ásgeirsson composed a compelling melody for it, and it was often sung in schools and children's homes. Halldór originally conceived of the poem as set to a popular German tune, and in his old age he once sang it to that tune on a radio programme.

Although he was so active in politics at this time, Halldór was preoccupied with his new character, the poor popular poet Ólafur Kárason, clearly modelled on Magnús Hjaltason Magnússon, a poet from the Westfjords. The lives of Ólafur and Magnús were alike in some ways: both of them were, for example, what would now be called convicted sex offenders, since in 1911 Magnús was imprisoned for having had intercourse with a teenage girl. But Halldór was interested in this person for a different reason. Magnús lived in horrific poverty and had experienced great personal tragedy, but he wrote constantly, no fewer than eleven thousand poems, an autobiography and diaries filling a total of four thousand three hundred and fifty pages. The diaries are a treasure-chest of descriptions of life and social circumstances in the Westfjords, though in many places they make for rather dull reading, especially when they, like so many other Icelandic diaries, give endless descriptions of the weather.

Halldór's notebooks show that he read Magnús' manuscripts at the National Library of Iceland and took notes on their contents. In the diaries one finds powerful expressions borrowed by Halldór, the most famous example being the "sonic revelation of the deity". But Halldór was most inspired by the fact that this orphan always let poetry occupy the highest place in his life.

In the second half of May, 1936, Halldór took an extended excursion to Magnús' home in the Westfjords, in the company of Vilmundur Jónsson, the Social Democrat Surgeon General and Member of Parliament, and his young son, Þórhallur. The trip was very useful, as he described it in the chapter "One Day at a Time," in *A Day's Journey in the Mountains*. He saw the places where Magnús had lived and worked, met numerous people, and heard stories that he fixed in his memory and used later. Only twenty years had passed since Magnús' death, and his fiancée, Guðrún Anna Magnúsdóttir, was still alive; the journal *Birtingur* published an interview with her in the year of her death, 1956. The conditions in which Magnús had lived were still evident in the struggle for existence and the primitive transport in the Westfjords, as can be seen in the account Halldór sent to Inga on 1 June:

> The trip has gone well, although it has been rather meandering and not precisely after the latest fashion. We went, that is, from Borgarnes by car to Stykkishólmur, from there by motorboat to Flatey in Breiðafjörður in tremendous wind and waves, which splashed over both sides of the boat; I stood on the forecastle, where some poor folk were vomiting; I stood in vomit up to my ankles. We both became seasick, although little Þórhallur did not. We stayed for two nights on Flatey in windy, wet weather. Then we took a motorboat to Brjánslækur on Barðarströnd, from there walked and rode horses to Hákon's at Hagi, where we stayed a night, then rode to Patreksfjörður . . . From Patreksfjörður we rode the best horses over two heaths to Bíldudalur, which is the most dull and wretched village that I have seen on our trip . . . Today we will hike over a very steep heath that is considered too difficult for horses . . .

Halldór wrote continually in his notebooks on this trip and used much of the material in "One Day at a Time". On 4 June the companions came to Skálavík, where Magnús had worked as a teacher. There he had begged people for bags of peat so that he could heat the schoolhouse, and had been denied everywhere; in his diary he wrote down the reply of one farmer who had a house full of firewood: "'You'll get damn-all peat from me! Those who can't make provision for themselves in the autumn can stew in their own juice,'" lines Halldór later used in *World Light*. Skálavík would become Bervík in the novel.

Halldór wrote down numerous stories that he heard, as can be seen in the episode "Dreary and Comical" in "One Day at a Time":

In Sæból in Aðalvík a red-haired pauper was sold for bait. He was tied to the mast and pieces were cut from him as needed; his screams could be heard on land for several days, and then the story ended.

One need not take such stories literally, but they illustrate the reality of an incredibly difficult struggle for existence. It was precisely because of Halldór's preoccupation with modernity that he was touched by this echo of days gone by; his writing was inspired by such contrasts. In "One Day at a Time", under the heading "Icelandic Life is Magnificent", is the following:

Everywhere one goes one meets people who are full of entertaining pseudo-sagelike twaddle and others who know off-the-wall stories. An Icelander has a definite dramatic streak, which has its roots both in this wretched country of his and his ridiculous struggle for existence. In the fate of the smallest man there is always something huge and grand: a man who is so small that hardly anyone notices him can easily be the close relative of some sort of extraordinary natural power and peril, raised in a society under the most pitiful of circumstances. This is also why Icelandic folk life is such an inexhaustible well of material for writing, no matter how one dips into it: life is everywhere just as magnificent, interesting and exceptional.

As a storyteller Halldór was enamoured of the grand spectacle of the old world. The realist movement in literature had been built on the contrast between old and new, just as the many realist writers in Europe who wrote about the corruption of urban life in the wake of mass relocations from the countryside to the city did so from personal experience.

At the end of June, when Halldór returned from the Westfjords, he wrote a tribute to Maxim Gorky, with whom he had in common a belief in socialism and a belief in the development of the people of his homeland:

During [Gorky's] roaming years he gathered a huge amount of knowledge about the people of Russia and Russian life, which was the same thing as knowledge of pauperism, suffering and the people's cultural darkness under the monarchy.

In July the *People's Paper* reported that *Independent People* had been published in Vienna and had received excellent reviews. The first volume had in fact been published by Zinnen Verlag. The company also had offices in Leipzig and Berlin, thus making the book available to all German-speaking areas.

The reviews of the German-language edition show that the first part of

Independent People did not convey the work's thematic unity, and that people read whatever they wanted to read into the novel. Rascism had inspired indulgence towards Iceland on the part of the Nazis, and it seems that the book benefited from this; it even received good reviews in *Völkischer Beobachter*. Later that summer Halldór wrote to Erlendur to tell him that a well-known Nazi had said that the book was "the absolute best that has ever been written about *Blut und Boden*!".

Because it was extremely difficult to move currency out of Germany, Halldór decided to go there to try to get some of his royalties. Halldór needed some cash because he had decided to attend the international P.E.N. meeting in Buenos Aires later that summer, and wanted to take Inga with him. He stopped in Copenhagen to see Hasselbalch, taking the opportunity to visit Jón and Þórunn and to dine with Martin Andersen Nexø. Halldór had thus come an extremely long way from Hamrendar and Skálavík in a very short time, and it seems that he had never felt more ashamed about the easy life in Denmark: "One seldom opens a Danish paper without seeing one or more pictures of fat citizens eating."

When Halldór arrived in Germany in 1936 Hitler had been in power for three years; all political opposition had been crushed and attacks against Jews were on the rise. The government was lenient to foreigners while the Olympic Games were taking place in Berlin. Jón Helgason and Þórunn went with Halldór to the Games, stopping first in Leipzig, where Zinnen Verlag had an office. According to Halldór, the company was preparing to print *Salka Valka*. His old friend Kippenberg had become a minor player at Insel, which had no further plans for publishing his work.

A man by the name of Erwin Magnus had taken it upon himself to translate *Salka* into German. This likely came about through the agency of Hasselbalch, since the Danish editions were used as the basis for both the English and German publications. Hasselbalch funded the German translation, but the money was actually drawn from Halldór's royalties, and while the Germans did not pay him, Halldór's debts to Hasselbalch were mounting.

Halldór's return to Leipzig was bittersweet, but he was delighted to show his companions the places where he and Jóhann Jónsson had spent time. Of course he was surprised at the changes implemented by the Nazis – the Aryan shops, the stupefying papers and so on – but if "One Day at a Time" is accurate, he like many other lovers of German culture could not reconcile these developments with the Germans he knew and loved.

On their way home from Leipzig the travellers stopped in Berlin for the Olympics. Although tickets for the events had sold out long before, a Jewish girl whom Halldór knew had managed to get them tickets. Halldór did not care much for the games and their competitive spirit; he felt that they encouraged the use of the body as a machine, with the competitors trying to squeeze as much as they could from it. He viewed the lacklustre performance of the Icelandic athletes differently from most of his countrymen:

> It can be said in praise of the Icelandic "athletes" who were taking their ease there, that none of them had even the lowest level of ability that was required for these games, but got to be there, as far as I could understand, because they belonged to the fairer race, as the Germans consider themselves, and the only way they drew attention to themselves was by giving the fascist salute on the field and denying at the same time the one thing that they could have shown: respect for their own nation.

Halldór continued on to London where Inga met him, and on 15 August they sailed for South America, with stops in Spain and the Canary Islands, aboard the luxury liner *Highland Brigade*. P.E.N. was never stingy in providing its guests with food, drink and other perks, and the writers all had first-class cabins.

Halldór published incongruous accounts of the trip in *A Poet's Time* and in a series of articles he sent to the *People's Paper* and republished later in *A Day's Journey in the Mountains*. He spoke well of the ship in a letter to his mother:

> The service on board is excellent and the ship is full of passengers, but one finds it tiring to have to dress oneself formally every single evening for dinner, but that is the English tradition, and the ship is English.

The day after this letter was written, the well-dressed passengers were given a harsh reminder of reality. The ship docked at Las Palmas in the Canary Islands, which were under the control of Franco's rebel army; the Spanish Civil War had started a month earlier. Policemen came aboard to arrest one of the passengers, Anibal Lamas, the leader of the Spanish popular front for the Orense district. After a lengthy delay the captain had no choice but to yield, Halldór says, and the fascists

> pointed the muzzles of their pistols first at his chest and then at his temples, dragged him and pushed him down the gangway and took turns kicking him with their army boots, threw him down into the boat like something dead, and continued to kick at him, especially at his head, there where he lay defenceless in the bottom of the boat, like a lamb being led to slaughter.

A large number of people witnessed this incident, among them the writers on their way to the P.E.N. conference, where Lamas had been going in order to muster support for the Spanish Republic. This was the first time that Halldór witnessed fascist methods, and the incident had a strong effect on him. Anibal Lamas was executed on 5 November, 1936.

The voyage was a long one. In the third week they stopped at Rio de Janeiro and Santos, from there going to São Paolo and Montevideo. In a series of articles published in the *People's Paper*, Halldór described how the writers' conference took place under the shadow of fascism and how the struggle against fascism was reflected at the conference. One of the writers that he had belittled in his article on modern bourgeois literature in *Red Pens* was especially memorable to Halldór: the Frenchman Jules Romains, who, in the conference's plenary address, remarked: "There is no literature against freedom, because there is no literature against the spirit." Romains, a supporter of the French popular-front movement, enjoyed a great deal of respect at the conference, which was attended by writers from forty-four countries. No German representatives attended, but fascism had a representative in the Italian delegation, with the Futurist Marinetti in its front ranks. The group also included Giuseppe Ungaretti, who supported the Italian Fascists at that time and later became one of Italy's most famous poets. Marinetti was involved in fierce arguments with other delegates, not least with Romains and Georges Duhamel, one of the most renowned novelists and poets in the French delegation.

The delegates ratified a proposal, authored by Romains and others, to challenge the governments of the world to work for peace. The proposal seemed innocent enough, but the Italian Fascists objected to it strenuously and Ungaretti shouted "*Canaille*" ("Bastard") over and over again at Romains, according to Halldór's account. After the proposal was ratified, Halldór presented another proposal according to which P.E.N. would oblige all of its chapters to accept the peace reso-lution as the prerequisite for membership of the international federation. The proposal was accepted with applause. At the conclusion of the conference Marinetti suggested that the next one be held in Italy, and at the final ceremony Ungaretti and his Fascist colleagues kissed Romains tearfully. This caught Halldór completely off-guard: "Personally, I must admit that I have never been as surprised by anything that I have ever witnessed among full-grown men in the middle of a meal."

Politics was not the only topic of discussion; one day was devoted to a discus-sion of "Human Knowledge and Life", which became extremely metaphysical. The trip was a memorable one, although it appears differently in *A Poet's Time* and *A Day's Journey in the Mountains*. He was now a valid conference participant who had published in several languages; the English edition of *Salka Valka* had even been available in the ship's library. And although he used the long voyage to write, making a great deal of progress on *Light of the World*, he also spent a considerable amount of time with his fellow writers. Especially memorable were Emil Ludwig and the Austrian Stefan Zweig. Zweig was a Jew and no favourite of the Nazis. The barbarism of Nazism was on Zweig's part the calamity from which he never recovered. In *A Poet's Time* Halldór says that during the evening entertainments on board the *Highland Brigade* Zweig had been:

> . . . the life and soul of the party despite his bearing, which was never expressly happy, much less frolicsome, but often slightly macabre, causing one to imagine that his conviviality hid a kind of gnawing gloom in his soul . . . All the same I enjoyed many pleasant conversations with this excellent man on all sorts of topics one might expect would interest two writers, one famous, the other unknown. I often recall one particular thing that he said to me because of the tragedy that it now reflects, a tragedy that might have been averted if he or I had paid more attention to the words that were spoken. We had been discussing the foreseeable ruin of Europe if war were to break out, but he insisted that Iceland would come out of it safe and sound, and concluded the discussion with these words: "When the next war breaks out I will send word to you to find me a little room somewhere in someone's house in Reykjavík . . ."

Unfortunately, when it came down to it, he never sent me this "word", but instead went, in a bottomless pit of ennui, with his youthful wife to Brazil, where they both killed themselves. I am of the futile opinion that had Zweig written to me as he had said he would, and had I got him a little room in someone's house in Reykjavík, things would have turned out differently.

One week into October Inga and Halldór returned to London, whence they planned to travel to The Hague, where an edition of *Salka Valka* was in preparation. In London Halldór received a message from Hasselbalch that caused him great concern. The Danish publisher had, as Halldór's agent, received a letter from the German company that was planning to publish *Salka Valka*. Zinnen Verlag had been sent serious criticisms by the German censors, because the book's author was a Communist. The company needed Halldór to send them proof of his political neutrality as a condition of publication and payment of royalties.

Halldór asked Hasselbalch to make it understood that he had no interest in explaining his philosophy to the Secret Police. It would be better for the Germans

to beware of fighting against the democratic spirit of Scandinavia, because that
would just bring them closer to lesser nations such as Italy and the Balkans.

It was not clear why Halldór was applying such peculiar reasoning to the situation, but he concluded his letter to Hasselbalch with these words:

> That individuals who work for the German censors should dare to use about
> me the most slanderous terms that now exist in the German language
> ("Communist" and suchlike) I consider not only to be an insult to me person-
> ally, but especially to the government of my country, which grants me a high
> yearly salary and allows its Cultural Fund to publish my books, such as *Salka
> Valka*, and which in the main I support politically.

Halldór was angry, but was trying to be tactful. The letter also reveals that he
was having trouble believing that it would not be possible to persuade the German
censors to listen to reason. Hasselbalch asked him to go to Berlin to speak to the
authorities and Halldór considered doing so, but also turned to Vilmundur with an
unusual request:

> I want to ask you to consider whether it might be possible on Iceland's part
> to take repressive measures in return as a symbolic act – for example, force
> the German exchange teacher at the university to stop teaching, recall the
> grant for Icelandic teaching at the university in Berlin, or, if it were techni-
> cally possible, prohibit, for example, sales of books and newspapers from
> Germany. Perhaps you can come up with a better sort of "answer", if they
> do in fact prohibit Icelandic literature in Germany.

There is no evidence to suggest that Halldór ever followed up these ideas, but he
did take Hasselbalch's advice and go to Berlin. It is not unlikely that while there he
contacted the Reichsschrifttumskammer, the Reich Chamber of Literature, established in 1933, and which answered to the Reichskulturkammer, the Reich
Chamber of Culture, run by Goebbels. The association, which writers, publishers
and booksellers were obliged to join, ensured the Nazis' ideological and practical
hold on publishing. They also had bureaux that oversaw book-publishing activities.

It would have been entertaining to have been present at the meetings between
Halldór and the Nazi censors. He would certainly have applied his considerable
charm to try to persuade them to change their minds, but he did not make any
headway. The case was unresolved when he left for Copenhagen, where Inga
awaited him. Zinnen Verlag did not publish *Salka*, but other companies made
offers and Hasselbalch signed with one of them, Henry Goverts in Hamburg.

Halldór had enough to do in Copenhagen: the second part of *Independent People* was published there, and the publisher staged the appropriate banquets and promotional events. Halldór also worked on completing the first volume of *World Light*, which he wanted to send home before Christmas. And he wanted to go to Russia, although he asked his friends to keep this confidential. It is not clear what business Halldór had in the Soviet Union at that time, but it is probable that he wanted to explore the possibility of publishing his work there. Kristinn E. Andrésson wrote to say that he probably did not need to contact Moscow regarding his visit, because Einar Olgeirsson had recently gone there and had said that Halldór was welcome at any time. As things turned out, Halldór's visa was delayed for some reason, and nothing came of it. It appears that the Soviets were not particularly interested in receiving a visit from this writer, who was not bound to Party discipline.

Kristinn asked Halldór to submit something for inclusion in *Red Pens*, but only received a chapter from *World Light*. Kristinn had now become Halldór's publisher in Iceland; Heimskringla, which he directed, intended to publish *The Light of the World* (the original title for the first part of *World Light*, changed to *The Revelation of the Deity* in later editions). Heimskringla, founded in 1934, had published, among other things, *Red Pens* and the play *Short Circuit*. Non-Communists lent support to the venture, including, in 1935, Ragnar Jónsson from Smári, an energetic businessman and great idealist.

Halldór was unable to finish *The Light of the World* quickly enough to guarantee publication before Christmas. At the end of November Inga went home, having been away from her son for so long. Halldór as always spent a great deal of time with Jón Helgason, and went to concerts and the theatre. He attended a special performance at the Royal Theatre of the ballet chanté *The Seven Deadly Sins* by Brecht and Weill and an opera from a fairy tale by Hans Christian Andersen, *The Little Match Girl*. About the opera Halldór wrote in his notebook: "An immoral and disgusting work". He had a great interest in Brecht, though. In 1931 he had read his poetry collection *Manual of Piety* (1927), and in 1935 published in *Réttur* his translation of Brecht's poem "The Infanticide, Maria Farrar".

Apart from his other projects that winter he worked a great deal on the first drafts of a novel about Jón Hreggviðsson conceived in the spirit of Marxism. Somewhat in the spirit of Brecht he notes to himself to make the officials in the novel always and without exception completely drunk. The notebook also contains the following comment: "I tip my hat to Bert Brecht in gratitude for these lines: '*Denn für dieses Leben ist der Mensch nicht schlecht genug*,'" lines that find echoes in both *Independent People* and *World Light*.

At the start of December Halldór wrote the final poems for *The Light of the World* and sent the manuscript home, telling Inga that he was "quite tired and heartsick after having completed the novel". There was still no word from Russia, so Halldór went over Erwin Magnus' translation of *Salka Valka*, hoping that the book would be published. Finally giving up on a response from the East, and because there were no ships going to Iceland until Christmas, he went to the small English town of Dewsbury to review J.A. Thompson's translation of *Independent People*:

> This is a small, sooty factory town in Yorkshire . . . Thompson has let me have a room in the house that he is renting, and I eat with him and his housekeeper. He is a teacher here. He has had great difficulty with the translation and is finishing the first part. We work all the time, when he is available, and read the translation together.

It is clear that Halldór worked extremely hard on the translations of his books. In this case it was well worth it. Thompson's work is thought to be excellent; he, unlike so many of Halldór's translators, had the advantage of knowing Icelandic, having among other things taught in a secondary school in Akureyri in 1931–2. Nevertheless, on almost every page of this book, in which the language is derived from a wide range of sources and particularly colourful, there are words or sentences that Thompson did not understand. When he finally completed the translation, he was apparently quite exhausted, according to Halldór in *A Poet's Time*, because

> the first thing he did after finishing the work was buy himself an apron, a brush and a bucket, and go and wash the steps of a certain fifth-class hotel in London; he thought such work a holiday after having translated Halldór Laxness for Sir Stanley, and never wanted to see another book after that.

Halldór is of course exaggerating here, though Thompson did actually run a hotel for a time in London. He may have been a one-translation man, but his translation of *Independent People* has been republished numerous times in both England and the United States.

Halldór spent Christmas in London in good spirits with the singer Eggert Stefánsson and his Italian wife, Lelja. As can be seen in *A Poet's Time* and elsewhere, Halldór never stopped admiring Eggert, especially his aristocratic bearing and elegance. His descriptions show how much of Eggert he put into the character of Garðar Hólm, because although he had his moments, his singing never came close to his cosmopolitan appearance and pomposity. But his friends adored him. The discrepancies between fame and skill, self-image and talent were always of interest to Halldór. In a 1933 notebook he wrote – in English – that his book about a "world singer" (*The Fish Can Sing*) should be a blend of various human types, among them Eggert Stefánsson, the man who made a mistake, as he puts it, the rambler Jón Pálsson, and the outlaw Grettir. It was also clear to him what the fundamental theme of the book should be, that is: "The beautiful exotic world, which lies by his side, without him being able to touch it." Throughout Halldór's life he was preoccupied with those Icelandic artists who existed on the boundary between the primitive and the erudite.

But Halldór found much to appreciate in Eggert's singing, as revealed in an interesting article he published in *Vísir* in the autumn of 1934, in fact a thank-you letter to Eggert, who had held a special concert for Halldór in the Old Cinema one morning since he could not attend the advertised concert. Halldór was actually not alone, since as he says in *A Poet's Time* the singer's mother was also there. The concert later became the inspiration for Garðar Hólm's in *The Fish Can Sing*.

Halldór did not stay long in the luxury of London. The next report that we have of him is in Berlin on New Year's Eve. From there he wrote to Jón Helgason:

> The flu has got hold of me, I have had a fever for several days, was completely bedridden yesterday, but needed to speak to a highly placed Nazi today; I had to crawl to my feet, and my health is as you might expect following that.

He had not, that is, completely given up trying to persuade the Nazis to change their minds. However, he started the new year by writing observations in his notebook on the necessity of a popular front against fascism, his visit to his previously favourite city having convinced him that National Socialism was insanity to a high degree. He returned to Denmark on 1 January and sailed home a fortnight later.

This time Halldór stayed in Iceland until the autumn, spending a good deal of energy on politics and other matters. He did not experience the depression or panic attacks of his youthful years, but he was restless and enterprising.

*

At the beginning of February the first volume of *World Light, The Light of the World*, was published. Two weeks earlier Halldór had told the *People's Paper* that the book was about "certain poets; their struggles, the sorrows that are a poet's lot, and the comfort that perhaps no-one is granted in richer measure than precisely a poet". Certainly many poets appear, but Ólafur Kárason towers over them all, though the interview suggests that Halldór's original idea had been to write more about the others and their destinies. He is cruel about Ólafur in his initial notes on the work (called there *The Outermost Sea*):

He constantly tries to flee under the protective wing of the power that he thinks is victorious, but makes excuses for his cowardice with love for "the spirit" and "beauty" . . . Youth lames him and makes him unfit to take any tangible position.

But if *The Light of the World* was supposed to display the cowardice of the poet who worships beauty in flight from the warring powers of the world, Halldór's sympathy for his protagonist grows, perhaps because in this first volume he provides him with so much of the thought and understanding of his own youth. They share a passion for writing, a feeling of being special, a love for books and the secrets they contain, and, last but not least, the experience of a youthful revelation. Many years later, in 1968, Halldór informed Magnús Magnússon that Ólafur was a description of himself, "a kind of flower-power baby".

Reaction to *The Light of the World* did not reach the same level as that to *Independent People*; *Morgunblaðið* had stopped reviewing Halldór's books for the time being. Apart from Halldór's closest colleagues, perhaps no-one understood better than his old friend, Sigurður Einarsson, what the publication of this book meant. In an article in the *People's Paper* Sigurður said: "There will come a day when Halldór will blow all our standards to bits." The book was well received by its readers; the first volume, in a print run of two thousand five hundred, sold out within a year and was reprinted. This had to have been good news in a sparsely populated rural country in which affluence was rare and books expensive.

At the end of February, 1937, the *Will of the People* announced that Halldór would speak at a meeting sponsored by the Communist Party about the preservation of culture in the face of fascism. On 2 March the paper published the speech's conclusion (it had been published in its entirety in *Réttur*) under the headline "A Strong Communist Party Can Lead to a United Front of the Icelandic Working People!". The headline said it all. Halldór exhorted the left to support the Communist Party so that the Social Democrats would be compelled to take part in the struggle for a popular front. The idea of collaboration between the workers' parties had widespread support at the time. It was no small matter for the Communists to have a supporter in Halldór.

Halldór delivered the same message on 1 May at an open-air meeting of the Communist Party on Lækjargata, in wind and rain. The *Will of the People* published this speech the next day under the title "Leftists, Stand Together!". There Halldór pointed out that a leftist coalition could gain a greater majority in Parliament, whereas schism could lead to Conservative rule. Before the elections in June he took an even more forceful stance and published a speech on the front page of the

Will of the People: "A Strong Communist Party is the Proviso for the Popular Front of the Icelandic People". The popular-front concept had changed since the early 1930s; emphasis was now placed on education and democracy, and just prior to the elections Halldór wrote an article in which he declared that the Communist Party was dedicated to democracy, and was not violent or dictatorial. The next day he published yet another article, to refute the opinion of the Social Democratic leader Stefán Jóhann Stefánsson that it was not possible to work with the Communist Party because it was controlled from Moscow. Halldór considered it just the opposite: it was an advantage to work with a party whose activities were based on the agenda of an international organization that functioned irrespective of the whims of "scratch-my-back, you-scratch-mine" businessmen. One might note there Sigurður Hróarsson's comment that these articles were totally inconsistent with what Halldór said later in *A Poet's Time*:

> I could not imagine joining a party that answered to the Comintern, that is to say, took orders from headquarters somewhere out in the world and in general limited the personal freedoms of its members.

Like many radical artists and intellectuals in the West who had experienced the post-war cultural crisis, Halldór bound his hopes to the "powerful international movement" that had its roots in the Soviet Revolution. For a time it occupied the place in his soul that the Catholic Church had earlier; its "scientific" theories shone with the same certainty as the doctrines of the Carthusians. Halldór's mind wavered between the rebelliousness of independent thinking and the will to surrender to a higher power. And at the same time that he preached narrow-minded politics with religious fervour in his articles, he explored his doubts in fiction.

Although Halldór was not bound to the Party, he did not conceal his position from his foreign friends. Shortly after the elections he informed Martin Andersen Nexø of the results:

> We have been engaged in a lively election campaign here recently, and we have truly been fighting. Now it has all been concluded happily . . . we have nicely got three Communist candidates seats in Parliament.

Halldór had not had time to write entertaining books recently, he added, because he was too busy with politics; he would probably need to go abroad to write a new novel.

Halldór's business with his Danish colleague was, however, not simply politically motivated. He wanted to thank Nexø for sending him the first volume of his autobiography, *Under the Open Sky* (1935), with an inscription that Halldór quotes in *A Poet's Time*. In the inscription Nexø says of the character of Bjartur in *Summerhouses*:

> Bjartur is a magnificent character: few writers have come so close to the truth as you have with this character. You are one hundred per cent modern and have more of a future than any other writer I know. You strengthen all our faith in the cause.

Halldór used this inscription often while attempting to promote his books, not least in the Soviet Union. In the letter he also voiced his concerns over the fact that his books were not selling well in Denmark, and that he had not heard from friends of his and Nexø's in the Soviet Union. It was now clear that Halldór's books were banned in Germany. An article published in the German censor's journal in 1937 called *Independent People*

> a sinister book, without a glimmer of light, merciless, almost fearsome . . . Its author is not favourable towards the Germans, especially the National Socialist Movement . . . We ask the publishing house, was it aware of the author's disposition when it decided to publish his work in German?

Zinnen Verlag hastened to reply:

> We are very eager to point out that when we bought the publishing rights to this work we naturally had no idea that this writer was in any way unfriendly towards Germany . . . Mr Laxness personally attended the Olympic Games here last year, and has publicly expressed his full acknowledgement of everything that he saw here. If Laxness had in fact at any time previously, because of his youth and immaturity, gone astray politically, it is certainly possible to reiterate that this stage in his development may now be considered to be long past.

At the same time that the State Bureau for the Promotion of German Booklore sent Halldór duplicates of these letters, it also gave him the opportunity to respond to the accusations levelled against him. He was asked to sign a declaration expressing regret that he had offended the National Socialists, denying that he had been a Catholic and afterwards divorced himself from the Church, and blaming his youth. It concluded: "For the German nation and its culture I bear the utmost respect, and especially for those who currently hold its banners." Hasselbalch asked Halldór to sign the declaration immediately, but Halldór sent Hasselbalch a brusque reply, asking him to hold on to the declaration for the next time that he needed to reach an agreement with fascists:

> If the officials of foreign government offices presume to tell me how I am to think about various spiritual matters, or about politics, and desire with my signature to bind me to the service of interests that are alien to me, then I am forced hereby, once and for all, to inform those who play any part in this matter that I reserve the right to speak for or against any opinion whatsoever, whenever, wherever, and in whatever way I deem necessary.

*

In the spring of 1937 Halldór became one of the founding members of the literary society Mál og menning (Language and Culture), which Kristinn E. Andrésson took the initiative in establishing. It was sponsored by the Union of Revolutionary Writers, which appointed three board members, Halldór, Eiríkur Magnússon and Halldór Stefánsson, and the publishing company Heimskringla, which appointed two others, Kristinn Andrésson and Sigurður Thorlacius. It was primarily intended as a book club that would sell by subscription, thereby guaranteeing lower retail prices. In its prospectus the society announced its goal of publishing six hundred-and-sixty-page books a year for only 10 krónur, if they could gain three thousand subscribers. This represented a great reduction in the price of a book, as the weekly wage of a worker was around 60 krónur. The book club was also concerned with critical contemporary issues: "The nation needs first and foremost books that it can use as weapons in the struggle for life." In other words, another of the society's duties was to circulate the joyful message of socialism. Yet from the beginning emphasis was placed on bringing into the society people who were not associated with the extreme left, for example the progressive Sigurður Thorlacius. Things went slowly at first: in its first year the company published *Red Pens* and a huge book by a Danish biologist, Niels Nielsen; their first novel was an edition of *Mother* (1906) by Maxim Gorky.

Halldór was involved with Mál og menning for many decades; he was on the company's board of directors until he was made an honorary partner in 1995, and during the company's first two decades he took an active part in its work. The idea for the company was well received; before a year had passed the goal of enrolling three thousand subscribers was reached. Books were highly sought-after since Icelanders had few other means of recreation. The self-image of the newly sovereign nation was inseparably connected with its literature, and the radical writers of the 1930s were influential. Sigfús Daðason, director of Mál og menning in the early 1970s, said later:

The political activities of these years cannot be separated from the cultural activities; this was the time of the struggle for the so-called popular front, and the optimism and confidence of those involved in the struggle was unquenchable; it was accompanied only by hope – the after-effects had not yet been felt.

A vigorous propaganda campaign for the newly established literary society was launched at a youth rally on 25 July; Halldór delivered the opening address: "The increased education of the public is the only guarantee of democracy. Let it be the work of the youth associations in every parish to secure democracy by supporting education." The writer Björn Th. Björnsson recounted sixty years later how he, then a fifteen-year-old boy from the countryside, travelled a long way to get to the rally:

> In a great clearing . . . by the Sogn River, there were Icelandic flags all around, while the crowds of people sat or lay in the grass or walked around congrat-ulating each other . . . The dais was on the edge of the clearing, and there Kiljan was concluding his righteous provocation of the people: "Books are your university, people of Iceland!"

Halldór was extremely busy that summer, since he had decided to publish his collection of essays *A Day's Journey in the Mountains* in the autumn. Early in July, however, he took a break and went north with Inga to Skagafjörður, where the bones of Solveig from Miklabær were being reinterred; she supposedly had demanded this through a medium in Reykjavík. Halldór could not refrain from writing an anonymous article for the *Will of the People*: "Reinterrment – New Life for the Church in Iceland". Otherwise Halldór spent the entire summer working while Inga went with Einar to Copenhagen in August. As Einar said:

> Mother and I had a very pleasant time in Copenhagen those summer days, where the sun shed its rays upon us in that paradise . . . We sauntered along the Strøget, lay on the beach, and went to Kjærstrupveg to visit Jón and Þórunn, where we were received with open arms.

Halldór was thinking of going to meet them in the autumn, because he longed to make another attempt to go to the Soviet Union with Inga.

In the meantime Halldór had started to think about the second part of *World Light*. In August he and Vilmundur hiked in the mountains and heaths in the north of Iceland. Halldór was still as energetic a hiker as he had been a decade before; he was a hiker all his life.

After travelling home to Reykjavík by ferry Halldór was told by the Ísafold printers that they had not started to print *A Day's Journey* because they needed paper for the job; he was certain that they were using their paper for another project. In consultation with Heimskringla, he nevertheless decided to hold interviews with the leftist newspapers in order to advertise the book. On 31 August the *Will of the People* published a conversation with him of the sort that was rather rare in those days, giving a kind of portrait of the interviewee. Halldór was asked about his interests, music and travels, as well as about his essays, which he said were mostly cultural critiques. His remarks about Ólafur Kárason are noteworthy:

> The Icelandic environment of the poor man living on parish alms is just an excuse, a reason for describing the position of the poet in the struggles of the modern world . . . What is human is universal. I put the poet into everyday life in Iceland because that is the everyday life that I know best. Otherwise the story could have taken place in any country.

Halldór says that he never considered becoming a writer in a foreign language, adding: "writers probably have to be professional nowadays, if they intend to achieve realistic results. The demands of the time are division of labour, specialization." His knowledge about sales figures and promotional matters are a part of his own professionalism.

In September Halldór went to Laugarvatn to start the next part of *World Light*. It felt good to be there mainly on his own, since the hotel was closed. However, he had a number of financial worries: Heimskringla could not pay him until his book had sold; he had debts in Copenhagen; Germany was closed to him; the Soviets were silent; Thompson had not yet delivered the translation of *Independent People*. He wrote a short story for *Red Pens* and asked for 100 krónur for it, and luckily things were going so well with the subscriptions for Mál og menning that he hoped the "entire undertaking" would "pay off substantially". (Another part of Halldór's professionalism was that he nearly always demanded to be paid well for his work.) The short story was the humorous "The Defeat of the Italian Air Force in Reykjavík, 1933". Written in the classic "David and Goliath" style, it has been translated into numerous languages.

Halldór spent most of his free time with Erlendur at Unuhús and Kristinn, and Einar Olgeirsson, meeting Unuhús' many guests, as well as Vilmundur and the widow of Jóhann Jónsson, Elisabet Göhlsdorf, who had moved to Iceland. But Halldór was restless. Brynjólfur Bjarnason had told him that he would be invited to Moscow on the occasion of the twentieth anniversary of the Revolution. Even though Halldór did not have any travel documents in hand, he decided to go anyway, and in October travelled to Copenhagen.

Adventures and Nightmares in Russia

> In 1938 the editors in Moscow said to me: "Our people have never seen Communists such as Arnald." I replied: "Of course they have, but you hang them."
>
> *Halldór Laxness*

At the start of December, 1937, Halldór took his second extended trip to the Soviet Union, staying there four months – the time when Stalin's reign of terror reached its savage peak. Halldór had no better grasp of what was happening than any other friendly visitor did. Although he could see that things were not what they seemed, he pushed his doubts aside and composed an ode to Stalin's Soviet Union, *The Russian Adventure*. If he ever regretted having written one of his books, this was it.

For October and most of November Halldór was with Inga in Copenhagen, awaiting the paperwork he needed. They did not receive approval for their visas in time to be present at the anniversary celebration and had to content themselves with attending a huge party held by the Soviet deputation in Copenhagen. Halldór used the time to immerse himself in *World Light*.

Early in October he received a letter from Martin Andersen Nexø, who asked whether he might be interested in setting up an Icelandic chapter of Red Aid; Nexø was chairman of the Danish chapter. He also said that he would do what he could to encourage the state publishing house (Goslitizdat) in Moscow to publish Halldór's work, and advised him to send several books to Leningrad, in particular to Anna Hansen, Goslitizdat's chief translator and adviser on Scandinavian literature.

Halldór visited Nexø in October, doubtless to discuss this further, and they considered travelling together to Moscow, although nothing came of this. But Halldór did send some of his books in Danish translation to Anna Hansen with an accompanying letter.

Anna Hansen was in fact Anna Vasiliyevna Vasiliyeva, not a Dane but a Russian. With her husband, Peter Emanuel Hansen, she translated various works of literature. He, however, was out of the country when the Bolsheviks revolted, and was never allowed to return. He became a friend of Martin Andersen Nexø, and supported him in his dealings with Russian publishing companies. Anna became Nexø's main translator.

Anna Hansen received Halldór's books just before Christmas, 1937, and was possibly asked to translate *Independent People* when contracts were drawn up for it in March, 1938. Whether Anna Hansen completed the translation, we shall never know. She died of hunger during the German siege of Leningrad in 1942. Seven hundred and fifty thousand inhabitants of the city shared her fate.

Hansen had for some time been Nexø's translator; few foreign writers enjoyed as much respect in the Soviet Union during Stalin's reign as he did. There is nothing further about her in Halldór's correspondence, however. On his trip Halldór reached an agreement with the Soviet State Publishing House for the publication of *Independent People*. It was said that the book would be translated shortly, but when he returned to the Soviet Union in 1949 and asked what had become of it he received no answer: "There was one story that the translation had certainly been prepared, but was burnt in the German attack on Leningrad during the great siege." When the book was finally published in the 1960s, it was translated anew.

But had it ever been translated in Leningrad? The All-Soviet Society for Cultural Relations Overseas wrote to the Soviet embassy in Reykjavík in 1945 to say that it had been. In 1953 Halldór mentioned that a part of it had been found, but that the translator was dead. So it seems likely that Anna Hansen did translate the work from Danish, and that her fate determined its fate as well.

While Halldór was waiting for his Soviet visa and a formal invitation to travel to Russia, he also needed money, so he tried to get an advance from Heimskringla and a travel grant from the Fund for Danish–Icelandic Relations. At the start of December he received conditional permission to travel, as well as some money, and Inga went to meet him in Stockholm. They travelled together through Finland to Leningrad, where they stayed for twenty-four hours in cold, stormy weather, arriving in Moscow on 9 December. Halldór wrote to his mother:

> We are doing splendidly here. I especially notice the great advances that have been made, since my last visit, in the outer appearances of all the great cities of Russia: the people are better clothed and happier than they were then, large numbers of new huge buildings have been built, and much of what was falling apart has now been made anew. An enormous quantity of huge department stores has been built, all of them naturally government and cooperative stores, and many of them are extremely beautiful and of fine quality. A great many products of all types are now available that were not seen before.

Halldór enjoyed the hospitality and care of Mikhail Apletin, the deputy head of the Foreign Commission of the Soviet Writers' Union; the two men became good friends. Halldór was given an interpreter by the name of Burmeister. His hosts from his 1932 trip were nowhere to be seen, and it would have meant little to wave a paper from Willy Münzenberg, who had fallen out of favour.

Halldór and Inga saw the sights of Moscow and went to concerts and the theatre. A special programme was designed for Inga, who planned to visit children's homes and learn about the educational system; perhaps she wanted to see with her own eyes the obedient Soviet children of whom Halldór had spoken. She left for home before Christmas, since she wanted to return to Einar. Travelling alone by train to Finland at the height of winter, sharing a cabin with four men. She said later: "Almighty God, how awful that was, and how angry I was with Halldór for putting me in a compartment with those strangers". But she had good things to say about the journey in an interview with the *Will of the People* in January:

> Of all that I saw there in the East I was most fond of the theatre. We went as often to the theatre and the cinema as we could. But that was no easy task, because all the theatres, cinemas, and in general all the places of entertainment were jam-packed every single night; it was obvious that people had enough money to spend.

The *Will of the People* was pleased to have this testimony, which contradicted the so-called "bourgeois lie" about famine in the Soviet Union.

Halldór was invited to travel to a writers' conference in Tbilisi in Georgia, which was to commemorate the seven hundred and fiftieth anniversary of the birth of the Georgian national poet, Shota Rustaveli. A five-member delegation departed from Moscow on Christmas Eve for the three-day train trip. On New Year's Eve Halldór sent Jón Helgason a letter from Tbilisi:

> The most important news from me is that I have now, for the preceding five days, been attending a writers' conference in Tbilisi, and have for five–six hours a day listened to people deliver lectures in Tabasaran, Kumik . . . Tajik, Lezgi, Mongolian, Nogai, Kabardian, Karakalpak, Uzbek, Chechen . . . Kazakh, Armenian, Laz, Kalmyk, Ingush, Karaim, Adyghe, Assyrian, Tuvan, Bashkir, Slovenian, Tatar, Marathi, Megrelian, Punjabi, Urdu . . . Bulgarian, Uighur, Ukrainian, Georgian, and Azerbaijani. I myself held a lecture in one of these languages, although it is not entirely clear to me which one, and the lecture was then printed here in the papers in an alphabet that I have never seen before. There was one ninety-year-old ruffian here from a country that

is said to be the size of Europe without the peninsulas, and is called Kazakhstan. These were former shepherds and horsemen: he was wearing riding boots, a silk gown and an appalling lambskin hood. He staggered up on to the platform and played on his guitar a kind of accompaniment to the wind of the steppes, singing to it a poem that he had composed; I felt as if it were the first time that I beheld a skald. He did not know how to read or write, but his poems were interpreted for me, and I found them incredibly ingenious: I particularly remember this continually repeated refrain: "A hundred years on horseback race quickly by."

Halldór's address, for the most part courteous blather, is preserved in Russian in the Soviet Archives. The shepherd from Kazakhstan was Zhambyl, about whom Halldór wrote in *The Russian Adventure*, reproducing his songs over many pages. Zhambyl Zhabaev was one of those men whom the Soviet government made into a living legend; as he was made to sing the praises of Stalin, it is difficult to determine what was genuine and what illusion. Halldór saw in the aged representative at the writers' conference a kind of archetypal poet.

Halldór never stopped writing during this trip, planning a book about his experiences, and also working on the second volume of *World Light*. The figure of the poet from a primitive country was coming to occupy an even larger place in his mind. In his notebook he wrote comments about the new novel, which he called *Folk For Sale*, but which later became *The Palace of the Summerland*. As always when Halldór was writing, he thought about beauty. Under the date New Year's Eve, 1937, in Gori in the Caucasus, he remarked:

> A boy in a car park, his perfect beauty, despite being clad in rags. How quickly I understood Thomas Mann's novel, *Death in Venice*. Fascination with beauty itself, without any sexual feelings, just an urge to do something for the beautiful, to give one's life for the beautiful. Beauty comes before everything.

The members of the delegation continued their journey through the south of the Soviet Union in January, 1938, travelling to Batum on the Black Sea, and from there aboard ship to Sukhumi in Abkhazia, where they stayed for several days at a writers' conference. Everywhere they went they were shown hospitality and kindness, says Halldór in his letters to Inga, and everywhere they went the writers returned the favours with lectures and interviews, addresses and visits to collective farms. Halldór describes such a day in a letter written after he returned to Moscow in the middle of the month:

I particularly remember one day in Batum, which began at seven and continued in uninterrupted slavery the whole day – always at intervals of a few hours a new "team" took over, and we always had to be interested and enthusiastic about being given newer and newer information and demonstrations; among other things we drove approximately 100 kilometers in a car to collectives and state farms, to inspect tobacco and tea plantations, and in the evening we attended a meeting that went from eight to twelve, and we had to deliver lectures there without preparation (I spoke in German and Burmeister translated for me simultaneously); then, when the meeting was over, a play was performed, starting at half-past midnight: it was a special performance in honour of our visit (and of the visit of the Russian writers who had come with us from Tbilisi), so we were obliged to sit in the front-row seats next to the government ministers from Ajaristan. The play continued until three-thirty. Then waiting for us at the Hotel International was a magnificent banquet, which went on until morning, but I must say that by the middle of the banquet I was dead-tired, and was in the worst of moods, and went up to my room to sleep. The next day at nine-thirty the cars stood honking outside the hotel to take us to yet another wondrous show, but I went on strike.

It is difficult to tell who worked harder, the delegation or the hosts, and it is actually incredible how much the Soviets did for writers whom Halldór describes as follows in *A Poet's Time*:

One crippled factory poet from Spain whom no-one in the group knew to have ever published anything; a Bulgarian who was so intensely overburdened by Marxist bombast that he could neither be called a speaker nor a writer; and finally one insignificant person from a country that seemed not to have existed on this planet or any other.

The Soviets made an art of organizing trips for delegations early on and had perfected the form by the time the Soviet Union collapsed.

In the final week of January Halldór wrote to Inga again from Moscow, where he had arrived in minus-20-degree weather with a box full of oranges, mandarins and lemons from the shores of the Black Sea; he was working avidly, he said, on the final chapters of *The Palace of Summerland*. He preferred not to return home until he was finished, because he knew that he would be overwhelmed by work on the popular front. But there was another reason why he wanted to stay on: his books were being seriously considered by two publishing houses. He had heard how the Soviets printed books in enormous numbers, and the royalties were quite good, although the problem of exchanging currency would prevent him from taking more than a small portion out of the country. Halldór wrote: "No matter what, I am not leaving here until I have received a yes or no reply from them about either [*Salka Valka* or *Independent People*]."

Besides working on his writing, Halldór took short trips with his interpreter every day at three o'clock; this description of the five-man group was included in the same letter to Inga:

> The poor woman is a complete nervous wreck, but she is so virtuous and conscientious and wants to do everything she can to please us that I always forgive her for it. Apletin is a thoroughly unique and excellent man. The little Spaniard is now setting off for home tomorrow by way of Scandinavia, completely helpless regarding languages; I wrote to Habba [Inga's sister] for him and asked her to help him in Stockholm. He is a beautiful soul. On the other hand the Bulgarian is unbearable, and his cheekiness has alienated everyone.

Halldór was so concerned about his crippled Spanish travelling companion that one can find in his correspondence a draft of a letter to Aksel Larsen, the leader of the Danish Communists, in which he says that it will be necessary for someone who speaks Spanish to meet the poet at the station in Copenhagen. Halldór admired the Russians' warmth and generosity when their publicly prescribed demeanours were set aside, and that admiration becomes even stronger after he has given up on their social system. And he repaid their hospitality when they visited Iceland.

On this second trip to the Soviet Union Halldór found none of the people to whom he had spoken five years previously, except for one woman, Nina Krymova, who was to become one of his best friends. In *A Poet's Time* he writes:

> She was one of those frenetic workers on the cultural battlefield who could never be parted from her projects, like old countrywomen in Iceland who walk from farm to farm continually knitting and never sleep, as far as anyone knows.

Nina Krymova, born in 1902, studied theatre in Moscow, but her great talent for languages earned her a position in the Soviet diplomatic service. In 1929 she was transferred to the embassy in Oslo and worked there with the famous Soviet revolutionary Alexandra Kollontai. Krymova went on to interpret for the Comintern's international conferences, and from 1935 she was supervisor of Scandinavian literature at Glavit, the Soviet censor. She survived the political turmoil to work in Soviet radio and television, where she remained for thirty-four years.

She was especially fond of Nexø and spent a huge amount of time translating and publicizing his books. She was the first to introduce Halldór's writing to the Soviet Union with the publication of two articles in the journal *International Literature* in 1939. When Halldór's books were finally accepted for publication in the Soviet Union in 1953, it was she who set to work on the translations.

Auður Laxness, who visited Moscow in 1965, later recalled Krymova: "She was an extremely pleasant woman. One time she wrote Halldór a letter that ended like this: 'Halldór, I love you. Regards to your wife.'" In May, 1982, a large gathering was held in Moscow in celebration of Halldór's eightieth birthday, at which Krymova delivered a speech. The next day she had a heart attack from which she never fully recovered. She died in 1983.

*

At the start of February Halldór wrote to Inga again and described his trips to the theatre. He had seen Gogol's *Dead Souls* in the Theatre of the Arts and was so moved that it took him a long time to recover; he was equally enamoured of *King Lear* at the Jewish Theatre. The play was in Yiddish, and the director, Solomon Mikhoels, played Lear, as Halldór writes in *A Poet's Time*. There he also tells of how Stalin had Mikhoels murdered in 1948 and the theatre closed a year later. Halldór told Inga that he was planning to leave for a sightseeing trip to the Ukraine, but otherwise was sticking to his plan of staying in Russia until his publishing business was successfully completed. But things did not look good for *Salka Valka*:

> *Salka Valka* is thought to be half counter-revolutionary because the representative of socialism in the book is supposedly portrayed as a coward, but *Independent People* seems to have more of a chance . . . As you can understand, however, I prefer not to leave until something has been decided in this matter, because it is of great professional and financial interest to me."

In fact *Salka Valka* was rejected in the end.

Halldór visited Kiev and continued south to Sebastopol in the Crimea. From there he sent Jón Helgason a letter containing, among other things, a commentary on the Scandinavians' visits to Kiev in the Middle Ages; he also asked Jón to send him some paper:

> This Russian paper is too coarse for me; it is torture for me to write on it . . . I am almost finished with the novel, which is now called *The Palace of the*

Summerland. The book has been written under rather uneasy circumstances, mainly in very different hotels, some of it scrawled in train carriages.

The next day he was in Yalta, and wrote to Inga about the beauty of the Black Sea shores. But he added that he had grown tired of his travels in the East, although they were informative and Soviet life had grown on him. He wanted to return to Moscow, conclude his business and go home.

On 2 March Halldór wrote to Inga again from Moscow, informing her that he still had not received a reply about *Independent People*. But he had news of a remarkable tribunal that was commencing in Moscow, against a "conspiracy of dangerous men and Soviet enemies, who have sneaked into all divisions of the government apparatus; this is one of the busiest criminal organizations in history." Adding that fascism was apparently at work he said: "They are trying to get me a ticket to the trial but it is in fact difficult; all the same it appears hopeful that it will happen."

At first it seemed that he would not be able to attend, but Wilhelm Florin wrote to Dimitrov, the leader of the Comintern, saying that he could not understand why Halldór had not received an admission pass. Sympathetic writers had been specially invited to the previous show trials, but here was one such writer who was not being admitted. Florin's arguments were effective, and thus it happened that Halldór was present at one of the most famous trials of the twentieth century, that of Bukharin and his colleagues. It lasted twelve days, and Halldór sat the whole time on a bench intended for foreign journalists and guests, following the proceedings with the help of an interpreter. The courtroom was the scene of the final phase of Stalin's showdown with the leaders of the Russian Revolution. And the reader can look through Halldór's letters into the darkened face of history.

The persecutions reached their peak in 1937 and 1938. According to conservative figures based on documents that were made accessible with the opening of the Russian archives in the last decade, nearly seven hundred thousand people were condemned to death and shot in the Soviet Union during just those two years; two and a half million were arrested, and in 1938 two million were incarcerated in gulags. Some historians, such as Robert Conquest, believe that the numbers of victims during this time were even higher.

Halldór took his role as sympathetic witness very seriously. Later he said in *A Poet's Time*:

It was one of the most peculiar sights that I had ever witnessed. The trial had an air of unreality, as if the participants were mere shadows; there was a hollow sound to everything that was said. The Marxist terminology that was as much in the mouths of the judges as the defendants, like the theological nonsense of the Inquisition in the Middle Ages, gave the trial a mechanical quality – it had been sheared of all humanity, making me feel partly as if I were in the company of spectral men.

This was how Halldór saw the trials in hindsight. But at the time, he experienced them differently, writing to Inga on 18 March:

I attended the whole trial here of the conspirators . . . It was a poignant moment in the history of the world – for example, the fascist Yagoda worked here for years as the Commissar for Internal Affairs and the Deputy of the GPU! The trial lasted eight hours a day for twelve days. All but three of them were shot.

While Halldór was attending the trials, news arrived that concerned him directly:

Finally two [Soviet] publishing companies have purchased *Independent People*. One of them is a mass publisher that prints large impressions, and the other is a bibliophile publisher. The first one plans to print twenty-five thousand copies, the other ten thousand.

Around the middle of March all the contracts were ready for signing, and he was convinced that they would strengthen his position greatly on the international stage. It was difficult to say what caused the Soviet publishers to make this decision. Doubtless their assessment had been favourable, but it was surely a precondition that Halldór should be a supporter of the government. In the Russian archives there are German translations of his speeches, for example, one that he delivered for the Communist Party on 1 March, 1937, and another that he delivered on the anniversary of the granting of Iceland's sovereignty in 1935. It is likely that Halldór's compatriots translated the speeches and sent them to Moscow to strengthen his position there. Martin Andersen Nexø also wrote a letter to Apletin on 5 February, 1938, in which he recommended that *Independent People* be published.

Now there was no longer any need for Halldór to put off going home, and he waited only for the necessary departure stamp for his passport. By 26 March he had left Moscow; he wrote from a hotel in Leningrad to the international office of the Writers' Union in Moscow, thanking them for their hospitality; the next day he was in Helsinki. He also expressed his appreciation publicly. On 26 March the *Will of the People* announced that Halldór would speak on the radio in Moscow. Obviously this speech must have been pre-recorded; most likely it was the same one that can be found in German in the Russian archives, repeating the Soviet explanations that the defendants at the show trials had been criminals, spies, fascist envoys and murderers.

If Halldór had naively believed the propaganda that his friends and hosts fed him, had he simply been deceived, as he claims in *A Poet's Time*? He certainly took the official explanations at face value. He believed them because he wanted to believe them. However, it must have become clear to him that things were not as they should have been on the night of 14 March, when Vera Hertzsch had been arrested in his presence.

In *A Poet's Time* Halldór tells of how he was invited to Hertzsch's home just before leaving Moscow in March, 1938. She lived with her young daughter in a small apartment in the Arbat district. Around midnight there was a knock on the door, and into the room came "an unfamiliar man, pale and long-faced, clad in the obligatory black overcoat of all Russian clerks of that period". The man asked Vera for identification, told her to come with him and said that the child would be well looked after in a state orphanage. The police officer took Halldór's papers as well, but returned them an hour later, saying that he was free to go, since he had a departure stamp on his passport. He caught the last tram back to his hotel: "I stared out of the window at the wet, heavy snowfall driving down in long white diagonal streaks and melting."

Here a definite discrepancy must be pointed out. According to Halldór's account, Vera was arrested on 24 March, because he left for home on 26 March. Newly discovered Soviet documents confirm indisputably, on the other hand, that Vera was arrested on 14 March. According to Halldór's letter to Inga, he did not receive the departure stamp for his passport until 18 March. An explanation for this discrepancy has never been found.

Who was Vera Hertzsch, and why was Halldór visiting her? Born in Meissen, Germany, in 1904, she moved to the Soviet Union in 1927. There she married a Polish Jew and Communist, Abram Rosenblum, but by 1935 they were separated. Vera lived first in Leningrad, but later moved to Moscow, where she worked until 1936 for the Communist University for National Minorities of the West. The Icelander Benjamín Eiriksson was studying in Moscow at the time and he and Vera were drawn to each other. Benjamín described her later as follows: "Vera was a pretty woman . . . rather tall, with a lovely forehead, dark wavy hair, incredibly beautiful teeth, a southern look . . . a wonderful person."

Benjamín applied for permission to go home in 1936, and at the beginning of December travelled from Moscow to the West. Vera was six months pregnant with their child. Theirs was a love in the shadow of persecution. Her husband Abram had worked with revolutionaries in Palestine, France and Germany before taking up employment with a publishing company in the Soviet Union. On 15 August, 1936, he was arrested, convicted of belonging to the "Trotskyite-Zinovievite" terrorist group and shot on 29 March, 1937.

There is no doubt that the arrest of her husband increased Vera's difficulties. From 1936 she had worked at the German-language Moscow paper *Deutsche Zentral-Zeitung* (DZZ). Suspicions of foreign "revolutionaries" were growing daily. At the end of July and the beginning of August, 1937, orders were given for the "purging" of Poles and Germans deemed to be working against the interests of the Soviet Union. Vera was visited in connection with this in the summer, because on 2 August, 1937, she wrote to Benjamín: "I am again in the most anxious situation . . . because of the child I am still at home." Her daughter, Erla Sólveig, had been born on 22 March, 1937.

On 9 September, 1937, Vera was sentenced to eight years in prison – only for having been Rosenblum's wife. However, it is apparent that she was not in prison that autumn, perhaps because of the child. In Stockholm, before Halldór and Inga went to Moscow, Benjamín asked Halldór to take a package to her. Halldór says in *A Poet's Time* that they delivered the package as soon as they arrived, which fits with Vera's thanking Benjamín in a letter of 8 December.

When Halldór returned from the Caucasus he met Vera by chance, and had considerable contact with her in the next few weeks. He says that she had been incredibly loyal to the Party, extremely well educated in doctrine, and always took the official political line. As Benjamín has pointed out, in that poisoned atmosphere of suspicion Vera as a foreigner had to be careful. *DZZ* was still under the authorities' microscope and twenty of the paper's employees were arrested between February and March, 1938.

For a long time no-one knew what had happened to Vera after her arrest. The Russian Red Cross has now confirmed that Vera Hertzsch died in the Karaganda labour camp in Kazakhstan on 14 March, 1943. The fate of her daughter remains uncertain; but she was probably reunited with her mother shortly after the arrest and perished with her in the gulag.

*

Halldór returned to Stockholm on 28 March, 1938. His publishing future was in some doubt, since Bonniers was not interested in publishing any more of his work. While in Stockholm he told Benjamín what had happened to Vera, though he said nothing publicly until twenty-five years later, in *A Poet's Time*. What was the justification for his silence? Benjamín, who like Halldór joined the new Socialist Party in the autumn of 1938, explains in his autobiography that people like Halldór considered themselves participants in a world war, and "had to beware of saying things that could be used to empower the enemies of the Soviet Union . . ." Benjamín himself had written sympathetically about the Soviet Union soon after his return from there, though he had avoided distorting the truth. He says that Halldór did not do the same.

News spread quickly of Halldór's attendance at the trials, which had been discussed in the Icelandic papers; The *Will of the People* interviewed him about them in April. He described the incredible progress in the Soviet Union and the peaceful way of life in Moscow, denying all the rumours of show trials and torture. The old revolutionaries were not counter-revolutionaries, but fascists: they were guilty of treason.

That Halldór was concerned about the situation in the Soviet Union is clear from a conversation he had with Jakob Benediktsson, one of his translators. But he had convinced himself that he had to defend the Soviet Union unconditionally; anything else would have been fuel for the fascists' fire and would have damaged the popular-front movement. His defence of Stalin had a strong impact on Iceland. Few supporters of Communism and the popular front had ever been out of the country; they did not know much about the Soviet Union, except that people there were fighting for their rights and better conditions. When Halldór defended the Soviet Union, people accepted what he said: he must have known what he was talking about.

Halldór understood this. He also was a believer and an idealist, and was single-minded when he set himself a goal. His search for the truth in his youth was never moderate or tactful. His articles were polemical and ironic in style; his wording was often offensive, and when he was young he was unafraid of ridiculing people if need be. He was convinced that ideals were higher than men – even after he professed his faith in man. By this he meant man as a symbol of life – an ideal, as he said in *The Book of the People*, not as a wearying reality of flesh and blood. Early in the 1930s he had convinced himself that the Soviet Union was attempting to turn the most splendid conception of the perfect society into reality. And he decided to support this magnificent attempt come what may, to defend it tooth and nail. It was his support of the Soviet Union, like his resolute and unreserved support of the Catholic Church for a time, that determined his position, much more than the struggle against fascism. But did he not also have interests to protect? Was he not hoping that the Soviet Union would provide his path to international fame? Unfortunately, despite the contract made in 1938, none of his books were published in the Soviet Union for the next fifteen years, precisely the years when he was the Soviets' most energetic spokesman.

Halldór's doubts caused him, as sometimes happens, to become even more out-spoken. *The Russian Adventure* is the clearest testimony to this. Much better written than *Going East*, its style is inspired at times, and the narrative is powerful. But it is also more insolent. Halldór had lost his childish faith in the Soviet Union; now he fought with the weapons of a political spokesman.

In his forceful prefatory remarks he says that now it is in his power to write a book that will secure him glory in the West for its exposure of the hunger and destitution in Russia and Stalin's betrayal of the old Bolsheviks:

> If I were, on the other hand, to publish this disjointed memoir of mine from Russia, as a witness to my sympathy for the people fighting their way out of the darkness of immorality into culture and freedom, with the support of the socialist movement and under the leadership of the Communist Party, then I need not have any concerns about the question of world renown in the future; I will not be troubled by large royalty cheques; people more deserving than I will move into my residence on the shores of the Mediterranean; ships will sail around the world without me; I will take walking trips in the summer instead of drives in Rolls-Royces. The small number of my books printed in various splendid countries will decrease rather than increase. And my name will be spoken of far less than it ever has been.

Halldór then turns to André Gide, a supporter of the Soviet Union who had been disappointed by his visit there in 1936. Halldór mocks Gide mercilessly as a typical Western aesthete who does not understand the difficulties with which the Russians have to contend. He criticizes those who had written about the Soviet Union but not seen the realities of life there. As he described the book to Apletin in the late summer of 1938: "I do my best to see things from a standpoint of human interest, which many of the leftist thinkers fail to do when they write about the Soviet Union."

He also writes about the trials, which he sees as an expression of the gigantic conflict between world powers in which the guilt or innocence of particular men becomes insignificant, petty. His description of the defendants is entirely Stalinist: they are the worst puppets of Nazism. And he spares nothing in his description of Bukharin:

> A small, bowed, bald, schoolteacherish meddler, drawn up entirely into a Mephistophelian point, a sharp nose, sharp ears, pointed-arched eyebrows,

a Napoleon forelock, with his arguments like some kind of extension of his buck teeth . . .

On the other hand Halldór speaks of Lenin with religious fervour: "Men such as . . . Lenin are not born more often than at thousand-year intervals." Here Lenin takes the place on the pedestal of the man in Halldór's mind when he was twenty: a man born approximately two thousand years earlier.

The book contains numerous entertaining observations, not least on literature. And one suddenly finds this statement about Icelanders: ". . . the Icelanders are, as is well known, first and foremost circus animals in Scandinavia . . ." Finally there is Halldór's poem about Stalin: "I know a farm there in the East/ which once though ruined land/ brings naught but bounty now beneath/ the Kremlin Farmer's hand."

In a radio interview in 1963, following the publication of *A Poet's Time*, Matthías Jóhannessen asked Halldór: "How could you go from Vera Hertzsch's room to Scandinavia and write *The Russian Adventure*?" Halldór replied:

Vera Hertzsch was a German Communist who was a Russian citizen. I witnessed her being taken away from her home and handing her child to her maid so that the child could be turned over to an orphanage. I have always looked on this as if I had been witness to an accident. I have frequently witnessed accidents, for example, on the streets of huge cities, and I have always looked on this as one of them. But this was at the time when Stalin's system was so strong, so sovereign, that I had never heard of any country securing the release of prisoners from Russia under Stalin. Foreigners there were arrested, Communists, and sent to gulags, among others one Danish Communist M.P. It was as inconceivable to tear Russian Communist prisoners from the hands of Stalin as it is to lift up a man alive after a train has flattened him. The only thing that I was able to do was to tell persons concerned what had happened, people who were connected to the case. There was nothing else that I could do.

Halldór does not answer the question directly; no-one thought that he could have saved Vera Hertzsch.

In *The Russian Adventure* there is one sentence that is particularly telling: "The desire for beauty that has not made a contract with reason and reality must cross over the border of the sorrowful, all the way out into the horrific." Halldór is here criticizing Gide and at the same time admonishing himself, because there was no desire stronger in him than the desire for beauty. One might even take out the phrase "desire for beauty" and replace it with "political ideal". The political ideal that has not made a contract with reason and reality must cross over the boundary of the sorrowful, all the way out into the horrific.

A writer's life must always be one of the keys to his works, particularly when that life crosses paths with a century's extremes. At the same time that Halldór was a witness to historical events, and sunk as deeply as possible into the swamp of Stalinism in his essays, his fiction reached its highest level: "The last chapters in *The Palace of the Summerland* were written during breaks in the trials of Bukharin and the Trotskyites," he says in *The Russian Adventure. World Light*, in which Halldór most passionately expresses a desire for beauty, was composed during these years. It was his ability to give voice to these opposites that made him a great writer.

When the Soviet publishers rejected *Salka Valka* in 1938 it became clear to Halldór that his literary partnership with the Soviets could only go so far; now both the Communists and the Nazis had rejected the book for political reasons. The first Eastern bloc company to publish *Salka Valka* was Dietz in East Germany in 1951. The company's directors were rebuked, so they contacted Halldór to ask whether he could not write an addendum to clarify what happened to Salka. Halldór, who at the time was still publicly devoted to the Soviets, replied angrily, pointing to the period during which *Salka Valka* had been written. Addenda were out of the question; one did not write novels that way:

> In 1938 the editors in Moscow said to me: "Our people have never seen Communists such as Arnald." I replied: "Of course they have, but you hang them." (I had then been present at the trial in Moscow of Yagoda, Bukharin, & Co.) Write a final chapter to be added to the end of the book, in which the people hang Arnald and make Salka Valka the leader of the glorious and victorious Communist Party of Iceland, and then you will think the book good. You call yourselves socialist realists, but I am unfortunately just a realist.

⤳ *The Story of the Fur Coat* ⤶

In amongst the earnestness of *A Poet's Time* there is a tragicomic story about the payment Halldór received for the contract he made in March 1938 with Anisimov at Goslitizdat for *Independent People*. The company had paid him 10,000 rubles upon signing, but all that he could do with this money was spend it on something he could take out of the country and sell: "I bought a fur coat, which, according to the current exchange rate, was worth well over 20,000 Danish kroner." But then the tragic story takes over: when the fur coat reached Reykjavík it turned out to be so poorly made that no-one would look at it. It was impossible to sell in Copenhagen as well, and after it was sent back to Moscow its equivalent value in rubles was deposited in a Soviet bank account that had vanished when the writer tried to locate it on his next trip in 1949. Such was the fate of the payment he received for *Independent People.*

Contracts that Soviet publishers made with foreign writers in those years stipulated a predetermined number of impressions, with half of the payment made in rubles on signing, 40 per cent on publication, and 10 per cent in foreign currency during the period of the contract. It was thus clear that foreign writers who intended to leave Russia had to spend their money on something there, and Halldór made an early decision about what he would buy, as he wrote to Inga: "Well, my dear, if I get a contract, you get a fur!"

Halldór bought what he thought was beaver-skin coat: ". . . very expensive; I spent nearly all my Russian honorarium on it, but I did it in a very good mood, because the fur is truly a beautiful sight . . ."

On 1 April, Halldór wrote to Inga from Uppsala:

> My beloved, it so happened that at the Soviet border I was prohibited from leaving the country with your fur, because it was against the rules that a man should travel with women's clothing . . . only with permission from the highest authority . . . I had to leave it behind . . .

With his friend Apletin's help the fur was eventually sent to Iceland. In October Halldór wrote to Apletin to report that things were not going too well. In Iceland there was no specialist who could value the coat so they had to try Copenhagen. There the best furriers, Levinsky, told them that the coat was not beaver but otter fur, of the cheapest quality, and besides that so poorly tailored that it was beyond alteration. (The coat was much too big for Inga; furthermore of a style that had gone out of fashion twenty years earlier.) The fur had been meant as a present to Inga to make up for their eternal poverty: he bought her a fine new tiger-pelt of the latest fashion to make up for it.

Halldór explained to Apletin that they had tried all the furriers in Copenhagen. The days of otter-fur coats were over. The fur might sell best as a rug; although this was unlikely. Eventually they placed an advert in the newspaper, but those few who came to view the coat found the object repulsive, and the best offer they received was 75 krónur. All Inga could think of doing was returning to Iceland with the fur and trying to get a refund of customs tax.

To send the fur back to Russia or not? How would they get it across the border?

On 11 January, 1939, a letter arrived from Apletin. The shop in Moscow would indeed take the fur back and the refund would be deposited in Halldór's account. In the meantime he was sending Halldór a copy of *The History of the Communist Party in the USSR*, (1939). Halldór received this on 8 March, in exchange sending Apletin the coat the same day. It was not until 17 May that Apletin wrote to confirm the fur coat's arrival. The shop had taken it back, the rubles had been deposited.

Thus the fur that Halldór had bought for Inga to wear at the expected Soviet publication of the novel about Bjartur had gone from Moscow to the border of Finland, from there back to Moscow, from Moscow to Reykjavík to Copenhagen, then back to Iceland and then back to Moscow. But *Independent People* was not published in Russian until 1954, a year after the death of the great farmer and furrier in the Kremlin.

On 1 May, 1938, Halldór's political dreams were achieved, when the Federation of Labour Unions, the Social Democratic Party and the Communist Party held a joint open-air meeting in Reykjavík. Halldór gave a speech urging a popular front against conservatism and fascism, while singing the praises of democracy. However, Halldór did not jump back into political activity at this time, since he had to prepare *The Palace of the Summerland*, the second volume of *World Light*, for publication on 10 June. Not much was written about the book, though Halldór's colleagues and admirers received it well. The artist Jóhannes Kjarval, for example, wrote these inspired words in *Vísir*: "From the book's open pages waft all sorts of luxurious fragrances – peculiarities cap verses, as do strange flavours from the most unlikely directions – or the most unlikely changes in temper." On the other hand, Guðmundur Friðjónsson said of the first two volumes of *World Light* that they were "from beginning to end hot air and malice, and a disgrace to Icelanders, both in Iceland and abroad". In fact *The Palace of the Summerland* is a brilliant book, into which, as Peter Hallberg has shown, Halldór gathers every possible type of character from his environment, emulating a technique that has always been used by the great writers of small societies: Aristophanes in Athens, Dante in Florence, Joyce in Dublin or Strindberg in Stockholm.

An important debate takes place in the book that is carried into the next volume, namely that between Ólafur and a character called Örn Úlfar, a "Red Pen" who thinks that a poet should, before anything else, support the workers. Örn Úlfar says to Ólafur: "Beauty and human life are two lovers who are never allowed to meet." This sentiment sounds as if it originated in Halldór's description of André Gide in *The Russian Adventure*, although the context is different. Örn Úlfar resembles

Halldór in his newspaper articles, but Ólafur is an aesthete, like Gide. Thus, what Ólafur says to Örn in the next volume of the work is much more interesting: "Hasn't it occurred to you that it's possible to fight for justice until there's no-one left alive on earth?" To Halldór, the novel was a stage for the expression of human doubts and questions, not simple propaganda. In this regard he resembled Ólafur, "the only focus and switchboard for the emotions here on this estate".

Around the middle of May Halldór returned to Laugarvatn, where he stayed long into the summer writing *The Russian Adventure*. He wanted to finish the book while the trip was still fresh in his mind and before he turned to the third volume about Ólafur. Halldór stood firm in regard to the Soviet Union, perhaps because he needed to conquer his doubts. When *Nordeuropa*, a Scandinavian journal dedicated to the spirit of the popular front, was published for the first time, he was on the editorial board. Communist influence was strong, but nevertheless the first issue included an article by the Swedish writer Vilhelm Moberg, in which he described his disappointment at developments within the Soviet Union, saying: "Stalin's reign of terror resembles more and more the reign of terror of the French Revolution." Halldór became quite angry:

> If I am to be connected in any way with *Nordeuropa* in the future, I demand that the anti-Soviet element be removed from the editorial board, since anti-Soviet sentiment means, in fact, the same thing as pro-fascist sentiment.

Halldór worked hard to get *The Russian Adventure* published in Scandinavia. Jakob Benediktsson's wife, Grethe, took it upon herself to translate the book, but Halldór was unhappy with the translation and asked Jakob to redo it. The book did not suit Hasselbalch, and Halldór tried to interest Monde in Denmark, which was controlled by Communists; this company published the book in 1939.

While it did not sell well, it had an effect, according to Morten Thing, an expert on the Communist movement in Denmark:

> The book was considered so weighty because Laxness began by surprising everyone with his criticism of "Soviet boasting". By doing so he put himself in the position of *informer*. In interviews with old Communists, many of them named this particular book by Laxness as an example of a work that had had a great influence on them.

Around Christmas, 1938, Halldór met the editors of *Nordeuropa* to explore the possibilities of publishing the book in Swedish. But this did not happen.

That summer at Laugarvatn Halldór met up with many of his comrades and friends. He enjoyed walking and swimming when he was not working in the library.

At the beginning of October, 1938, Halldór decided to go to Scandinavia, Paris and London on publishing business. Inga and he went first to Copenhagen, as they had done so often previously. *The Russian Adventure* had just been published, and Halldór took first copies with him and sent one to Apletin. Naturally, the book sparked debate in the papers, with opinions divided along political lines. It also had a strong influence on Halldór's fellow-socialists; as the poet Jón Óskar put it, he and many others had "come to possess, with this book, the dream of revolution".

Halldór went on alone to Paris at the end of October. By this time Professor Jolivet had translated *Salka Valka*, as well as the play *Short Circuit*, in which the director of L'Oeuvre, Paulette Pax, had shown an interest. But Halldór did not like the look of things, as he wrote to Inga:

> I am not impressed by the publishing world here, and I think that the publishers are miserable. It seems to me that Jolivet is very averse to approaching people regarding business issues, but I intend to take advantage of the few relationships that I have here.

Halldór contacted French people whom he had met at the P.E.N. conference in Argentina in 1936, including Georges Duhamel, who edited *Mercure de France*, and the secretary for the French chapter of P.E.N., Cremieux, who was an adviser at Gallimard. Halldór attended a dinner sponsored by P.E.N. at which he was an honoured guest; Cremieux and Jules Romains were clearly well disposed.

As in Moscow, Halldór had no intention of leaving until he had accomplished something. By accident he met up with an old friend:

> I was sitting here the other day in a café reading the papers, and who . . . should turn up but Kristján Albertsson? It was an extremely joyful meeting, and since then we have been together every day . . . until yesterday, when he left to return to Berlin.

Kristján was an exchange teacher in Berlin at this time, and although he and Halldór were worlds apart politically, their friendship was clearly unchanged.

It was decided that a special "P.E.N. Evening" would be held in Halldór's honour on 23 November; a hundred guests would be invited, and Jolivet would introduce Halldór's books. Halldór felt that his publishing future hung in the balance and decided to remain in Paris although he was broke and currency transfers were nearly impossible. He wrote to Inga:

... it is extraordinarily difficult for a Nordic writer to be accepted in France. You understand that I am in no position not to do everything that I possibly can for my books, although it might be expensive and boring.

This proved to be correct. The P.E.N. evening went well; it was well attended, an actor read from *Salka*, and Jolivet lectured about Halldór's writing. After he had finished,

> Cremieux ... announced that he had the pleasure of personally informing Monsieur Laxness that his book *Salka Valka petite fille en Islande* had the day before been accepted for publication by Gallimard ... there was a tremendous amount of applause.

Halldór wrote proudly to Inga that this was the first modern Icelandic work of fiction to have been translated into French, and from the original language besides: "It is a victory for Icelandic and Icelandic literature to achieve such a result in the most fastidious literary country in the world." At the end of November he returned to Copenhagen, having scraped together the money for the journey.

While Halldór was abroad, the Communists had managed to drive a wedge into the Social Democratic Party in Iceland with the result that the left wing of the party joined the Communists. A new party, the Socialists Party, was founded, and the Communist Party was formally disbanded. Those who had fought for the popular front viewed this development as the achievement of their dream. Halldór showed his support by joining the Socialist Party. He explained his behaviour in an interview in the *Will of the People* in 1952:

> I never joined the old Communist Party, but I worked to unite the leftist socialists and Communists into one party, and after the work was finished I felt obliged to join the new party, although I had neither time nor reason to be an active Party member.

Inga returned home from Copenhagen around mid-December, but Halldór stayed on and worked on the translation of *The Russian Adventure* and other projects; around Christmas he moved back to their old hotel, Goldsmith's House. His most difficult task was to get going on the next volume of *World Light*: "Over and over again this week, while I was wrestling once more with Ólafur Kárason, I decided to give up and stop writing and never go near him again."

As in the past, Halldór spent most of his evenings with Jón and Þórunn, but he also worked with Jakob Benediktsson on the translation of *The Russian Adventure*, and his mood was heavy as it always was when he was starting a new novel. He told Inga that anyone who did not have to be near him in this condition was blessed. On the other hand it was extremely important that he succeed in writing the conclusion of Ólafur's story; he envisioned one huge concluding volume, which in fact became two. This was, he said, not just an artistic necessity, but also a financial one.

At the end of January Halldór returned home from Copenhagen, having improved his financial situation a little by writing an overview of Icelandic literary heritage for an outstanding cultural journal, *Tilskueren*. As usual in his articles for foreign publications Halldór was more cautious and patriotic than in the ones he published at home. Most interesting were his comments on the position of writers in Iceland. He said that they could not live on the income of their book sales but depended on grants from the government, without becoming dependent on individual political parties. Respect for literature came before other concerns, and no Member of Parliament would ever let party interests dictate the decisions made about grants. If this had ever been the case, Halldór stood to learn a hard lesson.

In this article and another that Halldór published in the *Will of the People* on 17 March, he presented himself as a radical socialist supporter of the confederation between Iceland and Denmark. In 1918, Iceland had agreed to a twenty-five-year act of confederation with the Danes, which stipulated that the two peoples would have the same king; the Danes were to remain in charge of Iceland's foreign affairs, and the citizens of both states enjoyed reciprocal rights. It meant a great deal for Icelandic citizens to have full rights in another country, especially regarding work, education and cultural activities. Shortly after Halldór returned to Iceland, Sigurður Guðmundsson, an editor for the *Will of the People*, interviewed him; they discussed foreign editions of Halldór's books, the necessity of education for young writers, and even schools that might be established specifically for them. Halldór commented:

> They could teach people to write faultlessly, although of course it is not possible to create genius in such a way. Serious artistic work is always single-handed; every writer has to scratch and claw at his demons on his own.

In May Halldór returned to Laugarvatn, where he remained for the better part of the summer and into the autumn. Ólafur Kárason occupied his mind completely. He did, however, deliver a speech at the Þingvellir Meeting of the Youth Coalition at the end of May, expressing his views on cultural heritage and nationalism. He still had strong reservations about people he called "hurrah patriots" and "fatherland ranters":

The man is not the greatest patriot who praises his nation's heroic tales the loudest and is most unstinting in dropping the most famous names, but rather the one who also understands the suffering of his nation, the silent battles of the numerous nameless people who were never considered story material . . . The patriot esteems not only the strength of his people and their achievements, he also knows better than others where their wounds have cut deepest, where their degradation has been bitterest, where their defeats have been worst.

Halldór's extended stay at Laugarvatn that summer was not solely dictated by his work on *The House of the Poet*, the third volume of *World Light*. A crack had appeared in the foundations of his marriage. Halldór and Inga had been married for just over nine years. Despite many happy times it was not easy to be Halldór's wife. He travelled constantly, and always put his writing first. The family's finances remained uncertain, and Halldór had little interest in raising children or other aspects of traditional family life; he wanted his family to be secure, but if he did not have to have too much to do with it that would be the best thing. Inga for her part was interested in a career in the theatre and she was, as she worded it, "no wife-type . . ."

Nothing indicates that Halldór was himself considering a change, because on 17 January, 1939, he wrote to Inga from Copenhagen:

Although I am very fond of solitude, I cannot live without you but for a short time, and often I think that in fact no man could be better married than I am – so long as I am married.

But Inga fell for another man:

He was married but moved out, and I planned to divorce Halldór and marry him. I did not want to behave dishonourably in any way or hide this from Halldór, and we separated.

Inga's affair with Dr Bjarni Bjarnason began that summer, although she and Halldór lived together until late winter, 1940. In the autumn of 1939, of course, war broke out. And Halldór fell in love.

FOUR

Hot and Cold War

The Years
1939–1955

One starts off as a poet and ends up a travelling salesman:
that is the tragedy of being a writer.

Halldór Laxness in an interview

War Against Mankind

IN AUGUST, 1939, HALLDÓR WAS AT LAUGARVATN WRITING *THE HOUSE of the Poet*, the third volume of *World Light*. At the end of the month a young woman called Auður Sveinsdóttir was also there. Auður and one of her girlfriends were on holiday from their jobs at the radiology department of the National Hospital. Just over twenty at the time, she had dark hair, strong features and a cheerful countenance. She and Halldór had met at Laugarvatn in the summer of 1936, and those brief meetings had been memorable: "It was as if people forgot everything but him when he was present."

During those late-summer days in 1939, Halldór and Auður fell in love: "Halldór and I went out for a walk one evening ... Halldór reached over my shoulder to pick a flower, and our fate was sealed." This was summer love. The relationship was strengthened during the war years by trips to various parts of the country. Halldór wrote to Auður around Whit Sunday, 1940, telling her that he could not sleep:

I ... rather listened to the rain falling outside my open window, and to the redwing, and thought about you – about our first early-summer nights, the mornings when I heard your footsteps growing distant on the street just as the pigeons started to coo, and how I felt that everything I might encounter during the coming days would be wonderful because you were with me.

At first they proceeded with care: Halldór's marriage was disintegrating and he was fearful of binding himself immediately to someone else; it was not until a year later that he made the relationship known publicly, after he and Inga had parted for good.

Other things also occupied Halldór's mind in August, 1939. The debate about the relationship between Iceland and Denmark continued, and he added his voice to it with an article in which he adopted another tone to that of his article written the previous spring. Now he was of the opinion that the time was right for renouncing the king of Iceland, for dissolving the union with Denmark. There were two reasons for this. One was that in the summer the Danes had made a "non-aggression pact" with Germany. The other was that Danish politicians had visited Iceland in the summer and delivered a staunch anti-Communist message, which Halldór said was inspired by Hitler. The events of the next few weeks would change the writer's position entirely.

Halldór and Auður were both at Laugarvatn on 1 September, 1939, when the Germans invaded Poland. The guests at the hotel, among them Germans and British, gathered around the radio. Halldór and the Danish ambassador, de Fontenay, helped to translate the news for the foreign guests, who quickly packed their belongings and rushed back to town. At the start of the war Iceland was neutral, but it also had no army, and everyone knew that the Danes could not offer much protection. The atmosphere in Reykjavík was uncertain.

The war looked different to the Icelandic Communists and their supporters than to most other Icelanders. After Hitler and Stalin signed their non-aggression pact on 23 August, the *People's Paper* asked Halldór what his position was now, he replied that he supported Soviet foreign policy wholeheartedly, stating that the British and the Germans, "the two greatest pillars of the Western capitalist system", had adopted a policy of mutual extermination, which must have been a shock to anyone who had hoped that they would ally themselves against Bolshevism. The non-aggression pact allowed the Soviets to break this anti-Communist axis, and the imperialist war between the Western powers handed them the key to controlling Europe and the Far East.

Halldór again praised the non-aggression pact in an article at the end of September, when Poland was divided after the Soviet army reached the Weichsel River. The article showed how absurd Halldór's logic had become, though in his favour it might be noted that he did not try to conceal this. In fact he rejoiced over the news that "Bolsheviks" were on the river bank:

> . . . fifteen million people in a medieval feudal state, which was famous for
> the most miserable rural destitution in the West, have, with very little struggle

and without any real bloodshed to speak of, made the leap into a Soviet society of workers and farmers.

At the same time he considered it one of the best results of the non-aggression pact that German fascism's cornerstone had been kicked out from under it – its struggle against Communism: "What is left is a tame old dog, which no Bolshevik would consider worthy of kicking . . ." To call Hitler a tame old dog at the start of the Second World War was nothing but short-sightedness, and Halldór did not include this article in his essay collection *The Contemporary Scene* in 1942.

Many of Halldór's contemporaries must have been startled to see one of the main leaders of the front against fascism adopt this position. But in his eyes support of the Soviet Union had taken priority: if the Soviets felt that the struggle against fascism was no longer their primary concern, this was his position as well. Above all else they had to protect the future socialist state.

The expressions used by the supporters of the Soviet Union now started to resemble those used around 1930: the war was simply an imperialist conflict in which they played no part. Observations that Halldór wrote for the twenty-second anniversary of the Russian Revolution, entitled "The Imperialist War and Socialism", reflected this position.:

> It does not matter whether the representatives of imperialism are called English or German: imperialism has nothing to do with nationality; instead, it is by nature an international conspiracy of crooks, who are eternally prepared to fight and quarrel about who has the licence to rob and plunder the world, subjugate innocent peoples, usurp people's values, enslave them; and the method that they employ to pursue this beautiful interest of theirs is to drown the nations in blood.

Although Iceland's neutrality policy enjoyed widespread support among its citizens, the Socialist Party's position was not widely understood. One of those who criticized Halldór harshly for his position regarding the non-aggression pact was his old friend Guðmundur G. Hagalín. Rifts were developing between friends, rifts that would widen significantly during the Cold War.

Opposition to the Socialists would increase throughout the world after the Soviet invasion of Finland on 30 November, 1939, marking the start of the Winter War. Those Socialist leaders in Iceland who came from the Communist Party continued to support the Soviets and refused to condemn the invasion, but this was more than the Party could bear, and after fierce quarrels the Party chairman, Héðinn Valdimarsson, left it along with several of his chief supporters. On 4

December the M.P.s for the other parties resolved that the seating of Socialist M.P.s was a disgrace to the Alþingi. All of the other parties had joined to form a government in the spring of 1939, and now attempts were made to silence the Socialist M.P.s whenever they tried to voice their opinions in parliamentary debates.

These events were recorded in the history of the Icelandic Socialist Party as persecutions in which the Socialists were made to pay for their neutrality towards a war that was waged over the national security needs of the U.S.S.R. Halldór interpreted the conflict in the same way. But he also admitted that the war "depressed many people, not least the friends that the workers' state in the East has throughout the world".

In mid-December, 1939, Halldór published *The House of the Poet*, which received little attention in the papers. The *Will of the People* published a positive review by Björn Sigfússon, later Head Librarian of the University Library, and several months later Jóhannes Kjarval published another review in *Vísir*, in which he calls the book a puzzle while also observing that it "deserves as much respect as the most beautiful painting" – a huge compliment from the painter. The book is about a poet in horrendous difficulty; Ólafur is torn between his calling and the class struggle. In the service of Pétur Þríhross, he composes, on order, love poems and marriage proposals, congratulatory poems, birthday poems, marriage poems and epitaphs, becoming the switchboard for the emotions of other people. But the conflict between the workers and Pétur prevents Ólafur from whiling away his time writing poetry; he is forced to take a stand. In the end he delivers a speech for the workers that has often been quoted, since it can be taken as an outline of Halldór's own agenda at that time:

> The fact is that it is much more difficult to be a poet and write poetry about the world than it is to be a man and live out in the world. You hump rocks for next to no pay and have lost your livelihood to thieves, but the poet is the emotion of the world, and it is in the poet that all men suffer. "From the hoof of this damned world, O Lord, remove the small nails," says the old hymn. The poet is the quick in this hoof, and there is no stroke of luck, neither higher wages nor better catches, that can cure the poet of suffering – nothing but a better world. On the day the world becomes good, the poet will cease to suffer, and not before; but at the same time he will also cease to be a poet.

Throughout the country the role of fiction was being discussed by the "Red Pens". Was it possible for fiction to serve a cause? As always, Halldór did not want to bind fiction to politics. Halldór's vision of the world of beauty strengthened his faith that fiction had independent value and its own laws, even when he himself was the most ruthless political fighter.

Notwithstanding this, the reader of *The House of the Poet* never knows for sure whether Ólafur supports the workers' struggle because he believes in its cause or because he is in love with a radical girl, Jórunn. This ambiguity does not change the fact that the novel is a strong social critique or that it satirizes political events in Iceland. This did not escape the notice of those in power.

At the start of 1940 Halldór felt the authorities' wrath. For several years he had been receiving a 5,000-krónur grant from the Alþingi, roughly the annual salary of an office worker. Meanwhile the director of the Cultural Council, Jónas from Hriflu, was becoming more staunchly anti-Communist with each passing year; the hysteria in the anti-Communist camp was sometimes hardly less intense than the Communists' attachment to the Soviet Union. At the time of the Winter War Jónas felt that he was justified in punishing the main writers in the Socialist camp, and the grants to both Þórbergur Þórðarson and Halldór Laxness were lowered significantly. Jónas made no attempt to conceal the fact that the decision was political. At the time Halldór was at the peak of his writing career.

The *Will of the People* protested the Cultural Council's actions vociferously and called on various people to witness the fact that Halldór was both the most respected and the most widely read Icelandic writer, but to no effect.

Halldór was in the process of moving out of the house he had shared with Inga, and the reduction of his grant came as a shock. The war made publication of his books in Europe uncertain. *Independent People* had not yet appeared in the Soviet Union, and although Apletin and his colleagues assured him that it would be published later, Halldór had his doubts. In early December, 1939, he wrote to Apletin and told him about the isolation of the Communists, who were basically being viewed as traitors. He said that he was certain that he would be deprived of his government grant "on the grounds that I am a Russian and an enemy of the Icelandic people . . ." and concluded by asking whether it might be possible to transfer the money that he had on account in Moscow to a Danish or Swedish bank in foreign currency. Goslitizdat, which planned to publish *Independent People*, responded positively and sent Halldór payment equivalent to approximately 1,000 krónur in royalties.

Halldór's books sold well in Iceland – each volume of *World Light* sold between two and three thousand copies – but this was far from sufficient to cover his living expenses. Nevertheless, he decided not to accept the reduced grant from the

Cultural Council. In a newspaper interview he said: "This money was allotted to me as a punishment and a warning, in order to humble me . . ." In the light of this he said that he was thinking of depositing the grant money into a fund for the protection of the spiritual freedom of Icelandic writers, "no matter what views they hold". This marked the start of a battle between the authorities, under the leadership of Jónas from Hrifla, and radical and liberal artists and intellectuals, a war that lasted for several years and that took on an increasingly fanatical form.

Writers and intellectuals who supported the Socialist Party felt strongly that they needed to break free from their isolation, and that now, after the conclusion of the Winter War, they had an opportunity to do so. In order to accomplish this they made use of the literary society Mál og menning. An agreement was made with Sigurður Nordal for the writing of a great work on Icelandic heritage (the book was published under the title *Icelandic Culture* (1942)). This work bore witness to the fact that conservative and socialist intellectuals trod the same path when it came to the interpretation of cultural history. The group tried to gain the cooperation of Gunnar Gunnarsson, who was asked to write the preface to an edition of the works of Jóhann Sigurjónsson. And in the spring of 1940 a board of forty well-known intellectuals was established in order to strengthen Mál og menning and encourage people from outside the Socialist camp to join the society. A meeting was held at Hotel Borg on 4 May, which was attended not only by old "Red Pens", but also by Sigurður Nordal, Páll Ísólfsson and Ragnar Jónsson. Halldór attended this meeting, just as he attended most of the board meetings of Mál og menning during the war years. Their journal, *Mál og menning*, was established in early 1940, and from the start he wrote a great deal for it about issues close to his heart.

Kristinn E. Andrésson did not attend the meeting at Hotel Borg, however, having undertaken a long trip abroad, among other reasons to procure paper for *Icelandic Culture*. Kristinn went first to Denmark, where he negotiated with Gunnar Gunnarsson for the publication of his collected works by Landnáma. Upon receiving Gunnar's consent, Kristinn sent Halldór a telegram and asked him to translate *The Church on the Mountain*, which Halldór agreed to do immediately, doubtless feeling he owed it to Gunnar, beside the fact that the project was financially appealing. Kristinn went next to Sweden, but his route back was closed when the Germans occupied Denmark and attacked Norway at the start of April. Kristinn decided instead to go to Moscow, where he gave Florin at the Comintern a detailed report of the situation in Iceland, telling him proudly about *Icelandic Culture*. Kristinn also asked for financial support for Heimskringla to publish the *History of the Communist Party of the USSR* and other works by Lenin and Stalin. This request was denied, although he had previously been promised 1,000 dollars.

Halldór was at Laugarvatn when the British occupied Iceland on 10 May. Although the government protested, it cooperated with the British, and many people were doubtless happy that it was the British and not the Germans who reached Iceland first.

The British occupation would change the appearance of the land and its culture completely. After a year there were twenty-five thousand soldiers in Iceland. The invasion of modernity had certainly started earlier, but with the military occupation it became clear that it could neither be stopped nor controlled, despite the dreams of many. Reykjavík was changed, as the historian Þór Whitehead's citation of Gísli Kristjánsson attests:

> Before the occupation everyone knew everyone else, even the cars by the sounds of their engines, and there was an air of calm to the life of the city. Then came the army: there was always something new to see; the old days were gone and would never return.

The war years were boom years: the price of fish products was high in Britain and a great deal of employment was created by the occupation. The depression lifted and unemployment disappeared. The war years also marked the beginning of the end of Iceland's farming society; farming in the isolated places that Halldór had visited simply ended. Urban culture received a boost, spending power increased, and the position of women changed completely as many of them could now work outside the home. But the Icelanders were not unaffected by the tragedies of the war, and numerous seamen lost their lives when their ships sank, either in convoys or when sailing to Britain with fish.

In the spring of 1940, however, few people had any idea of what was ahead; the Icelanders could do nothing but wait for what would happen in the conflict between the superpowers. And most Icelanders were condemned to remain at home. The war years became the longest continuous period during which Halldór would remain in Iceland. When he needed a change or peace for writing, he went to Laugarvatn or visited friends in the countryside.

This unavoidable house arrest, if it can be called that, came at an appropriate time. Halldór had started to redirect his sights towards Icelandic culture and history by delving into the Icelandic sagas, and his great project during the war years was the historical novel *Iceland's Bell*. He was more content with his nationality than ever: for the time being the Icelander had the upper hand over the cosmopolitan.

There exists a remarkable source for the daily activities of the radical artists in Reykjavík during the war years: the diaries of Þóra Vigfúsdóttir. Þóra, the wife of Kristinn Andrésson, was a fiery idealist and intensely emotional. She and her poor, idealistic friends met almost daily, drank coffee and talked about writing and politics far into the night, fearful of the news on the radio: Halldór Stefánsson and Gunnþórunn Karlsdóttir, Steinn Steinarr, Ólafur Jóhann Sigurðsson, Erlendur Guðmundsson, Þórbergur and Margrét – and Halldór. Þóra's admiration for Halldór is obvious: "It was as if half the world arrived when he turned up".

From Þóra's diaries of May, 1940, one gathers that Halldór was in high spirits. Although she was concerned that Kristinn had not yet returned from his long journey, on 13 May she wrote: "Then Kiljan phoned . . . [he] had completed *The Beauty of the Heavens* [the final volume of *World Light*], and I suddenly felt as if everything were normal again." Two days later there is this entry: "Kiljan came in the afternoon and said that he had finished moving, and seemed to be very content with life. He plans to be in town for some time . . ." Halldór was renting a top-floor apartment at Vesturgata 28, where he lived throughout the war years, though he had not yet introduced Auður to his friends.

On 1 August *The Beauty of the Heavens* was published, the fourth and final volume of *World Light*, Halldór's most lyrical novel and one of his greatest works. As Gunnar Benediktsson put it in the *Will of the People*:

> The greatest work of art that has been written in the form of a novel in the Icelandic language one hears said, and I for my part feel that every word of this is true.

In a review for *Morgunblaðið*'s *Lesbók*, Sigurður Nordal calls the work the writer's most beautiful and true book: "And I am sometimes in doubt as to whether any living novelist I know has a richer or more varied talent." There was a hitch, however: Sigurður was also writing about *Sólon Íslandus* by Davíð Stefánsson, and in order to maintain critical balance the review was entitled "Two Great Novels". A quarter of a century later it provided Halldór with the occasion for the following comments:

> In an Icelandic paper one does not mention the name of a tolerable writer unless he is connected with a certain group of people that require special protection . . . I know of one highly respected Icelandic paper that would not review a novel by a well-known novelist unless a novel by another writer, who was a novelist neither in his own eyes nor the eyes of anyone else, received an even better mark in the same review.

Such a statement is an excellent example of Halldór's sensitivity to reviews.

With the fourth volume of *World Light*, the part of Halldór's writing career that can be associated with the social-realist novel came to an end. Ólafur Kárason walks up the glacier at the end of the book, and the lyrical takes over. The plot slows; realism gives way to dreaminess, until suddenly there is no more story.

Halldór's working methods are revealed by comments made in his notebooks: "Read great lyrics while rewriting *The Beauty*. Holderlin, Stefan George, Verlaine, Baudelaire – translate the beautiful images and use them Icelandicized." Ólafur's desire for beauty reaches its apex in this volume. The girl he desires is a symbol of beauty, and the discovery of beauty awakens sorrow because it was "the hurt that could never be assuaged, the tear that could never be dried". The girl has told Ólafur to think of her when he is in glorious sunshine, and so he hikes up the glacier in order to find his love when the sun is directly overhead. Halldór turns to the Old Icelandic narrative of the Virgin Mary to find similes for the sun and brightness, and then writes the concluding words over and over again in his notebooks, cutting and replacing words until they are completely lucid.

Ólafur Kárason is partly a Christ-figure, as Reverend Gunnar Kristjánsson has said, and Halldór uses religious references to strengthen the work. In this final volume he stops several times at the outer limits of the emotional scale, but saves himself from going over the edge by simplifying his narrative: he has left behind the wordy style and obtrusive narrator that occasionally characterized his previous novels. In the first draft he wrote: "Always clear, directly simple, as if everything were easily understandable precisely to emphasize the rare and the precious."

Satire and humour, Halldór's familiar tools, are of course present, but this is his most sorrowful work in which he encapsulates his views on the role of fiction. Ólafur Kárason comes to a farm at the foot of the glacier, occupied by people who in their stance toward life resemble characters who become more common in his later books, and that are associated with the Tao: philosophical, peaceful people. At the farm is a bedridden wretch who has a mirror over her bed so that she can see the glacier, because to her it is life. A long time later a mirror shows up again in the novel, when Ólafur Kárason discovers that the girl he desires has left her mirror on board the ship on which they once travelled together: "It certainly could not have cost more than a few aurar; on the other hand, it had mirrored the most beautiful picture in the life of mortal man." Ólafur composes a poem about the mirror, in which there is the line: "In this your mirror dwells both One and All." The night before his final walk Ólafur returns to the farm under the glacier: the poor girl is weeping; she has broken her mirror. He gives her his girl's mirror and fastens it to the bedhead. These words can be read as an example of fiction: fiction is not beauty itself, but a mirror image of beauty. Beauty does not have a place of refuge in human life, but can appear to humans in this mirror. The writer guards this mirror and gives it to the most wretched people on earth.

Halldór never comes closer to the world of beauty that had appeared to him in his youth than in this book.

*

Whenever Halldór completed a great work he was often beset by loneliness, which he sometimes overcame by taking a trip. But where could he go now? Instead of travelling he turned to translation: besides *The Church on the Mountain* he translated Hemingway's *A Farewell to Arms* for Mál og menning, and thus during 1941 Halldór published no original work.

Halldór continued to be involved in politics, and on 7 November, 1940, he spoke at a meeting of the Socialist Society of Reykjavík in honour of the anniversary of the Russian Revolution. The speech was published in the *Will of the People* under the title "War Against Mankind"; in it Halldór interpreted the World War just as he had done when the Germans and Russians had made their non-aggression pact, as a struggle among the four chief representatives of capitalism for control of the world:

> The day that war, genocide, and the annihilation of human worth cease to be the nature and goal of capitalism and its imperialist policies, is the day that capitalism and imperialism are finished.

The U.S.S.R. had, beyond anything else, to protect its borders so that war-mongering capitalism could not attack "this peaceful and happy republic of workers, intellectuals, and farmers".

Halldór wrote shorter articles about literature and various cultural matters, such as his favourite dislike, Icelanders' drinking habits, mainly for the *Mál og menning* journal. His viewpoint often took unexpected turns, for example, when he wrote:

> Alcoholism is a disease and a tragedy, if not both, and there is no more reason to put a man who is suffering from alcohol poisoning in prison than a man who has gone into a seizure on the street or been involved in a car accident.

Here Halldór proceeded as he often did when party politics were not involved: he was far ahead of most of his contemporaries.

Halldór's relationship with National Radio was tense at this time, as it would continue to be. Icelandic National Radio was in a difficult position as the country's only station: everyone who had something to say wanted to speak on the radio. And it was impossible to heed the laws on neutrality in a way that would please everyone. That Halldór himself was sensitive to what was said about him on the radio was made evident in December, 1940. At that time the meteorologist Jón Eyþórsson was the chairman of the Radio Board and gave a regular talk entitled "Daily Topics". On 2 December he spoke, among other things, about Halldór's work, saying:

> And this is how it is for many people when they read Kiljan's books: they feel that he is often lying about both the settings and the characters, even though they might occasionally find in the midst of this other things that are fairly amusing and that hit the nail on the head.

Jón's comments inspired a heated correspondence. Halldór complained to the Radio Board on 15 December that the "National Radio's weatherman" was "harping endlessly on . . . with the abusive term 'to lie'". Jón replied on 23 December and challenged Halldór to publish his letter: "In that way you gain the chance to break the marked silence that hangs over your latest books." Halldór was furious and refused to allow "this weatherman" to read from any of his books on the radio, in addition to requesting that he not be allowed to discuss them. Jón responded at the end of the year, reminding his listeners that a weatherman, having complete freedom of speech, could discuss literature just as a writer could discuss politics.

At the time Halldór's sensitivity was even greater than usual, because of the political isolation of the Socialists and the accusations that were being levelled against them. His battle with National Radio reached its peak in 1944, when he refused to pay the full licence fee because he missed parts of programmes due to interference. The Radio's director refused to grant him a discount.

*

Halldór's translation of *A Farewell to Arms* was published as a "book club" edition by Mál og menning, which guaranteed it a wide circulation. Kristinn E. Andrésson said that Halldór's brilliant translation, as he called it, played a significant role in the work's popularity, even though certain people had been finding fault with the translator's eccentricities. Here Kristinn was handling a difficult matter carefully. Numerous people had criticized the translation's language, meaning Halldór's spelling and neologisms. *A Farewell to Arms* became one of the most debated translations of contemporary literature in Icelandic; once again it was up to Halldór to open new doors.

Readers of *World Light* had already seen Halldór depart from standardized spelling at times; he generally tried to approximate spoken language. *Salka Valka* and *Independent People* had been published with standardized spelling, but *World Light* took readers by surprise in this regard. In fact Halldór had adopted "practical spelling" early on in his private writing.

When to this was added the fact that he was unafraid of creating neologisms, inserting borrowed foreign words and slang, the language purists had to respond. For example, a physician named Sigurjón Jónsson wrote in *Morgunblaðið*'s *Lesbók* that Halldór was clearly a "language abuser".

A modern reader might find this laughable, but it was quite serious. The teacher Halldór Guðjónsson reviewed *A Farewell to Arms* for *Tíminn* in May, 1941, saying that he felt it impossible that the book had been translated into Icelandic: "It would be more correct to call it 'Kiljanic', and people in general joke that it is a collection of obscenities, verbal burlesques, and all kinds of barbarisms . . . The Teachers' Union of Southern Þingeyrar District announced a resolution concerning the abuses of language in recent books:

> The Union finds particular reason to name the latest book from the literary society Mál og menning: *A Farewell to Arms* in the translation of Halldór Kiljan Laxness, in which the language is such that it can hardly be called Icelandic.

Halldór responded to his critics in *Mál og menning* journal in 1941, taking polemical shots in all directions. About Dr Sigurjón Jónsson he said that he had "hardly fluttered his eyelids in forty years". Halldór made a connection between criticism of his language and the contemporary political struggle and said that he did not wish to compete with those who, in order to increase their standing with the authorities, claimed that Stalin was a murderer. Nothing had changed in Halldór's position towards the Soviet dictator.

Turning to his work as a writer, he replies:

> What matters is this: in the eyes of a writer no word is ridiculous except the one that does not belong in a particular context – and it is in general not possible to become a writer until one has grown out of the idea that there is such a thing as a ridiculous word. No word is ridiculous if it is put in the right place.

He discusses the problems of diction and style:

> In some ways, every work of fiction has its own special landscape, a particular collection of types of people or characters, and, it must never be

forgotten, a unique language, its own unique language. A work of fiction that does not have, in addition to everything else, this unique, specialized quality, can hardly be any good, and perhaps not at all.

The general and the particular are always associated in fiction. To write is an eternally unsolved problem, and the use of punctuation is a part of the writer's artistry. Halldór details his method for translating *A Farewell to Arms* and suggests that it might be healthy for children to begin their reading with books they do not completely understand:

New and unfamiliar words, even inaccessible material, an exotic quality to a book – all of this awakens a child's curiosity, encourages it to think and demand explanations: but even the explanations that are difficult to understand act as mediums for new ideas, open up new views, often in many directions at once; and this is the path towards education.

The debate over the language in Halldór's translation was a good example of the growing importance of modern Icelandic. Following the same path as when he wrote *The Great Weaver from Kashmir*, Halldór showed that Icelandic could accommodate modernity.

Halldór's preface to *A Farewell to Arms* shows his admiration for the master American storyteller, all the more remarkable considering how sparing he was in his praise of contemporary novelists. Hemingway's expressiveness, writes Halldór, is found in

... the carelessness of games or entertainment in the midst of suffering; a childish, healthy honesty combined with the cold impertinence of a highwayman; the incisive and concrete trust of a realist in facts, even if everything around him is in disorder, coincident with a limitless contempt for loquacity and emotional mire; finally a hidden certainty, marked by fear and yet fearless, that everything is being lost. But beyond all else the book's power lies perhaps in how its writer is constantly able to sharpen the concept of love with the concept of death.

In the latter regard, Hemingway and Halldór had much in common.

Halldór wrote a great deal about literature during the war years. When one reads his literary essays, it becomes apparent that they are offshoots of a larger cultural struggle: the conflict over the control of Icelandic literature and publishing. He strongly criticizes the publishing work of the Cultural Fund, which Jónas from Hrifla was manipulating at that time, among other things to oppose the influence of Mál og menning. Halldór also found fault with most of the books published by the Cultural Fund, though he never went as far as Jónas, who started acting as an editor himself. For Halldór Jónas was devoid of the ability to write about writers and writing: "He does not know how to distinguish things, but instead blurs everything; he blunts what he should sharpen, flattens what he should taper, banalizes instead of characterizes."

In the struggle for the control of culture and the arts during the 1940s, Halldór had little support to speak of, except among the Socialists, who were themselves not doing very well. After a strike by the union of unskilled labourers (Daybreak) in January 1941, their supporters distributed leaflets to British soldiers, encouraging them not to take the jobs of Icelandic workers; for this Socialist leaders were arrested and sent to prison. The Socialists continued to struggle, not least on the pages of the *Will of the People*, and at the end of April the British army arrested two of the paper's editors and one reporter and sent them to prison in Britain. These included Einar Olgeirsson and Sigurður Guðmundsson, who had interviewed Halldór for the paper. The *Will of the People* was also banned.

Although translations and articles took a great deal of Halldór's time in 1941, he also wrote fiction, among other things the short story "Temuchin Returns Home", first published in *Mál og menning* journal and then in the collection *Seven Magicians* (1942). Here Halldór introduced his readers to the nomad and warrior-king Temuchin, in other words Genghis Khan, and the master Sing-Sing-Ho, who preached in the spirit of Lao-Tzu.

The story's style is disciplined, and it has the feel of old sagas or fairy tales, with the exception of cutting comments about Temuchin's warmongering, which are references to the World War. The characters are given life through their actions and conversations, but the writer refuses to give any psychological descriptions: this method approximates the one that Halldór used for *Iceland's Bell* more closely than in any of his previous stories. For a long time he had been intending to compose a work on the contrasts between Genghis Khan and Lao-Tzu, but in the preface he said that he had given up on the idea because of his poor knowledge of the Far East.

This is the first story Halldór wrote entirely in the spirit of Taoism. It is based largely on *Genghis Khan* (1936) by Ralph Fox, as Halldór makes clear in the preface to the second edition. He said of it in a letter to Peter Hallberg:

Of all my short stories I am most fond of "Temuchin Returns Home", probably because I spent fifteen years writing it in spite of all its flaws, which I myself can see – and in spite of the fact that the smallest part of what is in it comes from me.

His position regarding Taoism was more ambiguous than is sometimes thought; his ambition was great and his will to fight was strong. Thus his path was not the path of the Tao. This position appears clearly in a review that he wrote a year later about a new translation of the Book of the Way and its power, in which he favourably cites a Chinese scholar who says that the book preaches "the philosophy of ignorance, the advantages of banality and the importance of giving a false impression of oneself". Nevertheless he was fond of Taoist philosophy since it challenged him with its lack of concern for "such vanity as freeing one's soul".

On the Other Hand There Was Another War

> Fiction is a language that the contemporary spirit writes on
> a human heart.
>
> *Halldór Laxness*

Having completed three great novels, about a girl in a fishing village, a farmer on the heath, and a poet in the world, Halldór was at the peak of his creative powers. He had started to plan his next great work, the story of the seventeenth-century criminal Jón Hreggvidsson. In Denmark Jakob Benediktsson was looking after his business interest, which was not easy since telegrams had to go through Lisbon.

Halldór's relationship with Auður was good and it gave him strength during his long stay in Iceland. In a letter most likely written in the spring of 1941, he told her about his work:

> Now I translate over ten pages a day, yesterday fourteen; I want to be finished
> around the middle of next month, and also to be able to have time left over
> for you when you come out east in a few days. Otherwise it is a bit depressing
> to be translating books by others, and I hope that I will need to do as little
> of it as possible from now on.

He says that he has a photograph of her on his table: "When I think about your beauty and feminine charm, which you have in the richest measure, then I am often unbelievably happy, even though you are somewhat far away".

Despite her relative youth, Auður had grown confident, and accepted what befell her with equanimity, an ability that served her well throughout her life. At Easter, 1941, she and Halldór were at Laugarvatn along with Þóra and Kristinn; Inga was there as well, with her mother and family. Þóra wrote in her diary:

> . . . everything seems to be pleasant on the surface. Auður has a special atten-
> tiveness. It seems not to affect her even though Kiljan's former wife, his son,

his mother-in-law and sister-in-law are so close by. She sits with her knitting, takes an active part in all the conversations, and is cheerful and outgoing. I find myself admiring her.

This description shows Auður's confidence; for many years Inga missed Halldór and would have taken him back, her relationship with the doctor having lasted only a short time.

On Whit Sunday, 1941, Halldór, Auður and Asdis, Auður's sister, went with Kristinn and Þóra on a two-week trip around Snaefellsnes:

It was an unforgettable trip [said Auður]. We went hiking every day for a fortnight, in sunshine and good weather, and one day when we thought it was bright enough we hiked on to the glacier. On this trip I prepared food for the first time in my life.

Halldór himself recalled the trip in a letter that summer:

Do you remember the plover, who spoke alone to us for so long up by the glacier huts under Snaefell Glacier, and kept posing in front of us on the slope – why in fact does this come to my mind now? Because that was such a beautiful and happy moment, and this bird was so wonderful there in its pure solitude, almost holy. My dear Auður, be with me always.

The travellers returned to Reykjavík on 15 June, and Þóra remained so enchanted that it took her a long time to turn her mind back to her work. On 22 June, though, Haukur Thorleifsson called to say that the Germans had declared war on the Russians: "The whole world had suddenly changed".

With the German invasion of the Soviet Union, supporters of the Soviets throughout the world had become participants in the war. The Socialists in Iceland sat anxiously by their radios every evening to follow the news from the front, and for a long time it seemed that nothing could stop the Germans. Halldór interpreted this new situation in a long article in the *New Daily* (which had replaced the *Will of the People*) later in the summer. The article was originally written in English at the request of Alexander Fadeyev, the director of the Soviet Writers' Union, which was looking to Western writers to provide material for a book against German fascism, as it was now called. On the morning of 22 June, said Halldór, the war

was no longer an unscrupulous sports match between two hostile imperialist cliques . . . The understanding of the fact that the struggle against a capitalist dictatorship, fascism, was, the way things were, the most urgent necessity for mankind, made political opponents into comrades in one instant.

The article was telegraphed to Moscow at the end of July and the writer received an appreciative reply from Fadeyev.

Halldór continued to defend the Soviet Union on all fronts, and in an article published at the end of August even criticized the economist Benjamín Eiríksson – Vera Hertzsch's lover and his comrade for a short time – in an exchange of views about the workings of Soviet Communism. This exchange was triggered by the Icelandic publication of Richard Krebs' autobiography. Krebs was a Comintern–Gestapo double agent.

Another event changed the image of the war in Iceland that summer. On 7 July the American army arrived as a result of an agreement between the British and American governments concerning the island's defence. Step by step the Americans took this over, bringing a new era with them. They were better armed than the British, more advanced technologically, and there were many more of them – approximately fifty thousand soldiers at the peak of the occupation in June 1943, at a time when the local population numbered approximately a hundred and twenty thousand. The political winds also changed, and the editors of the *Will of the People* were allowed to return home from prison in Britain.

The period of isolation was at an end, but the cultural war was just beginning.

The Story of the Spelling War, or The Struggle for Cultural Heritage

At the start of October, 1941, there appeared in the daily *Vísir* news about upcoming books from Viking Printers, a publishing company owned by Ragnar Jónsson, who also ran a margarine-production company called Smari. The announcement told of plans to "publish the Icelandic sagas in new editions, in which their language will be brought into modern form, and the dry genealogical lists left out". It was also announced that *Laxdæla Saga* would be the first book in the series. This harmless news set off a violent storm that lasted for two years.

The first one to protest was, naturally, Jónas Jónsson from Hrifla. Several days after the appearance of the advertisement he wrote an article in *Tíminn* under the title "Ancient Literature in the Mire". He stated that this proposed edition was a part of the cultural terrorism of the Communists and that the Alþingi must react immediately. Halldór replied with an announcement in which he said, among other things: "I have taken it upon myself to publish *Laxdæla Saga* in the form of the so-called Official Spelling." Otherwise the wording of the texts, their style or language, would not be changed. Halldór was not publishing the old sagas with the spelling that he himself used, but simply with the common school spelling. He pointed out that the standardized spelling that the linguists of the nineteenth century had come up with, commonly used in saga editions and defended by Jónas, was no closer to the ancient texts than the spelling of modern Icelandic. There was a need for two kinds of editions: scholarly editions or facsimiles, and reading editions intended for the public. This may seem innocent enough, but in the minds of people like Jónas from Hrifla, the nation's cultural heritage and self-image were at stake. He wrote: "The ancient works are being attacked like a battlement that the enemy army wishes to raze to the ground in order to make it easier to invade the country."

Jónas proposed a bill at the Alpingi, whereby the Icelandic government would be granted exclusive rights to the publication of Icelandic works composed before 1400.

The trio behind the prospective *Laxdæla Saga* edition responded by speeding up their work, and the book was published on 11 November, just before the Alpingi passed the law. They then went on to publish *Hrafnkels Saga* but now the government decided to sue them for violating the new law. The case was heard in the Reykjavík Criminal Court in September, 1942, with Valdimar Stefánsson presiding. In November the trio were sentenced to pay 1,000 krónur each to the government; a forty-five day prison sentence would replace the fee if it was not paid within four weeks.

The ruling was appealed in the Supreme Court; neither the Communists nor the margarine grocer would budge an inch, nor did Jónas' party give way. In the spring of 1943 he submitted a report to the Alpingi, an "overview of the endeavours of the Icelandic Bolsheviks to gain control of the spiritual affairs of the nation". It was doubtless correct of Jónas to say that the leaders of the Socialists wanted to maintain the strongest hold that they could over the cultural life of the nation. But the struggle was not only over Iceland's cultural heritage, but also over the power of politicians in Icelandic cultural life, which Jónas did not understand.

The Supreme Court put an end to the "spelling" war in June, 1943, when it acquitted the trio. Two of the court's three judges came to the simple conclusion that the ancient-text laws violated the constitution. The spelling war served to help Halldór renew and strengthen his acquaintance with Old Icelandic literature. He would subsequently write many articles on the topic, with more knowledge, insight and wealth of ideas than most of his contemporaries. After Jónas' defeat there was complete enmity between him and Halldór; perhaps Halldór found in the conflict an echo of the relationship between Sing-Sing-Ho and Temuchin, in the way that two completely opposing views of life met.

The cultural war was all-pervasive, and the discontent among artists intensified in 1942. Younger visual artists were even more dependent on public funding than writers, since the market for their work was still small.

In March, 1942, Jónas from Hrifla organized an exhibition in the Alþingi Building of government-owned art by the modern painters Jón Stefánsson, Gunnlaugur Scheving, Þorvaldur Skúlason, Jóhann Briem and Jón Engilberts. The nation should see the handiwork of these "daubers", as Jónas called them. However, Jónas was forced to move his exhibition of modern art to the display window of a shop in the city centre after protests by the leaders of the Alþingi.

The similarities to Hitler's 1937 exhibition of degenerate art in Germany were apparent to everyone. But now it was not just Halldór and his Communist associates who spoke out against Jónas; at the end of March sixty-six members of the Federation of Icelandic Artists, including Halldór, sent a strongly worded letter to the Alþingi in which they criticized the methods of the Cultural Council and its chairman.

Jónas from Hrifla was not a Nazi. But he was a domineering politician who did not hesitate to employ governmental power in contentious issues such as this, and he was simply opposed to any kind of modernism. Halldór, on the other hand, strongly supported painters who rejected the notion that art had to imitate nature. In a glowing article about the first exhibition of work by Nína Tryggvadóttir, he observed:

> ... any man can, if only he is unlearned enough, become the kind of artist who sits down and starts in on the endless production of imitations of mountains, imitations of the blue sky, mirror-smooth water and things of that sort.

In an article written in 1943 he summarized his view in clear, direct language:

> The laws of the arts are not subject to the laws of nature, but rather are, like all civilization, the suppression of nature. The artist takes a royal stance towards reality, uses it as his possession according to his will, but reality must bend under the rules that the artist sets for his work. The painter does not paint nature, but rather his relationship with the world. He does not imitate nature, but rather creates a world: his own world.

Beauty had its own world, and the arts followed their own laws; Halldór was preaching this message with more self-confidence than ever before.

*

In the spring of 1942 Halldór turned forty. He celebrated the occasion by publishing *Seven Magicians*, a collection of short stories from various periods: the oldest, "The Phenomenon in the Deep", from Taormina, and the latest, "Temuchin Returns Home", just a year old. Many different notes were struck, from the proletarian to the humorous. One such story, about the Old Icelandic poem the "Völuspá" in Hebrew, shows Halldór's fascination throughout his life with his contemporaries who resolutely followed their own paths, like the Jew Stein in the story who translated the "Völuspá" in the winter of 1938. It has no simple message and is partly based on Halldór's memories.

The same may be said of "The Flute Player" from 1939, which tells of a boy whom a mysterious man puts in a bag and takes on a long fantasy trip. This tale can be read as a kind of consecration to the art of writing, as Peter Hallberg has said. The boy is fascinated by the charm of the man's words:

> From the time that I learnt to read, those stories irritated me that contained moralistic teachings, secretive attempts to edify or other agendas behind their wonderful first words, or that were in the guise of fairy tales. I always felt as if such abuse of the letter were a betrayal, and I automatically stopped reading or listening when it came to the point at which I felt that . . . the story was peddling some kind of wisdom some other person felt interesting, a virtue that others thought fair – instead of telling me a story, which is, however, the most magnificent thing possible to tell.

Halldór repeats this idea many years later in the chapter on children's books in *In the Fields of Home*.

Gunnar Gunnarsson wrote an article in honour of Halldór's fortieth birthday in *Mál og menning* journal, and so admired *Seven Magicians* that he called its writer the "eighth magician": "This is the book of a full-grown man, but a man who does not know how to grow up.

Halldór felt young that spring. Several days before his birthday he had written to Auður from Laugarvatn:

> Often when we are together I feel as if our happiness were like an entire ocean. Some people say that all women are the same – and all men – but I did not think that the woman existed who could be such a perfect wife to me

as you; nor for that matter the woman with whom a man could be as perfectly
in love from a distance.

Halldór was never so much in love as from a distance, and his love was possessive, as perhaps all love is.

He and Auður had discussed marriage, and in the letter he says that he needs
time: "Just don't be impatient with me, my dear Auður. I have never loved a woman
like this and I could never imagine leaving you or losing you."

At this time Halldór also travelled around Iceland in order to refresh himself
and be inspired by a change of scene, as was his habit. In June he went north by
plane, and wrote to Auður from Akureyri:

> It was a great deal of fun to fly north, like a dream . . . After a short time we
> were crossing slantwise over Skjaldbreiður in such a way that I felt as if I
> could reach out my hand and scratch the mountain on its head.

Halldór worked well in Akureyri: "Ten pages, sunshine," it says in the same
letter. He also was making plans for his future with Auður:

> Now I know that we are industrious each in his own way; it is fun to relax
> as we often do, but one has to be industrious between times – such are we
> also, my love . . . But we must never let any shadow come between us, my
> dear Auður.

Halldór was writing the first draft of the first volume of *Iceland's Bell*, which he
completed at Laugarvatn at the start of September. This first volume is also entitled *Iceland's Bell*.

While Halldór was in the north a legendary figure among radical Scandinavian
literati gave a reading in Reykjavík: the dramatist and poet Nordahl Grieg. The
Norwegian had been held up as an example in *Red Pens* of a socialist writer who
supported Stalin's Soviet Union in peace and war. In the eyes of the Icelanders he
represented the Norwegians' heroic struggle against the superior strength of the
Nazis, and he was received extraordinarily well. Later in the summer he and Halldór
met in Reykjavík, as Halldór recalled in an article. To Halldór, he brought to mind
the concluding words of Auden's famous poem on the Spanish Civil War: "But
today the struggle." Nothing else would do.

Later that summer Grieg's wife, the actress Gerd Grieg, arrived to appear as
Hedda Gabler in Iðnó. It was likely in connection with this visit that the Norwegian
ambassador held a banquet, about which Auður wrote:

Halldór was invited to attend, and could bring a companion. I thought for sure that he would invite me. I started to think about what I could wear. In a splendid shop up in the attic of Haraldur's I tried on a beautiful, long black dress with red trim, and bought it to wear to the banquet. But when it came to it, Halldór did not invite me to go with him.

Halldór was in the habit of keeping his private life to himself when it seemed appropriate to do so. He became better acquainted with Gerd Grieg during the war years, even reading *Short Circuit* to her; apparently she wanted to translate the play into English and play the female lead. Nothing came of this, however, though it shows that Halldór was, as before, constantly trying to promote his work. When Nordahl Grieg was shot down over Berlin in December, 1943, the reaction of his friends in Iceland was strong; some people composed poems for him and the Norwegians.

*

In November, 1942, the first Artists' Congress was held in Iceland; a broad-based cooperative had been created in opposition to Jónas from Hrifla. The Federation of Icelandic Artists sponsored the Congress; Gunnar Gunnarsson became president and the Governor Sveinn Björnsson patron. Addressing the Congress, Sveinn noted that the construction of the National Theatre had not yet been finished, and that there was no art gallery in the whole country. There was a lot of work to be done.

The Congress ratified proposals concerning the necessity of artistic freedom from authoritarian interference. It also passed a vote of no-confidence in the Cultural Council. National Radio broadcast some of the events, among them a programme entitled "The Writer and His Work", in which Halldór was one of the speakers. He delivered a passionate speech about the work of writing, a job that could never be made to bend rules, least of all concerning spelling and language, because a "book is an illusion and a book can never be good unless it is a secondary matter that it is a book." Most important were to write in a living language and have some understanding of contemporary topics. This was why poets were both national and international; the fascists were wrong to insist otherwise: "Man is, especially these days, at least as international as the birds . . . A good book written in China is written for Iceland."

With the exception of additions to his articles that he had written in foreign languages, this speech was the final item to be included in a large collection of essays he published in December, *The Contemporary Scene*. In it were most of his articles written after *A Day's Journey in the Mountains* was published in 1937, long as well as short. One of these, entitled "Agricultural Issues", inspired a good deal of debate.

In it Halldór says that Icelandic agriculture was run in such a way that it served neither producers' nor consumers' financial needs. Farmers' living conditions were substandard, and people were flocking to the city; agriculture survived only by means of endless loans and government grants. Most to blame was the Progressive Party, which could not imagine any other system in Iceland than cottage farming. But cottage farming had nothing in common with modern business activity; it resembled an expensive sport supported by endless government contributions.

These views had doubtless been taking shape while Halldór was writing *Independent People*, and during the next few years he wrote further articles on the same subject, as can be seen in the collection *Self-Evident Things* (1946). Around mid-December, 1942, he reiterated his views in the *Will of the People* with "The War Against Consumers", in which he compared the price of agricultural products and the purchasing power of workers in Reykjavík and purchasing power of workers New York.

The year 1942 did not end without Jónas from Hrifla and Halldór going head-to-head one more time. In the wake of the Artists' Congress, Jónas felt that he was becoming isolated as the chairman of the Cultural Council. He wrote an open letter in *Tíminn* on 7 November in order to explain why the grant to Halldór had been reduced: in his recent books Halldór had slandered the country's farming class and fishing industry: "The Cultural Council came to the conclusion that this sort of fiction could not be supported by the government."

Halldór was furious. He questioned in the *Will of the People* whether it was usual outside Iceland to turn individuals' personal financial details into newspaper fodder. And he added. "A man can speak words of endearment for a short time to a good-natured dog before he suddenly orders him to shut up and piss off home . . ."

Halldór had his revenge when Jónas' reign of power came to an end due to opposition to his policies. His understanding of politics belonged to the interwar years; his understanding of the arts had its bases in the nineteenth century; his polemical methods were sometimes like a storm in a teacup. Halldór and Jónas had found worthy opponents in each other, but had not always fought with weapons of which they were worthy.

Many years later, Jónas wrote about Halldór in a friendly way and even visited him at his home.

For Whom the Bell Tolls

In this impractical society each person has to install himself
as practically as possible.

Halldór Laxness

In 1943 war continued to rage in Europe, but it was becoming clear where things
were heading. Stalingrad confirmed people's belief in the Soviet army, and the
Icelandic Socialists were no longer as isolated as they had been.

Conditions for artists had changed as well. The proposals passed at the Artists'
Congress had a real influence on the Alþingi. The member unions of the
Federation of Icelandic Artists were given the task of allotting the artists' grants.
The earmarked funds were not increased, however, remaining approximately two-
thousandths of the state budget. It cannot be said that the government had set
aside a great deal of money for culture. But what mattered most was that the atmosphere had changed. *Icelandic Culture* by Sigurður Nordal had finally been published,
and it sold thousands of copies. The wars, the huge one out in the world and the
small one at home, had brought people together.

The allotment of writers' grants was never a simple matter, though. The Writers'
Union committee in the Federation of Icelandic Artists tried to compensate for the
actions of the Cultural Council by granting Halldór 5,000 krónur for 1943. He had
received no grant for three years and had been made to pay for his opinions. Others
thought to be important writers received either 3,000 or 3,600 krónur.

This special treatment was viewed with disgust by Gunnar Gunnarsson, who left
the Writers' Union as a result. Gunnar thought that Halldór was being elevated at
his expense; he was, with the exception of Nonni, by far the most widely read
Icelandic writer abroad during the 1920s. But in fact Gunnar's popularity had
passed for the time being. He never regained his position in Europe, although he
always had admirers in Iceland. He belonged to the generation who had tried to
make their names by writing in Danish, but in the end disappeared from Danish
literary history.

The year 1943 was a good one for Halldór. He could accept his public grant
once again, and *Iceland's Bell* was published at the start of September, enjoying an
immensely good reception. The work's subject matter inspired a large number of
people to accept Halldór's worth. The story is one of pride, obstinacy and beauty
in the midst of savagery and ugliness.

Halldór had no interest in jingoism; the cosmopolitan still lived within him. But

Iceland's independence became increasingly more important to him. So choosing a theme from Danish colonial times, when sovereignty was centuries away and national identity seemed to have been lost, made good sense. For a long time *Iceland's Bell* benefited from having been read from the perspective of nationalism and the struggle for independence, but it has perhaps paid for this in recent years. Some of the dialogue has been quoted so often that it has become both idiomatic and anonymous: "Rather the worst than the next-best," says Snæfríður, before marrying Magnús from Bræðratunga. "A fat servant is not much of a man," says Árni to the German Uffelen. When nationalism waned, *Iceland's Bell* fell into the shadow of Halldór's other books.

But it, like Halldór's other great novels, is much more than a simple propagandistic work. The focus is different in each volume, and each has its main character: in the first volume, *Iceland's Bell*, it is the criminal Jón Hreggviðsson, in the second, Snæfríður, and in the third, *Fire in Copenhagen*, the scholar Arnas Arnæus. The commoner, the proud and enchanting aristocratic woman and the intellectual who has to choose between ideals and love – the trio appears often in Halldór's books. Arnas, the educated sceptic and cosmopolitan, is not weak-willed like Arnaldur in *Salka Valka*, and thus his story becomes more tragic. He sacrifices love for his ideals, his collection of the ancient manuscripts of Iceland, which later burn – just as he sacrifices his personal advancement for his national pride – but questions of nationalism are his concern. His ideals are higher than men; the country's books are more important than its inhabitants: "Their one and only task is to retain their stories in memory until a better day."

In Snæfríður appears the dream within the nightmarish reality. She is proud, and her character has its roots in the sagas; in the things she says she appears more like a study of Guðrún Ósvífursdóttir in *Laxdæla Saga*. Jón Hreggviðsson is the oppressed man who cannot permit himself the luxury of an emotional life, as can be seen when Arni's Danish upper-class wife asks him about his health: "Jón Hreggviðsson replied that he'd never had any physical or spiritual health, neither good nor ill – he was an Icelander, after all." Thus the basic themes of class struggle, love and nationalism all provide the reader with opportunities for insight.

Halldór's interest in the sagas was not just a response to the growing nationalism of the war years: it had its roots in his struggles with narrative methods. With the writing of *World Light* he deviated in some ways from the style of *Independent People*, where he tried to avoid over-explanation and wordiness. While working on *Iceland's Bell* he became determined to make the narrative much less bulky. It was the objective style of the sagas that he was aiming at so that the reader became acquainted with the characters' thoughts and emotional life only indirectly. In a 1944 interview about *Iceland's Bell* he said that he had been "trying to describe things from the exterior rather than the interior", and added: "Thoughts and feelings are conveyed through dialogues and physical reactions". He compared it to what he called material psychology, by which he meant behavioural psychology. Thus he connected his narrative method to both the ancient sagas and the newest sciences.

He spoke in a similar way in Matthías Jóhannessen's *Interviews with Halldór Laxness* (1972), when he described his compositional methods for *Iceland's Bell*:

Unnecessary loquacity is avoided; what a man is thinking is never expressed, because if one were to describe everything that everyone was thinking, there would be no end to it, and it would result in nonsense, contrary to the story.

This statement also shows the influence of Hemingway. It is a method that makes great demands on a writer and Halldór gained a good grasp of it. Description of the secondary characters, always one of Halldór's strengths, becomes even better under such constraints, and more humorous, as when he describes a character as resembling "two twigs stuck into a cream puff". From the same stylistic root comes Halldór's method of employing understatement more frequently than in his previous works, as when Jón Hreggviðsson fights with ghosts in a German dungeon and they recite to him "dubious assertions".

Luckily Halldór had not become a sedate, nationalistic narrator: his books were still characterized by a nonchalant, revolutionary spirit, but they were subject to a different type of discipline than before.

Iceland's Bell was Halldór's first work based on history, though he did not wish it to be thought of as "'a historical novel,' but rather that its characters, events and style bow solely to the laws of the work itself". All of the main characters in the work, except for Snaefridur, have clear historical models, as do large number of the secondary characters.

Peter Hallberg studied the background to the creation of *Iceland's Bell*, and the work's sources are scrutinized in Eiríkur Jónsson's *The Roots of Iceland's Bell* (1981). The inspiration for the story was a letter written by Jón Hreggviðsson on 31 July, 1708, to Árni Magnússon and preserved in Danish in Árni's correspondence. Jón Helgason had told Halldór about the letter in 1924; in the 1930s Halldór started to go systematically through sources concerning the novel's period in the National Library of Iceland. He redrafted many times. This method gave the novel more power, as Eiríkur Jónsson has pointed out:

Although *Iceland's Bell* transports the reader into the costume of a particular

historical period, it is as if the life of the people is timeless. In the novel the
unity of Icelandic literature through the centuries is confirmed.

If *Iceland's Bell* marked a turning point in Halldór's narrative art, it also marked
a turning point in his relationship with the people of Iceland. The publisher Ragnar
Jónsson called it Halldór's most popular book of all time. The work's contents
and style were most important in this regard, but external circumstances such as
the increased sense of nationalism also played a part. Not everyone, however, was
fond of the work; Jónas from Hrifla thought that it had been a poor choice to
take as a subject the worst period in Iceland's history.

Not only did Halldór redraft his books over and over again, but he also made
revealing adjustments to his texts on the typesetter's proofs he received from his
publishers. It so happens that his set of proofs of *Iceland's Bell* has been preserved.
The few corrections show his precision and sensitivity. In Chapter 8, Jón
Marteinsson and Jón Hreggviðsson are getting drunk in Copenhagen, and
Marteinsson tells Hreggviðsson that Iceland has no future.

They ordered venison with French red wine, but no sooner had they started
to tear into the steak than Jón Hreggviðsson came to his senses, grabbed the
shaft of the knife with one hand and stuck it into the table with a strong
blow, the point sticking up.
"Huh, sunk?" he said, and looked at Jón Marteinsson.

Halldór made several changes to the proofs, shown here in italics:

They ordered venison with French red wine, but no sooner had they *torn*
into the steak than Jón Hreggviðsson came to his senses, grabbed the knife
with one hand and *drove the shaft on to* the table with a *great* blow, the point
sticking up.
"*Never, never,*" he said, and looked at Jón Marteinsson.

But then he wrote a completely new version in the margin:

They ordered venison and French red wine. Jón Hreggviðsson ate for a while,
then drove his knife into the table with a great blow and said: "There, at last
I've had something good to eat. Now the land is slowly starting to rise again.

In the final proof Halldór deleted "with a great blow", and with that gesture
perfected the sentence.

Iceland's Bell was not published by Heimskringla but by Helgafell, Ragnar
Jónsson's new company. Ragnar and Kristinn E. Andrésson had owned and run

Heimskringla since 1937, publishing *World Light* and various of Halldór's other books. They worked well together: Ragnar sat for a time on the board of Mál og menning, and he and Kristinn collaborated in founding Landnáma in order to publish Gunnar Gunnarsson in Icelandic. But Helgafell was Ragnar's own creation.

Ragnar was a legendary figure in Icelandic cultural life, and became a publisher and friend of many of the country's greatest writers. He did not like office work and was known for driving around town in his jeep and collecting people with whom he had business, which could mean that anyone trying to get in touch with him had to chase after the jeep; it happened that one or two manuscripts went missing as a result. In 1954 Halldór described Ragnar's company offices:

> . . . the famous publishing company had its home in among the whirring printing presses and the shrieking binding machines; one had to push one's way past the stacks of paper on the stairs and in the hall; the venerable editors . . . were in the most literal sense . . . constantly doing cartwheels back and forth across the hall, the stairs and the machine rooms, looking for some shelter or corner in which to hide, like a vexed bird in a winter storm, where they could find peace to correct as much as one error . . . the bookshop was set up in side-rooms . . . without any visible sign of a cash register, a counter, a ledger – or even a cashier.

Although the description might seem dubious, this article was a congratulatory address to Ragnar on his fiftieth birthday. Halldór said that Ragnar had revolutionized bookselling in Iceland, besides starting the tradition of paying writers properly for their work. Being properly paid had, of course, always been Halldór's goal. His collaborations with Ragnar continued until 1980, when Ragnar had to retire due to poor health. Around that time Halldór said that he had never made a written contract with Ragnar: payment mostly depended on how things were going for the company, but the two men enjoyed perfect trust and never had a disagreement.

As time went by both parties profited from this association. During the war years it meant a great deal to Halldór to have dependable support from an Icelandic publishing company. His publications abroad were uncertain, the public grants had failed, and he had taken up translation, among other things, to support himself. But now he had a public grant, a popular book, an extremely energetic publisher, and the increased goodwill of the Icelanders, who besides going to parties in town had little to do other than read books. Halldór started to think about fulfilling his old dream and building himself a house in the vicinity of his youthful haunts.

But why did Halldór not have his work published by Mál og menning? In fact Kristinn E. Andrésson was overwhelmed with various projects at that time, so he agreed that Ragnar would take Halldór on. This was a wise move on Halldór's part. Mál og menning had a cultural and political agenda, and his hands would have been tied, as one of the society's founders and board members, by a conflict of interest between the society's agenda and his own financial concerns.

The parting of ways was not entirely without pain, however, as is clear from the diary of Þóra Vigfúsdóttir, who felt that the writers who had signed with Ragnar at that time were thinking about money, not ideals. This changed nothing between Halldór, Þóra and Kristinn; Þóra had simply come to understand what everyone else knew: in matters of publishing Halldór always placed his financial concerns as a writer above everything else. As Þóra put it: "Kiljan . . . swings towards the bourgeois as an individual, but is a great thinker and opens new perspectives with his art."

In the autumn of 1943 the *Will of the People* was bulked up to eight pages, among the new additions being a column called "The Contemporary Scene". It was published weekly; Kristinn and Halldór took turns writing it. Halldór's articles, many of them published in 1946 in *Self-Evident Things*, did not have the same severe political tone as his articles from the latter part of the 1930s but were closer to his articles from twenty years earlier. Now he was not as childish and insolent, but his mission was the same: to cultivate modern civilization at home.

In the first article in this group, "Criticism and Culture", Halldór took stock of the situation in Iceland from the time that it had been granted sovereignty, claiming that now the primitive culture of the rural poor was disappearing. In the course of shifting to an urban society, Icelanders needed to be ever-attentive to cultural criticism:

> We Icelanders are, so to speak, still country folk in the towns; the towns, especially the capital, are the exterior wrapping of a type of human life no previous Icelander has ever known . . . We cannot gain the respect of the world with weapons, gold or numbers of inhabitants, or with the recognition of our independence, only with the culture of our nation.

Halldór's other articles covered a wide range of subjects, from local history to the new National Theatre building. Some of his views were well ahead of the times. For example, he recommended the establishment of an anthropological institute that would keep a register of all Icelanders ever. Such a register would be invaluable to anyone researching Icelandic life from the time of the first settlements. As Halldór put it:

We are lacking the lives of farmers, the lives of workers, the lives of cottars, the lives of sheep-thieves, the lives of orphans living on the parish, the lives of itinerants at the fishing stations, and the lives of men who return to haunt others as ghosts – and it is of men of these classes that the nation was first and foremost composed.

This was of course way before computer technology, databases and personal privacy laws, and Halldór's ideas were coloured by his literary interest in Iceland in the seventeenth century.

*

For most of 1944 Halldór was writing the second volume of *Iceland's Bell, The Fair Maiden*, which was published that December. In the next few months he continued to write cultural critiques for the *Will of the People*.

*

Throughout the war years Halldór and Auður spent a great deal of time together; she was waiting patiently to see what would happen next. She shared many of Halldór's political views, and was very concerned with social issues. Þóra Vigfúsdóttir had awakened her interest in women's rights, which "received a blast of inspiration when Rannveig Kristjánsdóttir came home in 1942 from her studies in Sweden, full of new ideas", as Auður wrote. Rannveig started by editing the women's page of the *Will of the People* and got Auður to write for it, especially about weaving and other crafts. She was also, along with Þóra Vigfúsdóttir, among the supporters of the journal *Melkorka*, founded under Rannveig's guidance. Rannveig's husband was Peter Hallberg, who became Halldór's greatest translator in Sweden and a specialist in his literary oeuvre.

In 1944 the Icelanders founded their Republic at Þingvellir on 17 June. As we have seen, Halldór, the radical socialist, had written about the relationship between Iceland and Denmark in the spring of 1939, recommending that the agreement between the countries be renewed. He was among those who signed a petition to the Alþingi supporting this position in August, 1942. A year later another petition was delivered to the Alþingi, but Halldór did not sign it. In November, 1943, he published an article in the *Mál og menning* journal in which he celebrated the fact that the separation of the two countries had come about because of external circumstances, without bad feelings. Halldór wanted the mutual civil rights enjoyed by the two countries to be maintained, since they were convenient for students, artists and anyone else who wished to seek spiritual nourishment abroad, which was vital for Icelanders given the sparsity of their population and their remoteness. And he wanted an agreement to be made with Denmark for the return of Iceland's greatest cultural treasures, its ancient manuscripts. Negotiations over these demands would shape the relationship between the two nations during the next decade.

The secession of Iceland from Denmark inspired Halldór to write in March that the hymn composed for the national celebration in 1874 was useless as a national anthem: "... emphasis is placed on how the nation is insignificant in relationship to its God; the mystic elation of self-deprecation associated with saints and visionaries illuminates the hymn," and this had nothing at all to do with modernity. Iceland needed a new anthem.

Only those who lived through it can understand what Iceland was like in June, 1944, the "hoped-for hour of the nation", as Halldór called those days: "It was remarkable how every single Icelandic individual felt ... as if the life of the nation were his own life ..." Although Halldór was doubtless exaggerating, the feeling had been strong, and several days before the celebration of the Republic he went on a long hike through the countryside, "because I wanted to discover the land and its people at this turning point, when history itself had come to life in the heart of every man".

In the summer of 1944 Halldór was at Hotel Goðafoss in Akureyri writing *The Fair Maiden*. He returned in the middle of August and had good things to say about the experience; Auður had visited him and they had hiked in the mountains. These conditions matched his personality: he was a city-dweller, but wanted to be able to enjoy the countryside, just as later on he enjoyed family life much more because he could always leave when it suited him.

In September he continued to write at Þingvellir, oscillating between total happiness and despair – typical mood swings for a writer.

In the same month Ólafur Thors formed a coalition government of Independence Party members, Socialists and Social Democrats, with the Progressives excluded. The alliance that had been formed among the artists now took on political form. The Socialists, whom everyone would have preferred to see in prison three years earlier, were prepared to work with their chief opponents as well as the fishing-industry capitalists. The atmosphere had changed radically. This development was not uniquely Icelandic; the end of the war saw a resurgence of the left in the West and Communists accepted into the governments of many countries.

The Fair Maiden was received extremely well. It is interesting that at the start of this volume several contextual strands are derived from *Bishop Jón Vídalín* (1892–3) by Torfhildur Hólm. The relationship between Snæfríður/Þórdís and Arnas was in fact created by Torfhildur, as Helga Kress has pointed out. Halldór's youthful dream of writing a novel to compete with Torfhildur Hólm was finally fulfilled.

To celebrate the book's publication, the *Will of the People* interviewed Halldór on 23 December. He spoke in detail about his views on fiction, where he made clear the influence of the sagas on *Iceland's Bell*.

Just before *The Fair Maiden* was published, on 13 December, 1944, Dr Jónas Sveinsson, the owner of the Laxnes farm, sold Halldór a triangular piece of his land at Kaldakvísl for 1,000 krónur. Halldór had achieved his dream: bought land in the place where he had grown up, land around the holy stone where he had experienced a vision as a child. He had the land fenced and all that remained was to build on it. Auður learnt of these plans when she returned from a trip to Viðey; she and her sister had been toying with the idea of setting up a children's home there.

Disagreement over the allotment of writers' grants had increased again, even with the Writers' Union in charge. The union was riven by such disagreement at its meeting in March, 1945, that Guðmundur Hagalín and his colleagues broke away and formed the Union of Icelandic Writers. This rift later became a symbol of the Cold War in Icelandic literature. Seeing an opening, the Alþingi took the grant allotment back into its own hands. Halldór was in the Writers' Union and supported its work, but after the war did not involve himself to any great degree in union matters.

Although the final volume of *Iceland's Bell* was Halldór's main project that year, he had others in the works. He published *Burnt-Njál's Saga* and its epilogue, finally having the opportunity, with the support of Ragnar Jónsson, to publish a book with no expense spared. Gunnlaugur Scheving, Snorri Arinbjarnar and Þorvaldur Skúlason did the illustrations; the latter also designed the covers for the volumes of *Iceland's Bell*. In the epilogue Halldór explained his views regarding the saga as a work of fiction: it was an important source of cultural history, evidence of Norse belief in fate, and a unique medieval work because of its depiction of different personality types. Halldór repeated the view that Dante had discovered the individual in European literature, but said that in his opinion the author of *Burnt-Njál's Saga* had upstaged the Italian genius. He said of the idealistic world of *Burnt-Njál's Saga*:

This idealism, inseparable from the idea of fate, is an unconditional worship of the heroic personality without reference to whether a character's position is good or evil; it is the praise of the man who reacts neither to pain nor death, the type of manhood that no defeat can touch and who is strongest in his own death.

In the same year Halldór was also responsible for an edition of *Alexander's Saga*, one of the first books to be translated into Icelandic. Halldór's progress in the publication and promotion of ancient literature shows that he still thought along the same lines as he expressed in *The Book of the People*: a new revolution had taken place in the psychology of the writer, and he offered the Icelandic public the chance to enjoy its fruits.

A writer finds material everywhere and uses it in his own way. A writer does not keep secrets, but he can disguise them. Halldór was at this time a writer for a newly freed people who had only books to show for themselves. He occupied the place of the national poet; many were displeased by him, but everyone reacted to what he wrote.

In 1945 Halldór published a translation that he had done two years earlier in twelve days at the Ski Hut in Hveradalir, according to his own account: Voltaire's *Candide* (1759). In the preface he said that he had "Icelandicized" the work rather than translated it, in doing so employing the methods of medieval writers. The names of the characters show more than anything else the delight he took in the work. His translation of Voltaire, like that of Hemingway, benefited Halldór's own writing, as Peter Hallberg has said. The French philosopher's ironical criticism of militarism in the name of wisdom and the common man is seen clearly in the story of Jón Hreggviðsson.

*

In the spring of 1945 the war in Europe finally came to an end. Icelanders had profited from the war, the coalition government had brought opponents together and considered itself to be performing great deeds; the establishment of the Republic had strengthened Icelanders' ambition both at home and abroad. The old times had gone. Many excellent writers had also passed away, including Einar H. Kvaran and Nonni. Halldór wrote tributes to both of them. In Halldór's mind Nonni represented the best in Catholicism, and he had benefited from the help Nonni had given him twenty years earlier.

Halldór held fast to the theory that fascism was the "reasoning used by capitalism against socialism in countries where other reasoning no longer worked". In the struggle against fascism, however, another power had arisen that was even stronger than socialism: the conscience of the world, with Churchill and Roosevelt as its representatives. In a speech he made on 13 May Halldór echoes the ambiguous position adopted by the Communists when the defeat of the Nazis was in view: Roosevelt was the representative of progressive powers in the United States that struggled against the conservative powers on Wall Street, which threatened small nations with their imperialist policies.

That month, Halldór's mind was preoccupied with house-building, however. It was clear that the cost would be greater than he had expected, but his financial situation was better than it had ever been; he said in a 1945 letter to Hasselbalch that his income had increased significantly in Iceland. A book that had previously earned him 1,000 krónur now earned him 45,000. Besides this, the outside world had opened up again, so he could attend to his publishing matters abroad.

The cosmopolitan lived on within Halldór, but he became convinced that he could live in Iceland. It may well be that Gunnar Gunnarsson's decision to return home and build a large house had encouraged him in the same direction, but there were also other reasons. Iceland's cultural heritage was closer to his heart than ever before, and *Iceland's Bell* was in part his peace treaty with the nation. It also meant a great deal that he had met a woman who was prepared to sacrifice herself for him as he sacrificed himself for his writer's ideals, as he had worded it in that letter to Inga in 1931. Auður was the wife of whom he had always dreamed.

That year Auður had displayed her ability to lighten his load of practical concerns so that he could devote himself to his writing. Shortly after she saw the designs for the house by the architect Ágúst Pálsson she went to work. They had agreed on a country house that was not a farmhouse, appropriately large but unostentatious. On the anniversary of the Republic, Auður typed out a building contract. It also fell to her to think about fixtures and fittings, and in this she benefited significantly from the assistance of her father, who was skilled in such matters.

Later, Halldór spoke about this summer in an interview with Matthías Jóhannessen:

> I went east to Eyrarbakki while Gljúfrasteinn was being built, so that I could have peace from the builders who were always asking me for direction. I was bad about building and it meant nothing to ask me. At Eyrarbakki I wrote the book *Fire in Copenhagen* . . . It was a rather uneventful summer. I worked in the later part of the day and past midnight. That was in June and July. I was sometimes fed by Mrs Ragnhildur from Háteig, who owned the house. I often went on long hikes along the sea, gathered dulse and dried it on the steps and chewed on it while I was working. Or else I went for hikes up on to the land, sometimes entire mornings, alone and with everyone in Flói asleep. Around ten I would visit my old woman who lived in a little house next door. It was her job to light the stove . . . She lit the stove with coal and

I did not get up until the fire was blazing. When I left Eyrarbakki, I still had one bag of coal, which I gave the woman as a reward for her excellent work. I have seldom or never received such blessings for me and my family throughout time and eternity as I did for this bag of coal. I imagine that these prayers will pull me a long way towards heaven.

In the autumn Halldór returned to Reykjavík and started writing short articles for the *Will of the People* in the column "The Contemporary Scene", which had not been published for some time. Turning yet again to the drunks on the city's streets, as so often before, he expressed the view that Iceland, unlike Southern Europe, lacked a wine culture. He was always on the lookout for the chance to educate his nation. He wrote again about the high price of agricultural produce and about government subsidies for farmers.

In October a topic arose of which Halldór would become fonder than any other. The American government had asked to be allowed to maintain a military base in Iceland for ninety-nine years. Although this was not confirmed officially, a huge number of people rose up in opposition. In November an issue of the *Mál og menning* journal was devoted to this "Matter of Icelandic Independence". Included was Halldór's article "Against the Sale of the Rights to the Country and the Destruction of the People". If Icelanders were to hand over their country to a superpower for military use, he argued, the land would become a battlefield during the next war, a target for nuclear attack. This was a direct violation of the nation's neutrality and an affront to its newly achieved independence. Halldór described his vision of the future:

Iceland can have no foreign policy except to support the position of the United Nations, to prevent the world from being divided into two warring factions: two dominant, hostile political coalitions, who seek to wage war, wiping out the civilization of the world.

Halldór's article drew the main lines of the Cold War in Iceland. The ideal of Icelandic independence became increasingly important to him over the next several years, displacing Soviet Communism in his mind. In the meantime the Icelandic government rejected the Americans' request for the time being.

*

The construction of Gljúfrasteinn continued briskly even though building materials were difficult to obtain, and Auður had to remain extremely practical in order to keep things running smoothly. The plan was to move to the countryside at Christmas, 1945. Shortly before this Halldór suggested that they get married.

Halldór's friend, Bergur Jónsson, was to perform the ceremony but was unable to do so, and when the wedding day, Christmas Eve, arrived, it fell to his successor, Guðmundur Í. Guðmundsson, to marry the couple. Auður recalled: "I was half-dazed . . . When the Justice of the Peace took my hand and said 'Congratulations', I answered, 'Thanks, same to you.'" Their next encounter would not be so pleasant.

Only Halldór and Auður's closest relatives knew about the wedding; neither their friends nor Auður's workmates heard about it until a long time afterwards. That evening after dinner, Auður went with her cousin Ívar to Gljúfrasteinn to learn how to work the lighting and the boiler; and Halldór came the next day with their Christmas guests. When they moved in, the house had no electricity and was to be heated with coal, which was difficult to get at the time; power was to be supplied by a diesel motor. When the house was finally lit, it illuminated half the valley. In this regard Halldór and Auður proved to be innovators, as had Halldór's father forty years previously, because the area was not electrified until two years later.

There was only a primus stove in the kitchen, making it difficult to cater for numerous dinner guests, but everything went well. Þóra and Kristinn were among those invited, though Þóra had no idea until 8 January that Halldór and Auður were newly married. This was evidence of Halldór's growing need to keep his emotional life closed to others.

The newly-weds were happy with their house, and started to think about furnishing it. In January Ragnar Jónsson had a piano sent to Gljúfrasteinn, and Halldór took great delight in playing it. Þóra wrote in her dairy: "Halldór has . . . in general an interest in nothing but furniture for the moment." Halldór had noted down around this time: "In this impractical society every person has to provide for himself as practically as possible."

Þóra's comments were not entirely true, because on 23 January Halldór spoke at an "Intellectual Meeting" of the Socialists, criticizing the Social Democratic Party for taking the part of the warmongering American right-wingers over that of the U.S.S.R. He maintained, as was now common among supporters of the Soviet Union, that certain Western politicians had been threatening them with the atomic bomb. Halldór disliked it very much that opponents of the Socialists should sing the praises of Arthur Koestler; in this he spoke as a loyal supporter of the Socialist Party.

Halldór published two books in the first part of 1946. *Self-Evident Things* takes up the thread of *The Contemporary Scene*, yet here critiques of art and culture were much more to the fore. The *Will of the People* published a positive review signed

M.K. for Magnús Kjartansson, who had recently arrived from Scandinavia and who would become Halldór's greatest supporter at that paper and later in Mál og menning. In June the final volume of *Iceland's Bell, Fire in Copenhagen*, was published; just as influential as the previous volumes, it contained more references to modern times and the new independence struggle.

The final volume of *Iceland's Bell* had hardly been published before the peace was shattered. Halldór's writer's grant was decreased by the Alþingi from 6,000 to 4,000 krónur, and he refused to accept it. On a much larger front, the Cold War had begun.

Expensive Atom Station

The only thing that matters – and all the rest is vanity.
Halldór Laxness on the Military Base Issue

During the immediate post-war years, the foreign military occupation and risk of a new world war never left Halldór's mind. Nearly all of his writing, articles as well as fiction, centred on these issues. When one looks back on the Cold War from the distance of half a century, one cannot help but yield to the fatalism Halldór expressed in the epilogue of *Burnt-Njál's Saga*; despite their heated domestic disputes, it was not within the Icelanders' power to influence events in a significant way.

In the West many of the coalition that had led their countries out of the war dissolved; the Communist parties were pushed out from governments that sought support from the United States, and would not get the chance to return again for many decades. The coalition government in Iceland went the same way despite the excellent cooperation between Ólafur Thors and the Socialist leaders.

The Western powers were determined to secure their authority over the Atlantic Ocean, and although the United States had, for the time being, rescinded its request for a base in Iceland, it was clear that it would make the request again in a different form. For its part the Soviet Union felt that Iceland was within the American sphere of influence. Thus Icelandic authorities were able to secure Marshall Plan aid, even though Iceland had profited from the war, and was able to sail through the economic depression of the post-war years. In addition, throughout the 1950s the Icelanders earned approximately 15 per cent of their income from work at the American base near Keflavík. Whether or not the young Republic was proud of this fact, *realpolitik* was the order of the day.

Of course people did not take such things into consideration in 1946. The

Socialists considered those who wanted a long-term American military base in Iceland to be traitors, while the Socialists opponents accused them of preparing to seize power according to a Soviet plan. It seems that both parties were equally far from the truth. The Americans delayed presenting their new request until after the elections on 30 June. Halldór wrote an article for the *Will of the People* in which he said that only one issue was of any importance: "Iceland shall never become an atomic station for foreign warmongers."

His friend Kristinn E. Andrésson followed with a harsh attack on the Social Democratic Party and the Independence Party for not giving a clear response on the matter. *Morgunblaðið* replied: "Kristinn E. Andrésson, the editor of the *Will of the People*, has for many years been the servant of foreign military powers." The political climate was cooling off quickly.

In the summer of 1946 Halldór's publishing situation changed outside of Iceland when Knopf's edition of *Independent People* was selected for the Book of the Month Club in America. Knopf, one of the best-known publishers in the United States, had published *Independent People* in the spring, in a print run of seven thousand five hundred copies. The Book Club selection, however, meant a print run of at least four hundred thousand, and Knopf added that 60,000 dollars would be deposited into an account with Stanley Unwin's agent in New York.

When Halldór's Icelandic detractors started to calculate the income that he would receive from this deal, they forgot to take into account the fact that Knopf would of course take his share, as had the literary agent Curtis Brown in New York. After taxes and everything else, there appeared to remain 24,000 dollars for Halldór. This was a handsome amount, but not the end of the matter, as he would soon find out.

The story of Bjartur enjoyed good reviews in the United States. On 28 July an article was published in the *New York Times Book Review* by Robert Gorham Davies, while a well-known literary critic, Henry Seidel Canby, published an extremely positive review in the *Saturday Review of Literature*. Despite this shining reception and good sales, no further books of Halldór's were published by Knopf. According to letters sent by Curtis Brown to Halldór during the 1950s, Knopf had told him that he had no readers in Scandinavian languages that he could trust. Of course such a thing mattered a great deal, and it must also be remembered that translations often had a difficult time in the American market. But most of all, the Cold War atmosphere made it difficult for Halldór in the United States. At least indirectly, if not directly, he was blacklisted, as we shall see. Nearly half a century passed before *Independent People* made its magnificent return to the American market.

Halldór himself finally made it abroad in the summer of 1946. He described the trip in "A Little Travel Diary", which was published in the *Will of the People* in the autumn, and also in the paper of the Danish Communists, *Land and People*. Halldór and Auður sailed to Copenhagen, where they stayed for several days, and there she met Jón Helgason and Þórunn for the first time. From there the couple went to Stockholm, and in June they flew to Czechoslovakia, where they were the guests of the government, which had invited writers from different countries to visit.

Auður described the trip in her biography, and her and Halldór's opinions are amusingly dissimilar. Halldór has things to say about the difficulties faced by travellers there, such as the strict border control and customs security, currency restrictions, other red tape to wade through and the difficulty of obtaining decent accommodation. Auður meanwhile, was tired: "Every time I sat down on this trip I slept, after the difficult experience of the first winter at Gljúfrasteinn. It was as if I had not slept for years."

Halldór had planned the trip to Scandinavia to take care of publishing business. The first volume of *Iceland's Bell* was published in Denmark in the autumn, this time by the largest publisher in the country, Gyldendal. For some time Halldór had had doubts about Hasselbalch, feeling that he did not pull his weight where sales were concerned; friends had helped him find Gyldendal. Halldór thought he could sense some pessimism among the Danes, as well as unnecessary rancour towards the Icelanders, though he personally only had positive experiences to report.

Things were not going as well for him with Bonniers in Sweden, where he was told that "in general, books were not much read". Luckily Johannes Lindberg, the director of the Kooperativa Bokforlaget, the publishing company for the Cooperative Movement, contacted Halldór during this trip and expressed his interest in publishing all of his works in Sweden. The contracts were signed in the autumn of 1947. Halldór's comments about the Swedes are rather ironical: "These people appeared to be considerably free from so-called spiritual turbulence and were not particularly intelligent." And he felt that there was not much of interest in Swedish writing, with one exception: "Their style lacks nuance. It also lacks sharpness; boldness; exertion . . . Except for Strindberg . . ." Observations like this are not remarkable because they contain deep truths about Swedish literature, but because they reveal Halldór's position towards literature – it had to be bold.

Halldór and Auður's week in Czechoslovakia as government guests included banquets, speeches and a daily itinerary. In his accounts of these aspects Halldór's tone is more serious. The tragic consequences of the war are apparent everywhere. He and Auður went to Lidice, where the Germans had murdered the inhabitants and razed the houses. They were told that members of the German minority were being driven out of the country. At the same time the Czech government was trying to support culture, and Halldór was fascinated by how the nation loved books. *Salka Valka* had sold twenty thousand copies in a few days, having been published in Czech in 1941, under the radar of the German censors. There was a great deal of interest in the continued publication of Halldór's books in Czechoslovakia. In an interview after his return to Iceland he said: ". . . it was especially interesting to notice the enormous amount of courage, strength, optimism, pacifism, and work ethic possessed by the Czech people."

Halldór and Auður returned to Sweden from Czechoslovakia and afterwards went to Denmark, where they stayed for several weeks, first in an apartment and then in a hotel that became Halldór's refuge in Copenhagen, the d'Angleterre. The guest houses of the 1930s were a thing of the past, and from now on Halldór only stayed in the most expensive hotels. Halldór also visited a respected law firm and spoke to the Supreme Court lawyer, Hartvig Jacobsen. During the next four decades he, his son and others from the firm handled Halldór's contracts with foreign publishers.

Before the war, Halldór had made many publishing agreements himself. Hasselbalch had handled contractual matters for him for a time, as had Stanley Unwin in the English-speaking world, and there were agents in some other countries. It could be a complicated mess to untangle. Hartvig Jacobsen had acted on behalf of Gunnar Gunnarsson and was knowledgeable of these matters, but he did not run a literary agency. When Halldór finally tried to hire an agent later on, interest in his books had dropped off to a significant extent.

Another reason that Halldór let the Danish firm handle his contracts was that all his royalties would go through it and then be deposited into a bank account. Halldór had received, including foreign sales, nearly 15,000 Danish kroner that year, mostly from Hasselbalch. In later years Halldór received an annual statement from the firm. The firm also paid various expenses on his behalf and provided cash when he and Auður were in Copenhagen. Foreign currency was hard to come by for Icelanders; if you had earnings abroad you kept them there.

At the start of September, 1946, Halldór and Auður returned home, and later in the month the first of a number of concerts was held at Gljúfrasteinn, with Rudolf Serkin playing piano. These concerts were held to benefit the Music Academy, and Ragnar Jónsson managed to get a number of good musicians to visit Iceland to meet Halldór and give concerts. Guests generally numbered between thirty and fifty, and Auður always had her hands full.

Halldór was a devoted music lover, but it did not escape the notice of his old comrades that he had started to keep a different kind of company. Þóra and Kristinn were invited to the Serkin concert, and although Þóra could not attend, her diary gives evidence of the sorts of remarks being exchanged: "It seems to me that Smári Ragnar is the main man behind these musical events at the writer's house. I do not wish to let myself be drafted into the margarine-manufacturer's war party."

*

In fact military matters were on everyone's lips. The Americans had delivered their new request for a military base. The Prime Minister Ólafur Thors headed the negotiations on Iceland's behalf. The intensity of the battles was not lessened by the fact that the coalition government was still in power, and that Ólafur enjoyed working with the Socialist. The result of the negotiations, the so-called Keflavík Agreement, was announced at the Alþingi on 19 September. It stipulated that the Military Protection Agreement of 1941 would be rescinded, that the Icelanders would own Keflavík Airport, and that the American army would leave within six months. On the other hand, the Americans would have full use of Keflavík Airport for five years, to support their occupying forces in Germany.

Compared to the Americans' earlier request this agreement did not look bad at all, as its supporters pointed out. But the Socialists, along with many nationalists and pacifists, were convinced that this was the beginning of a permanent American military presence, and they were right.

The Socialist Party at once engaged in a difficult struggle against the Alþingi's ratification of the agreement, enjoying the support of the Federation of Labour Unions and the Patriotic Party, as well as a number of voices within the Progressive and Social Democratic Parties. Halldór, very involved in this struggle, was never more sharp-tongued. On 22 September a well-attended protest meeting was held in Reykjavík, and the next day Halldór published an article in the *Will of the People*:

> We Icelanders wish to have total control over our whole country, not over Iceland with the exception of Keflavík Airport – or those other places within Iceland that will likely be demanded of us in the next round. The relinquishment of this right, whether in small part or large, signifies the surrender of Icelandic independence.

Ólafur Thors and his companions paid little heed to the protests or to the Socialists' threats to dissolve the government. The Americans, however, had grave

Hot and Cold War

concerns that the agreement would not be ratified, and for support they looked to the British government, which sent a threatening message to the Icelandic authorities. This message inspired Halldór to write another article, "We Are Not Impressed," stating that the Icelandic nation was too small to have any respect for superpowers, and so defenceless that it considered weapons to be ridiculous, but that the Icelanders would never betray their country to support the warmongering of the superpowers.

The Alþingi made its decision on 5 October, 1946. The Socialist Party demanded a national referendum, the Federation of Labour Unions called for a general strike, and Halldór published an angry article on the front page of the *Will of the People*, "Has the Moment for Parting Arrived?", which began with the words:

> Is it today or will it be tomorrow that we stand over the rubble of Icelandic sovereignty, the sovereignty that was recognized by the Anglo-Saxon superpowers and that we celebrated three summers ago, 17 June, 1944?

But the agreement was ratified, and the general strike failed. Ólafur Thors' argument that the agreement guaranteed the eventual withdrawal of the American military from Iceland definitely influenced the outcome.

While Halldór had been researching Icelandic culture and literary heritage and writing *Iceland's Bell*, he had become ever more inclined towards a kind of enlightened nationalism. Iceland's independence had become his most important ideal, more important even than the struggle for a socialist economic system. In a certain sense he had not changed at all from his Catholic period, or from the time of the writing of *Salka Valka*: he was still just as preoccupied by treachery, and all the talk of political betrayal resonated in his heart.

As often before, Halldór was invited to speak on the anniversary of the Russian Revolution, this time at Iðnó. In his speech he discussed the latest events in Iceland, without ever mentioning the Russian Revolution. Under discussion was

> the tragic topic that has struck us all and nearly robbed us of our voices for a time, deprived us of our joy at being a nation, inflicted every single Icelander with a deep and painful wound, so that we are no longer the same people.

Iceland was no longer an independent state except in name, wrote Halldór; it was an American air base. The Americans were not to be blamed – they could have whatever they wanted – rather the traitors who had sold them Iceland's sovereignty were to blame. The struggle ahead was no longer a class struggle in the strictest sense of the term, not a conflict between capitalism and socialism, but rather hinged on a single question: "Will Iceland remain a foreign military base or not?"

Interestingly the Soviets were disappointed about the Iðnó meeting. The acting ambassador, Vassily Rybakov, sent the Central Committee of the Soviet Communist Party a long report in the middle of 1947, saying that he had been scandalized by it; Halldór Laxness had spoken but never mentioned the Soviet Union:

> It is indisputable that the question of Iceland's independence is both important and pressing to the Icelanders, but not to mention the achievement of the Soviet Union and its role on the international scene as the protector of small nations in a special address devoted to the celebration of the Soviet Union bears clear witness to Icelanders' contempt for and complete underestimation of socialist propaganda.

With the ratification of the Keflavík Agreement the coalition government was finished. After a hundred-day crisis, the Independence Party, the Progressive Party and the Social Democratic Party formed a new government under the leadership of the latter. The Socialists were isolated once more.

*

In all likelihood Halldór was referring to *Atom Station* when he wrote to Jón Helgason on 16 February, 1947: "Otherwise I have done no work of any sort all winter, except for preparing to write a criminal potboiler, regardless of whether I finish it or not." Apart from this Halldór had translated two novels by Gunnar Gunnarsson, *On the House of the Blind* (1933) and *Vikivaki* (1932). Halldór was greatly disappointed at the outcome of the struggle against the Keflavík Agreement. In another letter to Jón he said that Iceland had become "'the Atom Station Keflavík' and the Republic only an appendix to it". His mood was worsened by the death, on 13 February, 1947, of Erlendur Guðmundsson from Unuhús, his long-time friend. Halldór wrote a beautiful piece in Erlendur's honour in the *Will of the People*, "After the Banquet". It concluded:

> We who walked away from this banquet took with us a great deal of wealth that will last us as long as we live: we have our memories of a man who was so precious to us that just to have met him made our lives worth living.

Though only ten years older than Halldór, Erlendur had been a father figure to him. He had provided the young writer with insight into world culture, and at the same time had remained one of his ties to Iceland; Erlendur had saved him from trouble numerous times, and had been a patient listener. Halldór took his death so hard that more than a year later he wrote to Jón Helgason:

> ... I have in some ways been living almost in a daze here since old Erlendur from Unuhús went up to heaven. I have felt as if everything were some sort of alien dream, and as if I were missing something, even my other half, and that all my days had been blessed while he was alive. But it is slowly getting better.

Erlendur had a profound influence on *Atom Station*, which Halldór was working on that year.

Halldór was a professional role model for writers in Iceland, not only in his relentless labour on his own behalf, but also in the way he introduced customs from the foreign book world. For example, Iceland was not party to the Berne Convention for the Protection of Literary and Artistic Works, which guaranteed the protection of writers in all its member countries. Icelandic laws applicable to writers were modelled after Danish ones, but generally translations were published without the rights being paid for. Halldór himself was hurt by this. In May, 1946, he had chastised the Booksellers' Union, which had passed a resolution against Iceland's membership of an international copyright convention, and in March, 1947, he wrote two long articles criticizing the lawyer Einar Ásmundsson, who had spoken out against Iceland's membership of the Berne Convention in *Morgunblaðið*. Halldór's arguments in support of Icelanders paying for foreign rights were clear and now seem perfectly self-evident. Iceland became a party to the Berne Convention that same year, the last of the Scandinavian countries to do so.

In the spring of 1947, writers' grants were once again allotted by the Alþingi. Halldór received 4,000 krónur, the same as the year before. This time he reacted in an unexpected way. In *Morgunblaðið* and the *Will of the People*, he announced that he was planning to use the grant as the prize in an essay competition on the recent "relinquishment of Icelandic national rights". The judging committee would consist of three people, named by the Icelandic Federation of Labour Unions, the Reykjavík Student Union and the Patriotic Society, and essays were to be submitted under pseudonyms before the end of the year.

The acting American ambassador to Iceland, William Trimble, was not best pleased. Trimble, who had become Chargé d'Affaires early in 1947, was extremely belligerent in his struggle against the influence of the Socialists, insisting for instance that the Communists be ousted from positions of influence in the government. He had good connections with the leaders of the Independence and Social Democratic parties.

On 12 June Trimble sent a message to his supervisors in the State Department reporting that a competition was being advertised for essays that would attack the Icelandic authorities, especially the Minister for Foreign Affairs, Bjarni Benediktsson. Trimble described Halldór as "Iceland's most prominent author, one of whose books, *Independent People*, was a Book of the Month Club selection, and a long-time member of the Icelandic Communist Party."

Four days later, Trimble sent another message, marked confidential, in which he said that he had discussed the matter with Bjarni Benediktsson, and the Minister for Foreign Affairs had said that he would like very much to know how much Halldór had received in royalties for *Independent People* in the United States. This data would be useful to the government in its efforts to identify the principal contributors to the Icelandic Communist Party.

The State Department transferred Trimble's request to J. Edgar Hoover, head of the F.B.I., in September, asking the Bureau to investigate the payments discreetly. Hoover wrote to New York asking whether it was possible to get information on all payments made by Knopf. Nothing came of this, so the State Department turned to the Internal Revenue Service. In November Trimble had become impatient, stating in a telegram that the Minister for Foreign Affairs desperately needed this information "in view increased tempo Laxness attacks on government for its pro-U.S. attitude". He was informed that no payments from Knopf to Halldór had been recorded for 1946 and that the accounts for 1947 would not be recorded for another year. The investigation was put on hold.

Halldór of course had no idea what Trimble was doing, or indeed that his own government had enlisted the American's help against him. Thus commenced a case that would only be concluded with a Supreme Court ruling in 1955. It is even more interesting that the envoys of the superpowers in Iceland were absolutely agreed about one thing: they were shocked by Icelanders' nationalism and complacency and considered them more or less to be living in the past.

Although Halldór's American royalties for *Independent People* were mostly deposited into U.S. banks, he was able to use some of the money to buy himself a car, which he took on his travels abroad. The first car that Auður and Halldór owned was a little black Ford, but in the spring of 1947 they bought a Willys Jeep. In the latter part of his life Halldór permitted himself the luxury of owning elegant cars, just as he had his clothing tailored and stayed in expensive hotels. The Willys was not a top-flight car of the type that he owned later, but an extremely practical car for travelling on his country's poor roads. The first foreigner to travel with Halldór around the country that summer was Zdenek Nemecek, the Czech ambassador in Copenhagen. Halldór and Zdenek spent three weeks together, visiting, among others, Gunnar Gunnarsson. Nemecek enjoyed himself royally, but told Auður when they returned that he had thought Halldór quite misogynistic.

Nemecek wrote an entertaining book about this trip, *Letters from Iceland* (1948), first published in Czechoslovakia. In form the book is not unlike the collection of letters written by W.H. Auden and Louis MacNeice from Iceland in 1937, full of information about the land and people, much of it received from Halldór. The framework is their trip around the country, and some of the things that the author says about Halldór's way of driving are witness to the fact that he'd only been driving for two years and stuck to the simple, basic rule: Drive as if everyone you meet on the road is a madman.

In the autumn of 1947 Halldór returned to Scandinavia on publishing business and to attend a writers' conference in Stockholm. He encountered rough weather on the voyage to Copenhagen, "but then a whole day of sunshine and blue sea and sky, this simple vision that inspires me most and makes me think how wonderful it is to sail", as he wrote to Auður. In the same letter he said that he had met his best friends, Jón Helgason and Kristinn E. Andrésson, in Copenhagen, and that they had enjoyed themselves; Kristinn was living abroad for health reasons, and was working on his literary history. Halldór stayed at the d'Angleterre and worked for four hours a day on *Atom Station*. In early October he went to Stockholm, staying just outside town at the Grand Hotel Saltsjöbaden: "This is a delightful place right next to the sea, and here I can work literally untroubled all day." Afterwards, whenever Halldór had business in Stockholm, he would stay at the same place. While there he met Jón Leifs and attended a concert by Yehudi Menuhin.

Halldór did not have much publishing business in Norway, but he did hold a press conference in Oslo. He sent Auður clippings of interviews in Norwegian and Swedish papers, stating that more or less everything that they reported him to have said was nonsense: "Newspaper reporters are, of all the types of workers that I know, the most unsuited to their jobs!"

One such misquotation sparked a debate at home. The Norwegian paper *Friheten*, the organ of the Communists, discussing the Keflavík Agreement in a detailed interview with Halldór, quoted him as saying that the Icelanders were required to obtain stamps in their passports from the American authorities if they wanted to travel abroad. When Agnar Klemens Jónsson at the Icelandic Foreign Ministry heard of this he sent an enquiry to the Icelandic embassy in Oslo, which in its reply called the interview "a collection of lies and insolence. Deemed nonsense here. People recognize Communist blather."

Morgunblaðið responded gruffly to Halldór's alleged statements and published numerous articles about the matter. Halldór responded by saying that he had been misquoted, and the *Will of the People* finally published the interview in full, along with prefatory remarks by him.

A shortage of goods and problems with currency in Iceland assured that no-one went overseas in the first decade after the war without being enjoined by his friends and family to buy things for them. Halldór's shopping list grew longer and longer every year in proportion to his expanding finances and the size of his family. Meanwhile Auður was finding it extraordinarily difficult to live at Gljúfrasteinn. She was in dire need of petrol to drive to work at the National Hospital: ". . . spoke to the quartermaster about an extra ration . . . but was told that I would just have to move into town!" There was no electricity yet, there were mice in the house, so on. She decided to leave the radiology department and in the autumn started a course at the painting and handicraft school. No matter how difficult things were, though, her and Halldór's letters that autumn are light-hearted and romantic. The fact that she did not take things terribly seriously certainly helped, as when she told Halldór:

> I am supposed to give in an essay about *antipathy* in ten days' time. I can do nothing about the fact that I always find classroom psychology somewhat ridiculous and spiteful. I would much rather have written about levity.

Halldór is appreciative in his reply:

> I feel much lighter to have escaped from daily troubles this nearly a month. It is good to wake up in the morning without having domestic worries; but then everything lands on you instead.

Slowly this became their pattern, the pattern that Halldór had always desired. But he was more than willing to help in some areas:

> When I come home I shall do all I can to try to procure petrol. I shall use all of my connections: I am a close personal friend of the directors of the major oil companies; perhaps it will be possible to warm them up with dollars.

While in Copenhagen Halldór read a chapter from his unpublished novel, *Atom Station*, to the Icelandic Students' Union there, something he did regularly. At the writers' conference in Stockholm, plans were afoot for the establishment of an international writers' federation in support of world peace. At the peak of the

Cold War the Communists and their supporters were trying to appeal to leftist and liberal intellectuals and artists by waving the banner of world peace. Halldór was active in this movement for a number of years.

Halldór spoke about his trip in an interview with Magnús Kjartansson in the *Will of the People* on his return home. Most remarkable were his comments on literature. Halldór declared that the most popular literary genre of the last century, the "social" novel, was on the decline, among other things because the workers were not fond of such novels and could not be persuaded to read them:

> Naturally, the workers know quite well that there is a class struggle, but fiction concerning the basic facts of the class struggle works on them as if they were reading the alphabet over and over again. And it will be proven in literature, as Picasso has said about painting, that it is not necessary to paint a gun to show that a man is a revolutionary; it would do just as well to paint an apple.

Halldór always emphasized the independence of the arts, yet *Atom Station* was his first novel set in contemporary Reykjavík and contained direct political references. The authorities' reaction was severe.

Atom Station was published on 22 March, 1948. Chargé d'Affaires Trimble informed his supervisors on 21 February that Halldór's book was expected to be published within two weeks; the embassy had heard that the book had an acrid anti-American tone. Trimble added:

> Consider Laxness' prestige would suffer materially if we let it be known that he is an income-tax evader. Accordingly suggest further investigation be made into matter of royalties, presumably received on *Independent People*.

Trimble did not let up, and on 16 March an employee at the State Department registered a phone conversation he had concerning the matter with a certain Gorrell at the I.R.S. Gorrell pointed out that it was the duty of those who paid Halldór's royalties to withhold the amounts that the American tax office was supposed to receive, not the writer's. Two days later the State Department sent the embassy in Iceland a precise account of Halldór's royalties from the agency Curtis Brown; included was confirmation from the Manhattan Bank that the writer still had 21,000 dollars in an account there. An investigation would be made into whether all Halldór's taxes had been paid, but any negligence was the responsibility of the publishing company, not his.

Trimble discussed the matter with Bjarni Benediktsson, who could now investigate whether Halldór had declared these earnings on his tax return in Iceland.

There was a catch, however, in that Bjarni had received the information informally rather than "officially". Trimble suggested to the State Department that Thor Thors, the Icelandic ambassador to the United States, be brought into the matter.

In May of the same year, the State Department disappointed the embassy by informing it that the I.R.S. did not see any reason for further investigations into the matter. But the Icelandic authorities did not give up. The investigations by the American government concerning Halldór's royalties, made in cooperation with the Icelandic authorities and with the goal of diminishing his reputation as a writer just as *Atom Station* was being published, might have come straight from that novel. It is probable, however, that the events would not have been considered believable.

Atom Station was much more energetic and fast-paced than Halldór's previous novels, and is satirical in tone. With this novel Halldór lost the sympathy that *Iceland's Bell* had gained for him: many people were angry about the book, and later it was agreed that it was among Halldór's weaker works. He himself had little to say about it in later years.

The book was not a haphazard concoction, however. Halldór wrote the first outline for it in the autumn of 1946. Besides that there are two handwritten versions and two typescripts. At the end of January, 1948, Halldór wrote to Jón Helgason:

> The novel is now for the most part complete. I have worked on it for fourteen months and have done absolutely nothing else during that time. This is hardly a great work of fiction; but it is a somewhat interesting book in many ways.

This is probably a correct estimation. The book is surprisingly effective at times, especially when one considers the political strife that was at its peak when it was being written.

Its form is traditional, but the style is lively, full of neologisms and puns. Halldór had not written in such a youthful manner since *The Great Weaver from Kashmir* and *Salka Valka*. The book's structure is simple: there are two righteous and two degenerate settings. But the narrative works in opposition to this simplicity.

Once again Halldór shows us love awakening between the earth-bound Icelandic girl and the refined yet treacherous intellectual. Ugla cannot accept Búi because she wants to be:

> Neither an unpaid bondswoman like the wives of the poor, nor a bought madam like the wives of the rich, much less a paid mistress, or the prisoner of a child society has disowned.

She would rather be a man.

The book's romantic element is understated and has a tragic tone, in contrast to the passages of loud debate. Búi is a worthy counterpart to Ugla, and *Atom Station* is far from being crude propaganda.

Atom Station generated an enormous amount of interest and its first print run sold out in a day. Halldór's opponents were angry about the image he created of the nation's authorities as underhanded rogues and traitors. A month after the book was published, the representatives of the Independence Party and the Social Democratic Party on the committee responsible for artists' grants rescinded Halldór's entire grant after a split-decision vote. One of those who voted to have the grant rescinded, Þorsteinn Þorsteinsson of the Independence Party, explained his decision by saying that the rescindment of Halldór's grant was clearly a political gesture. Þorsteinn also felt that there was no longer any reason for the committee to grant Halldór money, since there was no evidence to suggest that he desired a grant. The Student Council of the University of Iceland said that it would grant Halldór a special honorarium itself.

Atom Station brought back to the table the question of the connection between literature and reality. For example, the book contains a powerful chapter in which a girl is sent to have an abortion. An increasing incidence of abortion had recently been the subject of public debate, and a representative of the Criminal Court of Reykjavík launched an investigation. Halldór, among others, was called into court, and was asked what was behind the chapter on abortion in his book. Many years later Halldór said in *An Essay on Icelanders* (1967):

> A great travesty in court in Reykjavík: the same man who wanted to subpoena the fictional character Búi Árland, M.P., for abortion, had several years earlier sentenced me to prison for using the wrong spelling in books that I wrote.

The novelist could offer little assistance to the investigation without betraying his characters.

The Cold War also put relationships to the test. Halldór's old friend Kristján Albertsson wrote about *Atom Station* on 12 June, 1948, under the title "Dirty Clay". Kristján felt that Icelandic society was doing itself no favours by not taking account of the disgrace perpetrated by its chief writer by "boiling together a novel that is in many ways nothing other than insolent and tasteless lying rubbish". It is clear that Kristján was deeply insulted by the image that Halldór had created of Iceland's Prime Minister in the book; in reality that was Ólafur Thors, Kristján's cousin and benefactor:

From whom is hidden the nearly unlimited possibility for slander and lies that a political roman-à-clef has in far greater measure than newspaper articles, simply because a roman-à-clef does not need to reveal the true identities of those it attacks or libels, and yet can make it absolutely clear as to whom it refers? Does Icelandic culture profit from such literature?

Kristján's pain is understandable, but his perception belongs to a forgotten time; nothing is sacred in satire.

Before his piece was published, Kristján sent Halldór a letter to warn him about it: "Everything that my article says, you deserve – but you do not deserve it from me. Yet I had to write it."

Halldór replied to Kristján in a friendly way, saying that there was no hope for capitalism in the battles ahead. He also said that while Iceland's innocent rural culture and its lack of understanding of world developments had been used as excuses by those who had signed the Keflavík Agreement, that was little comfort:

> . . . I tried to avoid hitting these unlucky men personally, did all I could in order to ensure that there was no resemblance between the authors of the agreement and the criminals in the book, even drew forth all the best that exists in the bourgeois class in the midst of its unsalvageable putrefaction, and what's more I doubt that any Icelandic writer could have created as sympathetic a picture of an upper-class man as I have in Búi Árland . . . Criticize me as much as you possibly can, it touches me as much as if you were beating a fish up north in Langanes.

This is a remarkable dispute between old friends, one of whom proves to be more prophetic in politics and the other to have a clearer understanding of literature, with each trying to defeat the other on his own ground.

But there were more sides to the issue. At the time, Kristján was information officer at the Icelandic embassy in Paris, and the *Will of the People* suspected him of having used his position to try to hinder the publication of *Atom Station* in Denmark. Thus far all of Halldór's novels since *Salka Valka* had been published in Denmark, generally as soon as translations were completed. But the publication of *Atom Station* by Gyldendal dragged on and on, and the book did not appear until 1952, and then under another title, *The Home of the Organist*. Martin Larsen, an exchange teacher at the University of Iceland and a part-time employee of the Danish embassy, had taken it upon himself to translate the book, but had stopped. Was this because of political pressure?

Kristján responded to these accusations at the end of 1952, saying that he had resolutely advised Halldór not to let the book be translated and expressing his amazement that Larsen had agreed to translate it. A short time later he said that he had met Bodil Begtrup, who had been appointed Danish ambassador to Iceland, and that Begtrup had expressed his doubts about whether it was desirable that a man in Larsen's position should translate the book. Kristján said, however, that the main point was that Larsen had come to this conclusion on his own.

It is not entirely clear that Martin Larsen made his decision without assistance. In a letter that he wrote to the departing ambassador on 23 December, 1948, he states that he would not translate *Atom Station* because of his position at the Danish embassy. However, he might finish a translation of *On the Way to My Beloved* (1938) by Þórbergur Þórðarson, since it was an apolitical book.

Martin Larsen informed Gyldendal of his decision on 29 January, 1949. This put Gyldendal into a difficult position: the company tried to get various people to translate the book, but without success. In correspondence with Halldór, the director of the publishing company, Ingeborg Andersen, also stated that the title *Atom Station* might put readers off.

Halldór himself came up with the title *The Home of the Organist* to replace it. Benediktsson Jakob and his wife, Grethe, finally accepted the translation job, which they finished in March, 1950; plans were made to publish in the autumn. But publication was delayed twice more. It should be noted that Gyldendal experienced significant financial difficulties at the start of the 1950s and also that nothing in the correspondence suggests that the company was subjected to political pressure.

The American State Department continued to ask questions about Halldór after the publication of *Atom Station*. On 12 April, 1948, the Consul General in Winnipeg received instructions to gather information on Halldór's activities while he lived in Canada, since he was a known Communist who fought against American foreign policy. This was accompanied by a description of Halldór from the American embassy in Iceland, dated 6 December, 1945: "Halldór Kiljan Laxness is a most mild-mannered gentleman, particularly polite and thoughtful of others, but when he touches pen to paper he can be most vitriolic."

The consul, Walter H. McKinney, immediately started to investigate the situation and replied to the State Department on 22 April, saying that unfortunately the individual in question had no record with the police in Canada. Then he added:

From a leading member of the Icelandic community in Winnipeg it is learnt, however, that Laxness made a brief visit to this city many years ago, apparently following the First World War. Those who knew him at the time report that he was even then an avowed Communist. He writes brilliantly but his writings are invective to the point of obscenity. The suggestion is made that between his personality and his writings he is subject to some type of schizophrenia. My informant adds that he hopes that Laxness will not be considered as typical of the Icelandic people in general.

Halldór held fast to his own position while all this was going on, delivering speeches and writing essays. In the autumn he and Auður took a long trip to France, Switzerland and Italy, about which he sent articles to the *Will of the People*, which were later published in *A Little Travel Diary* (1950). Halldór found the situation in France rather miserable, but in these articles he wrote mostly about the warmongering of the right-wingers, as he called them. He seemed to think that the victims of Auschwitz had mainly been Communists and suspected Communists.

An article Halldór sent from Rome focused primarily on modern art: "To view Picasso is to view modernity, to examine him in detail is to examine the century in detail; whether his paintings are bad or good, beautiful or ugly." His concluding words were about the photograph, the machine-made image, "which has fettered mankind's vision and overlords it even today, making all modern art one of two things, either a war against its great power or nonsense". This may mark a change in emphasis from Halldór's articles written during the interwar years, in that he was playing the arts off against the automation and technology of modernity. His interest in technology, so strong during the 1930s, was on the decline. Indeed his thinking as a whole was changing.

When Halldór and Auður returned to Denmark, Auður spent some time with her relatives in Århus, but Halldór went to Store Kro in Fredensborg to find peace and quiet:

> I sit here with a sweaty brow, no-one could possibly believe how difficult it is for me to start a new book, and how distant is the feeling that I am able to write . . . But it is coming little by little, and in the next several months I intend to do all I can to close myself off from imposition and extra work, whether I am at home or away.

Halldór was starting work on what became his most difficult book, *The Happy Warriors*, a reckoning with the heroism of the Icelandic sagas and much more besides. Auður replied to him in the spirit of support: "I shall do all that I can so that you can work on your writing in peace, my love."

At the end of January Auður went home, but Halldór stayed in Sweden and Denmark, mostly writing. Auður's news from home included the information that electricity had come to Hraðastaðir (the farm next door) and that constant protest meetings were being held over the Keflavík Agreement. Auður also told Halldór that his lawyer, Ragnar Ólafsson, had talked to the Tax Bureau and informed her that Halldór would likely be made to pay an additional 40,000 krónur:

> People here still believe that you have millions of dollars. They quote a certain report published by Guðmundur Hagalín about the sale of your books in America, in which he said that you received 1 dollar per book and that *Independent People* alone had sold five hundred thousand copies.

It was not easy to be a great writer in a small society. But behind Ragnar's meeting lurked serious matters. The District Tax Authority had written the Ministry of Justice a letter on 11 November, 1948, in which attention was directed to the fact that Halldór had not accounted for his income from the publication of his books abroad. On 1 March the Ministry ordered an investigation, which turned to matters concerning Halldór's assets in foreign currency, while the tax investigation continued along other lines. The Minister of Justice at the time was Bjarni Benediktsson.

That month military defence was once again at the top of the agenda: Iceland's joining N.A.T.O. was being debated. At the beginning of March the *Will of the People* published an interview with Halldór concerning his trips abroad in which he was asked about warmongering in Europe; Halldór said that it was on the decline everywhere except Scandinavia. The capitalist camp was nowhere more in evidence than in Iceland, though. Halldór, when asked about European literature, declared Sartre to be the most widely read author of that time. He enjoyed Sartre's shorter works, but had doubts about his philosophy:

> . . . in a certain way derived from Søren Kierkegaard, who continues to be the only Scandinavian writer of whom there is any sign in France and Italy, causing one to chuckle involuntarily at the thought that this old Danish eccentric and Lutheran sectarian should be well considered in other countries.

Halldór also described his troubles with foreign publishers: he found it especially difficult in Germany, where six of his novels had been translated without anyone having agreed to publish them: "It is as I told a Danish reporter: one starts as a poet and ends as a travelling salesman; that is the tragedy of being a writer."

A long essay about outlaws published in the *Mál og menning* journal in May showed that Halldór was still investigating Icelandic history and the sagas. This interest served him well in *The Happy Warriors*. Nationalist issues continued to interest him, and he took part in protests against Iceland's joining N.A.T.O. and continued to lecture in favour of peace: "To commit ourselves to declaring war on other nations is and must be nonsense . . . although politicians might lend their names to such an agreement."

The protests, as before, were ineffectual. Joining N.A.T.O. was approved by a great majority of the Alþingi, followed by the greatest riot in the history of the sovereign state, on Austurvöllur in front of the Alþingi building on 30 March, 1949. The Socialists and their allies experienced a huge defeat, and Halldór's will to fight gradually diminished.

In the meantime Halldór had received an invitation to visit the Soviet Union along with other foreign writers and intellectuals to celebrate the hundred and fiftieth anniversary of Pushkin's birth. Halldór travelled to Copenhagen in mid-May; his main business was to meet Jón Helgason:

> [I want to] go over with him the chapters that I have written . . . and discuss with him various matters in connection with this type of book, since he is far more educated in these matters than I am.

The Happy Warriors is without doubt the book for which Jón provided the most assistance; they discussed its contents and language time and again. From Copenhagen Halldór travelled through Stockholm and Finland to Russia. That year *Iceland's Bell* was published in Finnish, and the local papers took the opportunity to interview Halldór. On 4 June he arrived in Moscow, from where he wrote to Auður:

> I have returned after eleven years to my old hotel, the National, and have met my old friend, Apletin, who kissed me on both cheeks with that most delightful Slavic cordiality.

Halldór was, like the other guests, under the supervision of both V.O.K.S., the bureau that supervised the Soviet Union's cultural connections with other countries, and the Writers' Union, and he was treated extremely well. Besides the celebrations he attended the ballet and the opera, but he excused himself from sightseeing trips; he had already travelled widely in the Soviet Union, and was not a man for delegations.

Halldór's most enjoyed hearing and meeting the American singer Paul Robeson, the foreign guest about whom the Soviets made the most fuss in those days. Halldór had taken great delight in Black music ever since his days in Los Angeles, and had great things to say about Robeson:

He is one of the cleverest people to whom I have ever spoken. He reads and speaks Russian perfectly. He is eager to come to Iceland in the autumn – Icelanders must come to understand that there is a different America than the one with whom they signed the N.A.T.O. treaty.

This was a man after Halldór's own heart.

Among the other guests was Martin Andersen Nexø, who displayed his usual kindness to his Icelandic comrade, calling Halldór "one of the greatest contemporary proletarian writers" in a speech he delivered at one of the banquets. Halldór wrote to Auður: "I was of course speechless, but went up to him at the main table and toasted him in Danish and said, '*For meget*' ['Too much']." Halldór got the chance to repay the compliment at a banquet held in honour of Nexø's eightieth birthday later in the month.

The Russians had not invited Halldór out of sheer goodwill, of course; they also wanted to make use of him. In an interview for *Pravda*, he was asked what he felt about the Soviet Union now:

I am most amazed by the fact that one can scarcely see any marks of the war here. The people are calm and optimistic and do not fear for the next day. In the Soviet Union there is no propaganda trumpeting a new war, no-one tries to instil fear of war into the public. Because of this the trip here has been both energizing and restful. I have the feeling that I am being healed after having lived in a huge mental hospital, into which the conservative forces have changed Western Europe in recent times.

Yet there was a shadow over Halldór's relationship with the Soviets, as he explained to Auður:

The manuscript of *Independent People* went to Leningrad during the war, and 6,000 rubles that I had in the bank here went to the state, because it was not checked on in ten years, but the Writers' Union has now raised a case to try to free up this money again, and is hopeful that it can do so.

On his return home Halldór spoke again to Korchagin, who was in charge of the Soviet embassy in Reykjavík. Korchagin sent a report of their conversation to V.O.K.S. It is likely that Halldór retrieved the money in the end, doubtless with the proviso that it be used inside the Soviet Union. There was, however, no further movement in his publishing matters in the East until 1953.

Halldór returned to Copenhagen on 26 June. Martin Andersen Nexø's birthday was celebrated with a great feast in the city's main park. Halldór sent a congratulatory message saying that Denmark was "a world power to have a son such as you, to whom all of working humankind feels it owes a great debt". Nexø suggested publishing companies in East Germany with whom Halldór should make contact, among them his own company, Dietz. Halldór wrote an article about this trip, "Thoughts in Moscow", which includes all the usual clichés about the Soviets' pacifism, but interestingly is in large part a criticism of Soviet aesthetics, especially painting. Halldór took issue with certain gallery directors' views about Picasso and Matisse, saying, "The logic of some of the cultural representatives of the Soviet Union regarding modern painting does not strike us Western socialists as reasoning, but rather Russian eccentricity". He was also dissatisfied with the concept of "socialist realism", because it diminished the sense of "realism", as if there could be capitalist realism or some other sort of realism. This was the first time he directly criticized the country's official ideology.

While he was in Moscow the annual artists' grants were allotted, and Halldór once again received nothing. Magnús Kjartansson, who sat on the grants committee, wrote a summary of grants awarded during the previous ten years, and showed how various left-wing associates of Halldór had been punished by having their grants decreased or rescinded.

In the summer Halldór's tax problems in Iceland reached a head. The Justice of the Peace for the Districts of Gullbringa and Kjós, Guðmundur Í. Guðmundsson, announced that Gljúfrasteinn had been seized and would be offered for sale at auction on 30 September, along with a jeep and a Mercury car, to pay off Halldór's 1947 tax debt of 225,000 krónur. The *People's Paper* took this announcement as a clear indication that Halldór had avoided paying a huge amount of tax; it had been rumoured that he had earned 100,000 dollars (then 650,000 krónur) from the publication of *Independent People* in the West. *Morgunblaðið* asked why the *Will of the People* had not mentioned the matter, since the *Will* had for some time been demanding an investigation into the earnings of Icelanders doing business abroad. The *People's Paper* accused him of gross hypocrisy.

Iceland's laws governing earnings in foreign currency were strict, so his opponents felt as if they finally had him where they wanted him. On the same day *Morgunblaðið* published a full-page article under the title "The Communists' Concern with Smugglers, Financial Criminals and Tax Evaders."

How had this come about? The problem had to do with Halldór's tax assessments for 1948 as compared with 1947. Tax had already been deducted from his royalties in America, and he had probably hoped not to pay taxes on those same earnings in Iceland. However, the law required that he do so. He appealed to the

Government Tax Bureau, but his appeal was rejected. His Icelandic tax bill was increased and a distraint order was placed on the house.

Now the government needed to gain official access to the information that Bjarni Benediktsson had obtained covertly, so the embassy in Washington was brought into the matter. On 12 August Thor Thors was finally able to reply to his superiors back in Iceland:

> This case has been delayed a great deal by the State Department, since infor-
> mation of this sort is usually not given. It became necessary for the Secretary
> of State to write to the Treasury Department . . . Yesterday the embassy
> finally received a confidential letter from Mr Benjamin M. Hulley, the director
> of the Northern European bureau of the State Department. His letter states
> that the information is for the eyes of the Icelandic government only.
> Enclosed are the original copy of Mr Hulley's letter and the report of the
> I.R.S. . . . [The report] stipulates that Mr Laxness has paid all the necessary
> taxes here in the United States, and that his agents in London, Allen and
> Unwin Ltd, will be able to give information about his earnings from the
> publication of his books.

A huge dust cloud had been stirred up, leaving no doubt that Halldór was being made to pay for his political opinions. Ironically, the one Icelandic paper that reported on the case in a moderate vein was the right-wing *Vísir*, which pointed out the obvious lack of fairness in double-taxing individuals with income from abroad: "Such a man should not be destroyed financially through a narrow-minded interpretation of the law – nor should any taxpayer for that matter."

Vísir's words fell on deaf ears, however. On 30 September, Guðmundur Í. Guðmundsson's representatives went tó Gljúfrasteinn. Halldór described their activities to Jón Helgason:

> Some representatives of the Justice of the Peace were wandering about here
> yesterday; they were so riled that they drove into my fence and broke it all
> down and tore up the posts, and then sat there without moving until some
> people who were visiting went out and saved them . . . My lawyer was there
> to hand them a Supreme Court subpoena, and that subpoena was enough to
> prevent them from doing what they had planned, as when one person trumps
> the high card that another has laid on the table.

The case appears to have been concluded when Halldór paid 70,000 krónur on his earnings in the United States, a third of what the Tax Bureau had demanded.

But other lawsuits against Halldór for infractions of the regulations governing earnings in foreign currency continued. In 1955 the Supreme Court fined him 1,500 krónur, besides court costs. The yield of a six-year legal entanglement was that scanty. As a result Halldór became ever more doubtful about the Icelandic authorities and about politicians, believing that the gulf between them and the public was ever more important than that between capitalists and workers. Twelve years later he said:

> From this lawsuit there survives nothing but one sentence, which has also become famous among Icelandic lawyers . . . "Is it correct that you have tried to conceal the fact that your books have been published in hundreds of thousands of copies in America?"

The Happy Warriors

The Cold War made none of us better people.

Matthías Jóhannessen

In the autumn of 1948 Halldór was nominated for the Nobel Prize for Literature for the first time.

When the Academy's Nobel Committee had gone over the nominations received at the start of February, 1948, thirty-one valid nominations, among them Halldór Laxness, had remained. He had been nominated by three Icelandic scholars: Sigurður Nordal and Einar Ólafur Sveinsson, both professors at the University of Iceland, and Jón Helgason, professor at the University of Copenhagen. The specialist opinion on Halldór was written by Per Hallström, who had been the Committee's spokesman for twenty-four years. His conclusion, accepted by the Nobel Committee, was that Halldór did not fulfil the necessary requirements. There was no further discussion of his merits, and T.S. Eliot was awarded the prize that year.

In 1949 Halldór was nominated again, this time only by Jón Helgason. Hallström rejected the nomination. But now Halldór's name was being mentioned in public debate in Sweden. The critic Stig Carlson wrote in *Morgon Tidningen*: "A more suitable Nobel Prize author than Halldór Laxness will be hard to find . . . Among living writers throughout the world he has hardly any equals." In the next few years Swedish critics and other literati became more and more vocal in their support of Halldór; Sweden being a neutral country, people were not as concerned about his political views.

In a letter to Jón Helgason written on 1 October, 1949, Halldór told of his work that autumn. Jón had done some proofreading for him, among other things of *Collected Poetry* – which was to be reprinted – and the translation of Gunnar Gunnarsson; Halldór thanked him and added:

> I think that it has always been one of my better qualities as a writer that I am always eager, and even keen, to let the people I trust make as many comments as they can stand to on my manuscripts; and that is because it has often been proved to me that the manuscripts improve immensely under such a procedure.

Halldór also mentioned that he and the writer Ólafur Jóhann Sigurðsson had been working on proofs of *A Little Travel Diary*, which was published early the next year. Ólafur acted as a reader for Helgafell, and often worked closely with Halldór. When completing work on a project Halldór could be very demanding. For example, when it was time to reprint *Salka Valka* in 1951, Ólafur was hard at work on his own novel, *Clockwork* (1955), and did not want to undertake the proof-reading. Halldór became quite angry, and their relationship was never the same.

Halldór had concerns about *A Little Travel Diary* since the essays had been written so quickly. As he wrote to Jón:

> . . . they were teeming with sloppy expressions, but I have no voice, as you know: my voice is made up of all sorts of things from different directions, and you can't predict when there'll be a good spurt from me and when some sort of gibberish.

Halldór made numerous changes on the proofs following Jón's recommendations, especially regarding editions of the sagas. Jón advised him to dispense with any commentary on standardized spellings and Halldór agreed:

> I know very well that my opinions there were vulgar and construed and combative, but I was hard-pressed and fighting tooth-and-nail alone against full-blown idiots, with no linguist available to support me because they all feared Hrifla and Thors, although they knew for sure that I was right, and it is simply grotesque to be archaizing the spelling of small words in such contemporary literature as the Icelandic sagas.

Thus did Halldór write the obituary for the spelling war.

On 7 November Halldór spoke at a meeting in honour of the anniversary of the Russian Revolution, delivering a speech entitled "Peace – the Only Thing that

Matters". Slowly but surely peace was becoming Halldór's most closely held political ideal. He believed that the people of both the United States and the Soviet
Union were devoted to the ideal of peace in contrast to the warmongering of the
capitalist leaders:

> I think that there is nothing more important in our day than to support the
> cause of freedom, against those apostles of death who are currently trying
> to buy up all the media outlets and take control of all the propaganda
> machines in order to preach war and genocide.

In this interpretation of international politics Halldór was still following the
same course as the Soviets, who considered it in their best interests to inspire,
support and finance the work of the pacifist movement in the West.

The struggle for peace and cultural work went hand in hand for Halldór and his
colleagues. After Iceland's entry into N.A.T.O., the view was strengthened among
the Socialists in Iceland that a cultural counterweight to the United States had to
be created; nothing had been seen of the Soviet Friendship Society for some time,
and in any case it was difficult to defend the Soviet Union during the Cold War.
Thus there was a need for a society dedicated to cultural connections between the
two countries.

For several years the Soviets had wanted to start such a society in Iceland, and
had their eyes on Halldór as its leader. In a letter from March, 1945, to Korchagin
at the Soviet embassy in Reykjavík, Kyslova at V.O.K.S. expressed the hope that
Halldór could be persuaded to found such a society, but Korchagin replied by
saying that Halldór was disappointed that his books had not been published in
Russian, and that he had no interest in working on behalf of such a society. Kyslova
said that she would try to press for the publication of Halldór's books, but nothing
came of this for a time.

In March, 1950, however, the Cultural Exchange Between Iceland and the
U.S.S.R. (M.Í.R.) was established. Because so many people attended the organiza-
tional meeting, it had to be repeated. Halldór was elected the society's president and
Þórbergur Þórðarson vice-president. In the 1950s the society, with Soviet support,
was responsible for, among other things, the visits of numerous artists and musicians to Iceland, many of whom were invited to Gljúfrasteinn.

The Socialist leaders Einar Olgeirsson and Kristinn E. Andrésson encouraged
the Soviets at an early stage to finance the work of M.Í.R., saying that it could not
function without such support. It was not long before the society received regular
payments from V.O.K.S.

A month after the founding of M.Í.R., on 20 April, 1950, the National Theatre was opened in Reykjavík. Construction had begun twenty-two years earlier, and during the war years the building had been used by the occupation forces. Guðlaugur Rósinkranz was the theatre's director and the first three plays on the schedule were all Icelandic: *New Year's Night* by Indriði Einarsson, *Fjalla-Eyvindur* by Jóhann Sigurjónsson and Halldór's *Iceland's Bell*. Halldór himself was appointed to the Theatre Board in 1948, a seat he held for twenty years.

Iceland's Bell was incredibly popular, running for an entire year, with a total audience of twenty-eight thousand. Most of the dialogue was reproduced word-for-word from the book. Lárus Pálsson worked with Halldór on the adaptation and directed the play. Sveinn Einarsson attributed the popularity of *Iceland's Bell* to that of the novel itself, and also to the fact that Lárus Pálsson was able

> through his sensitivity to fiction, to bring the novel's dialogue to life on the stage in what was at once a living language and at the same time something that bowed to the laws of fiction and was above and beyond everyday existence.

The opening of the National Theatre was symbolic of the great achievements in a half-century of Icelandic cultural life. That same year the Symphony Orchestra of Iceland commenced performances. Little by little Reykjavík was gaining the accoutrements of a major international city. At the end of April the third Artists' Congress was held, at which Halldór delivered a speech, saying, among other things: "Everything that helps to increase the nation's cultural wealth is inexpensive, whether it costs a great deal or not."

That spring the grants committee unanimously awarded Halldór 5,000 krónur. As the *Will of the People* put it: "The conservatives have given up their attacks on Halldór Kiljan Laxness." His popularity was so strong that it no longer made sense to decrease or rescind his grant.

Around the same time Peter Hallberg proposed his idea to Halldór for a book about his life and work. That Halldór responded favourably is revealed in a letter in which he conveys an unexpected picture of his life:

> . . . I shall do everything in my power to inform you, according to what I remember, of all of my criminal career; it seems to me that others have hardly written with more understanding of me than you have done – I just simply do not understand why you should imagine wasting so much time on such an unattractive and banal project; although it is a shame to admit it, nothing has ever happened to me that is worth putting in a book: I have

never landed in any significant adventure or ended up in a tight situation –
my whole life has somehow been smooth, ordinary and happy . . . I am the
laziest writer . . . although that might seem unbelievable, and I try to avoid
all unnecessary writing; that's why I would rather speak to you about this
material than have to write anything.

With Halldór's help, Hallberg wrote a short book about the writer that was
published in 1952, and then two long books, *The Great Weaver* (1954), and *The House
of the Poet* (1956), both of which were translated from the Swedish into Icelandic
and published in two volumes each. He also wrote a shorter book about Halldór
for an American publisher in 1971, and a summary work that was published in
Icelandic in 1975, as well as numerous essays. Hallberg benefited a great deal
from Stefán Einarsson's manuscripts and documents, but his best source was his
almost unlimited access to Halldór's letters and manuscripts. There is no doubt
that Hallberg played a huge role in making Halldór's name in Sweden, thus helping to pave the way for the writer's receiving of the Nobel Prize. It was thus
wise and prescient of Halldór to assist him. Many years later Peter Hallberg said
in an interview that what he had always found most remarkable about Halldór
was how he wrote about the uniquely Icelandic in such a way that it became
universal.

*

In May, 1950, Halldór went to Copenhagen, and in the decade that followed he
nearly always made at least two trips abroad each year, in the spring and autumn.
As in the past he needed peace and quiet for his writing, and he also needed
distance to endure the proximity of married life. When a new novel was in the
works and Halldór wanted to apply himself completely he left the country, regardless of what else was happening.

    Halldór used his time in Copenhagen well, sitting for long hours with Jón
Helgason over *The Happy Warriors*, which is set in the eleventh century. Halldór
wanted the book to have a language that belonged to the past. He also wanted to
see historical sites and landscapes on which to base the book's settings. When
Auður arrived at the end of the month they took a long trip through Norway,
north to Trondalag and from there to Jamtland in Sweden, and then south to
Copenhagen again; everywhere Halldór measured his characters against the
landscape.

    Early in 1950 a confederation was founded in Warsaw that called itself the World
Peace Council, its president being the French scientist, Frederic Joliot-Curie. One
of its first tasks was to gather signatures in support of the Stockholm Appeal,

which enjoined the nations of the world to ban nuclear weapons. The Stockholm Appeal enjoyed widespread support, but the confederation was said to be supported by the Soviet Union, if not directly sponsored by it; Joliot-Curie himself had been a member of the French Communist Party. Numerous artists and intellectuals who had nothing to do with Communism signed the appeal, but their opponents considered them Communist fellow-travellers. Halldór was an ardent supporter of the Appeal.

In the late summer of 1950 the *Will of the People* reported that Halldór had been included in a list of the world's best hundred writers in a book published by Dial Press. Then a French studio contacted him about filming *Salka Valka*. It seemed that many of his dreams were coming true all at once. In the autumn he was once again nominated for the Nobel Prize and, what mattered most, was publicly recommended for it. Among the writers who felt that Halldór should receive the prize was Karen Blixen.

The winter of 1950–1 found Halldór and Auður expecting a child. They had been together for nearly a decade, had been married for five years and had established a handsome home. Of course life at Gljúfrasteinn was not always easy; Halldór was away much of the time and Auður was sometimes plagued with worries, as can be seen from their correspondence. She had to leave her course at the painting and handicraft school and return to work in the radiology department of the National Hospital. As sensitive as Halldór could be to the psychology of women and children in his books, it was sometimes opaque to him in the real world. He did not find it easy to be with pregnant women, and was never one for cuddling babies. Perhaps he found it difficult to be so close to the origin of life: it was better to deal with such a thing in the imagination.

Halldór was mostly at home that winter. Besides writing *The Happy Warriors*, he went over the German translation of *Iceland's Bell* early in 1951; finally there was some activity on the publishing front in Germany. Dietz had decided to publish *Salka Valka* in the translation by Elisabet Göhlsdorf, who had moved back to East Germany from Iceland. The company was interested in other novels by Halldór and contacted a German translator who lived in Sweden, Ernst Harthern.

More things went well for Halldór that year. In March his artist's grant was raised to 15,000 krónur. That same month M.Í.R. sponsored a festival, including an art exhibition, a general assembly, and the visit of a large delegation of writers and artists from the Soviet Union; heading the delegation was the composer Aram Khachaturian. The opera singer Nadyezhda Kasantsyeva came as well, and

Auður gave a dinner at which Khachaturian performed a Russian dance to piano accompaniment.

The Soviet musicians also visited work places, thus occasioning the following comments in *Morgunblaðið*:

It must have been a great relief and inspiration for orthodox Communists among the Reykjavík workers to have seen and heard these Russian guests. Because this must have worked to strengthen the belief of the Reykjavík toadies of Stalin that, if Stalin were to gain hold of the Icelandic nation, as both he and his Fifth Army here certainly hope happens, the workers here in this country could still, even as they were denied all human rights in the Communistic way, maintain the hope of being able to enjoy instrumental music in their oppression . . .

There now commenced a written debate typical of the tone of the Cold War in Iceland throughout the 1950s. Of Halldór *Morgunblaðið* said:

The next step might be for Kiljan to choose to excuse his servility to the Moscow powers by saying that he had not given any thought as to how the leaders of the Communists, the clique of dictators in the Kremlin, imagined themselves taking over the world, robbing every nation and every man of his freedom and personality.

Tempers got hotter and hotter, until Halldór wrote an article in his biting polemical style, asking the *Morgunblaðið* editor Valtýr Stefánsson:

Do you consider me in reality to be more of a simpleton than anyone else, my dear Valtýr, to think that I take note of anything that is said in that blend of drunken blather, hysterical hot air, and general childishness that spews from you, pure and holy, about Communism?

Halldór always had the last word in such debates.

"The Cold War did not make any of us better people," said the poet Matthías Jóhannessen, who had started work as a reporter for *Morgunblaðið* that same year. The international situation seemed unsalvageable: Stalin was still in power and his persecutions were becoming ever more savage; the Korean War had been raging for nearly a year; McCarthyism was in full swing. On 5 May, 1951, the governments of Iceland and the United States signed an agreement stating that America would take on Iceland's military defence on behalf of N.A.T.O. The Alþingi was not convened, but the Social Democratic Party, the Independence Party and the

Progressive Party declared their support. When the Alþingi voted just before the new year, only the Socialist M.P.s were opposed. A foreign military presence had become permanent.

In May, 1951, Halldór travelled through southern England and northern France to research the settings for *The Happy Warriors*. It had originally been planned that Auður would go with him, but she was so far along in her pregnancy that she did not want to. Halldór visited Stanley Unwin in London, and engaged in a long correspondence with Ernst Harthern, who wanted to secure him a publisher in West Germany. Harthern himself visited several companies in West Germany in the spring and returned with some offers. Finally he and Halldór accepted an offer from Suhrkamp, who published Brecht, Mann and Hesse. *Iceland's Bell* was published in West Germany before Christmas, 1951.

Harthern, who spent ten years doing nothing but translate Halldór's works into German, was a German Jew. Early on he had become interested in Scandinavian languages and literature and had started to work as a translator before the First World War. He was confident, and his letters to Halldór show that he was unafraid of suggesting changes to the novels that he was translating. He wanted Halldór, for example, to change the ending of *Salka Valka*; the reader had to know what became of Salka.

Having settled in Copenhagen in the 1930s, in 1943 Harthern was among the Jews who went by boat over the Øresund to Sweden under the surveillance of the German border guards before mass arrests began. He quickly started translating again, including books by Martin Andersen Nexø, which is when Dietz contacted him about translating Halldór. His translation of *Iceland's Bell* received excellent reviews in West Germany, although sales were somewhat disappointing. Suhrkamp also published *World Light*. Wishing to promote Halldór as best he could, Harthern sent a copy of *Iceland's Bell* to an acquaintance, Thomas Mann, who replied by saying that he looked forward to indulging in "this great and extremely significant work of a storyteller who up until now had been unknown to me".

Harthern was doubtless an accomplished translator. He described his views in a letter to Halldór, using a familiar simile:

> To me translations are like women. If they are beautiful, they are not always faithful. If they are faithful, they are not always beautiful. This is an old truth. Hopefully my translation is somewhere in between.

Harthern knew Danish, Swedish and Norwegian, but not Icelandic, and he had never visited the country. Because of this various errors found their way into his translations. At the end of the 1950s Halldór exchanged letters with his new publisher in West Germany, Rowohlt, concerning a change of translator. Halldór always said that he had to spend too much time on Harthern's translations and had to correct numerous errors. Harthern heard of this and was quite angry. Fame, he said, had gone to Halldór's head: "You love money, and everything that it is possible to buy with it."

It took almost two years for Harthern to come to terms with this, and he wrote Halldór a parting letter:

> And bless you now, dear Laxness – after a ten-year cooperation. This Moor here has done his duty, he is scarcely fit for travel any longer . . . We shall let the great swamp cover over the path that he might have left behind. Amen.

> Ernst Harthern died in 1969.

*

Sigríður, Auður and Halldór's eldest daughter, was born on 26 May, 1951; her father was still abroad and only returned home several weeks later. Auður wrote:

> I became unwell, had a varicose vein in my leg, and made a mess of breast-feeding, so I was feeling very low and quite anxious when Halldór came home a short time later. After several weeks we agreed that I should go to Sweden . . . to get back on track. My mother took on the job of looking after the girl . . .

The stay in Sweden proved beneficial, and after Auður returned in the autumn she left her job, gradually becoming a full-time housewife. In her memoirs she says that Sigga (as the little girl was known) had likely saved her marriage, as she and Halldór had not been seeing eye-to-eye. So, as is often the case, the child became the ballast for the family. Halldór chose, as always, to have things his own way, to leave when it suited him and to be away as long as he felt necessary. But when he was in Iceland he wanted to have a comfortable, cultured and elegant home. No matter how radical he was in politics and the arts, in this particular arena he was a conservative.

That summer *Salka Valka* was published in East Germany in a run of twenty thousand copies. There was not much domestic activity at Gljúfrasteinn as Halldór was there alone, Auður having gone to Sweden. He worked on *The Happy Warriors* and corresponded with foreign publishers and translators. On 10 September he sent Ernst Harthern some interesting comments about *Atom Station*, which had been translated into several languages but not yet been published abroad:

Atom Station has been translated into Danish, German, Czech and Russian, but it has not been printed in the West because of its content, in the East because of its form; all my publishers in the Marshall Aid countries have orders not to print it; but in the East it is considered un-Marxist, a formalist work. This position works well on my sense of humour; there these two worlds have found a shared misfortune and a stumbling block (the book is otherwise my finest in an artistic sense).

Eventually *Atom Station* was published in all these languages, but the letter gives a good indication of Halldór's doubts about his old comrades to the east of the Iron Curtain; he did not trust their artistic sense, and deeper within him were even stronger doubts.

On 17 September, Halldór's mother died. She had been a constant support during the decades when he was travelling around Europe and North America, sending him money when she had any to spare, taking care of his daughter María, and sheltering Halldór when he had nowhere to stay. Halldór wrote to her frequently while on his travels, always starting with "Dear Mother", and ending with "Your Dori", long after he stopped using that name with anyone else. When he wrote about her in *In the Fields of Home* he mentioned a characteristic that he himself shared in his old age: "It was her habit to speak in fresh, laconic terms and bold comments, which sometimes came as if from an unexpected direction . . ." He added:

> One time during these final days of hers a woman was speaking on the radio about thrift in cooking, and when she came to discussing how one could be most sparing with margarine, my mother said: "Do you think we could turn the old woman off now?"

Four years later Halldór was shown a picture of his mother at a party. He looked at it for a long time before saying: "In fact I never knew this woman. She was a fairy. But I was fonder of her than any other woman."

*

At the end of September Halldór went to Sweden to see Auður, visiting Harthern in Sigtuna and meeting his German publisher, Peter Suhrkamp, there. In October Auður went home to Iceland via Copenhagen, but Halldór remained behind to write.

Among the West German reviews of *Iceland's Bell* was one by Rudolf Kramer-Badoni, who wrote that the book should be considered "one of the most important Scandinavian novels that has ever been written". The *Frankfurter*

Allgemeine declared that Halldór's eloquence was on a par with Joyce and Mann. That the book inspired a great deal of attention despite not becoming a bestseller was made clear when the Swiss paper *Weltwoche* asked several well-known writers in German what book they would give as a Christmas present. Hermann Hesse named *Iceland's Bell* and declared it the most important work of fiction that he had read that year, a true Icelandic saga, a modern version of *Egil's Saga* and *Grettir's Saga*. (It is worth nothing that in 1960 George Lukács named *Iceland's Bell* as important contemporary proof of his theory that historical realism was still valid.)

At the start of December, 1951, Halldór attended a peace congress in Stockholm in the company of more than six hundred representatives from all over Scandinavia. At the opening session representatives of the various delegations spoke: Errki Saloma, an editor from Finland; Jacob Friis, a Social Democratic M.P. from Norway; Reverend Uffe Hansen from Denmark; and Halldór on behalf of Iceland. Halldór's speech, later published in the *Will of the People*, was in the spirit of his previous articles about the necessity for peace, and yet more moderate and with more emphasis on Scandinavian solidarity. It concluded with the words:

> We have come here today in order to work to strengthen Scandinavian national unity against the prophets of war, against the three sages of the atom bomb, against the twelve apostles of mass murder.

In the midst of the Cold War few people noted the fact that Halldór's politics were marked by a new tone: there was less constant praise of everything that happened in the East, and sometimes he spoke as if he were a kind of independent leftist.

In the autumn of 1951 the Danish newspaper *Berlingske Tidende* interviewed Halldór, who said that he had grown tired of fiction and preferred a huge book about sparrows to belles-lettres. He said that he had little interest in the theatre and always fell asleep in the cinema; concerning Icelandic writers he declared that they had never reached true maturity. At the same time he made some serious points, acknowledging his debt to Hemingway, Dreiser and Upton Sinclair. He found Faulkner, on the other hand, too pinched, deliberate, complicated. Halldór also stated that he was not a Communist, did not belong to any party, but was a socialist in the spirit of the *New Statesman* in Britain. This was a new tone for Halldór, one he chose to air in a conservative foreign paper.

The press in Iceland picked up the interview, since many people there followed the news from Denmark. The *Will of the People* asked Halldór for details several months later, and he repeated that he had never been a member of the Communist Party. This was true, but the remark glosses over his contribution to the work of the Icelandic Communists during the 1930s.

At the start of December Halldór went to Copenhagen to visit Jón Helgason, having sent on ahead the latest chapters of *The Happy Warriors* with a letter:

> I have worked for nearly a month to complete these few pages . . . although I previously sat over them for much longer than that. I cannot do any better for the time being. You must have them although they are poor, and perhaps completely lifeless; I have simply lost my talent for writing. Now not even half a word from some good man I respect would suffice to make me cast to hell all the dirty work that I have been struggling with for three years. I am quite on the edge of giving up for good.

Halldór did not go home that Christmas; that he let the book take precedence was no doubt difficult for Auður.

Halldór went to Ireland to research historical background in January, 1952, in bad weather. The well-known Irish folklorist James Hamilton Delargy met him in Dublin and showed him round. Halldór was fascinated by such national treasures as the *Book of Kells*, as well as by the graves of ancient Irishmen. He wrote to Jón Helgason: "They wrote better in Ireland in the days of Ingólfur Arnarson than anyone in Europe since – and likely in all the world." That was a great deal coming from an Icelandic writer.

Halldór returned to Iceland around mid-February. Awaiting him was a letter from Dietz about the trouble they were having with *Salka Valka*: the book had not been well received; Arnaldur's political development was too negative and it was unclear what became of Salka at the end. Just like the book's translator, they would have preferred to see another conclusion to the book. They also felt uncomfortable about *Atom Station* and thought that *Iceland's Bell* was too weighty. They therefore referred Halldór to a company called Aufbau, which took over the publishing of his work in East Germany for the next few decades. Although all East German companies had to bow to the will of the Party, there were nuanced differences between them. Aufbau was a decent literary company, making it a more natural home for Halldór.

The fact that Halldór's comrades at home were happy to have him in their ranks was apparent in April, when he turned fifty. Numerous old friends and fellow-activists wrote about him in the *Will of the People*, and special greetings came from the central committee of the Socialist Party. Other supporters wrote about him in the papers or composed poetry for him: "You are this wonderword, with a bright distant sound – how dear you are to your nation," wrote one. An article written by Þórbergur Þórðarson for the *Will of the People* took a light-hearted tone and retold humorous stories from their years together at Unuhús.

In the new isolation of the Cold War the Icelandic Socialists felt fortunate to have Halldór on their side. Halldór was also popular with the public. A literary event held in Reykjavík had to be repeated because of the huge turnout: nearly one and a half thousand people came.

Halldór also received greetings from abroad. The Danish Communist paper *Land and People* published birthday wishes from Danish writers and intellectuals, including Karen Blixen, who wrote:

> When not feeling well I have taken out your books. And there the clear, genuine sound received me, firmly and powerfully, from the first page. I have read *Iceland's Bell*, *The Fair Maiden*, and *Fire in Copenhagen* many times. I wept over *Fire in Copenhagen* – and had otherwise shed my last tear over a book before you were born.

Like most artists Halldór enjoyed being praised. He had long fought for recognition as a writer in Iceland and in Icelandic. He had experienced "being nothing" and endured political persecution; he had been deprived of grants, been involved in endless tax troubles. He remained refined and courteous in his behaviour, and generally kind to people who sought him out. But as a fifty-year-old he was not as eager to meet new people as in his younger years; he could often be stand-offish to strangers. To this was added the fact that a famous man in a small society will often have to "play himself", and thus can sometimes become a caricature. Society started little by little to ripple with stories about Halldór, things he said and his idiosyncrasies, and he became a popular subject for ventriloquists and cartoonists.

Halldór's publishing company, Helgafell, made great inroads into the distribution of his books in Iceland that year. *Independent People* was reprinted in the summer with a new epilogue, and in the autumn most of his collected works were published in a set of thirteen volumes. He also published *When I Left Home*, which he had written in the mid-1920s and which had been in the keeping of Stefán Einarsson.

At the Socialists' Midsummer Celebration he delivered a speech exhorting the Americans to work towards spiritual achievements on the world stage and to give up their faith in war machines, while on the thirty-fifth anniversary of the Russian Revolution M.Í.R. sponsored a meeting at which Halldór delivered a speech that was perfectly in keeping with the Soviet political agenda:

> The socialist peace, the peace of the worker, is the highest moral power of our century, and in the state that is founded on this ideal of peace, all men who celebrate good will play a part . . .

In December the World Peace Council sponsored a so-called international peace congress, on the occasion of which Halldór published an article about the Korean War in the *Will of the People*. At the congress it was announced that he and seven other artists would receive special prizes "for their work of writing in the service of peace". It was unclear as to whether this meant a nomination or the actual prize, because the *Will of the People* published the news again six months later, calling the recognition the Literary Prize of the World Peace Council, and naming the artists who were to receive it along with Halldór. This prize was accompanied by a medal, which Halldór received at the end of November, 1953.

It may have been the Soviet connections of the World Peace Council that caused Icelandic newspapers and American encyclopaedias to state that Halldór had received a prize associated with Stalin; this was simply not the case but rather represented a confusing of Halldórs prize with the Stalin Prize for Peace and Friendship Between Nations, awarded, for example, to the Brazilian writer Jorge Amado.

Halldór's priority in 1952 was to finish and publish *The Happy Warriors*. In the autumn he sent proofs to Jón Helgason, who returned them with comments that he found invaluable. This time he was fighting to get his book on to the Christmas market. He wrote to Jón:

> It is very important that the book does not get held up, especially because all my finances for now depend on its selling before Christmas. If it does not make it on to this Christmas market, it will perhaps have to wait a whole year, which would be very bad for me since I have not had any income here since 1948 [when *Atom Station* had been published].

The Happy Warriors is a modern Icelandic saga turned upside down, picking up threads from both *Iceland's Bell* and *Atom Station*. It may be read as a sharp criticism of warmongering and preposterous heroic ideals, a kind of portrait of the Second World War, even though it is set in the eleventh century. The work clearly displays the mental wrestling match with the sagas that had engaged Halldór for a number of years, because "an Icelandic writer cannot live without thinking constantly about the old books". But, as he put it in an interview with Matthías Jóhannessen: "What I wanted to do . . . was to create an archaic work of art for modern people."

Halldór worked very hard to give the work the air of an old text, making use of *The Saga of the Foster-Brothers* and the *Saga of St Ólafur* by Snorri Sturluson, besides numerous foreign period sources. But he devoted most of his energy to the novel's language, which he learnt as he wrote it: "My rule was, in general, never to use words that could be proved not to have existed in the language in the eleventh century." This would scarcely have been possible in other European languages since the book would have been incomprehensible to ordinary readers. In a letter to Peter Hallberg almost ten years later Halldór said:

> It might only have been the language, but it took me far more work to master it than anything else in the book. I would certainly have been able to learn Chinese and many other languages during the six years that it took me to learn this language.

The obsolete nature of the language gives the book an exotic quality, and its criticisms of ancient heroic ideals are all the more telling since they come "from within": the story is a kind of anti-saga. It is curious that very few modern Icelandic authors, with the exception of Halldór and Gunnar Gunnarsson, should have managed to write a modern saga, or focused on material from the sagas' period. Perhaps people were too careful regarding the sagas, too reluctant to challenge them. It might not seem controversial now, but in the newly established Republic there were those who considered the ideals of the ancients to be the very cornerstone of society, and resented the message of the book.

The foster-brothers of the novel are the offspring of heroic ideals. Þorgeir Hávarsson is overbearing and ridiculous in his heroism, and the poignant discrepancy between ideals and reality is underlined early on in the description of his appearance: "At that time most men in Iceland were stunted and bow-legged, gaunt and swollen-jointed, knotty and twisted with gout, wrinkled and blue-faced." From infancy he is a victim of the ideological world of murder and rape. His foster-brother, Þormóður Bessason, is not as simplistic a character, but he holds to the same ideals and tries to honour them with poetry. The poet's role is to praise warriors and kings, delivering ballads about their achievements and excellence. No king is a more worthy subject of praise than Ólafur Haraldsson the Stout, to whom the author has lent qualities taken from Hitler.

Þormóður's problem is that he has become acquainted with another kind of life through his relationships with women: Kolbrún the Dark, who lives in the netherworld, and Þórdís the Bright, who is rich and provides Þormóður with a handsome home for a time. Kolbrún is more closely related to the common people, lives on the boundary, in the dark world of human instincts and urges, and is connected to Greenland. Halldór's description of Inuit society has a utopian air:

hunters live in a kind of collective society, in harmony with nature, though naturally not in peace due to attacks by the Vikings. It suits Halldór to site Utopia in a place he has never seen. This may be an indication of why he becomes – at least in his fiction – doubtful about radical social struggle: he transports the ideal of a better society to the dream world that is inaccessible to human beings.

At the end of the book Þormóður achieves his goal to present himself to the king and recite a poem to him. By then, however, the dazzle of the heroic ideal has abandoned him completely. The book ends as follows:

> "Now bear your king up, skald," said Olaf Haraldsson, "and let me hear this night by the cairn your lay of The Happy Warriors."

The Happy Warriors displays a great deal of the critical power of Halldór's earlier books, and its clear message amplifies the tragedies of the Second World War and the hope of peace. More specifically, there are parallels between the poet who honours the wrong king and Halldór the poet who had honoured Stalin. Later Halldór would flirt with such interpretations, although he did not want to go too far with them, believing that books should speak for themselves.

The book was published at the start of December, 1952, and its reception exceeded all expectations. On 19 December Helgafell hosted a splendid promotional event at which Jakob Benediktsson delivered a lecture and well-known actors performed scenes from Halldór's fiction. He himself read from the book. In the autumn of 1968 *Morgunblaðið* reported that *The Happy Warriors* had sold twenty-five thousand copies in Iceland.

The Nobel Prize

In mid-February, 1953, Halldór went to Scandinavia on business until the end of April. It was probably at the start of this trip that the Justice of the Peace Guðmundur Í. Guðmundsson denied him a passport because he had still not cleared up his tax problems. Ragnar Jónsson, his publisher, saved him by paying his debt, thus allowing Halldór to leave the country. *Vísir* noted, in cheerful anticipation: "With regard to this, he is going, as we know, to receive his Stalin Prize, and it remains to be seen how much it will be worth in taxes." Ragnar was mystified because his company had taken over Halldór's tax payments some time ago, and any suggestion of mismanagement was absolutely inconceivable to him. In any case Guðmundur Í. Guðmundsson, later Minister for Foreign Affairs, never spared Halldór during these years. Auður's remembers:

The ship waited a quarter of an hour past its scheduled departure time, while Ragnar Ólafsson, Halldór's lawyer, went up to the Government Building to speak to the Minister. "No, a travel ban won't be placed on Kiljan," said Eysteinn Jónsson. "They can express their opinion of him in some other way." And the ship sailed away.

In Copenhagen Halldór met the new director of Gyldendal, Otto B. Lindhardt, who still remembers him with respect, although he always found the writer somewhat distant and difficult to approach even though Lindhardt was Halldór's publisher for a decade. In Sweden Halldór spent almost a week meeting representatives of Nordisk Tonefilm. The Swedes wanted to film *Salka Valka*. The company in France that had previously shown interest could not raise enough money. According to Auður, things had progressed to the point that:

> the French had already sent red wine to Iceland, which they wanted to drink, in addition to camp beds that people were going to sleep on while the filming was taking place . . . I don't know what happened to the beds, but the wine was given to the State Alcohol Monopoly, bottled here with labels reading '*Salka Valka*', and sold to the public." The Swedes did not send any wine, but set to work straight away.

Rune Lindström wrote the script, which Halldór liked.

Halldór attended a meeting on behalf of the Stockholm Committee of the World Peace Council, where he saw his Soviet acquaintance Sofronov. From there he went to Finland on contractual business and to meet writers and translators. He described the visit in a letter to Peter Hallberg:

> I do not intend to count up the huge numbers of people with whom I have spent time on this trip. And things did not go any better here in Helsinki – it started when I arrived, when the bosses in my publishing company . . . took me to lunch at Vapuna, followed by an extremely long press conference, and immediately afterwards a radio interview, then the theatre; the next morning there were business meetings at the company and the signing of a contract for Ólafur Kárason, and then endless lunches and teas with people from the papers, societies, and institutes, besides private individuals, telephone calls, bouquets, book gifts etc., which I do not intend to count up, among them tea with a famous Finnish poetess, the Communist and millionaire Hella Wuolijoki; moreover, I received a visit from an extraordinarily pleasant Swedish chauvinist, Dr Ekhammer from Uppsala, who wanted me

to assist him in driving all the Finns from power in Helsingfors [the Swedish name for Helsinki] . . .

Halldór's later trips to Scandinavia followed the same pattern. When he had finished with the public functions, he would often take a break at a hotel just outside town and write alone and untroubled.

Halldór appeared on these visits as an elegant cosmopolitan, impeccable in appearance, well versed in all the manners pertaining to banquets and an accomplished linguist. He drank little, and found few things more boring than when his compatriots behaved themselves immoderately abroad, no matter whether that included friends and artists whom he respected.

While Halldór was abroad, on 5 March, Stalin died. He was remembered with respect in the *Will of the People*, which published among other things a chapter from *The Russian Adventure*. Auður told Halldór in a letter that numerous people went to the Soviet embassy to sign their names in a book of remembrance, but she could not bring herself to go. Thus concluded a poignant and violent period in the history of Russia; at the same time, the period of Halldór's staunch support for Soviet policies was coming to an end.

This change occurred slowly and without fanfare over the next ten years, alongside other changes in Halldór's ideas and interests. He continued to support the Peace Council for a time, and in the spring wrote an article, "A Voice From Iceland", for its organ in Paris, in which he said:

I have lived for a longer time in America than in any other country. My books have been read in the hundreds of thousands in America. I shall always feel indebted to the country that made me a socialist.

He made a clear distinction between the American public and its politicians. His thinking followed this formula: the pacifism of the public as opposed to the warmongering of the politicians.

In a similar spirit was the speech "Great Nations and Small Nations", which Halldór delivered that summer in the Icelandic countryside. Employing logic that many Icelanders accepted, he noted:

I should add here that the people the Northern Hemisphere should thank for its education, the ancient Greeks and the Jews, were, approximately two thousand five hundred years ago, when their culture stood at its highest, not much greater in number than we Icelanders are now.

Halldór also wrote about literature that summer, tried to get himself going on a new novel and composed the first drafts of the play *The Silver Moon* (1954). At the end of September he travelled to the Soviet Union, having accepted an invitation from the Writers' Union for a month-long stay. He took *The Silver Moon* with him in manuscript form and showed it to his friends en route to Moscow to gauge their reactions. From Helsinki, Halldór wrote to Auður:

> One of the best pieces of news that I received in Stockholm was that Churchill was going to receive the Nobel Prize. As you can guess it lightens my load a great deal to know this, because I am always being harassed by this prize.

Halldór doubtless found it uncomfortable to be asked every time he went to Sweden whether he thought he might receive the prize. Ivar Harrie in the Swedish newspaper *Expressen* remarked: "In the world right now there exists an epic writer on a par with Homer, who writes in a language the Academy has never been fond of: Halldór Laxness."

That year he came closer to receiving it than ever before. According to Anders Österling, the spokesman for the Nobel Committee, Robert Frost, Walter de la Mare and Halldór were next in line to receive the Prize after Churchill. Österling expressed his high opinion of Halldór's narrative talents, but he felt that the books' weightiness worked against them. What he meant was that Halldór's political position informed his writing – it was still the Cold War after all.

Halldór was welcomed in Moscow with open arms. His old friend Apletin was still working there, and they had a joyful reunion. And there was some progress on the publishing front. Krymova was translating *Atom Station*, and now, fifteen years after a contract had been signed, *Independent People* was published. Halldór was extremely pleased. But for a man accustomed to staying at the d'Angleterre in Copenhagen, the hotels in the Soviet Union were not wonderful:

> They took me to a hotel – and the hotels here are as poor as they have always been, decrepit, dilapidated aristocrats' hotels from the time of the Tsar, absolutely horrible to see in every way.

Halldór stayed for three weeks at a health resort in Sotsi on the Black Sea. He was pleased to be living a life of luxury, and had been working on his Russian so diligently that he could stumble through *Pravda*. With him was an interpreter, Valentina Morosova, "a wise and gracious woman", as Halldór wrote to Auður. When Halldór returned to Moscow the writer Polevoi held a huge party for him, and Halldór spoke on the radio as he had on all of his previous visits. He left for Germany and Vienna on 17 November.

Morosova, the wise and gracious one, wrote a detailed report to her supervisors in V.O.K.S. and perhaps elsewhere. Clearly she did not think it inappropriate to record Halldór's various criticisms, since there had been something of a thaw in Russia after the death of Stalin. She first explained that Halldór would be going to a congress of the World Peace Council in Vienna, where an exhibition was to be held of the work of writers who had received the Peace Council's prize. Halldór was displeased that it would not be possible to exhibit any Russian translations of his works, as such an omission might inspire talk about his lack of political reliability. Halldór had asked which Western writers were published in translation in the Soviet Union, and had expressed his amazement at how few they were.

Halldór told Morosova that writers had to compromise when it came to form, and that he considered many Communist writers far too stiff: they shut themselves off in their different camps and thus failed to reach a wider audience. What mattered most was for writers to get as many people as possible to listen to them.

Halldór added that a cultural exchange between West and East was extremely important, but had to be realistic and mutual. Declarations made by the Peace Council were only clichés, and the contribution of the Soviet representatives was not uplifting. Cultural exchange could be of use to both sides, said Halldór, and he reiterated his discontent with the official position of Soviet gallery directors towards Picasso and his colleagues.

Halldór asked whether M.Í.R. could not choose the artists' delegations that came to Iceland in the future. And he added that he found the Soviets much more liberal and humanistic when they were abroad than when they were at home. He also thought that it would help if an Icelandic scholar were allowed to stay in the Soviet Union and assist translators and scholars, and that it would be a worthy project if the sagas could be published in the Soviet Union.

Finally Halldór reiterated that he needed to have his royalties paid in transferable currency, since writing was his livelihood. He said that he had always defended the Soviet Union, and had sometimes suffered financial injury because of it. He was told during the trip that this wish would be granted. And he left *The Silver Moon* behind for his hosts' perusal.

Morosova added her own conclusions, saying that she had got the impression that a battle was being waged over Halldór. He had a chance to win the Nobel Prize if he changed his political views. Thus it was extremely important that the connections with him be strengthened, and that his books be published.

This is an interesting report. It is hard to know how critical this visit was, but during the next years work began in the Soviet Union on publishing Halldór's books, and also the sagas. *Atom Station* and *Independent People* were both published in two editions. The print runs were not large initially (thirty thousand for *Independent People*), but two short stories also appeared in the weekly *Ogonyok*, which had a circulation of two million. *Independent People* was published in a total of four hundred and thirty thousand copies in Russian, and in a hundred and thirty thousand copies in six other languages in the former Soviet Union. Thus the combined print run in the United States and the Soviet Union was over a million copies.

Shortly after his homecoming Halldór wrote "Peace in the East", in which he described the consequences of the war in the Soviet Union, the unbelievable damage the nation had to endure and the horrific loss of life. Because of this the Soviet public was more interested in peace than anything else. Halldór also wrote about his friendships with Russians, which were to endure even if his pro-Communist feelings did not.

From Moscow Halldór went to Vienna, and on 27 November, 1953, he accepted the World Peace Council Prize. On this occasion he delivered a short address: ". . . never before has an international literary award found its way to Iceland." It was as if this were a dress rehearsal for the Nobel Prize:

> When I was a teenager I decided to become a writer, which is of course no great story in a country where every other person feels obliged to compose poetry. But I wanted to make the calling to be a writer my life's work, so that I could devote my time undivided to literature; as such, I determined to compose fiction in the epic form about the powerful life that has been lived with all its incredible contrasts on my weatherbeaten island, which thunders alone in the middle of the North Atlantic, and in the eyes of distant viewers must represent the image of the most remote desolation . . . My ambition was from the beginning only to follow in the footsteps of the ordinary poets and storytellers of Iceland, the writers of former times who didn't usually attach their names to their creations, and in every century in the life of the nation sat up at night by a little light at the conclusion of the day's work, often in cold turf hovels, and wrote books – and although their hands were sometimes cold, they did not lay down their pens while their hearts were warm.

After Halldór returned home, Magnús Kjartansson interviewed him on Christmas Eve for the *Will of the People*, asking for news from the literary world. Halldór made particular mention of the Cuban poet Nicolás Guillén and the

Brazilian novelist Jorge Amado, whom he had recently met. He had seen *Mr Puntila and His Man Matti* by Brecht in Berlin and enjoyed it very much:

> The play was full of imaginative power, without a single dead minute, although in a certain way it did not contain any dramatic conflict in the ordinary sense. Brecht is an excellent writer in his own way, and different from most other people.

These writers had in common the radicalism of their political views, a connection with the World Peace Council, a desire for formal innovation and brilliance in the field of literature. Halldór wanted to belong to their world.

*

Auður and Halldór had another daughter, Guðný, on 23 January, 1954. Conditions were different from when Sigríður was born: Halldór was at home, and domestic life at Gljúfrasteinn was more serene. He had tamed the restlessness of his youthful years without suppressing his creative power, made an ordinary life for himself in which he could work unhampered. And he had married a woman who dedicated herself to him so that he could write, as he had dreamed of in the early 1930s. Of course the situation was not entirely free from difficulty. Some time after the birth of Guðný, Auður said:

> Halldór went abroad in the spring, and the next day I stopped breast-feeding her. I was so sensitive, even though I didn't feel bad that he had gone – I had become used to that.

But before Halldór went abroad, he took on an unusual project: he translated *Wild Duck* by Ibsen for the National Theatre. Gerd Grieg produced the work, and it was previewed on 29 April. Halldór described his admiration for the play in a preface, saying that it was difficult "to point out a more merciless critic of so-called holy moral values" than Ibsen, who loved life all the same. No matter how great an artist might be, "if he hated human life, he [could] not compose works of fiction".

Halldór's mind was on the theatre because he was trying to promote *The Silver Moon*. The National Theatre decided to put on the play in the autumn, and the Maly Theatre in Moscow also wanted to do so; there was talk of productions in Helsinki and Oslo as well. Halldór proudly wrote to Peter Hallberg:

> I have also tried my hand at writing a play, which is perhaps only mediocre, although it has the virtue (or deficiency) of enchanting all the actors who read it and causing them to want to act in it immediately.

Hallberg, though, was not fond of *The Silver Moon*; he found its gambits somewhat coarse and obtrusive: "It also lacks that overtone, that multifarious and
sparkling nuance that characterizes his novels."

This statement says a lot. The drama, a kind of variation on *Atom Station*, tells
of an innocent young girl who falls prey to a greedy agent; its main topic is the relationship between art and commerce. When there is no narrator's voice or magical
stylistic playfulness, the message is delivered bluntly: it becomes somewhat
lugubrious and obvious.

At the start of May, 1954, Halldór went to Oslo to lecture at the Norsk
Studentersamfund on "The Problem of Literature in Our Times". He took this
task seriously and was anxious about his delivery. The next day he wrote to
Auður:

I have been apprehensive the whole time because of my lecture, which I
finally gave last night, thereby lifting from me a heavy load. I was writing it
up until the last minute in fact, and felt as if I would never finish it, and actually never did. Then I spoke for an hour and fifteen minutes to a full house,
an attentive audience, who gave me a huge amount of applause and appreciation afterwards.

The lecture in fact summarizes his opinions on literature and the arts. He main-
tains that he is not much of a philosopher, any more than most Icelanders are:

The Icelandic mind is little inclined towards philosophy; at least it is distant
from any sort of philosophical discipline. We, as you know, are in the first
place a storytelling people and are inspired by palpable images; we create
from our existence.

Here Halldór touches on the view that Páll Skúlason and other Icelandic
philosophers wrote about later. He had no interest in approaching his work from
a theoretical angle, though he believed that a novelist had to have some kind of
foundation in rational thought.

The lecture has no prominent political aspect except when Halldór turns to the
struggle against war: "Only one thing can give our discussion about culture some
meaning, and that is peace." And he added: "Many poets and writers try to approximate the cadence of the politicians by becoming the envoys of all kinds of
pessimistic theories, especially here in the West."

Halldór is taking a stand here against much contemporary art; in fact he is
extremely critical of most fashionable fiction, which seemed to be influenced by

what was in vogue in his youth, namely surrealism and psychoanalysis. But he also criticizes the artistic doctrine being preached in the Soviet Union.

Most interesting is Halldór's understanding of realism:

Realism in my eyes is not a particularly special form; it can be all forms; it is beyond all else an artistic movement or literary movement that can influence reality because it has its roots in reality and serves a specific purpose there; it is an artistic movement that can influence the century because it expresses the century, the face of the century, the soul of the century, the suffering of the century, the desire of the century. If I were to name a creator of realistic art in our time, then I would name Picasso. In poetry I would name Neruda, in drama Brecht, in film Chaplin. Among the representatives of the spirit of the age that bears the characteristics of Anglo-Catholicism, classical education and royalism, I would consider T.S. Eliot the greatest realist, so great that if one had merely been a regular reader of *The* (London) *Times* for twenty-five years, one would understand his poetry immediately, without any explanation.

This was a remarkable statement from a man considered to be a staunch supporter of the Soviet agenda. And here one can see the continuity in Halldór's thinking: these were basically the aesthetics that he espoused for most of his life, once he abandoned the experimental fiction of his youth.

Halldór knew how his words would be understood in the East. In a letter to Auður he wrote that the speech belonged

first and foremost to the East – and although it was delivered in Oslo and Copenhagen, it was conceived of as a contribution to the discussion in the East – now just before the Soviets' great writers' congress, which is nearly upon us.

The speech was published in Denmark in *Dialog*, a scholarly journal of the Danish Communists that had turned gradually away from the orthodox line.

Halldór delivered the same lecture in Iceland on 20 September, 1954, at the Reykjavík Student Union. *Morgunblaðið*'s interpretation is a clear indication of how the Cold War had made people deaf: Halldór, the paper claimed, had made a "fierce attack against young writers and poets in Iceland today". This ought not to have been surprising:

Communists hate personal independence and originality like the plague. Art that is not built on "socialist realism" is in their understanding "degenerate capitalist art". And where can "socialist realism" be found? Only in art that casts a romantic light over the tyranny of Communism. Art that does not serve this goal is "degenerate" and useless.

This was not what Halldór had said, however.

In Norway Halldór met his publisher, his friend Gerd Grieg, and the writer Johan Borgen, whom he considered among the best men in the country. From there he went to Hälsingborg and met Maria Wine, the wife of Artur Lundkvist, and invited the couple to visit Iceland. He wrote to Auður:

> Artur Lundkvist . . . is one of my best friends and benefactors in Scandinavia, and it was directly through his agency and agitation that I received the World Peace Council Prize. Because of this I am planning to receive him and his wife as best I can, and I promised them that they would be welcome at our home; and besides that got rooms with a kitchen for them in town, and I promised to show them round, even drive them myself to the north of Iceland.

Halldór was still cultivating any relationship that he felt would benefit him.

In mid-May he went to Germany and visited his old friend, Elisabet Göhlsdorf, in Konstanz. Things were difficult for her: she was unwell and poor, and had been forced to leave East Germany: "She bungled by letting herself be forced out . . . there is no end to her thinking of herself as a grande dame, and how this gets her into extraordinary trouble," wrote Halldór to Auður. The difficulties experienced by Göhlsdorf were shared by many Germans who were driven into exile after the Nazis seized power.

Around the time that Halldór returned home, the Swedish film-makers and actors arrived in Grindavík to start on *Salka Valka*. Although there are no mountains in Grindavík, it was a good location, as it was where Halldór had gone to find the atmosphere of a seaside town when he had written the book. It was noteworthy for a motion picture to be filmed in Iceland, and the papers wrote a great deal about it. Elín Pálmadóttir went to the film set, and informed her readers that film-making mainly meant one thing: "Waiting and waiting some more." Arne Mattsson directed the film, and the cinematography was in the hands of Sven Nykvist, who later became chief photographer for Ingmar Bergman. The main role, Salka in her adult years, was played by Gunnel Broström.

Auður held a dinner party for the film-makers at Gljúfrasteinn:

> I remember that we were standing round the dining-room table, when Inga, the wife of Vilhjálmur Þ. Gíslason, then the acting director of National

Radio, asked: "Don't you find it somewhat lonely here?" "Yes," I replied. "Absolutely incredibly lonely sometimes. I can't deny it." Halldór was standing next to me and heard this. He was so surprised that he asked: "Do you really mean that? Do you find it lonely here?" Sometimes he didn't realize what things were like here when he was away from home.

In June Halldór's short stories were reprinted in a single volume, *Short Stories*, which includes commentaries on their origins and contents. On the Icelandic national holiday Halldór wrote an essay for the *Will of the People*, sharply criticizing the Americans for the military occupation and for not having stood by their promise to leave when the war ended. Old wounds would not be healed until the last American soldier had left Iceland.

At the start of June Halldór's old friend and comrade Martin Andersen Nexø died. Halldór bid farewell to his beloved and highly respected friend in an article in *Land and People*. It was not until *A Poet's Time* that Halldór´s tone regarding Nexø became tainted with irony.

The summer was devoted to visits from young friends; besides Artur Lundkvist and Maria Wine, there was the English art historian Mary Sorrell, whom Halldór had first met shortly before the war. Sorrell and Wine were completely different: the latter was an elegant and fashionable woman of the world and a writer of erotic poetry, while Sorrell was less elegant and more of a moralist; Halldór and Auður sometimes called her Mary Sorry behind her back. They all took a trip to the north of Iceland in two cars; the chemistry turned out to be problematic, according to Auður: "Maria Wine and Mary Sorrell had started to exchange such awful looks that the latter threw up once."

Halldór received more guests in the autumn. M.Í.R. hosted a conference in September, and on behalf of the society two world-class musicians, the pianist Tamara Guseva and the cellist Mstislav Rostropovich, visited Iceland; a dinner was held in their honour at Gljúfrasteinn.

*

The Silver Moon opened at the National Theatre on 9 October, 1954, the same day that it was published in book form. If nothing else, it inspired a strong reaction. The *Will of the People* reported that the usual audience was deeply scandalized. The drama critics followed political lines: the reviews in *Tíminn*, the *Will of the People* and the *People's Paper* were positive, but those in *Vísir* and *Morgunblaðið* were critical.

The Silver Moon's reception on the international stage disappointed Halldór. It met with a rather dull response in Helsinki; the Moscow production was of course successful; everywhere else the play was snubbed. With the exception of

Short Circuit, which had been written quickly and which Halldór never took too seriously, *The Silver Moon* was his first serious attempt at drama, and he tried to promote it everywhere, as he had done with his short stories in the 1930s. He particularly wanted to see it performed at Brecht's theatre in Berlin, but this never happened.

After he had returned home, Artur Lundkvist tried to gain support for Halldór in the Swedish papers as a Nobel Prize candidate. On 28 October it was announced that Hemingway had received the prize. The *Will of the People* cited the Swedish papers concerning the fierce debate that had raged in the Academy about who should receive the prize, Laxness or Hemingway, and said that the decision had been close. Many Swedish papers hoped that Halldór would receive the prize this time, and had prepared articles to run. Halldór's old friend, Þórður Sigtryggsson, also expected it and had written to him earlier in the summer:

> Now it is definitely decided that you will receive the Nobel Prize in the autumn. It costs a lot to film *Salka Valka*, and in order to guarantee the sale of the film the Swedes will finally be forced to grant you the prize.

The Icelandic embassy in Stockholm stated that it had proof that Halldór and Hemingway had received equal numbers of votes in the Academy, and that an unusually high amount of people had nominated Halldór this time. These included Wilhelm, the brother of the Swedish king, on behalf of Swedish P.E.N.; the Writers' Union of Finland; and Professors Kuhn from Kiel, Turville-Petre from England and Kemp Malone from Baltimore.

After Hemingway was awarded the prize, *Vísir* printed a statement on its front page that was said to be written by Halldór, who had recently gone abroad: "It Is All the Same to Me." Halldór had apparently told reporters:

> I have grown tired of listening to this endless talk saying I should receive the prize . . . I have no interest in it, because it would only mean that I would have to pay much higher taxes in Iceland.

Hemingway was not present at the award ceremony due to poor health, but *Vísir* said that he had told reporters "that he was sorry that Laxness did not receive the award, but on the other hand he could borrow from him if he needed to". In Halldór's family the story went that Hemingway had sent Halldór a telegram saying: "Don't worry, you'll get it next time" – which proved to be true.

At the end of October Halldór went to Prague on one of his "official" visits, as he described it to Auður:

One never gets time to scratch one's head in peace; yesterday I was made to run the gamut between some excellent representatives of the government, and then I was taken to the opera, although I hadn't slept for the last twenty-four hours.

He was replete with his familiar old impatience, but a week later he was completely exhausted:

You know how it is to be an official guest here in Czechoslovakia. It is not exactly a blissful position: one is woken in the mornings and rattled around well into the night . . . Here they take one from place to place without pause, and one has to talk to everyone, some new energetic workers take over at intervals of a few hours to "show" one some wonder (everything rather ordinary, however); yesterday I realized that I had had to give seven lectures.

Of his female guide he said:

. . . the most boring and least charming woman in Europe; it is nothing but nerve-wracking to hear her speaking this Swedish of hers with difficulty, always in falsetto. But she is so incredibly good-natured that one can't help but forgive her.

It must have been a matter of interest to Halldór on his trip that most of his friends in the country, like Nemecek, had been exiled.

From Prague Halldór travelled through Germany to Stockholm, where the film *Salka Valka* was premiered on 15 November. A great deal was written about the premiere in the papers, the reviews being rather positive. Halldór was happy, as he told Auður:

The film is the best that it is possible to hope for from films of this kind: they are somewhat heavy and humourless, but a lot of effort has been put in . . . and only those parts of the book filmed that mattered.

Halldór was in the news in Sweden that autumn; *The Happy Warriors* had been published at the start of November and had received outstanding reviews. In addition to numerous newspaper interviews, a television documentary was made about Halldór, in which he spoke to the scholar and Icelandophile Sven B.F. Jansson. He also attended a World Peace Council congress in Stockholm as one of five Icelandic representatives, and met both his Russian translator, Krymova, and Frau Janka, the wife of his East German publisher.

ᕔ *Jorge Amado on Halldór* ᕽ

The Brazilian writer Jorge Amado was a Communist for a time but was expelled from the Party in 1956. At the start of the 1950s he was very influential in the World Peace Council and met Halldór in connection with that organization. His biography, *Coastal Sailing* (1992), contains a chapter about Halldór, entitled "In the Baltic Sea, 1951 – Storm". The date was obviously mistaken, because this was in 1954:

On the ferry that brought us from Germany to Sweden Halldór Laxness was eating raw fish from a plate in front of him; the portions could hardly have been called miserly. The night was as black as a fish; a winter wind blew over the Baltic. Writers chatted enthusiastically around the Icelander: the Frenchmen Vercors and Jean Laffitte, the Argentinian Alfredo Varela, the Romanian Sadoveanu, the Chinese Emi Siao, and the Uruguayan Gravina. We were all on our way to a meeting of the World Peace Council. Varela and Laffitte followed Halldór's example and ate raw fish. I kept a low profile.

The storm increased in strength as it approached the ship: it was like a cat playing with a ball of yarn, the ship a nutshell in the midst of the waves . . . People started to go down below. Zelia [Amado's wife] went first, and the wind very nearly tossed her into the sea. One sailor close at hand grabbed her and helped her down into the cabin: our hold was in the belly of the ferry. Emi, the sailor of fiction, followed her example; Vercors and Gravina went after them. Varela asked for a vomit bucket. Laffitte was obstinate: he was fond of raw fish. He suddenly stood up in great haste and vomited on the deck.

I was insensitive to the waves, thanks to the trips that I took in my youth . . . I continued to sit on deck with Halldór, but did not join him in his meal. The Swedish aquavit put a fire in my belly. The novelist looked sideways at me: how long would his Brazilian comrade last?

I read Laxness first during the years that I was in exile in Rio de la Plata. I read the Argentine editions of *Salka Valka* and *Independent People*: I have a great deal of respect for his books and announced that to the audience when I presented Laxness with the International Peace Prize of the World Peace Council . . . A Brazilian translation of *Atom Station* was published in the series "International Novels" by the Communist company Vitoria, but it did not pay him any royalties. I also received no royalties from my publisher in Reykjavík, which at Halldór's advice translated *Sea of Death* into Icelandic. He had read the book in German.

The storm tossed the ferry, the wind howled, the waves gushed over the deck: we were completely soaked. Halldór gave me a look that suggested the evening meal was finished; he offered me his arm as we walked down the deck. I took it, I was drunk, I laughed like a madman: I am perhaps not a good novelist, but I am on the other hand an old sailor, a real ship's captain . . .

In Stockholm Halldór went with us to see the movie version of *Salka Valka* in Swedish. Zelia clapped. I preferred the novel. In 1958 we were, Laxness and I, the first writers among those most closely connected to the Soviet Union to protest the attacks in Moscow (filthy) against Pasternak, who had received the Nobel Prize . . . I became a great friend of Laxness, and we maintained a good friendship during the time that we fought for peace. When I recall him I see him in my mind on board the ship, with the plate of raw fish in front of him; storms meant nothing to this Icelandic novelist.

The autumn of 1954 also saw the publication in Sweden of Peter Hallberg's major study of Halldór's youth, *The Great Weaver*. Hallberg had sent Halldór proofs of the book, which the writer read on board the *Gullfoss* in October. He was grateful for Hallberg's meticulousness and effort, but it concerned him that Hallberg had used "the psychological stirrings of puberty" to explain his characteristics as an adult writer:

> The same goes for all sorts of fears that naturally have their place in young-sters with normal "health" and a moralistic upbringing: fear of sex, fear of living, fear of dying, and so forth. In my case, I am somewhat opposed to these being called my characterics as a writer – these are simply the normal characteristics of a thinking boy in his puberty.

Halldór stated that few adult men were as free of phobias as he was. Luckily Hallberg did not pay much attention to these comments. It may well be that all teenagers experience these psychological stirrings, but in Halldór's case they proved to be the antecedents to great artistic creation.

Halldór complained about Swedish banquets and the constant activity that prevented him from being able to manage his own time, but he was certainly happy: he was reaping the benefits not only of his career as a writer, but also of his cease-less work as his own agent. His books were being published in ever-increasing numbers of languages, huge markets had opened up to him, and he was one of the most well-respected writers in Scandinavia.

He was, however, prone to sadness at times, and he said of his daughters in a letter to Auður:

I am trying not to be too sensitive about them, but my mind is always with them, and that is a great comfort when I think about how to you I am a worthless and useless husband, constantly in disarray – there is so much crashing around in my head, despite the fact that I never get the chance to put words to paper. And now I need to be able to start on a new novel.

This time Halldór went to the hotel Store Kro in Fredensborg. But it was not always easy for his wife to read the news of Halldór's progress in foreign countries in the papers; some of the news became distorted along the way. In *Vísir* she read that Halldór intended to stay in Sweden for a year, and in "the *People's Paper* yesterday I read that you could not work at all at home because of the crowds of visitors here." Halldór replied:

I believe that all kinds of damned rubbish is written in the papers about me; I avoid reading all those newspaper interviews – they are more or less nonsense, misunderstandings, misquotations, mishearings, sensational rubbish. Of course I have not told any Swedish reporter that I plan to stay longer than a week in Sweden . . .

The same letters discuss the heated debates that occurred in Iceland because of a speech that Gunnar Gunnarsson delivered at a meeting of young conservatives on 14 November, "Western Culture and Communism". *Morgunblaðið* and the *Will of the People* naturally used the occasion for their usual bickering, and Gunnar brought a charge of libel against Magnús Kjartansson, the editor of the Socialist daily. Halldór and Auður were both shocked that Gunnar should have started such a passionate conflict in Iceland in his old age, and they recalled his dubious position towards the Nazis; the letters also reveal that they were not in agreement with their friend, the publisher Ragnar Jónsson, and regretted his political position. When Gunnar's speech is read now it seems very old-fashioned; although his basic facts concerning freedom of speech and democratic rights east of the Iron Curtain were obviously correct. On these matters Halldór had had little to say, taking his former position and not criticizing the Soviet Union in public.

After the first week in December Halldór started thinking about returning home. Prior to this he sent Auður a warm letter ("You are the sword and shield of domesticity at Gljúfrasteinn"), made some remarks about the reception of the film version of *Salka* at home, and added: "I think that it hardly matters what I do in

Iceland at this time: everything is thought bad. Even *The Silver Moon* is an attack on Bjarni Benediktsson." And then he told an entertaining story about fame. It was good to be in Store Kro; he had worked well and met no-one:

> ... except once I called Gunnel Broström in Hälsingborg and asked her to lunch – she is currently acting in Hälsingborg. I felt in some way that she had been neglected regarding all the celebrations for *Salka Valka*: she was not invited to the premiere, and it actually turned out that she was acting every night, but she said that she could have had that changed if she had been invited. We hadn't been sitting in the restaurant for more than five minutes when I received a phone call from a Swedish newspaper, asking whether it could send a photographer to take a photo of us – Gunnel had said inadvertently at the theatre that she was having lunch with me, and this news was immediately reported throughout Sweden. We certainly did not want our photographs taken there as we ate, and I refused my permission on the phone. Despite this, three press photographers suddenly turned up, pushed their way into the crowded dining room and started taking photos of us, which in fact made me quite angry, and I asked the manager to have them removed. Publicity can be so noxious here. Gunnel Broström is a very likeable girl.

The first Icelandic celebrity was born.

Halldór had a new novel in the works; though he was unable to concentrate on it in the New Year and decided to finish preparing a new collection of essays for publication first. The collection, *A Day at a Time*, which was published in July, contained speeches and articles from the years 1950–4 that mainly bore the marks of the peace movement and the Cold War.

At the start of April, 1955, Halldór returned to Denmark. He planned to stay in Saltsjöbaden to write, and then to go to Moscow to attend the premiere of *The Silver Moon*. At the home of Hans Kirk he met a large Soviet delegation that included both Krymova and the artistic director of the Maly Theatre, who wanted to bring Halldór to Russia for several weeks before the premiere to work with the company. In Sweden he met his translator Harthern and the director Arne Mattsson. The atmosphere in the country surprised him, as he wrote to Auður:

> Here one is unsparingly made to understand that one would receive the Nobel Prize if one were to change both one's opinions and one's travels. It is a hostile, oppressive atmosphere. Both Kuhn and Harthern reported to me rumours from the circles of the Swedish Academy (which they heard

second hand) that I was being strongly opposed *on behalf of Iceland* "on the basis of politics" – and that there was little likelihood that I would receive the Nobel Prize unless I were to change my position. For the love of God, do not go to Moscow now, not until after November . . . that's the message that I get here! It is difficult to imagine anything that could work on me so contrarily to the purpose than such concerns. To tell the truth, I find the atmosphere here in Sweden so hostile that I look forward to leaving.

Rumours like this can never be confirmed, but Halldór's political position was certainly a point of contention for the Swedish Academy. He was also reminded of the other side of the reality of the Cold War on his trip. While in Uppsala he telephoned his "old acquaintance Dr Emil Walter" who worked as a poorly paid teacher: "I tremble at the thought of seeing this vain man and pleasantly talented cosmopolitan in obvious poverty and helplessness." Walter was shattered; he could not publish his translations of the sagas in his homeland of Czechoslovakia. One after another Halldór was encountering people whom the changing political winds of the twentieth century had left empty-handed.

Halldór was present at the Maly Theatre's premiere of *The Silver Moon*, which ran for two years. In order to make things as clear as possible, the play, which was also published in book form in Russian, was given the title *Lullaby Sold*. The play's theme came to Auður and Halldór's minds many years later when they encountered Janis Joplin in the foyer of the Tre Falke Hotel in Copenhagen.

Leading Soviet cultural figures must have read Morosova's report about Halldór's previous visit, because much was made of him this time: well-attended promotional events were held in factories, and he was honoured in numerous ways. The Soviets were not ready to admit defeat. He himself spoke highly of the Maly company's production in an interview with the Swedish Paper *Ny dag*.

Halldór's allies in Sweden, Peter Hallberg and Ernst Harthern, reacted differently to *The Silver Moon*. Hallberg wrote a critique in *Svenska dagbladet*, but Harthern was pleased. He translated the play to send to Brecht's wife, Helena Weigel, and their theatre company, Berliner Ensemble, but it turned out that a young East German student, Wilhelm Friese, had already translated it and sent it to the company. This marked the start of a long correspondence, in which Harthern said that he saw himself as a kind of private agent for Halldór throughout Germany. It appears that Brecht had been considering *The Silver Moon*, and that Rowohlt was eager to publish *Atom Station* in a large run. Halldór and Harthern decided to travel together to Germany in the autumn to clarity matters there.

Atom Station was published in both East and West Germany in 1955, the year that the formal division between the two countries became a reality. In the East the book was celebrated, while in the West many critics thought it a rather unpleasant contribution to the Cold War. A review intended for West German libraries stated that the book should only be lent to mature readers who would not be scandalized by its "heathen origins".

On 26 June, 1955, on Martin Andersen Nexø's birthday, Halldór was awarded a prize named after him. Hans Kirk wrote an article in the *Will of the People* that is evidence of Kirk's lack of foresight:

> Of course there exists another literary prize that neither Gorky nor Martin Andersen Nexø was ever granted, and there is little likelihood that Laxness will ever receive it. That is the Nobel Prize, granted by members of a gang of aged, petit-bourgeois, even fascist, men known as the Swedish Academy.

As we have seen, Halldór had begun to have doubts about Soviet Communism, but he did not want to disappoint those in Iceland who had stood by him during difficult times.

In late summer he wrote an article in defence of Magnús Kjartansson, the editor of the *Will of the People*, who had been imprisoned for libel due to charges brought by the *Will of the People*. The Minister of Justice, Bjarni Benediktsson, had ordered Magnús' incarceration. The libel laws were strict in this outspoken nation, but punishment had seldom been applied. Now this was happening, causing Halldór and others to react strongly:

> It is interesting to witness the conflict between these two types of Icelanders: on the one hand a man such as Magnús Kjartansson, who presents his case based on the cold grounds of reality, a man of the sort for which there has been an eternal need in Iceland simply to make it possible to continue living here; on the other hand a man such as Bjarni Benediktsson, who is supposed to have some sort of intelligence below the surface, but who seems to lack the qualities of a normal adult man in a civilized society, and only under-stands one logic – prison, prison.

The government certainly did not have much to gain from the case, and the *Will of the People* had a martyr many would support. Magnús in fact only went to prison for a few days, saved as he was by representatives of the Daybreak Labour Union who paid his fines.

The article in defence of Magnús was one of Halldór's last stinging critiques of Icelandic politicians. His tone became gentler, and he chose his battles with care.

There was, however, no hesitation apparent in his struggle to promote his books abroad. In September he went to Copenhagen and from there to Germany with Harthern. They travelled almost 3,000 kilometres in Halldór's Buick, visiting both Rowohlt and Suhrkamp, and Halldór did not forget his old friends, such as Elisabet Göhlsdorf, who was in hospital. They arrived in East Berlin after the usual difficulties with the border police: "We drove into East Berlin late in the evening through a kind of shitty little village on the backside of reality. But got a good reception from Janka." Walter Janka was the director of Aufbau.

Halldór wrote to Auður that he and Harthern went to the theatre:

We saw a poor and boring play by Brecht, an extremely fossilized work [*Timpani and Trumpets*]. I did not feel well about leaving *The Silver Moon* in Brecht's hands, because it would be transformed by him into something unrecognizable. We agreed . . . that it should be left in the hands of Langstorff, who runs the . . . Deutsches Theater.

Although Halldór was not fond of Brecht's "boring play", he wanted to visit the writer whom he esteemed most east of the Iron Curtain. He described this visit to Auður:

Then I went to find Brecht. I have never spoken to him before. He is somehow warm and cold at the same time, full of abstract theories, mixed in with peculiar anecdotes. Although he sometimes goes awry, he is probably the most talented German writer after Thomas Mann; we spoke for two hours on various of the main problems of modern fiction, and it was as if we had known each other all our lives.

In *A Poet's Time* Halldór described their meeting in detail, as a conversation between leftist writers who both had doubts about the orthodox Communist understanding of literature and the arts. Halldór heard from Brecht that a book was often judged in the Party offices by the formula *gut aber nicht richtig* – good but not correct – and would thus fall under the axe of the censors. This formula is a kind of bad joke. Another book is shown mercy and published with pomp on the basis of its being *schlecht aber doch richtig* – poor but at the same time correct. Discussion of this sort was increasing among writers in the Eastern bloc after the death of Stalin.

Brecht found *The Silver Moon* neither correct nor good. Later he rejected it and recommended in the literary journal *Sinn und Form* that it should not be published, because it was inappropriate for performance under current conditions in the

Democratic Republic. For a long time there existed at Gljúfrasteinn a manuscript of *The Silver Moon* in German, upon which Brecht had written, "Anti-Nora stuff". Here he was citing the heroine of Ibsen's *A Doll's House*, who was locked up in her own home; it seems that Brecht had viewed *The Silver Moon* as a kind of response to that work; a conservative contribution to the debate about women's rights.

From Germany Halldór went to Denmark on 10 October, staying for nearly a week. *The Happy Warriors* was published in Danish at that time and received good reviews. Halldór gave a reading at a well-attended meeting of Icelandic students and wrote to Auður that he was thinking of going to meet Peter Hallberg in Göteborg. Hallberg was engrossed in his next book about Halldór, *The House of the Poet*, besides articles about the writer, and they had things to discuss.

Halldór was hesitant about going to Sweden, as he wrote to Hallberg:

> ... Sweden has been ruined for me with this useless chatter about the Nobel Prize for so many years. I have not a minute's peace there on my travels because of all the reporters. If I come, I come only to say hello to you, and would prefer to stay incognito at the Park Avenue Hotel.

There was also a great deal of talk about the Nobel Prize in Iceland that October. The Nobel Laureate William Faulkner visited the country and wanted to meet Halldór, but that did not happen. Many people thought it was Halldór's turn with the Academy. An article on the front page of *Morgunblaðið* on 22 October asked: "Will Gunnar Gunnarsson and Halldór Kiljan Share the Nobel Prize?" The U.P. news bureau stated that Halldór had more of a chance of winning the prize than ever before. But it also suggested that he might find himself sharing it with Gunnar.

Auður wrote to Halldór about all of this, also giving an excellent description of a gathering of Icelandic cultural boffins in the midst of the Cold War:

> On Saturday evening there was a great banquet for [a Russian] delegation at the home of Helgi Guðmundsson: forty-three people and a lot of alcohol. I heard that Einar Olgeirsson's wife Sigríður chastised Ragnar from Smári terribly for planning to start philandering with Russians again now, after having already sold out. Páll Ísólfsson moved from one corner to another as he recited the poem "Látrabjarg" by Jón Helgason, and people commented that Jón was the best Icelandic poet since Jónas Hallgrímsson. Þóra Vigfúsdóttir chastised Sigrún, Páll's wife, for being a Nazi, and all sorts of other things.

But Auður added that the atmosphere was actually improving: for instance, both the Minister of Education and the President considered holding a party for the visiting Russians.

Halldór gave in and went to Sweden, tempted by the idea of being close by if the call were to come, and he spent 24–6 October in Göteborg with Hallberg, meeting a reporter for *Dagens Nyheter*, as well as Artur Lundkvist and Gunnel Broström. On 26 October he thought about going back to Copenhagen. When he arrived in Hälsingborg to take the ferry to Helsingör, the same ferry that he and Ísleifur Sigurjónsson had taken thirty-six years earlier, he received a message saying that an announcement was expected, so he spent the night in Hälsingborg before driving back to Göteborg the next morning. Thus it happened that he was at the home of Peter Hallberg around noon on Thursday 27 October, 1955, when Anders Österling, the chairman of the Nobel Committee, announced the Swedish Academy's decision to award Halldór the Nobel Prize for Literature.

The Swedish Academy keeps its documents on the events leading up to decisions on the Nobel Prize closed for fifty years, and in material it makes public, conflicts and votes are not mentioned. However, it is possible to reach a fair understanding of what went on in 1955 by reading the correspondence between Sten Selander and Dag Hammarskjöld stored in the Royal Library in Stockholm. Both were members of the Academy at the time, Sten Selander being a poet and literary critic, and Dag Hammarskjöld the Secretary General of the United Nations. The latter was living in New York, but his friend Sten, who was opposed to Halldór, kept him informed of the progress of the case in detailed letters.

Selander goes through all the nominated writers in a letter to Hammarskjöld on 4 February, and few of them make the cut: they simply churned out books (Maugham, Huxley), were too old (Claudel, Robert Frost), had absurd views (Pound), or were too pretentious (Blixen). As Selander put it: "The decision this year seems thus to stand between Sholokhov, Kazantzakis and Laxness, with Gunnarsson like a yawl in the wake of Laxness." Many in the Academy wanted the prize to go to Iceland:

Now I see that Harry [Martinson] wants to go so far as to recommend Gunnar Gunnarsson; but whether there is any reason for letting him have the Nobel Prize other than that he is an Icelander I absolutely cannot determine. I am also fond of *Burnt-Njál's Saga* and the poetry of Egill Skallagrimsson; but at this point, after *The Happy Warriors*, I find that a rather feeble reason to let Laxness have the Nobel Prize . . . Laxness is certainly a very remarkable writer and would be one of the greatest in modern times if only he could learn some restraint. But he can't. There are brilliant chapters in nearly all his books; but between the promising moments one has to wade through waffle and unbearable propaganda. His political position puts proportion, both artistic and human, entirely out of kilter. Otherwise, his public political statements bear witness to either complete lunacy or perfect obedience, neither of which is appropriate for a Nobel Laureate.

Selander admits that it was a ridiculous situation: "Eighteen elderly gentlemen from out-of-the-way Europe sit in a Gustavian palace and choose between modern, international geniuses," but such were the conditions.

Hammarskjöld agreed with most of the things Selander said; he had numerous doubts about Laxness, and was much more favourable towards Malraux and Perse. Selander thought it most promising to bet on Malraux if they were unable in the short run to prevent Laxness from being considered seriously; ". . . it may not be possible in the long run," he added, which is a remarkable confession. In September Selander thought that the prize would be divided between Halldór and Gunnar. Hammarskjöld told his friend: "I do not like Laxness, but it is even worse to divide the prize – the result in such a case is frequently that the sum of two is less than one." Notwithstanding Hammarskjöld's opinion of Halldór, it is remarkable to see the Secretary General of the United Nations write a long letter about contemporary literature, displaying his knowledge and admiration of younger writers, for example, James Baldwin.

The Nobel committee, consisting of Österling, Sigfrid Siwertz and Hjalmar Gullberg, decided on their recommendation to the Academy on 23 September. Österling and Siwertz suggested that the prize be divided between Halldór and Gunnar, but Gullberg thought that Laxness should have it alone. On 6 October the Academy held its first meeting regarding the final decision. Österling had started to seek a compromise, and members of the Academy were asked what solution they would settle for if it came down to it. On this occasion Hammarskjöld says about Laxness:

As concerns Laxness he has certain undoubted merits, but . . . a book like *The Happy Warriors* is anything but a merit. If it is a question of getting him out of the picture, I *could* vote for him, although reluctantly.

It is clear that some members of the Academy felt pressured to award Halldór the prize, and it should also be mentioned that his main Swedish supporters were not members of the Academy: Artur Lundkvist, for example, did not hold a seat until later.

Around mid-October there was another meeting at the Academy, which was characterized by fierce debate. The Scandinavian specialist Elias Wessén now supported Halldór, saying that he had made Icelandic a modern literary language. The Academy's position was surveyed informally, but the result was so unexpected that the vote was repeated, with these results: the Spanish writer Juan Ramón Jiménez received eight votes, Laxness four and the Spanish scholar Menéndez Pidal two. No-one voted to split the prize between Halldór and Gunnar. Selander now considered it very likely that Halldór would receive the prize, but a new result was obtained at the final meeting a week later. There the written votes of members voting *in absentia* were tallied, with Jiménez receiving five votes, Menéndez Pidal six and Laxness five. It appeared to Selander as if the Academy would perhaps not grant the prize that year. A compromise needed to be reached. First the possibility was investigated as to whether a majority vote could be gained for Jiménez, without success. Then Österling asked whether it might be possible to gain the majority for Laxness by having those who could at least settle for him grant him their votes. On this basis he received ten votes, with three members voting for Menéndez Pidal and three for Jiménez. A decision had been reached.

Selander was among those few who would not settle for Halldór, going even further than Hammarskjöld. Several weeks later Selander told Hammarskjöld in a letter:

> There has never been so little enthusiasm for any Nobel Laureate within the Academy . . . nor can it be said that he did anything to increase his popularity by his conduct after the decision. Perhaps you saw the comment that he made to the reporters that all writing Swedes after Strindberg were uninteresting imitators.

Selander found it incredible that Halldór should not have thanked the Academy but instead had requested forty tickets to the awards banquet!

The announcement of the award was accompanied by a statement of explanation: Halldór had received the award "for his vivid epic writing" that had "renewed the great Icelandic narrative art". The prize was 190,000 Swedish krona. A great celebration was held at the home of Peter Hallberg that evening, as one might expect, and many people came to greet the writer. Of course Halldór himself was happy in every way. The reward was a symbol of the fact that the dream of the country boy to write stories for the world had been achieved.

Numerous Swedish papers celebrated the award; in Scandinavia Halldór's position was strong, his books were being published everywhere, and he had scores of admirers. In Germany the prize was interpreted more politically. The East German papers celebrated the fact that a socialist had received it, but opinion was divided in the West. Some papers criticized the prize for political or artistic reasons, while others celebrated it and emphasized the fact that Laxness, while certainly a social critic, was not much of a Communist. The award was interpreted politically in numerous other countries as well. In France his old friend Professor Jolivet, who had translated the first part of *Salka*, wrote a long article in the conservative paper *Le Figaro*, despite Halldór's being virtually unknown there.

The *New York Times* reported on its front page that Halldór was little known in America despite the success of *Independent People* and that he "loves the Russians but practises a lot of the American way of life". Two attitudes characterized these reactions: the idea that the Swedish Academy was compensating for giving the prize to Churchill and thereby relieving the tension between East and West, and a friendly curiosity about the work of a storyteller from an island far away.

*

The Icelanders were thrilled with the news. Even Halldór's opponents viewed the prize as a kind of confirmation that here flourished an independent national culture; the President and the Minister of Education sent congratulatory messages. The *Will of the People* could hardly control its delight, speaking of "a great victory for modern Icelandic literature, the culture of the nation and the struggle for independence". *Morgunblaðið* had a problem, given its quarrels with Halldór, but nonetheless printed a huge headline on its front page. Further down the page it was mentioned that Gunnar Gunnarsson had also been a candidate and had been supported by the Swedish Writers' Union as well as one of the Academy's chief literary scholars.

Morgunblaðið got Kristján Albertsson to give them a quote. He praised Halldór, but also said:

> We who are not his fellows in politics would celebrate his award even more wholeheartedly if it were possible to forget that the writer has for a long period of time and with a great deal of effort used his pen to promote the worst causes in the life of the Icelandic nation in recent years, and often in a way least seemly to a great writer. At the same time as we join in celebrating the writer today we must clearly assert that in doing so we are not retracting our previous negative judgements of his writing and behaviour in matters concerning his nation.

On 28 October Halldór went from Göteborg to Copenhagen, where Gyldendal held a banquet for him, and the next day travelled on to Iceland aboard the *Gullfoss*. A huge crowd met him when the ship docked on 4 November, though it was not official Iceland that welcomed him – yet – but rather the Federation of Labour Unions and the Federation of Icelandic Artists. Hannibal Valdimarsson, who had once criticized Halldór sharply for his spelling, and Jón Leifs, who had tried very hard to cultivate him when he was young, addressed the writer, emphasizing the victory of the Icelandic nation. Halldór replied with a short address that is often rebroadcast on the radio, thanking the people of Iceland in the words of a poet who sent his love some poems. When she thanked him, the poet said: "Do not thank me for these poems; it was you who gave me all of them."

"Today all Icelanders are noble," said the singer Eggert Stefánsson, in honour of Halldór's homecoming: "They feel noble – you have knighted them with your victory . . ." The President of Iceland held a banquet and the Scandinavian Society sponsored a celebration on 15 November. On 1 December Halldór delivered a speech on Icelandic sovereignty to students for the first time in twenty years, referring to the military presence as "foreign military squatters . . . trampling the fields and meadows here". His criticism of the politicians who had allowed this to continue was severe. Halldór did not want to go to the Nobel ceremony without having his views heard beforehand.

The award ceremony took place in Stockholm on 10 December, 1955. This time Auður left before Halldór and spent several weeks with Jón Helgason and Þórunn in Copenhagen, "to get myself kitted out so I look like Lóa in *The Silver Moon*", she wrote to Halldór. She managed this quite well and many Swedish papers commented on her elegance at the ceremony and accompanying banquets. Halldór also worked to ensure that his publishers and translators were present, in addition to his Icelandic friends – this is why he had asked for so many tickets, annoying Sten Selander. From Germany came both Walter Janka, his publisher in the East, and Heinrich Maria Ledig-Rowohlt, his publisher in the West, though Peter Suhrkamp could not attend due to illness. Also present were Ernst Harthern, Peter Hallberg and Artur Lundkvist.

A great burden of work was placed on the Icelandic embassy in preparation for the event, especially on the attaché Birgi Möller, since there was no Icelandic ambassador in Sweden at that time: Helgi Briem had recently gone to Germany and his successor had not yet arrived. Helgi, Halldór's old friend, was thus recalled for two weeks to handle arrangements. Other friends such as Jón Helgason and Þórunn, his publisher Ragnar Jónsson and Sigurður Nordal attended.

It is remarkable that Halldór also invited his old adversaries. Jörundur

Brynjólfsson, then the President of the Alþingi, and Bjarni Benediktsson. Bjarni did not attend, though.

In his presentation speech Professor Wessén said among other things:

> There was a time when Icelandic authors chose another Scandinavian language for their art, not merely for economic reasons, but because they despaired of the Icelandic language as an instrument for artistic creation. Halldór Laxness has, in the field of prose, renewed the Icelandic language as an artistic means of expression . . . and by his example given the Icelandic writers courage to use their native tongue.

Wessén underlined his point by closing his speech in Icelandic, before Gustav Adolph VI presented Halldór with his award. It was reported in the Swedish papers that no award recipient had ever bowed as deeply as the Icelandic writer.

At the formal dinner the same evening, Halldór delivered his speech, telling of his parents and grandmother who had taught him poetry from ages past; now he, a poor wanderer from a remote island, had been called to step forth "in the bosom of the stage lights of the world". Most often cited are these words:

> But if an Icelandic writer forgets his origins in the depths of the nation where the story lives; if he forgets his relationship and duty to the life that is hard-pressed, the life that my old grandmother taught me to revere in my heart and mind – then fame is of little worth; along with happiness that is gained from wealth.

This beautiful speech contained no revolutionary undertones. Halldór surprised the Swedish papers by not making any Communist comments. *Svenska dagbladet* wrote:

> Laxness is a charmer. Nothing can make him angry. But as an interviewee he is afflicted by the unpleasant fault of never speaking about himself. He is a special blend of manliness and pretence, of audacity and diplomacy. There is something of the Anglo-Saxon in him.

It was in this manner, with Auður at his side, that Halldór sailed elegantly through the several days of ceremonies.

Ragnar from Smári described the dinner extremely well in a long letter to Sigríður Helgadóttir, the wife of his colleague (published in Jón Karl Helgason's *The Hero and the Writer*):

> Laxness was the first to deliver his speech, a magnificent speech that gripped me so much that I shed tears, and I saw some tears run down the cheeks of

Professor Jón Helgason, who was seated at the next table. The speech was received with unquenchable admiration. Then came one speech after another, in general, excellent speeches, but Laxness' was best of all – on that everyone was agreed.

It was a magnificent feast, which the Swedes alone know how to hold. It was inspirational just to see a hundred servants come in like sheep driven down a mountainside in Iceland. The food naturally resembled the most beautifully written poetry, and everything was decorated abundantly . . . even the arrangements and tablecloths were inspirational, since they were serving such a good purpose. My heart was full of vibrant sunshine despite the two exotic women on either side of me, who had no place in my soul. If that matter had been better arranged, this would have been a day of the afterlife lived within this life.

*

The ultimate goal achieved, it was time to chart a new course. From Stockholm Halldór and Auður went to Copenhagen, whence she went home, while Halldór remained for Christmas and then continued to Italy. He wanted, beyond all else, to have the leisure to write. The happy days in Stockholm had had a good effect on both him and Auður, who wrote on her return home:

And, my beloved Halldór, I do not know how to say how thankful I am to you. It was not just the ceremonies and the banquets that lifted me so much, but rather, first and foremost, your behaviour towards me, which gladdened me so unspeakably much and made me so secure and happy.

But then everyday life took over. Auður wrote from Gljúfrasteinn the day after Christmas to say how cold it was in the house, how the roads were impassable, how the men pushing the car had given up at the drive. On New Year's Eve: Halldór wrote from Rome:

I started working the morning after my arrival and have been working since then. It is going well, although I am extremely disappointed with what I am doing, and feel that I am on a kind of wayward path in writing it . . . I am truly having a great deal of difficulty with the new book: trying to write a draft of the conclusion . . . And I thank you sincerely for how you held your-self so well, how you were so elegant, honouring our land and people with your presence. It was truly important to me.

Halldór was at work on *The Fish Can Sing*.

FIVE

Shattered Hopes and New Perspectives

The Years
1956–1969

These mornings when we were seeing to the lumpfish in
Skerjafjörður (and they were really all one and the same
morning) – suddenly they were over. Their stars faded: your
Chinese idyll ended.

Halldór Laxness, The Fish Can Sing

Ode to the Hidden People

JANUARY, 1956: THE BOY FROM MOSFELLSDALUR SAT WRITING IN A
hotel in Rome. Was his mission out in the world accomplished? Were there any
victories left to be won? And, what mattered most, did he have any more stories
to tell?

Halldór had felt as if he could not go straight home after the Nobel ceremony
and continue to bask in the limelight. He had to get away to work. The book he
was writing had been germinating for a long time; it was about the inconstancy of
beauty and the fate of those who live an illusion. It was also a book that derived
much from the writer's own youth.

During the first weeks of January Halldór wrote to Auður:

It is absolutely unbelievable how well it has gone for me to work here in the
quiet of the large city, where everyone leaves one alone and the phone doesn't
ring. Now I have two chapters remaining of the new book, the draft of which
has reached five hundred pages. This will be a book of the size of *The Happy
Warriors*. But I am very tired and often have chest pains for hours at a time,
and the pain in my chest is always accompanied by the fear that I am dying,
and then my desire to come home to my little jewels becomes almost unbear-

able. In the approximately two weeks since I came here I have written over
seventy pages.

This was no small amount of work, but all the same Halldór felt powerless and
unwell, experiencing the same chest pains he had twenty years earlier when he
started *World Light*. Back then he had given up smoking and hiked through
Snæfellsnes National Park. In this sense the pains were a good sign; he only felt
them when he was writing. "I was not aware that I had a heart – it is peculiar that
it should always make its presence felt when I am starting to work."

Halldór turned out not to be the only Icelander in Rome in January:

One day I went down to St Peter's in sunshine and mild weather, and stood
before the toeless Peter (his toes have been kissed off) and spoke to some
Germans about how this was the one image that was disappearing in all of
St Peter's, when I suddenly heard someone say to me in Icelandic: "I am
happy to see you in this place". It was Gunnar Eyjólfsson, the actor and
airline steward, who had come from Teheran the evening before and was
going to Beirut and then to New York the day after.

It was fortuitous that Gunnar and Halldór should meet in Rome; they were lifelong friends, and in Halldór's old age Gunnar accompanied him to mass at the
Catholic Landakot Church.

From Rome Halldór went to Helsinki to attend the premiere of *The Silver Moon*
on 11 January, which he found only "so-so", as he wrote to Auður. The reviews
were not particularly good, and in the same month the Deutsches Theater in Berlin
declined the work; its readers had given it a negative appraisal. Easy victories did
not necessarily go hand in hand with the Nobel Prize.

But Halldór was greeted enthusiastically when he returned home in February.
The Dawn Youth Society in Mosfellsdalur sponsored a well-attended torchlight
procession to Gljúfrasteinn, a special performance of *Iceland's Bell* was held at
the National Theatre, a dinner was held at Hlégarður, and there was a party at the
National Theatre Cellar, where Bjarni Benediktsson and others delivered speeches.
Bjarni sat next to Auður at the latter party and they chatted animatedly; this was
the start of his reconciliation with Halldór.

The same month witnessed a shake-up in international politics when
Khrushchev delivered his famous Secret Speech at the Twentieth Congress of the
Soviet Communist Party, attacking the personality cult of Stalin and disclosing
various of the tyrant's crimes. The speech inspired discussion in the West, causing
serious trouble for supporters of the Soviet Union throughout the world. Men

like Halldór, however, who had turned against the one-party system in the Eastern bloc, gained new hope that the Soviets could clean out their stables and make the necessary improvements. There was still hope for socialism.

In the mid-1950s there was a general feeling in Iceland that the Cold War was abating, also that Iceland would be best served without a military force during times of peace. The Progressive Party and the Social Democratic Party changed their opinions on the Keflavík Agreement, and at the end of March the Socialists and the Patriots agreed to a parliamentary proposal that the American army leave the country. In the wake of elections in June a leftist government was formed, with among other things the army's departure on its agenda. The Socialists had broken free from their isolation once again and were feeling energetic.

Though a member of the Socialist Party, Halldór took a much less active part in politics than before. Later his old comrades spoke as if he had been "bought" with the Nobel Prize, or that it had blunted his teeth. This is incorrect. The Nobel Prize fell into his lap in the middle of his career but did not change its course, any more than it changed Halldór himself.

His fiction did change, however. His works from the 1920s bore the mark of so-called modernism; during the 1930s Halldór wrote "social" novels; the 1940s up until and including *The Happy Warriors* were devoted to a study of Icelandic nationality, its traditions and history. But the book at the same time points to *The Fish Can Sing* and *Paradise Reclaimed*, which are characterized by sorrow and a feeling of shattered hope. This feeling had nothing to do with artistic surrender, because Halldór always invested his writing with the same cultivation and meticulousness. But most of the political hotheadedness and narrow-mindedness had left him.

Halldór continued to promote his work abroad, in April going to both London and Paris. In London he met his old friend Stanley Unwin, though Halldór received no explanation as to why Unwin would not publish him. As paradoxical as it might seem, Halldór was not published in the English-speaking world for a long time after the success of *Independent People*. *Atom Station*, for example, was not published until 1961, and *Iceland's Bell* did not appear in English until 2003. Financial issues doubtless played a part, but as we have seen, the Cold War prevented his entry into the American market. Typical of the atmosphere was a headline that appeared in an American paper: "Anti-American Wins '55 Nobel Prize".

Halldór's visit to Paris yielded few results: Jolivet had been paid the majority of his royalties for the translation of *O Thou Pure Vine*, due to the rather poor contract that he had made. Gallimard were sympathetic: *Pure Vine* was republished (although *The Bird on the Beach*, the second part of *Salka Valka*, was never published in French), and politics did not get in the way as they did in America; for example, *Atom Station* was published in 1957. But Halldór was no star in France. He met Icelandic friends in Paris, such as the young poet Sigfús Daðason and the painter Nína Tryggvadóttir, but mostly he wanted to find himself a quiet place and continue working. As he wrote to Auður from London: "My skin is itching to continue writing my novel, which lives in me like a separate world."

Halldór's last stop was Prague, where he had been invited to a writers' conference. The conference showed all the signs of the new thaw, as he described in a letter to Auður:

> The conference has been a conflict between politicians and writers. The writers try to tear themselves out from under the constraints and interference of the politicians who have paralysed Czech literature for eight years. Finally now after the Twentieth Congress in Moscow these blessed wretches have gained a voice. The President of the Republic gave a speech and tried to defend the government. It is as if everyone is starting to gain a voice here to the east of the Iron Curtain. I must say that it has been extraordinarily informative to witness the ice breaking here.

The description is typical of the hope felt by many leftist intellectuals that year. Governments were moving towards the idea of independent rule – for example, in Poland – and it was in keeping with his views that Halldór should interpret this as people breaking away from the rule of politicians. But these hopes did not last long.

Halldór was at home that summer. Life there depended on his having as much peace to work as possible. Jytte Eiberg, who went as a young girl to Gljúfrasteinn with her mother Thea, a housekeeper there, described Halldór's routine (which he maintained for the rest of his working life) as follows:

> He worked in the mornings all those years I was there. Around twelve o'clock he went out for a walk. He took his stick with him for long hikes; I see in my mind how he would cross the river, and he always came home by two when lunch was served ... After lunch Halldór often went into town. When he was abroad there was something of a different arrangement ... Auður and I would often eat in the kitchen.

In September Halldór went abroad again. He had business with his lawyer, Per Finn Jacobsen, in Copenhagen and he wanted to buy some furniture; he also needed to visit Peter Hallberg in Göteborg because he had started to read the manuscript of *The House of the Poet*. Overall he was pleased, as he said in a letter to Auður: "I would never have dreamt that such a good book would be written about me while I was alive."

His main business, however, was to go to Bonn to speak to the Indian ambassador. Having been invited to visit India, he wanted to discuss his itinerary. Halldór had also received an invitation to visit China and imagined combining the two trips. Auður was to come with him, and he planned to take a secretary along as well. Halldór's travels had started to take on the air of state visits.

An edition of *Independent People* had been published in English in Bombay, and a year later the book was published in Orija, one of the subcontinent's many languages. Halldór decided to postpone his trip until the following year due to the Suez Crisis.

While Halldór was abroad, the *People's Paper* published an interview with the poet Steinn Steinarr that received a great deal of attention. Steinn had recently returned from Russia and was not happy with what he had seen. He thought the government distant from his concept of socialism: "I think that it is a kind of violence: coarse, insipid, and inhumane. And we so-called Western men would probably find that intolerable." He had nothing good to say about literature and the arts in Russia, nor about the clichés spouted by so-called intellectuals. Stalin had trampled on Lenin's great ideals, and there still had been no proper reckoning. Soviet Russia was not the model for the future, said Steinn; it was certainly not socialist.

The reason this was so shocking was that Steinn was the first of the "Red Pens" to speak out about the Soviet Union. Many old friends were hurt by what he said. Auður sent Halldór the interview, and his reaction shows clearly how much he had distanced himself from the social order that he had praised in two books:

Steinn's comments are "correct", apart from failing to mention the friendly nature of the Russians, which it is not possible to avoid noticing when one gets to know them, and not giving the recognition the Soviet government deserves on behalf of all reasonable men for its attempts to improve the lot and increase the cultural level of the people of Russia.

Halldór's thinking was now completely the opposite of what it had been when he had written *Going East*: now the people appeared better than the system.

Events that autumn would strengthen his new convictions. In the first days of November Hungary's attempt to break away from the influence of the Soviet Union was quashed by the Soviet army. On 7 November Halldór's article in the

Will of the People had a different tone from the speeches and articles he had written to mark the day in preceding decades:

> The misfortune that has been met by the authorities in Hungary affects me deeply as an Icelandic Socialist . . . From my knowledge of the friends of peace in the U.S.S.R. and the oft-preached pacifist agenda of the Soviet government, this war of the U.S.S.R. with the Hungarians is an incomprehensible misfortune, a setback so tragic that it equals only the shockingly sorrowful news that was published in Moscow in late winter [February] of this year . . . If I could come to terms with the events that have taken place in Hungary . . . I could never again permit myself to speak a word against the conduct of foreign armies in foreign countries, no matter how horrific they might be; I would at the same time become unsuited to opposing the continued presence of foreign armies in my own country.

This was the first time that Halldór publicly criticized the ruthless government of the Soviet Union. Later in November he sent, in his official capacity as the chairman of M.Í.R., a petition to Bulganin, the Soviet Prime Minister, urging the abandonment of military action in Hungary. Thereafter he distanced himself from the Soviet Union more and more with every passing year.

Many socialists and Communists in the West criticized the Soviet invasion of Hungary, and some of their companions in the Eastern bloc tried to do the same. One of these was Walter Janka. Janka could never have been condemned for capitalist servility. His brother was a Communist Member of Parliament and was murdered by the S.S. immediately following the Nazi rise to power, and Janka himself was arrested by the Gestapo and spent two years in a prison camp. He made it out of Germany on a false passport and went to Spain, where he fought with the international brigade, was wounded and sent to prison camp in France; finally he managed to flee to Mexico. In 1952 he was made director of Aufbau. After the invasion of Hungary Janka was arrested and convicted of conspiracy to overthrow the government of the German Democratic Republic.

In December, 1956, he was interrogated by the Stasi, among other things about his connections with Halldór. Janka admitted that he had maintained a correspondence with Halldór and Harthern and met them at the Nobel ceremonies, but reiterated that his foreign connections had only to do with literature and the work of his publishing company. During long interrogations, at his trial and in jail, Janka always maintained his innocence. When Halldór heard of his arrest, his doubts increased about the Eastern bloc.

On the home front the events of 1956 caused the Icelandic government to abandon its intention to revoke the Military Defence Agreement with the U.S. and instead agree to receive American loans and assistance.

*

During the next month Halldór worked on completing *The Fish Can Sing*, which was published in March, 1957. This was his first novel for five years, and it received good reviews. Kristján Albertsson wrote: "*The Fish Can Sing* is a magnificent novel. Laxness has never written more artistically." But the *Mál og menning* journal published an unusually sharp-worded critique by the writer Elías Mar. Elias said that the novel had to be criticized for what it was not: timely:

> We, who have hardly seen the light of day since H. K. L. wrote the timely book *The Great Weaver from Kashmir* – although it is defective – find *The Fish Can Sing* to be extremely far removed from the time and place in which we now live, and far from the ideals that now occupy our minds.

Elías' views were not simply political; he found the book too conservative as literature, in comparison with *The Great Weaver*. But he doubtless spoke on behalf of many socialists who missed the polemical writer, finding the work to be lacking teeth; they wanted Halldór to continue to wave firebrands at capitalism. But times had changed, not because Halldór had received the Nobel Prize, but because he had lost his faith in the foundation for his earlier polemics.

The Fish Can Sing is told in the first person, as is *Atom Station*, and like that book has a well-defined setting. But this time the narrator more closely approximates Halldór himself: there are memories from Melkot, the story of the grandmother and the clock, and the dream about lyrical victories out in the world. Here Halldór comes the closest to creating a traditional plot, and the narrative style is disciplined.

All the same the book contains many different stories: about growing up, but also about an artist and the arts. As we have seen, the idea to write a book about an international singer had long been germinating in Halldór's imagination. His creation involved two singers in the end, Garðar and his young disciple, Álfgrímur. *The Fish Can Sing* is not a book about the vanity of fame, but rather about the danger of illusion.

The social contrasts in the novel are in the spirit of the ideas to which Halldór was becoming more and more devoted. He wrote in a notebook:

> The Hidden People, the ordinary and unspoilt folk (indefinitely frail from the point of view of moral theology) . . . the book is to be a hymn of praise

to them, a proof that it is precisely these people, the ordinary folk, who foster all peaceful human virtues.

These are people who "accomplish all great deeds, yet do not pride themselves", as it says in one of Halldór's notebooks. Their conduct is characterized by endless kindness, coinciding with their lack of interest in preaching or intervening in the conduct of others. Their philosophy, if it can be called that, is expressed by the man who looks after the town toilet. He is asked:

"Do you never think it improper that a gifted man like you should be living your life in degradation, as the lowest of the low?"

"High and low, my friend," said the attendant, and tittered slightly, but almost inaudibly. "I don't know what that is."

In contrast to the "hidden people" are the people connected with the merchant Gúðmúnsen, who represents wealth and power, pitiable and cultureless at the same time. Halldór's notebook speaks of "the praise society" based on "the collective responsibility of microscopic local bigwigs to praise each other". Here speaks a man who knows what it means to be famous in a sparsely populated society.

Had the great envoy of modernity begun to romanticize Icelandic rural society? Things were not so simple. It is clear to Álfgrímur when he leaves Brekkukot that its world is disappearing: his departure marks his loss of paradise. The book's hope rests on him taking the values of youth out into the world, not entering the service of Gúðmúnsen. For the most part Halldór avoids the emotionalism that could conceal itself within such a narrative, and as so often before humour comes to his rescue. The sometimes smug narrator of his earlier books is gone, replaced by the scribe who refrains from judgements and pronouncements.

*

When the book was published in Iceland, Halldór gave some interviews, but then he was gone, to Denmark, Germany and France.

In Germany he met Rowohlt; in Paris he tried to strengthen his connection with Gallimard. Kristján Albertsson had not yet reviewed *The Fish Can Sing*, and Halldór wrote to Auður:

Nor can I bring myself to visit my old friend Kristján Albertsson, who can no longer write or say a word without going out of his way to criticize me. From now on if he wants to see me, he can come and find me . . .

The number of people with whom Halldór wished to spend time was decreasing, both at home and abroad.

The trip did not consist simply of meetings, however: he was with Jón Helgason and Þórunn in Copenhagen, and there he also met Reverend Bjarni Jónsson and and the daughters of Reverend Jóhann Þorkelsson, upon whom Halldór had based characters in *The Fish Can Sing* and elsewhere. He made this comment in a letter to Auður:

> [I] was so lucky to have copies of *The Fish Can Sing* to give to the daughters of Reverend Jóhann, with apologies for having always been writing novels about their father; and to Reverend Bjarni with a message that I should never have written a novel about him.

Auður cleaned the house from top to bottom while Halldór was abroad, because the Swedish king was expected. His visit at the end of June was for no other reason than that official Iceland wanted to profit from Halldór's success. Gustav Adolph VI, who six months previously had presented Halldór with the Nobel Prize, was taken to Gljúfrasteinn on his way to Þingvellir. Little by little Halldór was becoming a kind of cultural president of the nation, and visits to his home became a part of official visits; in this instance he was also invited to address the king at the University of Iceland.

Halldór continued to distance himself from the official Soviet line that year. In *The Book of Essays* (1959) one can find his correspondence with the editor of the Soviet journal *Culture and Life*, Georgy Pasternak; the journal was intended to introduce sympathetic Westerners to Soviet culture. Halldór sharply but genially criticised its clichés, its habit of quoting authorities like Lenin and its lack of understanding of the arts in the West – the editor still maintained that abstract art was misanthropic. Halldór also tried sending a petition and message of protest to the East, although it was doubtless clear to him that such a thing would have little effect. He sent a telegram to Janos Kadarin in Hungary on 1 July, 1957, to protest the persecution of writers, since Kadar was at that time crushing his opponents mercilessly.

At the end of that month Walter Janka was sentenced to five years' solitary confinement. His wife was allowed to visit him for two hours each year. Their conversations were of course bugged. A Stasi report about the first conversation says that Janka maintained his innocence, wanted to know whether his friends were standing by him and asked his wife to extend warm wishes to Halldór.

In July, 1957, the entire Laxness family went abroad, first to Sweden, where Halldór remained behind to write. Auður went with their daughters to Germany. Halldór followed later and the family went together to Schio in Italy, where Lelja

Stefánsson, the wife of the singer Eggert Stefánsson, lived. Auður and the girls stayed with her but Halldór stayed at a hotel in town. This arrangement pleased him, and he made the same arrangement for his trips on the *Gullfoss*. Auður stayed with the girls in a "suite" and was often seasick, while Halldór had a little cabin with a desk. He could be with the family when it suited him and by himself when he wanted. This suited his needs, and those closest to him had to content themselves with it. Intimacy had always to be tempered by distance; he felt that he needed this freedom to write.

Halldór was in Venice with his family when he replied to a question from the American magazine *Books Abroad* about the death of the novel. Halldór objected loudly to this fashionable topic:

> In my opinion, telling a story about the great things that have taken place in the world is inherent in humanity and will never be outmoded. The art of telling a story in the right way is indeed one of the most difficult things imaginable . . .

To Halldór's mind most modern novels were a kind of sickening subjectivist expectoration:

> There is no reason to be sorry for the "downgrading" of this nauseating rubbish that calls itself modern novel-writing. But the difficult epic way of facing a subject – or an object, if you will – will never become outmoded or "downgraded".

Halldór remained as ever a spokesman for the epic novel.

*

In the autumn Halldór went to Copenhagen, where he met Per Finn Jacobsen, and they drove together to Stockholm. Their plan was to review Halldór's finances and investigate the possibility of transferring his Nobel Prize money to accounts in America. Interviewed by the present author in 2004, when he was in his nineties, Per Finn remembered Halldór as larger than life and the trip as unforgettable. Halldór had recently purchased a big Lincoln; they found themselves in difficulty as soon as they reached the ferry to Hälsingborg, because the car was too large for the usual berth. When they arrived in Sweden Halldór drove so fast that he was stopped by the police. Per Finn said that one local newspaper had printed across the whole of the front page: "Nobel Laureate Arrested for Speeding".

Halldór did not trust the Swedish krona or the Icelandic tax authority, although the government had agreed that the prize money would be tax-free. Per Finn was nervous about meeting the Swedish bankers. A man at the next table saw how nervous he was and cheered him up by offering him a cognac. This was Rémy Martin, whose family had produced that excellent drink for three hundred years. Whether a glass of cognac offered by its own producer had anything to do with it or not, Per Finn got his way, and the Nobel Prize was transferred into dollars. Nearly three years later this would prove to be an extremely lucky move.

In mid-September Auður returned home with the girls. Halldór, having been invited to the United States on behalf of the American–Scandinavian Foundation, thought he would connect that trip with the one to India and China, so now he needed to think about inoculations, visas and other such matters. Gylfi Þ. Gíslason, the Education Minister for the leftist government, offered him Halla Bergs as secretary for the trip. Halldór thought that Halla could do some of his paperwork on the long sea voyages. According to Auður not much came of this, but Halla was an elegant individual and Halldór liked having beautiful women around him.

Halldór also read a book by the Norwegian Agnar Mykle, *The Song of the Red Ruby* (1956), at the time the most discussed book in Scandinavia, its author being brought up on charges of pornography. Halldór wrote to Auður:

> Here there is a great deal written about Mykle's book: I opened it the other day and fell on a description of how a certain man (the narrator) is struggling to pick the pieces of a torn condom out of a woman. This is of course excellent. All the same it is a bore to find oneself in court for describing one's love affairs.

Halldór was never an "outspoken and daring" writer in this sense, although some of his compatriots felt that he had written pornography in the 1920s.

Around mid-October, 1957, Halldór arrived in the United States on his first visit in twenty-eight years. His world tour had begun and he travelled around like a head of state, delivering speeches in New York, Peking and New Delhi, appearing everywhere as an elegant cosmopolitan. The speeches – which Halldór published in English in *The Book of Essays* – reflect the nature of the trip: they are diplomatic and friendly, but show that in his mind he was on a fast track towards a kind of Scandinavian social democracy. The American papers that mentioned the trip were surprised that this notorious Communist could have such good things to say about America, although he did not want their military base in his country. He also wrote articles for the major Scandinavian papers such as *Svenska dagbladet* and *Politiken* on this journey.

Auður met Halldór in New York and over the next months they travelled around the world with Halla Bergs; Auður has described the trip in detail in her memoirs. Of course it was not all reunions in America, because Halldór had never been to New York. About the skyscrapers in Manhattan he said:

> These high towers express a worldly power that is at once realistic and transitory . . . As before, people's cheerful, carefree demeanour is one of the most sympathetic traits of the Americans; everyone is the same to them.

Upon closer inspection one can see that Halldór has started to view Americans as he did the Russians, preferring the people to the social order, although he did not have as many good friends in the West as in the East.

Both Halldór's article and Auður's memoirs indicate that they were constantly being entertained in America by professors and millionaires. The ambassador Thor Thors, who of old had investigated Halldór's earnings and taxes, held a banquet for them, and they met many Icelanders. From New York they took a two-hour train trip to Wilmington to visit Thomas Brittingham Jr and his wife Peggy; Brittingham had donated a great deal of money to research on the Vikings and was respected in Scandinavia. They also visited Chicago and Madison, and then took a train across America to Salt Lake City in Utah, where the Mormon bishop John Bearnson received them.

Halldór had started to think about his next novel and planned to use the books of Eiríkur from Brúnar, who had travelled to Utah long before him, as source material. The Mormons were very helpful and he acquainted himself with the fate of Icelanders and their descendants in those parts, most of whom were poor.

Halldór wrote a detailed article for the magazine *Samvinnan* based on his acquaintance with the Mormon faith. He did not conceal his respect for the Mormons' religious devotion, their elegant architecture and their values. But the reader gets the feeling that this was in some ways a sterile community: "Their social life seems . . . scrupulous and chaste . . . one is often reminded of the atmosphere prevalent in Sunday schools and Communist countries." This is an interesting assertion for 1958, when most of Halldór's countrymen still thought that he was a Communist. His interest had been awakened by the Mormon belief in a soon to come Promised Land, a belief shared by many Communists. However, he was not exactly enthusiastic in Utah: it did not sit well with him to spend a lot of time with people who offered neither coffee nor alcohol. Halldór always thought water an unofferable drink when people gathered.

Most enjoyable for Halldór was returning to San Francisco, according to Auður; they walked the streets and Halldór showed her the places that he had visited twenty-eight years earlier, humming old songs to himself. The couple did not go to Los Angeles, but instead set off for the Far East on 10 November, arriving in Japan on 23 November. Halldór was happy on the journey: having succeeded in writing stories for the world, now he was seeing it. China was particularly interesting to him, as might be expected. Besides visiting one of the most densely populated countries in the world as a representative of one of its most sparsely populated ones, he was seeking the roots of the Tao, the philosophy that was now dearest to him. As he expressed it several years later:

> I was on a trip round the world. There were two holy temples that I wanted to see on that trip: the Mormon tabernacle in Salt Lake City and the chief temple of those who follow the Tao in Peking.

Around the same time Halldór started to speak of Marxism as a nineteenth-century economic theory invented in London, but about himself as if he had been a Taoist for most of his life. A writer not only creates a story about himself, he can change it just as quickly.

Halldór and Auður were well looked after in China, where they were the guests of the bureau in charge of cultural exchanges with foreign countries and writers' unions. It was still uncommon for Western writers to visit Mao's China, and large numbers of reporters flocked around Halldór in Hong Kong, both when he arrived and when he returned after spending almost all of December in China. Halldór and Auður spent most of their time in Peking and the vicinity, on sight-seeing trips and at receptions and banquets, yet he seemed to perceive a peculiar silence when he asked about the Tao or Taoist priests and their temples. He turned to the Book of the Way and its Power in an address at a banquet held by the cultural exchange bureau and said that this book had always meant a great deal to him, regardless of what other turns his life had taken, and sometimes he had thought it the best of all books. He spoke of himself as a European Taoist who found it difficult to understand how such an anti-spiritual book could have become the foundation for a religion in China.

Later Halldór's host bent to his wishes and took him to a restored Taoist monastery in a rather shabby suburb; the route there was long and winding, which caused Halldór to think about The Book of the Way: "Whoever seeks the Tao will not find it." But the monastery was found and the head priest showed Halldór round, and as always when one reaches a place that one has dreamt of visiting, his perception of it became stronger than words. The adventure was perfected when Halldór stood opposite a tall old wooden sculpture at the grave of the Taoist monk K'iu Ch'ang Ch'un (K'iu Chuji). Halldór had written about him, calling him Sing-Sing-Ho, in "Temuchin Returns Home". This was his Chinese reunion.

In Hong Kong Halldór and Auður once again boarded a huge passenger liner, and sailed to Singapore over New Year, 1958. Halldór used the time for writing essays as well as reading. Among the books that he read on the voyage was one by Alexander Orlov, a Soviet general and spy who had fled to the West; his *The Secret History of Stalin's Crimes* (1953) attracted international attention. The book had a strong effect on Halldór: Kristinn E. Andrésson later told Árni Bergmann that the book had "turned" Halldór.

Halldór and Auður stopped in Sri Lanka before arriving in Bombay. There they were guests of the government, and envoys came on board and placed huge garlands round their necks. The reception Halldór and Auður received was fit for royalty: there were great banquets, and – unlike in China – Halldór got to meet the country's political leaders. They were invited to a lunch at the home of Prime Minister Nehru, attended only by his closest family members, including his daughter, Indira Gandhi.

Halldór was inspired by the political leaders of India: "[They are] among the philosophers of our century, highly educated philanthropists, who have devoted themselves to much of the most excellent in Eastern and Western thought." In Delhi he delivered a speech on Old Icelandic literature to a packed house – almost eight hundred people came to listen to him. He and Auður were taken to see many of the holy places, were invited to a sitar concert by Ravi Shankar, and met numerous writers and cultural representatives.

It is difficult to know why Halldór received such a royal reception in India, because he was largely unknown, although *Independent People* had been published in Delhi and he had a few old friends there. In one place he was introduced as the writer of a new book about India, *The Great Weaver from Kashmir*, in another his hosts announced him as Aldous Huxley, since there were similarities in the sounds of their names. India was, of course, as a newly independent country, interested in promoting understanding and support in the West – and Halldór was a Nobel Prize-winner. Such a man might be useful later.

On the way home Halldór wrote an article in English about the virtues and vices of India and China; but his main purpose was to exhort the West to try to relieve the needs of these huge proletarian countries that represented the core of mankind. He concluded the article with these prophetic words:

> The absence of a reasonable Western response to Eastern needs will mean that in the future, "class struggle" will be fought on a world scale, between the "haves" and the "have nots" of the world.

From India Halldór and Auður sailed aboard a luxury liner to Italy through the Suez Canal, and had the chance to visit Cairo and view the Pyramids. The trip ended in Naples, and from there Halldór and Auður went straight to Rome, where a Catholic prelate had invited Halldór to a great feast. The face of Fru Dinesen, the hotel manager in Rome, must have paled when the couple turned up at her door with twenty-five trunks. To their luggage had been added numerous gifts, not least books; Halldór and Auður had for their part given Old Icelandic bibles to the Chinese Minister of Education and his counterpart in India. Halldór and Auður arrived home in February, 1958.

*

Sacks of letters awaited Halldór on his return and there was no way that he could reply to all of them. One he did answer in March was from his old friend, Hans Kirk, who had written asking him to write something for the World Peace Council. Halldór's response is interesting. He says that the World Peace Council had of course once awarded him a prize at the encouragement of Artur Lundkvist, but no-one on the Council had ever heard of him:

> The enforced silence of the Council when people heard this peculiar name was finally broken when Bishop Hewlett-Johnson from London said that, if in fact there really was a country somewhere in the Atlantic Ocean halfway between Europe and America, and if in this country there did in fact exist a writer, he deserved the prize.

Halldór added that later the World Peace Council had frequently asked him to give his opinion on various topics that the Council liked to rehash over and over again. Halldór said that at first he had responded by sending articles, entreaties and telegrams. But although his name had been used on the Council's petitions, none of his articles had been published, not even the acceptance speech he had delivered in Vienna in 1953. It had been explained to him that the Council never published articles unless they were first abridged and translated into a kind of party language that all writers despised and that made ordinary people sick. In sum, Halldór had no further interest in writing for this organization.

Halldór did not stay long in Iceland. In April he went to London to attend to publishing business: although Stanley Unwin no longer published Halldór's books, he always had some money for him. Unwin had sold the rights to *Independent People* to Argentina, for example, and the royalties went through him. Around that time a new publisher, Methuen, published Halldór in English, so that finally there was some movement in the English-speaking countries.

Halldór was in an excellent mood following his world tour and financially well off after the Nobel Prize. Although for many years he had accustomed himself to being thrifty, he could be generous when necessary. Mary Sorrell tells in her memoirs of how Halldór unexpectedly came to visit her in London that April and invited her to visit Gljúfrasteinn: "'We will take care of everything,' he said. 'The entire visit from beginning to end will be a gift from us.'" Thus Mary, who was still recovering from a stroke, was able to take a six-week, carefree trip to Iceland.

Following the war, it was an exception if Halldór was at home on his birthday. It was as if he did not want to let his psychological balance be disturbed. The family always sent him a telegram, and that spring in London was no exception. Halldór wrote to Auður and thanked her for the telegram ". . . always as equally welcomed and enjoyed each year, and always just as delightful, as it is my only birthday party, and a huge one at that."

After London Halldór went to Paris and then to Hamburg to visit Rowohlt. But he did not like the looks of things, he told Auður: the boring atmosphere, everything topsy-turvy, an interest only in bestsellers, the publisher telling endless "stories of his drinking revelries with famous people". But there was something else:

> . . . it made me very happy, and was one of the few times that a man's words
> do any sort of good, when in the winter I met a man about getting Janka's
> former secretary, Fräulein Bernhardt, something to do; she had fled from
> East Berlin to West Berlin to escape impending prison, and was living there
> on welfare support with her decrepit mother. Now Rowohlt has made her a
> secretary on a starter's salary in his company. I spoke to her for a long time
> about the situation in the East . . . I have now decided to write to Pieck to
> ask for mercy for Janka; of course I have no expectation of any result, but
> at least then one cannot blame oneself.

After this Halldór visited Fräulein Bernhardt whenever he went to Hamburg.

On 19 June, 1958, Halldór sent a letter to Wilhelm Pieck, the President of the German Democratic Republic, in which he asked for a pardon for Janka; Ernst Harthern had, among other things, encouraged him to do this. Halldór praised Janka as an honourable and upright man, although he made it clear that he did not wish to involve himself in internal political matters.

Janka was finally released at Christmas, 1960, after serving four of the five years of his sentence. It is thought that international protest, led by Katya Mann, the widow of Thomas Mann, Lion Feuchtwanger and, later, his widow, played the greatest part in achieving this goal; Halldór had merely lent his weight to the issue. Janka later worked at translating and dubbing movies, under a pseudonym. In the summer of 1961 he wrote Halldór a letter that he obviously had needed to clear with the censors, saying that he had never been plagued by moral doubts, although he had spent ten years in prison and prison camps: "Whoever has a clear conscience is strengthened by such circumstances, no matter what difficulties he encounters." At the time of the fall of the Berlin Wall Janka wrote a book about his experience, *Struggles with the Truth* (1989), which encouraged many others who had fallen foul of the East German judicial system to tell their stories.

Halldór's mind was not only on politics and publishing matters that year; he was preoccupied with a new book. In May he wrote to Auður from Copenhagen, informing her that invitations rained down on him:

> I do not want to attend, and keep myself away from people and decline visits, am always collecting material for this new book of mine – the material is magnificent and fine, but I am unsettled because I don't have control over it yet. When I am home in the summer I must ask you to protect me well from visits and disturbances; peace and quiet and perfect concentration, without disturbances from people, is the first requirement, especially while this is in its beginning stages.

Auður's role was expanding steadily. She looked after the girls and the house and was to arrange things so her husband could work – even when they had already invited a friend to visit for the whole summer. At the same time she increasingly did Halldór's typing. His demands were endless, and the same may be said of Auður's industriousness.

In the autumn Halldór took another long trip, this time on invitation to Poland. He travelled through Copenhagen and Berlin, where he met the new director of Aufbau. A faithful Party member now occupied Janka's seat: Klaus Gysi, father of the politician Gregor Gysi. Gysi had been given the responsibility of getting the company to toe the Party line and did not say a single word to Halldór about his predecessor. Halldór did not like the man or the Democratic Republic, as he wrote to Auður:

> It is the same tiresome atmosphere in East Germany. I think that East Germany would take the award for the shabbiest shitland that I have ever visited – and it is not normal that in just a few years three million people have fled the country. When you think of the population of Scandinavia, this is equivalent to all the Norwegians fleeing in ten years.

Halldór had a much better opinion of the Poles:

I find people here thoroughly and uniquely charming, affable and humane.
I feel everywhere here as if I am at home – even the waiters in restaurants
approach me familiarly and address me by name.

Otherwise the visit had an official feeling: Halldór had to sit through interviews
and attend numerous parties, with an interpreter and organizer in tow. He still felt
that he needed to accept such invitations now and then, not least to promote
himself abroad, and he was also still curious about the places he got to visit. But
he was always thinking about writing: "What is torturing me is that I never get the
chance to work; it is as if one were transported outside oneself."

After receiving the Nobel Prize, Halldór was sent more invitations than he could
possibly accept. For example, when he returned to Stockholm from Poland at the
end of September, awaiting him was an invitation to a writer's conference in
Tashkent in Uzbekistan. But he had had enough for the time being: "I wish that
these gentlemen were as efficient in paying a man his royalties as they were eager
to pay for a man's propaganda trip."

About his visit to Poland, Halldór wrote "The Seven Wonders of the Prairie",
and although he complained to Auður that it was difficult to write such articles
because of how many different things he needed to take into account, it was a
success. He had stopped penning apologia like those he had written following his
stays in the Soviet Union in the 1930s; now he wrote as an educated inhabitant of
the West who, in this instance, knew what the Poles had had to endure. The consequences of the war were evident everywhere. And Halldór had visited Auschwitz,
"the most horrific murder factory in history". He concluded the article by
defending a young dissident writer, Marek Hlasko:

We would hope that it will not be forgotten in Poland that things are fine
when writers are able to attend to their primary duty of criticizing social
conditions and governments, each in his own country. When writers stop
doing this, then it is better to have no literature.

After Poland Halldór returned to Sweden and met Harthern, although their
relationship was becoming more difficult with each passing year. He also met old
friends as well as new ones:

I was invited to tea with the poet Sara Lidman, which of course was coffee
on the day that I was leaving; she is a nice country woman, with an extraordinarily large mouth, and she revolts against her fellow-poet Maria Wine by

having her hair cut short. Female poets often seem to be more unlike normal people than any male poet of any time.

From Sweden Halldór returned to Germany, going from there to Belgium, where, among other things, he was made an honourary citizen of Ghent. Apparently this had become too much of a good thing, because in a letter to Auður he said that the trip to Belgium was

> perfect slavery and torture, rushing from one end of the country to the other from early in the morning long into the night . . . I tried to stay in the best mood on the surface although I was constantly cursing to myself, because the whole time that I was there I did not once get time to read the newspaper, or better still write a few words.

Halldór was no longer the breathless admirer of modern, urban culture as he had been during the 1920s. For example, he was bored with the world exhibition in Brussels, but inspired by the medieval towns of Flanders:

> It is entertaining to discover old areas like these that are regaining life. These are the true cultural sites of Europe, not those damned huge cities, the capital cities that gape over everything, but that are exactly the same everywhere.

This traveller had stopped singing the praises of factories and power plants: Halldór now preferred the man to the ideal and also the past to the present.

Halldór went home at the end of October. Around the same time, the Swedish Academy announced that it would award the Nobel Prize to Boris Pasternak. The Soviet authorities reacted in the worst way, since Pasternak was in disfavour due to his novel *Doctor Zhivago*, which had first been published in Italy the year before. Pasternak was expelled from the Writers' Union and ordered to decline the award. Halldór sent Khrushchev a protest telegram. Jorge Amado did the same.

Where is the Promised Land?

> Between the garden from which you set out and the garden
> to which you return lie not only the many kingdoms, but also
> the big oceans and the big deserts of the world – and the
> Promised Land itself as well.
>
> *Halldór Laxness,* The Origins of Paradise Reclaimed

In 1959 Halldór was in no mood for political debate. The World Peace Council turned to him yet again that spring, but he had no inclination to oblige: "[It] has become one of those isolated Soviet organizations that have never managed to establish a relationship with any other party, and consequently it only speaks to itself," he wrote to Auður. Apart from writing, most of his time was spent on publishing business. There were endless discussions with Rowohlt, who preferred to stop using Harthern as a translator. Under discussion was the translation of *The Fish Can Sing*, and an attempt was made at an agreement with a woman called Ute Pehlemann-Jacobshagen to correct Harthern's translation and possibly take over as Halldór's translator. Rowohlt and Halldór met Frau Jacobshagen in Hamburg: "She is a painfully boring *Schulmeisterin* and gave me a one-hour lecture about a lopsided theme in *The Happy Warriors*, causing Ledig-Rowohlt to scowl like Reverend Sigurður Einarsson in Holt," wrote Halldór to Auður. Good Icelandic translators were hard to find.

Halldór went to Switzerland to visit the publisher Kummerly & Frey, which wanted to produce a book of photographs of Iceland with texts by Halldór and his friend, the geologist Sigurður Þórarinsson. This is one of the first travel books about Iceland, with photographs by Alfred Nawrath. It contains more than enough stony landscapes, and Halldór's text can be quite sentimental at times:

> On clear summer days and still, bright nights when the tiny, richly coloured terrain of the world's northern end is in bloom, then the blue of the sky, the sea and the land is sometimes so absolute that it numbs all one's senses. It only takes one such day for an Icelander to forget a hundred storms.

In the summer Halldór continued his work on *Paradise Reclaimed*, a book about an Icelandic farmer who went to Utah in the late nineteenth century in search of the Promised Land. Halldór himself had made a similar pilgrimage during the 1930s and written inspired books because of it. To gain a good grasp of the material, in the autumn he returned to Utah, for a longer visit.

"New York has been just as much of a wonder for me as before, and there is no other city like it," wrote Halldór to Auður from America. "During one's first few days one walks around here half in a trance . . ." Halldór met Icelanders in New York, and he tried to apply some pressure concerning the publication of his work by visiting Nellie Sukerman, an agent at Curtis Brown, although he was not optimistic about the situation.

Unexpected people were in New York at the same time:

> Khrushchev and his wife are here. She is thought to be the most shabbily dressed woman that has ever been seen in public in America from the time the land was inhabited, and the papers say that nowhere in all of America can

as bad a dress as her formal gown be bought. But Krusy is extremely elegant and charms everyone more than any other official guest that the Americans can remember.

Cracks had finally appeared in the Iron Curtain and the threat of war seemed to be diminishing:

Khrushchev certainly seems to be making a victorious trip here, letting himself in a certain sense be defeated, which, according to circumstances, might be called good; but his wife works away steadily and inspires everyone's respect and sympathy, although her appearance is so poor. There is no longer anything but praise for her talents and virtues in every paper.

Halldór cultivated liberal people in New York, like the judge Julius Isaacs, who was one of the leaders of American P.E.N. and whom Halldór and Auður had met at the start of their world tour two years earlier. Isaacs was a good friend of many American writers, including Saul Bellow and Edward Albee. His wife, Betty, was a sculptor, and they knew another good friend of Halldór's, Nína Tryggvadóttir, and her husband, the scientist and painter L. Alcopley. Judge Isaacs and his wife became good friends with both Halldór and Auður and visited them in Iceland.

Friends like Isaacs are perhaps symbolic of Halldór's changed world view – he did not seek out any American socialists. That autumn he wrote an article for the Danish paper *Politiken* in honour of its seventy-fifth anniversary, calling it a defender of democracy and freedom and praising it for its support of Brandesianism, which he termed a humanitarian intellectual movement independent of religious formulas. Halldór himself had adopted a similar position, although he still had warm words for the basic ideologies of socialism: he had become doubtful about grand ideals, because from them it was only a short distance to illusion.

From New York Halldór went to Salt Lake City, where he spent two weeks collecting material with his usual energy:

I . . . spoke to people in Spanish Forks, Provo and Springville, most of them of Icelandic descent, dozens of them; some days I was visiting people from morning to night, one after another. It was tremendously informative and I gained a great quantity of reliable information about Icelandic immigrant life here . . .

He also went to the Mormon tabernacle early one morning to listen to the famous choir and thought the singing good, but the programme rather poor:

I do not understand how it is possible to wake up so many good singers at eight in the morning and make them sing "The Londonderry Air" and things like that.

A good reception and people's helpfulness did not affect Halldór's doubts concerning the Mormon community. But the visit was the deciding factor for *Paradise Reclaimed*, because afterwards the book lay open before him, as he said in his letters, and he did not hesitate to incorporate what he had learnt into new chapters.

In Salt Lake City Halldór wrote the preface to the Indian edition of *Doctor Zhivago*, having been asked by its publisher, Prafulla Chandra Das, to do so. It had been Chandra Das who had published *Independent People* in the Oriya language in his series of books by Nobel Laureates, and he was very fond of Halldór; he wrote to him constantly throughout the 1960s to get him to write the prefaces to various books, and his letters are extremely courteous and charmingly insistent. When the Indian's mother died in 1973 he decided to publish a collection of essays called *The Role of the Mother in the Strengthening of World Peace and Her Influence on the Ever-Changing World*, and asked Halldór for a contribution.

In his preface to *Doctor Zhivago* Halldór avoids saying what he thought of Pasternak's novel; he is interested in what inspires a novelist to write the story of people who are cheated of their rightful share of history. If a novelist is true to his calling, all of his characters are equally distinguished. "Positive heroes" do not exist in literature, other than those that the writer is able to endow with the life and colour of human reality. In the name of humanism he expresses his admiration for Pasternak's endeavour to tell the story of people destroyed by the Revolution. There was now more harmony between Halldór's articles and his fiction than there had been during the 1930s and 1940s.

Pasternak's written reaction to this preface still exists. His Indian publisher got it to him via the writer Ilya Ehrenburg, and Pasternak thanked the publisher in a letter that he later copied and sent to Halldór.

The preface of Halldór Laxness fills me with joy and pride and makes me a great honour. Laxness is an artist of the highest level, an author of the kind I dreamed ever of to second myself. I like him as I liked Knut Hamsun; this is the deepest praise on my lips.

Early in October, 1959, Halldór went to Los Angeles for the first time in thirty years to visit old friends including Jón Þorbergsson and Upton Sinclair. And he doubtless recalled Valgerður Einarsdóttir. "When I drove through the city," he said in a letter to Auður, "I felt as if I had been here yesterday, so well did I recognize the atmosphere, the streets, the architectural style, the advertisements, the people."

Halldór spent an entire day with Upton Sinclair, who appeared not to have aged even though he was now eighty-one, had written eighty books, and had another six in manuscript. He had donated his papers (weighing 8 tons) to a university in Indiana: "Upton never stops talking and is extremely pleasant and I find it much more interesting to speak to him than to read his books."

It is clear from Halldór's letters that he was in high spirits that autumn. Halldór met one "Western Icelander" at a party at the home of Judge Isaacs in late October: ". . . the writer Holger Cahill, who speaks the most beautiful Icelandic, grammatically correct and without an accent, although he said that he had denied being an Icelander until ten years ago."

Cahill, one of the best-known art critics in America, had been influential as the chief cultural adviser of President Roosevelt during the 1930s. Although he kept it secret almost all his life, his real name was Sveinn Kristján Bjarnason, and he had been born on Skógarströnd on Snæfellsnes in 1887, moving to America with his parents when he was a year old. At the end of his life he began reacquainting himself with his origins, and Halldór did not realize at first whom he was meeting at the party:

> He was a thin old man and at that time actually in poor health, but bright of appearance, slightly red-haired, vivacious and liberal in that American sort of way. He walked straight over to me with his hand extended and said with a smile, in pure Saskatchewan-Icelandic: "Hello, Mr Laxness, I am glad to meet you, my name is Sveinn Bjarnarson, from Skógarströnd."

Halldór met Marcel Duchamp at the same party, but the meeting with Cahill was much more memorable, because of the book he was writing about Icleanders in Utah.

Halldór spent little time in Iceland that winter. He was away when the *Book of Essays* was published that autumn. In late October he took the *Queen Elizabeth* from New York to London and arranged to meet Auður and the girls in Lugano in Switzerland. He went first to Copenhagen, because he trusted his lawyer Per Finn Jacobsen completely when it came to his finances and practical matters concerning the family's move abroad.

It was difficult for Auður to get herself, their daughters and nineteen pieces of luggage to Switzerland, but she was met in Lugano by Halldór and their German friend, Ute Raizner. Halldór planned to use the months in Switzerland to complete

Paradise Reclaimed, but he continued to take trips here and there, to find peace to write and to pursue publishing business.

At the start of December he went to Hamburg to sign a contract with Rowohlt, visiting Fräulein Bernhardt on the way:

> When Fräulein Bernhardt, who is in fact a middle-aged woman, was in East Germany, she was a hardline Communist, and a kind of spy who oversaw the doings of the company, but now everything has turned around for her, the poor woman, causing her to say that she chastises herself thoroughly for all her horrific devotedness to the Party.

This woman might well have reminded Halldór of Vera Hertzsch, and he probably felt no worse to have taken the trouble to save her from a fate in the East German one-party state.

In Lugano, besides maintaining a household, Auður had to get the girls to a school and nursery in the morning and collect them in the afternoon. Between times she typed *Paradise Reclaimed*. Eggert Stefánsson and Lelja visited at Christmas. Later an old friend of Auður's, Nanna Ólafsdóttir, came to visit and they went to Milan together: "For the first and only time in his life Halldór took care of the home and the children. It all went excellently," says Auður in her memoirs.

In March they went to Denmark for nearly two months; Halldór completed, and Auður typed, *Paradise Reclaimed* there. Halldór having gone off to Holland, Auður suddenly fell ill with a bad tooth infection. She tried to contact Per Finn Jacobsen to get some money to pay for domestic help, but he seemed rather upset when they finally made contact.

The reason for his behaviour soon became clear. At the start of the year he had been forced to resign from the huge law firm at Gammel Torv because of irregularities in his working methods. His former colleagues did not suspect how serious things had become until on 15 May, 1960, *Politiken* reported that he had been arrested, suspected of having defrauded his clients and used investment funds for personal gain. The fraud was discovered when the lawyer himself was seriously ill; he turned out to be bankrupt, even though he had had a large inheritance from his father. It was thought that he had been addicted to betting on horses and speculating.

Halldór and his family returned to Gljúfrasteinn when Auður became seriously ill again early in the summer, this time suffering internal bleeding from a second miscarriage. The doctors at Landakot Hospital saved her life, and she recovered well.

On 21 July *Paradise Reclaimed* was published. Halldór had high hopes for the book, and the manuscript was sent quickly to Rabén and Sjögren, his publishers in Sweden, in the hope that the book might be published simultaneously in several countries. It received a great deal of attention and enjoyed vigorous sales. Helgafell promoted it energetically and Halldór was widely interviewed. But few reviews appeared. Kristján Karlsson wrote a detailed one for *Morgunblaðið*, discussing the novel as a philosophical allegory. Halldór was disappointed, as he wrote to Auður, who had gone to Copenhagen for dental surgery:

> I send you a clipping from yesterday's *Morgunblaðið*; it is the first review in the entire world of *Paradise Reclaimed*. I find it somewhat problematic and a bit dull, although its author is actually trying to display a tiny bit of learning, some of which is, however, derived from dictionaries, like this bit of wisdom about the picaresque.

Halldór's disappointment sprang not least from the difficulty he had writing this story and how close it was to his own heart, in the sense that it was a reckoning with his intellectual history. It might perhaps be said that the novel had more significance for Halldór than for his readers. Nearly a decade later he told a Swiss newspaper:

> *Paradise Reclaimed* is in true measure derived from the course of my life. I ran away from home, followed different ideologies and passed through completely different stages. What I thought was right proved to be wrong.

Paradise Reclaimed takes place in the 1880s; the one date mentioned specifically is 1874, when the thousandth anniversary of the settlement of Iceland was celebrated, giving the writer an opportunity for the ironic pun that Iceland had become a thousand-year-old kingdom. This was the time of emigration to North America and the disintegration of Icelandic agriculture.

At the start of the book the farmer, Steinar, lives in poor conditions on a farm with his family. It is as though he inhabits the bygone world of the sagas. When the Danish King comes to Iceland, Steinar follows the example of his forefathers and gives him a horse, the family's greatest treasure. After this his own story is marked by tragedy. Encountering Þjóðrekur, a Mormon bishop, he decides to visit the Promised Land of Utah, with his family to follow later. As the bishop explains to Steinar:

> No-one will bring the Promised Land to you. You must trek across the wilderness yourself. You must renounce homeland, family and possessions.

That is a Mormon. And if you have nothing but the flowers that people in Iceland call weeds, you must take your leave of them. You lead your young and rosy-cheeked sweetheart out into the wilderness. That is a Mormon.

While Steinar is away, his family loses everything, having fallen victim to the new commercial era. When the family finally follows Steinar to America, his wife dies aboard ship, while three young men take advantage of his daughter's gullibility and take her to bed.

Naturally, the Promised Land proves to be no such thing. It is built on a Mormon orthodoxy whose certainty mirrors that of the Soviet dictatorship. When the Mormon bishop Þjóðrekur points out the ruins of his childhood home to Steinar's wife and says: "'These ruins bear witness that every dwelling shall be laid waste if the people do not have correct opinions,'" the woman replies: "'And there were farms where people had neither [food nor clothing], but that wasn't because they didn't have correct opinions . . .'" Here we have an echo of Halldór's scepticism about the idea of universal truth, to which he had been so devoted in his youth.

Halldór is not entirely pessimistic in his depiction of Utah, but many kinds of battles are waged. In fact, in *Paradise Reclaimed* Halldór pulls together many threads from his previous books. In the end Steinar returns to Iceland and his ruined farm, which he starts to rebuild. A passer-by asks him who he is, and Steinar replies: "'I have found the truth, and the land in which it lives.'" The story reminds one of *The Happy Warriors*; both books tell of men who undertake painful journeys and make sacrifices for ideals that turn out to be illusions.

Paradise Reclaimed is sometimes dark and depressing, and lacks Halldór's usual light-heartedness. Pain is always close at hand, although the writer sometimes seems distant; the pain has its roots in the connection Halldór felt to his main character. He himself had searched for the Promised Land:

And between the field whence one set out and the field whither one returned is not only the kingdom and the seas surrounding it, along with the deserts of the world, but also the Promised Land itself.

With *Paradise Reclaimed*, Halldór divorced himself entirely from his old conviction that ideals were higher than human beings. Paradoxically, after this he lost some of his ability to create flesh-and-blood characters. It was as if he had been distanced from human life.

A Poetical Time and Mirror of the Century

A book that is magnificent reading about a magnificent time.
Benjamín Eiríksson on A Poet's Time

It was while Auður was in Copenhagen for her dental operation that she happened to see a newspaper article about Per Finn Jacobsen. The press had discovered that he had emptied the accounts he was meant to be looking after, among them the royalty accounts of Halldór Laxness and Gunnar Gunnarsson. Auður told Halldór, who contacted Gammel Torv.

Per Finn's arrest was a huge setback for Halldór, not only because of the 40,000 Danish kroner that had been stolen from his Danish royalties account, but also because of the trust he had placed in his lawyer. Luckily Per Finn himself had sent the Nobel Prize money to America. For a time it seemed that Halldór's Danish money was entirely lost, but after several years most of it was repaid from the Danish lawyers' insurance fund. The office at Gammel Torv took over his business affairs, but Halldór's relationship with the firm was never the same as it had been with Per Finn. It should be mentioned that when Per Finn had served his sentence he was hired by Gyldendal, where he was later made manager of the contracts department. He earned a great deal of respect for his work in this field, building on his experience with Halldór.

Around this time increasing numbers of people began to turn up at the Laxness home; whole busloads sometimes stopped outside. Halldór wrote to Auður:

> The other day when I came out an incredibly huge woman, the largest I have ever seen, sat at the piano; she was American and had pushed her way into the house to speak to me – about what, I do not know.

It would be wrong to deduce from *Paradise Reclaimed* that Halldór had renounced all of his political opinions. He was as before opposed to the American military presence in Iceland, as is revealed in his letters to Auður. The base's opponents were, for example, preparing for a so-called Þingvellir Meeting, and Halldór spent time discussing with Kristinn Andrésson and Þóra how it might be possible to reach beyond the ranks of the Socialist Party. The leftist government had fallen in the meantime. When Jónas Árnason looked to Halldór to support the Þingvellir Meeting financially, Halldór happily made a donation.

In the autumn of 1960 *Paradise Reclaimed* was published simultaneously in Norwegian, Danish and Swedish; Halldór's position was still very strong in

Scandinavia, and the book was quickly translated into other languages. It received generally good reviews but did not sell very well, and once again did not produce the results Halldór had hoped for. Readers who were interested in the newest literary movements thought it old-fashioned. Halldór understood that there was not much demand for epic novels at this time, and eight years passed before he published his next one.

At the end of September, 1960, Halldór went to the Soviet Union at the invitation of the Writers' Union. Five years had passed since his previous visit and there had been a great deal of movement in his publishing affairs, but he had received few royalties.

His old friends received him joyfully: these included Morozova and Krymova, the writers Polevoy and Sofronov, and Markov, the director of *The Silver Moon*. The Icelandic ambassador in Moscow and his wife were old friends, so Halldór was treated royally everywhere. He felt that Moscow had grown larger and more beautiful, the people dressed better than before, but what mattered most was this: "People's demeanour is always just as charming and winning as I knew from the previous trip, when their difficulties seemed to be insurmountable." The hospitality was magnificent, and people everywhere took the time to speak to Halldór.

When he returned to Copenhagen he summarized the trip in a letter to Auður:

> I think that the Russia trip was very necessary. Neglected connections with numerous parties were renewed. I reached agreements with three companies, all of the money in my accounts I have actually managed to have converted into Western money, and finally my royalties for *Salka Valka* were transferred to Stockholm. The fetters were cut from *Iceland's Bell*. The manuscript had been put to sleep because of defects; it had slept for two years and it had been decided to let it sleep for an additional two, but I persuaded them to get people to correct it and worked myself on corrections in dubious places with Morozova the final days. *Independent People* has now been sent to the printers to make a hundred thousand copies of it in a new edition etc. I met and was invited to a banquet by Polevoy, Kasanteva and Sofronov, and by three publishing companies, and did newspaper interviews and other publicity.

One of Halldór's interviews was with the literary journal *Literaturnaya Gazeta*. In it Halldór said that his *Paradise Reclaimed* was above all a rural novel, and that he had tried to avoid creating characters influenced by education and culture: "I have no interest in man as an offspring of culture, but rather am interested in human nature." This is similar to what he had done in *Independent People*, and a comparison between these books is suggestive. But in the interview Halldór downplays the new work's political aspects.

In October Halldór was in Copenhagen, where he attended long meetings with his new lawyer, Sonne-Holm. A good deal needed sorting out in the wake of Per Finn's arrest. Stanley Unwin stirred and said that he wanted to publish *Paradise Reclaimed*, as did Methuen, whom Halldór preferred. He also needed to negotiate with Rowohlt, because Harthern wanted to be paid well for his translation of *The Fish Can Sing*, but finally agreed to let an Icelander correct his translation against the original text.

Halldór did not confine his activities to business in Copenhagen. He called Kirsten Jacobsen, Per Finn's wife, to express his sympathy while her husband was in jail. And he visited his friend Svavar Guðnason, who was setting up an exhibition in Kunstforeningen. At first Halldór was worried because the painter was drinking:

> I scolded that wretched Svabbi like a dog and said that I would not come to the opening if I heard that he was drunk, told him that he did not have the right to wreck his personality in this way in front of the Danes, when he was appearing publicly on behalf of Icelandic art and culture – along with other such perfectly reprehensible moralizings.

The moralizing bore results and Svavar was in good form at the opening. Halldór was born when Iceland was still a Danish colony, and he always thought it important that Icelanders not behave in Denmark in any way that would allow the Danes to look down on them. A letter he wrote to Auður the next autumn shows how much it mattered to him that Icelanders make a good impression on foreign soil. An Icelandic composer had given a lecture in Copenhagen that Halldór thought extremely bad:

> It was typical of the type of speech Icelanders make to order for foreigners, when they think the main point is to take the money and let their sun of grace shine. He also received a free round-trip to Denmark and free lodging at the Hotel Palace for this event. It was the type of lecture that will always work to create the opinion in foreign countries that Icelanders are the most ridiculous people in the world . . . The speaker neither wanted to think nor had any clue about his topic, which was Icelandic folk songs. It is a great harm that Icelanders when abroad are so eager to make themselves more foolish than they are: just do everything with the least amount of effort;

just get the money fast – even though everyone who is there to learn something stands gaping after the lecture, wondering at the fact that such ignoramuses should exist on this earth . . . It is extraordinary to produce so many idiots in such a sparsely populated country . . . Garðar Hólm over and over again.

In 1960 Halldór turned to drama more seriously than ever before, in the autumn writing *The Chimney Play* (1961). Whatever his convictions were about the worth of narrative fiction, he was sensitive to the discussion about the death of the novel. As a young man he had listened to the rhythm of the times; as a writer from a remote island he hated to be viewed abroad as a representative of a bygone era. This is a classic problem for modern writers, for whom the demands of originality and innovation are stronger than anything else. When Strindberg's *Miss Julie* was premiered in Scandinavia in 1888 it was called one of the first naturalist dramas, but when its author introduced it in Paris six years later he called it a symbolic work, because symbolic drama was new there. In the same way, Halldór wanted to use his play to move closer to avant-garde theatre in the West.

Halldór's doubts penetrated not only his political ideals, but also the literary genres in which he had worked. He was re-experiencing his old restlessness, and he wrote numerous articles for foreign papers and spent a lot of time abroad. It was as if the cosmopolitan once again had the upper hand in the ongoing wrestling match with the Icelander.

In the spring of 1961 Halldór was invited to Romania. En route he stopped in Copenhagen, Hamburg and Göteborg on business. And he left Auður with an assignment: "Have a swimming pool built while I am away." Shortly before his birthday Halldór wrote from Copenhagen: "Renovations work best under your control when I am away and not there to trouble you with squabblings and interference." But of course he expressed various opinions, at the same time telling her that they had enough money for the project.

However, actually getting hold of this money was a challenge. Halldór enlisted the support of both Rowohlt and his new lawyer in Denmark to demand payment from Aufbau in East Berlin, where he had 30,000 marks on account. Despite Gysi's hardline politics, Halldór did get some money out of him, though it was only sufficient for about half of the swimming pool. But he was happy to hear that his friend Janka had finally been released from prison.

Despite having a swimming pool, Halldór thought about going abroad with his family the following winter, or renting an apartment in town; he was fed up with driving to and from Gljúfrasteinn in bad weather. On his birthday he was in

Göteborg, where he made a remarkable announcement, as he wrote to Auður: "I was somewhat irritated as usual on my birthday and said that I would never write another novel."

Halldór's impatience regarding clichés and stagnant thinking explains why he was unusually averse to the propaganda directed at him in Romania. He found the entire trip ridiculous. Twenty years later he wrote a hilarious travel diary from the notebooks that he kept in Romania, in which he told of the reception he received immediately after his arrival:

> Two honourable gentlemen the same age as I from the pacifist movement came to find me at the hotel and praised me to the skies as a magnificent warrior for peace. I had to take a drink from my coffee cup in order to think of something to say; but could not think of anything except for, "Turkish coffee is best."

Everything went downhill from there. His interpreter was a respectable lecturer in English literature, Profeta by name: "She said that she had never been much for literature although she had unfortunately become a teacher in it. I was sympathetic." The trip confirmed all his worst fears about the Socialist Republic.

Halldór had one good friend in the country, the writer Zaharia Stancu, whom he had met at various pacifist meetings. He told Auður that Stancu was:

> . . . writer and theatre director and M.P. and much more besides. In such a country people can be all sorts of different things and everything all at once without needing to think at all, because the Party does all the thinking for them.

In his travel diary, however, he spoke well of Stancu, whose most renowned work, *Barefoot* (1948), had been published in Icelandic.

Halldór found the country's medieval atmosphere interesting, with hardly a car to be seen, but carts and gaunt horses instead. "But they feel well and have their own homes," he wrote to Auður, "which are certainly just as pleasant as ours; and much calmer. I want most of all to be a shepherd here."

The travel diary makes it clear that Halldór could no longer be deceived by propagandistic babble: "Too much talk of peace, when there is only one war-party present, works on me like a wedding in which either the bride or the groom lives in Akranes." Notwithstanding Halldór's friendly attitude towards Russia, he had grown tired of the Eastern bloc. When he returned to Denmark he found an invitation awaiting him for a two-week trip to Bulgaria. He expressed his opinion in a letter to Auður: "No thank you, those Balkan states are downright medieval despite a little socialist glimmer on the surface."

But the Russians remained loyal. Halldór was still president of M.Í.R. in name, although he had few dealings with it except when Soviet artists came for visits. At the end of the 1950s the Reykjavík chapter contacted a representative of the Soviet commission and asked for the same sort of grant as that given to the national organization. The Reykjavík chapter consisted of staunch Soviet supporters, and its leaders had good connections with the Soviet embassy. They attacked Kristinn E. Andrésson who lost his position in the chapter as a result, due to problems over official trips and other perks.

Despite this setback, Kristinn maintained his relationships in the East, in the summer hosting a visit by three translators, including Morozova. Halldór accompanied the delegation on a trip to the north. Two of the delegates wrote reports expressing their delight at their reception, though the embassy had tried beforehand to spoil their connection with their hosts, referring to Kristinn E. Andrésson as a "cunning hypocrite" and to Halldór as a "morally dubious alcoholic". The hardliners' attack missed its target, however, and Halldór continued to maintain his reputation with the Soviets.

*

On 11 October *The Chimney Play* opened at the National Theatre. There was a great deal of interest and a large demand for tickets. Several days before the opening a press conference was held, at which Halldór made absurd comments. Although the play is fantastical and the events it describes far-fetched, it is not Absurdist. It is concerned in part with the commercialization of art, a subject which had been of interest to Halldór for some time, and with a society that has become more affluent, but which is built on falsehood and illusion: "The world is a bluff, but the blow is real," the main character says.

Halldór may have been flirting with the theatre of the Absurd, and the drama of Brecht, but *The Chimney Play* displays a distinct disharmony between form and content, the latter being rather old-fashioned and reminiscent of *The Silver Moon*. One can detect a note of rancour in the portrayal of the role of the artist. *The Chimney Play* received positive reviews except in *Morgunblaðið*. At the press conference Halldór stated that the play had been translated into English and German and that there was wide interest in it, but that he was letting his agents take care the details, since it was not up to him to do so. In fact the agents, including Curtis Brown, had difficulty promoting the play, and it was never produced abroad. But Halldór was not about to give up and wrote two more plays during the next few years.

In the same month that *The Chimney Play* had its premiere Halldór went abroad with his family, as he had been planning to do. They spent the winter in Vienna, where he wrote another play, *The Knitting Workshop Called "The Sun"* (1962). Rögnvaldur Sigurjónsson, the pianist, and his wife, Helga Egilson, were Auður's anchors in Vienna, where she did not know many people. Halldór meanwhile travelled to Paris, Denmark and Italy.

Rögnvaldur met Halldór often that winter. They occasionally went to a little restaurant for lunch; Halldór would have an aperitif beforehand and a Czech beer with his meal, and they spoke a great deal about the situation in the Eastern bloc. Rögnvaldur thought that Halldór had began to think about writing *A Poet's Time* that winter. As he said later:

> Halldór enjoyed people, was curious about them, but he himself was mysterious in his way. If he was asked about his work it would be just like him to ask in turn, while raising his eyebrows: "What, did I write that?"

Halldór and Auður went to Bratislava and Prague at the end of January, and Auður said that they often stayed up late talking to writers, because Halldór wanted to express his increasing doubts about the Czech political system. At the start of March they took a typical "official" trip to Budapest, with a predetermined schedule lasting from morning until night.

*

Although Halldór's plays are often viewed as lesser projects, especially considering their lack of success, it is clear from his letters that he took them just as seriously as his books, putting everything he had into them and experiencing crises of composition. In February, 1962, he was at Tre Falke Hotel in Copenhagen, working on *The Knitting Workshop*. At the same time he was thinking about the prospects for his plays abroad, and he wrote to Auður: "I think that my next play should not be premiered at home, because it will be just like them to kill it." He considered sending Peter Hallberg the manuscript for translation. But then he felt stranded and thought of discarding his winter's work. As before, he could do nothing else when he was engrossed in a project:

> I have no motivation for anything . . . when I am wrestling with such great problems in my mind; everything that happens is in some way remote and irrelevant to me; I try to be pleasant to people, but hardly hear what they are saying.

In the middle of this project, however, Halldór rushed off to Florence to attend a conference of a new European writers' federation, the Comunità Europea degli scrittori (C.O.M.E.S.). The creator of this federation and its secretary general was the art critic and writer Giancarlo Vigorelli; its goal was cooperation among European writers. Vigorelli was a workhorse and got big names to sign the original invitation letter, such as Albert Camus and T.S. Eliot; he also managed to procure funds to allow the federation to hold meetings at the most luxurious venues.

The reason the society received such enthusiastic support is simple: this was an opportunity to create relationships between writers in the middle of the Cold War. Western writers were given the opportunity to meet the most important Russian writers; Vigorelli even managed to gain the society an invitation to visit Khrushchev.

Around three hundred writers attended the C.O.M.E.S. meeting in March, 1962, and the election of the executive body says a great deal about the political balance they were attempting to create. The Italian Ungaretti, who had attended the P.E.N. conference with Halldór twenty-six years earlier, was elected president; there were three vice-presidents: Jean-Paul Sartre, Nikolai Bayan from the Soviet Union and Halldór. Halldór did not go on to take a very active part in such conferences but he was always well respected. He was delighted that the society's headquarters was in Italy. He wrote to Auður:

When one comes to these wonderful historically renowned Italian cities, and to Italy itself, one asks oneself automatically: how the devil have I been able to be so far away from here for so long? I am absolutely determined to settle down here sometime, whatever time it is that I have left.

Halldór did not seek out the great names at conferences such as this. Perhaps because of recent political and literary disappointments, he preferred to be with people he knew. In Florence he went with the aged Anders Österling, the secretary of the Swedish Academy, to a café that Österling had first visited in 1897. He also spent time with his good Danish friend, Hans Hartvig Seedorff, and thanked him for a little book that the Dane had sent him about birds: "I . . . told him that this little book was so good that if the birds had for their part written a book about him, they could not have done any better."

From Florence Halldór returned to Vienna, after stopping to visit Fru Dinesen in Rome. In April the family moved to Copenhagen, which was where they wanted to be for Halldór's sixtieth birthday. The Icelandic ambassador, Stefán Jóhann Stefánsson, held a luncheon in honour of the day, and in the evening Halldór read *The Knitting Workshop* at a meeting sponsored by the Icelandic Student's Union.

On the occasion of Halldór's sixtieth birthday an article by Tom Kristensen was published in *Politiken*, entitled "The Man of Many Minds". Halldór was extremely pleased and said the article described him well. Kristensen expressed his admiration for Halldór's control of variety, comparing him to Cervantes and saying that like most great artists his mind possessed a quantity of different compartments, which made it possible for him to create an extremely wide range of characters and styles.

A Writer's Work: Plus X

In 1962, at the request of the Soviet magazine *Literaturnaya Gazeta*, Halldór wrote an article that is a unique source for his views on fiction at that time: "Personal Notes on Novels and Plays". It is very apparent here that great doubts plagued Halldór about what he knew best: how to tell stories. Talk of the "death of the novel" had doubtless had more influence on him than one might think, but his opinions were also coloured by doubts about the ideals and ideological systems to which he had devoted himself.

In this article he points his spear at the inescapable component of all narrative art: the narrator. When a story is told there is always someone telling it, of course. But the narrator can be more or less obtrusive. Sometimes he makes his presence felt by means of incessant comments about the progress of the story; sometimes he is almost silent. This is what Halldór was aiming for in his later books: a less obtrusive narrator and greater economy. He had divorced himself from the loquacious style of his former works:

> When one is writing a novel, it is healthy to use the telephone book's table on the price of international calls; for instance, to the Falkland Islands. The fear of having to pay for every single word according to the cost of such a call would protect many writers from loquacity.

In *The Great Weaver from Kashmir* the narrator is more prominent than the story itself; but from *Iceland's Bell* onwards, Halldór was more sparing with his words and more trusting of the material. Now he wanted to do away with the narrator (Plus X) entirely:

> For a long time the present writer has struggled with the question of how he should deal with a certain person who we shall call Plus X. Who is Plus X? He is that interloper with no name and a dubious passport who is eternally present like a peeping Tom wherever one opens the novel. This person is

never so condescending as to take his place at the end of a line of characters – he is content with nothing less than the throne at the centre of the narrative, even in a story in which the writer takes great pains not to identify himself with the narrator.

There is a literary form in which the story proceeds and the characters interact without the narrator ever coming near them: the play. Against Plus X is the disciplined dramatic form, in which the writer needs to keep himself in check. Drama is the logical conclusion in the development of Halldór's narrative style.

On the other hand, this aversion to the narrator who constantly makes his presence felt stems from the doubts that assailed Halldór in other areas. The man who had lost faith in an entire ideological system had also lost the hill upon which the narrator could stand to view the wide world and pass judgement on it.

———

After Halldór's birthday celebration, the family returned to Iceland. At the end of May he sent Peter Hallberg *The Knitting Workshop*:

> The National Theatre here in Reykjavík has ruined two premieres for me, one after the other in the space of only a couple of years, because they cannot perform my plays at all, and I would really prefer to have the premiere of *The Knitting Workshop* somewhere outside of Iceland, preferably in a smaller city that has a cultural heritage, either in England, Sweden or Germany. Perhaps Göteborg . . .

In the summer Hallberg translated the play into Swedish, and Erik Sønderholm translated it into Danish. But Halldór was not optimistic: he had no theatrical connections and felt as if the Scandinavians had turned their backs on him. He seemed both disappointed and irresolute; it was as if his self-confidence had dwindled. Twenty years earlier he would have knocked vivaciously on the doors of the major theatres, but he did not want to waste time doing so now. Nor did his agents work miracles, and nearly four years passed before *The Knitting Workshop Called "The Sun"* was premiered – in Iceland. It has still never been produced abroad.

In September Halldór and Auður went to the Soviet Union at the invitation of the Soviet Writers' Union. They sailed aboard the *Gullfoss*, as always, and stopped at Leith to visit Sigursteinn Magnússon and his wife Ingibjörg, whose son Magnús Magnússon had started to translate Halldór's books. They then went on to Sweden and Finland.

From the Soviet trip Auður particularly remembered the plays and concerts, as well as Halldór's frankness with his hosts in his criticism. Ilya Ehrenburg invited them to his home, and the two writers talked for a long time. Their conversation took place to a great degree in French, to the translator Morosova's distress. They had known each other for a quarter-century and had seen each other at peace conferences, and they discussed politics and history in detail. Auður says:

> When we left Morosova said, pale and reserved: "I have never in my life heard anything like it." She was a great partisan and highly placed in the Writers' Union, and thus was always controlled "from above".

Several years later Ehrenburg asked Halldór to sign a request to participate in the International Peace Congress in Helsinki. Halldór replied:

> Peace Congresses as a Patent of Left-wing Intellectuals, Amateur Politicians, Professional Propagandists, Theologians, Novelists and Painters seem academic as long as actual antagonists are not represented. Hoping you will find means bringing together war agencies of both sides for negotations before they succeed in widening their game into a general world conflagration. Welcoming any serious peace [initiative], tentative I sign with all good wishes.

These were likely Halldór's final interactions with the World Peace Council.

After their visit to Russia, Halldór and Auður went to England, where Halldór visited Methuen, who were preparing *Paradise Reclaimed* for publication. From there Auður went home, but Halldór went to Germany. He had long talks with Rowohlt, because the slow sales of his books in West Germany were of concern to him. He wrote to Auður about Ledig-Rowohlt, the company director:

> He explained that it was difficult in West Germany to sell an Icelandic writer, especially one who was vilified as a Communist, but said that the ice was melting – I wonder if it might be completely melted only when I've stopped writing books!

Halldór was right, because soon after he stopped writing, Steidl was responsible for his comeback in Germany.

In late autumn *The Knitting Workshop Called "The Sun"* was published, by both Helgafell and Mál og menning, the latter having received permission to publish it in a limited edition on the occasion of the company's twenty-fifth anniversary. The work is one of the most peculiar and perhaps most original of Halldór's plays. It contains many unfathomable symbols and is strongly critical of consumerism; its plot becomes increasingly absurd as it unfolds. In a notebook Halldór wrote that the work was about invalids and beauty queens who go to war over a comic anecdote.

Halldór was a believer in humanism and did not hold the view that all value was gone from the world, as did some Absurdist writers. Stefán Baldursson has said that in Halldór's plays the representatives of two worlds collide:

> ... what [the plays] concern is, on the one hand, the unpolluted and orig-
> inal world of sufficiency, the commonplace and modesty, and on the other
> hand the mixed-up world of the morally blind, commercialism and material
> affluence.

This is the same basic conflict expressed in *The Fish Can Sing*, and is most evident in his plays *The Silver Moon* and the later *The Pigeon Banquet* (1966), but in *The Chimney Play* and *The Knitting Workshop* there are other matters at stake, as the critic Jón Viðar Jónsson has indicated, "because their worlds are so transparently unhealthy and false that there can scarcely be found any realistic glimmer of light within them".

Halldór wrote to Peter Hallberg in December, 1962, that he had started to think about a new play. He felt that his slack publishers in Sweden and other countries deserved to be ignored and that he would turn entirely to drama. Yet he was disappointed with how little people understood of his plays:

> ... I have often been amazed at how the aesthetic in *The Chimney Play* (which
> is a much more serious thing than *The Knitting Workshop*) has gone completely
> over people's heads. Yet I thought that the three triangles that I set up there
> around the overwhelming idea of deception, and the sacrifices that moder-
> nity makes to that idea, should have been understandable – even here at
> home, since we are so thoroughly out of focus and always live, probably for
> geographical reasons, with something of a skewed perspective.

Hallberg had to disappoint Halldór with the news that the theatre in Göteborg had rejected *The Knitting Workshop*. Halldór replied with a detailed letter in January, 1963, about his plans. He wanted to offer Dramaten in Stockholm the work, but first to remove from the translation all references to Icelandic reality, as such things meant nothing to Scandinavian audiences:

> Then I think that we should let someone we know investigate whether there
> might be any interest in producing an avant-garde drama by Laxness. If there
> is any interest in it, that interest will be based on my name. Because an old
> Nobel Laureate is naturally no newcomer it would be fun to try out, to take

an interest in and experiment with. First of all people need to decide whether they want to work with this man or not. New men, new talents are objects of speculation, not half-rusted figures that have been around for, I have to admit, generations, like some kind of Eiffel Tower . . .

*

Not surprisingly he wrote to Auður at the start of March, on the way to Rome: "I am extremely happy to leave this grey, wet, bad Scandinavian weather, and I look forward to being able to work a great deal and well for some time." Halldór was in an excellent mood and sent Auður a large number of letters.

He attended a conference that the Food and Agricultural Organization of the United Nations held to launch a new campaign, Freedom from Hunger. The previous evening several selected representatives appeared on television and announced their support for the campaign. As well as Halldór, these included the Indian Sen, the director of F.A.O.; Dr Tatur, the Nobel Laureate in Medicine; Zafrullah Khan, the President of the General Assembly of the United Nations; and Aldous Huxley and Salvatore Quasimodo, the 1959 Nobel Laureate.

Of this broadcast Halldór recalled how long it took to get everyone made up and to set up the cameras, and the fact that Quasimodo overslept during his siesta.

Halldór was delighted to sit next to the representative of the Pope at the conference. His doubts about politics had not changed, as can be seen from his description of the former French Prime Minister, Pierre Mendes-France:

He is, it seems to me, one of these pale, power-hungry politicians who see nothing and hear nothing other than power and bow only to power, and besides that a typical French snob, but handsome and elegant.

The delegates were granted an audience with Pope John XXIII, whom Halldór admired, as did many liberals and leftists. This is how Halldór described the Pope to Auður:

It was quite an elegant show. His guards, walking both before him and behind, looked just as if they were from an opera or even an operetta, because of the way they were adorned. And then the old man came walking awkwardly in his cream-coloured silk cowl with gold and red on both the stole around his neck and his skullcap. He sat on his throne and let the Hindu Dr Sen greet him and kiss his ring, always smiling a bit to himself as if he did not think much of such ceremony. Then he delivered a speech from his throne, in French, which was excellent in the sense that it was the right words in the right places from the right man; and at the right moment, do not forget that. He is an excellent pope, I think.

Halldór's speech at the conference was a challenge to collective human responsibility, but he also showed that he had lost his faith in public solutions to social problems: "I may have occasionally been shown otherwise, but now I would not dare to assert that there is an elixir of life." Although Halldór did not have a magic potion, he was proud to take part in this particular conference.

When it was over, Halldór moved to Hotel Dinesen to work on *A Poet's Time*. He did not intend to leave Italy until he had got the manuscript into some sort of shape: "I have the best work conditions possible for the time being, absolutely free from any trouble of any sort, and I am in a very good mood." There was good food to be had at Fru Dinesen's, and the old woman, who would be ninety that year, was still on fine form, telling Halldór that dogs and Germans were not permitted in the hotel.

Halldór expected that he would need a secretary's help during the summer to finish the book, which he wanted to publish in the autumn. Barbara Bünger, who had previously looked after the house and children, had contacted Auður to see whether she could find work for her in Iceland, and Halldór wanted to hire Bünger so that Auður could help him finish the book. On the way home he thought about stopping in Sweden to investigate theatrical possibilities: "I still do not believe that my plays, for example, *The Knitting Workshop*, are as boring, unactable, chaotic, and idiotic as they think in Sweden and Denmark."

Halldór rushed through *A Poet's Time*, and had so much energy that for the first time in many years he wrote a short story, "The Pigeon Banquet". He planned to turn it into a play, but felt that he had encountered so much enmity in Scandinavia that he decided not to for the time being. In a letter to Auður he expressed his doubt that any dilettante or beginner would have such a difficult start in the theatre in Scandinavia: "Perhaps I am just an incredibly bad dramatist."

Early in April, 1963, Halldór went to Copenhagen, visited Jón and Þórunn and had news of Kristinn E. Andrésson:

Kristinn was here the other day to find some Chinese, and word is that he will be backing out on the Russians and throwing in his lot with Mao, who would be the right man to pay the losses of Mál og menning . . . At least it looks as if the Russians have betrayed Kristinn's hopes and there is nothing that he can expect from them any longer. But this has all been said in fun, and in confidence.

Halldór and Auður were now looking for a new apartment in Reykjavík. They decided to buy one in a house that was being built at Falkagata 17 and which was completed a year later.

While Auður was clearing out their old apartment, Halldór was in Sweden involving himself in theatre matters. He wanted to meet Ingmar Bergman, but received a message that Bergman would not be available until 2 May: "These small popes in Scandinavia are harder to deal with than the Pope in Rome himself," he wrote to Auður. It turned out later that Bergman had been shooting a film. Halldór publicized the situation in an interview with the Göteborg paper *G.T.*, which printed a headline stating that no-one cared about the Nobel Laureate's plays.

In the interview Halldór said that he was finished with writing novels and was now writing mainly humorous pieces and newspaper articles: "I think that I can imagine a future writing in Danish, German or English. English is a magnificent language, the best tool that a writer can imagine." Here Halldór was presenting himself as a struggling cosmopolitan. It required a strong sense of self to make such pronouncements in the papers, and Halldór probably did not fully consider the impression he would give; he had hoped that the Swedish theatrical world would react quickly. But nothing happened.

At the end of April Halldór returned to Copenhagen; Gyldendal was publishing a collection of his essays and he held a press conference in which he was asked about all sorts of things. He clearly enjoyed surprising, even dumbfounding, the reporters with his replies. Even in Scandinavia people had not followed Halldór's ideological development closely.

Nor had people in the Eastern bloc, despite advanced methods of surveillance. For example, a journal that was published in English in Prague, *Facts of Peace and Socialism*, asked him for an article that spring. Halldór responded by writing "The Origin of Humanism" at Gljúfrasteinn in the summer while completing *A Poet's Time* with Auður's help, and he sent the article to Czechoslovakia at the end of July.

The article is an apology for liberalism, tolerance and humanism as opposed to totalitarianism and censorship. Halldór took as his starting point the questions thrown at a writer on a trip around the world, such as what was the "chief obligation of a writer today". He said that he could not answer this except to say that: "The highest obligation of 'a writer today' is to write what he feels and to see other writers in peace." He says that he wrote what he saw and would not let others influence him, and because of this he could be considered a writer. It was the application of a universal theory to the foundation of society and everything that was written, he argued, that led to the Spanish Inquisition:

It would not surprise me if some people found parallels in those parts of the world where liberal writers still have to fight "the truth" of powerful, armed institutions, as was the case before humanism.

The editors of the journal now had something of a problem. The Icelandic philosopher Jóhann Páll Árnason, who lived in Czechoslovakia during the 1960s, wrote in a letter to the present author:

This was not a Czech journal, but rather an international organ of the Communist movement, with an office in Prague. It is incredible that they should have considered requesting an article from Halldór at that time, and entirely unthinkable that it should ever have been published.

In Halldór's collected correspondence it can be seen that he exchanged several letters with one of the journal's editors, Jiri Zuzanek, who said that he did not understand Halldór's response very well. The journal bore a heavy responsibility, because Halldór had been kept from his work on an important book in order to write the article. Finally Halldór asked in a telegram what nonsense this actually was: now he had been asked to delete a huge part of the article and write a new one, about problems in the arts!

*

On 9 October, 1963, *A Poet's Time* was published. Readers were intrigued by the way in which the book marked a break with the author's political past; they would sometimes forget that it discussed many other things. It is an invaluable source on Halldór's search for truth in the 1920s, on his Catholicism and the writing of *The Great Weaver from Kashmir*, on writers and books that he read as a young man, and on his discovery of the "social" novel. The narrative is condensed and has a suitably nonchalant tone that is the product of great meticulousness.

Halldór now views himself as a humanist and a sceptic. He is averse to all grandiose theoretical systems; one of his targets in the book is German philosophy and the literature written under its influence. On the other hand the technological advances of the 1960s hold great interest: he suggests that psychology and sociology will not exist in the future except as subdivisions of physics and chemistry. His opposition to theoretical systems includes religious and political movements: *A Poet's Time* was Halldór's first book in Iceland in forty years that gave his name as "Halldór Laxness" on the title page; "Kiljan" had gone. By dropping it he was displaying his disengagement from Catholicism.

His rejection of Soviet socialism is absolute: "National Socialism is just as unthinkable without Marx as Stalinism. It was no accident that these two became companions." Of course the man who supported Hitler and Stalin's non-aggression pact and defended the Moscow trials had a lot of explaining to do:

> I would not have written as I did about Bukharin if I had not believed what I was told, but unfortunately no-one is excused from believing what one is told; all lies are lies to oneself . . . the greatest defect of us socialists was our gullibility. It is in most cases more of a crime to be gullible than to be a liar. We were inspired by the Revolution and bound our hopes to socialism.

The book closes with the narrative about the arrest of Vera Hertzsch.

A Poet's Time would not have surprised those who had followed Halldór's political and ideological development during the preceding decade; one might have asked why he did not write this confession earlier. Halldór was not writing about "the God that failed". The conflicts that he had experienced with the Icelandic right-wingers probably had some influence in this regard. During difficult times most of his support came from the Icelandic Socialists and Communists, and he did not want to stab his old friends in the back. But when the book is read in the larger context of Halldór's life, one gets the feeling that it is not free from evasiveness. Halldór was not simply a gullible idealist during the 1930s and 1940s. He was without question one of the greatest supporters of Stalin and the Soviet Union in Iceland. For a time he supported the Soviet Union in everything, and he did not draw a lesson from the arrest of Vera Hertzsch. But then every man tries to create a story of himself with which he can live.

Naturally, *A Poet's Time* inspired an enormous amount of discussion. Never before had *Morgunblaðið* covered any book of Halldór's in such detail. Emphasis was laid on the book's political aspects, and an editorial commented on Halldór's linking of Nazism and Stalinism: "There is certainly great reason for Icelanders to celebrate this remarkable writer's perceptions of Communism. Here Laxness does not beat around the bush."

At first Halldór was dismayed that interest in the book was directed so sharply at its political element. He and Auður left for Israel three days after it was published, and in a short interview with *Morgunblaðið* before he embarked he said:

> If we take stock of the newspapers, we see that there is no interest in literature in Iceland, only politics . . . Prevalent here is something called political neurosis or political psychosis. Literary interest has not existed here for a long time. It seems that the literary nation went to Canada in 1880.

Halldór was uncomfortable with *Morgunblaðið*'s gloating over the book, but he certainly knew that he had political gunpowder in his hands. In his correspondence one can see that when he described the book to foreigners he always mentioned the chapter on Vera Hertzsch, and some papers and journals published it separately.

Morgunblaðið continued its discussion, publishing the reactions of well-known Icelanders to the book. There one could see the difficulties it posed for Halldór's old friends his fellow-socialists were not called upon to answer the paper's questions. It is interesting that Benjamín Eiríksson, the father of Vera's child, is very fond of the book, comparing it to blue sky after stormy weather. Aðalbjörg Sigurðardóttir, a teacher and women's rights activist, doubtless spoke for many when she said that she wished Halldór had declared this understanding of Russia when he had realized it:

> I feel as if I and others who believed in him as a writer and at the same time trusted him as a man deserved not to have been wilfully deceived by him.

Many of Halldór's old companions from the Socialist Party found it difficult to swallow the contents of *A Poet's Time*. It may seem surprising now, since the writer describes himself as a socialist in the book, and much of what he says about the Soviet Union contains what are now long-established truths. But unlike its brother-parties in Scandinavia, the Icelandic Social Democratic Party became no great power after the war, and the leadership of the Socialist Party still consisted of people who allied themselves with the Soviet Union. On 17 November the *Will of the People* published a review in which Gunnar Benediktsson spoke harshly about *A Poet's Time*: "This last essay collection is the most meagre of all of them, in the same way that *The Book of The People* is the most ample." Worst for Gunnar was Halldór's treatment of the Soviet Union, and he stated that Vera Hertzsch was alive and happy, regardless of what Halldór's story suggested. The disappointment felt by middle-aged Icelandic Socialists was understandable, especially considering what a book like *The Russian Adventure* had done for them.

A year later *Mál og menning* journal published the most famous reply to *A Poet's Time*, the well-written article "Misguided Humanism" by Þórbergur Þórðarson. Its inspiration is Halldór's description of Erlendur from Unuhús in *A Poet's Time*. Þórbergur discusses the image of Erlendur point by point: his world view, his behaviour, his appearance. Þórbergur's emphasis is political:

> About Erlendur's "endorsement" of politics there is only this to say: he was a very determined and completely unhesitant socialist, and there would have been no other way to define his "position" regarding politics except by falsifying it.

Þórbergur adds that Halldór is possibly trying to drag Erlendur "down into the political darkness in which he himself has been fumbling in recent years".

There is a great difference between Þórbergur's precise essay and Halldór's creation of a legend – which of course more than anything else is a description of what Erlendur had been to and for him. Comparison leads to the feeling that Þórbergur is correct in the details, but Halldór in the overall picture.

Halldór did not reply to Þórbergur's essay except indirectly, in the short story "Jón of Breadhouses", which is about two disciples who debate Christ's appearance and disagree about everything. Through their short conversation Halldór manages to convey his and Þórbergur's differences of opinion. Perhaps Halldór was also thinking about these differences when he wrote to Peter Hallberg several years later:

I also think that it is quite impossible for me to create a character based on reality. If I had that talent I would definitely start writing biographies. But instead, when I try to create an image of a real person, even for an obituary, I create a fictional character – and I see this myself after I have finished creating an image, but I can't do anything about it.

In *A Poet's Time* Halldór made his confession; he had by now become what he would be for the rest of his life, and what he experienced afterwards did not change his view to any great degree. But he still had things left undone, and the debate about him continued.

Stone Wall of Dunces

Halldór had received several invitations to visit Israel, but only decided to go there in 1963. He and Auður sailed on an Israeli ship from Genoa, which in Naples and Marseille took on hundreds of refugees from North Africa and Eastern Europe. This reminded Halldór of the poor European emigrants to North America in earlier times, except that the people on Halldór's ship were welcomed joyfully on board and given sets of new clothes as part of Israel's ingathering of Jewish refugees from all over the world.

Halldór's admiration for the Israeli nation was clear. Besides his visits to biblical sites, two other things affected him: the educated people from all over the world whom he met at meetings and dinners, all of whom had a story to tell and who spoke several languages, and the kibbutzim, which reminded him of the Communist collective farms he had seen – only without the aspect of compulsion. Israelis were free to leave a kibbutz if they wished to.

Halldór met the President, Zalman Shazar, and the Minister for Foreign Affairs, Abba Eban, who later visited Iceland. He delivered a well-attended lecture at the university in Tel Aviv, referencing the article he had written about the origin of humanism; the speech was later published in Hebrew.

From Israel Halldór and Auður went to Greece. Halldór had met the writer Georgios Athanasiadis-Novas at the C.O.M.E.S. conference, and contacted him beforehand. While the couple was en route from Haifa, Novas was named President of Parliament. Halldór and Auður were welcomed with limousines and banquets; they enjoyed guided tours of historical sites, and a visit to the poet George Seferis, who had received the Nobel Prize that year. Halldór delivered his lecture about humanism at the Academy in Athens.

Salka Valka, World Light and *Iceland's Bell* had been published in Greek, besides several short stories, without Halldór ever having seen a contract, and he was unable to meet the publishers of these pirate editions. (Per Finn Jacobsen recalled investigating such unauthorized editions on Halldór's behalf, even in Norway.)

From Greece Halldór and Auður went to Italy and stayed for several days with Fru Dinesen. One afternoon, when Halldór was going to be interviewed by *Corriere della Sera*, the reporter telephoned to excuse himself: John F. Kennedy had been shot. Halldór took the news quite hard: many liberal intellectuals had bound up their hopes with Kennedy, who had, for better or worse, become a symbol of the end of the Cold War.

In the winter Halldór was at Gljúfrasteinn, working on short stories he had started in Italy, in preparation for a collected edition. He went abroad in the spring of 1964, though this time he wrote to Auður:

I have become more discontented on trips abroad, and often wish so much that you were with me, my dear, and that my girls, who have quickly become so big, were around me. It is peculiar to be in one's sixties.

This is one of the first indications that Halldór was feeling his age.

Halldór delivered his lecture about humanism to a well-attended meeting of the Danish Student Society in Copenhagen. As usual, he was apprehensive:

I am always extremely nervous for many days before I am to appear in public like this, and I think of those peculiar people from my mother's side of the family, who were pretty much hidden people, such as my mother and grand-mother and sister Sigga. But then when it comes to it, its alright.

It made sense that Halldór spoke about the women from his mother's side of the family as "hidden people" in his life. He names his sister Sigríður only once in his memoirs, and his sister Helga never. Halldór's family was too personal a topic for him to write about in any detail, with the exception of his grandmother.

When Halldór was setting out his ideas for *The Fish Can Sing* and wrote in his notebook about the hidden people who are not prideful but who do everything that needs doing in life, he had these women in mind. Perhaps he thought of them as followers of the Tao which was close to his heart but distant from his behaviour.

*

When Halldór was in Copenhagen in the spring of 1964 he attended a banquet hosted by the rector of the university, where he met some of his old Communist comrades from the 1930s such as Mogens Fog, who later awarded him the Sonning Prize. Most memorable from this trip to Denmark was his visit to the actor Poul Reumert; a year had passed since Reumert's wife, Anna Borg, who had read a poem by Jóhann Sigurjónsson for Halldór many years before, had died in a plane crash. Halldór and Reumert sat up late into the night talking. Halldór wrote to Auður:

> What a great madcap is this immensely talented and experienced man in art and life, speaking such pure gold when he opens up his mind and heart, and forgets to act – or perhaps acts so well. I don't think I've ever lost track of time so much as I did in this night-time conversation with Poul Reumert.

Halldór's mind was still on his plays. At the end of April he wrote Peter Hallberg a long letter from Copenhagen, analysing *The Knitting Workshop Called "The Sun"*, which he calls a turning point in his career. It was rare for Halldór to explain his own work, but he felt as if no-one else had interpreted the play properly:

> What is "lacking" . . . are the two chief "ideologies" that the modern educational system, way of thinking and view of the world depend on more than anything else, especially and particularly in the West: Freudianism and Marxism. *The Knitting Workshop*'s rebelliousness is found in its ignoring of these two "truths", of which the upbringing of the last two generations consisted to such an unbelievably great extent. I have therefore not been surprised that the play, which is a denial of both Freudianism and Marxism, has had a difficult time and that people find it at once incomprehensible, annoying and foolish.

So *The Knitting Workshop* is a work in which he denies the theories that had gripped him so strongly in his twenties.

The 1960s was a rather quiet period for Halldór. Perhaps indicative of the situation was an article about the Nobel Prize published in 1967 in *Time* magazine: "And then there are the unknowns – the Icelandic novelist or Italian poet, each of whom only a handful of people know, even in their own countries." This was of course wrong, but when an employee at the American embassy in Iceland protested to *Time*'s editorial board, its representative admitted that Halldór's books had enjoyed good reviews, but maintained that the reading public had not known who he was when he had received the Nobel Prize. This was doubtless correct as far as the English-speaking world was concerned.

Several books of Halldór's were available in French, Italian and Spanish (in Argentina), mainly published in the years after he won the Nobel Prize. That books travel widely is well known. In Havana in the summer of 1962, Che Guevara asked Magnús Kjartansson: "I have read one Icelandic novel, *Atom Station*; does it give the correct picture of life in Iceland?" Kristján Albertsson's concerns that *Atom Station* could damage Iceland's reputation were perhaps not entirely unfounded.

In Halldór's collected correspondence there are numerous courteous letters of rejection from foreign publishers dating from the 1960s. His name was connected with social-realist novels and an interwar socialist perspective that was in disfavour with Western publishers at that time. Halldór realized this and tried to improve his situation through his agents. For example, he contacted a Dutch woman, Grete Baars-Jelgersma, who had translated several of his books from Danish, sending her all kinds of advice and repeating the general opinion that *The Happy Warriors* was his best book. It was clear that Halldór had hoped that *A Poet's Time* would free him from the shadow of social realism. As he wrote to Baars-Jelgersma:

> Regarding *A Poet's Time*, you tell me that the French are waiting for an English translation and the English are waiting for a German translation. And thus these gentlemen are trapped in a vicious circle regarding this material. This was a book written in the heat of the moment, and now there are other problems and other ideas in the foreground. It could take an enlightened publisher . . . nine years to struggle through this vicious circle that they themselves have created around a book that took me only nine weeks to write. And in the time that it takes them to stop waiting for each other I could write another nine books.

A Poet's Time was quickly published in Scandinavia, but was not published in German until 1976, and it has never been published in English or in French.

Halldór nevertheless constantly received fan letters and requests for autographs, especially from Scandinavia and Germany. As a young man he had intended to step forth on to the stage of the world, but now it was as if he were disappearing behind the curtains again. His writings throughout the 1960s reveal his increasing bitterness.

*

The new apartment on Falkagata was ready in the autumn of 1964. Auður was happy to have a home in town, and she and Halldór thought about staying there through the winter – which proved to be somewhat complicated. She had agreed to teach knitting at a school in the Mosfell district for two years, which meant having to go back there for two-day stretches while Halldór and the daughters wanted to be at Gljúfrasteinn at weekends. Auður was thus constantly packing. The family spent a total of three winters at Falkagata.

Halldór went to Scandinavia and Italy that autumn to finish a collection of short stories, *The Book of Seven Signs* (1964). In Copenhagen the "case of the Icelandic manuscripts" was in the news. Like other Icelanders, Halldór wanted the Danes to send the manuscripts home, but was – perhaps under the influence of Jón Helgason – not certain about whether his countrymen could rise to the task of researching them. He wrote to Auður:

> As one might have expected, it has come down to this: that the incompetence of Icelanders in their own area of speciality, historical research, is the main stumbling block in this matter. Pretension, coupled with uselessness, will be our undoing there as it is everywhere else.

In Copenhagen and Göteborg Halldór finished the two last stories in the collection, "Bird on the Fence" and "Jón of Breadhouses". He wrote to Auður that it had cost him a great deal of mental exertion and concentration, but he was happy with the result.

Halldór went to Saltsjöbaden, taking the opportunity to meet the writer and editor Olof Lagercrantz and his wife Martina, as well as Artur Lundkvist and Maria Wine: "In the desolation and neglect that seems to be my lot in Sweden, it is necessary for me to maintain such good relationships, which are first and foremost friendships." It was much less interesting to meet his publisher, Hans Rabén, who declared himself to be tired of all this book-bother; Halldór found it a dismal idea to have a man who had grown bored with books publish his. In a letter to Peter Hallberg he said that no-one at the company seemed to have read *A Poet's Time*, although they were publishing the book, thinking that it was an essay collection until he told them otherwise.

Halldór still had enough energy to pursue such matters, and from Copenhagen went to Italy, stopping in Frankfurt to meet Siegfried Unseld, the new director of Suhrkamp, to try to reinvigorate that connection. Through Aufbau in East Berlin a new translator from Icelandic had entered the picture, Professor Bruno Kress.

At the end of his autumn trip Halldór spent several days in Rome with Fru Dinesen. Vigorelli wanted him to take a more active part in the work of C.O.M.E.S., but Halldór found it impossible to participate from Iceland. He preferred that Thor Vilhjálmsson, whom he also met in Rome, take on this task. He wrote to Auður that Thor found no place more enjoyable than Italy, was a good friend of writers and artists there, and spoke Italian better than he did; however, he lacked authority because of the shortage of translations of his work.

It is hardly possible to imagine more different types of literature from the post-war years than those by Halldór and Thor, the pioneer of modernism in Icelandic prose. It is a good indicator of Halldór's role in the history of Icelandic literature that, when they were together in Rome, Thor told him about the euphoria he had felt when he read *The Great Weaver from Kashmir* as a young man.

In Italy Halldór finished preparing his essay "The Origin of Humanism" for the C.O.M.E.S. journal *L'Europa litteraria*. He returned home in mid-November, and *The Book of Seven Signs* was published before Christmas. He had not composed any short stories for nearly twenty years, with the exception of "Visit on Þorri", which was published in 1956, and the new collection showed that he was exploring new ground, his narrative style approximating drama. The viewpoint is often limited, since most of the stories are told in the first person, and dialogue plays a large part. The title is influenced by *The Book of Seven Words*, a seventeenth-century Icelandic theological work, and Halldór imagined that the stories were related as variations are in a symphony.

Halldór's stories are discussed more now than they were in the past. Some of them work like *romans-à-clef* to which the writer has thrown away the key. A good example is "A Capital Error in the Westfjords", a variation on visionary literature of the Middle Ages with a hint of the modern world. It contains veiled references to religious literature, and the dedication ("*Si me vis esse in tenebris*") is taken from a book Halldór knew inside out, *De Imitatione Christi* by Thomas à Kempis.

It is understandable that some of Halldór's readers were left speechless by stories whose message was difficult to find. But most people at least understood the humour in them, and they showed that Halldór was regaining his energy as a writer of fiction, although he claimed to have stopped writing novels.

In April, 1965, Halldór went to Copenhagen. He was there for his birthday and received a telegram from Auður and the girls, for which he thanked them in the words of his German teacher Jón Ofeigsson: "*Immer gleich schön.*" Despite decreasing sales, Halldór was still being published widely enough to have thousands of Danish kroner in his Copenhagen account, allowing him to purchase government bonds, since he did not want to stuff his foreign royalties into the maw of inflation at home. He had similar sums in banks in Sweden, along with the money he had in America.

His tax report for the year showed income of 380,000 krónur, almost half of it abroad; he and Auður owned a house, an apartment and two cars, and had 600,000 krónur in overseas accounts. Besides everything else, Halldór had become the highest-paid latter-day Icelandic writer; Snorri Sturluson, however, had probably been a wealthier man. Although Halldór was in the habit of giving generous gifts and allowing himself luxuries, clothes and cars, he was always thrifty, remembering how things had been during the first twenty years of his career.

In May Auður went to Denmark to meet Halldór, and together they took another trip to the Soviet Union: Auður found it almost an exact replica of their previous one. Yet one thing was different: for the first time they were invited to people's homes, including those of Morozova and Krymova, whom Halldór had known for more than three decades. These invitations displayed a great deal of trust, and perhaps a wish to speak more openly about a book of which his Russian friends were extremely fond: *A Poet's Time*. Chapters in Russian were being passed around as a kind of samizdat.

Although *A Poet's Time* was not published in Russia, the book did nothing to slow down the publication of Halldór's other work in the Soviet Union, which reached its peak in the 1960s and 1970s. The Russians now saw him as a Nordic storyteller, a representative of the old traditions, not as a social realist. During the years following *A Poet's Time* he was published in Armenian, Georgian, Lithuanian, Latvian and Estonian.

In a book that Krymova and Prodogin wrote about Halldór in 1970 they admitted that he had been disappointed by the Soviet Union, and not without good reason. He had, however, become a part of the Soviet literary canon. This was most apparent in 1977, when *Iceland's Bell* and *Independent People* were published in the World Literature Collection in three hundred thousand copies, and *Atom Station*, *The Fish Can Sing* and *Paradise Reclaimed* in the Masters of Contemporary Literature series in a hundred thousand copies. The Soviets' viewpoint was expressed by the artist Werejski at a party held in honour of Halldór's eightieth birthday in 1982:

"Laxness often criticizes us, digging at things he does not like – and this makes his friendship even more precious."

That same spring Halldór's articles from the previous five years were published in the collection *The Origin of Humanism*. This was a more purposeful and unified collection than some of his previous ones, and provided a clear image of his transformed views on politics and literature.

*

In the autumn of 1965 Halldór travelled from Denmark to Rome. After his usual financial business in Copenhagen, he attended the C.O.M.E.S. conference at the start of October:

> Of all people I am worst suited to sitting in a conference, and can barely stand it due to boredom, but they really want me here and today re-elected me as one of three vice-presidents of this society, for which I received a round of applause.

The Russians barely made their presence felt and there were very few English-speaking representatives; all of the discussions were held in Romance languages and Halldór missed Thor, who had been unable to attend.

He did meet the Guatemalan writer Miguel Ángel Asturias, author of *Mr President* (1946), and had good things to say about him and his wife, who was an Argentinian Indian. But he was not fond of one of the other vice-presidents of the society:

> Attending the conference is also one of the greatest asses in Europe: Sartre, who has been dragged here to deliver a speech about avant-gardism at the meeting tomorrow – I am thinking about skipping as much as I can of the meeting.

To Halldór, Sartre's high-flown philosophy was a kind of extension of the German ideological system he had completely rejected. Instead of attending Sartre's lecture he had a whisky with Fru Dinesen.

At the start of December Halldór took one more short trip, this time to Belgium. It was there that Father Dominique Pire, who received the Nobel Peace Prize in 1958 for assisting refugees in Europe after the war, had founded the Peace University in 1960. Five years later he decided to seek out several people to be the face of a society that he called the Friends of the Peace University. Halldór received a letter from Father Pire asking if he would like to join and responded favourably by sending a copy of his 1964 message to Ilya Ehrenburg, saying that it best described his position on the subject.

Dominique Pire was adamant that the pacifist work of the university be independent of all governments and ideologies, and that it not bow to Soviet influence. Albert Schweitzer was a staunch supporter, though he died around the time that Pire contacted Halldór.

Halldór felt that it was difficult to participate in European work from Iceland, among other things because he preferred to sail rather than to fly, but he went to Belgium and attended a ceremony in honour of the founding of the Friends of the Peace University. The Friends included Nobel Prize laureates, mainly in the sciences, and one writer besides Halldór, Salvatore Quasimodo.

Dominique Pire had received the Danish Sonning Prize that year, and after the establishment of the society – little more than a name – he and Halldór exchanged several friendly letters. But after Pire's death in 1969, Halldór's relationship with the university grew more distant. He still viewed himself as a friend of peace, although he had lost his faith in the working methods of the World Peace Council.

In the winter Halldór completed *The Pigeon Banquet*, the play that had its origins in the short story of the same name in *The Book of Seven Signs*. The play premiered in the spring of 1966 at the same time as *The Knitting Workshop*. Halldór had long intended to write this play, and Sveinn Einarsson, then the director of the Reykjavík Theatre Company, played a part in his finishing it. He had first contacted Halldór and asked him to turn *Atom Station* into a play, but Halldór did not wish to do so. Sveinn then asked him about adapting *The Knitting Workshop*:

> Halldór gave me a most pleasant reception and said that we were extremely welcome to produce it if we saw something in it. But at the end of the conversation he added: "Otherwise I have a little piece of writing that perhaps could become a play, another play."

This was the first act of *The Pigeon Banquet*. Halldór and Auður then visited Sveinn and his wife Þóra, and they read what Halldór had written. Sveinn was enthusiastic and encouraged Halldór to finish the work.

Here he finally got the good reception he had been hoping for. He finished writing *The Pigeon Banquet* while the play was already in rehearsal. Halldór still held a seat on the Board of the National Theatre, and the director, Guðlaugur Rósenkranz, tried to acquire *The Pigeon Banquet* when he heard about it. But Halldór wanted to honour his promise to Sveinn, whom he had known for a long time and who was the son of one of his childhood friends, Einar Ólafur Sveinsson. As things turned out, the National Theatre produced *The Knitting Workshop*, and thus it happened that both works were premiered in Reykjavík at the same time. This was a large boost for Halldór's plays, and he wrote to his friends abroad encouraging them to come and see them.

The Knitting Workshop Called "The Sun", as we have seen, was thought to be the most problematic and obscure of Halldór's plays. *The Pigeon Banquet* was much more accessible. It also dealt with affluence, illusion, commercialism and the problems of daily life, but the characters are closer to the audience, perhaps because the work is akin to *The Fish Can Sing*. Two worlds met, as Halldór said himself. Despite mixed reviews, *The Pigeon Banquet* was extremely popular and ran for two years.

In an interview with Matthías Jóhannessen, Halldór went along with the idea that the drama was a satire, although its purpose was to express "thoughts in a form that people would find entertaining". In hindsight one can see that the play was in accord with the 1960s Western critique of consumerism and affluence, falsehood and ambiguity, rather than being an exposé of capitalist oppression. Despite the popularity of *The Pigeon Banquet* in Reykjavík, it achieved no success elsewhere, though it was performed in Århus in 1970.

The same year saw the publication of Halldór's translation of Hemingway's *A Moveable Feast* (1964), done at the request of Geir Björnsson of the Oddur Björnsson Printshop in Akureyri. When Geir had first asked Halldór to do this in 1964, he had received a reply that adequately summarizes Halldór's views of his countrymen in the mid-1960s. Unfortunately he did not have time to translate the book:

And anyway such a book is over the heads of modern Icelanders, isolated, dull and degenerate as they are from concerns about food. I think that it will prove difficult here in this country to find some worthy group of readers with any understanding of the book's topic. We are unfortunately trapped in a kind of childishness, and despite all our schools, or perhaps because of them, we have become greater islanders than at any other time in our history. Our understanding of European education is less here than at any other time, and besides that, everything American is a closed book to us – except perhaps for chewing gum and certain kinds of kitchen gadgets. The only thing that we can focus our minds on besides our bellies ("politics") in the newspapers (and naturally cement and the fishing catch) is a kind of habitual moaning about the old sagas and a kind of absolutely irrelevant poetry that reminds one of the flight of hens whose heads have been cut off. The present generation in Iceland, and especially its writers, has lost all its ability to distinguish between well and poorly written books, and is thereby legally excused for not understanding the man who resembles a medieval Icelandic writer in the way that he searches for *le mot juste* – and no other – the man who holds the pen in *A Moveable Feast.*

Six months later, however, Halldór did translate the book by the man who was always searching for the right word. Halldór's last translation, it was not as hotly debated as that of *A Farewell to Arms.*

In September, 1966, Halldór returned to Copenhagen. His old haunts were becoming a bit empty. In the spring Jón Helgason's wife Þórunn died. Halldór paid tribute to her in an article, citing a letter she had written to him during her last winter:

> At home everything is the same: we seldom have guests, seldom go out, the housewife quite lazy and indolent to start with, and the master of the house the same at those times that are intended for the home, those few waking hours.

Halldór visited Jón and also went to see his lawyer. His accounts were in excellent shape and he looked in on his tailor, Eyvind Jessen. On the other hand he was extremely unhappy with his Swedish publisher, who sold a total of five hundred and thirty copies of *A Poet's Time* that year, misadvertising the book as a collection of essays. Halldór made his feelings known, prompting Rabén and Sjögren to offer to reissue the book if Halldór would write an additional chapter about Iceland for it; this became the inspiration for *An Essay on Icelanders*, published in Iceland as a separate book.

An invitation to Bulgaria awaited Halldór, but he did not want to go there, as he wrote to Auður: "The atmosphere in the countries that call themselves socialist is the same everywhere, and everywhere one finds the same boredom and soullessness, and one knows it by heart." It appears that the Bulgarians had been inviting him for a number of years, and had published five of his books in translation.

With Auður he travelled through Europe, ending up in Paris. Halldór had accepted an invitation to attend a conference of the Confédération Internationale des Sociétés d'Auteurs et Compositeurs, the international copyright commission. The conference was held at the end of October, and Halldór chaired a meeting of the drama division and was chosen as its president. The Confédération was party to the Berne Convention and had done a lot of important work in the area of copyright. Halldór accepted the presidency on the recommendation of his old friend Jón Leifs, who helped to establish the Union of Musicians and Owners of Performance Rights in Iceland, and who was a great fighter for musicians' and writers' rights.

Thus three Icelandic pioneers who had known each other for more than thirty-five years spent a week together in Paris: Jón, Gunnar Gunnarsson and Halldór. Auður recalled how much they enjoyed meeting up again, not least Halldór and Gunnar, who were no longer on opposite sides in the Cold War.

Halldór was not entirely suited to being the president of the drama division: the group was purely a financial watchdog and he did not know anyone on its governing board. During the next year he received sackfuls of letters and other printed material; he resigned at the end of the year.

Halldór and the family spent Christmas at Gljúfrasteinn, and it was there that he wrote *An Essay on Icelanders*, all in one go. To Hallberg he said:

My best working days are around Christmas, and Christmas is usually the best working day of the year, and this Christmas was better than any other, because there was such a storm for thirty-six hours that it was not even possible to open the outer doors at Gljúfrasteinn, because by the time morning came the drift was higher than the door. All the same I have not missed anything this Christmas and the family was happy to spend the Christmas holiday at home.

Halldór's displeasure with Hans Rabén left its mark on *An Essay on Icelanders*. The book contains numerous brilliant comments and funny anecdotes, but its tone sometimes suggests the author's feelings of rejection. At the start of the book Halldór introduces foreign readers to his country and its ancient literature with pride and comments that no writer needed to starve any longer in Iceland. Print runs were comparable to those in large nations, which always surprised foreigners; this could perhaps be explained by the facts that popular literature was a pastime and there were far fewer titles printed in Iceland than elsewhere.

Halldór then turns to the Academy of the Icelandic Language, which he locates in the nation's countryside, where every writer should live – an idea that is completely contrary to what he felt when he was young. Turning to his own role, he pulls out the stops:

For decades I was entirely taboo in homes, reading groups and libraries throughout the country, driven out by cultural institutes and cultural leaders, and whole districts and counties organized themselves against this poor writer. That entire time it was virtually only the Icelandic Stalinists who praised the things that I was writing, perhaps not so much because they thought them good, but rather because they hoped that I was as loyal a Stalinist as they were.

He adds that he had never really had a breakthrough in Iceland, and was "now rightly forgotten by those few friends who once hoped that I would achieve such a thing". His disappointment borders on self-pity. His publishing history in Iceland after *Iceland's Bell* had been a nearly unbroken success; *A Poet's Time* had sold five thousand copies on publication.

But here what he remembers most are antagonisms and disappointments such as the tax case. Guðmundur Í. Guðmundsson, who in the meantime had become both Minister for Foreign Affairs and Ambassador, gets an earful:

> When the authorities had lost all of these cases, in addition to many other far worse things, it was not possible to save the man in any other way than to kick him up stairs, in a political way, according to familiar rules. Somehow he managed to gather the coals of the fire to his head in his new position until this extremely everyday character had become the most hated man in the country. When it started to pour over him in Iceland he decided to appoint himself Ambassador to London – the Icelandic complement to the Court . . . A French philosopher has said that ingratitude to men of accomplishment is the mark of strong nations. Perhaps a strong enough wall of dunces will be more useful in the war than one or two straggling men of accomplishment.

Halldór was still changing his own story, and now he spoke as if he had never been recognized in his own homeland.

Work to Be Done

An Essay on Icelanders gave Halldór some sense of release. He could have stopped there and, little by little, passed into bitter old age. But he had expressed what he felt, and no-one realized better than him that he had come to a crossroads. Such was the power of renewal that Halldór possessed as a writer.

As always the renewal began with a trip abroad, or, to be more precise, to Rome, where Halldór had been invited to attend a C.O.M.E.S. meeting. He sailed to Copenhagen early in March, 1967; there were few people aboard and the weather was bad; he only made a short stop. But he was contemplating his next work:

> In such pleasant solitude puzzles that I have about my work are often solved, and things open up to me that have stood unbending and tortured me for months on end. Yet a horrible amount of the things that I am thinking about now are unsolved, and I am not bold enough to take further steps with these

things until the clouds disperse. I feel how extremely deadly it is for the development of the work when the writer always has his mind and interest and
perception on something else, although it is good to go to such a writer's
convention, where no demands are made on one's mind.

The work that was taking shape within Halldór was *Under the Glacier*.

Several days later he arrived in Rome. Dinesen was livelier than ever, and Halldór
was making notes for his new book.

Halldór did not escape entirely from thinking at the C.O.M.E.S. meeting, which
was stormier than usual. For an entire year its members had found no common
ground. The reason for this was that two young Soviet writers, Andrei Sinyavsky
and Yuli Daniel, had been arrested for publishing critical books in the West and
sentenced to prison. Zhurkov and Tvardovsky, the representatives of the Soviet
Writers' Union at the assembly, were attacked for this. Halldór was sympathetic
towards the Russian representatives, and he was also upset that writers from East
and West had stopped communicating. In conclusion the meeting agreed to a
proposal he supported, whereby the Soviet representatives would take the case up
with the highest authorities in their country:

> But after the main work was finished yesterday, a huge argument boiled up
> and Vigorelli and Yeskevitch from Poland were on the verge of blows, and
> no-one knew how this was going to end up, and I think that I can pride
> myself on having said enough to calm them down and end this devilish
> enmity. The Russians were moved and thanked me for this.

It is clear that Halldór took the original aim of C.O.M.E.S. seriously, and he
was elected vice-president once again.

As before, Halldór's letters from Italy during the 1960s discuss his purchases and
the latest fashions. Halldór seemed just as conscious of such things as he had been
forty years earlier. That spring he shuddered: ". . . shoe styles have become so ugly,
nothing suits my taste, everything is somewhat deliberately ugly and awkward."
But he had his shopping list and bought clothes for his wife and daughters. "All the
time we sisters were growing up he took care of purchasing most of our clothes
on his trips: after we had grown up he continued to oblige us," wrote Sigríður
Halldórsdóttir. Sometimes Fru Dinesen went along to help the shopper. They must
have been quite a sight in the fashion boutiques of Rome: the Nobel Laureate in
his tweed jacket and the hotel manager in her nineties.

~~~ *The Father of Young Daughters* ~~~

Halldór was around fifty when his two daughters, Sigríður and Guðný, were born. He was by then well known in Iceland and played a public role. When he was at home he needed peace and quiet in which to write. He was often away, mostly on trips abroad; the family didn't often join him. His role in bringing up his daughters was thus limited by these conditions. Furthermore, he was no man for housework and did not pretend to be. Sigríður Halldórsdóttir paints this vivid picture of her father:

> We sat at the kitchen table and stared at the big man stooping over the little fridge; finally he took out a milk bottle and before he could get a firm hold it dropped to the floor. Milk and pieces of glass went everywhere. This was followed by a deathly silence. Then he looked at us with a dazed expression, gesticulated violently and asked: "What the blazes was that?" Then he walked out and closed the kitchen door quietly behind him. At that we knew that this was a man we could trust . . . It would not have occurred to our father to look in the fridge for himself for something to drink. He would have called Mother, and stood there just like his friend Jón [Helgason] and asked for the life of him whether it was possible to get something other than tap water when a person was thirsty.

Practical matters were under Auður's supervision; the same can be said for the girls' schooling. When Halldór wanted to take Auður with him overseas it fell to someone else to care for the children, sometimes for months at a time, such as when their parents travelled round the world.

Halldór had specific ideas about bringing up children. In *An Essay on Icelanders* he wrote:

> Disobedience such as I practised in my teenage years is a double-edged sword and perhaps a triple-edged one, damn it. I think that a rigid upbringing, though it might not suit one, is better than no upbringing at all or simply bringing up yourself.

When it came down to it, Halldór seldom followed this advice, being some-what compliant and laissez-faire with his daughters. He didn't always get through to them: children do not understand dissimulation and ambiguity. But they had freedom there in the countryside, just as Halldór had enjoyed in the same place half a century earlier, and they had their way when Auður's discipline slackened.

Early on Halldór started to send his daughters cards and letters, sometimes about domestic matters. Sigga wanted a horse, and her father wrote to her that it was no problem to buy one – the problem lay in looking after it. His letters reveal that he was a good friend to the girls in their teenage years and later; they would confide in him. His replies are amusing and affectionate. Yet he had his principles. Sigga, for example, was not allowed to be confirmed, even though she wanted to be. He said that she could be confirmed when she was sixteen and could decide then which religion she wanted to follow. When they lived abroad she went to a Catholic school, but she was expected to form her own opinions of Catholicism.

Halldór's granddaughter, the author Auður Jónsdóttir, writes: ". . . we all remember him as being playful, warm, distracted and inventive." He was not particularly demonstrative, but always caring. His ideas and attitudes made a strong impression on his children. Perhaps writers are always partly children themselves.

In the summer of 1967 Halldór's mind was completely focused on *Under the Glacier*. He wrote to Peter Hallberg:

> I have a book in the works that makes stringent demands on me; a battle has been going on within me as to whether I have the necessary power to conclude it or not; and again and again I have been on the point of destroying it and giving up. It is still not clear how it will go. Because of that I can't get anything else done, and letters full of the problems of societies, institutes and individuals throughout the world remain unanswered . . .

In the autumn Halldór took a break and finally decided to go to Bulgaria. With Auður he went first to Paris, taking *A Moveable Feast* so that they could visit its settings like true culture-tourists. Halldór went to the Bulgarian embassy to take care of formal details for the trip, yet this turned into endless waiting and paperwork, according to Auður. Finally he walked up to the desk and said that he could not wait any longer: the trip was off. The Bulgarian visit never happened.

After Auður had set off for home, Halldór went to Utrecht to see his agent, Greta Baars-Jelgersma, who had brought order to bear on his contractual affairs, including his royalties from East Germany.

He was in Utrecht when the fiftieth anniversary of the Russian Revolution was celebrated. On the day before he sent the Soviet–Icelandic Friendship Society in Moscow a formal congratulatory message, but he did not want to make any public statements concerning the anniversary. Matthías Jóhannessen, who became the editor of *Morgunblaðið* in 1959 and wished to improve the paper's relationship with the writer, asked him for an article, but Halldór declined. As he explained to Matthías:

> ... perhaps the Russian writers Sinyavsky and Daniel will be set free ... If this happens, it means that the situation has changed, and there will be no cause for further protests in this matter. If our hopes are dashed, our protests will continue, making known how the Soviet government prefers to try to destroy its good relationship with the writers of the world, like me and others like me who have never fought against it, instead of sparing these two poor prisoners of theirs.

The European writers' wish was not granted, and it was not surprising that Halldór thereafter harboured no hope that the Soviet government would ever change course.

From Utrecht Halldór returned to Copenhagen; he had become less enthusiastic about visiting people and going to parties, but by accident met the painter Asger Jorn at his hotel, and they sat for a long time over drinks and cigars. These were his people, the abstract painters who belonged to the so-called Cobra Group. One of them was a friend of Svavar Guðnason; Halldór wrote a long introduction to a book about Svavar that was published by Gyldendal in 1968. There he says that after Svavar's 1945 exhibition Icelandic art had never been the same: an Icelandic artist had brought contemporary art home and given it an Icelandic twist. The same idea can be applied to the author of *The Great Weaver from Kashmir*.

During the winter of 1967 Halldór worked on *Under the Glacier*. He wrote to Peter Hallberg in February, 1968:

> I have been working the whole winter, started a play, but the material I've gathered for the play is so bulky that I could write an entire novel from it in addition. I have enough material in my hands to last me well into the summer.

This suggests that he had originally conceived of *Under the Glacier* as a play, but that he had abandoned this plan and put the material into novel form. In the same letter he tells Hallberg that he will not be sending the play to a Scandinavian theatre: their interest in such things had already been put to the test.

*

While French students were turning the world upside down in May, 1968, Halldór was made an honorary doctor at the University of Abo in Finland. He always listened to the news at home and was a great reader of daily newspapers, so he was fully aware of what was happening in the world. But from his correspondence it can be seen that the 1968 "revolution" did not have any real impact on him: he doubtless felt as if he had seen it all before. But like other thinking people he had concerns about the Vietnam War, and at the start of 1967 he wrote to his friend Julias Isaacs in New York that he did not want to go to America for the time being: "America's image among its friends is getting worse. This is all almost too heavy to bear, compared to how hopeful everyone was while Kennedy was in charge."

In 1967 Halldór had actually been encouraged to become involved in Icelandic national affairs, and the encouragement had come from an unexpected direction. Bjarni Benediktsson, who had made peace with Halldór, asked Matthías Jóhannessen to go to Gljúfrasteinn and offer the writer his support should he wish to become President of Iceland. The elections were to be held in June, 1968, and many people announced their candidacy. Matthías found the writer's amazement at the offer unforgettable: ". . . Halldór refused the offer cheerfully, and we had a very long conversation about how difficult it might be if the President of Iceland were to write controversial books." In a certain way he had already become the country's President, at least in a cultural sense, and he could play the role well when he felt like it. In the end the archaeologist Kristján Eldjárn was elected in a landslide victory.

Complete concentration on *Under the Glacier* was Halldór's method for dealing with the changing times. Before he went to Finland he wrote to Hallberg:

> I have now been working almost non-stop on the same idea for fifteen months, and have been hampered by having two ways of using the material in my mind at once; but now I have determined that the novel should come first, and I may find that I have exhausted myself and will not continue with the play. This will be a little novel, since it becomes smaller and smaller as I rewrite it. I am now "cutting it down" for the sixth time, and there will be very little left using my current method.

Halldór's method had not changed; he was just as precise as he had been when writing *Independent People*.

In May he went through Copenhagen and Sweden to Finland to accept his doctorate. For many years he had an energetic spokesman there, the editor and translator, Toini Havu. Ten of Halldór's books had been translated into Finnish and he was well respected. It had been a long time since he had scoffed at the honorary professorships granted to Guðmundur Kamban and Gunnar Gunnarsson.

Halldór returned home at the start of June. That month an old friend of

Auður's, the painter Nína Tryggvadóttir, died. Nína had gone back to Iceland at the start of the war after several years of study in Denmark and Paris, and she spent time at Unuhús. Afterwards she went to New York. As Halldór worded it in an obituary: "Although she had taken on the appearance of a worldly woman, the basis of her personality was similar to that of many Icelanders, international and aristocratic at the same time." The days had come when most of what Halldór published in the papers was obituaries for friends or addresses on the occasion of important birthdays.

During the summer Halldór continued his work on *Under the Glacier*, despite the great numbers of visitors to Gljúfrasteinn, Icelandic as well as foreign; the novel was published at the start of October. Halldór wrote to Auður from the Tre Falke Hotel in Copenhagen:

> I enjoy being by myself and prefer to let no-one know about me, because in some ways I still have not gathered my strength after *Under the Glacier*; it was a little bit like falling off the Goðafoss.

Thus he was far away when the Icelandic papers praised the book, almost with one voice.

> Whoever sees a photograph of Sigríður from Vogar in her heyday cannot doubt that the person in the picture is one of those elegant and outstanding women that have always existed in Iceland, and not just in the ancient sagas; although not more perhaps than one or two per century . . . this was the photograph of the woman I imagined when I was making an attempt to describe Úa in *Under the Glacier*.

Sigríður Jónsdóttir was the mother of the writer Nonni. To Halldór, her image expressed the feminine power he had so often tried to understand in his books; the eternal feminine, as Goethe called it. This was one of the themes explored in *Under the Glacier*.

In the novel Halldór tries to diminish narrative dilemmas by employing techniques derived from drama; some chapters consist entirely of dialogue. The narrator, a young theologian, takes a tape recorder with him to an isolated district and writes dry reports about what he sees, making no attempt at interpretation. This framework allows Halldór to limit the presence of the narrator, the notorious peeping Tom, Plus X.

No report, however, can capture the variety of human life. As one of the characters puts it:

"I merely think that words, words, words and the Creation of the World are two different things, two incompatible things. I do not see how the Creation can be turned into words, let alone letters, hardly even a fiction. History is always entirely different to what has happened . . . The difference between a novelist and a historian is this: the former tells lies deliberately and for the fun of it; the historian tells lies in his simplicity and imagines he is telling the truth."

A writer plays the wordless art, music, against the limitations of words. Birds are used to symbolize it, as occasionally before: "'It's a pity we don't whistle at each other, like birds. Words are misleading.'" And in another place Jón Prímus says: "'It is pleasant to listen to the birds chirping. But it would be anything but pleasant if the birds were always chirping the truth.'"

Halldór brings the rationalism of *A Poet's Time* into doubt. Jón Prímus is a sceptical man; but he is also a representative of sorrow.

The character of Úa represents life, just like many of his other female characters, but she is more mystical than any of them. Elements of her relationship with the much younger Embi recall the Spanish mystics of the sixteenth century, John of the Cross and St Teresa of Avila. The young man falls in love with Úa, and his love awakens him to life. He experiences love for an instant, just like Arnaldur and Salka; in a certain sense that instant is eternal.

There are parallels between *World Light* and *Under the Glacier*; in both, the glacier is a symbol of the mystery of existence. The chapter entitled "The Glacier" in the later novel closes with these words:

At night when the sun is off the mountains the glacier becomes a tranquil silhouette that rests in itself and breathes upon man and beast the word "never", which perhaps means always. "Come, waft of death".

In later years *Under the Glacier* became Halldór's most heavily studied novel. One reason for this is that the work is partly a novel of ideas. The characters discuss their views within a framework that reminds one of a play. The discussion reflects Halldór's own inner conflicts; the characters are vehicles for ideas: they do not exist in the same way as the characters in his previous books. Sympathy, which, according to *Independent People*, is the origin of poetry, is discussed here, but not shown. This is a different kind of book. Its melancholic tone is rooted in the writer's failed belief in the power of the novel to awaken sympathy for Bjartur's daughter Ásta Sóllilja on earth.

*

On his autumn trip Halldór travelled to Copenhagen, Utrecht and Saltsjöbaden. He feared his countrymen's reactions to the new book and wrote to Auður from Sweden:

I am devoting myself completely to rest and relaxation and am slowly recovering myself after *Glacier*. I am happy to hear that Jón Helgason has been reading the book over and over again: it has been a long time since he has spoken to me with such great interest and curiosity about a book.

Peter Hallberg wrote to him:

I read the book at one go on Sunday, and thought it one of the most remarkable that you have written. It is realistic and mysterious at once, enchanting in a unique way.

Auður wrote to Halldór about the book's good reception:

It was so pleasant to take books to your friends; everyone was so pleased for you and fond of you. I sat for a short time with Kristinn and Þóra and Kristinn was so impressed that he said he had to abandon us to go and read. He was delighted. The same can be said of Sigurður Nordal; he laughed out loud and said that's how it is with Halldór: he's so reliable and excellent, and now he's just waiting for you to write to him, if God permits, as they say.

Halldór was pleased to hear all this, although at the same time he said that no-one knew better than he how deficient the book was.

Under the Glacier charmed the Icelandic literary world. At the start of 1969 critics awarded Halldór the Silver Horse, the Icelandic print media's literary prize. Halldór expressed his appreciation with these words: "It is remarkable that the critics should hold any book in enough esteem to give it a prize. If I were a critic, I would hate all books."

With *Glacier* the doubtful voices were silenced. No matter what people felt about the book, Halldór had proved his creative worth.

Regardless of Halldór's Icelandic victory, he, who had stepped forth as the determined spokesman for modernity, was outside the prevailing trends in literature. Hallberg wrote to him at the start of 1969 to report his conversation with Ake Lofgren, the editorial director of Rabén and Sjögren:

In their day your books and articles were considered by respected citizens to be too radical, but now the new readers and critics feel as if your recent books lack the radicalism that inspired both the fondness of your previous

admirers and dispute over your name. In that connection Lofgren pointed
out negative reviews by radical critics such as Folke Isaksson in *Dagens Nyheter*
– who is for example a very staunch opponent of the Americans in Vietnam.
(In general Vietnam is the main topic of interest for youth at this time, and
more often than not the younger literati discuss world politics rather than
aesthetics.)

It was one thing for Halldór to be thought rather conservative in literary matters,
a different thing entirely to be put right by young readers regarding politics. This
shortly became even more apparent.

Halldór's position in Denmark remained strong. *A Poet's Time* had reawakened
real interest, not least because Halldór had many friends among the Danish
Communists and had written articles for *Land and People*. On 2 February, 1969, it
was announced that Halldór would receive that year's Sonning Prize, a sum of
150,000 Danish kroner. *Politiken* reported the news first, placing a great deal of
emphasis on Halldór's strong sense of social justice, especially regarding poverty
in the Third World. This article may have inspired the protests that followed, as the
literary historian Haukur Ingvarsson has suggested. The prize, which Leonie
Sonning had established in honour of her husband, was funded by income made
from renting property, and administered by the University of Copenhagen.
Sonning had owned a large amount of property in Copenhagen and had earned
enormous amounts of money from rents; the property, however, had not always
been in the best condition, and there were rumours of extortion and profiteering.

The Sonning Prize had been granted eleven times for outstanding contributions to European culture. Among the laureates were Winston Churchill, Bertrand
Russell, Arthur Koestler, Albert Schweitzer, Laurence Olivier and Dominique Pire.

Now, for the first time, the prize was harshly protested. The Student Council of
the University of Copenhagen wrote Halldór an open letter on 5 March, 1969,
informing him that the prize money had been acquired by immoral means, in other
words by taking advantage of the Danish housing shortage. Halldór was challenged
not to take the money, but to deliver another lecture to the university instead, on
the subject of slums, about which he had written in 1962.

Halldór reacted gruffly:

What does Leonie Sonning mean to me? The university granted me the prize,
and I am moved by the honour . . . But I know the Danes. They do not know
what an honour is. For them this is just money, money, money . . . they can
keep the money themselves.

The paper asked if that meant he was refusing the prize, to which he replied:

I have thought about donating the money to a special cause in Denmark. But if this is to be done because of threats, I will think twice about it. I will not let these terrorists control my actions.

An old acquaintance of Halldór's among the Danish Communists, the writer Hans Scherfig, teased him about the prize in *Land and People*. Scherfig discussed the preface to *The Russian Adventure*, recalling its statement that that book would guarantee its writer neither honour nor money from the bourgeoisie, then turned to *A Poet's Time* as an example of a book that was agreeable to the bourgeoisie. The Sonning Prize had thus become like the prize the writer of *The Russian Adventure* had not wished to receive.

Many people agreed that Halldór should refuse the prize. It was mentioned particularly that Halldór would be receiving it from Mogens Fog, the former member of the resistance and former Communist. Tage Voss wrote in *Ekstrabladet*: "These are two great men who have grown old and after long hardship bent and stopped saying no. They say yes – and bow and smile old men's smiles of surrender."

One of those who defended Halldór was Aksel Larsen, for a long time one of his political fellow-travellers. Larsen was the leader of the Socialist People's Party, which had broken away from the Communist Party in 1958. His position was clear: "I am pleased that you refuse to succumb to the pressure from the ideologues who want someone else to receive the money – because that would be a facile solution."

Ekstrabladet contacted Halldór when he arrived in Denmark to accept the prize and asked him about his views on the "youth revolution". Halldór replied:

Youth revolution! What youth revolution is that? I don't know of any youth making more of a revolution today than they have always done. Do you speak of the youth revolution here when some radicals try to terrorize an individual? I'm not much impressed by that sort of youth revolution!

The protests, he said, were simply anti-Icelandic.

Ironically, Halldór and Auður were at the time of the award ceremony staying in the same hotel as Janis Joplin, the youth revolution personified.

The award ceremony took place on 19 April at the old university building in the city centre. Several hundred invited guests did no more than half fill the auditorium, while from outside came the echoes of the loud protests of three thousand students and their supporters. Things got violent when the protesters pushed their way into the courtyard, and the disturbance did not abate until the police, with helmets and clubs, intervened. That was the first time that the police had been deployed on the university grounds. The photos in the papers the next day seemed to come from two worlds: inside, the rector in robes and Halldór in his finest, Leonie Sonning on his arm, wearing a feathered hat and over-large sunglasses, as if from a wax museum of a vanished ruling class; outside, long-haired protesters with banners and red flags fighting with the police.

Halldór took it particularly hard that Icelandic students participated in the protests. He had read on numerous occasions at the Icelandic Students' Union in Copenhagen, sometimes from unpublished works. He did not do so again until the spring of 1983. In Iceland discussion about the prize was focused for the most part on whether it should be tax-free or not. The former was approved after some debate. And because so much surrounding the prize was paradoxical, it should be mentioned that Skúli Guðmundsson, an M.P. for the Progressive Party, turned in the minority report against the prize being made tax-free in poetic form ("Let's take a bit of the Danish gold from Gljúfrasteinn"), while the Minister of Education, Gylfi Þ. Gíslason, who wanted the prize to be tax-free, responded in kind ("Skúli through fair poetry gave his spirit word/ though his lack of wisdom were better left unheard"). Danish students fought with the police while Icelandic M.P.s exchanged verses.

The demand that Halldór return the prize was unfair. Most European universities were earning "dirty" money. Halldór was a victim of the times: radical students were searching for good causes, and they thought that they could count on Halldór as an old revolutionary. However, the voices of protest were quickly silenced, and far more determined leftists than Halldór had ever been, such as Dario Fo, received the prize in later years.

What is more interesting is that Halldór seems not to have understood the point of the protests, feeling as if they were directed against him personally. For the first time in his life he did not understand the spirit of the times.

*

After the award ceremony Auður went home, but Halldór remained in Copenhagen for several days. On 24 April he wrote to Auður: "Yesterday on my birthday I sat alone in my hotel the whole evening. It was extremely pleasant and calm." The next evening he went to a dinner with Mogens Fog and Aksel Larsen, who agreed that the protests had been absolutely unnecessary.

Halldór had his mind on Old Norse topics and that spring prepared several long essays about them, calling the collection *Some Remarks on Vinland* (1969); among other things he explained how the so-called Vinland Map was in fact a forgery. On these topics Halldór expressed numerous unexpected ideas, not least concerning the Middle Ages, going much too far in the opinion of some scholars. In the preface to the collection he wrote:

> This book is composed particularly for people who do not know much more than myself, and it is refreshing to think about the Middle Ages with wisdom and not according to stony orthodoxy that inclines itself towards shunning provable facts.

During the 1920s Halldór sometimes gave the impression that he wanted to hear nothing about Old Icelandic literature. Now it occupied his mind completely.

Early in the autumn of 1969 Halldór returned to Denmark. *Under the Glacier* was being published there, and he was interviewed for television and took part in promotional events. He also went to Sweden to see old friends, telling Auður that Artur Lundkvist had completely turned his back on his acquaintances in the East and now wrote mostly popular history:

> Now he has become a member of the Swedish Academy and is right at the centre of culture as usual; as a writer I can't see his books going very far beyond his own borders, but then again, he's an extremely indispensable man in his own country.

Halldór had lost interest in meeting new people by now, as can happen as time goes by, but he kept faith with his old friends. Among them were people who had perhaps shown him interest or goodwill a long time ago and to whom he felt indebted. As well as Artur Lundkvist he visited the Swedish writer Lillemor Holmberg, who was a painter as well as a great idealist, but perhaps somewhat naïve. As can be seen in a letter to Auður, Halldór had not lost his ability to see the humorous side of things:

> Now [Holmberg and her mother] had bought a guest-book and a camera, and that was magnificent. The guest-book was a three hundred-page album, but no guests had signed it, and first I had to write my name and the day that I came a year earlier, then a hundred blank pages were skipped and I wrote my name again and the date in honour of this new visit; so now my name stands in two places in this enormous guest-book, which looks as if it belongs in the embassy of some huge nation. Hmmm, not a single guest had come to see them but me, and I urged them to invite about five hundred

people to a cocktail party so as to fill up this great space between my two visits. They were so thrilled by my visit that they looked me up and down, even taking a look at my socks . . . and they had for this occasion bought the camera, which they knew nothing about, in order to take pictures of me high and low, in front and behind, me stroking their cat, who was a stray. They could not have been more fascinated or enchanted if a zebra had walked into their house.

In order to be like great aristocrats they gave me tea in a cup that held approximately half a litre, and looked as if they could eat me alive while I was drinking from this and eating half a slice of French bread with cheese, although they did not join me in drinking tea, but each sat in her own corner and gaped at the beast with hands outstretched. Then they called for a taxi and we went to the theatre to see *The Seagull* by Chekhov . . .

Since they had bought cheap seats far from the stage, I heard nothing, and had to send Lillemor down to the first row to make a deal with someone to allow me to sit there, and the man with whom they made a deal would get to sit between them in the cheap seats. This they managed, making a deal with a Finnish man with a beard who had bought his way into the first row, and the man sat between them throughout the play while I peacocked in his seat in the first row. They asked me many times for forgiveness for having bought cheap seats, but that arose from their never having gone to the theatre before and from not knowing how to enjoy themselves there. The play was excellent and very well acted; it was one of the funniest, best times I've ever had in the theatre. That evening on the train on my way back to the Grand Hotel Saltsjöbaden I laughed to myself as if three people were tickling me.

This trip concluded in Italy in October with Fru Dinesen, who was ninety-seven but still lively enough to go with Halldór to the shops to buy shoes for the women at home. The city still worked on him like a drug, encouraging him to start a new project. That month he began on the second version of a book for which he had written a draft four years earlier, *A Parish Chronicle*. A new stage had begun in his career.

SIX

In the Fields of Home

The Years
1970–1998

I am a storyteller. God protect me from saving the world.

Halldór Laxness

A Countryside Annal

UNDER THE GLACIER PUT AN END TO HALLDÓR'S TIME OF DISAPPOINT-
ment and painful reckoning. His fear that the epic novel was of little value to the
world dwindled, and his reckoning with Soviet society was finished. He had abandoned his ambition to be a world-class playwright, and it was as if he were more
relaxed within the joy of writing. He was extremely productive in the 1970s.
Between 1970 and 1981 he wrote two novels, four linked autobiographical works
and four collections of essays. With *Under the Glacier* he had shown that he could
write a powerful modern novel, and his next books seemed to indicate that he had
little or no concern with contemporary movements in literature and politics;
instead, he simply wrote about what he saw and had seen, wrote as things appeared
to him. There is a free, expansive feel to these books, especially the autobiographical ones.

These were good years for Halldór, characterized by delight in his work and no
major conflicts; he travelled regularly, yet now Auður most often went with him,
and he had more peace of mind, was more contented than ever before. This
showed itself in the light-hearted, effortless tone of his writing.

There were readers who had a difficult time accepting this changed Halldór;
they wished that he would continue to fight for important causes, against conservative forces. In the late winter of 1970 he contemplated his position in a letter to
Peter Hallberg:

... I have had a little novel in the works since the autumn, driven on by the same need for renewal that has always plagued me and has now lost me most of the readers of mine who maintain their childhood faith like a stone baby in the womb ... Unfortunately many of my old readers have become incredibly stiff, simply wanting me to repeat the same old stuff from years ago (which of course was thought devilish by those who carried around stone babies from even older times). But I say as it says in an old rhyme: "No-one puts me in the ground/ before I am dead."

Halldór had been asked about this very topic earlier in the year in an interesting television interview by Matthías Jóhannessen. Halldór and Matthías were good friends, but Matthías came at things from a different direction and questioned Halldór more straightforwardly than most other Icelandic interviewers.

Halldór emphasized what he had said in *A Poet's Time*. When Matthías asked him whether he had betrayed his youthful ideals, he replied: "I hope so." He also said that his contemporaries in the Soviet Union had been betrayed by Stalin. He was happy with the interview and wrote to Hallberg a short time later:

There has been a great deal of discussion here about whether I am the one who has stiffened in my ways of thinking and stopped developing, or my readers. In a television interview here I said that it was only to be expected that readers my age, who had finished developing and were fully formed by forty (around 1942), found it difficult to follow the numerous changes that I underwent later ... This set in motion a discussion that is still going on here, about renewal versus stagnation.

At the same time that Halldór divorced himself publicly from his youthful ideals, he came closer to his origins in *A Parish Chronicle*, a story about the history of Christianity in Mosfellsdalur. As before, Jón Helgason read over the text. Halldór informed him in the spring that he had finished deleting half the novel and had run into trouble because he could not get the style right. At the same time he sent Jón the essay "Interesting Places in the Old Poetry", an investigation into Christian ideas that Halldór found in the Eddaic poems the "Hávamál" and the "Völuspá".

In April he went to Switzerland to attend to an unusual errand: "writing" a chapter of his novel on limestone for a gallery and publishing company called Erker. The idea came from Asger Jorn, who wanted to create a "book-work" of seven lithographs with texts by Halldór. Halldór wanted to use "The Bread of Life", a chapter from *A Parish Chronicle*. When Halldór and Jorn's work, *The Bread of Life*, was published two years later, it was accompanied by a vinyl recording of Halldór reading the chapter in Icelandic; a hundred and seventy-five copies were made, costing 1,650 Swiss francs each. A less expensive edition was made later. On the same trip Halldór visited Hamburg, where there was talk of filming *The Fish Can Sing*.

The director and writer Rolf Hädrich had been interested for some time in filming one of Halldór's books, and Jón Laxdal, an Icelandic actor living and working in Switzerland, introduced him to Halldór. Hädrich, who was familiar with Halldór's work from his school years, originally wanted to film *Atom Station*, but Halldór would not give him permission to do so. He said that he did not want people to use his ideas from that time to encode their own problems with the modern world: "Besides, I have heard for a fact that people are extremely content with their occupation forces in both parts of Germany." Walter Janka had first suggested having *Atom Station* filmed when he was working at the Babelsberg studio in East Berlin in 1963, after he was released from prison. Halldór refused, saying that *Atom Station* was concerned with political problems from a bygone era. East German television made another attempt in 1974, but Halldór refused again. It was clear that he did not want much made of this work during the 1960s and 1970s. So Hädrich chose *The Fish Can Sing* and contract negotiations were begun in the spring of 1970.

At the start of that summer Halldór was at home finishing *A Parish Chronicle*. On the night of 10 July Prime Minister Bjarni Benediktsson, his wife and their young grandson died when the Prime Minister's summer house at Þingvellir burned down. Halldór remembered him in a memorial article. In fact Halldór seemed to have made peace with many of his old opponents, like Jónas from Hrifla, who had in the early 1960s visited him at Gljúfrasteinn. For Halldór the Cold War was over.

*

The autumn of 1970 was generous to Halldór. The Actors' Union of Reykjavík premiered Sveinn Einarsson's adaptation of *Under the Glacier* on 12 September, 1970, the same day that *A Parish Chronicle* was published. Halldór trusted Sveinn most of all when it came to his plays and assisted him with the adaptation. The play was incredibly popular, not least due to the outstanding performance of Gísli Halldórsson in the role of Reverend Jón Prímus, and it ran for a record-breaking three years.

Halldór went to Denmark in September, where his daughter Guðný joined him for a time. Later in the autumn Auður came and they attended the first and only production that Halldór ever saw of one of his avant-garde works in a foreign country, when the Århus Theatre produced *The Pigeon Banquet*. Halldór and Auður attended a preview in Bergen on 17 October, and Auður was pleased even though the play was to be only middlingly successful. Six months later Halldór said in a letter that the rural Danish had not understood *The Pigeon Banquet* at all.

Halldór need not have feared for the reception of *A Parish Chronicle*, because the book received extremely good reviews, and was a bestseller that Christmas. It is an extremely modest work, as the title indicates, and when Matthías Jóhannessen told Halldór that he viewed it as a pearl Halldór hesitated, as if he had not taken the work as seriously himself. The book tells of the fate of a church that is torn down and then rebuilt centuries later. It is unique among Halldór's novels in that here he himself is the narrator.

Concerning his working methods while drafting the book, Halldór said:

Certain things in the narrative are more flexible in order to make it much more beautiful in form; the dates, the names and the places have been subject to some modification. I was looking backwards to the origin of the novel, to how it started as a chronicle or an imitation of a chronicle. The novel is edited history or the imitation of history. One pretends to speak of reality, but that is a reality ordered by the writer, a "correct" order, at least according to his best conscience.

Halldór plays around with the hagiographical form, but the book also contains elements from his earlier books such as *Salka Valka* and *Iceland's Bell*. But the story is told dispassionately and calmly, because its idea is simple: the people who fight for the church, preserve its relics or work for its restoration are not people of faith; they simply believe in themselves and their origins.

"The Bread of Life", the clever exemplum that is the most renowned part of the book, is about faith. The story tells of how Guðrún Jónsdóttir, an old working woman on the farm, is sent to fetch bread, but loses her way and is not found until four days later; despite having no other food, she had not touched the bread that she was entrusted to fetch. Guðrún spent many hours at Laxnes when Halldór was growing up, and in the book she is made to tell the annalist her story. He asks whether she would have cared whether she lived or died, as long as the bread was delivered: "'What one has been entrusted with, one has been entrusted with'" is her reply. "Question: 'But can't one ever be too faithful to one's employer?' The woman asked in return: 'Can one ever be faithful to anyone, if not to oneself?'"

Halldór was asked about the book's message in a Swedish interview in 1981, and he replied:

I am a storyteller. God protect me from saving the world. Guðrún was a magnificent woman. Went on to a heath and rambled around for days on end with the priest's bread – why didn't she just go home? This is an excellent story, which I had to tell. Guðrún as a saint – ha!

As before, he rebelled against the idea of reading simplistic messages into his work.

In *A Parish Chronicle* Halldór demonstrates what he admires in the Icelandic sagas of his ancestors. As he put it in an essay in 1962:

It may well be that the writers of the old sagas had been learned, talented men, if not philosophers and psychologists. But if so they avoided showing it like the plague. Vis-à-vis their topics, which in their enormity compelled them to write, they thought it taboo to stick into the sagas any other tricks than tell the story "correctly".

About Snorri Sturluson's *Heimskringla* he said: "Despite the appearance everywhere of the narrator, the story carries a learned irony beneath the surface." In many of his later books Halldór strives to attain more distance from the topic. He has divorced himself from the bulky narrator, placing more value on objectivity, letting the topic dictate the action. This results in an ironic distance, like in the story of the bread of life, one of the pearls of Halldór's oeuvre.

*

Halldór's changed political and ideological views are not only explained by his own development or by changes in international politics. Icelandic society had also changed. Problems that he had found compelling as a young man had vanished. The countryside had been electrified and the worst poverty had been eradicated; there was more of a bourgeois and cultural atmosphere in Reykjavík; writers and artists were being supported more and more. But this is not to say that Halldór was pleased with everything and everyone. The progress that he had previously landed, such as mechanization, technological advance and industrialization, he now viewed critically. At Christmas, 1970, he wrote his most famous article about these issues, "Warfare Against the Country". It could just as well have been written today.

Now Halldór was fighting against the consequences of industrialization, describing how Icelanders had been ruining their country for a thousand years. He discussed the effects of sheep farming and the tragic consequences of draining the moors, the country's respiratory system. And now, he argued, when the time had come to say stop, destructive powers were gaining greater strength than ever before from the construction of power plants in the service of heavy industry. Halldór pointed his spear not least at the National Energy Commission:

> Problems arise when the Commission, which deals with the disposition of power plants for some sort of prospective large industry, grants developers free hand to tramp around the country like a bull on turfless ground, and are even given the opportunity to destroy or lay to waste those special places which, because of their natural benefits, natural glory or historical significance, are not just dear to Icelandic hearts, but are also famed throughout the world as some of the most precious treasures on earth.

The places that Halldór wanted to protect, such as Laxárdalur and Þjórsárver, are still in danger, according to the Nature Conservation Association. In some ways, this article showed him to be far ahead of other conservationists, who were just beginning to make their voices heard. His article inspired varying responses, but as the journalist Illugi Jökulsson has shown, it was probably typical of Icelanders that the loudest protests came from those who felt that Halldór had spoken disrespectfully about sheep and their role in keeping down the undergrowth.

Now Halldór had cut his ties to technology, one of the stone babies. He had wanted to introduce modernity to Iceland, but, having done so, he wanted nothing to do with modern heavy industry and the destruction of the land.

*

When the ancient manuscripts were returned to Iceland on 21 April, 1971, Halldór was away from home. His spring trip that year took him through Germany, Switzerland and Italy. In Hamburg he met Hädrich and the directors of German television, N.D.R., to discuss filming *The Fish Can Sing*. They had grandiose plans that demanded a great deal of preparation, since very few people in Iceland had experience of film-making. From Hamburg Halldór went to Zurich, where Jón Laxdal put him in touch with theatre people and agents, having translated *The Pigeon Banquet* into German. As Halldór put it to Auður: "Jón plays a role as my servant and assistant in between playing Laertes in *Hamlet* in the evenings."

Halldór had actually made an excellent friend in the best-known writer in the country, Max Frisch, with whom he had attended C.O.M.E.S. meetings in Rome during the 1960s. C.O.M.E.S.' work was in decline; in 1970 it was gathering signatures in support of the Russian writer Solzhenitsyn and asked Halldór to sign the petition, which he did.

From Zurich Halldór went to Rome and visited old Dinesen, who was now ninety-eight years old, but graciously accepted Halldór's gifts of whisky, sweets and cigars; they sat over these refreshments and discussed the years between the wars, where the old woman's mind was now pretty much fixed. Halldór also turned his mind to the past, and it was during this period that he proposed to Auður the idea of pulling the stone up from Kaldakvísl and setting it down by the house. He also attended the Pope's Easter mass, but with only a moderate sense of piety. He told Auður of the huge crowd that had gathered, and that the Pope had addressed the congregation in a variety of languages:

> I felt, however, as if things really started to go too far when he started to speak Chinese and Arabic and to send his greetings to the nations that speak those languages. But the poor Israelis got nothing even though they contributed both the Saviour and the Holy Scripture, which I felt to be quite a gibe against the Jews (likely for having crucified the Saviour), although it would have cost the Pope nothing to say something, since all popes surely know Hebrew and it is in fact not just the Israelis' language, but the one and only language that God truly understands. The same went for one large golden butterfly that fluttered constantly over this throng of millions and could not find itself a place to land: it also got nothing, and even though this butterfly might perhaps have been the Holy Spirit in disguise, in my heart I forgave the poor Pope for not having known its language.

As so often in Rome, Halldór started a new novel, which also became his last novel: *God's Good Gifts* (1972).

As one might guess of such a well-dressed cosmopolitan, Halldór had no admiration for hippies, but he occasionally had sly fun with them. For instance, he says in the same letter to Auður that Italians on the Via Veneto were always beautiful ". . . elegant and charming . . . even in this new mode that makes people in other countries look like country bumpkins or bushmen". That spring Guðný asked him to buy her the double album of *Jesus Christ Superstar* on his trip abroad. The riots over the Sonning Prize had faded into the distance, and Halldór was calm about the changing times.

He had taken part in too many battles to support the new generation's struggle against the Vietnam War in any way that that generation would have wanted. On 18 March, 1971, an article by him was published in the *New York Times*, "Mankilling is the King's Game", in which his antipathy to war is made plain, and he expresses his disgust with all attempts to justify war. But the article is written from the viewpoint that war has accompanied human endeavour from the beginning, just like leprosy, and is in fact a kind of leprosy of the human spirit. The article has an undeniable tone of erudite irony.

It was the editor of the *New York Times*, Harrison Salisbury, who got Halldór to write the article, and he asked him for others in the following years. At the start of 1973 he wrote another one, "Auburn and Pink-Lilac Men: An Epitaph for the Vietnam War", in which his viewpoint was the same:

> The Indochina affair was just an ordinary mankilling game, like so many other wars, and did not have significance beyond showing that man is the beast that enjoys killing its own kin.

He wrote as one who had lost faith in the limitless victories of the good, as he put it later in an obituary for Tómas Guðmundsson.

Halldór was still loyal to the cause of conservation, however. In the summer of 1971 he supported those who wanted to protect the nineteenth-century block of houses in the centre of Reykjavík known as the Bernhöftstorfan:

> When people demand that these unpretentious houses of memories at Bernhöftstorfan be torn down simply because they are dilapidated, they do not have sufficient reason. These old houses are as pristine as if they had been built yesterday. On the other hand it is true that, as far as their mainte-nance goes, the same kind of political game has been played as when country girls let their teeth decay and grimace so that they can go south and buy false ones.

These protests inspired the foundation of an organization for the conservation of these houses.

The same cannot be said of another conflict two years later, when Halldór declared his support for the fight against the construction of new offices for the Central Bank at Arnarhóll. An open-air meeting was held on 10 September, 1973, in which addresses from Halldór and his old friends Gunnar Gunnarsson and Tómas Guðmundsson were given. Halldór said:

> I take part in the protests of the people of Iceland against the irresponsible vainglory of wasting public funds on the construction of a grotesque, conceited house for financial insecurity and inflation.

In this case protesters did not achieve the results they wanted.

A Swiss company, Bucher, had decided to publish Halldór's work in German, but there was a kind of sluggishness afoot in Scandinavia, although his books were still being published there. Halldór thought that things looked rather banal in Iceland, "where our great fisheries-romantic Guðmundur Hagalín has become the literary voice of the university". Halldór had never been quite happy with that institution and sometimes felt himself completely alone when writing about the relationship of Old Icelandic literature to the Middle Ages, despite his friendship with important scholars in the field. In the autumn of 1971 he published a collection of essays about the old literature and other topics, called *Overshadowed Places*. The name was taken from Jón Guðmundsson the Learned, a seventeenth-century scholar, who spoke of "hidden places and overshadowed valleys".

The following spring Halldór was reconciled to the University of Iceland, when he was made an honorary doctor on the occasion of his seventieth birthday. Halldór mentioned in his speech that this was the first time that his and the university's paths had crossed. Now all the battles had ceased in Halldór's struggle for recognition.

Icelanders celebrated the writer's seventieth birthday in various ways that spring. The National Theatre premiered Baldvin Halldórsson's adaptation of *Independent People* on its anniversary, the Reykjavík Theatre Company produced Sveinn Einarsson and Þorsteinn Gunnarsson's adaptation of *Atom Station* a month earlier, and *The Chimney Play* was produced by the Akureyri Theatre Company. The book of interviews with Halldór by Matthías Jóhannessen, *Conversations Through the Ages*, was published, and Halldór was made an honorary citizen of Mosfell parish.

Halldór was interested in the theatrical productions, attending, for example, the first reading of *Independent People*. The production had a social-realist emphasis, slightly contrary to the prevailing mood; a complete farm was constructed on stage. Although some critics did not like the look of it, the production was popular, as was *Atom Station* and other adaptations of Halldór's novels. Many saw a chance to renew their acquaintance with the novels, since the plays seemed to offer scenes from the books, spiced with words that were well known throughout the country, and it was entertaining to hear much-loved actors pronounce them.

Many things from the past were brought to Halldór's attention during those birthday weeks, some of which he had doubtless already forgotten. For example, an unusual question arose, which Auður relayed to him in a letter:

> A man by the name of Kristján Einarsson called here from the Government Tax Bureau to ask about the bank book of a fund that you established in 1940, called the Fund for the Protection of the Spiritual Freedom of Icelandic Writers. He said that he had found out that it was supposed to be kept with the General Fund of Iceland, but no-one knew about it there.

Now this fund was lost, along with the cause that it was meant to have served. But the government assessors were still doing their jobs, thirty years on.

*

Halldór was pleased with the respect he was shown in his homeland on the occasion of his birthday. But he was happier still when filming commenced in the summer for the television adaptation of *The Fish Can Sing*, under the direction of Rolf Hädrich. Halldór and Hädrich had got on well, discussing *The Fish Can Sing* over many cigars; Hädrich himself wrote the script.

The Fish Can Sing was the largest film project that had ever been undertaken in Iceland. Besides German television, all the Scandinavian television stations took part, and it fell to Icelandic television to oversee the production. The set designer Björn G. Björnsson said that they used approximately twenty locations to achieve the feel of Reykjavík at the start of the twentieth century. They had to build a turf farm by a little pond in the south, and an entire street in the north of Reykjavík. Shooting commenced in June and continued well into the autumn, but the weather gods took over from the director; it rained endlessly, scenery blew away, and many other related problems arose.

Jón Laxdal played Garðar Hólm, and an excellent group of Icelandic actors played the other roles. First among equals was Þorsteinn Ö. Stephensen, who played Björn from Brekkukot, and Sveinn Einarsson was assistant director to Hädrich. Halldór, who felt very positive about the production, played a supporting role in the film, with remarkable intensity, according to Björn. And Halldór lent the crew props, such as the eighteenth-century clock made in Edinburgh, and inscribed with the word "eternity". Perhaps Halldór recalled the plans being made in the summer of 1928 in Hollywood, when he had hoped to be able to go with Greta Garbo to Iceland to film *Salka Valka*. It is certain that his interest in movies, which had been very little for a long time, was reawakened. His daughter Guðný was given some work on the production and later made film her career. Film people were everywhere at Gljúfrasteinn, said Auður: "We were like a hotel; sometimes the costume department stayed here."

Halldór published *God's Good Gifts* that November. The book enjoyed outstanding reviews in the Icelandic papers, and was said to have sold in record numbers that Christmas. The reviews emphasized the book's humour, with Ólafur Jónsson saying that it had been a long time since he had laughed so much reading a book. The underlying story was the invasion of modernity seen from the viewpoint of the herring trade, and it allowed its writer to take potshots at many different aspects of Icelandic society. In a short epilogue Halldór wrote:

The book is a blend of various forms of writing, such as memoir, polemic, poetry, history, short story, historiography etc., etc.; but beyond all this it is a novel, fiction both in form and content. In a foreign language this form would most likely be called an essay-novel.

But there is a serious tone to the book in the way that Halldór brings together numerous themes from his earlier works. The herring dealer, Iceland's Bersi, has elements of previous well-to-do characters, but he awakens more sympathy, not only because the writer's views have become milder and less political, but also because Bersi has a daughter whom he loves more than anything else and whom he loses. Her luckless life becomes a reminder of the unrealistic life of Bersi in profiteering and speculation. The sorrowful connection between father and daughter appears in Halldór's books several times in a forty-year period, perhaps reflecting the fact that he had missed out on the childhood of his own daughters.

Iceland's Bersi searches for the one true note on the fiddle, the same note that is spoken of in *The Fish Can Sing*. It does not matter what he tries, he cannot find it any more than anyone else can who has given in to the power of commercialism. The home of the arts, as before, is on the other side of the real world, inaccessible to those who compromise.

In 1973 Matthías Jóhannessen wrote a detailed article about *God's Good Gifts*, based among other things on his conversations with Halldór. Halldór added all sorts of observations, comments and corrections to it, which showed how much he wanted the book to be understood.

As the article makes clear, some aspects of the book are based in reality, others are inventions, and yet others are somewhere in between. For example, the description of the meeting between the narrator and Iceland's Bersi is based on Halldór's having met the herring dealer Óskar Halldórsson at the Hotel Continental in Copenhagen in the autumn of 1919, and then again in 1920. Much of their interaction was as it is conveyed in the novel, as Halldór told Matthías:

> . . . Óskar never called me by name, as in the novel. . . . He called me "boy" and "friend", as in the novel, and when we said goodbye he said: "Friends for life," as in the novel. I think that he never read any book by me, and most probably thought that I was a fool . . . but he did like me.

On the other hand, much in the description of Iceland's Bersi is the writer's invention, such as his interaction with his daughter Bergrún. And another old friend filled out the character: the Los Angeles estate agent Haldor Haldorson.

Halldór thus made use in *God's Good Gifts* of various things he had seen and heard, just as he did in *A Parish Chronicle*. In that sense the book is a clear antecedent of the autobiographical books he started to write several years later. It was natural that a larger-than-life personality like Óskar would tempt Halldór as material. But he was also trying to draw an image of a speculator, a gambler. As he put it to Matthías:

> Those who understand the psychology of such people know that everything is vanity to them except for risk; they have a kind of nervousness in the pits of their stomachs that causes them to laugh at all normal human life. On the other hand such men are not just open-handed, they pour out their hearts. They don't keep anything up their sleeves. It's never a wine bottle to them, it's a case of whisky. On their part generosity is just as limitless as their gambling addiction. Perhaps no man is more of an individualist-anarchist than a gambler, and that is very clear to Bersi Hjálmarsson himself, because no matter what group he is in he never lets the opportunity go by to remind the others that he is the only anarchist there.

This is the core of the character description of Iceland's Bersi, and in some ways Halldór's interpretation of the history of the Icelandic nation in the twentieth century: speculation has driven it forward.

*

Halldór was abroad when *God's Good Gifts* was published. He wanted to spend the winter in Europe, and Auður and Guðný went with him, finding pleasant accommodation in a little village, Teufen, close to St Gallen in Switzerland. It was a calm winter, according to Auður. They were in contact with the directors of the Galerie Erker and Halldór read there at the start of December on the occasion of the publication of *The Bread of Life*. Among the guests, most of whom were artists, was Asger Jorn, who sat with his young German wife next to Halldór and Auður at the dinner and discussed many plans with his Icelandic friend. (Sadly Jorn died of cancer not long afterwards.)

Several days later Halldór wrote to Jón Helgason and described the magnificent library in St Gallen, adding:

> I sometimes think how pleasant it would be for a medievalist and Germanist from the north to come here and acquaint himself with this medieval school, which has an unbroken history in education, not to mention book production and art, since the sixth century.

And if this was not enough, Halldór added that the area was a "sausage paradise": throughout his life Halldór had a weakness for German food.

In February Halldór and Auður went to Hamburg and attended the premiere of *The Fish Can Sing*. Halldór was very proud of the film and wrote to Hädrich at Christmas:

It made me very happy to have been able to be present when this cinematic work was being put together little by little, and to have, although only indirectly, taken part in its coming into being.

The film, which was in two parts, received good reviews in both Germany and Scandinavia and was shown on television throughout Europe. As a film it can be considered somewhat old-fashioned, "filmed literature", perhaps. But it has, like the book, a nostalgic air. It was well received in Iceland.

The Field at Home

It is easy for the latecomer to invent the bang when others have already invented the gunpowder.

Halldór Laxness, The Greek Year

In the 1970s Halldór said farewell to many of his friends, most of whom were older than he was. Vilmundur Jónsson died in 1972, as did Jóhannes from Katlar, and Kristinn E. Andrésson died the following year. Halldór wrote a memorial piece about Kristinn, one of those men who never lost faith in the Soviet Union. The piece was also about men who never lost sight of their youthful ideals:

But men of faith, who heeded the call from such an unfathomable direction as the day and age, they are the ones that endured. For them a change of heart was not something done by luck or mistake, much less by the law of the conveyor belt; instead for them time stands still, in a certain sense, from the moment of their awakening, and illuminates the man within with the same strength until their final moment; such a man was Kristinn Andrésson. Only true men of faith complete works as he did.

Halldór had lost his faith, but he respected Kristinn, just as he respected the Catholic monks who devoted their lives to their faith.

Halldór wrote energetically throughout the 1970s. Besides the autobiographical novels, he composed numerous essays, the majority of which were dedicated to early Icelandic literature, but he also wrote many obituaries. His writing was thus bound to the past, although his style was often fresh and modern. He kept on reading, although it changed him very little. He was often amused by what he read, not least when it confirmed what he already felt. Then he would perhaps send a card, as he did to Matthías Jóhannessen, who had sent him a book of poetry:

Heartfelt thanks for the soul-stirring poems that achieve their goals. Your poems made me search for frames of reference in the English tradition rather than the French or German, but never reminded me of Scandinavia, luckily. It is a matter of life and death not to write or compose like the Scandinavians, who did not gain literature until the nineteenth century.

Halldór did not spend all his spare time reading, no more inclined to read in the evenings than a kindergarten teacher would be to look after children after work, as he sometimes put it. He enjoyed some of the books that his daughter Sigríður gave him, such as the stories of Isaac Bashevis Singer, and he was delighted when this Yiddish writer received the Nobel Prize in 1978. He also read history, ancient literature, social science and biology.

Halldór remained curious about young Icelandic writers and followed their progress in the papers and on the radio. Sigríður remembers having been with him in downtown Reykjavík in the early 1970s when they met the poet and rock-singer Megas. Halldór nodded his head to him and said to Sigríður afterwards: "This man will become one of the greatest Icelandic poets." But he often found the novels of new writers too light and even simply not long enough.

Halldór still enjoyed finding good writers in unusual places. He wrote the preface to a collection of stories by Kjartan Júlíusson, a farmer at Upper Skáldsstaðir in Eyjafjörður, entitled *Majestic Peaks on Autumn Nights* (1978). Kjartan lived in such an isolated place and the farm was so old and dilapidated that foreign guests who went to visit it with Halldór in the early 1970s asked Auður afterwards "Was Kjartan just acting?" . . . "Did he really live there?"

In the 1970s Halldór still kept a strict daily schedule. He got up around nine and took plenty of time to read the papers, then turned to his work, often standing at his desk for three or four hours; then it was time for a walk, preferably with his dog Lubbi, and then a good lunch. After lunch it was business in town, and the evenings were often spent peacefully at home. Halldór was jealous of his peace and quiet, whether for writing or for listening to the news. Writing still took priority, and he could sometimes be difficult to be around.

"Where is Auður?" he asked his daughter Sigríður once. "She went out to the clothesline." "Oh, always outside enjoying herself." His mood could change quickly, delighted as he was by diversion, and then he would be nothing but charming.

Jón Gunnar Ottósson, Halldór's son-in-law for almost twenty years, recalled that the writer enjoyed taking car trips around the countryside. Then he was often talkative and relaxed and always ready to stop for a hot dog just like everyone else. Context was everything. He could arrive at a hotel out in the countryside and chastise the waiters because no-one knew how to lay the table or serve food in a civilized way, but if he came to a farm where he was served overcooked meat and lukewarm milk he would beam with happiness and appreciation.

It was not always easy for such a sensitive person to be a public figure. He was still a favourite among impersonators and comedians, who mimicked his remarks, pronunciation and phrasing. Strangers would be overfamilar with him at a time when he was losing interest in meeting new people. Early in the 1980s he told the writer of this book that such peculiar people were visiting him that he could open a zoo outside the house. Many old friends died: Þórbergur Þórðarson and Guðmundur Böðvarsson in 1974, and Gunnar Gunnarsson a year later. Halldór gave no outward sign of how such things affected him.

Halldór sometimes reacted with determined formality and remoteness, guarding his feelings, and for the longest time he spoke very little of his private life. He had to play the role of poet laureate for a small nation, some part of which he had sought himself, but when it came down to it he was bored by unneccesary ceremoniousness, and self-importance was poison to him. His doubts about politicians had increased, if anything, and he did not spend time with many of the younger ones.

Sometimes – not least when cultural issues were at stake – he accepted invitations to deliver public speeches, such as at the Independence Day celebrations on 28 July, 1974, when he said that literature had always been the centre of gravity in the nation's life:

> Educated men say that no people have been, to their knowledge, as wrapped up in the art of the word from the start as the inhabitants of this country. One might say that both learned and laymen, regardless of mental capacity or finances, have been united in this, century after century . . .

But things had changed: "A hundred years ago we lived in the century of patriotic poems, now we live in the century of the car."

Halldór continued to go abroad in the spring and the autumn, and sometimes it was difficult for Auður when she did not go with him. For instance, she wrote to him at the start of April, 1974:

> Now I have heard your voice, dear, and when I do I am so floatingly light and happy, because I always find things so dull for the most part when you are

gone, and everything is so empty. On the other hand I get a very large amount of work done when I am alone like this and independent.

After their daughters left home, Auður found it rather boring to be alone at Gljúfrasteinn, but by then Halldór's trips had started to dwindle.

He had lost all desire to rush around pursuing his publishers and promoting himself. He was very helpful when people showed interest in his work, and would still help others to find good translators or appropriate publishers. But he did not waste any time making pointless trips. As he wrote to Peter Hallberg, having been invited to lecture in America:

> I know for a fact that in every club or university ten to fifteen people will turn up, only to start horrific debates about the old sagas or speak to me about Iceland as a kind of freak country, as it is in the eyes of the Americans. I made a living giving such lectures in California when I was a boy, and it is unthinkable to repeat that joke in old age. As a writer I am entirely forgotten in America.

In fact, Germany apart, Halldór has not been promoted as vigorously anywhere in the last few years as in America.

However, it was very important for Halldór to go to Scandinavia, and he spent some time in Copenhagen with his friend Jón and even some hours at the Arnamagnæan Institute writing. While there he received news that his oldest daughter María had lost her husband Kolbeinn. He had died suddenly as they sat in a clearing at Þingvellir, having stopped at Gljúfrasteinn along the way. Halldór wrote María a comforting letter, referring neither to faith nor to eternal life:

> I am reminded of your great-grandmother, Guðný Klængsdóttir, who lost five of her children and her husband in a very short time, and remained behind alone with a little girl by her side, my mother Sigríður and your grandmother, whom you knew well . . . I know how worthwhile it is to gain strength from old people, who came before us and lived with great constrictions and often painful sorrow, more than we, but never let themselves be discouraged.

Halldór's mind was with these old people in the later part of the 1970s; he wrote about them and about his youth in four autobiographical works: *In the Fields of Home, When I was Young, The Saga of the Seven Masters* and *The Greek Year. In the Fields of Home* covers the period from Halldór's earliest memories to when he went to Reykjavík as a thirteen-year-old; *The Saga of the Seven Masters* covers the years 1915–9;

When I was Young tells of Halldór's first winter in Denmark; and *The Greek Year* recounts his homecoming and his time spent teaching in Dilksnes. On the title pages of the second editions Halldór inserted a phrase stating that these were four linked stories in the form of an essay-novel. It made sense to speak of the books as fiction: although most of the characters are given their real names, Halldór wanted to take some liberties – and did so, saying that it would not be pleasant to listen to the birds chirping if they were always chirping the truth.

In an interview published in Sweden in 1981 Halldór said that he had become stronger after having written himself through the "crisis of the novel" with *Under the Glacier*, and had subsequently composed many novels, all in the first person. The memoirs are thus novels about how his consciousness came into being, unlike *A Poet's Time*, which is a writer's reckoning (the title of the Danish edition). There is a kind of cloudlessness to these books: the Taoist in them is the narrator himself.

In his story about Temuchin, his first "Taoist" work, when the nomad has conquered the world and become the most powerful king that ever existed, he turns round and goes home to the northern pine slopes, "where the water in the rivers is cold and clear and the sound of their streams happy like little bells". So it is with Halldór. Having told half the world his stories and having become the greatest Icelandic storyteller since the days of Snorri, he turns back to the fields of home, where he finds the "perfectly clear brook and the fragrance of reed". Though his autobiographical books sometimes have an air of sorrow, their often humorous tone reflects an inner peace. The narratives are built from many small images; Erik Sønderholm, Halldór's Danish translator and author of a book about him, likened them to a Byzantine icon: there are numerous characters, each of whom appears as a perfect painting and seems to be the main character when viewed in proximity, but as soon as some distance is placed between viewer and subject, the complete image comes into focus. This is the image of how the writer came into being; a story about the power that drove him to write, about the books he read and how the writing obsession took over little by little. The last book concludes when the narrator is twenty, when it has become clear that he will pursue a career as a writer. Autobiographies are always dramatic up until the point at which the writer discovers himself; afterwards their value is more cultural-historical than anything else.

But, as Halldór wrote in *When I was Young*, "No-one can tell the story of himself . . . it always becomes more nonsensical the more one tries to be truthful." These books can thus be considered risky sources; he highlights facts according to how

they suit his purpose. One example will suffice: in *The Greek Year* he includes a
letter from Þórður Sigtryggsson, which the narrator says that he received on his
twentieth birthday. The young writer takes this letter as an honour and an encouragement. But the letter was actually sent to Halldór forty years later, on his sixtieth
birthday.

In these books Halldór writes a great deal about the methods of the storyteller.
Thus he states in *The Greek Year*: "A well-written sentence 'sits' like a flower that
grows in earth: it fits. It is easy for the latecomer to invent the bang when others
have already invented the gunpowder." In another place he states that writing is like
ballet: there must be no visible effort; everything must come naturally. Main topics
should appear through secondary details; he tells the story of the writer's coming
into being through numerous small images of other people. He stops short when
it comes to the largest questions – love, death – because: "The art of writing is
contained in being silent about many things". His parents are described with great
tact and elegant nuance, and the death of his father is followed by the comment:
"At one point both history and fiction fall silent." Observations such as this are a
direct continuation of his ideas about the craft at the start of the 1960s.

In *When I was Young* Halldór recounts an Eastern story about a master in a
bamboo grove who sends his disciple down to a river to fetch a jug of water. At
the river the disciple sees a young girl combing her hair, falls in love, builds a hut
with her, and has a family. They live through war and all sorts of other tragedies;
everything falls apart and is lost, and in the end the disciple is alone, empty-handed
and destitute. He remembers his master and goes to find him: "The master looked
at him for a moment . . . and said: 'Friend, where is the water that I asked you to
fetch?'"

In his autobiographical novels Halldór has turned back to the Tao. He participated energetically in the wars of his times, but did not forget the fragrance of reed
and the clear spring of fiction.

*

The late 1970s were a time for reflection and also a time Halldór used to revisit
old friendships, whether repaying Ísleifur Sigurjónsson for the trip to Hälsingborg
of old or visiting Guðmundur Hagalín in Borgarfjörður while writing *The Saga of
the Seven Masters*. In the summer of 1976 Icelandic National Radio produced six
programmes in which he discussed his life with different interviewers, using the
same broad strokes he used in many interviews later on. Naturally, he embellished
a good deal and chose to forget certain things, but he also provided a good deal
of curious information. He did not want to speak about his political views of the

1930s, and, in conversation with his old friend, Jakob Benediktsson, barely remembered *The Russian Adventure*.

In the last interview, conducted by Helga Kress, he was asked about his faith. Halldór said that he was interested in many different religions: when he was young he had read Annie Besant and Krishnamurti, but they had no staying power. He also said that he had been a Catholic for two years: "But I do not profess anything other than what my little wisdom has taught me." And if he were offered a new universal theory, he would respectfully decline.

Peter Hassenstein, who had been Hädrich's cameraman for *The Fish Can Sing*, produced an excellent programme about Halldór in the spring of 1980 for N.D.R., German television. Hassenstein gave himself plenty of time for the production, and he and his crew enjoyed Auður's hospitality. In the interview Halldór eagerly discussed the radical views of his youthful years:

> I was devoted to all of it – religion as well – you name it I was devoted to it and I took part in all the "isms". But what is that now? A drawing on the wall, material for my novels.

All of the ideals that were higher than men had paled, but his writing remained. When one looks at Halldór's final years it sometimes seems as if they are one continuous celebration, either for his birthday or for a particular work, although he had never been much for such celebrations. In the spring of 1977 his seventy-fifth birthday was celebrated in various ways, and that year he received an honorary doctorate from Edinburgh University.

But Halldór had not become entirely tame. For example, he enjoyed taking part in a new spelling war – no wars have been of such great interest to the Icelanders since the Age of the Sturlungs. The occasion arose when Magnús Torfi Ólafsson, Education Minister for the leftist government of 1971–4, had the letter "z" removed from standard Icelandic spelling. There was a huge debate at the Alþingi, and the majority of M.P.s were opposed, but the Minister held his ground. One of those who wanted to keep the "z" was Sverrir Hermannsson, and on 8 May, 1974, he delivered the longest speech that has ever been delivered at the Alþingi, lasting for five hours; most of it centred on the laws governing elementary school, but Sverrir was also concerned about the letter "z".

This case was still being argued when a new government took over and Vihjálmur Hjálmarsson was appointed Education Minister. Halldór joined the battle with an article, "The New Z-Man Adventure", comparing the debates at the Alþingi with Jónas from Hrifla's persecutions in 1941, when matters concerning the life and death of the nation in the midst of a world war were forced to give way to this psychosis, as he called it. Halldór covered wide ground in his article, scoffing, for example, at the Icelandic ban on beer that he always thought ridiculous, and especially and particularly at the rationale for keeping the "z": that it would help Icelandic children to understand the origins of words:

> Might I be allowed to ask, what the hell does Sverrir Hermannsson care about the origins of words? And even if he did, why then only those words in which it is possible to put a "z"? Etymology is actually a specific scientific field, as everyone knows, and no-one with his wits about him would imagine pushing such a thing in elementary school; it would more likely render this generation of Icelanders speechless ... Might I ask the highly respected first self-appointed Z-scholar and etymologist Sverrir Hermannsson: What is the origin of the word "dog" or "cat"? And how and whence is a word like "zed" formed? And what is the original form of the word "idiot"? And beyond all else, who would be improved if he knew these things?

At the end of the article Halldór suggests that Icelanders should stop writing "y", as he himself tried doing fifty years earlier. The article shows that in the midst of all the ceremony Halldór sometimes needed to step out of his assigned role and tease people.

In the summer of 1979 Rolf Hädrich started work on a version of a new television series based on *Paradise Reclaimed*. It was a huge production and the filming took place in Copenhagen, Iceland and Utah, where an entire set had been built for the town of Spanish Forks. Icelandic actors took the most important roles. Halldór did not participate, yet he and his son Einar took a car trip to a remote part of eastern Iceland to watch the shooting. En route Halldór was in high spirits and talked about everything under the sun. When he took trips with his close relatives he did not need to engage in role-playing, and most often he was light-hearted. *Paradise Reclaimed* was premiered in December, 1980.

Quite a few films were made from Halldór's novels during those years. Baldvin Halldórson had directed a film based on the short story "Jón of Breadhouses" in 1969, and in 1975 Helgi Skúlason made a television film based on "Hunting Trip in the Wilderness". Hrafn Gunnlaugsson made a short film adaptation of the short story "Lily" in 1978, and also directed the television production of *The Silver Moon*, which premiered at Christmas, 1978. That drama was controversial, since it took liberties with Halldór's text. Concerning this, Halldór said in an interview several years later:

There is no ill-will between me and Hrafn. He is an extremely energetic man. In *The Silver Moon* he was so enthusiastic that he thought the play was written by him. That can happen to anyone.

Halldór finally permitted the filming of *Atom Station* in 1984. The director was Þorsteinn Jónsson and the producer was the film studio Óðinn; the production was the largest Icelandic one ever. Halldór was pleased with the result, but of all the film versions of his novels he thought *The Fish Can Sing* was the best.

In 1989, Guðný Halldórsdóttir's film adaptation of *Under the Glacier* was premiered, and although Halldór had become somewhat frail, he enjoyed the film and spoke a great deal to his daughter about it, saying that much of it could be understood as miraculous and completely realistic at one and the same time.

On Halldór's eightieth birthday there was once again a great deal of celebration. He received an honorary doctorate from the University of Tübingen, the Theatre Company of Reykjavík performed *Salka Valka*, the people of Mosfell honoured him, and a large ceremony was held at Hotel Saga.

State television produced three programmes about the eighty-year-old Halldór to which his contemporaries made contributions, men such as Jón Helgason and Kristján Albertsson, who does a fine job of describing *The Great Weaver from Kashmir* and states that Icelandic prose took a half-century leap forward with the book. The interviews with Halldór are curious: he is more relaxed than in the programmes made six years earlier, almost nonchalant. But sometimes his memory fails him, as when he says that he met Brecht as a young man in Denmark – the two actually only met once, in 1955. But Halldór says a lot about his work, including how he considered his curiosity to have helped him in his writing.

Halldór had reached the age when he was able to say what he felt, and reporters were sometimes made fun of. The Finnish reporter Taisto Jalamo, who interviewed him for *Svenska dagbladet* in the summer of 1984, said that Halldór started by expressing his disappointment with the Nobel Prize. It was no measure of the quality of literature, he said: "The gentlemen in Stockholm drag forward all sorts of writers of whom no-one has heard, or else they grant the prize to some 'pocket-philosopher' like William Golding." And when asked about the Norwegian writer Axel Sandemose, he said, after first saying "What?" and asking whether he was a Norwegian:

Yes, but I have always been afraid of alcoholics, in the same way that some people are afraid of dogs. And I have never seen that man sober. Besides that, I think he is too highly regarded as a writer.

During the 1980s, he permitted the republication of *The Russian Adventure* and *Going East*. On the other hand, he did not by any means wish to take part in new debates about old conflicts. For example, a young part-time reporter, Jakob F. Ásgeirsson, published an essay in *Morgunblaðið* on 11 July, 1982, under the title "Atom Station and the Keflavík Agreement". The essay was written from the point of view of a right-winger – Jakob felt that Halldór's political message had prevented *Atom Station* from achieving artistic unity – but it was neither fanatical nor ill-willed.

Halldór reacted gruffly. He felt that *Morgunblaðið* was stirring up old conflicts. The editorial board was informed, and editor Styrmir Gunnarsson decided to go up to Gljúfrasteinn to explain to Halldór that this piece by a young right-winger was not any sort of attack. Halldór chastised him for two hours, in a way that Styrmir said he had never experienced before. He was saved when he brought up his connection with the translator Magnús Ásgeirsson, who was from Borgar-fjörður, like Halldór's father's family. The writer changed his tone immediately and was nothing but charming. The matter of Jakob's essay was forgotten.

This story is not just evidence of Halldór's sensitivity, but of his temper. He could become angry very quickly, sometimes for little reason, and he could give an earful to those whom he felt deserved it, even when he was otherwise quite charming. These mood swings became more common with age, probably marked by his illness.

In the spring of 1983 he and Auður went to Copenhagen, where Halldór gave a reading to the Icelandic Students' Union for the first time since he had been given the Sonning Prize. That same year he wrote an obituary of his friend Tómas Guðmundsson, discussing how they had grown up as romantics and read each other's poetry. He also wrote about the distance that had opened up between them during the Cold War, when best friends had become strangers: "The worm that gnaws everything living down to the root, and competes to make the continents into desert, crept into the lives of us poets."

Halldór's last public reading was in 1984. In May he went with his son Einar to Akureyri and read for a group of senior citizens. He was in good spirits on the long drive north. Later in the summer he read from the opening of *Iceland's Bell* for the Þingvellir Trip of the Socialist People's Alliance, which was taken on the fortieth anniversary of the Republic. It was a long time since he had given a reading to a political group.

That year Halldór's close friend and publisher, Ragnar Jónsson from Smári, died. Halldór had often written about him, as he said in a short obituary:

There are not many people who have written about Ragnar from Smári more often than I – sometimes entire comic essays – or who have had substantial reason to do so. Now that he is dead I am speechless. A special thread in my life has been cut.

The obituary appeared in Halldór's final essay collection, *And the Years Pass By* (1984), which contained new articles and letters as well as older material. The same year saw the publication of Auður's memoirs, *At Gljúfrasteinn*, transcribed by Edda Andrésdóttir. Auður put a great deal of work into the book and was extremely busy that autumn. She had not expected Halldór to produce another collection of essays, and of course she had to type them; in that sense it was a two-book Christmas for her. *At Gljúfrasteinn* was the year's bestselling book; the public of course was thrilled to be invited through the doors of the most famous home in the country.

When Ragnar Jónsson died, his heirs decided to sell Helgafell. The buyer was Ólafur Ragnarsson, who just a short time earlier had founded Vaka, who published Auður's book. Ólafur took over the management of Helgafell in 1985 and made great strides in publishing Halldór's books in the following years. He even cut the ties with Halldór's Dutch agent, who had done little for him since the 1960s, and Licht and Licht took over his foreign rights.

Ólafur Ragnarsson is without a doubt the man who knew Halldór best in his old age outside his own family. When Ólafur took over Helgafell plans had been made to reissue *Going East*, but this was not the best choice to relaunch his collected works. A year later Ólafur published Halldór's articles from the 1920s under the title *On the Cultural Situation*. In the spring of 1987, when Halldór was eighty-five, an edition of *The Bread of Life* was published, with illustrations by Snorri Sveinn Friðriksson, and in the autumn Halldór's monastery diary came out under the title *Days with Monks*. The diary was published with a detailed introduction, the last thing that Halldór wrote.

Ólafur went nearly every week to Gljúfrasteinn. In the first year of their collaboration Halldór was still interested in publishing and in his book sales in Iceland and abroad, and always asked Ólafur: "What is the news from the book publishing world?" A man who had fought so firmly for the promotion of his books for nearly sixty years could surely be expected to take an interest in them while his health lasted.

Vaka-Helgafell, together with a literary society, sponsored a conference on Halldór's work in 1987, which he himself attended. Two years earlier he had written to Peter Hallberg for the last time to thank him for his work, while also looking back over his own career:

After researching my writing various good men have written essays and books, and I am appreciative of such men for often squandering on me more headaches and inspiration than I deserve. I have always been wary of having an influence on the work, methods and viewpoints of literary critics, since I myself am peculiarly blind to my own books, am at least unable to explain them otherwise than as they appear to me. Here in Iceland these books were actually considered among the most disgraceful handiwork, and the mob, supported by recognized cultural leaders, officials and farmers, remained in a fighting mood against me because of this vulgarity until I reached the age of seventy. Iceland was the one country that worked strongly against me on a political basis in connection with the Nobel Prize, said those in the know in Sweden . . . On the other hand I also had many good friends and well-wishers who could never understand that I was more of a simpleton or evil-doer than normal. But I am certain that you know this story as well as I, or even better. I myself have never borne animosity towards a man even when he considered me a poor writer; I have even forgiven them, though they are poor writers themselves . . .

My basic views concerning "the appearances of things" are strangely objective and not easy to explain, even if one had already found oneself a seat in heaven. I have no printable theory at my fingertips that is close to metaphysics. But perhaps we can meet, if I live as long as the summer, and establish a two-man universal congress.

The story here is not unlike the one in *An Essay on Icelanders*, but the tone is gentler. It is easy to visualize them now at their two-man universal congress, Halldór and Hallberg, speaking of the appearances of things.

In the Sunshine of Forgetfulness

When I die, I want to hear music.
Halldór Laxness, When I Left Home

It cannot be said with certainty what afflicted Halldór in the final decade of his life; many of the symptoms were the same as those of Alzheimer's disease, others were just down to old age. His closest family think that the brain damage, if that's what it was, may have taken hold earlier. For instance, Halldór sometimes experienced bouts of anger for little reason, which others would try to appease. For a long time it was not easy to distinguish slight derangement and forgetfulness from the idiosyncratic behaviour that Halldór had cultivated for a long time. If he suddenly asked, as in the Swedish interview: "William Heinesen, what has he written again?" was he asking in earnestness or teasing the interviewer, who was a great fan of the Faroese storyteller?

He enjoyed such games, as the present author became aware of in a long conversation with him at Christmas, 1983. And he said a lot about his fellow-writers that can be interpreted at will: "He was originally a printer, Jón Trausti, so he more or less approached literature from that direction, right?" or: "What was his name again, that bad painter who was spokesman for the surrealists – Breton?" But then he added serious observations, such as when he said that now that everyone wrote about sex it was impossible to write about it with the same explosive power as Weininger had in his youth.

Well into the 1980s Halldór had ready responses and reactions that saved him in numerous interviews. As late as 1989 he replied smoothly to questions put to him by the Icelandic press on the seventieth anniversary of his becoming a writer.

Halldór's daughters and their husbands built their houses either side of Gljúfrasteinn, and he and Auður spent many good moments with them and the grandchildren; he was loving and caring, although he did not spend much time holding the children. A hand to a hand, a kiss on the forehead, those were his ways of showing affection.

As the decade went on he once again became interested in Catholicism, the religion that had been "explained only by sages and understood only by simpletons", as he worded it in an interview in 1986. He sometimes attended mass at Landakot Church, and in the end even started using the name Kiljan again.

His oldest friend, Jón Helgason, died early in 1986. A short time later Halldór and Auður went to Copenhagen, where for the first time Auður felt that things were starting to become unclear to him. He had to be reminded that Jón was dead; every now and then he said that he wanted to go and visit him. Auður did not dare to leave him alone at the Tre Falke Hotel, and the one time that she did, he set off for town on his own.

By the spring of 1988 Halldór had started to be aware of his deterioration, and he was reluctant to go out, fearing that he would not recognize people he knew, or that he would forget what he wanted to say. Such a thought was hard to bear for a perfectionist like him. The bouts of anger that had sometimes gripped him began to diminish, but he became subject to episodes of fear and delusion. He thought that perhaps now the country's leaders were persecuting him, or that an editorial in the paper was directed personally at him. Around 1990 his difficulty in speaking became more pronounced: he forgot words, even the most simple ones, but strug-

gled to remember them and did not want to give up. Once he tried to ask his
daughter for a pen, struggling to find the word, until finally he came up with
"bureaucratic member".

*

When Halldór turned ninety in 1992 a candlelight procession took place at
Gljúfrasteinn; people carried placards displaying the names of his books; speeches
were made and songs were sung. He came outside and was happy, although his joy
was perhaps not completely of this world. That spring he was delighted by the
republication of *Poems*.

After this he declined quickly. Words disappeared from the master little by little,
though music lived on within him. Music, which came closest to the world of
beauty, was one of his first memories and likely also his last. He had always played
the piano; though the way that he played bore the marks of first having played the
organ, but he could read music well and preferred to play Bach. In the autobiographical novel *In the Fields of Home* he writes:

> I have never been in doubt that if I needed to answer that classic reporter's
> question, what book would you take to a desert island to last you the rest of
> your life, I would say without a shadow of a doubt *Das Wohltemperierte Klavier*
> by Johann Sebastian Bach.

When the letters disappeared from him, the notes remained, and still in place
on the open piano in the sitting room at Gljúfrasteinn is that book, which he would
have taken to a desert island where all other books would have been closed to him.

Halldór's final years were difficult for Auður and the other members of the
family. They had to watch over him constantly so that he would not leave the house,
and he always had to know that Auður was near by; otherwise he would become
frightened. In March, 1993, Guðný and her husband, Halldór Þorgeirsson, invited
Auður to join them at a film festival in France so that she could have a much-
needed break. Halldór was able to stay in Reykjalundur Nursing Home while she
was away. He was treated well there. He returned to Gljúfrasteinn but the family
knew that this could not go on for long. It became clear to the doctors and nurses
when he fell down the stairs there.

At the beginning of 1994 Halldór moved to Reykjalundur for good. Auður
visited him daily; he always recognized her and would light up when he saw
her. She would occasionally take him out in the car, sometimes to Gljúfrasteinn,
but these trips had to stop, because once there he did not want to return to the
nursing home.

Halldór lost the ability to speak altogether two years before he died on 8 February, 1998. Auður was with him to the last. Catholic mass was sung for him and he was buried in Mosfell, a short distance from the fields of home.

*

Halldór Laxness lived for nearly a whole century. His upbringing bore the signs of the stagnant rural society of the 1800s, but there quickened within him the ambition and creative energy that drove him as a young man into the swirling modernity of Europe and America. Although he sometimes lost his way, he led his nation into the twentieth century. His achievement was to create in his novels those characters that became the symbols of the nation and marked its path: Salka Valka, Bjartur and Snæfriður, Iceland's Sun. In his fiction he gave voice to the perceptions and feelings of his countrymen during the greatest uprooting in Icelandic history. His questions are classic, although some of his answers have been forgotten. In the end what survives is the true note, when all the meaning that words can grant is gone. And beauty reigns alone.

Note on the Sources

THIS ENGLISH LANGUAGE EDITION OF MY BIOGRAPHY OF HALLDÓR Laxness has been edited and abridged. It does not include, for example, all the endnotes and references of the original Icelandic edition. Where works published in English are quoted, the reader will of course find a reference. The appendix includes a bibliography of all of Halldór Laxness' books, including all published English translations. Most of my sources are, however, in Icelandic and most of the texts that I quote have not been published. This is true of all the letters, for the most part kept in Icelandic archives, either public or private. Readers who want to check my sources should refer to the original edition of my work: *Halldór Laxness – Ævisaga*, Reykjavík, 2004.

The most important sources of the book are:

Halldór Laxness' collection of letters and his manuscripts, now in the National and University Library of Iceland.

The many letters that Halldór wrote to his first wife, Ingibjörg Einarsdottir, access to which was granted to me by their son, Einar Laxness; as an historian, he was very supportive of this work. Halldór Laxness' widow, Auður, kindly allowed me to read and quote from all the correspondence between her and her husband, as did Halldór's daughters, Maria, Sigridur and Guðný. Peter Hallberg's son, Kristian, also generously sent me copies of all the letters that Halldor wrote to his father, Halldór Laxness' first biographer.

Letters and other material on Halldór is also to be found in the archives of the Icelandic Foreign Ministry, the Icelandic embassies in Copenhagen, Stockholm and Washington. Material on Halldór's tax case is also to be found in the archives of the State Department and the F.B.I. in the United States, and in obtaining these

I was greatly assisted by the historian Valur Ingimundarson and the researcher Chay Lemoine.

Documents on the award to Halldór Laxness of the Nobel Prize are in the archives of the Swedish Academy in Stockholm and correspondence between members of the Academy concerning the award is in the letters collections of the Royal Library in Stockholm.

Halldór's letters to his German translator Ernst Harthern are in the Archives of the Swedish Labour movement in Stockholm, and Halldór's letters to Danish authors are in the manuscript department of the Royal Library of Copenhagen.

The minutes of the questioning of Walter Janka by the East German security police are in the Stasi archives in Berlin.

I received invaluable assistance from the historian Reinhard Müller, who also introduced me to the Russian researcher Jakov Rokitchansky, who obtained documents and letters from the Russian archives R.G.A.L.I., R.G.A.S.P.I. and G.A.R.F. The Icelandic specialist in Russian affairs, Jón Olafsson, also gave me invaluable assistance.

Apart from these sources, I spoke to many of Halldór's relatives, friends and contemporaries. My heartfelt thanks to all of these people mentioned by name in the Icelandic edition and also to all of those who supplied information, photographs or other material for the book. My thanks also to my family, my original publishers, JPV of Reykjavík, my translator Philip Roughton and the people of the MacLehose Press at Quercus.

My deepest gratitude to Auður Laxness, who supported my work throughout and unconditionally, untroubled by any critical view on Halldór's life and work. She granted me access to all of Halldór's private letters and documents. Only the author, on the other hand, can be held responsible for any mistakes or flaws this work might contain.

H.G.

January 2008

Bibliography

Books by Halldór Laxness

The details of English translations have been given where available

Novels

Barn náttúrunnar (Child of Nature), 1919

Undir Helgahnúk (At the Foot of the Sacred Peak), 1924

Vefarinn mikli frá Kasmír, 1927
The Great Weaver from Kashmir, trans. Philip Roughton (Archipelago Books, 2008)

Þú vínviður hreini, first part of *Salka Valka,* 1931
O Thou Pure Vine, trans. F.H. Lyon (Allen & Unwin, 1936)

Fuglinn í fjörunni, second part of *Salka Valka,* 1932
The Bird on the Beach, trans. F.H. Lyon (Allen & Unwin, 1936)

Sjálfstætt fólk, first part, 1934, second part, 1935
Independent People, trans. J.A. Thompson (Allen & Unwin, 1945; Vintage International,
    1997; Harvill Press, 1999)

Ljós heimsins, first part of *World Light,* 1937
Light of the World, trans. Magnus Magnusson (University of Wisconsin Press, 1969;
    Vintage International, 2002)

Höll sumarlandsins, second part of *World Light,* 1938
The Palace of the Summerland, trans. Magnus Magnusson (University of Wisconsin Press,
    1969; Vintage International, 2002)

Hús skáldsins, third part of *World Light,* 1939
The House of the Poet, trans. Magnus Magnusson (University of Wisconsin Press, 1969;
    Vintage International, 2002)

Fegurð himinsins, fourth part of *World Light,* 1940
The Beauty of the Heavens, trans. Magnus Magnusson (University of Wisconsin Press,
    1969; Vintage International, 2002)

Íslandsklukkan, first part of *Íslandsklukkan,* 1943
Iceland's Bell, trans. Philip Roughton (Vintage International, 2003)

Hið ljósa man, second part of *Íslandsklukkan*, 1944
The Fair Maiden, trans. Philip Roughton (Vintage International, 2003)

Eldur í Kaupinhafn, third part of *Íslandsklukkan*, 1946
Fire in Copenhagen, trans. Philip Roughton (Vintage International, 2003)

Atómstöðin, 1948
The Atom Station, trans. Magnus Magnusson (Methuen, 1961; Harvill Press, 2003)

Heiman eg fór (When I Left Home), 1952 (written in 1924)

Gerpla, 1952
The Happy Warriors, trans. Katherine John (Methuen, 1958)

Brekkukotsannáll, 1957
The Fish Can Sing, trans. Magnus Magnusson (Methuen, 1966; Harvill Press, 2000)

Paradísarheimt, 1960
Paradise Reclaimed, trans. Magnus Magnusson (Methuen, 1962; Vintage International, 2002)

Kristnihald undir Jökli, 1968
Christianity at Glacier, trans. Magnus Magnusson (Helgafell, 1972; Vaka-Helgafell, 1990, 1996; Vintage International, 2004)

Innansveitarkronika (A Parish Chronicle), 1970

Guðsgjafaþula (God's Good Gifts), 1972

Short stories

Nokkrar sögur (Several Stories), 1923

Fótatak manna (Footsteps of Men), 1933

Sjö töframenn (Seven Magicians), 1942

Þættir (A collection of short stories), 1954

Sjöstafakverið, 1964
A Quire of Seven, trans. Alan Boucher (Iceland Review, 1974)

Poems

Kvæðakver (The Book of Poems), 1930

Plays

Straumrof (Short Circuit), 1934

Snæfríður Íslandssól (Play based on *Íslandsklukkan*), 1950

Silfurtúnglið (The Silver Moon), 1954

Strompleikurinn (The Chimney Play), 1961

Prjónastofan Sólin (The Knitting Workshop called 'The Sun'), 1962

Dúfnaveislan, 1966
The Pigeon Banquet: An Entertainment in Five Acts, trans. Alan Boucher (Universitetsforlaget, 1973)
Úa (Play based on *Kristnihald undir Jökli*), 1970
Norðanstúlkan (Play based on *Atómstöðin*), 1972

Essays

Kapólsk viðhorf (The Catholic View), 1925
Alþýðubókin (The Book of the People), 1929
Dagleið á fjöllum (A Day's Journey in the Mountains), 1937
Vettvangur dagsins (The Contemporary Scene), 1942
Sjálfsagðir hlutir (Self-Evident Things), 1946
Reisubókarkorn (A Little Travel Diary), 1950
Dagur í senn (A Day at a Time), 1955
Gjörníngabók (The Book of Essays), 1959
Upphaf mannúðarstefnu (The Origin of Humanism), 1965
Íslendíngaspjall (An Essay on Icelanders), 1967
Vínlandspúnktar (Some Remarks on Vinland), 1969
Yfirskygðir staðir (Overshadowed Places), 1971
Þjóðhátíðarrolla (A Rigmarole on the National Holiday), 1974
Seiseijú, mikil ósköp (Well, Well, Oh Yes), 1977
Við heygarðshornið (On Home Ground), 1981
Og árin líða (And the Years Pass By), 1984
Af menníngarástandi (On the Cultural Situation), 1986

Memoirs

Skáldatími (A Poet's Time), 1963
Í túninu heima (In the Fields of Home), 1975
Úngur eg var (When I Was Young), 1976
Sjömeistarasagan (Saga of the Seven Masters), 1978
Grikklandsárið (The Greek Year), 1980
Dagar hjá múnkum (Days with Monks), 1987

Travel Books

Í austurvegi (Going East), 1933
Gerska æfintýrið (The Russian Adventure), 1938

Index

Halldór with his parents in 1906

Halldór aged around fifty

María, Halldór's daughter, and Málfríður Jónsdóttir, her mother

Halldór at Clervaux Monastery in Luxembourg on the day he turned
to the Catholic faith in 1923

Sænautasel farm in 1939; probably the model for "Summerhouses"
in *Independent People*

Kristín Valgerður Einarsdóttir, Halldór's lover in Los Angeles, in 1930

Halldór in 1934. The photograph is by Inga, his first wife

Inga and Halldór in Nice in 1935

Halldór at the Bukharin trial in March 1938. Very few photographs exist showing the audience at the Moscow trials

Vera Hertzsch with Erla Sólveig in 1937

Auður Sveinsdóttir at the age of twenty

Halldór at the memorial sculpture to the Taoist monk K'iu Ch'ang Ch'un, 1957